Themantic Education's

IB Psychology

A Student's Guide

Travis Dixon

Thematic Education™

Building concrete foundations
for limitless horizons

Themantic Education™
Yokohama, Japan

Themantic Education™
Building concrete foundations
for limitless horizons

This book is for any student, past or present, who's ever felt bored, confused or lost in a class and just wanted to be thrown a few building blocks to play with.

First published July, 2017. Reprinted with minor changes, October 2017 and July 2018. Printed in China.

Cover & layout design by Kim Littani.

This book has been developed independently of the IB and Themantic Education has no affiliation with the IB. All opinions expressed in this work are those of the author and of Themantic Education.

All images are used with license from bigstockphoto.com or from creative commons media. Any infringement is accidental and if informed of any breach, we will happily make amendments to future editions of this work.

For orders and new products please visit our website: www.themantic-education.com
Facebook Group for Teachers: ThemEd's IB Psychology Teachers
Facebook Group for Students: ThemEd's IB Psychology Students
IB Psychology Blog: https://ibpsych.themantic-education.com/

ISBN: 978-0-473-39139-3

Preface

The goal of this textbook is to provide you (the student) with a tool that will support your study of IB Psychology, from comprehending the concrete to thinking in the abstract. After all, thinking about the big ideas starts with comprehending the basics.

What we know from cognitive science and neuroscience is that learning is about making connections: we learn something new by relating it to our existing knowledge when we're trying to answer a question or solve a problem. With enough repetition, this also creates changes in our brain structure that supports this learning. With this model of learning in mind, this book has been deliberately structured so that it facilitates a lesson-by-lesson, topic-by-topic, unit-by-unit approach.

Each lesson in this book, therefore, includes carefully selected content that is detailed enough to support your learning, but not so detailed that it will be too complex for you to understand. The guiding questions are also there in each lesson to help you grasp the significance of what you're learning about. Lessons are connected with one another, as are topics. In this way, the intention is that this textbook will facilitate a process of learning that's constructed from the ground up.

However, you are reminded that there is definitely more than one way to teach IB Psychology and while I am incredibly proud of the course this book supports, I by no means think it's perfect. Similarly, teaching is about sharing one's passion, and the topics I've included in this course are the ones I'm passionate about - I don't expect your teacher to share my same passions when it comes to teaching psychology. With this in mind, I welcome your teacher to swap lessons, topics or even whole units and you should trust these decisions, because they may disagree with the ideas and explanations I present, and might have even more interesting, relevant or suitable topics to teach.

While every effort has been made to ensure this book is accurate in terms of content, language, style, grammar etc., with a work of this magnitude some minor mistakes are inevitable. I can assure you that any errors are not a result of carelessness, and should serve as a reminder that all media (including textbooks) should be consumed critically.

Similarly, while every effort has been made to ensure that this book has enough material to prepare you to master the IB Psychology course, there is always an element of unpredictability with IB assessment. Therefore, it is important that you and your teacher are familiar with the IB assessment requirements and are open to the idea of supplementing and/or swapping content in this book with additional and/or alternative materials if you feel it's necessary.

My passion is working hard so I can help teachers teach and students learn; I sincerely hope this book can do both.

Cheers,

Travis Dixon
Yokohama, Japan.
June, 2017.

Psychology is an inherently fascinating and complex subject and if you complete this course with more answers than questions, I'll feel this book has failed.

Contents

Chapter 1
Introduction

Introduction

Welcome to the wonderful world of psychology – *the scientific study of individual human behaviour and mental processes*. This is a fancy way of saying that psychology is the study of how and why people think and act the way they do. While you probably haven't studied psychology in school as a subject yet, you may already be familiar with some aspects of psychological study like amnesia, conformity, and psychiatric disorders. You may have come across these ideas as psychology is such an interesting and popular subject that it appears everywhere in the media, including in films, TV shows and in the news.

Because psychology is not like other school subjects such as biology, maths or English, where you are familiar with what's involved in these courses and how to do well, it is important to take the time to learn a little about what this course is all about and how to succeed in IB Psychology *before* getting stuck into the heart of the course. This is the primary goal of this introductory chapter.

This book has been written and constructed to accompany the teaching and learning of the IB Psychology course. With this purpose in mind, it has been crafted in a way that is different to many other textbooks. For one, it's not written using language that is of a formal and academic style that is traditional for many textbooks. Instead, it's written in a conversational and informal tone, similar to how I would talk to my students in a classroom. As you're reading the explanations in this book, I hope they're like another voice helping to guide your study, supporting your teacher's explanations, and deepening your understanding of this intriguing subject.

You'll notice there are lots of anecdotal and everyday examples included throughout the book. These are designed to help you access the information and to build your knowledge. Sometimes it's tricky to think about psychological concepts in the abstract, so these examples help to make things a little more concrete. That being said, the *end goal* is that you will be able to understand the abstract concepts by themselves and explain them in a precise manner using correct terminology and with empirical evidence, not anecdotal evidence or examples.

We'll begin by breaking down the definition of psychology, the *scientific study of individual human behaviour and mental processes*, as this seems like a logical place to start. This thematic textbook is designed so that your learning builds over time and understanding one idea will deepen the next. The end result will hopefully be a deep understanding of important concepts and a desire to continue exploring this fascinating subject.

The IB Psychology course is immensely challenging, but if you are conscientious, ask questions, and work hard to develop your thinking skills, I'm sure you'll find it incredibly rewarding!

Psychology is the scientific study of behaviour and internal mental processes.

This textbook should always come second to your teacher's advice and guidance. Think of the book as a guide, but your teacher is the pilot.

1.1 Introduction to Psychology
What is "psychology"?

(a) Behaviour and Mental Processes

Let's ease into this course and begin your career as a psychologist by starting with a general introduction to what psychologists actually do. As mentioned in the introduction, psychology is the scientific study of individual behaviour and mental processes. A behaviour in a psychological sense is commonly defined as an action that can be observed. For instance, the way people go along with a group because of peer pressure is an example of a behaviour called conformity. Or when there is a person in need of help but everyone walks past and does nothing is another commonly observed human behaviour known as bystanderism. These are examples of behaviours because they're actions by humans that are *observable*.

Along with studying behaviour, psychologists also study mental processes. Other terms for mental processes include cognitive processes, cognition, mental processes or internal processes. These terms are used interchangeably and all mean the same thing. If we think about behaviour as being the way we *act*, cognition is the way we *think*.

Like many complex ideas, "behaviour" is rather difficult to define in a black-and-white sense and so it's important that you try to understand it conceptually. That is to say, think about real-life examples and get an understanding of the idea instead of trying to memorise the definition. Moreover, just to make things tricky the IB Psychology course considers mental processes as part of behaviour. For example, there are three approaches to understanding "behaviour" that form part of the core of the course: the biological, cognitive and sociocultural approaches. Cognition can be studied in these approaches to understanding "behaviour." So for now as you get started, let's think of behaviour as an umbrella term that includes observable actions *and* cognitive processes.

> **Psychology** is the scientific study of observable actions and internal mental processes.

Behaviour	
Observable Actions	*Mental Processes (Cognition)*
• Violence, aggression and violent crime • Conformity and compliance • Bystanderism • Attraction • Mate selection (choosing whom to marry and/or have children with) • Communication	• Processing • Judgement • Thinking • Decision making • Memory • Perception • Problem-solving • Attention • Language

Some psychologists focus primarily on studying observable behaviours, while others specialize in investigating cognitive processes. In the IB Psychology course

Cognition refers to the internal working functions of the mind.

you'll develop an understanding of *both*, including how they interact and can influence one another.

Cognition can be an abstract concept and like many abstract concepts you'll be introduced to, a good way to understand it is to make connections with what you already know. Try reflecting on your own cognitive processes. For example, how do you get from your house to school each morning? Picture yourself at the front door and then in your mind imagine the way you have to get to school. You will be able to see a lot of things in your mind, including the streets and buildings along the way. This is using your memory, which is a really important cognitive process. More specifically it's using visual-spatial memory, which is your ability to remember what things look like, a very helpful skill when you are trying to find your way around. Or use your imagination. Picture yourself holding an apple. Your ability to see that in your mind is a result of you cognitively processing information in your mind.

In the IB Psychology programme, all cognitive processes could be used in exam questions that ask about "behaviour." However, not all behaviours could be used in response to questions about cognitive processes.

It's important to remember that behaviour and cognitive processes are extremely closely related, and the differences between these are often not black and white. For instance, is feeling emotional a behaviour or a cognitive process? We can often see when someone is really happy or feeling depressed, but we can't see their feelings or their thoughts, which are equally important in experiencing emotion. Another example could be stereotypes: are these behaviours or cognitive processes? They involve thinking about people in a certain way, but they are closely related to how we might act towards them as well. Or what about attraction? This includes the way we think about someone, but also can affect how we act. Psychological disorders also encompass visible and cognitive symptoms.

The study of observable actions without focusing on internal processes is rather limited, because these processes are often at the heart of our behaviour. How we think, or don't think, in certain situations can have big effects on how we behave. For example, if we're trying to understand why some people are more likely to react violently in situations when they feel threatened, focusing only on their reactions would give us a limited understanding of *why* they reacted that way. By going deeper and trying to understand their thought processes that lead to their violent reactions, we can get a deeper understanding of their behaviour.

Attraction involves internal processes and observable actions. This is a good example of how our cognition and our behaviour interact (i.e. they can influence one another).

As you can see, distinguishing between behaviour and cognition is pretty tricky. For the most part, distinguishing between behaviour and cognitive processes isn't *essential* while progressing through this course. Having said that, as these two concepts are the core of psychology, it is essential that by the end of the course you have a firm understanding of a number of behaviours and cognitive processes, as well as multiple ways in which they interact.

Psychology is filled with these "grey areas" and things are not always black-and-white. In fact, they rarely are. Some of my students get frustrated and ask, "If there are no definitive answers in psychology why do we even study this subject?" As the course progresses it's hoped you'll be able to see your own answers to this question. If you can learn to appreciate grey areas and to think more deeply about them, rather than always trying to put the world in black-and-white terms, you'll be able to consider and grasp increasingly complex ideas, which is an underlying goal of the IB Diploma Programme.

Guiding Question:

Why do psychologists study behaviour *and* cognition?

Critical Thinking Extension:

It's already been explained how it's often very difficult to distinguish between behaviour and cognitive processes. Looking at the list of cognitive processes provided in this section, can you think of any relationships they may have with particular behaviours? For example, language includes speaking but speaking is an observable action. The thinking about what to say and forming the words is the cognition, while the act of speaking and the manner in which someone speaks (e.g. body language, volume, etc.) are the observable actions that constitute the behaviour. Can you think of other examples of areas of uncertainty between what is "behaviour" and what is "cognition"?

If you're interested…

There's so much to learn in IB Psychology and so little time to learn it all, that these sections provide you with opportunities to explore possible areas of interest. There is a great collection of some of the most influential ideas in psychology in *50 Psychology Classics: Who We Are, How We Think, What We Do: Insight and Inspiration from 50 Key Books* by Tom Butler-Bowdon. The fact that this book has each theory divided into individual sections makes it easy to read little and often.

(b)   *Studying Individuals*

The focus on *individuals* is where psychology is different to other fields of study, like sociology and anthropology. These subjects tend to focus on humans as they exist in groups, whereas psychology focuses on humans as they exist as *individuals*. That's not to say that our individual behaviour and cognitive processes aren't influenced by our social and cultural groups. In fact, the influence of our social and cultural environments is the subject of a whole unit in this textbook and is a recurring theme in other units as well. For instance, you will learn about how the culture you were brought up in may affect your way of thinking about certain things and this might also affect how you act in certain situations. But whereas anthropologists would look at the cultural influence as a whole, psychologists look at the effect of the cultural influence on the behaviour and cognitive processes of *individuals*.

This is why it's important to be very careful when making broad, sweeping statements and drawing generalized conclusions in Psychology: everybody's different and so while we can observe general trends and patterns across large groups of people, there are nearly always exceptions in particular individuals. For instance, compare the following two statements:

- In one of her answers, Sarah writes that "…because of their cultural values, Japanese people go along with the group."
- In one of his answers, Raffi writes that "…because of their cultural values, Japanese people may tend to go along with the group."

I really want to emphasize the importance of the difference between these two statements and why Raffi's is far more accurate and demonstrates a deeper understanding than Sarah's. Sarah is making a definitive claim about Japanese people that suggests she thinks of all Japanese people as being exactly the same and behaving the same way when in a group. Sarah is treating all 120 million + Japanese people as the same, which means she either hasn't thought carefully about the conclusion she is drawing, or she hasn't thought about the words she is using to show her conclusions.

Psychology is closely related to anthropology, sociology, biology and even philosophy.

While it's often very appealing to simplify the world and make generalizations, it's important that you understand that generalizations aren't always true. What happens in one culture, might not be the same in another.

Try to get in the habit of challenging your own conclusions. This is an important part of learning to think critically.

Variables and behaviours in psychology can interact, which means they influence one another.

Raffi, on the other hand, includes two very important clauses to his claim: "may" and "tend to". The word "may" is important in this conclusion because it recognizes that Japanese people won't behave the same way all the time, just like all humans. The phrase "tend to" also shows that while this is a pattern of behaviour, it leaves it open for exceptions. Later in this chapter you will be shown some guidelines when making conclusions about people's behaviour and/or cognitive processes so you can come to show similar levels of thinking like Raffi and avoid over-generalizations like Sarah's.

We've mentioned already that psychology involves studying cognition, behaviour and the social environment, but there's one major factor that is missing: biology. Our thinking and behaviour is influenced by our internal biological processes, such as the function of our brain, levels of hormones and other chemical messengers in our body. Part of studying individuals involves the investigation of biological factors that affect, and are affected by, our behaviour and mental processes.

Guiding Question:

How is psychology different to other social sciences, such as anthropology and sociology?

Critical Thinking Extension:

Psychology involves a combination of many other subjects, such as biology, chemistry, sociology, statistics and even philosophy. One area that involves a lot of overlap between these subjects is the human brain. Both biologists and psychologists study the brain. How do you think a biological study of the brain might differ from a psychological one?

If you're interested…

This introductory chapter doesn't go into the history of psychology, which some of you might find interesting. The work of arguably the most famous psychologists, Sigmund Freud, is not included in this text. If you know about Freud and are interested in learning about his ideas, there's a fascinating documentary called *The Century of the Self*. At time of writing this full documentary was available online. You can also find his full library online as well.

(c)   Psychologists are Scientific

The term "scientific" has many connotations. In psychology it refers to following a scientific method when studying behaviour and cognitive processes in order to gather empirical evidence. In other words, valid and reliable evidence needs to be gathered to test ideas and theories.

The scientific study in psychology typically follows this pattern:

1) Observations are made (relating to behaviour and/or cognitive processes)
2) Background research is conducted
3) Hypotheses are formulated
4) Experiments or tests are designed to test hypotheses
5) Data are gathered and analyzed
6) Conclusions are drawn based on the analysis of data

This is an important process to follow in psychology because humans are such complex creatures. Our thoughts, perceptions and interpretations of others' behaviour is also highly susceptible to our own biases, which is why a scientific method should be applied to develop valid conclusions. There is much more to know about the research process in psychology and understanding this process is a recurring theme throughout the course. Standard Level (SL) and Higher Level (HL) students need to have a firm grasp of experimental research methods as all IB Psychology students conduct experimental research for the Internal Assessment (IA). An understanding of research methods is also important for other areas of the course as well. HL students will go further in their studies of research methods, as this is a key point of difference between the SL and HL courses.

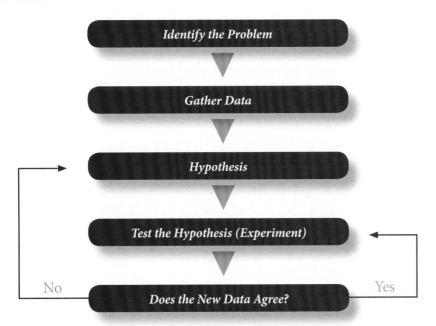

Psychology research is based on the scientific method.

It's essential that you work to develop a scientific and analytical approach to your own study of Psychology. Part of the scientific approach involves gathering and scrutinizing evidence to test ideas. As you come up with your own ideas and conclusions, it's essential that you analyze the evidence you have available to support your opinions.

You can read more about the concepts of validity and reliability later in this chapter. You might not be able to fully grasp what these mean this early in the course, but it is hoped that by the end of this course you will be able to.

Throughout this course you will be presented with a lot of studies to analyze and draw conclusions from.

There's a great TED Talk called "10 myths about psychology, debunked" that shows how ten common myths about psychology can be disproven through empirical research.

Many students make the mistake of ignoring the evidence or not thinking carefully enough about evidence before they make big claims in psychology.

In our course, the evidence is the research: the studies and the theories. The following sections aim to provide you with a brief introduction to these aspects of psychology and the further you progress through the course and the more studies you learn about, the more this will make sense. If you feel lost and confused now, try not to panic. A good strategy would be to make notes and write questions to yourself and then as you learn about more and more studies and you develop a deeper understanding of what psychology is all about, regularly revisit your notes until you have answered your own questions.

A beneficial habit to get into is trying to relate what you're learning about in class to your own personal experience and observations. The more you can connect what you're learning in the IB Psychology course to your existing knowledge, the more you will understand. This will help transform what you're learning about from abstract concepts to concrete examples. For instance, when studying criminology you learn about a theory of judgement and decision making. This theory includes two types of processing of information. Processing, judgement and decision making are all very similar and related, but slightly different, cognitive processes. The definitions of these will be hard to understand in the abstract, but if you can come up with your own concrete and real-life examples it will make them easier to understand.

Guiding Question:

Why is a scientific approach important when studying individual behaviour and/or cognitive processes?

Critical Thinking Extension:

Tolerating Uncertainty: When does research become scientific? In this course you need to become trained to tolerate uncertainty, which means acknowledging and understanding that often there are grey areas. Most concepts you will learn about in Psychology can't be viewed in black-and-white terms and scientific research is one of them. This textbook contains only psychological research that has been published in peer-reviewed journals, but does that mean that research that follows the scientific method that hasn't been published is any less valid and/or useful? To what extent is your own observation of other people a valuable way of "knowing" something in Psychology?

If you're interested…

Some of the most famous psychologists and their experiments have been summarized in Lauren Slater's book *Opening Skinner's Box*. This is written for a popular audience so it's generally pretty accessible for a student who is interested in reading more about some of the historical and groundbreaking studies in psychology.

1.2 Psychological Studies
How do we know what we know in Psychology? Part I

(a) Variables and Relationships

As you've already learned, psychology involves scientific investigations. In order to follow the scientific process, research must be conducted. Most psychological research is focused on studying relationships, but not relationships as in romances or friendship (although this is an area of study and one we'll look at in the "Love and Marriage" unit). Psychology involves the study of relationships between variables. A variable is something that can change or vary. Remember that as you are now a psychologist, one of your key goals is to understand *why* people behave and think the way they do. In order to understand "why" (i.e. the reason behind something) we have to investigate factors influencing behaviour and cognitive processes. Thus, psychological research focuses on studying the relationships between factors that may influence behaviour and/or cognitive processes.

> At the heart of psychology is the study of relationships between variables and behaviour.

I'm going to use a fictional example of a really basic idea to help my explanations of psychological studies. Let's imagine that I've invented a pill and I think this pill will help you remember more after reading. Put simply, it improves memory of what you've read. My pill's called Rememberol. Before I can make solid claims about Rememberol's effects on memory I need some scientific evidence, so I need to conduct some research. In this instance, I'm going to investigate the relationship between two variables: the pill (Rememberol) and memory.

If I got 20 students to take Rememberol and then did a test to see if it worked I couldn't make valid conclusions. Why not? I don't have anyone to compare them to. This is why in many psychological studies[1] there is an independent variable (IV). Hopefully you are already familiar with independent and dependent variables, but just in case we'll have a short refresher course here.

The IV is the variable that the researcher believes will have an effect and so it is what they manipulate. By having an independent

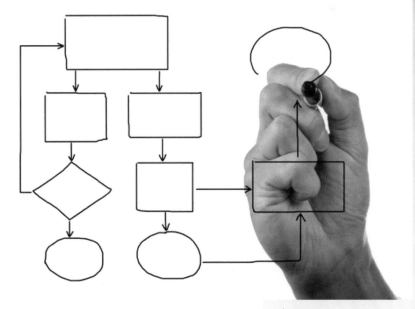

Analyzing psychological studies takes careful thinking and processing. You need to know the individual bits of information (building blocks) and then try to see how they relate.

---

[1] *I say "many" because qualitative research methodology doesn't have variables, but this is an extension topic. A vast majority of psychological research is quantitative in nature, and at this early point in the course we'll focus on just quantitative studies.*

variable we are able to make comparisons between groups and in making these comparisons we can draw conclusions about the effects of one variable on another. For example, I might conduct an experiment whereby ten of the students in my study take Rememberol and the other ten don't. Now I can make comparisons between the two groups: if the Rememberol condition has better memory scores on my test, I have some evidence that suggests it really works.

The dependent variable is the effect of the manipulation of the IV. It is what is measured by the researchers. So in my experiment on Rememberol, my DV would be the scores of the test because this is what was measured; it was what was affected by the IV.

When understanding studies, it can be helpful to identify the IV and DV in the study. This will help you identify the direction of the relationship being investigated. After you know the IV and DV, you will be able to draw conclusions.

There are many other important components to psychological research besides just the IV and DV and these will be explored in-depth later in the course.

It's also important to note that there are *many* components to conducting studies in psychology and this is a *very* brief introduction. The key point to understand at this stage is that by making comparisons between groups in studies, psychologists gather evidence and draw conclusions about cognition and behaviour.

You have probably learned about variables in science class already. Try to draw on your prior learning to understand how these are used in psychological research.

Guiding Question:

What's the difference between an independent variable and a dependent variable?

Critical Thinking Extension:

Is psychology a "science?" "Social Science" is a name commonly given to subjects like Economics, History, and Political Science. Natural Science is the name commonly given to subjects like Biology, Chemistry and Physics. From what you've learnt so far about Psychology, do you think it's more of a Social Science or a Natural Science?

If you're interested...

"Crash Course" is a YouTube channel that has many useful videos on a range of subjects. Their videos on psychology are really well done. If you're interested, they have one called "Episode 2: Research and Experimentation." This might provide you with more helpful explanations of research and studies in psychology, although be warned that they use a lot of jargon (which we'll explore later in the course).

(b) Applying Conclusions

The experiments explained throughout this textbook have important and significant relationships between variables and it's this relationship that you need to draw a conclusion about. The studies are used to help facilitate your acquisition of important conceptual understandings related to psychology. Some of those conceptual understandings are related to:

- How our physical environment can affect behaviour
- How culture can affect thinking
- How biology can affect thinking
- How thinking can affect behaviour
- Etc. etc.

You'll notice that these are very broad, but they're all about relationships. In particular, they're relationships between variables (e.g. biology, culture and our environment) and behaviour and/or mental processes (e.g. thinking).

In order to draw a conclusion about these relationships between variables, you need to first know the methodology used. The independent variables and dependent variables are important parts of this methodology, as have been explained in the previous section. Once you know the methodology, you need to understand how one variable affects another. Moreover, you'll need to *explain* your understanding of that relationship.

Sometimes you might find it helpful to identify the aim of a study. The aim of a study is simply a one or two-sentence statement that identifies the relationship being investigated between the IV and the DV in a particular study. For instance, the aim of my experiment was to see if Rememberol would have an impact on memory.

Two other key components of the methodology include:
- The Participants/Subjects: Who took part in the study? (e.g. age, gender, nationality, etc.)
- The Procedures: What were the participants asked to do?

A key component of drawing conclusions from studies are the results. The results are the measurement of the dependent variable. In my Rememberol study the results would be the scores the participants got on their tests. In order to see if my drug actually has an effect I need to compare the results from my treatment group (those that got the pill during revision) with my control group (those that didn't take the pill). If both groups' scores were the same it would suggest that my pill *doesn't* have an effect on memory.

After you have drawn the conclusion it is important that you can apply it to a particular question or problem being asked. Throughout this textbook you are provided with guiding questions

> It's important that you use the guiding questions in this textbook to help you draw conclusions about the research you are presented with. After you draw your conclusion, remember to go further and challenge your own conclusions by thinking critically.

> Methodology refers to the aims, procedures, participants and equipment used in the study.

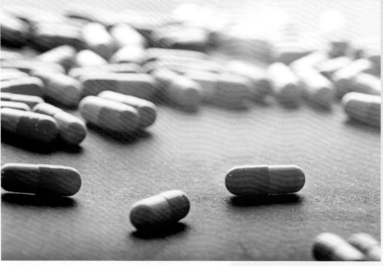

I'm using my fictional example of "Rememberol" just to help you understand a few basic ideas about psychological research. Hopefully as you learn about real research you'll be able to apply these concepts to real studies.

whenever a major piece of research is explained. These guiding questions are designed to help you think carefully about the research and the relationships they demonstrate. The overview of the IB course provided later in this chapter will show you more precisely the variables, behaviours and cognitive processes involved in the relationships that you need to understand.

Many students make the mistake of blindly memorizing as many details about a study as possible. You need to be focusing on understanding the relevant details that help you to draw conclusions about relationships between variables and behaviour.

There are *a lot* of other aspects involved in psychological research and these will be explained in more detail in later chapters. They are not explained here because they will probably make more sense *after* you have a good knowledge base of a range of studies first. At this stage, it's just important to know what to look for in studies and how to draw conclusions.

You will have *many* studies that you will need to remember by the end of this course. In order to remember which study is which, there are a couple of things you can do. Sometimes very famous studies become known by a common name. For instance, you may have heard of the famous psychological study, 'The Stanford Prison Experiment.' It can be helpful sometimes to give a study a name so it's easy to remember and identify what you're talking about, like 'The Iowa Gambling Study.' However, there are a number of different studies that use the Iowa Gambling Task and so calling it this might not make it clear what study you are referring to. Nevertheless, you can identify studies by referring to them by a common name, like 'Asch's Conformity Studies', 'The Bobo Doll Study', 'The Robber's Cave Experiment', 'The Iowa Gambling Study', etc. Another strategy to give you something concrete to remember is to refer to the researcher/s name/s, e.g. Milgram, Goetz et al., Sherif, Bandura, etc. and the year of the study. This is also helpful for examiners to identify the particular study you are referring to in exam answers.

Guiding Question:

How does understanding relationships between variables (e.g. IVs and DVs) assist in applying conclusions in psychology?

Critical Thinking Extension:

The Rememberol study I have explained is an example of a basic experiment: it manipulates an independent variable in a very controlled situation. You may have conducted many of these studies in your science classes. But what are the limitations of conducting experiments in very controlled environments?

If you're interested…

There's an interesting article on *Huffington Post* called "10 Psychological Studies That Will Change What You Think You Know About Yourself." Not only are these fascinating studies and many of which we'll learn about, it might give you a good chance to practice identifying IVs and DVs and drawing conclusions. The more you can familiarize yourself with some basic studies at this early stage, the more confidence you'll gain to tackle more difficult studies later.

(c)   Causation

There are two types of relationships that can be concluded from psychological studies: causal and correlational. As you learned in the previous section, when you are analyzing a study to draw conclusions you need to have a question or problem in mind that is guiding your analysis. As you analyze the results and draw conclusions in response to this question/problem, you will be deducing either a correlational or a causal relationship.

You might be familiar with these concepts already from other subjects, such as Science and Maths, but let's have an overview of these concepts just in case.

Causation means that one thing causes another. In psychology it refers to one variable *causing* a change in another variable. In order to claim a causal relationship between one factor and another, *all* other possible factors have to be eliminated so that one variable is shown to have a high probability to have a *direct* result on something. i.e. one variable *causes* an effect on another.

For example, in order for me to conclude that Rememberol *causes* improved memory I need to make sure that there were no other possible factors influencing the dependent variable in my experiment. That is to say, I need to make sure there was nothing else that might explain the differences between my treatment and control groups. For instance, what if one group just naturally had a better memory than the other group? Or what if just by taking a pill they *believed* that they were going to do better and this made them concentrate more?

This is one major advantage of the laboratory experiment: it enables researchers to carefully design experiments that have many controls in place. A control is something that helps isolate the IV as the only variable influencing the DV. If there are other possible factors that might influence the DV (e.g. the age of the participants, their general memory abilities, etc.) these are called extraneous variables. A variable that does have an effect on the DV that was not intended is called a confounding variable.

For example, the noise level in my testing room during my Rememberol experiment might be an extraneous variable because it might affect the concentration levels of participants. I can control this by having all participants in the same room at the same time. However, if half of my control group turned up late and had less time than everyone else and this affected their results, this would be a confounding variable because it is not the IV and it is affecting the DV.

Here's another example: in many countries cigarette packets come with warning labels that say "SMOKING *CAUSES* LUNG CANCER." This means that if you smoke cigarettes regularly, there is a very high chance that you will develop lung cancer. In this instance, the variable (smoking) has a direct result (lung cancer). Before governments could pass laws that required cigarette packets to have that warning label there would have been lots and lots of research and studies conducted to determine that there was a direct causal relationship between smoking and lung cancer. In fact, in some countries the word "may" has to be put in there so it reads: "Smoking may cause lung cancer" because even this relationship may not be definitively causal.

If a study showed that people who read more are smarter, could you say that reading causes people to be smarter?

A laboratory experiment is also called a true experiment, because they do not always happen in laboratories.

In psychology, causal relationships are concluded from laboratory experiments. In a laboratory, all extraneous variables are controlled for. That is to say, every variable that may affect the DV is kept constant so it's only the IV that is having an effect on the DV. It is only in a laboratory (i.e. highly controlled) environment that this can happen.

For instance, if I wanted to conclude that Rememberol *causes* an increase in test scores, I would need to design an experiment in a highly controlled environment that controlled for all extraneous variables so they wouldn't confound my results. Here is a list of some possible extraneous variables relating to my participants that may affect my DV (test scores) that I might need to control for:

- Hours of sleep
- Diet
- Prior knowledge
- Academic ability
- Interest in the subject
- Language
- Age

In order for me to conclude that my learning pill Rememberol *causes* grades to increase I would need to design and conduct numerous studies that controlled for possible extraneous variables so I could isolate the IV (my drug) as being the variable that is directly affecting the DV (memory, as measured by test scores). Again, there are many terms used to describe how laboratory experiments are designed and you'll learn more about these later in the course.

Throughout this course you will learn about laboratory experiments that investigate relationships between variables. Be wary, however, that just because an experiment is a laboratory experiment it doesn't always mean that the relationship is causal.

Guiding Question:

How can laboratory experiments demonstrate causal relationships?

Critical Thinking Extension:

Human behaviour doesn't occur in a laboratory and this is a major limitation of the laboratory experiment. You'll learn about many other types of research methods that are used to understand human behaviour, including case studies, natural experiments and correlational studies. What are some relationships between variables (e.g. cognitive processes and/or behaviours and factors influencing them) that you think could not be tested in a laboratory setting?

If you're interested…

There have been recent film adaptations of the stories of two of the most famous experiments conducted in Psychology: the Stanford Prison Experiment (Zimbardo) and Milgram's experiments on obedience to authority. The films are called *The Stanford Prison Experiment* and *Experimenter* respectively. Remember that Hollywood has a tendency to alter facts to make better stories, so be wary of treating these films as factual representations of what *really* happened.

(d) Correlation

This section aims to provide you with an understanding of the differences between causal relationships and correlational ones. However, it's important to note that it's not expected for you to fully grasp these differences so early in the course. The first step in understanding the research that you are going to study is to identify the obvious relationship first. That is to say, how one variable affects another and how this is shown in research. For example, how my drug Rememberol affects memory and how my experiment shows this. The next step *after* you draw this obvious conclusion, is to reflect on whether or not the relationship is causal or correlational. This requires really deep thinking and will take a lot of practice. A good strategy is to regularly review these introductory chapters throughout the course to keep a gauge on your own level of understanding of these tricky concepts.

Historically, laboratory experiments have been the most popular research method in psychology. And while there are still thousands of laboratory experiments conducted around the world every year, there are significant limitations is studying human behaviour only in the lab. One limitations is based on the fact that humans might not behave naturally in a laboratory because it's not a normal environment. This is one reason why field experiments are conducted. These are experiments where the independent variable is manipulated in a natural setting, for example a shopping mall, a summer camp or in a hospital. I might give my Rememberol drug and a placebo to two groups of IB students during their exam review session and then my DV would be their actual exam results.

But once you get into the "field" it's difficult to control for extraneous variables, so identifying causation becomes harder. For example, how do I know that all my IB students took Rememberol when they were supposed to? Perhaps some of the exams were more difficult than others. Researchers may have to make a compromise between ecological validity and establishing causal relationships. Ecological validity is a term used to describe how accurate an experiment's conditions are in replicating

Correlation and causation are two more examples of grey areas in psychology. Some studies might show a causation of effect, but not necessarily a causation of behaviour. For example, my study could show that my Rememberol causes increased activity in the memory part of the brain, but I may not be able to conclude that this causes improved memory.

It's often very difficult to draw causal relationships in human studies because there are so many differences (variables) from one person to the next, and from one group of people to the next.

what happens in the "real world". There's more about this concept and how to apply it properly later in this chapter.

Similarly, researchers can't always create the independent variable themselves in the laboratory or in the field. Let's say, for instance, that I wanted to study a relationship between brain damage and decision making. To do this I want to compare the difference between people with brain damage and people with healthy brains. I wouldn't find many volunteers who would want to have their brain damaged simply so I could study them. But I can find people who have *existing* brain damage and ask if they want to participate in my study. When the independent variable is naturally occurring it's called a natural experiment. But like with field experiments, the researcher in a natural experiment can't control for extraneous variables so establishing a causation is difficult as there are many possible variables that may be affecting the DV.

Maybe, for example, I have a hunch that Rememberol works better for boys than it does for girls. To test this, I can get 20 girls and boys in an experiment and then give them the drug followed by a test. I can then compare the results between the boys and the girls to test my idea. You can see from this example that the independent variable is the gender of the participant (boy or girl). But you could imagine how many extraneous variables there are. So even if girls did better on the test, I couldn't say necessarily that Rememberol *caused* this improvement in the test because it is possible girls are just better at taking tests than boys. Therefore, I can only say that the correlation exists because the test-taking ability of boys and girls is a potentially confounding variable.

Where we can't find a causation but we know that one variable might affect another variable, we call this a correlation. A correlation means that there's a relationship between two variables but we can't claim it to be causal. We *might* not be able to conclude that there is a cause-and-effect (i.e. causal) relationship because:

- There are too many extraneous and/or potentially confounding variables.
- We do not know the direction of the relationship (which variable is affecting which).

For instance, research has shown that on average the more fish a country eats the lower the rate of depression (Adams et al., 1996). This is a negative correlation as while one variable increases (eating fish) the other variable decreases (depression). From this statistic, can we say that not eating fish *causes* depression? No, we can't say that because there are too many other variables. For instance, perhaps countries that eat lots of fish live nearer to the ocean and those that don't live away from the ocean and it's this proximity to the ocean that affects depression, not the diet.

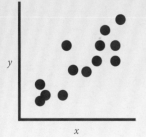

Positive correlation

Negative correlation

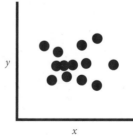

No correlation

A positive correlation is when as one variable increases, so does the other. For example, a positive correlation might be between hours studied and test scores: the more hours on average students study, the higher on average their test scores are.

Sometimes in correlational studies we don't know the direction of the relationship. Perhaps variable (a) is affecting variable (b), or variable (b) is affecting variable (a). For example, in the fish-depression relationship, it could be that the fact that the more fish a person eats

Many students early in their psychology career love to use the word "prove." Be warned: it's very rare in psychology that research *proves* anything. You'll realize through the course why other verbs such as suggest, demonstrate and show, are often more applicable.

the less likely they are to get depressed. Or, it could be that the more depressed a person is the less they want to eat fish. When the direction of the relationship is uncertain like this, it's called bidirectional ambiguity.

Laboratory, natural and field experiments all have independent and dependent variables, which is why they're called experiments. Some studies don't have *independent* and *dependent* variables, however, they just have variables. These are called correlational studies. This may seem quite confusing now and so it will be explained further later in the course. By this stage, it's simply hoped that you understand what you're looking for when reading studies and the general difference between a laboratory, field and natural experiment.

Guiding Question:

What is the difference between causation and correlation in psychology studies?

Critical Thinking Extension:

Understanding the difference between causation and correlation is a key to doing well in IB Psychology. Moreover, if you can clearly explain *how* specific studies demonstrate specific causal or correlational relationships between variables you will do very well in this course. One study mentioned in the TED talk in this section's "If you're interested" claims that people who use Google Chrome and Mozilla Firefox internet browsers are likely to stay in their jobs 15% longer than those who use Explorer or Safari. What's the obvious causal relationship to deduce from this finding? What's a possible argument that could counter the causal one?

If you're interested…

Adam Grant's TED Talk "The surprising habits of original thinkers" is where the above stat regarding internet browsers came from. This talk discusses some really interesting findings he's discovered through his work as an organizational psychologist. If you're a chronic procrastinator, you might find this talk interesting.

1.3 Psychological Theories
How do we know what we know in Psychology?
Part II

(a)   Psychological Theories

What we "know" in psychology comes from research. When students hear the word "research" they naturally think of studies, but I can't stress enough how important it can be to include theories as part of your understanding of the term "research" in psychology. One practical reason for this is that in your exams you need to demonstrate knowledge and understanding of *research*: many students forget that theories count.

In general, a theory is an attempt to explain a phenomenon. So in psychology, a theory is an attempt to explain a particular psychological phenomenon. The term phenomenon (plural – phenomena) is a useful one to know as you can use it as an umbrella term like I've just used it in my above definition of a psychological theory. A phenomenon is something that can be observed to occur, especially if there's some questions or uncertainty about its cause or origin. One example of a psychological phenomenon is confabulation. This is when you can remember something that never really happened. Another example of a biological phenomenon is neurogenesis: the brain's ability to grow new cells. You'll be exposed to a plethora of new terms throughout this course, but they all help you to explain things more clearly.

> A psychological phenomenon refers to an interesting behaviour or mental process that can be observed to occur. There may be some questions surrounding their origin, as well.

But I digress. Here are *some* of the theories that you will learn about in this course:

- Realistic Group Conflict Theory
  - *An attempt to explain how competition and co-operation between groups can influence conflict.*
- Social Identity Theory
  - *An attempt to explain how belonging to a group can influence individual thinking and behaviour.*
- Social Cognitive Theory
  - *An attempt to explain how an individual person's characteristics (including biology), their behaviour and their environment all influence one another.*

So when learning about psychological theories the first step is to figure out what the theory is trying to explain. In other words, what's it a theory of, exactly? A big part of knowing the theory involves knowing the behaviour and/or cognitive process involved.

> Psychological theories provide plausible explanations for relationships between variables and behaviour.

One example is Bandura's social cognitive theory (SCT). An important first step in understanding SCT is to figure out what it's attempting to describe and explain. This theory posits that behaviour, the environment and an individual's characteristics all influence one another. After you understand this tricky idea, it might then be necessary to figure out how SCT applies to the context of criminology. After you can explain how SCT is relevant in criminology, you can then start thinking about other fields of study that SCT might be applicable to. As you learn more throughout the course, you'll be able to make more and more connections, which leads to deeper understanding.

It's important to note that there are multiple times when psychological theories might be relevant, even if they're not what you're *immediately* studying. This is where practising your thinking skills is really important: you can make connections between various ideas even when they're not immediately obvious or concrete. For instance, after you learn about the dual processing model of decision making you may be able to apply it to numerous different areas of study. For example, you may begin to wonder if this could explain why some people gamble or why some can resist temptations better than others.

This is another reason why making connections and asking questions is really valuable: as you go through the course try to make connections with what you're learning in class to what you see in the "real world". Furthermore, try to make connections between what you have learned in one part of the course with another. Identifying and asking questions about these connections will help you develop an in-depth understanding of psychology and will lead you to enjoy the course a lot more. Moreover, as a teacher, I love hearing students ask questions that show their in-depth thinking about what they're learning and I'm sure your teacher will, too!

The relationship between theories and studies is important to understand, because studies form important pieces of evidence that can demonstrate and support, or challenge and contradict theories. Studies can be used to support key claims of theories if the relationships stated in the theory can be demonstrated by results of studies. For example, one interesting idea about social cognitive theory is that our behaviour can be influenced by our internal characteristics, including our biology. You'll find numerous examples throughout this course showing how our behaviour can be influenced by our biology. But the theory also states the relationship can happen in the other direction: our behaviour can influence our biology, and when you learn about neuroplasticity you'll see how this can happen.

To do well in IB Psychology you need to be actively thinking, processing and questioning.

Biological evidence for theories of cognition and behaviour are strong sources of supporting evidence. For example, when studying social identity theory you are going to see how there might be some biological evidence to explain discrimination and prejudice.

Understanding theories, therefore, still requires investigating relationships as theories include explanations of relationships between variables and behaviour. Moreover, being able to see how studies relate to theories is another important skill to develop as it helps to evaluate the validity of particular theories. There is more information later in this section about how to evaluate psychological theories.

In psychology we also study models of thinking and behaviour. Whereas a theory explains relationships between variables, models provide an illustration for how a cognitive process or behaviour might happen. Here are two examples of models that we will learn about in this course:

- Dual Processing Model of Decision Making
  - *A description of different types of thinking (fast and slow).*
- Multi-store Model of Memory
  - *An attempt to describe the process of memory formation.*

Guiding Question:

What do psychological studies and theories have in common?

Critical Thinking Extension:

An important reason to practice your abstract thinking skills is that many students treat theories as "facts" because they "read it in a textbook." The difference between a theory and a fact is quite subjective. For example, is the Theory of Evolution a theory or a fact? Is Climate Change a theory or a fact? These are highly debated questions and the same goes for psychological theories. Learning how to question and challenge ideas is another underlying goal of this course and is the primary objective of these Critical Thinking Extensions. After you can determine a relationship between two things (as directed by a guiding question), the next step is to think abstractly about that relationship. When evaluating theories you can first explain studies that support or demonstrate key claims of the theory, and then offer a counter claim that shows evidence that challenges or contradicts the theory.

If you're interested...

There's a good TED Talk by Ben Ambridge called "10 myths about psychology, debunked." This might be a good place to start your study and to give you a better idea of what this subject *isn't* about.

1.4 Evaluating Research
How do we evaluate studies and theories in Psychology?

The information provided in the rest of this chapter is for reference purposes. Much of this information may not be very useful or helpful early in this course because you won't have the context to make sense of it. Hopefully, it will be useful as you progress through the units and begin to develop more of an understanding of what is required in IB Psychology. Your learning in this course will compound, meaning it will grow over time as you continue to learn. Each piece of knowledge you acquire and relationship you understand will build on prior learning and will facilitate the learning of the next new topic. This text has been designed to facilitate this process so that each topic isn't taught as an individual entity, but that the themes running throughout each unit will enable this development of your learning. Reading these sections throughout the course could also make for excellent tasks to extend yourself and to prepare for important assessments.

(a)   Critical Thinking

After reading the material so far in this chapter, you should have a general idea of what you're supposed to understand in the psychology course. But you're also expected to be able to develop the skills to go further than understanding and to be able to reflect critically upon your own understanding. The IB Psychology guide provides several areas of your understanding that you can reflect upon:

- Research design and methodologies
- Triangulation
- Assumptions and biases
- Contradictory evidence, alternative theories or explanations
- Areas of uncertainty

Essentially, this means that after you demonstrate a conceptual understanding of a significant relationship in psychology, you then need to reflect on that understanding and this is an important next step to aim for. Coincidentally, it's also what the Critical Thinking Extensions are designed to help you with. You will learn more about what these areas of critical thinking mean as the course progresses, but here's a quick introduction to each concept and how it might be applied.

Critical thinking involves asking questions about significant relationships.

Research design and methodologies: you may demonstrate critical thinking about a study that you have used to demonstrate a significant relationship. This would involve analyzing and critiquing the methods of the study and explaining how this might affect the validity of the conclusions and applications of the study itself. For example, if a natural experimental method was used this could affect the types of conclusions that could be drawn and the applications of the findings. The next sections explain why some forms of methodological evaluation are more encouraged than others.

Triangulation: To triangulate data in psychology means to get information (data) from more than one source. It helps to strengthen the validity of conclusions. There are a few types of triangulation, including methodological triangulation, researcher triangulation and data triangulation. These are explained throughout the Critical Thinking Extensions. You can reflect on applications and conclusions regarding relationships by explaining how triangulation may affect their validity.

Assumptions and biases: An assumption is something that is believed, without necessarily having any proof or evidence. Bias could likely refer to researcher bias. Assumptions and biases can influence the validity of conclusions in many ways. It's hoped that you can learn to try to see where they *may* have influenced research or conclusions.

Contradictory evidence or alternative theories or explanations: There's often more than one way to explain a phenomenon in psychology so thinking critically could involve offering a different explanation for a relationship you've explained, or contradictory evidence that challenges that relationship in some way. If you focus on biological explanations of behaviour, for instance, you could counter with an explanation of how sociocultural factors may be influential.

The IB Psychology course is designed to develop your knowledge, understanding and thinking skills.

Areas of uncertainty: This is my favorite critical thinking criterion because it's so vague that it can be applied in so many ways. It really leaves you freedom to think critically in multiple possible ways. For example, a "discussion" can involve hypothesizing, so if you are discussing a relationship you could come up with interesting hypotheses as to how that relationship might be applied in multiple ways, but as it's only a hypothesis you can say that it's an "area of uncertainty." Correlation vs causation might also be relevant in a discussion of an area of uncertainty.

What all these criteria have in common is that they are encouraging you to think beyond the concrete information you are presented with. One major goal of the IB Psychology course is that after completing this course you will become more than just a passive receptor of information, more than just a sponge who is content to have information poured into their brain without questioning or challenging it. It's hoped that you will not only learn to understand ideas and complex concepts, but that you'll be able to go further and challenge them, including challenging the very evidence upon which they're based.

You will have multiple opportunities to practice your critical thinking throughout the course. It's important that you don't rush through learning the basics first.

You'll see that evaluating research only covers some of the ways you *might* demonstrate critical thinking. You can learn more about evaluation of studies and theories in various chapters. They are not included here because without the context of understanding the studies being evaluated, they wouldn't make much sense.

There is a very good possibility that you won't need to evaluate *any* studies in your exam answers. Spending copious amounts of time in the beginning of the course learning how to do this, therefore, might be counterproductive, confusing and a bit meaningless. Nevertheless, an important criterion for your essay answers is "critical thinking". Critical thinking can mean a lot of things. The IB Psychology subject guide defines it as having an "inquiring and reflective attitude to (your) understanding of psychology."

The IB defines evaluation as making "an appraisal by weighing up strengths and limitations." When evaluating studies and theories, there are some guidelines you can follow to make such an appraisal. Fundamentally, an evaluation involves clear explanations of the strengths and limitations. However, you will not be able to provide clear evaluations of a study unless you fully *understand* the relationship it is demonstrating and you can *apply* that study to a particular problem or question. That is to say, you need to be able to describe the study, then explain it, and only after this can you truly provide a valuable and insightful evaluation. Assessing the strength/s of a study, therefore, includes explaining why it's valuable in demonstrating a significant relationship. The limitations include explaining reasons why it might not be so applicable in demonstrating that significant relationship.

Investigating psychological studies, therefore, first involves *knowing* the study. What were the variables and the relationship investigated? Who took part? What were they asked to do? What did they find out? Etc. You need to know the aims, methods and results of the study.

The second step involves understanding and application. You have to know *how* the study demonstrates a significant relationship and you have to be able to apply that in response to a particular question or problem. Too many students focus on blindly memorizing aims, methods and results without thinking carefully about the significance or applications of the study in the first place. Knowing the methodology is only important if it helps you apply the study to show a conceptual understanding of a psychological phenomenon. Overviews of the relationships you need to understand are provided later.

After you understand the applications and significance of the relationship/s demonstrated in the study, you can then reflect critically about your own understanding of the evidence.

There are three primary ways you can think about evaluating studies:

- Internal Validity
- Reliability
- External Validity

Remember that the information in these sections is for reference only. It's not expected that you will be able to fully grasp these concepts at the beginning of the course.

(b) Internal Validity of Studies

The internal validity of a study refers to the extent to which the study *actually* demonstrates the relationship that it intended to. In this instance, an explanation of a limitation of a study could involve explaining possible confounding variables that might have affected the results. For example, if I conducted my Rememberol study on students and measured its effect on test scores in English, a critique of internal validity would involve investigating my methodology. Were the questions in my test fair? Was the test a good measure of memory? Were all extraneous variables controlled for, or might there be some other variables influencing my results?

Before I could say that my Rememberol experiment would have high internal validity, I would need to make sure that the pill was the only variable affecting my dependent variable (e.g. effectiveness of studying).

It is far easier to include explanations of the *strengths* of studies that we use in this course in relation to internal validity, than it is to explain potential *limitations*. After you learn about controls later in the course when you are designing and conducting your own experiment, you'll be able to identify controls more easily in other examples of research. When asked to evaluate a study, therefore, you'll be able to see how they aimed to ensure internal validity by employing such controls. This will allow you explain strengths of the study, which is an important part of evaluation.

It is extremely difficult to explain the limitations of the studies used in this course in terms of internal validity for a number of reasons. First of all, the studies that we use have been published in peer-reviewed articles, carefully designed by extremely professional and experienced researchers and highly scrutinized by other psychologists. It would be very difficult for a first year high school psychology student to notice a limitation that someone else hadn't already noticed. Therefore, the only real critique that you would be expected to offer in terms of internal validity would be one that was probably proposed by someone else (e.g. in a textbook). In this case, you are not demonstrating *your* critical thinking, you are demonstrating your ability to regurgitate someone else's.

Asking you to independently evaluate internal validity in all the studies we use in this course would be as challenging as asking you to evaluate Dickens' use of imagery in *Great Expectations* - not impossible, but very challenging.

Peer-reviewed journal articles are those that have been analyzed by a range of other psychologists before being published. This helps to ensure they are credible sources of information.

This is why explanations of evaluation cannot be found in this text. Telling you what others have concluded about the strengths and limitations of theories and studies would only increase the content of the course and limit the development of your own thinking skills. Trust me – it's far better to figure out how to think critically for yourself than it is to memorise all the possible statements of strengths and limitations of *all* the research you need to understand.

A second reason why I discourage trying to evaluate studies based on internal validity is that it requires an enormous increase in additional amount of methodology that you have to study. In this course you read about new studies almost every lesson In order to try to evaluate their methodology to assess internal validity would involve in-depth descriptions and scrutiny of their methodologies, and since our primary purpose in using studies in the first place is to develop conceptual understandings of significant relationships between variables, behaviours and cognitive processes, we only need to look at the methodology in as much detail as is required to show that relationship. Evaluating research is a secondary purpose to developing conceptual understandings of relationships, so internal validity simply adds a lot more potentially unnecessary content.

When you will be expected to critically evaluate a study based on its internal validity is when you conduct your own experiment for the internal assessment. It is during this chapter and the qualitative methods chapter that you will learn about evaluating methodology based on internal validity and in your report where you will be expected to demonstrate your ability to assess internal validity of research. Higher Level students may also demonstrate this in their third question in Paper Three.

(c)   Reliability of Studies

Reliability refers to the extent to which the study has been replicated (copied) and similar results have been obtained. If a study gets results one time and in one experiment, it might demonstrate a relationship but this may only have happened once. Perhaps it was a fluke or they just got lucky. A study can increase its reliability by having many different researchers conduct the study over and over, on different participants, in different locations and in different situations. If a study gets the same results over many replications it can be said to have test-retest reliability.

Much like the reasons for not evaluating studies based on internal validity, this textbook is not always crafted to help you evaluate studies based on their reliability. There are some good reasons for this. Firstly, the studies that have been included in this textbook, generally speaking, have been replicated and their results have been shown to be reliable. And much like internal validity, explaining strengths or limitations of reliability involves more content and more memorization - it doesn't necessarily demonstrate your critical thinking ability.

For example, the best explanation of test-retest reliability you could really hope for would be: "this study has been replicated many times and so it has test-retest reliability." This could be followed by describing a study that used the same or similar methodology and got the same (or different) results. Understanding reliability and adding more studies to do this would add more content that is highly likely to be unnecessary and counterproductive to developing other essential conceptual understandings. The major aim of this text is to reduce all unnecessary content to free up time to develop a deep understanding of important psychological concepts.

A study has high internal validity if it was only the IV that affected the DV. It would be very difficult for you to evaluate existing, peer-reviewed research for internal validity, so it's recommended that you focus on external validity instead.

Your teacher may disagree with my approach to teaching the evaluation of research. As always, you should always put your teacher's advice ahead of my personal opinions.

In order to know if a study has test-restest reliability you need to know of other studies that have investigated the same relationship. Discussing this concept in essay answers doesn't really demonstrate critical thinking: it demonstrates knowledge.

(d)   External Validity and Generalizability!

There are two more concepts to understand when evaluating research and they are the concepts that I believe are most useful to understand and apply when evaluating studies: external validity and generalizability. External validity means the extent to which the results of a study can be generalized to another context. By context, I mean time, place, situation, group of people, etc. Generalizability refers to the extent to which we could expect to observe the relationship demonstrated in the study in another context. There are key terms that are explained throughout the text in the Critical Thinking Extensions to help you develop your ability to consider generalizability. Three of these are ecological validity, mundane realism, and population validity.

Ecological validity refers to the nature of the environment, its ecology. Laboratory experiments are often criticized for lacking ecological validity. For example, if Rememberol was shown in a laboratory experiment to improve memory, could this really be generalized to real-life situations? Many students make the mistake of thinking that an evaluation of ecological validity simply includes making a claim as basic as: "This study took place in a lab so it lacks ecological validity." This does *not* demonstrate "critical thinking"; it shows that you know the research method and the term ecological validity.

A thorough evaluation and one that shows excellent critical thinking is providing an explanation for *why* the specific relationship demonstrated in the study might not apply beyond the situation of the study. After all, the reason we use lab experiments is to understand the human behaviour in the real world, so you have to think carefully and show you know the real world applications that studies may or may not apply to.

In my Rememberol example, perhaps taking a test in a laboratory condition where there was no real pressure and there wasn't any consequence riding on the participants' score of the memory test might limit the extent we could apply this to a real life situation. My explanation of this question regarding ecological validity needs to go further and provide an example. For instance, if students are using Rememberol to

Before I could say that my Rememberol experiment would have high internal validity, I would need to make sure that the pill was the only variable affecting my dependent variable (e.g. effectiveness of studying).

Many students oversimplify their evaluations of studies based on external validity. It is important that you offer well-developed explanations for your evaluations. The "Critical Thinking Extensions" will help you with this.

You can visit our blog at themantic-education.com to find lots of online resources to help your studies, including examples of evaluations in student essays.

study they are likely under a lot of pressure and their scores carry big consequences. Whether or not the stress and anxiety surrounding this situation would alter the effects of Rememberol could be questioned. This evaluation would be made even stronger if I could provide some evidence that suggests stress affects memory.

Here we see the ability to evaluate ecological validity relies on being able to question the extent to which a relationship demonstrated in a study could be applied to a new context, providing an explanation of the relationship between the new context and the characteristics of the study that raise this question. And that's something that's important to note: evaluation can involve asking questions. You don't always need to be making definitive claims like, "*this study lacks ecological validity*." You can phrase it like, "*perhaps we could question the ecological validity of this study because…*" This further shows your ability to think reflectively and in more ways than simply black-and-white.

While ecological validity refers to the environment, mundane realism refers to the actual task participants are being asked to perform. In other words, it refers to the extent to which the procedures in the study reflect what would happen in real life. For example, if I tested Rememberol by getting participants to read pages of an encyclopedia and then take a reading comprehension test, this may not be a good indication of what the effects the drug might have in more realistic situations because people don't read the encyclopedia and then take tests. Perhaps this design would lack mundane realism. Whereas, getting them to read a chapter of a novel they have chosen specifically might be a way to make sure the task was more reflective of everyday situations.

Population validity is another way to discuss generalizability of a study that involves very little additional information learnt and can truly demonstrate your critical thinking. Population validity refers to the extent to which the characteristics of the sample are reflective of a wider population or different population that the results might be abstracted to. For example, historically speaking most studies have been conducted in the United States on white, college-aged students. Can relationships demonstrated in these studies be applied to, say, African tribes or South East Asian cultures? Bear in mind that when you are explaining population validity, you need to provide clear and logical reasons for your conclusions. For instance, if you were to argue that the results from one study could not be applied to another specific group, you need to explain why or at least raise questions.

An explanation of population validity requires knowing an important characteristic of the participants in the sample that might affect the extent to which the results can be generalized to another important group, thus raising questions about the validity of the results. But like explaining ecological validity, a strong demonstration of critical thinking requires clear reasons. For example, if you're taking a sample from "healthy" participants and then trying to explain that to a group of people such as war veterans addicted to drugs, what factors about the latter might affect the generalizability of results from the former?

If one study used all females and showed a relationship between testosterone and aggression, could we apply these findings to males as well? Males naturally have higher levels of testosterone and perhaps this has led to other biological differences that might affect the processing of testosterone in the body. Moreover, if the findings of the study were being applied to explain high testosterone levels in prison populations, the all-female participants also raises the question of population validity as a majority of violent criminals (statistically speaking) are males. Thus, the nature of the sample in the study raises questions about the generalizability of the possible applications.

You will learn about a lot of studies that use modern technology. While they can provide some correlations, the nature of these machines means that mundane realism is often questionable.

Critical thinking is not easy - it takes time and serious effort.

(e)   Correlation vs. Causation

You'll hopefully learn through the course how and why a study demonstrates a causal relationship or a correlational one. This can be another valuable way to demonstrate your critical thinking about the relationships in studies you are explaining.

For example, if I used a natural experiment to test Rememberol's effects of different ethnicities, I could explain why this is a correlational relationship. A weak explanation would be something like, "this study used a natural experiment so it can only determine a correlational relationship." Once again, this doesn't demonstrate any reflective thinking, it simply shows you know the terms natural experiment and correlation.

A strong explanation would need to include *why* it's only correlational and offer alternative explanations for the relationship demonstrated. For example, if my study compared students in China and students in the UK, I could explain other possible explanations for why students in the UK achieved higher scores. I would need plausible reasons for my explanation. For example, British schools might have more tests for students based on reading comprehension, so perhaps these results could be explained by the fact that UK students are better at taking these types of tests than Chinese students. Or, the test would have had to be in two different languages so perhaps one test was easier. An even more abstract idea that would really show critical thinking and knowledge of psychological concepts is the fact that reading in Chinese characters might use different areas of the brain than in English because of the nature of their scripts (Chinese is based on characters, not letters), and so maybe Rememberol works better on one part of the brain than another.

It might seem like trying to take a short-cut by avoiding reliability and internal validity. However, this limited focus is necessary due to the nature of the IB Psychology course and its assessments: you are expected to develop conceptual understanding of such a wide range of relationships. The studies need to be applied first and foremost to develop these understandings. Secondly, many essay questions require you to "discuss" relationships or to determine "to what extent" one variable influences another, and in these cases there's a very good chance you won't need to evaluate the research. Furthermore, in questions where you discuss or contrast ethical considerations, for example, an evaluation of the research methodology in terms of the conclusions they drew between variables becomes rather redundant.

But this doesn't mean that aiming to develop evaluative skills in psychology isn't important. Far from it! Being able to critically assess information you are given and how you use it is an absolutely vital life skill and another underlying goal of this course.

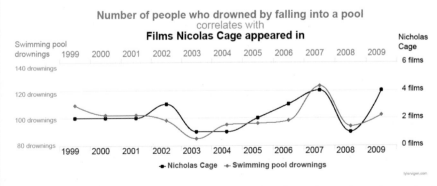

A favourite saying of psychologists and statisticians is "correlation does not equal causation." This is shown quite effectively in the graph above. (Image used with permission from Tyler Vigen @ tylervigen.com).

You absolutely *must* be working conscientiously to develop your thinking skills so by at least the second or third unit of the course you are able to know a study or theory, explain it and then question it! If you can't learn to question the validity of information you receive, you run the risk of going through life an open sponge ready to be influenced by any piece of manipulative media that floats your way.

More terms and concepts that are useful to know when evaluating studies are explained in the "Critical Thinking Extensions" included in each section of the text. The exam preparation materials also include more examples of evaluating studies and theories in exam answers. For most students in their first few weeks or months of studying IB Psychology, it might be difficult to evaluate studies because it takes time to become fluent in reading, analyzing and understanding them first. As the course progresses and you become more fluent in understanding studies you should be working more and more on developing your critical and abstract thinking skills.

Many students make the mistake of blindly memorizing evaluations of studies and then "dumping" them in their answers. However, through the thematic course structure you are going to learn about studies and the relationships they demonstrate in a way that will enable you to apply them to *multiple* possible questions to explain multiple possible relationships. The relationship you are applying the study to will affect *how* you evaluate the study. Moreover, the course and exams have been designed so that it makes it extremely difficult, nearly impossible, to memorize "critical thinking" and do well. There are simply too many possible exam questions that might be asked.

To summarize, the following questions can be used as guides when evaluating studies. To what extent…

- …can the results be generalized from the study to other contexts based on methodology?
- …are there alternative explanations for the results and/or conclusions in the study?
- …is there data from other sources that support or contradict the findings in the study?

(f) Evaluating Theories

It is just as important that you can critically assess theories as you can psychological studies. This is why it can be useful to begin your study of a theory by reminding yourself that it is a theory and it's up to you to determine to what extent you think the theory is valid.

Some of the most important evidence in assessing psychological theories comes from empirical studies. Therefore, when evaluating the validity of a theory (*after* you've understood what the theory is describing and explaining) you should determine to what extent the theory can be supported by evidence that comes from credible studies.

Another way to critique a theory is to determine the extent to which it can be applied to explain psychological phenomena. For instance, social identity theory can be used to explain a range of phenomena, such as stereotyping, conformity, prejudice and discrimination. Being able to apply theories to a range of behaviours is an important cognitive skill to develop and can be very useful when writing essay answers. If you are asked about a particular behaviour, for instance conformity or stereotyping, you could apply the social cognitive and/or social identity theory to these questions. The ability to use studies and theories in multiple different explanations is what is going to help you reduce the amount of content you need to memorise, which gives you more time to develop understanding and deeper critical thinking skills.

The first step in evaluating a theory is usually finding at least one study that can demonstrate the same relationship that the theory posits. You can then go further by evaluating the supporting evidence or by finding contradictory evidence.

Similarly, one way of critiquing a theory is through explaining how a study contradicts that theory. Perhaps you can find a study that actually gives evidence that goes against the major claims of the theory. For instance, some theories were developed before the invention of brain imaging technology so new information we can learn

Many theories of cognitive processes were devised before the invention of technology like the MRI and fMRI. These new methods can offer supporting and contradictory evidence for psychological theories.

about the brain can actually be used to critique some of these theories that were developed without the help of this technology. For example, the multi-store model of memory was developed in the 1960s. Results from studies using fMRI and other brain scanning technology may be used to contradict or support the memory processes that this study attempts to model.

Another way of critiquing the theory is to determine the extent to which the psychological phenomenon being explained by theory could be explained using an alternative explanation. A good way to begin thinking about this is to identify which approach is at the core of the theory (i.e. biological, cognitive or sociocultural). For instance, social identity theory ignores biological aspects of group behaviour, but while it attempts to describe and explain how belonging to a group can influence behaviour, you could provide alternative explanations for the behaviour in group situations based on biological factors.

One final way of evaluating a theory is to determine the extent to which it accurately describes and/or explains the phenomena in question. For example, the multi-store model of memory attempts to describe the process of memory formation and explain how attentional processes affect this formation. But does this apply to *all* types of memory? Perhaps there are some memories, such as fear-conditioned memories, that can't be explained using this model.

To summarise, the following guiding questions can help you think critically about theories. To what extent…

- …is the theory supported and/or contradicted by studies?
- …can the theory be applied to explain phenomena?
- …are there alternative explanations for the phenomena that the theory attempts to explain?

Charles Darwin's Theory of Evolution has considerable evidence to support it. You will learn about lots of psychological theories and you will need to consider evidence that supports and/or challenges these theories.

One aim of this textbook is to get you to develop your thinking skills to a point where you can come up with insightful, well-developed and clearly explained critical thinking points in your exams, including some that you've never thought of *before*. This is the same goal shared by the IB examiners: it's *not* hoped that you will pre-prepare your critical thinking points before exam day. This is why there are so many possible exam questions: it's hoped that you will be able to demonstrate novel critical thinking in the exam situation. If you were able to pre-prepare all your arguments, then the exams wouldn't be an accurate assessment of your critical thinking ability because there'd be no way for examiners to discern if the thoughts were your own, or if they were simply memorizations of someone else's thoughts. The exams are designed so an accurate assessment can be made as to the extent to which you have demonstrated an ability to demonstrate thinking skills that you are likely to be able to use *beyond* the IB programme.

This book follows Themantic Education's philosophy - education is about preparing you for success in life, not just about success in exams.

There is more information on how to demonstrate "critical thinking" in the Exam Preparation chapter. The strongest message I want you to take away from this is that learning how to *think* is absolutely vital in this course if you're hoping to do well.

1.5 IB Psychology Overview
What are the requirements of the IB Psychology course?

(a) Assessments

In IB Psychology, HL students have four major assessments whereas SL students have three.

Assessment	Time	Weighting	
		SL	HL
Internal Assessment (IA)	20 hrs	25%	20%
Paper 1	2 hrs	50%	40%
Paper 2	1 hr (SL) 2 hrs (HL)	25%	20%
Paper 3 (HL)	1 hr	-	20%

There is a lot more detail about these assessments in other relevant chapters. A useful strategy to make sure you're well-prepared for your exams is to regularly re-read the reference materials included in the Introduction and Exam Preparation chapters so you can be making sure that you are understanding how and why what you're learning is relevant for the exams.

Do note that the structure of the course is such that you don't need to revise *everything* for the exams. You will have a lot of choice as to what you want to revise. For example, by the end of the course you will have multiple ways to discuss evolution and behaviour. You can wait until all units have finished to decide which evolutionary explanation of behaviour you want to focus on. This means that throughout the course you can worry less about what you're going to write about in exams, and simply enjoy the process of studying psychology - leave most of your exam preparation for nearer the end of the course. The benefit of the thematic approach is that you should have more revision time to do this because overlaps can be found between the core and options.

(b) The "Core": Three Approaches to Psychology

The IB Psychology course identifies three ways of approaching the study of psychology. These are also known as the "core". The three approaches are:

- The Biological Approach
- The Cognitive Approach
- The Sociocultural Approach

The Biological Approach

This approach is designed to get you to understand how physiological factors can affect a range of mental processes and behaviours. Biological factors, including hormones, genetics, and brain function, have all been shown to affect our behaviour. Moreover, the study of neuroplasticity shows how in fact our behaviour can affect our brain, so the relationship can work in the opposite direction, too.

The Cognitive Approach

Not surprisingly, this approach focuses on developing an understanding of the cognitive processing side of psychology. You'll learn about theories of memory and how a range of factors can influence our cognition.

The Sociocultural Approach

The primary focus of the topics within this approach are designed to get you to understand how our thinking and behavior can be influenced by social and cultural factors.

You can see from the following table that many of the topics from the three approaches are covered in at least two different units. This takes much of the pressure off preparation for the exams because what you will learn in one unit might not be used in the exams. For example, if you didn't quite understand the localization of brain function topic when studying criminology, you get another chance when studying PTSD.

As the goal is to develop conceptual understandings of these areas of study and their relevant topics, you'll hopefully see why there's no reason we can't study them in any order we like!

This text combines all three approaches in understanding specific behaviours. This is designed to give you a more holistic understanding of the complex interaction of variables involved in human behaviour.

A good way to revise at the end of the course is to sort out all the studies into the diffferent approaches. You will find that some studies form part of two or even all three approaches.

Approach	Topic	Content	Covered In...
Biological	The Brain and Behaviour	Technology in research	• Criminology • Social Influence • PTSD
		Localization of brain function	• Criminology • Social Influence • PTSD
		Neuroplasticity	• Criminology • PTSD
		Neurotransmission	• Criminology • PTSD
	Hormones and Behaviour	Hormones	• Criminology • Love and Marriage
		Pheromones	• Love and Marriage
	Genetics and Behaviour	Genetics	• Criminology • PTSD
		Genetic Similarities	• Criminology • PTSD
		Evolution	• Criminology • Love and Marriage
Cognitive	Cognitive Processing	Models of memory	• PTSD
		Schema theory	• Social Influence
		Thinking and decision making	• Criminology
	Reliability of Cognitive Processing	Reconstructive memory	• Social Influence
		Cognitive bias	• PTSD • Social Influence
	Emotion and Cognition	The influence of emotion on other cognitive processes	• Criminology • PTSD
Sociocultural	The Individual and the Group	Social identity theory	• Social Influence
		Social cognitive theory	• Criminology
		Stereotypes	• Social Influence
	Cultural Origins of Behaviour and Cognition	Culture	• Criminology • Love and Marriage • Social Influence • PTSD
		Cultural dimension	• Social Influence • Love and Marriage
	Cultural Influences on Individual Attitudes, Identity and Behaviours	Enculturation	• Social Influence
		Acculturation	• Social Influence
Ethical Considerations and Research Methods	For all topics and areas of study in the three approaches you need to be aware of how and why research methodology (e.g. natural experiment, case study, etc.) and ethical considerations (e.g. informed consent, anonymity) are related to those particular areas of study.		

(c)   *Conceptual Understandings*

Throughout this chapter I've been using a term that you might not yet understand: conceptual understanding. A concept is an abstract idea, something that doesn't exist in the concrete. A conceptual understanding, therefore, is an understanding of an abstract idea and in psychology this often refers to relationships. The reason why it's valuable to develop this skill is that because the ideas are abstract, they have the power to be applied in many ways to the different areas. This increases the possibility of *actually* using what you learn in school.

For example, *causation* is an abstract idea. If you can understand the idea of causation in psychology, it's hoped that you could abstract this understanding and think about it in relation to your other subjects (e.g. causes of war in History). This is the goal of TOK: to get you making connections between ideas across subjects so you can develop your understanding of abstract ideas.

Developing these understandings of abstract concepts begins with concrete learning. So acquiring an understanding of key *psychological* concepts is one major goal of this course. From the earlier table that outlines the topic you know generally what it is you need to know about. But you need to go further than just knowing about these topics and areas of study.

In psychology, you need to develop knowledge and understanding of significant relationships between the following:

- Behaviours
- Cognitive processes
- Variables
- Research methods
- Ethical considerations

The examination questions are designed to assess your conceptual understanding of these significant relationships. The topics provide you with an indication of what you need to understand. The following table will also help guide your learning. The guiding questions for each section in the text are not necessarily the overarching conceptual understanding that you need to develop by the *end* of the course, but they do help provide you with an understanding that helps lead you towards developing that bigger understanding.

Developing an understanding requires you to figure out how things are significantly related in response to a question or problem. The more abstract these relationships become, the broader the concept that you're understanding becomes.

For example, you will learn about how levels of testosterone might increase aggression. Then, when you compare this concept with other hormones and their effect on behaviour, like the role of cortisol on memory, you can develop an understanding that "levels of hormones can influence behaviour". Then, when you connect this with other studies investigating biological variables, you will develop an understanding that "biological factors can influence our behaviour", and voila! You've developed a key conceptual understanding of the biological approach to studying psychology.

All of your IB courses encourage the development of conceptual understanding. This means doing more than just focusing on memorizing as much information as possible.

Psychology is the study of relationships. If you simply work hard to understand the relationships you're introduced to throughout this course, you will be developing conceptual understanding.

(d) Concepts in the Core

The following tables provide insights into the conceptual understandings you will develop by the end of this course. These are what the examination questions in Paper One are based on and what you need to demonstrate. In fact, that's one big thing examiners are looking for as they read your answers: they look for evidence that shows you have grasped and comprehend an important concept in this course. The exam preparation information will show you exactly how to demonstrate your understanding.

Underlying all of these is an understanding of how research methods and ethics relate to these approaches, areas of study, and topics. The ability to reflect upon these understandings and the evidence upon which they're based is another underlying goal for the course.

Conceptual understanding in IB Psychology is about understanding the interactions between variables, cognitive processes and behaviours. This text is designed to help you move from concrete knowledge to comprehending increasingly abstract ideas about these complex interactions.

Conceptual Understandings in the Biological Approach						
Biological factors can influence, and are influenced by, our mental processes and behaviour.						
Functioning of the brain can influence our behaviour and vice-versa.			Levels of hormones can influence our behaviour, and vice-versa.		Genetics can influence our behaviour and vice-versa.	
Levels of neurotrans-mitters can influence behaviour	Different parts of the brain have different functions	When studying the brain, particular techniques are used.	Levels of hormones can influence behaviour	Pheromone excretion may influence behaviour	Genetics can influence our biology, which influences our behaviour	Evolutionary processes can influence our behaviour
e.g. decreases in serotonin may influence aggression	e.g. the hippocampus plays a role in memory formation	e.g. MRIs enable the researcher to measure changes in brain structure	e.g. increases in testosterone may lead to aggressive reactions	e.g. phero-mones may give off signals of strength and health, influencing attraction.	e.g. the presence of a variation in the MAOA gene may affect violence.	e.g. the innate desire to have healthy babies may influence whom we're attracted to

Conceptual Understandings in the Cognitive Approach

Cognition influences, and can be influenced by, a number of processes and factors.

Cognitive processes can influence one-another, as well as be influenced by external factors.			Many factors may influence the reliability of our cognitive processes		Emotion can influence our cognitive processes
MSM and WMM provide explanations for how internal processes affect memory.	Schema theory describes how our mind organizes information. This can influence our behaviour and other cognitive processes.	Thinking and decision making can influence our behaviour.	Our memory may not always be reliable, and could be affected by various processes and factors.	Cognitive biases may occur in our thinking and decision making due to a range of factors.	Emotion can influence our memory, thinking and decision making.
e.g. the MSM explains how attention processes influence the formation of short term and long term memory formation.	e.g. stereotypes may be a result of forming a schema of a particular group of people.	e.g. inability to use System two processing may lead to rash decisions and impulsive actions.	e.g. schema processing may influence how well we remember details of certain people or events.	e.g. confirmation bias may occur to influence our self-esteem and increase positive distinctiveness between groups.	e.g. fear conditioning is a type of learning and is influenced by feelings of emotion and the biological factors associated with fear.

Conceptual Understandings in the Sociocultural Approach

Social and cultural factors can influence, and are influenced by, our cognition and behaviour.

Individuals can influence, and are influenced by, the group.			Culture can affect our mental processes and behaviour.	Cultural influences can affect identity, attitudes and behaviour.
Belonging to a group can influence our thinking and behaviour (SIT).	Our environment, behaviour and individual characteristics all influence one another (SCT).	Our way of thinking about others (stereotypes) can be influenced by social, biological and cognitive factors.	Cultural values can influence our cognition and behaviour.	People may change their ways of thinking and/or their behaviour based on their cultural environment (i.e. being acculturated or enculturated).
e.g. when we belong to a group we may look negatively towards out-groups, which can explain negative stereotypes.	e.g. we can learn attitudes and values by observing others, which can affect our behaviour and our biology (e.g. culture of honour).	e.g. stereotypes may form as a result of schema processes and/or the influence of group belonging.	e.g. our cultural values regarding thinking about our family before ourselves may influence what we look for in a potential mate.	e.g. sudanese refugees who arrived in the US without parents were able to combine aspects of their home culture and positive aspects of the US culture.

(e)   HL Extensions

For each of the approaches to understanding psychology, HL students have been allocated additional material to study. However, these are general themes that are covered in the core topics anyway, so new studies and information don't always need to be learned. The HL Extension Topics identifies exactly what these themes are and will help HL students focus on developing their understanding of the nature and importance of these themes. For example, the theme for the biological approach is "the role of animal research in understanding human behaviour." Through Criminology there are numerous animal studies included and so HL students will already know about how and why these studies were used, so the HL extension chapter just allows HL students some time to focus on these themes specifically and to solidify conceptual understandings. But new studies and ideas will be introduced to further your understanding of psychology. The concepts in these extensions are often more challenging than in the core in order to challenge HL students.

So the three themes are:

- Biological Approach: "the role of animal research in understanding human behaviour"
- Cognitive Approach: "cognitive processing in the digital world"
- Sociocultural Approach: "the influence of globalization on individual attitudes, identities and behaviour."

These may seem daunting right now, but they are not as confusing as they sound.

Two possible ways these HL extension topics may be addressed are:
a)   As a separate unit near the end of the course
b)   As the course progresses

Option (a) is recommended because it may prove easier to identify and understand these themes from topics and studies after they've been covered in the context of other units. However, your school's scheduling might mean that this is not always possible and so they can be taught as the course progresses. For instance, you could learn about animal research alongside criminology as there are many animal studies in this unit, and cognitive processing alongside social influence as the use of technology is often influenced by social factors. Your teacher will decide how you will approach these HL extension topics.

There are pros and cons to either approach. This book has tried to be structured in a way so either approach would be equally suited. The Biological Approach extensions are in line with Criminology, Sociocultural with Social Influence and Cognitive with PTSD. You can see an overview of the topics in the HL Extension chapter.

HL students have been given 30 hours to cover extensions to the core. However, this entire time may not be necessary and could be spent in other ways.

(f) The "Options"

There are four options topics available in IB Psychology. SL students are recommended to study one option and HL students need to study two.

Material that supports the other options will be published separately.

The two options topics that are the core focus in this thematic course are Abnormal Psychology and Human Relationships. These options topics are designed to teach you how biological, cognitive, social and cultural factors can all be influential in human behaviour. The PTSD unit is focused on addressing the topics in Abnormal Psychology, while the key concepts from the Human Relationships topic are addressed primarily in Social Influence and Love and Marriage.

When studying Human Relationships you will learn about how multiple factors may affect different types of interpersonal and inter-group relationships. For instance, you will learn about biological, cognitive and sociocultural factors that may influence attraction, marriage, conflict and altruism (helping others).

The theory behind the structure of the IB Psychology course is that you should start by developing an understanding of the individual approaches in the core, and this will prepare you for understanding the options topics. However, in reality this doesn't really work because it limits the time you have to develop an understanding that is comprehensive enough to do well in all aspects of both exam Papers One and Two.

Be sure to subscribe to our free blog for revision resources. You can also use our text *IB Psychology: A Revision Guide* for exam preparation.

Because you're studying psychology thematically, which means each chapter includes a combination of the three approaches and aspects of the options, your exam revision is very important. You will find that you will have a lot of choice as to what you write about in the exams. The exams are structured according to the approaches and the options, so The Exam Preparation materials (and the accompanying workbook) will help you identify what aspects of the course you'll be able to apply to each possible exam question.

Another reason why you don't need to study the options and core separately is because the ultimate goal is to develop the necessary conceptual understandings and these can be developed in a number of ways. For example, learning about biological origins and treatments of PTSD symptoms contributes to your understanding of how biological factors can influence behaviour.

By studying psychology through the narrow lens of individual approaches, you may only get a limited understanding of the complex interactions of variables involved in human behaviour and mental processes. This is why it makes sense to combine the options with the core.

The following table provides you with an overview of the Abnormal and Human Relationships topics.

Option	Topic	Content	Covered In...
Psychology of Human Relationships	Personal Relationships	Formation of personal relationships	Love and Marriage
		Role of communication	Love and Marriage
		Explanations for why relationships change or end	Love and Marriage
	Group Dynamics	Co-operation and competition	Social Influence Criminology
		Prejudice and discrimination	Social Influence
		Origins of conflict and conflict resolution	Social Influence Criminology
	Social Responsibility	Bystanderism	Social Influence
		Prosocial behaviour	Social Influence
		Promoting prosocial behaviour	Social Influence
Abnormal Psychology *While the PTSD unit covers this option, much of the concepts build upon learning from previous units (e.g. the role of the amgydala in the stress response, the role of the PFC in cognition and neuroplasticity).*	Factors Influencing Diagnosis	Normality versus abnormality	PTSD
		Classification systems	PTSD
		The role of clinical biases in diagnosis	PTSD
		Validity and reliability of diagnosis	PTSD
	Etiology of Abnormal Psychology	Explanations for disorders	PTSD
		Prevalence rates and disorders	PTSD
	Treatment of Disorders	Biological treatments	PTSD
		Psychological treatments	PTSD
		The role of culture in treatment	PTSD
		Assessing the effectiveness of treatment(s)	PTSD

As with the core, the themes of understanding approaches to research and ethical considerations are important to understand for each of the topics in the options.
In addition, understanding the extent to which these topics relate to biology, cognition and socio-cultural factors is also important.

You may be asked an essay on any one of these topics, so straight away you can see that it would be nearly impossible to develop an understanding that is detailed enough to write an essay about each of these in the time the IB allows (20 hours) if you were to try to study this course topic by topic. For abnormal psychology, there are 8 topics in 20 hours, which would leave you with just over two hours to develop knowledge of, and conceptual understandings regarding:

- The terminology and key concepts
- The relevant research (studies and/or theories)
- An evaluation of the research methods
- Relevant ethical considerations
- Relationships with biological, cognitive and sociocultural approaches

This is another deliberate ploy by the designers of the IB course to make it almost impossible to succeed by memorization alone, which aids major goals of the course: to develop understanding and critical thinking skills that require more than memorization of copious amounts of facts and details. In order to be well-prepared for the exams you simply must develop an in-depth understanding of key concepts in psychology.

(g)   Concepts in the Options

As with the core, the options topics and their corresponding exam (Paper Two) require you to develop and convey conceptual understandings of a range of topics. This is made a little easier by the fact that the exam will probably have one question from each of the areas of study, so you can choose an area of study that you want to excel at and focus your revision and exam preparation on that particular area of study.

Conceptual Understandings in Human Relationships

Human relationships are influenced by biological, cognitive and sociocultural factors.

Personal relationships can be influenced by a range of factors.			Group dynamics influence, and can be influenced by, a range of factors.			An individual's feelings of social responsibility may be influenced by a range of factors.		
The formation of personal relationships can be influenced by a range of factors.	Communication can influence personal relationships.	Relationships may change or end based on a number of factors.	Co-operation and competition influence, and are influenced by, many factors.	Prejudice and discrimination may be affected by, and affect, many factors.	Conflict may be the result of a number of factors, and strategies can be used to resolve conflict.	Bystanderism may be influenced by a range of factors.	Prosocial behaviour may be influenced by a range of factors.	Strategies can be used to promote prosocial behaviour.
e.g. cultural values may affect the type of person we want to marry.	e.g. Constant negative communication (e.g. criticism) can affect relationships, even at a biological level.	e.g. Marriage satisfaction is affected by the presence of negative communication styles.	e.g. Competition between groups for resources can increase conflict.	e.g. the belonging to a group and desire to increase self-esteem may increase feelings of prejudice and acts of discrimination.	e.g. competition for resources can cause conflict but working together can resolve it.	e.g. The presence of others and their actions may affect levels of bystanderism.	e.g. Cultural values may affect how inclined someone might be to help someone else.	e.g. Jigsaw activities in classroom can increase the likelihood kids will help one another.

Conceptual Understandings in Abnormal Psychology

The diagnosis and treatment of psychological disorders requires consideration of multiple variables

Diagnosis of disorders can be influenced by a range of factors.				There are multiple explanations for the origins of disorders, their symptoms and their prevalence.		Treatment of disorders needs to consider multiple factors and approaches.			
Disorders are difficult to define.	Classification systems help define disorders, but there are issues.	Clinical bias can influence diagnosis.	Validity and reliability of diagnosis can vary.	There are multiple possible explanations for psychological disorders.	Symptoms and prevalence rates can vary across cultures and genders.	Disorders can be treated biologically.	Disorders can be treated psychologically.	Culture influences treatment of disorders.	Treatments can vary in their effectiveness.
e.g. It's not always clear what a maladaptive behaviour is.	e.g. The DSM may be biased towards Western cultures.	e.g. confirmation bias may influence validity of diagnosis.	e.g. Distinguishing what is normal shock and what is PTSD may be difficult, affecting diagnosis.	e.g. PTSD may be a result of brain dysfunction and/or sociocultural environmental factors.	e.g. Veterans from different ethnic groups may experience different rates of PTSD for a number of reasons.	e.g. Drug therapy and medication could be used to treat symptoms of PTSD.	e.g. Cognitive-behaviour therapy could help treat PTSD	e.g. A veteran's cultural background may influence treatment.	e.g. Drug therapy may only target symptoms, whereas psychological therapy could target underlying neurological origins.

(h) Research Methodology

There are two underlying themes that thread throughout the approaches and the options: research methods and ethical considerations. These are important to understand and are addressed fully in later chapters.

If research is how we know what we know in psychology, critically assessing the nature and quality of this research is really important. There are two distinct types of research methodology in psychology:

I.   Quantitative
II.   Qualitative

Quantitative research is research that gathers numerical data. That is to say, it deals with numbers and figures. The most common of this type of research is experimental research, which deals in independent and dependent variables. You will learn about laboratory, natural and field experiments in the chapter on quantitative methods. It will be easier to understand these methods after you have had decent exposure to a range of studies, which is why it's recommend (if possible) to learn about these later in the course after you have a firm knowledge base on which to build.

The following are the topics involved in studying *quantitative* research:

Quantitative Research		
Quantitative Research Designs	Experiments	
	Field Experiments	
	Quasi Experiments	
	Natural Experiment	
	Correlational Research	
Elements of Quantitative Methods	Research Design	Matched pairs
		Independent samples
		Repeated measures
	Hypotheses	Null
		Experimental
	Independent and Dependent Variables	
	Sampling Techniques	Random
		Convenience/opportunity
		Volunteer/self-selected
	Controls	
	Ethical Considerations	
Analyzing Data	Data Presentation	
	Statistics	Descriptive
		Inferential
Evaluating Research	Reliability	Test-retest reliability
	External Validity	Ecological validity
		Population validity
	Internal Validity	Demand characteristics
		Inter-rater reliability
Drawing Conclusions	Correlation and Causation	
	Replication	
	Generalization	
	Triangulation	Researcher triangulation
		Methodological triangulation
		Data triangulation

Because humans are so complex, many modern psychologists believe that it's not always beneficial to reduce our behaviour and cognition down to numbers, so they take a qualitative approach. This approach involves gathering qualitative data, which means words and descriptions, *not* numbers.

The following are topics involved in studying *qualitative* research:

Qualitative Research		
Qualitative Research Designs	Case Studies	
	Observations	Covert and Overt
		Participant and non-participant
	Interviews	Unstructured
		Semi-structured
		Focus group
Elements of Qualitative Methods	Sampling Techniques	Purposive
		Snowball
	Ethical Considerations	
Analyzing Data	Inductive content analysis (thematic analysis)	
Evaluating Research	Credibility	
Drawing Conclusions	Transferability	
	Triangulation	Researcher triangulation
		Methodological triangulation
		Data triangulation

Both SL and HL students will learn about experimental methodology because it's essential for completion of the internal assessment. Understanding methodology may also be required in Paper One and/or Two.

Only HL students will study both qualitative *and* quantitative methodology in-depth, as either of these approaches to studying psychology may be the basis of Paper 3, which is the HL only exam.

You will see that there are a lot of new terms for you to remember. Trying to learn these terms without context (i.e. without developing detailed knowledge of a range of studies first) is difficult, which is why it's recommended to approach the understanding of these new terms and concepts in the following ways:

(a)   Read the Critical Thinking Extensions in each section to gradually acquire an understanding of these terms and concepts.

(b)   Read the additional explanations and links included at the end of each topic to help build your understanding of the connections between research methods, ethics and areas of study.

(c)   Study these terms, concepts and methods *after* first completing one or more units of study (e.g. Criminology, Social Influence, etc.) so you have a solid foundation of research knowledge to make connections with.

(i)   Ethical Considerations

Ethics are closely related to morals and the difference between ethics and morals is debatable and highly subjective, so note that the explanation of ethics here is *my* understanding of ethics and this is open to being challenged.

Morals typically refer to an inherent belief about what is right and wrong. People talk about their "moral compass" which refers to their ability to be directed by their understanding of the right and wrong ways to think and act. You may discuss morality in your TOK classes.

Ethics are closely related to morals in that they are related to appropriate and inappropriate ways of behaving. Where ethics often differ, however, is that they are connected with a particular group, field or situation. Many professions have particular ethical standards and codes that they are required to follow. For instance, if a doctor went on a date with her patient many people wouldn't consider this "immoral", but they might consider this "unethical."

Let's look at the words of someone who is an expert in the field of ethics, the Dalai Lama. He believes that "establishing binding ethical principles is possible when we take as our starting point the observation that we all desire happiness and not to suffer." (Ancient Wisdom, Modern World). It is this idea of preventing physical suffering, or harm, or any form of psychological stress or discomfort that lies at the heart of ethics in psychological research. Many students make the mistake of thinking that understanding ethical considerations in psychology involves making judgements about if research is ethical or not. You are not required, nor encouraged, to make such black-and-white judgments. You need to learn the guidelines that are in place and how they relate to particular studies and areas of study.

But beyond that it is hoped you will develop a deeper understanding of how ethical considerations are simply that: to be considered. What is ethical and what is not is not always black and white. Moreover, sometimes harm or suffering is required in research to get valid results. Thus, considering the balance between ethics and research is a difficult one, and this is a relationship that you should be contemplating deeply throughout the course.

Ethical guidelines have been put in place to guide psychologists in their design of studies using animals and humans. Before conducting research, psychologists often need to present their research proposal to an ethics review committee who will approve or decline their research based on ethical grounds. They make judgments, but you don't need to.

There are numerous ethical guidelines that are different depending on the psychological association the researchers (i.e. psychologists) are registered with. Common ethical guidelines for researching using humans are:

- Informed Consent
    This involves having participants agree to participate (consent) in the study beforehand. They need to be provided some information regarding the nature of the study (they're informed). They can provide consent through checking an online form, signing a paper, verbal agreement, etc. Retrospective consent is a particular ethical consideration that replaces informed consent in covert observations: it is when consent to analyze data and publish findings is gathered after the study.
- Considerations regarding deception
    To deceive means to lead someone to believe something that's not true.

This can cause psychological damage, but is sometimes necessary in psychological research, so researchers may need to carefully consider issues involved in deception, such as justification of the deception and the extent to which it will cause harm.

- Justification

    Sometimes inducing harm, stress or other undesirable effects is essential in research studies. Where this is the case, there must be appropriate justification for such measures, as well as measures taken after the study to ensure that there are no long-term negative effects as a result of the research.

- The right to withdraw

    Participants are given the right to stop participating in the study at any time.

- Debriefing

    Providing participants with all the details of the study after it has finished, including the aims and results and possibly even the significance of the findings.

- Anonymity

    To be anonymous means not having your name known. In studies the names of participants are not revealed (i.e. participants are anonymous) to protect their privacy and to avoid embarrassment or other potential issues.

- Approval from an ethics review board

    Modern psychological research is subjected to review by a group of members of the relevant psychological organisation (e.g. American Psychological Association for studies in America, or the Chinese Psychological Society in China). This review board will consider the proposed research and determine if it meets ethical standards and can be approved.

You will learn about many studies that involve the use of animals. Naturally, the ethical considerations surrounding the use of animals are slightly different. For instance, it's impossible to get informed consent from a rat and a debriefing of the results of an autopsy on a rabbit would be a rather one-sided (and pointless) discussion.

HL students may be asked about the ethics of animal research as part of their extension material for the biological approach. Here are some common ethical considerations regarding animal research:

- Animal welfare

    Animal welfare should be a primary concern for researchers who are using animals in their studies.

    Animal welfare includes avoiding any unnecessary harm or suffering. If it is expected that animals may experience long-term suffering as a result of an experiment, euthanization needs to be considered.

- Justification

    Where there is harm, stress or suffering inflicted upon an animal, just as with human research there should be sufficient justification for this to occur. For example, if a study is being carried out that involves stress and physical injury to animals just to replicate findings that have been replicated many times, is this sufficient justification?

Another interesting ethical consideration surrounding animal research is that regarding the cognitive capabilities of animals and whether or not that affects their treatment. For example, should the same set of rules be applied to sea snails as to chimpanzees? Should all animals have the same set of considerations, or does the ability for some animals to experience greater levels of consciousness affect how we should treat them? This is perhaps beyond the scope of our studies, but it's an interesting consideration nonetheless.

Conclusion

"Why am I learning this?"

This is the most powerful question you can be asking yourself as you are studying IB Psychology. All the information, materials and resources provided in this book are designed to have an impact on your learning that is going to be meaningful in some way. The more you can figure out for yourself the relevance, significance and importance of what you're learning, the deeper your understanding of psychology will become.

As you begin this course, much of this information may not make too much sense as you have not had enough experience with the course. However, as you practice writing exam-style questions and you become more familiar with the study of Psychology, it would be wise to regularly refer back to the information provided in this introductory chapter.

It's important to try to find a nice balance between learning in an authentic way and learning in preparation for assessments. It is hoped that the concepts and material included in this text will provide you with an interesting variety of topics and ideas so that you will naturally enjoy the study of Psychology and get a little lost in the subject. It's also a reality that students, teachers, and parents are very aware of examination and IB assessment requirements, as these are important for the next steps in your life. Thus, your approach to this course will hopefully aim to strike a balance between learning because it's interesting as well as being well-prepared to exceed your potential.

The text has been carefully designed so everything you would need to know in order to succeed in the exams has been included. However, if you are curious and/or want to seek out more information, especially about the studies that have been explained and referenced, you are encouraged to do so.

It's important to remember that this text is flexible and is not prescriptive by any means. I have included information in a sequence that makes sense to me, but your teacher may decide that they have an even better way of teaching the course. Similarly, your teacher might have better and more relevant topics to study than those that I have included. As always, this text is a "student's guide" and not a "student's bible."

Remember that school isn't just about preparing you to be successful in tests and exams; it's about preparing you to be successful in *life*.

Chapter 2
Criminology

Introduction

In the middle of the night on August 1st, 1966, 26-year-old Charles Whitman sat down at his typewriter in his house and began typing a letter.

It begins:

"…I don't really understand myself these days. I am supposed to be an average reasonable and intelligent young man. However, lately (I don't recall when it started) I have been a victim of very unusual and irrational thoughts." Later that night, Whitman drove to his mother's house and killed her. Before leaving, he wrote a note and left it next to her on the bed:

"TO WHOM IT MAY CONCERN,

I've just taken my mother's life. I am very upset over having done it. However I feel that if there is a heaven she is definitely there now…"

Later that night Whitman murdered his young wife, Kathy, while she lay sleeping in bed. He stabbed her numerous times in the chest. Before he did this he wrote another letter…"…It was after much thought that I decided to kill my wife, Kathy, tonight after I pick her up from work at the telephone company. I love her dearly, and she has been as fine a wife to me as any man could ever hope to have. I cannot rationally pinpoint any specific reason for doing this." (Austin History Centre)

Later that day Whitman drove to the University of Texas at Austin campus, where he was a student. He had packed a huge case filled with guns, ammunition, food, water and enough supplies to last for a few days. He climbed to the top of the observation tower that looks out over the campus and the city. Whitman killed the receptionist with the butt of a rifle. He then set up his sniper rifle on the tower and began taking aim at innocent people as they walked around the campus.

In two hours of what must have been horrific terror for the people of Austin, Whitman killed 14 people, and injured over 30 others.

What are your thoughts when you hear the story of Charles Whitman?

Whitman's case was and still is a mystery, like many murderers and

Charles Whitman. (Image from wikimedia commons)

serial killers who seem to kill without reason. But your job as a psychologist isn't necessarily to judge people's behaviour, it's to investigate the research in order to understand it. In this chapter you are going to be introduced to the fascinating subject of psychology by looking at criminal behaviour.

In understanding how and why people behave and think the way they do, we have to consider multiple factors – including biological, environmental, cultural and social influences. By the end of this chapter, you're going to be challenged to answer this question: How might a variation of the MAOA gene increase an individual's probability of being violent?

If you can keep up with the guiding questions and you understand the significant relationships explained in each section, by the time you reach the topic of genetics you will hopefully be able to answer this really difficult question. In doing so you'll realise that understanding human behaviour is rarely simple.

2.1 The Brain and Behaviour
How might brain damage affect our behaviour?

(a) The Frontal Lobe

In this first introduction to understanding violent crime, we're going to focus on the most important organ in our bodies – the brain. As you'll remember from the introduction, it's always important that you analyze the evidence when making conclusions about behaviour. Remember that understanding human behaviour and mental processes is about understanding relationships, and research (studies and theories) can demonstrate those relationships.

Numerous studies have shown that there are correlations found between brain function and violent behaviour. Moreover, there are specific parts of the brain that appear to be different in some violent criminals than in non-violent, ordinary people. In order to fully understand these concepts, it's important to have a general understanding of some of the functions of important parts of the brain first.

When discussing the brain in psychology, researchers refer to specific areas of the brain. Different areas of the brain perform different functions, a concept known as localization of brain function.

The brain is generally divided into different lobes, as shown in the image. To begin with, we're going to begin our focus on what I think is one of the most interesting parts of the brain – the frontal lobe.

One important function of the frontal lobe is to regulate our impulsive behaviour and decision making. When the frontal lobe is functioning normally it kind of acts like a "break" on our impulsive behaviour. So when you get really angry at your teacher/parent/friend and you want to yell and scream at them but don't because you know that it might get you in trouble - you have your frontal lobe to thank. Or if you're walking down the street and you see an attractive person and you think, "Wow! They're gorgeous!" and you keep that thought to yourself

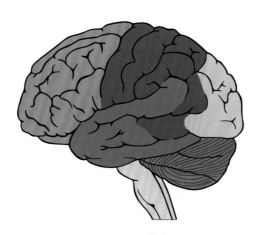

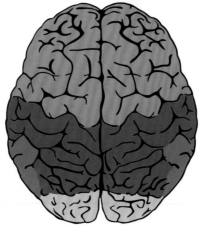

Our brain is made up of different lobes. For now we are going to focus on the frontal lobe (in red) and later in this chapter you will learn about the temporal lobe (in green).

Localization of Brain Function: This describes the concept of different parts of the brain having different functions.

– once again, you have your trusted frontal lobe to thank. Teenagers' frontal lobes are still developing and are not fully formed until later in adult life, which might explain why teenagers can be more impulsive and more likely to take risks than boring adults.

But how do we know about the functions of the frontal lobe? Well, how do we "know" anything in psychology? We always have to consult the research. And there is a lot of research on the frontal lobe.

One of the most famous studies of a man who had severe damage to his frontal lobe was that of Phineas Gage. I'm going to tell you Gage's story because it's really interesting and I'll guarantee you that you remember this story for a long time, probably because of its gory details. But I will also say that it's best if you forget about him come exam day. We're going to investigate far better evidence regarding the functions of the brain, and the frontal lobe. I introduce Gage here because it's a fascinating story, but also because it generally marks the beginning of studies into understanding neuropsychology.

Neuropsychology: The study of the complex relationships between the brain and behaviour.

Gage was a railroad worker who was putting dynamite into rocks while working with a team to lay train tracks. As he used a six-foot bar to pound the dynamite powder into the rocks it ignited, essentially making the long steel pole a bullet that fired up through his left eye socket, through the top of his skull and landed about 50ft away. Gage survived and was even conscious while he rode on the cart to the nearest town to get help. He went to see the doctor and probably said something like, "can you help me with this?"

As a result of the incident, Gage's behaviour seemed to change as he went from being a rather mild-mannered man to "no longer Gage" as his friends said. Reports have even said that he was no longer allowed to be around women because he would often say rude things to them. This was in 1848 and Harlow, the doctor who treated Gage, made a few observations about the change in Gage's behaviour that has made him one of the first and most famous cases that links brain damage to our personality, our "sense of self"

Phineas Gage posing with the steel rod that shot through his frontal lobe.

and also to our ability to regulate (control) our behaviour (Smithsonian Magazine). It is this final function that we're going to explore further.

> ### Guiding Question:
> How does Phineas Gage's case suggest that damage to the frontal lobe affects impulsive behaviour?

Critical Thinking Extension:
Causation v Correlation: Many students make the mistake of jumping to conclusions like, "Phineas Gage's study proves that damage to the frontal lobe causes impulsive behaviour." In order to deduce causation we need to eliminate the possibility of other factors other than the brain damage affecting Gage's behaviour. What other alternative explanations could there be for the change in Gage's behaviour?

(b)   The Prefrontal Cortex and Aggression

Aggression:
Feelings of anger and hostility towards someone or something, often resulting in violent actions.

Since Gage there has been a lot more research into the functions of frontal lobe, especially the area within the frontal lobe called the prefrontal cortex (PFC). The prefrontal cortex is a more specific area within the frontal lobe. It's at the very front of the frontal lobe; it's the area of the brain just above the eyebrows beneath the forehead. The term lobe refers to the whole section of the brain, whereas cortex refers to the dense outer layer of the brain.

Like Gage's study first suggested, lots of recent research has shown that an important function of the prefrontal cortex is to regulate our impulsive decision making and our emotion. This has been shown partly through studies that show people with prefrontal cortex damage lack an ability to inhibit their impulsive behaviour, may not be able to behave in socially appropriate manners and may be easily provoked into aggression. Studies have also shown that there is a correlation between low functioning frontal lobes and criminal behaviour. (Clark et al., 2008; Blair, 2010)

Understanding the biology behind criminal behaviour is a popular and important field of study. British criminologist Adrian Raine has conducted many studies investigating biological correlates of criminal behaviour. He and some of his colleagues carried out a study in 1997 with the aim of comparing the brains of convicted murderers with those of healthy controls (i.e. people who had never been convicted of violent crime). The results showed that there was less activity in particular areas of the brains of the murderers, including less activity in the prefrontal cortex. (Raine, Buchsbaum & Lacasse, 1997)

Raine's studies, like many others, can show us that the brains of violent criminals are different to "normal" controls. But it only suggests a correlation and leaves a lot of uncertainty. Another way of studying how the brain can influence behaviour is to find people who have existing brain damage in particular areas of the brain and to compare them with control groups.

During the Vietnam War many soldiers received injuries to their brains from a variety of factors (e.g. bullets, explosions, land mines, etc.). The use of brain imaging technology (e.g. MRI – see section on brain imaging technology for more information) allows researchers to pinpoint the exact location of the damage and to find those participants who have damage in areas of specific interest, like the prefrontal cortex.

The Vietnam Head Injury Study (VHIS) is a longitudinal study of over 1,000 American veterans of the Vietnam War that aims to research the impact brain injury has on behaviour. One such report from the VHIS came from investigating the connections between frontal lobe damage and the influence this damage had on the aggressive tendencies of the patients. (Grafman et al., 1996)

Based on prior research, the researchers hypothesized that the prefrontal cortex helps exert control over automatic reactions to environmental provocation. In other words, when something makes us emotional, our prefrontal cortex functions to help stop us from reacting in a violent or aggressive manner. To test this idea, the researchers compared Vietnam War veterans who had suffered brain injuries with healthy controls (people with no brain injury). The veterans were also divided into those who had injuries specifically in the prefrontal cortex, and those who had damage to other areas

Many war veterans end up with brain injuries. The Vietnam Head Injury Study uses this naturally occurring variable to further our understanding of brain function. (Image credit: Fotoshop Tofs, on pixabay.com).

of the brain. MRI machines were used to locate the damage in their brains.

The researchers hypothesized that because of the role of the prefrontal cortex in inhibiting impulsive behaviours (e.g. reacting violently to someone who makes you angry) those veterans with damage in the prefrontal cortices would demonstrate more aggression than those with no damage or damage to other parts of their brain.

The researchers gathered data on a range of aggressive and violent attitudes and behaviours of the participants using self-report forms (e.g. questionnaires) and family observations. This means they measured aggression by asking questions such as, "How often do you react with physical aggression when someone makes you angry?" (Never, Sometimes, Always, etc.) Or, "How often do you swear or shout at people who make you angry?" Etc.

The results showed that those veterans who had damage to their prefrontal cortex had higher levels of reported violence and aggression than the controls or veterans with damage to other parts of the brain. By using MRI technology and being able to compare the three groups in the study, the researchers were able to draw the conclusion that damage to the prefrontal cortex is more likely to lead to aggressive behaviours than no damage or damage to other areas of the brain.

This is an interesting finding and it's a good basic introduction to the study of the brain and behaviour. However, the issue with this study is that it doesn't tell us how damage to the prefrontal cortex might influence our behaviour: we'll get to that in the next section.

Guiding Question:

How does the Vietnam Head Injury Study show that damage to the prefrontal cortex may affect aggression?

Critical Thinking Extension:

Evaluating Methodology: On the surface, it appears this study may show a relationship between prefrontal cortex damage and aggression. But you have to think critically about the methodology. They measured aggression and violence by using self-report forms, which are the participants' own answers to the questions. When evaluating research methods, we have to think about their effectiveness in investigating the specific relationship we're investigating. So in this study, to what extent are self-report of violence and aggression useful ways of gathering data? In studying aggression, would people always be honest?

If you're interested…

The magazine The New Yorker has an article called "Vietnam's Neuroscientific Legacy" that goes into more detail explaining this longitudinal study on Vietnam war veterans and the significance of its findings.

Relevant Topics

- Ethics
- Research Methods
- Localization of Brain Function
- Origins of conflict

Practice Exam Questions

- Outline one method used in a study related to localization of brain function.
- Evaluate one origin of conflict.
- Discuss ethical considerations related to studying the brain and behaviour.

Research Methods

When studying the relationship between brain damage and behaviour researchers may use correlational studies. In Grafman et al.'s study the two variables being correlated were the size of the lesion in the brain and the extent of aggressive behaviour. Conducting correlational analyses and finding correlational coefficients can enable conclusions to be drawn between naturally occurring brain damage and changes in behaviour.

Ethical Considerations

When studying sensitive subjects like aggression, anonymity is an important consideration. Individuals who display high levels of aggression, especially in family situations, would probably not want their level of aggressiveness made public. Informed consent is also important when investigating such sensitive issues and using tools like questionnaires: participants would want to know why the researchers were asking such personal questions *before* they participated. Not knowing this information beforehand could lead to stress, embarrassment or frustration.

2.2 The Brain and Decision Making
How might brain damage affect the way we think?

(a) Judgement, Processing and Decision Making

Hopefully you have started to see how the research paints a pretty strong picture of the effect damage to the prefrontal cortex can have on our behaviour. But so far the evidence we've looked at can't really tell us exactly how the prefrontal cortex influences behaviour, only that it does. In order to know exactly how damage to the prefrontal cortex can influence aggression, we need to go deeper inside the brain.

But first, we need to move beyond just the brain, and look inside the mind!

Let's first look at an interesting experimental paradigm that involves a child, a marshmallow and a ten-minute wait with the prospect of two marshmallows. A paradigm is a pattern or typical example of something; in psychology there are many experimental paradigms which means a general design of a study that is often used. This experimental paradigm involves putting a child in a room and giving them one marshmallow. A researcher tells the child that they have to wait ten minutes and then if when the researcher comes back the marshmallow is still there, they'll be given a second marshmallow and they can eat both. Could you imagine the poor little kids having to resist this temptation? Some kids can, and others can't (e.g. Mischel, Shoda, & Rodriguez, 1989; Mischel et al., 2011).

These experiments with marshmallows are typically done on small children because if we tried it on teenagers, the prospect of having two marshmallows might not

If you were a young kid, do you think you'd be able to wait ten minutes for another marshmallow? Try to imagine what kinds of thoughts would be going through a child's head as they wrestle with this problem.

be that enticing. But would you have a hard time waiting to get something you really loved right now, if it meant by waiting you could get more of that awesome thing? We're going to see how the ability to control our initial impulse and to think more about the future is a key function of the prefrontal cortex. As you learn more about this fascinating part of the brain, perhaps you'll be able to hypothesize explanations for why studies have shown that those kids who can wait for two marshmallows are more likely to grow up to be successful in school.

First, let's try to understand the decision making process that might be happening in this scenario. There are many theories of how and why decisions are made, but here we're going to look at a pretty basic one that might help us understand human behaviour a little better. After all, we can't understand behavior (the way we act) without thinking about cognition (the way we think).

Deciding how to behave in a particular situation first involves processing the information available to you before making a judgement about that information and then making a decision. If we think about this in terms of the research we've just seen on the Vietnam veterans, imagine the door bell ringing at dinner time. The family is around the table, everything's peaceful, and then "ding-dong"! Dad reacts by storming across the room and shouting down the hallway, "don't you know it's dinner time???!!!!" But Dad didn't do this without thinking – his brain didn't automatically just make him do it. He had to perform a series of mental processes that lead to his shouting and getting angry. First, he needed to process the information (the door bell ringing, the time of day), then make a judgement (no-one should be knocking at this time) and then make a decision (to shout at the person knocking).

Here we see that to understand the behaviour (e.g. being angry) we have to also understand the thinking. The cognitive processes involved here are processing, judgement and decision making. While this seems like a basic concept, knowing how these three relate to one another is key to understanding the rather complex theory explained in the next section.

Guiding Question:

How might processing be influencing the judgement and decision making of the children in the marshmallow study?

Critical Thinking Extension:

One of the studies you will study later in this section about judgement and decision making involves a gambling task. Think of a type of gambling that you are familiar with (e.g. betting on sports, horse races, playing poker, slot machines, etc.). Can you explain the relationship between processing, judgement and decision making involved in that particular type of gambling?

If you're interested…

There are some interesting TED talks about the marshmallow experiment that you can watch. One is called "The Marshmallow Test and Why We Want Instant Gratification" by Silvia Barcellos.

(b)   A Dual Process Model of Decision Making

"Dual" means two, so in psychological theories, a dual theory means there are two factors involved. The following theory about how we make decisions is based on how we process the information available to us in order to make the decision. The less we process the faster we make a decision. Conversely, the more we process the longer it takes for us to make a decision.

So for Dad's example when the doorbell rings at dinner time, some Dads might not process much at all and hear the bell (or knock) and **snap!** They get angry. Another Dad might hear the bell ring, become irritated, but then think "maybe that's Grandma coming to tell us how Grandad's operation was."

Kahneman (2003, 2011) has proposed a dual process model of thinking to explain two types of processing involved when making a decision.

They are appropriately known as:
* System One Processing
* System Two Processing

When we process information using system one it's fast and automatic. It's also often based on emotion (Kahneman, 2003). In other words, when processing information using system one we make a decision without really thinking about it. So getting angry and snapping at the doorbell is processing information using system one. The information in this example is the doorbell ringing – processing involves thinking about that information.

System Two is "slower…effortful and deliberately controlled" (Kahneman). When processing information using system two, we take our time and consider more factors. So processing the doorbell ringing using system two requires a little more thought, taking into consideration more factors like "who might this be?"

The dual process model is a general description of how we process information by using different systems when making decisions.

Two Systems of Processing Involved in Thinking and Decision Making	
System One	**System Two**
• Fast • Nonconscious • Automatic • Based on experiences	• Slow • Conscious • Controlled • Based on consequences

Let's go back to the kids and the marshmallows. Some kids probably ate the marshmallow straight away as soon as the researcher left the room. But others struggled, they agonized, they fought the temptation. They were probably continually trying to think about the prospect of getting two marshmallows for their efforts. According to the dual processing model of decision making, they were processing using system two, again and again and again for ten whole minutes – thinking about those other factors like how great it will feel to have two marshmallows. Here we see the decision making isn't just applicable to one situation (aggression) and we could apply this theory to many types of behaviours. In fact, findings from the Stanford Marshmallow Experiments have found that kids that can resist the temptation have a higher chance to grow up to be successful in many ways, including higher SAT scores, lower stress and lower chances of becoming addicted to drugs (Mischel et al., 2011).

Let's look at one more possible example of what this might look like: you're sitting in a test with 20 multiple choice questions and you really want to do well. You're at the front of the class and the supervising teacher has fallen asleep with the answers sitting in front of him. You need to pass the test in order to pass the class and you can simply sneak a peek and see the answers. Processing the information available using system one would involve not thinking past the "need to pass, see answers, get answers!" Using only this system might lead you to look at the answers and copy them into your test so you could pass the class. You've made this decision quickly and haven't thought too much about it. However, using system two processing might override this initial response as you think more carefully about the possible long-term consequences of your actions: "what if the teacher wakes up and I get caught?" "What if I pass but then I might feel guilty for the rest of my life?" "What if they're not even the actual answers?"

What the dual-process model allows us to do when explaining people's behaviour, is to hypothesize (based on the theory) how the person might have made the decision to act. You'll learn in later sections how damage to the brain might influence the ability to use system two processing.

Guiding Question:

How can the system used in processing influence judgement and decision making?

Critical Thinking Extension:
Evaluating Psychological Theories by Challenging Assertions: when learning about new **theories** (e.g. Dual Process Model), it's always tempting for students to think of these as facts and to talk about them as facts because "I read it in the textbook so it must be true." It's true that the dual process model is *one* explanation of decision making, but it is not the only explanation. Try to see if you can come up with examples of decision making that can't be explained by this model. I.e. test the theory! This is one way of critically assessing psychological theories: examining to what extent they are accurate in explaining the **phenomenon** in question.

If you're interested…

The American Psychological Association (APA) has many interesting resources related to all fields of psychology. In particular, they have an article available called "Delaying Gratification" which goes into detail about the Stanford Marshmallow Experiments, including research using fMRIs to test the function of the prefrontal cortex when people are presented with something tempting. You might also be interested to read Daniel Kahneman's book, *Thinking, Fast and Slow*.

(c) PFC Damage and Decision Making

We're now going to examine the role the prefrontal cortex has on our decision making and how it might influence our ability to use the systems outlined in the dual processing model of thinking and decision making in the previous section. The study that we're about to look at suggests that one role of the prefrontal cortex is that it allows us to plan and make decisions based on long-term consequences. In other words, it allows us to process information using system two. We have other areas of the brain that allow immediate responses without much thought, but it's the prefrontal cortex that allows us to exercise control over those initial responses based on consideration of other factors. For example, studies have shown that people who are able to resist temptation and show self-control (using paradigms like the marshmallow test) have higher function in their prefrontal cortex than those that can't (Casey et al., 2011).

Based on these two systems involved in decision making and what we know about the prefrontal cortex already, it seems plausible that people with dysfunction in the prefrontal cortex may have an impairment in their ability to use system two processing and rely more on system one when making decisions. We could hypothesize about this in the Vietnam Head Injury Study, as I've done so far with the Dad and the doorbell example. But these are just my hypotheses made up in my imagination – we need strong, solid, empirical evidence from studies that can clearly show the connection between our prefrontal cortex and our ability to process information.

Many studies have shown that people with lesions in their prefrontal cortices are primarily guided by immediate rewards and may not think about long-term rewards or punishments (Kim & Lee, 2011).

Within the prefrontal cortex there is a more specific region called the ventromedial prefrontal cortex. The parts of the brain are often named for their location. Frontal – front. Medial – in the middle. Ventral – means on the bottom. So this very specific name – ventromedial prefrontal cortex, means it's in the cortex (outside), in the prefrontal region (front) towards the middle (medial) and the bottom (ventral). We began broadly but you'll begin to see that the brain is so complex and the function is very specific in very specific areas.

If you can't remember ventromedial prefrontal cortex, you can skip out the ventromedial part. But the more specific terminology you can learn and use, the clearer your explanations in psychology are going to be. Many studies have

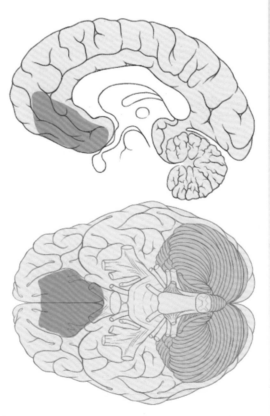

The ventromedial prefrontal cortex is a specific area within the PFC. It is highlighted in red in the image. (Image by Patrick J. Lynch from wikicommons).

Empirical Evidence: Information and knowledge gathered through observation and experimentation.

Cognitive capabilities: This refers to one's ability to perform cognitive tasks.

investigated patients who have damage to the ventromedial prefrontal cortex and they have shown an inability to learn from previous mistakes and to continue to repeat behaviours even when they result in negative consequences. Other aspects of their cognitive capabilities (intellect, problem-solving, memory, etc.) remain normal.

Before we consult the research into the relationship between the function of our brain and our ability to process information, it's important to understand how cognitive processes are investigated in experimental situations. Of course we can't see the mind (at least not yet!). I don't know what's happening inside your mind, for instance. So how can we investigate this in psychology? What happens is that psychologists design an experiment and their dependent variable is the behaviour – that's what they measure. So they have to design really clever experiments to see the relationship between the thinking and the behaviour. Their independent variable might be a type of task that they think requires different types of thinking, and then they measure the product of that thinking by doing some kind of test.

To test the dual process model, for instance, they design experiments that require the participant to process two different types of information and then they time how it takes them to respond. While the study in the next section did not have the specific aim of testing the dual processing model, it is a good example of how behavioural measures in studies can provide insight into cognitive processes.

Guiding Question:

How might damage to the prefrontal cortex influence decision making?

Critical Thinking Extension:
One way of abstracting relationships is to apply them to a different context. If you can understand how damage to the prefrontal cortex could influence decision making, how could this relationship explain the correlation between PFC damage and aggression? Or PFC function and future success in things like the IB exams or standardised tests? The ability to devise hypotheses that abstract one relationship to various contexts is a valuable thinking skill and one you should work on developing as you progress through this course.

If you're interested…

There's a book called *The Teenage Brain: A Neuroscientist's Survival Guide to Raising Adolescents and Young Adults*. As you're a teenager, you might like to know how your brain is different now from when you were a little kid and how your brain is going to change over the future years. There is a lot of research in the field of the brains of teenagers, especially that which focuses on why teens tend to engage in more risky behaviours than us boring old adults.

(d) Processing and Decision Making while Gambling

In the following study researchers measured the gambling behaviour of partici-pants in order to draw conclusions about the role of a particular area of the prefrontal cortex in decision making. Based on previous studies the researchers hypothesized that patients with damage to their ventromedial prefrontal cortices may not consider future consequences of their behaviour. This could be because of the ventromedial prefrontal cortex's role in processing information.

One study compared 17 healthy controls with 8 patients who had lesions in their ventromedial prefrontal cortices. By comparing the healthy controls with the patients with damage, they could focus on one variable – the proper functioning of the ventro-medial prefrontal cortex (Bechara, Tranel & Damasio, 2000).

They played what has come to be known as the Iowa Card Game or Iowa Gambling Task (named after the university where the research took place). This has been used in many studies and you can play it for yourself online.

It's tricky to describe, but basically there are four decks of cards and participant are told they can choose from any deck of cards. They start with $2,000 (*not* real money) and they win money randomly when they pick cards from either deck. But sometimes they might have to pay back money – this is why it's gambling.

There are two decks whereby the initial money won is rather small (e.g. $50) and two decks where the money won is larger (e.g. $100). But the smaller reward deck also has smaller penalties (so you might have to pay back $50 every fifth turn), but the larger initial reward deck has bigger penalties (e.g. you have to pay back $1,250 after nth turn). So in the long run it makes more sense and you'll win more money if you can resist the initial big reward and go for the shorter initial payment with the better long-term gain. There is no real strategy involved[1] except learning to go for low rewards. The game is designed to see how people adjust their thinking (and behaviour) based on learning from experience. Perhaps it's important to note that this was *play money* and they were not really gambling with figures this high – it might have been a very expensive experiment to run if they were!

So there are four decks of cards like below. The cards are just red or black – it's not about what card they turn over that determines how much money they win. There are just two different types of decks: low reward – long term gain (A and C) or high reward but higher long-term losses (B and D). It's important to know that the participants weren't told which deck was which. *They had to learn from experience.*

So the participants had to process information using two systems. According to

The Iowa Card Game has been used in many studies. Originally they used real playing cards, but changed to having just red and black cards as people tried to overthink the possible patterns.

Deck A	Deck B	Deck C	Deck D
Win $50 nine out of ten times	Choose from here and win $100 7/10	Win $50 nine out of ten times	Choose from here and win $100 7/10
One out of ten times pay back $50	Pay back $100 2/10 times	One out of ten times pay back $50	Pay back $100 2/10 times
	Pay back $1250 1/10 ten times		Pay back $1250 1/10 ten times

[1] In fact, the researchers began by using actual playing cards but they found this to be a confounding variable because people thought too much about the possible patterns and it took too long to realise the obvious differ-ence between the two decks.

This gambling study can show biological evidence to support the dual processing model of decision making. It also demonstrates one localized function of the ventromedial prefrontal cortex.

the dual processing model, system one processing would lead to a fast and automatic decision because it would be based on instinct. Not many factors would be considered except for something like, "Go for high reward!" But system two processing would require more careful consideration – I want money, but actually I might have to pay back more money so is it the best option? More factors would have to be considered.

The results showed that the healthy controls slowly learned to avoid the decks of cards with high rewards but bigger long-term punishments, and opted instead for the low immediate reward but with longer long-term gains (due to less punishments).

However, the patients with damage to their ventromedial prefrontal areas chose the decks with the higher immediate rewards which had long-term punishments. This pattern took a few trials to emerge but generally remained throughout the remaining trials. The patients were less able to consider the long-term factors and consequences of their impulsive decisions, unlike the healthy controls.

Guiding Question:

How does this study suggest that the vmPFC plays a role in system two processing?

Critical Thinking Extension:

Transfer: It's important that you are able to transfer your learning from one context to another. If what you learn in IB Psychology is only ever going to be useful within the context of IB Psychology, this will be a rather big waste of two years of your life. But if you can begin to transfer what you learn and use it in new ways, suddenly what you learn can stay with you for a long time. While the theme of criminology isn't always immediately relevant, and in fact, there's a good chance you won't even mention criminology in your exam answers, it's still valuable thinking practice to be trying to abstract significant relationships and to think about how they might be applied in various fields. As you've learned more about the role of the PFC in system two decision making, could this be relevant in areas of human thinking and behaviour that aren't related to criminology? How could PFC function affect learning or studying or addiction, etc.?

If you're interested...

At time of writing there is an online version of the Iowa Gambling Task available. Playing this game for yourself is a good way to learn about the methodology of the study.

Relevant Topics

- Thinking and Decision Making
- Ethics and Research Methods (BA and CA)
- Localization of brain function
- Origins of conflict

Practice Exam Questions

- Outline one theory of thinking and decision making.
- Explain two ethical considerations related to research on thinking and decision making.
- Discuss research into localization of brain function.
- Evaluate one theory of thinking and decision making.

Research Methods

The natural experiment is valuable when studying biological correlates in thinking and decision making. Neuropsychology involves the study of the relationship between biological factors and cognitive processes like thinking and decision making, so using the experimental method where participants have naturally occurring brain damage allow researchers to focus on the relationship between particular areas of the brain and cognitive processes.

Ethical Considerations

Debriefing would be an important consideration in studies using the Iowa Gambling Task because participants may be curious to know why they were being asked to gamble. Moreover, the results of the study and their impact on patients with vPFC damage may have particular relevance for them: they would want to know that their decision making might be impaired. This is a significant finding and knowing about it (or not) could have a major impact on their life.

2.3 The Brain and Emotion
How might our brain affect our experience of emotion?

(a) Fear and the Amygdala

In the previous section you learnt about the frontal lobe and the prefrontal cortex, a section of the outer layer of the frontal lobe. We're now going to look deeper beneath the cortex within the temporal lobe at a part of the brain called the amygdala.

Another important area of study in psychology that involves brain function and mental processes is emotion. Emotions are universal and there's no single common definition of emotion or even types of emotions. For instance, could you objectively tell the difference between people who are "depressed" and people who are just "unhappy"? Or at what point does mild amusement become happiness and then jubilation? The feeling of emotion is a complex human experience and we need to always remember that when learning about it and drawing conclusions from research.

In order to understand this complex human experience, we have to investigate the relationship between the brain, thinking and emotion. To do this we're going to first look at the biological factors influencing one particular emotion – fear.

We're going to investigate fear because it's an important aspect of human behaviour that has many implications. Moreover, our response to fear is a type of response to a threat, which is an important idea in understanding violent crime. What may be useful to note is that criminals have been characterized as having a lack of fear and an inability to recognise fear in other people's faces (Herpertz, Werth and Lukas, 2001).

For some types of crime, this seems to make sense. For example, if someone cannot feel fear then they may be more inclined to do something dangerous, like participate in a shoot-out with a rival gang or get involved in a street brawl. Not being able to detect emotion in others may also inhibit experiencing empathy for victims. If one can feel empathy they may be less likely to inflict suffering on others.

There is also a lot of evidence that dysfunction and abnormalities in the amygdala can be found in violent criminals (E.g. Raine, 1997). Later in this chapter you will learn more about possible relationships between fear and crime, but first it's important to understand where fear might come from[2].

The word amygdala comes from the Latin for almond because the amygdalae are almond-shaped.

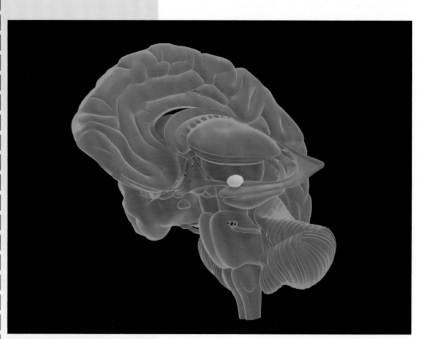

Unlike the prefrontal cortex on the outer layer of our brain, the amygdala is deep within the temporal lobes of the brain.

Our experience of fear is reliant on a few things. First, we need something to be afraid of. When talking about any emotion we call this the emotional stimulus. To keep it simple to start with, we'll be looking at *external* emotional stimuli related to fear. In other words, things in our environment that make us scared.

As usual, try to make connections to your own life. We've all felt fear before. When was the last time you were really scared!? What were the physical reactions in your body?

Spiders are an emotional stimuli for many people. Could you hold a tarantula on your hand without feeling scared?

Guiding Question:

How might a lack of response to an emotional stimulus explain violence?

Critical Thinking Extension:
Generalizability: Does a lack of an emotional response explain all types of violence? The ability to think abstractly about relationships involves thinking carefully about the individual components of the relationship you are explaining. In this case, thinking abstractly about what violence means would enable you to assess the extent to which a lack of fear or emotional response might explain all types of violence. Types of violence include punching, stabbing, shooting, rape, etc.

If you're interested…

If the study of criminology interests you, Adrian Raine has a book called *The Anatomy of Violence: The Biological Roots of Crime.* As the title suggests, this book devotes itself entirely to studying the biological correlates of crime. We are merely skimming the surface of this fascinating topic in this course; reading books of this nature in your own time is a valuable way of pursuing your interests further.

---

² We'll also study fear in more detail when we investigate origins of Post-Traumatic Stress Disorder

(b)   SM: The Woman with No Fear

Studies on the functions of the amygdala go back as far as the late 1800s. Early studies on rhesus monkeys involved removing their entire temporal lobes. After this removal they found a change in a number of behaviours, including the fact that the monkeys lost emotional reactivity, meaning they didn't react in emotional ways to environmental stimuli. But this involved the removal of the whole temporal lobe – the amygdala is just one part of the temporal lobe. So further replication of these findings was carried out and the monkeys' amygdalae specifically were lesioned and the changes in behaviour were recorded. The results gathered were similar: damage to the amygdalae resulted in emotional blunting, a reduction in emotional reactions (Weiskrantz, 1956).

Numerous animal studies like this have suggested that the amygdala plays an important role in threat perception. But what about in humans? It is very difficult to study damage to such specific parts of the brain as the amygdala in humans. Unlike the prefrontal cortex, that is located near the skull and easily damaged, the amygdalae are located deep within the brain and so it's rarer to find people with damage in this area. Moreover, often when people do experience damage in this area (e.g. through a stroke or disease), they also have damage in other areas. However, there are some rare exceptions and when people with particular areas of brain damage occur, often they are the subjects of case studies. One such patient is known as SM, who the media have called "the woman with no fear" (Feinstein, Adolphs, Damasio & Tranel, 2011).

Most people would find walking through an abandoned hospital in the middle of the night very scary, but not SM. Her study helps to show the important function the amygdala plays in experiencing fear.

Like the monkey experiments, numerous studies on people with damaged amygdalae have shown that lesions in amygdalae of human patients result in a lack of fear. One such study was carried out on a patient called SM, a 44 year old woman with bilateral lesions in her amygdalae that were the result of a genetic disorder. Previous research has shown that she has an impairment in fear conditioning (learning to be afraid) and fear recognition (recognizing fear in others' faces). This was the first study on SM that tried to see if the amygdala played a role in the induction of fear - being made to feel scared. In all other ways SM is a normal person - her scores in IQ, memory, language tests and other tests of general cognitive function are as good as healthy controls.

One way they tested her fear was to take her to an exotic pet store where there were lots of snakes and spiders. These are two of the most common fears people have and from an evolutionary view a healthy fear of these animals is a good thing (because of their potential danger). SM had also told the researchers that she didn't like snakes and spiders and "tried to stay away from them." So they went to a pet store and made notes on her behaviour as they walked around the store. But even though she had told them she didn't like snakes and spiders, SM showed no fear. She held one snake for over three minutes and the researchers noticed that she was curious and inquisitive, touching its skin and its scales, but that she didn't

Fear conditioning means learning to be afraid of something. This serves important purposes for our survival and you'll learn more about this process when you study PTSD.

show any fear. In fact, she said things like "This is so cool" and she even kept asking if she could hold the bigger snakes, but the store owner continually told her they were too dangerous.

We can see that SM had no fear of something that most people are afraid of. And to test her fear response further they then took her to a haunted house. Every year at Halloween one of the "most haunted places in America", an old psychiatric hospital called Waverly Hills Sanatorium is turned into a haunted house. So even though it wasn't Halloween the researchers created the Haunted House and to make sure their house was in fact scary they invited a few other people to join the group so they could make comparisons between their fear response to the haunted house and SM's. They noted that while walking through the house SM never showed any fear. "Monsters" would jump out from behind dark spaces and SM never seemed to show any physical signs of fear, but would do things like touch their faces instead. Ironically, she even scared one of the "monsters"!

So this case study suggests that the amygdala might play an important role in the experiences of fear in scary and threatening situations. If we have damage to this area of the brain, perhaps we won't be able to experience fear.

Guiding Question:

How does SM's case study demonstrate the role of the amygdala in experiencing fear?

Critical Thinking Extension:

Generalizability: Thinking critically about research involves assessing to what extent the results from the study can be applied beyond the study itself. One way to assess this is to look at the nature of the subjects of the research. In this case, the subjects in the research mentioned are animals and one woman. To what extent can findings from these studies be used to explain human behaviour? It's important that you provide reasons for your answer: simply saying "one limitation of this study is that it was carried out on animals and can't be generalised to humans" is pointless, and is not demonstrating abstract thinking – it is description. You must show you understand the specific factors involved that influence the generalizability. Part of your explanation, therefore, should include reasons why findings may not be generalised. Can you explain some specific reasons that might influence the generalizability of SM's case study or the animal studies?

If you're interested…

Neurosciencenews.com is an interesting website that has regular stories and articles about the fascinating world of studying the brain. They have an article on SM called "The Fearless SM: Woman Missing Amygdala" in which this case study is explained further.

(c)   The Amygdala and the Fear Response

So you've had an introduction to the amygdala and seen in research that it is a necessary component of fear, it's time to look a little more closely at how the amygdala may cause us to feel fear. In this section we'll focus only on the biological processes involved after we perceive a threat.

With modern technology, we can now see the functioning of the amygdala when people are exposed to scary or threatening stimuli. When images of snakes, spiders, or angry faces appear on the screen our amygdala is activated. One study used a PET scan to compare the responses in the brains of women being exposed to images of snakes or spiders (things they said they were afraid of) and things they weren't afraid of. The results showed that when looking at the snakes and spiders their amygdala activation was higher than when looking at non-threatening stimuli (Ahs et al., 2009).

Research also suggests that our amygdala plays a particular role in situations when we feel *socially* threatened. A social threat is one that comes from another person or group of people, for example someone swearing at you, challenging you to a fight, etc. It's an emotional stimulus that is separate from a natural threat, such as seeing a dangerous animal or being trapped in a burning building. If someone is threatening us, we might need to defend ourselves: this is why we have evolved to have biological reactions that can facilitate aggression.

If we think back to the theme of our chapter, knowing about a fear of snakes and spiders has little applicability to something like murder. This is why knowing the term social threat is a key concept to understand in this chapter as it is important to really explain what might provoke someone into committing violent crime.

One study that we'll look closely at later in the chapter showed that when people are threatened socially their amygdala is activated. They can see this by putting people in fMRI machines and flashing images of happy, neutral or sad faces and then measuring the activation of the amygdala. When people perceive angry faces their amygdala is activated. But here's my favourite part: the researchers give the instructions to the participants that they are to push a button as soon as they see an emotional stimuli (in this case the picture of the face). FMRI studies show that the amygdala activates before the person has even consciously realised that they have seen a face (e.g. Williams et al., 2004). Studies have also shown that our amygdala may activate upon perceiving a face from a race different to our own (Chekroud et al., 2014). This will be explored when you learn about social influence and prejudice.

How does that happen? When there's something threatening in our environment (i.e. something that might scare us) it is perceived by the amygdala. We have seen this already in the existing research. But in order to understand the physiological response caused by fear (the increased heart rate, heavy breathing, etc.) we need to know what happens after the amygdala is activated. After a threat is perceived by the amygdala a message is sent to another part of the brain called the hypothalamus. The hypothalamus is below the thalamus (hypo = below) and is like a control centre (imagine an air-traffic controller sitting at a large desk with a whole bunch of buttons or switches, or those little people in the heads of the characters in that Pixar film, Inside-Out). As the hypothalamus receives a signal from the amygdala it needs to get the body ready physically to deal with the threat.

The hypothalamus is involved in activating the fight-flight response (Steimer, 2002). It sends a signal to the adrenal glands, which are small glands that sit on top of your kidneys and trigger the release of adrenaline into our blood stream. You may know

One function of the amygdala is to perceive threatening stimuli and prepare our body to react accordingly.

Emotion and aggression are closely related because an individual is unlikely to be aggressive without feeling emotional. Emotion includes the physiological arousal associated with the stress response.

a little bit about this hormone in our bodies, or just you have heard the word before. The term "adrenaline junkie" is a popular one to describe people who love doing those extreme sports like bungee jumping, sky diving, parasailing, jetboating, white-water rafting, etc. When we receive adrenaline in our bodies our heart races, blood pumps faster, we get more oxygen, and we get more instant energy. The reason these sports increase adrenaline is because they trigger in us a natural fear response as we haven't evolved to be used to the feeling of jumping head first off a 200metre high bridge!

But this response serves an important evolutionary purpose: when we are threatened and feel afraid, we need to have the energy to either stand our ground and fight or to run away really fast to escape danger. This is why it's known as the fight-flight response. Another name for this is the stress response.

Understanding the role of the amygdala in emotion is relevant for the study of criminology, as well as origins of prejudice and possible causes of PTSD.

We'll explore more about the significance of this later.

Many people like to participate in sports that activate our stress response. Are you an adrenaline junkie?

Guiding Question:

How does perception lead to the physiological arousal associated with fear?

Critical Thinking Extension:

Assumptions: This explanation of fear being a product of the physiological processes activated by the perception of emotional stimuli in our environment doesn't include explanations of how we can generate emotion internally. Can we feel fear without having to perceive a fear inducing stimulus? What about other emotions: do you think the explanations of the physiology of fear can be applied to emotions like sadness, anxiety and joy?

If you're interested…

There are many different theories of emotion that you can read about if you're interested. One particular theory of emotion from the 1960s is called "The Two Factor Theory." This theory was originally included in this chapter but its relevance to the current IB Psychology syllabus was questionable and it's a rather complex theory with a more complex experiment associated with it so it was removed. However, if you're interested it does provide an explanation of how emotion could be influenced through internal cognitive processes.

Relevant Topics

- Localization of brain function
- Emotion and Cognition
- Evolution
- Techniques used to study the brain
- Ethics and Research Methods (BA)
- HL Animal studies

Practice Exam Questions

- Contrast two studies related to localization of brain function.
- Describe one technique used to study the brain and behaviour.
- Discuss techniques used to study the brain and behaviour.
- HL To what extent are animal studies models useful in understanding human behaviour?

Research Methods

Case studies on individuals with unique characteristics are valuable for psychologists investigating relationships between the brain and behaviour. It is rare to have people with bilateral amygdala damage and so the findings from case studies using patients like SM can be used to corroborate findings from animal studies.

Ethical Considerations

The right to withdraw would be a particular consideration involved in the unique methodology of SM's case study as they were deliberately putting her in potentially stressful situations. Participants should always be given the right to withdraw, but this is of particular relevance when the methodology involves potentially high levels of anxiety.

2.4 Hormones and Behaviour
Why are men more aggressive than women?

(a)   Testosterone and Aggression

So far we've talked pretty generally about the brain and areas of the brain. It's time now to delve a little deeper into the actual chemical functioning of our body and our brain so we can develop our understanding of how biological factors can influence our behaviour.

A key biological factor in psychology is the endocrine system, and its role in releasing hormones in our body. Hormones are chemical messengers that are transported through our blood as a result of activation of different glands in the endocrine system. These chemicals perform a number of functions on our physiological processes. Put simply, they are chemicals that can spark physical reactions throughout the body. We've already looked briefly at the way one hormone (adrenaline) might play an important role in the experience of emotion through its impact on the physiological processes involved in emotion.

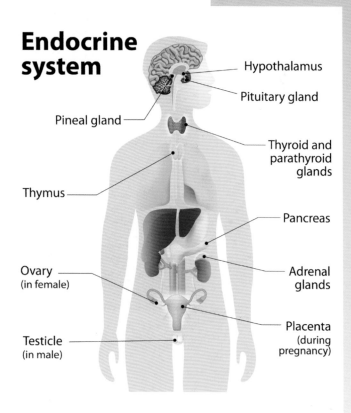

Testosterone is another hormone that has been studied extensively and particularly in relation to its influence on aggression. Many studies have shown that criminals in prison have high levels of testosterone (e.g. Dabbs et al., 1997 as cited in Batrinos, 2012). More evidence that suggests testosterone might affect aggression can be found in numerous animal studies. These studies follow a similar experimental design as the monkey studies on lesions in the amygdala, but typically they remove the testicles from male animals (often rats) and compare the differences in their aggressive behaviour before and after castration.

Testosterone is the male sex hormone and is produced in the testes (and in the ovaries to a lesser extent in females).

An example of this can be seen in Albert et al. (1986). In this study they wanted to investigate the effects of changing testosterone levels on the aggressiveness of male rats. They placed rats in cages and identified the alpha males. An alpha male is the leader of the colony. In animals, this is typically the biggest and strongest. The term can be applied to any animal group, including humans. So the researchers identified the alpha males and they measured their aggression levels when there was a nonaggressive rat placed in the same cage. They measured aggression by recording behaviours such as biting.

After they measured the aggression levels they divided the alpha males into four separate groups to undergo four separate surgeries:

A.   Castration

B.   Castration followed by implanting of tubes with testosterone

C.   Castration followed by implanting of empty tubes

D.   A "sham" castration followed by implanting of empty tubes (this means they would have cut open the rat and sewn it back up without actually removing the testicles).

They then measured the change in aggression when nonaggressive rats were introduced to the cage. Those that had the operations that reduced testosterone levels (e.g. Group A and C) had a decrease in aggressiveness (e.g. attacking and biting) but those that had the operations that kept testosterone levels in tact (Group B and D) didn't have a significant change in aggression levels.

You can see the advantages of using a laboratory experiment to manipulate variables in Albert et al.'s study. By measuring effects of aggression on manipulations of testosterone levels, a clear cause-effect relationship can be determined.

By experimenting on rats, researchers are able to determine correlations between biological factors and behaviour. Albert et al. were able to manipulate levels of testosterone and conclude that levels of testosterone affect aggression.

This evidence by itself demonstrates a correlation between testosterone and aggression. It was followed by a second operation so that those that had the surgery that decreased testosterone had another operation that increased testosterone (e.g. Group C had their tubes filled with testosterone). Those alpha rats that had their testosterone replaced showed returned levels of aggressiveness similar to those in the "sham" castration group.

Moreover, the researchers observed that when a subordinate male (one that is not the alpha) is placed in the same cage as an alpha rat that has been castrated the lower rat (subordinate) becomes the dominant (alpha) rat in the cage. Also, when a rat that had the sham operation is put in a cage with a castrated rat, the sham operation rat shows higher levels of aggression. This suggests that testosterone may facilitate behaviour associated with social dominance in rats.

By comparing the before and after changes of aggression, as well as comparing the results of the different operations, this experiment suggests that testosterone levels influence aggression. The researchers concluded that the role of testosterone in aggression influences social dominance in that those rats that have reduced testosterone lose their place as alpha males.

Much like with the monkey studies, we can see here how animal studies can show us that there is a relationship between testosterone and aggression, but it doesn't tell us much more than that. We want to go deeper into understanding aggression. Moreover, rats and humans are pretty different animals with different brain structures, so can we really generalize from an aggressive rat in a lab to a serial killer?

Guiding Question:

How does Albert et al.'s study show a causal relationship between testosterone and aggression?

Critical Thinking Extension:

Analysing Questions: If you are asked to "explain how testosterone influences behaviour, the above research is rather limited. It suggests that testosterone does influence aggression but it doesn't provide much insight into how it does. However, if you are asked to explain how research suggests testosterone influences behaviour, the above research can be used in a very good explanation of how the research demonstrates testosterone's role in aggression. However, it's limited to animal studies so the generalizability to humans needs to be questioned. Analysing the demands of the question in order to identify the explanation/s required to demonstrate your understanding is really important, especially in exam situations.

If you're interested…

While rather gory and gruesome, and especially unsettling for boys, there's a rich and fascinating history behind castration that could be worth researching. Castration is used extensively in farming to control livestock while a castrato is the name given to the singing voice and the boy who had that particular singing voice through castration. This was a popular practice in Europe as was chemical castration to treat homosexuality. One famous case of the latter was that of the famous mathematician Alan Turing.

(b) Aggression: An Evolutionary Adaptation

In the previous section we investigated some basic evidence that suggests testosterone influences aggression. In order to explore more deeply *how* high levels of testosterone could increase aggressive behaviour we need to look again at the way many factors may be involved in this complex behaviour.

Albert et al.'s the study did identify an important concept: social dominance. The role of social dominance and having a strong position within a social group is one that we will explore throughout the following sections. So before we investigate the connection between testosterone and aggression further, perhaps we may need to take a moment and reconsider our thoughts on aggression. In modern society being overly aggressive is generally considered bad because it's anti-social. But has this always been the case? A big part of understanding functions of the brain and other biological components is that we have to think about things from an evolutionary standpoint. The development of our cortices, for instance, enabled us to develop language, make tools, form social groups, etc., which helped us rise to the top of the food chain. We've also seen that the amygdala plays an important evolutionary role in perceiving danger and preparing our body physically to deal with the danger. This is another adaptation that has helped us to survive.

Similarly, aggression may be an adaptive behaviour because it enables us to defend ourselves when we are threatened. Shows of aggression don't always mean actually making physical contact. Sometimes shows of aggression without resorting to *physical* violence could be enough to defeat the threat. Dogs show aggression through gnarling and growling, for instance, and many males show aggression by clenching fists, puffing up their chests and offering verbal assaults. These signs of aggression might be important in maintaining our social dominance (i.e. maintaining a high social status). Social status refers to your rank in society. In cavemen times social status might mean being the toughest and the best hunter, which would mean you would have access to more resources. Social status in a modern, industrialized society might mean having a high-powered and high-paying job. In both of these situations, shows of aggression might help to retain status. Status is achieved in many ways across social groups, cultures and genders, so the value of aggression in these situations will vary from situation to situation. Having and retaining social status is key to our survival, because it ensures that when the food and berries are shared around the tribe, we'll get our fair share (we need to eat to live!). If we look weak and we're scared it might be easier for our foes to defeat us, take our hunk of mammoth meat or copulate with our mate.

Displaying signs of aggression may serve an evolutionary advantage. By being aggressive and willing to confront threats and competitors, an individual may be able to keep or improve their social status.

Evolution is about survival of the fittest, but what this means is not who can run the fastest; it doesn't mean fit in that sense. In general biological terms it means the organisms that have the best characteristics (physical and otherwise) for their environment and so are most likely to be able to pass on their genetic material. In animals we pass on our genes by procreating (having babies). Much like other biological aspects in our psychology course, evolution is another one we have to skim over. The key concept for

Natural selection is the process of organisms better adapted to their environment surviving and passing down their genes to their offspring. Over time, this results in significant changes in a species.

Having and maintaining social status is important because it can increase chances of getting resources that are key to survival and passing on genetic material.

you to understand is that genes will be more likely to be passed on if they affect us in a way that increases our chances of survival and/or reproduction. This may be through an influence on our behaviour. Thus, some behaviour can be explained through understanding how biological traits are a result of evolutionary pressures. That sounds complex, but it is the key to understanding evolutionary explanations of behaviour. The process of evolution works by mutations (small changes) happening in the genetic material that are passed on from parents to kids. If a mutation helps an organism to survive, it increases the chances that it will be passed on and so over hundreds of thousands of years those slight mutations add up to mean significant changes. The process of evolution, therefore, is a slow one that takes tens of thousands of years.

Understanding the evolutionary advantage of aggression is important because it helps to explain the effects of testosterone on the amygdala that will be explored in the following sections.

Once more we find ourselves delving deep into the biological aspect, which is fascinating, but we must stop ourselves at some point and begin focusing on the psychology (i.e. the relationships between the biology, the mental processes and the behaviour). The key idea from this section to understand is that our brains have evolved to allow us to think and behave in ways that are likely to increase our chances of survival. Displaying aggression is one of those behaviours because in situations when we are being challenged or threatened, reacting aggressively is a valuable function as it can help us maintain our social status.

Evolutionary explanations of behaviour should include how the behaviour might help an individual to survive and/or pass on their genetic material.

Guiding Question:

How might aggressive tendencies be an evolutionary adaptation?

Critical Thinking Extension:

Hypothesizing: In the following sections you are going to learn more about how testosterone impacts the brain and how this might be an evolutionary adaptation. However, you won't always be provided with the follow-up explanations to questions you may have, so devising your own hypothesis can be valuable in exploring concepts and conducting your own research to further your knowledge and understanding. You can also hypothesize in "discussions" in essay answers in exams. Based on what you have learned already about aggression and criminology, can you make a hypothesis as to how and why testosterone levels may affect particular parts of the brain?

If you're interested...

If human biology and evolution interests you, Desmond Morris' book *The Naked Ape* is a recommended read. In this classic non-fiction text, Morris talks about the human species as if they were like any other animal being observed from a biological perspective. It's really quite interesting reading about humans from this perspective.

(c)   *Testosterone and Social Threat Part I*

Studies using fMRIs have shown that levels of testosterone in our body can affect the functioning of the amygdala, which is a key piece in the testosterone and aggression relationship. So it seems plausible that aggression might be an evolutionarily adaptive behaviour and so the role of testosterone actually helps to ensure our own survival in times of social threat by reacting with the amygdala. If the amygdala can stimulate the process of pumping adrenaline in our body to get us ready to fight (i.e. act aggressively), it is plausible that the testosterone may impact the function of the amygdala to stimulate this reaction.

This can be seen in one study where the researchers gave 16 healthy young men doses of testosterone on one day and a placebo the next. In both conditions they showed them images of various types of faces, including neutral, sad and angry faces. While they viewed the images their brains were being scanned in an fMRI, much like the similar studies already discussed earlier in the chapter. The results showed that when participants were injected with testosterone they showed increased reactivity of the amygdala and the hypothalamus when they were viewing images of the angry faces. Testosterone was not shown to have the same influence when observing other types of emotional faces. (Goetz et al., 2016).

This study reinforces what we've learned in earlier sections about the amygdala: it plays an important role in social threat perception. Seeing an angry face is threatening and we need to be aware of someone who might be ready to do us harm, whereas a sad or neutral face, while activating perhaps a different emotion, doesn't require us to get ready to fight. The activation of the hypothalamus also suggests that the body will release adrenaline as the hypothalamus triggers the adrenal glands during the fight/flight response.

This study quite simply shows that the function of the amygdala can be affected by testosterone levels. Saying aggression is caused by increased activation of the amygdala leaves a lot of questions unanswered. Just because we have more activation in our amygdala doesn't really help explain clearly how that might lead to aggression.

A social threat is when another person, or group of people, pose a potential challenge to us in a way that may be scary, frightening or dangerous. Testosterone's impact on the amygdala at times of social threat may be an evolutionary adaptation.

We could say that when seeing an angry face the testosterone increases the activation of the amygdala and the hypothalamus will trigger the adrenal glands to release adrenaline and we will be ready to fight, but it does provide a rather overly simplistic explanation because it misses an important component: cognition.

Aggressive actions and reactions in situations are not simply robotic performances based on biological functions. As we've seen, we can't ignore mental processes when providing a full explanation of human behaviour, so it is important that these are also explored. This will be the subject of the next section.

Perception means to become aware of something. We perceive information in our environment through our sensory organs. Social threat perception means becoming aware of a social threat.

Critical Thinking Extension:

Application, Causation and Correlation: Prison populations have been shown to have high levels of testosterone. Does this suggest **causation** or **correlation**? Perhaps people arrive in prison because they have high testosterone levels and this was what led them to commit violence acts. Or, prisons are such environments where there are many alphas who are competing for social dominance in that highly competitive environment. It's not hard to imagine testosterone levels spiking in situations where you place many alpha males in a cage (literally, in many cases) where they are left to establish their own social structures.

If you're interested…

There is a plethora of research on the role of testosterone in social situations, especially those involving competition. Numerous studies have investigated the role of testosterone in sports matches and how even the observation of victory and defeat can affect spectators' testosterone levels. This would be well worth investigating, if you are interested.

(d)   Testosterone and Social Threat Part II

In order to investigate the relationships between perceiving a social threat, testosterone and the amygdala, Radke et al. (2015) designed a pretty complicated, but clever experiment. They hypothesized that the amygdala wasn't just involved in the *perception* of the threat, but the effect of *motivation* to deal with the threat was an important aspect to consider. Now we're getting a little closer to making the connection to aggression. If someone threatens us personally (i.e. they're a social threat) from an evolutionary perspective we need to be able to respond to the threat to keep our social status. If we are in danger of being harmed, we need to be able to protect ourselves. In other words, in real life when we're threatened we feel motivated to defend ourselves and our social status. In the following study, the researchers suggest that it isn't just about experiencing emotion that sparks the activation of the amygdala, but it is about motivation to respond in some way. The results suggest that testosterone works by increasing the activation of the amygdala when we are motivated to retaliate to a social threat, which in turn prepares our body physically for that defense.

In this study half of the participants (54 healthy females) were given a small dose of testosterone and the other half were given a placebo. As in similar studies, lots of pictures of faces that were either angry or happy were shown one at a time while the participant lays down in an fMRI scanner. For each face that appears on the screen, the participants have to "avoid" or "approach" the face. As they have to lie perfectly still in the fMRI, they avoid/approach the face by moving a joystick with their hand. When pushed one way the stick will make the face gradually appear larger (approach) and when moved another way it will make it gradually appear smaller (avoid). The "approach" is when the face is made to look like it's coming towards the person (i.e. it gets bigger), and vice-versa for avoidance. The faces appeared on the screen one at a time and the participants followed the instructions (approach or avoid). The motivation factor was the following of the researcher's instructions to approach or avoid the faces (which is important to note: the participants didn't get to choose to avoid or approach, they were instructed). While in the scanner the activity of the participants' amygdala and prefrontal cortices were measured.

The results showed that the group with testosterone had more activation in their amygdala when they were *approaching angry faces* when they were told to do so and the activation was higher than when they approached happy faces. So here we can see that perhaps in a situation that involves a social threat (an angry face) and we are motivated to defend ourselves against that threat, testosterone levels play an important function in increasing the activation of our amygdala which will result in more emotional and physical readiness to react aggressively. The activation of the amygdala may help us get physically prepared for the confrontation by triggering the release of adrenaline into our bodies that will give us the instant energy to fight. And the role of testosterone may be to help prepare for that confrontation, as shown by the fact that the testosterone condition had higher amygdala activation when they were moving the joystick forwards and making the angry face become larger.

But while testosterone might influence aggression at times when we are socially threatened by increasing the activation of the amygdala when we are *approaching* a threat, that alone doesn't yet give us the full picture of how that might lead to acting in a violent manner, like punching or shooting someone.

The study showed that there wasn't a significant difference in the activation of the prefrontal cortex across groups. We've looked at the key role in the prefrontal cortex in being able to process information and make judgements based on long-term consequences, and so it's important not to overlook this function when you are explaining

While Goetz et al. showed that testosterone affects the amygdala, Radke et al. can show how motivation is an important influence as well. The influence of motivation is key in being able to link the amygdala activation with aggression.

Remember that emotion, amygdala activation and aggression are all related. The activation of the amygdala enables experiencing emotion through its role in the stress response. High levels of emotion could easily lead to aggressive reactions to social threats.

In this experiment, motivation was defined as following the experimenters instructions.

acts of aggression that have serious consequences. If we have high levels of testosterone, perhaps we won't necessarily react aggressively when we're threatened because we'll be able to regulate that emotional reaction and we'll be able to think through our decisions. However, individuals with existing damage or low functioning of the prefrontal cortex may not be able to do so, which could explain why studies have shown low prefrontal cortex activity and high levels of testosterone in prison populations. In this section I hope you've realised even more how behaviours like violence, aggression and crime are complex and that drawing broad conclusions that ignore specific factors leads to erroneous statements and uninformed opinions.

Radke et al.'s study showed that testosterone impacted the amygdala when participants were motivated to approach the angry face. How might this help explain the connection between testosterone and aggression?

So in this section we've gone further with our understanding of the amygdala and seen how the many correlations shown between testosterone and aggression could be explained through the effects it has on other parts of the brain. We've also introduced the value of using evolutionary explanations for biology to help with our understanding of human behaviour.

You've also been introduced to the idea that human behaviour involves one more element that we haven't explored much until now: social influences. We will explore this later in the chapter, as humans are naturally social animals and it is our sociability that can impact our behaviour and mental processes in many ways. It's important that when we're applying our understanding of behaviour to explanations of violence that we have to try to test our abstract understandings by applying them to real life examples. This thought process is imperative if you are to develop a full understanding of the applications, and limitations, of psychological research.

If you don't understand how testosterone influences the behaviour of aggression, there are other topics covered that will allow you to explain how testosterone may affect behaviour (e.g. competition and attraction).

Guiding Question:

How can Radke et al.'s study demonstrate how high testosterone levels may influence aggression?

Critical Thinking Extension:

Ecological Validity and Operational Definitions: An operational definition is how a variable is defined in a particular study. In this example, one operational definition was that of "social threat". In this study they defined this as a face being moved closer or further away on a computer screen. But to what extent does this resemble social threat in a real life situation? A good discussion of the ecological validity of this study would include examples of social threat that this study's operational definition might not apply to, but yet might still result in aggressive reactions. For instance, receiving a threatening email (or Facebook post, tweet or other form of communication) from someone that attacks you personally is still a social threat, but does not involve the perception of an angry face. So ecological validity could be questioned here based on the limited operational definition of the social threat variable. More research into multiple forms of threat and its influence on the amygdala would be required in order to test the generalizability of these conclusions.

If you're interested…

radiolab.org has an interesting podcast called "Forget about Blame?" In this podcast the hosts talk with neuroscientist David Eagleman, who is very much about the biological approach to understanding criminal behaviour. They have some interesting discussions about biological origins of behaviour and culpability.

Relevant Topics

- Ethics and Research Methods (BA)
- Origins of conflict
- Hormones and behaviour
- Evolution

Practice Exam Questions

- Evaluate one study related to hormones and behaviour.
- Outline one ethical consideration related to hormones and behaviour.
- Discuss one origin of conflict.
- Evaluate one evolutionary explanation of behaviour.

Research Methods

The laboratory experiment is valuable for isolating an independent variable's effect on a dependent variable. In the studies involving injections of testosterone in samples that have been controlled for other characteristics (e.g a history of violence or antisocial behaviour) we can see the effect that the testosterone levels have on brain function. It's important to note the causation here, however: the causation regarding the role of testosterone on the function of the amygdala in particular situations can be deduced. This does not infer a causal relationship between other relationships, such as testosterone and violent crime.

Ethical Considerations

The right to withdraw is an important consideration in any study using technology like fMRIs. These machines are incredibly noisy, cramped and uncomfortable. Participants need to have the right to stop participating if they are feeling uncomfortable. For instance, they may begin to have feelings of claustrophobia.

2.5 Culture and Biology
How can culture affect testosterone levels?

(a) Culture and Cultural Values

In nature we don't have injections that increase our testosterone, so if we want to develop our understanding of how testosterone can influence aggression we need to investigate possible factors that may *naturally* influence testosterone levels.

This has been the source of numerous studies, including some that have shown that testosterone levels can increase as a result of our environment. For instance, if you're watching your favourite sports team play and they win, your testosterone levels may increase more than if they lost (Bernhardt, 1998). And it's not just physical sports, testosterone has also been shown to rise in competitive chess tournaments (Mazur et al., 1992). A lot of research has suggested that testosterone plays an important role in getting the body ready for competition, and that displays of dominance and might facilitate displays of aggression that make someone look and act tougher (Cohen et al., 1996). There are many possible factors that can influence testosterone levels, but in this section we'll look at the interaction of cultural values and social threat.

A value is something that is believed to be important to an individual; a cultural value is something that a cultural group commonly believes to be important. For instance, in some cultures individual expression and the freedom to make your own decisions is highly valued, whereas in other cultures there might be more of a higher value placed on maintaining good relationships within your family even if this means not doing what you want. So while values are individual beliefs of what is important, these individual beliefs are highly influenced by our social and cultural environment.

> A cultural value is a term used to describe something that a particular cultural group believes is important. For example, having respect for elders is a cultural value in Japan and is reflected in Japanese language. What cultural values exist in a cultural group you belong to?

Comparisons between cultural values and their effect on our biology, cognition and behaviour was the subject of a study in the United States that compared males from different states in the US (Cohen et al., 1996). The actual details of the study will be explored in more depth in the next section, but in order to fully understand the study it is important to understand its cultural context. The Eastern border of the United States is roughly divided by the "South" and the "North". If you've learnt about American history and in particular the American Civil War, you may already be familiar with the general differences between these two areas within the USA. Cohen et al.'s preliminary research findings suggested that the South is generally more violent than the North and so they wanted to investigate a possible hypothesis as to why this might be.

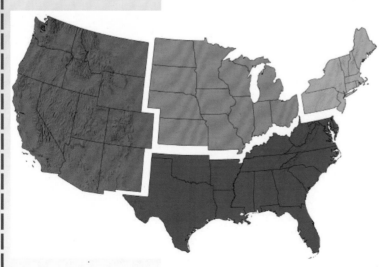

The area of the US coloured in red is typically what is referred to when people talk about the "southern states."

Their explanation for the existence for increased violence in the South is based on what they term a "culture of honour". This culture of honour, the researchers claim, exists in the Southern States, but not the North. In the South in the USA when America was a young country (having broken away from England) the main economy was based on herding (farming animals). As there wasn't a lot of law enforcement or government in the South during this time, men who wanted to survive had to rely on themselves. For instance, if someone tried to steal their cows or their sheep they couldn't go to the police as there often weren't any to protect their herds, so they needed to look out for themselves. In order to do this, a man would have to present an image of toughness, a stern façade that showed he couldn't be messed with. However, this wasn't the case in the North as their economy was more industrial with more cities and less farming and agriculture. There was also more law enforcement (e.g. sheriffs and police officers) so Northerners didn't have to take the law into their own hands.

Interestingly, even though modern society no longer relies on such "Wild West" type behaviour, the values and beliefs associated with the culture of honour seem to have persisted in the South. For instance, Southerners are more likely to condone and approve violence, especially if it is in defense and "…the South exceeds the North only in homicides that are argument-or-conflict related, not in homicides that are committed while another felony, such as robbery or burglary, is being performed." (Cohen et al., p.946). This suggests that Southerners might be more likely to use violence when confronted, perhaps in defense of one's honour.

Cohen et al. hypothesize that being able to defend one's honour is a value that is particular to Southerners because of historical influences. In the next section you'll learn about how this cultural value may have biological effects during times of social threat.

Cohen et al. provide many possible reasons why the culture of honour emerged in southern states in the USA. The idea of herding and law enforcement is just one. You can read the full article to learn about the others.

> ### Guiding Question:
> Why are cultural values different between Northern and Southern white Americans?

Critical Thinking Extension:
Avoiding Generalizations: Whenever we discuss culture and cultural values it is very tempting to make broad generalizations about a culture and overlook the fact that cultures are made up of individuals and individuals are very different from one another. One way to avoid doing this is to identify a culture you belong to and one or two cultural values that could be said to exist in that particular cultural group, but that you do not hold personally.

If you're interested…

The original article that describes the culture of honour and how it came to be in the Southern States is available online. The language is relatively accessible for high school students so if you're interested in learning about this more, or if the explanation here needs clarifying, you'll be able to find this article online using google and the title: "Insult, Aggression and the Southern Culture of Honor".

(b)   Cultural Values and Testosterone

To test their hypotheses regarding cultural values and responses to confrontations, Cohen et al. devised a fascinating experiment that involved insulting Northern and Southern males and testing their responses, including the differences in testosterone levels. The study compares the reactions of American college students to a situation where they were insulted and challenged. The researchers wanted to compare the reactions of college students from Northern states in the USA (e.g. New York, Massachusetts) and Southern States of the USA (e.g. Texas, Georgia, Kentucky).

There were many different variations of a similar experimental paradigm. In one of the experiments the researchers gathered Northern white male participants and Southern white male participants who were told they were taking part in an experiment on judgement. They took saliva samples in order to measure their levels of testosterone so they could compare the changes in testosterone levels (they told the participants they were measuring blood-sugar levels). After an introduction to the experiment, participants filled out a questionnaire and were told to walk down a long hallway to put the questionnaire on a table. As they walked back from putting down the piece of paper, a confederate of the study was pretending to organise a file cabinet in the middle of the hallway. As the participant walked past, the confederate bumped the participant and called him an "a**hole."

Cohen et al. had numerous experiments with subtly different conditions. It's pretty interesting to read the other variations as well. For example, they also measured cortisol levels (a hormone released during times of stress).

How would you react to someone insulting you? Would you feel a need to defend your honour, or would you be able to brush it off?

The researchers had many dependent variables (which are interesting and you can read more about in the original), but the important one for us is that the testosterone levels of Southern white males increased by 12% from before the experiment began, compared with 4% from the Northern males.

So our level of testosterone that rises getting us ready for conflict in a social situation may be influenced by our cultural values.

Due to the increase in testosterone the Southern white males were more primed for competitive and even aggressive actions. This may be because of their cultural values in that when they are confronted and offended they think about that threat differently because of the value they place on defending their honour. Northerners on the other hand, may find it easier to dismiss the offensive remark, which means there is little increase in testosterone getting them ready to be aggressive.

It's important to note that these results by themselves don't show that testosterone can cause aggression. The earlier research showed that relationship. This study provides a possible explanation for why some people might have higher testosterone levels than others.

This could have important implications in the study of violent crime. We've seen how testosterone can increase the body's physiological readiness for aggressive actions and that violent criminals have higher levels of testosterone, but we can't simply put the blame on these biological factors. Our social and cultural environment may affect our values and our thinking, which could in turn affect our physiological processes in certain circumstances. Here we see once more the complex interactions between social, biological and cognitive influences when trying to understand complex human behaviours such as aggression, violence and criminal behaviour.

Guiding Question:

How might cultural values influence aggression?

Critical Thinking Extension:

Population Validity: Population validity is the extent to which findings from one study can be valid in terms of applying to a larger population (it affects generalizability). This research focused specifically on southern white males. Why do you think they focused only on southern white males? Why not males from other cultures? Based on this limited sample, to what extent can these findings be generalized to other situations where social factors may influence cognition, biology and aggression? Are there other social environments that exist in society today that might pass on values similar to the "culture of honour" which may have similar to effects to the one explained above?

If you're interested…

There's an interesting article called "The Role of Testosterone in Social Interaction" by Eisenegger, Haushofer and Fehr that is available online. This article goes further into explaining the role that testosterone plays in social interactions.

Relevant Topics

- Ethics and Research Methods (BA, SCA)
- Origins of conflict
- Hormones and behaviour
- Culture and behaviour

Practice Exam Questions

- Explain one study related to hormones and behaviour.
- Discuss one ethical consideration related to hormones and behaviour.
- Describe one study related to culture and behaviour.

Research Methods

Social psychologists like Dov Cohen also use the experimental method. This is another study that is difficult to categorize, but there's definitely a variable (cultural background) that is being studied in relation to another variable (aggression and testosterone levels in response to insult). Experiments in social psychology enable researchers to investigate the effects of social variables on behaviour.

Ethical Considerations

Informed consent would need to be considered carefully in Cohen et al.'s study. On the one hand, you probably need informed consent in order to ensure your experimental design can be approved by ethical review committees. However, they would have had to carefully consider just how much information to provide participants so as to ensure the validity of their results. For example, they can't tell them that an actor will insult them because this would affect the behaviour of the participant and could be a confounding variable. Here we can see that the combination of informed consent and debriefing is often important in research.

2.6 Neurotransmission
Can chemicals in our brain cause violent crime?

(a)   *Neurotransmission*

We've looked at one type of chemical messenger in the body, hormones, and now we're going to look at a second type of chemical messenger, neurotransmitters. Whereas hormones are chemicals transmitted through our bloodstream, neurotransmitters are chemicals transmitted through cells in our body called neurons. Remember we have *billions* of neurons in our brain. We also have neurons throughout our central nervous system (CNS) and our peripheral nervous system (PNS). The central nervous system is our brain and our spinal cord, while the PNS consists of nerves outside of the CNS. These nervous systems are how we receive and respond to sensory information, like external emotional stimuli.

Our nervous systems perceive and interpret environmental stimuli through our sensory organs: our ears, eyes, skin, tongue and nose. These organs are responsible for sensory perception: detecting environmental stimuli such as what we see, hear, taste, touch and smell. When an environmental stimuli is detected, our sensory organs send messages to our brain through a process called neurotransmission. Neurotransmission is the process of neurotransmitters being sent from one neuron to the next at a speed of anywhere from one to over 200mph. This rapid transmission of chemicals throughout the nervous system allows you to perform complex behaviours and cognitive processes quickly. In psychology when we're talking about the level of brain *function* or brain *activity* we are referring to the level of neurotransmission happening in particular areas of the brain. This is what brain scanning technology like fMRIs and PETs measure.

When sensory information is detected through our sensory organs, neurons in the stimulated area are activated and send messages along neural pathways through particular areas of the brain. A neural pathway is a series of connected neurons that go through the process of neurotransmission between particular areas of the nervous system. Sensory information is sent along neural pathways to the relevant area of the brain that processes that type of information. For example, you have a particular area of your brain that processes hearing spoken language and a different part for processing written language (i.e. when you are reading). You even have a particular area of your brain that processes drawing, watching and imagining cartoons. This is the concept of localization of brain function that was introduced earlier in the chapter.

I like to think of neural pathways as kind of like roads of neurons. If we continually practice something and have lots of repeated experience with receiving sensory stimulation and responding to it in a certain way (e.g. catching and throwing a ball, typing on a computer, listening to and understanding a new language) the neural pathway will become well-developed and strong, like a big highway of chemical and electrical

Understanding the process of how our environment can affect brain function will be helpful when learning about neuroplasticity in the next topic.

Hormones and neurotransmitters are quite similar. In fact, some chemicals can be both neurotransmitters *and* hormones.

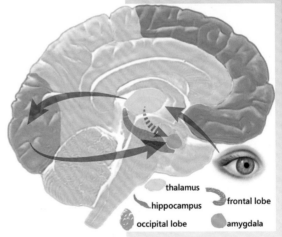

thalamus

hippocampus

frontal lobe

occipital lobe

amygdala

This is an illustration of how emotional information perceived through our visual sensory organ (our eyes) may be transmitted through various parts of the brain related to processing emotional stimuli.

97

signals being fired through the brain. If we don't use a particular neural pathway often or the sensory perception is new, it's a bit more like cutting a way through an overgrown jungle path. This is why when we begin a new task like learning a new sport, instrument or a language, we feel slow and clumsy – our neural pathways are underdeveloped. We will learn more about this later when we study neuroplasticity.

Particular neural pathways and areas of the brain also have various levels of specific neurotransmitters. Neuropsychology often involves the correlations between levels of specific neurotransmitters in particular areas of the brain and our behaviour. Here are some neurotransmitters and their correlates:

A neural pathway is a series of connected neurons that send signals throughout different areas of the brain and the body.

Neurotransmitter	Behaviour/Cognitive Process
Serotonin	Mood, sleep, impulsive behaviour, violence.
Dopamine	Love, motivation, pleasure, learning.
Acetylcholine	Muscle movement, learning, memory.

You can see from the wide range of behaviours that these chemicals are associated with that the relationships between neurotransmission, the brain, and behaviour is rarely simple. In the next section we will look at a very specific relationship: how levels of serotonin may influence violence through its effect on the prefrontal cortex during times of social threat.

There are many factors that can influence neurotransmitter levels, including sleep, diet, exercise, medication and drug use, genetics, and other environmental influences. In the next section you will see how perhaps diet, levels of serotonin and violence may be related.

The process of neurotransmission can be quite complex. In biology class you might learn more about this process. This topic focuses on how one specific neurotransmitter, serotonin, might affect behaviour.

Guiding Question:

How do particular areas of our brain receive relevant information about environmental stimuli?

Critical Thinking Extension:

Over a hundred years of neuropsychological research has shown that our ability to process information and perform cognitive processes is a result of the biological process of neurotransmission. These findings may challenge existing notions of what happens when we die. Our ability to remember, think and feel makes us who we are. So if we lose the biological ability to perform these tasks (e.g. when we die and our neurons stop firing), can we have perceptions and perform cognitive processes in the afterlife? If so, how? If not, what type of afterlife are we going to experience without sensory experience or cognition?

If you're interested…

There is a very famous book of case studies with people with brain abnormalities called *The man who mistook his wife for a hat* by the late, great Oliver Sacks. If you're interested in learning about the brain and how abnormalities and dysfunction in particular areas of the brain can affect our behaviour, this is a fascinating book to read. You can also watch Sacks' TED Talk about hallucinations and the brain. It is in this talk that he mentions the very specific area of the brain responsible for processing cartoons.

(b)   Serotonin, Threat and the Prefrontal Cortex

The neuropsychological world of neurotransmission is extremely complex, so in this section we're going to focus specifically on how changes in levels of serotonin may affect our behaviour. Serotonin has been shown to affect many behaviours, but we'll focus on how it might be correlated with aggression and violent crime.

Numerous research studies have shown that violent criminals tend to have low levels of serotonin (e.g. Moi and Jessel, 1995; Scerbo and Raine, 1993). Studies have also shown that serotonin is associated with controlling impulsive behaviour (Pattij, 2008). Hopefully from what you've learned already in this chapter you'll be able to start making predictions about the areas of the brain that might be associated with serotonin levels and impulsive behaviour.

Many experiments using rats and other animals have shown that changes in serotonin levels affect aggression (e.g. Annemoon et al., 2000). But the same problems exist in these studies as with other animal studies we've looked at: they don't show *how* serotonin can affect aggression, they just show that it does. Because of the complex nature of the way serotonin is communicated through the brain and the difficulty of manipulating aggression in a lab, it's been difficult to explain *how* serotonin affects violence. With modern technology, however, researchers can now investigate the relationship between areas of the brain and neurotransmission in ways they couldn't before. The following study provides one possible answer for explaining the relationship between neurotransmission (serotonin levels) and violent behaviour by measuring brain activity in an fMRI when participants' serotonin levels are manipulated and they are exposed to emotional faces.

Passamonti et al. (2012) gathered healthy volunteers for an experiment where their serotonin levels were manipulated by altering their diet. A repeated measures design was used where on one day they were given a drink that lacked tryptophan. Tryptophan is an important amino acid that helps build serotonin and so a lack of tryptophan in the diet will reduce levels of serotonin available in the brain. In the control condition they were given a placebo, which was the same type of drink to consume but contained normal amounts of tryptophan. The expected effect of the reduced tryptophan would be reduced serotonin levels. The participants were then put in fMRIs and their brain activity was measured while they were seeing images of happy, angry and neutral faces. The researchers could see the activation of the brain, including the amygdala and the prefrontal cortex.

A common experimental paradigm involves the use of images of faces that are expressing different emotions. Researchers compare brain activity when processing different types of emotions.

The results showed that there was reduced activity in the frontal lobe during the low serotonin conditions. Importantly, the disruption occurred during the angry faces, but not during the sad and neutral faces. Which means that it's not just any stimulus that is affected by serotonin, but a *threatening* stimulus in particular. The reduced activation of the prefrontal cortex might affect violence through our inability to regulate impulsive actions and/or reactions to social threat. If someone has low levels of serotonin and they are threatened, they may not

Serotonin is associated with many different behaviours. Impulsive, antisocial and aggressive behaviour are only some of the behaviours that research has correlated with serotonin.

There is currently no way of measuring serotonin levels in the brains of living people. It is measured using spinal fluid or in this case, assumed by measuring levels of tryptophan.

Tryptophan is an amino acid found in food. It helps to build serotonin. Passamonti et al.'s study suggests that diet could be a contributing factor to aggressive behaviour.

By reducing the communication between the amygdala and the prefrontal cortex during perception of threatening stimuli, serotonin may affect an individual's ability to regulate their emotional reaction.

Remember that these topics are all interrelated. You should be trying to apply what you already know about topics such as the PFC, the amygdala and emotion to this new topic, serotonin.

have the function in the PFC to enable them to think through their actions and might react impulsively.

The results also showed that there was disruption of the communication between the amygdala and the frontal lobe. The researchers concluded that this evidence supports the idea that the serotonin impacts the prefrontal cortex role in suppressing negative emotions generated in the amygdala as a response to the threatening face. In other words, when we perceive an angry face we might instinctively feel a negative emotion in response to that angry person. This emotional response is instinctively generated in the amygdala and may be the basis of aggressive and other highly emotional reactions. If our PFC is functioning properly we may be able to suppress (reduce) our negative reaction to someone's anger towards us. However, with low functioning PFC our amygdala may activate in reaction to perceiving the angry face and we may not be able to reduce our emotion or behavioral response to the angry face, thus increasing the likelihood of an aggressive or violent reaction.

> ### Guiding Question:
>
> How can the results of Passamonti et al.'s study explain the correlation between serotonin and violence?

Critical Thinking Extension:

Areas of Uncertainty: When applying correlations like the one shown in the above study there are often areas of uncertainty as to the extent to which a single relationship (i.e. between serotonin and perceiving an angry face) can be applied to explain a complex behaviour like violent crime. Often a single explanation is not strong enough, or it could be made stronger by combining another concept. Here we can see that serotonin can influence the prefrontal cortex and the amygdala. After you've explained this relationship, the next could be to explain hypotheses about how the combination of low serotonin and high testosterone might influence aggression. This could be an example of triangulation: using more than one data point to explain a relationship.

If you're interested…

Dr Molly Crockett was a co-author of this study. You can watch her give a TED talk about the importance of being aware of publications of psychological research in the popular media called "Beware neuro-bunk." She also gives another TED talk called "Understanding the Brain" where she talks about the implications and applications of neuropsychology.

Relevant Topics

- Neurotransmission
- Ethics and Research Methods (BA)
- Origins of Conflict
- Evolution

Practice Exam Questions

- Explain how one study demonstrates an effect of neurotransmission on human behaviour.
- Outline one ethical consideration related to research on neurotransmission.
- Describe one study related to evolution and behaviour.

Research Methods

Much like the testosterone studies, manipulating physiology (as Passamonti et al. have done with tryptophan and serotonin) is an important characteristic in many true experiments that aim to investigate relationships between the brain and behaviour. By designing careful experiments, researchers can further investigate causal relationships between variables like neurotransmitters and their effect on particular areas of the brain in particular circumstances. But remember that just because it causes an effect on the brain, doesn't mean to say it *causes* behaviour.

Ethical Considerations

Whenever participants are going to be ingested with substances (like the drink they had to consume in Passamonti et al.'s study) informed consent and debriefing are important. They should be made to feel confident that the substance they are ingesting will not have any long-term side-effects. Moreover, if they are deceived of the nature of the substance they need to be debriefed about what it was they actually consumed and why.

2.7 Neuroplasticity
How can the way we think affect our brain?

(a) Environment and Brain Development

Neuroplasticity is the phenomenon of the brain developing new neural pathways as a result of repeated experience of something. This ability of the brain to grow and change as a result of experience is a relatively new concept discovered in psychology. For many decades researchers believed that the structure of the brain was fixed and could not change. Early animal studies and recent studies using the invention of technology like the MRI show that this is not the case.

Neuroplasticity refers to the brain's ability to demonstrate plasticity: the quality of being easily shaped or moulded. Repeated sensory stimulation, such as what we see, feel and touch, will affect the extent to which neural pathways are developed between particular areas of the brain. The construction and maintenance of these neural pathways is what leads to changes in our brain's function and structure.

When learning about serotonin earlier, you learnt about the internal process of sensory organs receiving information and connecting different parts of the brain. With this understanding it is now possible to begin investigating in more depth just how our environment can affect our neurological development, i.e. how neuroplasticity occurs.

The more sensory stimulation we have in our environment, the more input our sensory organs will detect and want to respond to. Moreover, lots of different types of sensory stimulation will require many different areas of our brain all activating and communicating with one another through neurotransmission. The more our brains are active, the more connections (neural pathways) will require developing. Some of the first studies investigating the effects of sensory stimulation on brain development were carried out by Rosenzweig and Bennet in the 1960s (as reviewed in Rosenzweig and Bennett, 1996). Like we've seen before, they used animals to test their initial hypothesis about correlations between the brain and behavior.

Rats in cages with other rats and more toys end up having heavier brains. The stimulation they receive by social and environmental action is causing their brains to make more neural connections, which is why their brains become heavier.

In one of these experiments male rats were chosen from different litters to be randomly allocated to two different conditions: an enriched condition and a deprived condition. In the enriched environment there were about 10-12 rats with a range of toys that the rats could play with. This group also received "maze training". The deprived cage was slightly smaller, the rat was alone and the cage was isolated in a separate room from the other cages. Both conditions had adequate food and water. The rats lived in these different conditions for four to ten week periods (approximately 30-60 days). After these treatment periods, the rats were autopsied in order to determine if any differences had developed. To reduce researcher bias, a blind procedure was used where the scientist doing the autopsy on the rats did not know which type of cage they had been in. The rat's brains were dissected and various sections were measured, weighed and analyzed to determine the amount of cell growth and levels of neurotransmitter activity.

They found that rats living in the enriched cages developed heavier and thicker frontal lobes. Replications and further studies found that the brain weight of rats in enriched environments were 7 to 10% heavier than those in deprived ones. The results were quite groundbreaking at the time as they challenged the long standing idea that brain growth was fixed from birth. These researchers were so surprised by the results that they replicated the research numerous times and with each replication the same results were obtained, demonstrating the study's test-retest reliability.

Here we can see that sensory enrichment and deprivation might influence brain development. Sensory deprivation simply means not having much information coming through your senses (what you see, hear, think, feel, taste, etc.) All of this sensory information stimulates the brain and increased stimulation of senses means that multiple areas of our brain can be functioning and increased practice (or lack of) over time can have a profound effect on our brain's development.

The rats in the enriched environment would have been socially interacting with other rats. Not quite talking, but communicating, playing, bonding, smelling, etc. This social interaction would have required numerous areas of the brain to function. Playing with toys, running wheels and receiving the maze training would have also required plenty of regions of the brain to activate and communicate with one another. In order to learn and perform these tasks, the rats' neurons would need to be making more connections, resulting in growth in those areas of the brain (e.g. the frontal lobe).

Another exciting new discovery in neuropsychology is that research findings suggest we are able to grow new neurons in our brain: this was previously thought impossible. This phenomenon is called neurogenesis. Research into neurogenesis is in its infancy, but it has exciting possibilities.

Guiding Question:

How does this experiment show that our environment can influence brain development?

Critical Thinking Extension:

Triangulation: The relationships demonstrated in studies can be determined to be more reliable if the same procedures are replicated many times and the same results are gathered. When this happens it's called **test-retest** reliability. The above study could be said to have test-retest reliability because they replicated the experiment numerous times before publishing their findings. Getting data from more than one source is an example of **data triangulation**. How could Passamonti et al. increase the reliability of their conclusions?

If you're interested…

If you're interested in neuroplasticity and neuroscience, I highly recommend the fascinating book called The Brain That Changes Itself: Stories of Personal Triumph from the Frontiers of Brain Science by Norman Doidge. This is a collection of stories about how principles and practices relating to neuroplasticity can be applied to benefit people who suffer from brain dysfunction.

(b)   Childhood and Brain Development

With Roswenzweig and Bennet's research we see the problem again of generalizing results from animal studies to humans. We have seen that having enriched experiences can influence the brain development in rats, but can we really apply this to humans?

All mammals have neurons and the basic structure is similar across species. In fact, early research into the functioning of neurons used a type of sea snail that has abnormally large neurons, so it was easier to examine their structure and function.

When new learning is occurring neurons need to create more synapses, so connection between and growth of more dendrites and axon terminals (the branch-like things that connect neurons with one another) are necessary to connect more neurons throughout the brain. Connections will be weak when we are learning something new because areas of the brain involved in learning the new task or skill haven't had to communicate with one another before. Neurons need to create more synapses in order for the neurotransmission to occur. In the previously mentioned rat study by Rosenzweig and Bennett, synapses increased by about 20% when the rats were in enriched cages (Rosenzweig and Bennett, 1996). This shows that the dendrites and axon terminals were making more connections as a result of having more sensory stimulation. This would allow faster and more fluent neurotransmission to occur between different areas of the brain.

In this image you can see a neuron communicating with another neuron (insert) and a close-up view of how this is happening at the synapse. (courtesy of OpenStax via wikicommons)

Perry and Pollard's full text (1997) is available online if you are interested in reading the full article.

But how can we test the effects of environmental stimulation and deprivation on humans? There are obvious ethical issues with conducting such an experiment on humans: most people wouldn't agree to being locked in a cage for a month and definitely wouldn't agree to this being done to their child. So we see the value of the natural experiment. Sometimes these experimental conditions (being in an enriched or deprived environment) occur in the natural world and this allows researchers to investigate the same types of factors affecting our biology as have been investigated on animals in the laboratory.

Researchers made the use of one natural occurring form of environmental deprivation by using MRI scans to compare the brains of neglected children aged 0 – 17 years old (Perry and Pollard, 1997). They investigated many types of neglect, including social, physical, cognitive and emotional. They compared some kids who experienced global neglect, meaning they experienced multiple types of neglect. MRI results showed that the children who experienced global neglect tended to have less volume in their cortices (i.e. their cortices were smaller on average). MRIs tend to measure volume in particular areas of the brain. Volume simply refers to capacity: the more volume the more connections you have between neurons.

Being neglected as a child leads to having less sensory stimulation. Less stimulation will lead to a lack of connections being made in important areas of your brain and poor brain function in key areas has been correlated with anti-social behaviours like aggression and violence. Interestingly, one punishment commonly used in prisons is solitary confinement, where the inmate is locked in a small, dark, cell away from other inmates and any form of social interaction. This is designed to reduce bad behaviour, but perhaps it only further weakens important areas of the brain that are needed to control violent impulses and antisocial behaviour in the first place.

From what you know about the interaction of the brain and our environment, you can hopefully provide explanations as to why neglect may have damaging effects on the brain.

Poverty is another environment variable that has that has been correlated with brain development. A number of studies have investigated correlations between socioeconomic status and brain development and similar results are found: children from poorer areas tend to have less volume in their hippocampi and amygdalae (e.g. Luby et al., 2013). The hippocampus is another important area of the temporal lobe associated with learning and memory. Studies have shown that it plays an important role in transferring short-term memory into long-term memory. You'll learn more about this part of the brain when studying PTSD. You'll also learn about how exposure to traumatic experiences in childhood and adulthood can negatively affect brain function and structure.

We're now moving into combining our understanding of origins of behaviour with treatments. If we can better understand underlying causes of antisocial behaviour, this allows for more effective treatment and prevention strategies to be developed.

In summary, this research on humans seems to corroborate what earlier animal studies suggested about the effects of the environment on brain development.

Guiding Question:

How does research show that childhood environment can influence brain development?

Critical Thinking Extension:

Alternative Explanations: The guiding question above is leading towards developing an explanation of how neglect and poverty might affect brain development. An important abstract thinking skill is being able to offer alternative explanations for relationships. The correlation between poverty and brain development could be explained through the fact that if people don't have enough money to provide stimulating toys and experiences for children their brains might not develop as well as those kids who do have plenty of enriching experiences. But can you offer a counter-explanation for this relationship? For instance, could genetics or stress be factors involved in the correlation between poverty and brain development?

If you're interested...

A documentary was made about Norman Doidge's book (mentioned in the previous "If you're interested…") and can be found online. In this documentary you can watch examples of neuroplasticity being put into practice to help people who suffer from brain dysfunction. My favourite part of the film is when Doidge tries to count to ten while having mild electric shocks being sent to the parts of his brain associated with language processing.

(c)   *Meditation and Mindfulness*

From these results we can see that enriched and deprived environmental experiences in childhood can affect the brain development of children. But how does this apply to criminology? The simple answer is that if violent criminals have poor brain function in key areas such as the prefrontal cortex, perhaps this is a result of their childhood experiences. This raises interesting questions surrounding culpability in criminals: If a person commits a violent crime that can be explained through poor brain function, and their poor brain function can be explained as a result of environmental experiences beyond their control (e.g. childhood poverty, neglect, trauma, etc.), to what extent can we blame them for their actions?

This question is sure to raise some heated responses and it makes for an excellent classroom debate if enough students feel strongly about the discussion. But even if we can't come to an agreement about where the blame lies for violence in society, surely we can agree that we should be implementing strategies to reduce it. This is where the field of neuroplasticity can have significant implications and applications: if we understand the brain structures and biological correlates of violence, and we know that the brain can change as a result of experience, can we develop strategies to improve functions in areas of the brain like the prefrontal cortex in people prone to violence?

There are many factors that influence the brain's development, including stress, diet, exercise, genetics, and as we've already learned, experience. Let's look at one new idea that is slowly beginning to influence the justice system: mindfulness and meditation. Some prisons are beginning to implement strategies in mindfulness for their inmates. Mindfulness is a kind of meditation.

There are many different ways to practice mindfulness but it essentially involves a deep concentration that focuses on being aware of yourself and your thoughts. Usually when we try to clear our mind and relax, we encounter one of two problems. Sometimes we become bored. Other times our mind jumps to agitating thoughts, for example we might remember a text message we need to send. Either way we allow our thoughts to stray and sometimes it's hard to get our concentration back. Mindfulness challenges us to keep our minds from being distracted and to focus instead on being completely present. Essentially, we turn our attention to our minds themselves, and think about where our thoughts come from, and where they go. This is no easy feat, but there are many well documented health benefits associated with mindfulness, including significant reductions in stress and anxiety. When you try being mindful you'll realise it involves significant concentration, which is a function of the prefrontal cortex. Repeated use of the prefrontal cortex in this way can lead to connections in the prefrontal cortex strengthening and even an increase in volume.

The best way to learn about mindfulness is to practice it. After a mindfulness session, try to reflect on the level of effort you needed to apply in order to maintain concentration. This effort requires your prefrontal cortex. If you practice this type of high-level concentration for extended periods and over a long period of time, your neurons in this area will improve connections and neurotransmission will happen faster and more easily along newly developed neural pathways. For instance, studies on monks have shown correlations between meditation and brain structure. One study found a correlation between the density of the prefrontal cortex and mediation practice (Lazar et al., 2005).

Here we can see that our brain doesn't just change as a result of *external* stimuli – we can induce changes in our brain structure through mental processes that we initiate in our minds. The way we think over long periods of time can really change our brains.

Are there any circumstances you feel that a criminal could be excused for their actions?

Meditation has many forms. It essentially involves intense focus and concentration on particular thought patterns. Mindfulness could be viewed as a type of meditation whereby one's thought patterns try to focus on being in the present moment.

How might meditation and/or mindfulness improve the functions of the prefrontal cortex?

Critical Thinking Extension:

Hypothesizing: One of the exciting processes involved in studying psychology is generating questions and possible areas to inquire for yourself. Do other behaviours affect the prefrontal cortex? Do other behaviours and/or cognitive processes rely on function of the prefrontal cortex? Can you maintain concentration in class for long periods of time? Could the rise in diagnosis of disorders like ADHD be correlated with the prefrontal cortex? Unfortunately, we don't have the time to explore all your possible questions, but generating these questions and hypotheses can make the study of psychology more interesting and can enliven class discussions. It's important to note that often these questions just lead to more questions, and there aren't always definitive answers in psychology.

If you're interested...

The most difficult part about writing this topic on neuroplasticity is all the fascinating research I've had to leave out. There are heaps of studies investigating the relationship between experience and the brain. If you can think of a behaviour or cognitive process, chances are it's been studied in relation to neuroplasticity. Playing video games, using social media, and learning to juggle are just some of the areas of study in the effects of experience on the brain. These could make interesting EE topics.

(d)   Mindfulness and Emotion

If people who have dysfunction in their prefrontal cortices and amygdalae can be trained in meditative practices, perhaps they will be able to better regulate their emotional and behavioural reactions when they are in threatening situations and feel the impulse to react aggressively.

Evidence for the possible effects of such training comes from a study by Desbordes et al. (2012) where they compared the effects of mindfulness training on the response of the amygdala to emotional stimuli. There were two control groups and one treatment group. The treatment group received eight weeks of mindfulness training. One of the control groups received no training while the other control group received cognitive training that wasn't related to mindfulness. After eight weeks they had the participants return to the lab and undergo more fMRI testing.

Earlier studies showed that the activation of the amygdala is reduced when viewing emotional stimuli when people are in a meditative state: this study wanted to see if the effects of mindfulness training would still last even when people weren't consciously being mindful at the time they were viewing emotional stimuli. Participants lay in an fMRI and the activity of their amygdala was recorded as they were shown various images of stimuli that were hoped to get an emotional reaction (positive, negative or no reaction). These would have just been pictures of things that would stimulate a happy response (e.g. people smiling), a negative response (e.g. a car crash) or a neutral response (e.g. a loaf of bread).

This study was based on initial findings that suggested that activation of the amygdala in response to emotional stimuli is reduced when participants are in a mindful state. The results of the study showed that that there was a reduction in the activation of the amygdala of the group that underwent the mindfulness training when they were viewing the negative emotional stimuli.

There are numerous sources available online that can be used to help you practice mindfulness.

Desbordes et al.'s study shows that extended practice at mindfulness could help reduce activation of the amygdala during perception of emotional stimuli. This could have applications in criminology as well as other fields. After learning about PTSD, it would be hoped that you could see potential benefits of such training to help treat PTSD symptoms.

What this study shows is that the effect of mindfulness training can be transferrable to situations when people with mindfulness experience are in a non-meditative state (meaning, they're just laying down in the fMRI machine normally).

As you've learned, violence may be a result of a lack of prefrontal cortex function during times of social threat when our amygdala activates in response to the negative emotional stimuli. This increases physiological arousal and readiness to fight, which could lead to people acting violently. Mindfulness training could have potential applications to help people prone to violence by reducing their physiological reactions to emotional stimuli.

The term neuroplasticity can be used to describe any change in the brain's structure, function or activity as a result of experience. The neuroplasticity demonstrated in this study is the change in the neural pathway that has occurred in the mindful group in response to negative emotional stimuli. The perception of the negative emotional stimuli would not be travelling along a neural pathway through the amygdala at the same rate as the other groups. Perhaps a new pathway has been developed whereby the neural pathway perceiving negative emotional stimuli is better connected to the prefrontal cortex, thus reducing total activation of the amygdala.

After learning about some of the potential underlying biological correlates of criminal behaviour, hopefully you can see how studying the origins of behaviour can help us develop more effective strategies to address causes of antisocial behaviour. At the moment a common strategy is to address the symptom, without targeting the cause. This will be another important concept to think about when you learn about treatments for people with psychological disorders such as PTSD.

Being able to explain how mindfulness might be applicable to the study of criminology makes for good "discussion" in essays. You probably wouldn't have time to explain these connections in a short answer response (in Paper One, Part A), but you might be able to in essays.

Guiding Question:

How might the neuroplasticity benefits of mindfulness be used to reduce violence?

Critical Thinking Extension:
Research Methodology – External Validity - Sampling – Population Validity:
External validity involves being able to abstract a relationship demonstrated in one study and apply it to a wider field. The nature of the sample used in the study might affect the extent to which the findings can be generalized to a wider population because of characteristics of that sample. This is called "population validity". If we are trying to abstract the relationship between mindfulness and reduced amygdala activation in situations with negative emotional stimuli, you need to think about how the participants in the study might be different to those you want to abstract the relationship and apply it to. For instance, this study used healthy volunteers. What characteristics of people prone to violence might influence the extent to which we could expect to get the same results with them?

If you're interested...

There's a fascinating article written in *The Atlantic* by neuroscientist David Eagleman called "The Brain on Trial" that includes the case of Whitman and others to raise questions about culpability and crime. The relationship between neuroscientific findings and their implications in criminal justice is a fascinating field and one I recommend reading more into if you're interested.

Relevant Topics

- Neuroplasticity
- Conflict prevention strategies

Practice Exam Questions

- Discuss neuroplasticity.
- Explain how and why one research method was used to study neuroplasticity.
- Discuss strategies to reduce conflict.
- HL: To what extent are animal models useful for understanding relationships between the brain and behaviour?

Research Methods

Desbordes et al.'s study is a good example of how true experiments don't always happen in the laboratory. In this experiment, the participants were randomly allocated to a particular condition and extraneous variables were controlled for. The study was investigating a cause-and-effect relationship between mindfulness training and structural changes in the brain, even though this didn't happen in a laboratory. True experiments in neuroplasticity studies enable the variable of experience to be isolated as a significant factor in structural changes in the brain as a result of experience.

Ethical Considerations

There's an interesting consideration surrounding informed consent in studies where one group will have to experience a condition that is anticipated *not* to have an effect. For example, in some studies testing out the effectiveness of drugs on disorders, there's a control group that receives a placebo. But this means that they are going to be denied a possible treatment for their disorder. Researchers need to consider whether or not to tell them that they might or might not be in one group or the other (to be ethical), but then this has the potential effect of disrupting the results. Similarly, in the mindfulness training in Desbordes et al., three groups are experiencing conditions anticipated not to have an effect. Do researchers inform them that they *may* be in a control group to ensure the study is ethical, or do they not because this jeopardizes validity? Here you can hopefully see that explaining *considerations* doesn't need to involve making *judgements*.

2.8 Genetics and Behaviour
Are people born violent?

(a)   Twin and Adoption Studies

Think of something about you that you share with one or both of your parents. For example, an interest, dislike, passion, hobby, fear, personality trait, etc. Do you think you inherited that from your parents biologically, or are you similar in that way because of how you've been raised?

For much of the 20th century, many psychologists argued over the "nature vs. nurture" debate. Is behaviour a product of our genetics, or is it a product of our environment? Do humans think and act the way we do because they were born that way, or because they were raised that way?

Throughout this chapter we've indirectly been discussing this classic debate by investigating how biological, environmental, cognitive and social factors can all interact in aggressive or violent behaviour. Psychologists now generally agree that behaviour cannot be singularly explained by nature or nurture. There is overwhelming evidence that suggests how we think and act is a product of the interaction of environmental and biological factors.

The role of genetics in explaining human behaviour is a popular field of study. Researchers investigate multiple behaviours and their connections with genetics to see if particular behaviours are a result of genetic or environmental factors. Research in this areas regularly comes to the conclusion that *both* genes and environmental factors play a role in behaviour. Research into behaviours like antisocial behaviour, violence, aggression and crime are no different: these studies regularly show that both genetics and the environment can affect these behaviours.

The extent to which a behaviour can be attributed to genetics is called heritability. For instance, if a behaviour is 100% a product of our genetics, it is said to have 100% heritability. If it has 40% heritability, this means that the behaviour is 40% genetics and that the environment explains the other 60%.

Genetic studies often involve using twins. Twin studies rely on the fact that identical twins (monozygotic - MZ) have 100% of their genetic material in common, whereas fraternal twins (dizygotic - DZ) have 50% in common. What happens in these studies is that they get a bunch of identical and fraternal twins together and they measure a particular behaviour. For example, they might see how aggressive or violent they are, or their rate of committing violent crimes. What they do is they see how similar the identical twins are to each other, and then calculate this average similarity across *all* the identical twins. Then, they see how similar the fraternal twins are to one another and again calculate the overall average. What the researchers now have are two sets of figures: how similar the identical twins are on average, and how similar the fraternal twins are. They then compare the averages between the identical twins and fraternal twins. The statistical analyses they use to do this are pretty complicated, so we won't go into that here. But basically by comparing the average similarity between the identical and fraternal twins, they can determine the heritability of a particular behaviour.

There is more on epigenetics (how the environment and genes interact) in the HL extension on animal studies.

Heritability is the extent to which particular characteristics (e.g. behaviours) are attributable to genetic factors. More specifically, it is the extent to which variability can be attributed to genetics.

111

The methodology used in twin and adoption studies may take some time to comprehend. It is important that you can describe the process and that you can explain how this process can allow researchers to draw conclusions about the extent to which genetic factors influence behaviour.

Raine and Baker (2007) conducted one such twin study that used 1,210 twins in California, USA. Their particular area of study was antisocial behaviour (e.g. bullying, cruelty, stealing, skipping school, etc.) Antisocial behaviour in young children is a good predictor of later criminal activity, which is why studies on children and adolescents are often focused on these types of behaviours.

Genetic similarities between identical and fraternal twins make them valuable sources of data for genetics research.

The researchers gathered data using questionnaires. The child, their teacher and a caregiver (i.e. parent or whoever took care of them at home) filled out a range of questionnaires to test the kids' personalities, behaviours, and social skills. All these were designed to provide a measure of the kids' level of antisocial behaviour. This could then be statistically analysed, making comparisons between fraternal and identical twins and correlations compared. Regardless of which measure they used (the kid's, the teacher's or the caregiver's), the heritability always came at around 50%. The conclusion they drew from this was that antisocial behaviour in these kids was about half a product of genetics and half explained by environmental factors.

Antisocial behaviour is often used in studies investigating early childhood influences in later criminal behaviour. Kids don't usually commit violent crimes such as murder, rape or arson, but there are higher probabilities that they might if they demonstrate antisocial behaviour as children.

One limitation of making conclusions about genetics from twin studies is that perhaps the similarities between the identical twins could be explained because they are treated more the same than fraternal twins, because they look exactly the same (Raine, 2013). Thus, their environment might be affecting their behaviour in a more similar way than for fraternal twins. For instance, in fraternal twins one might be a boy and the other a girl. Perhaps they are raised differently because of their gender. This might affect the results of studies comparing identical and fraternal twins.

Studying identical twins who have been separated and adopted at birth is one way to isolate the genetics as the variable that's influencing the behaviour. Grove et al. (1990) gathered data from 32 sets of identical twins who were separated shortly after being born as they were adopted into different families. Because their genetic material is 100% similar, but their environments are completely different, researchers can use statistical analyses tests to determine the extent to which their antisocial behaviour can be explained through genetics. They first need to measure their antisocial behaviour by having a range of interviews, tests and questionnaires. Then their scores are gathered and the data are analysed. The results of this study were that the heritability of antisocial behaviour in adults was 28% and 41% in children. This is more evidence that while genetics can influence antisocial behaviour, our environment is still an important influence.

From this research, it is hoped you can see how researchers measure the extent to which genetic factors can explain behaviour. In the next section you will learn about a particular gene that has been correlated with violence.

Guiding Question:

How do studies on twins suggest antisocial behaviour is influenced by genetics *and* the environment?

Critical Thinking Extension:
Triangulation: Raine and Baker's study uses data triangulation by combining results from the kids, their caregivers and their teachers. This increases the credibility of the results as it reduces the influence that the individual bias of any one of these people may have on the results. Another form of triangulation is methodological triangulation: getting data by more than one method. How could methodological triangulation be used to further increase the credibility of Raine and Baker's study? What might be the limitations of using this method of triangulation?

If you're interested…

There's a centre in Minnesota that is devoted to studying genetics. It's called the Minnesota Centre for Twin and Family Research. This institute is carrying out two longitudinal studies on thousands of twins. There are multiple studies that they have published and you can read more about their research on their website. One particular field of study of the MCTFR is intelligence. You may be interested to research more about the extent to which IQ is influenced by genetics or environment.

(b)   The MAOA "Warrior" Gene

The previous section introduced you to the idea that our behaviour can be a result of genetics as well as our environment.

Due to the work of the Human Genome Project researchers are discovering specific genes that can be correlated with specific biological functions and behaviours. Once these genes are found their influence can be investigated; that is to say, they can use the specific gene as a variable in the research and see the relationship between this gene and particular behaviours.

The functions of genes are a very complex biological process. Our focus is partly on the gene, but mostly on how it *might affect behaviour*, since that's our role as psychologists to understand. So for now let's focus on one gene called the MAOA gene. The MAOA gene has been nicknamed the "warrior gene" because recent studies suggest there is a correlation between people with a variation of this gene and antisocial behaviour. MAOA is an acronym that's short for monoamine oxidase A. Monoamine oxidase A is an enzyme that affects levels of neurotransmitters. The MAOA gene produces the monoamine oxidase A enzyme, but some people have a mutation in this gene so they don't produce enough of this enzyme, and so the levels of neurotransmitters (e.g. serotonin) in their brain are affected.

However, the combination of genetics and environment cannot be ignored as studies also show that the presence of the variation of the MAOA gene coupled with abuse as a child, increased the likelihood of displaying antisocial behaviours (Caspi et al., 2002). This might explain why not every child that suffers abuse as a child grows up to be violent themselves: perhaps they have a perfectly normally functioning MAOA gene without the mutation, so the abuse may not affect them.

Here's one key finding about the MAOA gene that can help you solve the problem you were introduced to at the very beginning of this chapter:

> Males with a variation of the MAOA gene show greater activity in their amygdala during emotional arousal and they also show less activity in their ventromedial prefrontal cortex compared with people with the normal MAOA gene. (Raine, 2008; Meyer-Lindenberg, 2006).

There's enough in this chapter to write a whole new book explaining how this might affect our behaviour. The key is to make connections between this new knowledge about the MAOA gene mutation back to what you know about the amygdala, prefrontal cortex, decision making, emotion and situations involving social threat.

So here's the problem you can now try to solve, drawing on your learning throughout this chapter to help you:

How might a variation of the MAOA gene increase an individual's probability of being violent?

If you could take your time and think carefully about this problem, you could easily write an excellent and well-developed answer. But solving this problem might take a good hour, or even three hours. It's not simple. But the reward you'll feel when you come up with your own answer to this problem and you have the evidence that clearly supports your explanation will be well worth it. There are many possible answers to this question, which is the purpose of this chapter: providing you with multiple possible explanations for behaviour like aggression, violence and violent crime. Moreover,

You may be able to hypothesize other explanations for the MAOA gene's apparent effect on violent behaviour based on your learning from this chapter. For example, could its effect on serotonin levels be a possible explanation for its correlation with antisocial behaviour?

you should have enough research and evidence to support your explanations and hypotheses.

Here are a few steps in the problem-solving process that might help you:

1. Identify the problem
2. Identify the key details in the problem
3. Propose a possible hypothesis
4. Test your hypothesis by consulting the evidence (e.g. studies and theories)
   a. If there is not enough evidence, go back to step two and try again
5. Gather your notes and evidence
6. Organize your notes and evidence and continually make sure you are answering the question
7. Present and discuss your findings.

Answering the question above isn't going to be easy, but if you take the time to *think* about how it might be answered, your fascination with psychology will flourish.

You can find a full explanation of how the MAOA-L gene (the variation) might influence behaviour on our blog.

Guiding Question:

How might a variation of the MAOA gene increase an individual's probability of being violent?

Critical Thinking Extension:

Evaluation: If we never move past the *possible* explanations of relationships (e.g. between variations of the MAOA gene and violent crime) we run the risk of making massively erroneous statements like: "people with variations of the MAOA gene will become criminals." This just simply isn't the cast: your answer to this section's guiding question should include an explanation in a very specific context. It is hoped that you can also consider factors that influence the extent to which the relationship between the MAOA gene and violence could be applied to *all* forms of violent crime.

If you're interested…

Jim Fallon, a neuroscientist, gives a TED talk called "Exploring the mind of a killer." In this talk he discusses the MAOA gene and how he accidentally discovered that it ran in his family.

Relevant Topics

- Genetics
- Origins of conflict

Practice Exam Questions

- To what extent do genes influence behaviour?
- Outline ethical considerations related to research on genetics and behaviour?

Research Methods

Questionnaires are valuable methods to gather data from a wide range of samples and are often used as part of correlational studies, such as those investigating genetics. Raine and Baker's study used over 1,000 participants. This large sample can increase the probability of generalizability but it would be difficult to gather this data by other methods such as observations. Questionnaires can enable researchers to gather data from huge samples relatively easily. While triangulation can reduce bias, self-report methods like questionnaires always come with the chance of bias.

Ethical Considerations

Any study involving sensitive areas like antisocial behaviour requires informed consent and anonymity. Moreover, parental consent is particularly important when studying kids (the cut-off is usually under 16 years old).

Measuring behaviours like antisocial behaviour in kids can also make considerations surrounding debriefing rather complex. If, for instance, researchers know of a correlation between antisocial behaviour as a child and the probability of committing more serious crimes later in life, if they found kids had high levels of antisocial behaviour, should they share this with the child and/or their caregiver?

There are many ethical considerations surrounding the applications of findings from genetic studies as well: what if you could undergo genetic testing to find out if you had the MAOA gene: would you want to?

What if behaviour like murder could be sourced to one particular gene: what are the possible implications of making discoveries like this?

Understanding ethics is not always black and white, which is why you need to understand considerations and not just guidelines.

2.9 Social Cognitive Theory
How can nature affect nurture and vice-versa?

(a) Bandura's Social Cognitive Theory

One of the major goals of this chapter was to help you see how individuals, their behaviour and their environment all interact in complex ways. This is the crux of a theory developed in the 1980s by Albert Bandura called social cognitive theory: individuals, their behaviour and their environment all interact. Bandura calls the interaction of biology, behaviour, thinking and our environment, triadic reciprocal determinism. Let's take a moment to break down this key term, as it is the heart of social cognitive theory STC (Bandura, 1989).

Triadic: The key prefix here is tri, or three. SCT is comprised of three variables: the person, the behaviour and the environment. The person includes their beliefs, values, personality, thoughts, etc., as well as their biology (e.g. genes, brain function, hormones, etc.)

Reciprocal: To reciprocate means to return. In this instance it's referring to how behaviours, cognitions, personal factors and environmental influences all influence each other in a bidirectional manner. As you will see in the diagram, each factor can influence the other: bidirectionality refers to how an effect can work in both directions. For example, our social environment can affect our behaviour, but our behaviour can also affect our social environment.

Determinism: This refers to the *result* or the *effect*. Each of the three factors may determine another factor.

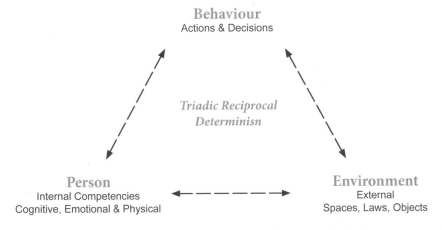

In short, triadic reciprocal determinism explains how individuals, their actions and their environment all interact. Let's look at some examples:

Cognition → Behaviour: what we think, believe and feel can influence our behaviour. For example, those that believe they should defend their honour when they are insulted will behave differently when they are threatened compared to those that hold no such belief.

Behaviour → Cognition: The results of our behaviour, including rewards, punishments and effects, may affect how we think in the future. For example, if we are rewarded and praised for acting in a tough and aggressive manner, this might lead us to think that this is an acceptable way to act.

Biology → Behaviour: Bandura considers biological factors as part of social cognitive theory as well and these fall within the individual aspect of the triad. We've already seen multiple examples of how our biology can influence our cognition, and how this effect on our cognition can influence our behaviour.

Behaviour → Biology: You learned about how this effect is bidirectional when you studied neuroplasticity. In short, repeated thought processes and actions can actually alter the structure and functioning of the brain. So behaviour can lead to changes in the brain, and these changes can in turn affect behaviour.

Environment → Behaviour: The environmental factors is where the "social" aspect of Bandura's theory comes in. By "environment," he is not just referring to our physical environment, but the effect of social influences as well. Some of these influences including modelling (learning by observing others), instruction and social persuasion (e.g. peer pressure).

Individual → Environment: This is an interesting direction of causality that few would consider. Characteristics as basic as size, age, gender, or race can affect people's reactions to an individual. These reactions, in turn, could affect a person in many ways. If a child, for instance, is viewed as being a bully or overly aggressive, other children may react differently to them than they would a meeker and more mild-mannered child. These reactions could, in turn, affect the children differently.

Bandura's social cognitive theory is a development of an earlier theory of his which he called social *learning* theory. But whereas SLT focused primarily on the effect of the environment on the individual, SCT is concerned with providing an explanation for how individual, behavioral and environmental factors all interact and influence one-another. As you go through this course, you'll be able to see many examples of Bandura's triadic reciprocal determinism. Moreover, understanding this complex relationship is one of the key ideas that you'll acquire by the end of this course.

While most studies show a relationship between two variables, the whole purpose of the structure and contents of this chapter was to enable you to understand multiple interacting relationships. When explaining social cognitive theory, try to think of a supporting explanation that demonstrates all three points of the triad.

Guiding Question:

How can triadic reciprocal determinism be demonstrated in research?

Critical Thinking Extension:
Supporting Evidence: In the next section you'll have one famous experimental paradigm that Bandura developed to test his social learning theory. Social cognitive theory, however, could be supported by almost *any* study in psychology. Can you find one or two studies that would explain a triadic explanation of behaviour? That is to say, they show how all three factors can be included in the same behaviour?

If you're interested...

Bandura's theories have been applied to many fields, including education and entertainment. Moreover, these fields have been combined whereby TV shows, films, radio programmes and other forms of media are created with the hope of educating whilst entertaining. The APA has an interesting article on this called "The Theory Heard 'Round the World."

(b) Vicarious Learning and Bandura's Bobo Doll Study

Before the following experiment is explained it's important to note that this experiment was conducted over twenty years *before* Bandura presented his social cognitive theory. There are numerous studies that we look at throughout this course that could be used to support an explanation of Bandura's triadic reciprocal determinism, which is at the heart of social cognitive theory.

For example, aggression could be explained through the effects of a lack of prefrontal cortex function to regulate impulsive reactions to social threats. In this instance, the behaviour (aggression) is an effect of brain activity (internal) and decision making (also internal) in reaction to the social threat (the environment).

Two other key elements of SCT are observational learning and vicarious learning. Observational learning quite simply refers to the process of learning by observing others, whereas vicarious learning means being able to learn through the observation of how others are rewarded or punished for their actions. This was the key claim in Bandura's social learning theory, but SCT was renamed to increase the focus on the internal aspects associated with this learning.

Bandura conducted many experiments in the 1960s to test his ideas regarding the effects of modelling on vicarious learning. In these experiments, young children around three to four years old were placed in a room and watched an adult playing with a big inflatable Bobo Doll. In one condition a child watched an adult beating, kicking, hitting with a hammer and generally behaving aggressively towards the doll. In another condition, the kids watched an adult playing nicely with the doll and in the control condition the kids didn't watch any model. The researchers made observations while standing behind double-sided mirrors and counted the number of "aggressive acts" the kids made (like punching, hitting, etc). The results showed that watching the violent adult did in fact lead to an increase in aggressive acts. Those kids that watched the aggressive adult performed more similarly aggressive acts than those that didn't (Bandura, Ross & Ross, 1963).

> Modelling is having someone demonstrate a particular behaviour and then the learner copying. This is one way children learn certain attitudes. While Bandura's theories can be used to explain attitudes and behaviours surrounding aggression and violence, they could also be used to explain other phenomena, like stereotypes, prejudice and discrimination.

In a follow-up study, Bandura replicated this but had four conditions:
- Real life model
- TV Model
- Cartoon Cat Model (the model was dressed up as a cartoon cat)
- Control condition (no observation of a model).

This study was in 1963 when television was becoming really common in American households and Bandura wanted to see if children would be more likely to copy televised aggression (i.e. by watching it on TV) or a model in real life. The adult "model" was told to behave the same as in the first studies, the difference was in how they saw the model. The real life condition was the same as in the original study, but in the TV condition the model was filmed. The cartoon cat version was the same behaviours but the model was dressed as a cartoon cat. Interestingly, the cartoon cat had the most influence on the children's behaviour. All three aggressive model conditions, however, lead to higher aggressive behaviours in the children than the control group.

In both of these studies, and many similar replications, the effect of the social environment (observing a model) on behaviour (aggression) can be witnessed. The children are learning how to behave vicariously through the observation of the model. Other variations of this experimental paradigm involved the children watching an adult being rewarded or punished for their actions. The results of these studies, not

The effect of violent media (including TV) on aggression and antisocial behaviour in children is a long-standing debate with a lot of research on either side.

surprisingly, was that the imitation of the observed behaviour increased when the children viewed a model who was rewarded for their actions (Bandura, 1971).

However, one limitation of the bobo doll studies is there is no measure of internal effects of the modelling. The "cognition" aspect of social cognitive theory is not directly measured in these experiments and can only be inferred. The kids in the Bobo Doll experiments may have been developing attitudes about aggression and violence, including what is acceptable and unacceptable behaviour. One reason why Bandura developed SLT to become social cognitive theory was that he wanted to highlight internal factors in the relationship between behaviour and the social environment.

Bandura's theories and studies can be used to explain how social factors, such as modelling, can influence our behaviour. This could explain, for example, how the cultural values of the "Culture of Honour" may still be prevalent in modern society: they are passed down from generation to generation through the effects of modelling and other social influences.

Guiding Question:

How does this bobo doll study support one or more claims of social cognitive theory?

Critical Thinking Extension:

Generalizability - Time: In evaluating studies, one key aspect to consider is the time period when they were conducted. Bandura's early Bobo Doll experiments were conducted in the 1960s. A lot has changed in the past 50+ years. Would you anticipate getting the same or similar results if these experiments were conducted today? A good explanation of generalizability would include explaining specific factors related to time that might affect the reliability of the results. What factors might affect the extent to which we could generalize Bandura's results from the 1960s to today's modern kids?

If you're interested…

Numerous videos, including footage from Bandura's studies, are available online. One example is an extract from the BBC's three-part documentary "The Brain: A Secret History."

Relevant Topics

- Social cognitive theory
- Origins of conflict
- Culture and behaviour

Practice Exam Questions

- Describe social cognitive theory.
- Discuss social and/or biological origins of conflict.

Research Methods

Bandura's Bobo Doll experiments are examples of how social factors can be isolated and observed under controlled situations in true experiments. In his studies he had numerous researchers observe and measure the childrens' behaviour quantitatively. By using a matched pairs design, he was also able to reduce the chances that participant variability in traits like aggressiveness would affect the results. The ability to assign participants to conditions randomly or by matched pairs is an important characteristic of laboratory experiments because it can control for extraneous variables, such as participant variability.

Ethical Considerations

When studying children as young as three years old there's obviously parental consent to consider. But another ethical consideration is simply taking into consideration the long-term impact the study might have (when studying ethical considerations, you can simply describe what you think the researchers might have to consider without having to label it with one of the standard guidelines). For instance, could the observation of aggressive models have long-term impacts on the kids? What if they grew up to hate clowns? That is perhaps an exaggeration, but it's still important to consider.

Conclusion

Remember the story of Charles Whitman you heard at the beginning of this chapter? Perhaps go back and re-read the story of Charles. Do the questions or thoughts you have about Whitman change now you've learned a little more about possible correlations of violence?

You didn't hear the whole story. In his letter Whitman writes…

"I don't really understand myself these days. I am supposed to be an average reasonable and intelligent young man. However, lately (I don't recall when it started) I have been a victim of very unusual and irrational thoughts. These thoughts constantly recur, and it requires a tremendous mental effort to concentrate on useful and progressive tasks. In May when my parents made a physical break I noticed a great deal of stress. I consulted a Dr. Cochrum at the University Health Center and asked him to recommend someone that I could consult with about some psychiatric disorders I felt I had. I talked with a Doctor once for about two hours and tried to convey to him my fears that I felt come (sic) overwhelming violent impulses. After one session I never saw the Doctor again, and since that I have been fighting my mental turmoil alone, and seemingly to no avail. After my death I wish that an autopsy would be performed on me to see if there is any visible physical disorder. I have had some tremendous headaches in the past and have consumed two large bottles of Excedrin in the past three months."

In fact, an autopsy was performed on Whitman and they found a tumour impacting his amygdala. Could this have influenced his actions? Or was it the excess amount of medication he was consuming? Perhaps it was his high levels of stress, his military training or trauma he may have suffered from the hands of his abusive father.

My hope from this chapter is that you've learnt how our brain can influence our cognition which can influence our behaviour which may influence our brain, but our environment might also influence our brain which could influence our cognition, but the role of emotion plays a part in our behaviour, which is affected by our cognition and our biology, which may be affected by our environment, which may influence other biological factors…….

Don't panic! You do not need to be able to explain the above. The reason the study of criminology (and psychology) is so fascinating, is that the path to understanding a complex human behaviour like violent crime is a complicated one. The study of psychology is about investigating complex relationships and multiple explanations, while continually scrutinizing the evidence used to support such explanations. Humans aren't simple animals, so explanations for our behaviour are rarely simple.

As this is early in your psychology career, all you'll need to do is explain straight forward relationships between two factors, with a possible effect of that relationship. These relationships are the basis of the guiding questions and will be the basis of your exam questions. For instance,

- How can hormones influence behaviour?
- How can neurotransmission influence behaviour?

- How can research demonstrate localization of brain function?
- HL: How and why are animal studies used?

If you can answer these questions and use psychological evidence to support your answers, you've taken a huge first step in becoming a great psychologist! And if you're not quite there with all these relationships yet, don't worry – there's plenty of time left in the course. This chapter has provided you with many building blocks of knowledge that will be useful in later chapters.

Chapter 3
Social Influence

Introduction

In the middle of the night on Friday the 13th of March, 1964, Catherine "Kitty" Genovese was coming home from work in the suburb of Queens, New York City. But she never made it home. Waiting in the dark was Winston Moseley, the man who would murder her. Genovese's murder was reported in a local newspaper, but it wasn't much of a headline as murders were pretty common in NYC at this time. However, one aspect of the story grabbed the attention of a reporter at *The New York Times*, who wrote an article called "37 who saw murder and didn't call the police" (Gainsberg, 1964). This later story *did* get national attention as people were outraged that so many witnesses could stand by and allow an innocent young woman to be murdered.

Many reported details of the story have since been questioned, but its impact remains: after the reporting of Genovese's murder and the witnesses who let it happen by failing to help, social psychologists Bibb Latane and John Darley began devising theories and conducting research into why people might not have helped Genovese. The phenomenon of people not acting in situations requiring attention has come to be known as the bystander effect. One reason why people may not help is because they're influenced by the actions, or inaction, of others. Even having other people present may make someone less likely to help. Bystanderism is just one example of how social influence can affect our behaviour.

Humans are naturally social animals. In fact, it is our social nature and ability to work in groups that helped our ancestors rise to the top of the food chain. It's not surprising then that we are susceptible to being influenced in many ways by the people around us: this influence of our social and cultural environment is one of the primary themes of this chapter.

Belonging to a group can have many positive effects, like providing us with a sense of who we are, a social identity. It can also raise our self-esteem. But at what cost? You'll learn in this chapter how belonging to a group may naturally lead us towards behaving negatively towards others in the form of stereotypes, prejudice and discrimination.

You might be able to make connections to what you're learning about social psychology to other subjects, such as the study of history or literature. History is filled with stories of inter-group conflict and many novels focus on characters' struggles in and against cultural and societal influences. But as with all explanations of behaviour, we need to broaden our perspective and consider alternative explanations. Thus, the role of biology and cognition is not ignored in the topics within this chapter.

The fact that you are often able to see many real life examples of the phenomena you're learning about is one of most interesting and enjoyable facets of social psychology. While you're learning about things like bystanderism, inter-group conflict, and conformity, try to connect these concepts and the relevant research to your own experiences. Making these connections regularly is sure to develop your interest and deepen your understanding of psychology.

3.1 Conformity
Why do people go along with the group?

(a) Normative Social Influence

Conformity may be one of the most interesting and popular phenomena to study. To conform means you are behaving in a way that is socially acceptable; you're following the norms and standards of your social environment. For many teenagers, peer pressure is often a source of social influence that is used to pressure them into doing something that they're not sure about. The social influence of having friends pressure you into doing something could cause conformity to the norms of your social group.

People often change their behaviour in order to fit in with the norms of their social environment through a fear of being ostracized - left out of the group. Social psychologists call this normative social influence. A social norm is what is "normal" in a particular social situation - it's an expected way to think, act or behave. It's important to remember also that the term social can mean many things. It's an umbrella term that means anything to do with other people or society.

For example, normative social influence might occur if you were at a party and someone hands you a beer to drink, but you don't like the taste of beer and you don't want to drink; you're quite happy with water. You look around and see your friends talking and laughing but they suddenly stop and notice you looking at your beer with a blank look on your face. At this moment you may be feeling some indirect social influence from your friends: you may be thinking, "…they're judging me and might not think I'm cool if I don't drink." The social norm in this case is that you drink beer because you're at a party and that's just what happens at parties: it's how you're expected to act. By having others present and indirectly putting pressure on you to conform to this social norm, you are experiencing normative social influence.

The effects of normative social influence on behaviour was famously demonstrated in a series of studies by Asch in the 1950s. Asch developed what is known as the Asch Paradigm, which is an experimental procedure that has been replicated in hundreds of studies around the world. The experiments were first conducted in the US on male college students. The procedure involves one subject being in a group of around 6 - 8 confederates and there's a researcher at the front of the room. The researcher explains that the study is about visual perception, gives the instructions on what to do, and then the tests begin. The confederates and the subject sit in a row and view two cards that the researcher holds up. They have to match one line, the target line, with one of the other three lines. This happens around 15 times.

In his early experiments, Asch wanted to see if he could put pressure on the subject to offer the wrong answer by having the confederates deliberately give the wrong answer, even though the correct answer is obvious.

The control for the experiment was that one group of subjects were asked to do this alone. Asch found that when alone they could get the right answer over 99% of

Normative social influence involves two concepts: pressure from others and this pressure results in changing one's behaviour to fit in with the social norms.

A confederate is someone who is working alongside the researcher. In other words, they're an "actor."

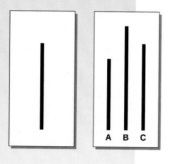

Would you be able to give the right answer if the rest of the group said "A"?

the time. This demonstrates that the task itself is easy and that if subjects can resist the influence of the group, they will be also be able to get the right answer.

In one series of experiments, Asch (1955) found that 74% of the subjects conformed at least once, which means that only 26% of the subjects were able to resist the normative social influence of the group and provide the correct responses in every test. On average, the subject conformed to the group norm and gave the incorrect response on 36.8% of the critical trials.

After the study Asch interviewed the people who conformed to the groups' incorrect answers and asked them why they did this. Some gave reasons like "I didn't want to spoil your results." Others were quick to draw the conclusion that they must be wrong and the group must be right, so they would trust the group's answer.

Asch replicated the same design in later experiments but he varied the size of the group. When there was just two people in the trial, one confederate who contradicted the subject's answers, it didn't have much of an effect. However, when there were two confederates in opposition to one subject, the subject gave in around 13% of the time. When there were three confederates, all in agreement with one another about the correct answer, the incorrect answers from the subject jumped to over 30%. The change in the size of the group may have increased the social influence the subject was feeling, leading them to change their answer.

By comparing the accuracy in the control condition of the original experiment with the effects of the group pressure in Asch's studies, the effects of normative social influence can be observed. Another variation had one confederate that broke the unanimity of the group. If all the confederates weren't in agreement and gave different answers, the normative social influence is reduced because there is no norm established, so the conformity decreases. When the normative social influence is restored by having a majority putting pressure on the minority, conformity rises again.

> *Do you think we could expect the same results in today's modern society?*

> *Interestingly, the rates of conformity did not continue to increase as the group grew in size and began to decrease at around seven confederates.*

Guiding Question:

How does Asch's study demonstrate the effects of normative social influence on behaviour?

Critical Thinking Extension:

Tolerating Uncertainty: From studies like Asch's, many students are quick to make judgements such as "group pressure increases conformity." It's really important that you can learn to look *beyond* the immediate and obvious conclusions that you are being led to form about these studies. Asch's study does suggest normative social influence can affect conformity. But if you look more closely at the results you should see that they do not "prove" that group pressure will cause conformity to social norms. How can the results of Asch's study be interpreted in a way that suggests group pressure might *not* cause conformity?

If you're interested…

There are many different sources of information about Asch's study, all with slightly different information because there are so many articles about this research. The above material comes from a very interesting article written by Asch and the language is accessible for high school students. It's called "Opinions and Social Pressure." There are also numerous clips online of replications of Asch's studies. It's easier to understand the study by viewing it than by reading descriptions of it.

(b) Cultural Dimensions

One major limitation of Asch's research is that its population validity and generalizability are questionable. The study took place on college campuses, in the United States, and all participants were males and it happened in the 1950s. Would different gender, age, ethnic, racial or cultural groups display the same levels of conformity? There has been a lot of research conducted in this area, particularly in regards to the differences in conformity rates across cultures. This will be explored in the next section. Before you begin discussing cultural influences on conformity, it's important to become familiar with a very influential concept in cross-cultural research - cultural dimensions.

Geert Hofstede is an organizational psychologist who conducted his early research when he was working for IBM between the late 60s and early 70s. Hofstede was investigating how values in the workplace are influenced by culture and to do this he gathered data from IBM employees from more than 70 countries. What came out of this cross-cultural research was his description of different cultural dimensions. A cultural dimension is a set of cultural values that are held by a particular cultural group. A value is something that is believed to be important, so a cultural value is a common belief about the value of something that is shared by members of a cultural group. In other words, what that culture thinks is important.

In total, Hofstede described six different cultural dimensions that describe a range of cultural values. We will focus on only one of these as it has become the most influential in cross-cultural research. This cultural dimension is known as Individualism – Collectivism.

According to Hofstede, individualistic cultures *tend* to place higher value on independence and stress the importance of individuals taking care of themselves and their immediate family. Individuals are viewed as unique and competitiveness is important. Moreover, having the power to make your own decisions (individual autonomy) and self-expression are highly valued. There is more focus on the "I", the individual, in individualistic cultures.

Collectivist cultures are on the other end of the continuum from individualistic cultures. They value close-knit family and social groups and place more value on identifying with the group than individual achievements. A person in a collectivist culture is more defined by their relationships and their obligations than they are by their personal achievements. Individual autonomy and self-expression may not be encouraged and group harmony is more important than individual achievement. Individuals in collectivist cultures can expect their relatives or in-group members to look after them in exchange for loyalty to the group. A society's point on this continuum is reflected in what has more emphasis – "I" or "We" (geert-hofstede.com; Buss, 1989).

Recent research carried out in China has tested a theory that differences in values of collectivism versus individualism may be a result of agriculture. Generally speaking, Western countries tend to be more individualistic, while Asian cultures tend to be more collectivist. Growing rice requires a lot of cooperation from a whole village as water networks need to be shared and planting and harvesting are labour intensive. This would result in collectivist attitudes being more beneficial and may explain why Asian cultures tend to be more collectivist. Growing wheat, on the other hand, doesn't rely on as much interdependence between societal group members and might encourage more individualistic values (Talhelm et al., 2014).

When asked about how cultural dimensions affect behaviour, you should really be explaining how the cultural values associated with that dimension may affect behaviour.

While generalizations are important, it's imperative that you recognize that they are generalizations.

Characteristics of Individualism	Characteristics of Collectivism
• Focus on the "I". • Have an identity that comes from their individuality. • Loose ties between individuals - look after yourself and your immediate family • Competition exists between individuals and is encouraged. • When carrying out a task, the task comes first, the relationship may come afterwards. • Confrontations are OK and can sometimes be healthy.	• Focus on the "we". • Identity is defined by relationships with others and belonging to various groups. • Form strong in-groups. This could be the immediate family, extended family, tribe, village or whole community. • Competition is between whole groups. • When carrying out a task, relationships come first, task comes second. • Value harmony in the in-group, even if some members disagree. The group harmony is important.

Here are some scores on the individualism-collectivism scale (clearlycultural.com). Note that the top score is 120 and the lowest is 0.

United States = 91 (most individualistic), Australia = 90, Spain = 51, Japan = 46, Malaysia = 26, China = 20, Guatemala = 6 (most collectivist).

It's really important point to note that countries are ranked on a continuum – they are not divided in black-and-white terms and labelled as individualistic or collectivist. Many students oversimplify this idea and discuss all cultures as being at one end of the continuum or the other, and this leads to erroneous and oversimplified explanations. While it does make it easier to discuss this dimension in terms of individualism or collectivism, it is really important to remember that countries are not categorized into one of two dimensions – they are scored along a continuum.

Also remember that just because a person comes from a culture with a particular rating on the individualism scale, doesn't necessarily mean that person will share those same values. For example, when you talk about the United States you are referring to around 400 million people in a *very* multi-cultural society. To make an overly simplified statement like "Americans focus on their own achievements and don't worry about the concerns of others", would be highly inaccurate, not to mention possibly very offensive.

In order to draw any conclusions regarding cultural influences on behaviour, it is inevitable that cross-cultural research will make some generalizations. It is imperative that you recognize these are generalizations that are prone to exceptions.

Guiding Question:

How do the cultural values of individualism and collectivism differ?

Critical Thinking Extension:

Hofstede's theory developed out of cross-cultural research from IBM employees. Can this sample provide generalizable descriptions of cultural values? IBM is a high-tech multi-national company and employees are presumably very well educated and they're all employed by a large multi-national company. Perhaps these characteristics might influence the extent to which these values are consistent across socioeconomic groups within each country. To what extent do you think the original sample of Hofstede's research influences the validity and/or value of his descriptions? Do these still exist today?

If you're interested…

You can check out geert-hofstede.com to find out more about cultural dimensions. Some of the others include "Masculinity-Femininity" and "Long-Term – Short-Term Orientation". There's a tool where you may be able to find your country and see your country's scores on the scales and compare it to other countries.

(c)   Culture and Conformity

Asch's early research into conformity raised a lot of questions and has inspired research in this area for the past 60 years. For instance, what personal differences, if any, exist between the 26% of people who could maintain their beliefs and voice their opinions in opposition to the group, compared to those who caved to the normative social influence? Could a person's cultural values influence their behaviour when put in such situations?

The influence of cultural values on behaviour is a common field of study and many studies compare countries with various scores on the individualism-collectivism scale. Conformity is one such behaviour that has been the subject of this type of research. It may not come as much of a surprise that the research suggests countries that have more collectivist values, also tend to demonstrate higher levels of conformity.

Early research in the 1950s and 60s in this area focused on comparing cultures with different types of food gathering practices. For example, they would compare a culture that focuses mainly on hunting, gathering and fishing compared with other cultures that rely on agriculture and farming. One study (Berry, 1967) compared a tribe in Africa (the Temne people of Sierra Leone) with the Inuit in Northern America (on Baffin Island). The results showed that the Temne people had higher rates of conformity than the Inuit. This is because, Berry argued, the Temne people were an agricultural society and so they needed higher rates of cooperation in order to survive. The Inuit, on the other hand, encourage more individualism as their method of gathering food doesn't require as much cooperation as agricultural societies (Berry, 1967 as referenced in Bond and Smith, 1997).

To conform means to act in a way that is socially acceptable and follows social norms.

From this research we can see that the cultural and economic environment can influence how much people might value something like cooperation, and how this value can influence the extent to which they demonstrate conformity. But a critique of this research is that these cultures are very traditional and haven't been modernized. They also have little contact with outside influences, so could these results really be generalized to other cultural environments?

Addressing this issue was one aim of the meta-analysis carried out by Bond and Smith (1997). They used surveys to measure the relative individualism-collectivism rating of 17 different countries. They then

Here we see Mongolian hunters using eagles. Their method of acquiring food may influence their cultural values.

gathered the results from 133 studies that had been conducted in those cultures using the Asch Paradigm. The results showed significant correlations between the cultural values of collectivism-individualism and rates of conformity. Individualistic cultures, such as the United States, UK and France demonstrated lower levels of conformity than countries such as Hong Kong and Brazil.

Collectivist values may influence an individual's thinking when put in situations like the Asch paradigm procedure. A person who has been raised to value thoughts and opinions of the group and to put group relations before their individual beliefs and opinions, may be reluctant to speak out against the group. People raised to have

You can check out our blog to find more interesting findings from this meta-analysis, including how conformity has changed in America since Asch's first studies.

values more associated with individualism, on the other hand, may be less inclined to worry about what others might think of them if they were to voice their own opinion.

From the research explained in this section you can hopefully see that multiple cultural factors can influence conformity. These include economic and socio-political factors, as well as cultural values.

Guiding Question:

How might cultural values influence conformity?

Critical Thinking Extension:

The studies above provide possible explanations for the changing rates of conformity over time and across different cultures. Would you suspect higher, lower or similar rates of conformity as Asch found if you were to replicate his experiments using a similar sample in your city/country?

If you're interested…

You can watch a series of interviews with Geert Hofstede on the YouTube channel called "ten minutes with…" You can get explanations from the man himself about the cultural dimensions.

Relevant Topics

- Culture and its influence on behaviour and cognition
- Cultural dimensions

Practice Exam Questions

- Discuss how one or more cultural dimensions may influence behaviour.
- Discuss cultural influences on behaviour and cognition.
- Evaluate research related to cultural influences on behaviour.
- Outline one study related to cultural dimensions.

Research Methods

Asch's experiment is a good example of a laboratory, "true" experiment and the benefits of using this method in social psychology. There are numerous possible extraneous variables that might affect behaviour if we were to investigate social influences in real life situations, so being able to isolate the effects of particular variables on behaviour in a controlled environment can allow researchers to draw cause and effect relationships. In this instance Asch was able to manipulate variables such as group size and unanimity, which allowed him to draw conclusions regarding the influence of these variables on conformity.

Ethical Considerations

Studies involving conformity have numerous ethical considerations. Deception is a necessary component in these studies because if participants were aware of the aims of the experiment and that the others were actors the validity of the study would be jeopardized. For this reason, debriefing becomes essential.

3.2 Enculturation
How can our cultural environment affect our behaviour?

(a) Enculturation: An Introduction

The normative effect of social influence shown in Asch's research is just one example of how social factors can affect our thinking and behaviour. As Bond and Smith showed, our cultural values may also play a role in behaviours like conformity. But how do we acquire cultural values in the first place? Addressing this question is the subject of this section.

There are multiple ways in which we learn from our cultural environment and this learning shapes our values. For example, our childhood experiences play a large part in shaping who we are. How we're raised and the values we're taught from a young age will probably have an effect on how we think and act throughout our lives. Bandura's early theories on social learning can also explain how we acquire values: we observe others and imitate their behaviour and learn to adopt their attitudes. Our friends and peers are also a source of information and influence. The media (e.g. TV, films, and the internet) may also affect our understanding of social and cultural norms.

By living in a particular cultural environment and belonging to various social groups we're constantly perceiving and learning about norms and appropriate ways to behave. In cross-cultural psychology this process is called enculturation. More specifically, enculturation describes of the process of being enveloped and surrounded by cultural influences that will enable us to understand the cultural norms and values of our primary ("home") culture. As you've seen, this can then affect how we behave in certain situations like conforming with the group even when we know they're wrong.

Enculturation is a very broad term that includes "…all forms of cultural learning…" (Berry, 2002). Enculturation is an important process because it gives us the knowledge and skills we need to be a healthy and productive member of society. There are numerous ways that enculturation occurs and cultural learning is transmitted, including observing the common behaviour of others and learning about what counts as socially acceptable behaviour. Direct teaching of cultural norms from parents and in schools is another way that cultural learning happens.

Another term used to describe the process of learning cultural norms is cultural transmission. The

> A cultural norm is the same as a social norm, but applied to a cultural group. It is a belief shared by a cultural group about the appropriate ways to think and act.

> For this psychology course it's not necessary for you to distinguish between social and cultural norms, as these concepts are very similar.

Parenting practices (how we raise our children and the values we instill) is one way that cultural transmission (i.e. enculturation) occurs.

information is transmitted to us from various sources, including peers, parents, school and the media.

Social learning is one factor that may contribute to the process of cultural transmission and enculturation. In the following sections we'll look at how economics may influence what a particular culture values and how this is reflected in parenting and child raising practices. Whereas earlier we saw that cultural values can influence conformity, in the next section we'll look at some research that uncovers just where those cultural values come from in the first place.

Guiding Question:

How might enculturation influence our behaviour?

Critical Thinking Extension:
Area of Uncertainty: The IB Psychology course focuses on sociocultural influences on human behaviour. You have been introduced to the idea of a social norm and a cultural norm. What do you think distinguishes a social influence from a cultural influence?

If you're interested...

Margaret Mead was a famous anthropologist who studied people and cultures from all around the world. If you're interested in anthropology and cross-cultural studies, BBC Four has a three-part documentary series about her research called "Tales from the Jungle."

(b) Economics and Cultural Values

In the previous section you were introduced to the concept of enculturation. This is a term used by anthropologists and cross-cultural psychologists to describe the process of learning the cultural norms and values of one's primary culture. There are multiple factors contributing to the process of enculturation, including how we're raised, our exposure to media, and what we learn in school and from our peers.

You've already read about early research by Barry that investigated different rates of conformity across cultures and provided possible explanations for these differences. Economic factors such as how a cultural group acquires food can influence values, which might affect behaviour. In this section we're going to look at where these differing values might come from in the first place.

Barry et al. (1959) used cross-cultural data to compare approaches to parenting. In this classic cross-cultural study they wanted to see if child training practices were correlated with economic factors in different cultural groups. Similar to Berry's research, at one end of the continuum they placed pastoralism (raising animals for food) and agriculture (raising crops for food). These were categorized as high food accumulation cultures because they rely on the gathering and storing of food over long periods of time.

> Cultural values can be influenced by economic factors. Can you think of how economic factors may influence the cultural values of your home culture?

Barry et al. hypothesized that if a cultural group primarily relied on raising animals for meat and food then they would raise their children in a way that would increase their compliance - the following of established rules and norms. One reason for this is because there may be a risk in trying something new or being innovative because it could damage the health of the animals or the crops and this would jeopardize their food supply. Being obedient and compliant by following daily routines and established procedures would be preferable in these societies because this will ensure successful food production. If a method of growing corn, for instance, has shown to be successful, it would be risky to try a new strategy in case it didn't work and this could have damaging long-term consequences. Similarly, if a member of a pastoral society isn't dutiful and responsible in taking care of animals, the animals may get sick or even die. These practical considerations may be influential in the enculturation process as they would influence the types of characteristics that are encouraged and nourished in children by parents and other societal influences.

> To accumulate means to gather an increasing amount over a long period of time.

At the other end of the economic scale is a subsistence economy, which means producing just enough to survive on a day-to-day basis and without being able to store food long-term. This is a low food accumulation culture. Groups that rely on hunting and fishing are subsistent and to procure food they may value initiative and innovation because they are not thinking about the long-term. Their daily catch is what is important and because they may not be able to store food, they rely more on their individual skills to get food on a daily basis.

Living in a community that requires high food accumulation may influence the types of values that parents try to instill in their children. This could influence thinking and behaviour.

Barry et al. argue that in these cultures, initiative may be encouraged because if a hunter/fisherman tries out a new technique or method to get food and it doesn't work, they can still revert back to the old system without having lost much. But if it does work, they would benefit from being able to use this new tool or technique. For example, a hunter may walk a great distance on a hunch that they can find new and better hunting grounds. If they don't find anything one day, they can simply return to the old hunting grounds the next. Or a fisherman might try to improve his hooks or nets with a new design. If it works he can catch more fish. If it doesn't, he's still got the old tools that he knows will work.

In summary trying new ideas may not be valued as much in a pastoral or agricultural society, because if something new is tried their sole source of food (their animals or crops) may die or produce poor harvests. This wouldn't just have consequences for one day, but would have long-term consequences (like having less food for the coming weeks and months).

The results of Barry et al's research will be discussed in the next section. For now it's hoped that you can see how economic factors can play a role in the types of characteristics that particular cultures value in an individual.

Guiding Question:

How might economic factors influence cultural values?

Critical Thinking Extension:

Alternative Explanations: This section only provided you with two extremes of economic structures in different cultures. But the world is not black and white like this. In their original article, Barry et al identified possible exceptions to these extremes of food production. Can you think of how some cultures may fall in the middle of these two categories? For instance, how might a subsistence culture have aspects of a high food accumulation culture?

If you're interested...

Anthropology and sociology are closely related to psychology and these may be particular areas of interest for you. There are numerous documentaries you can watch online. One good documentary about early human history, evolution and different ways of living across the world is called "Great Human Odyssey" and is available online.

(c) Parenting and Enculturation

The previous section elaborated on the idea that economic factors can affect the extent to which a particular culture may place emphasis on certain traits and values. This might explain why some cultures place value on traits like compliance and responsibility, while others value initiative and innovation. Growing up in cultural environments that encourage or discourage particular traits and values could explain differing levels of conformity across cultures. But a question still remains regarding precisely how these cultural values are transmitted from one generation to the next.

Based on their hypotheses, Barry et al. wanted to see if there was a correlation between economic systems and child training practices. They identified different types of child training practices for kids from around 5 years old until adolescence. Their categories were based on the values and characteristics that were the focus of child training. They measured a range of areas related to child training, including obedience, responsibility, self-reliance, achievement and independence. In other words, they wanted to know if there was a relationship between a culture's primary economic system (pastoral, fishing, etc.,) and how they raised their children.

The practices were measured across 46 societies from around the world. They used existing data to categorize societies as high food accumulating (pastoral or agricultural) or low food accumulating (hunting and fishing).

When correlating child training with food accumulation, their results showed a positive correlation for high food accumulation cultures and child training practices related to responsibility training and obedience training. If a culture requires adults who are going to be responsible in taking care of crops and animals, they need to teach these values from a young age. Similarly, obedience may be a valued quality because it will ensure that an individual follows the rules and can maintain the practices that will ensure healthy animals and crops.

On the other hand, low food accumulating societies showed a greater emphasis on child training related to independence, achievement and self-reliance. As hunting and fishing are largely independent activities that rely on individual skill and achievement, cultures may raise their kids in a way that gives them these values and qualities.

Barry et al.'s study provides plausible explanations for how economic factors may influence cultural transmission: child rearing is an important way in which cultural values are transmitted from one generation to the next. The process of enculturation is influenced by child raising practices, including how kids are taught at school and at home. The focus on particular values may differ across cultures to reflect the skills and attitudes that are necessary for the individual and the cultural group to survive and thrive in that

Child training practices in low food accumulating societies may be more likely to encourage self-reliance and independence, as these are important attributes for success in such a culture. This may explain Berry's early findings on different levels of conformity between different cultural groups (e.g. Inuit and Temne).

Child training is a broad term that covers any type of practice that ensures cultural transmission of cultural norms (Berry et al., 2002). An example would be direct instruction from a parent, or what is taught in schools.

Explaining how enculturation may affect conformity is similar to explaining how cultural values affect behaviour; you simply need to begin by explaining where those cultural values come from in the first place.

particular cultural and economic environment. As you've already seen, the values that are a product of our childhood experiences and how we're raised may influence other behaviours, such as independence or conformity.

In summary, enculturation through parenting and other child raising practices can influence an individual's values. Those values could be the result of enculturation processes that help prepare an individual to be a productive member of a particular cultural group.

Guiding Question:

How might enculturation influence behaviour? Use evidence to support your answer.

Critical Thinking Extension:
Generalizability: This study was conducted in 1959. Are these results applicable to today's societies? To what extent can we generalize these findings to modern societies? Consider the factors that may be different in industrialized and modern societies that could be different from the cultures that Barry et al. studied.

If you're interested…

You may wish to do some research into your own culture and its values. Could you think of some ways that the social, physical and/or economic environment of your local culture may influence enculturation processes? Think about the history of your culture as well; perhaps there are historical influences that may have encouraged the transmission of some values over others.

Relevant Topics

- Culture and its influence on behaviour and cognition
- Cultural dimensions
- Enculturation

Practice Exam Questions

- Explain the effect of enculturation on one behaviour.
- Discuss cultural influences on individual attitudes, identity and/or behaviour.

Research Methods

Barry et al.'s (1959) study demonstrates the value of the use of correlational studies in cross-cultural research. Cultural psychologists are interested in looking at how variables associated with culture can influence our thinking and behaviour. But these are incredibly difficult to create in a laboratory environment. For example, how would you design an experiment to create two different conditions of parenting styles? Cultural values and parenting practices are two examples of variables that would be difficult, if not impossible to manipulate in a laboratory but are still of interest to study. Correlational methods can provide insight into relationships between these variables and behaviours, like conformity.

Ethical Considerations

Whenever you are identifying potential ethical considerations in research it's important to think about the potential for the research to inflict psychological (or physical) harm. This is especially important when the nature of the subject matter in the research is extremely personal. Parenting practice is a very personal area of study, which means the "informed" part of informed consent becomes very important. In order to reduce the stress or anxiety for participants, the researchers may want to think about providing them with the full information as to why they are gathering data on their parenting practices. Whenever a researcher is providing information of the aims and subject matter of the research they should also consider how it might impact the validity of the research.

3.3 Acculturation

How can adapting to a new culture affect our behaviour?

(a) Acculturation: An Introduction

The previous topic's aim was to show you why some cultures may have different values than others: our cultural environment shapes and molds who we are in many different ways and how we're raised from an early age is just one way that this can happen.

But in our modern world people are more mobile than they have ever been. It's common for people to migrate between countries and even across whole continents. This may happen at any age and for any number of reasons. As the movement of people across cultures is common and can have significant effects on people's behaviour, it is a popular field of study for cultural and social psychologists.

While enculturation refers to the process of adopting cultural norms as a result of living within an original cultural environment (for example, where you were born), acculturation refers to the process of changes to an individual as a result of interaction and contact with other cultures (e.g. moving from one culture to another) (Berry et al., 2002). Naturally, this process of acculturation can have an influence on our thinking and our behaviour.

Acculturation can have many different outcomes, both positive and negative. There are also different acculturation strategies that people may adopt as they come into contact with a new culture. Some people may assimilate, which means they do not wish to maintain their original culture's norms or values and choose to adapt the values and norms of their new culture. Other people may prefer separation, which means they might reject the new culture that they're living in and develop a stronger sense of their original cultural identity. Another acculturation strategy is integration, which means someone maintains their original culture *and* participates in the new culture (Berry, 2002).

If you're an international student or have parents who were migrants, you will probably already know that the process of interacting with a new culture can be stressful. For example, if you have to learn a new language or customs that are unfamiliar and you feel pressured to do so, it might bring about negative psychological outcomes, like depression and anxiety. It's common to experience negative reactions to the process of acculturation and this is called acculturative stress. This stress that results from negative experiences and pressures of acculturation is one of many ways that acculturation may influence behaviour.

There are also many factors that may contribute to acculturative stress. As discrimination is a common theme that runs throughout this chapter, we'll look at how discrimination may affect acculturative stress and the psychological effects this could have on an individual.

Discrimination can be defined as any "...negative attitude, judgment, or unfair treatment of members of a particular group" (Williams, Spencer, & Jackson, 1999).

It is important to note that acculturation refers to any change in attitudes or values as a result of interaction with a new culture. It is not synonymous with assimilation, which means to adopt the norms of the new culture and remove oneself from the original culture.

Discrimination is an unfortunate yet common aspect to the acculturation process for many individuals and it is a common source of acculturative stress. New migrants to a country, for example, may experience outward and overt racism like people calling them names or making them feel unwelcome. It might be difficult to find a place to live or even a job, especially in communities where discrimination is common. As you can imagine, this acculturative stress might have negative psychological effects on an individual. It may even result in developing psychiatric disorders, such as depression.

In this text, we will focus on discrimination as being the unfair treatment of people from particular groups. People are often discriminated against because of the group they belong to, such as their race, cultural background, gender, sexuality, or age. Poor green fishy.

To summarize, the term acculturation in psychology refers to the psychological change to an individual as a result of contact with a new culture, not necessarily an adoption of new cultural values. As there are multiple ways that acculturation processes can affect behaviour, in this topic we'll focus on just one: how integration may reduce acculturative stress and feelings of depression for people who experience discrimination. The research investigating this idea will be explored in the following section.

Guiding Question:

How might acculturation influence acculturative stress?

Critical Thinking Extension:

Reflection: An important part of being able to think critically is to be able to reflect on conclusions. It might be easy to explain how acculturation could lead to acculturative stress for migrant workers or refugees. Can you think of other people who may experience acculturative stress as a result of interacting with a new culture?

If you're interested…

Ben Huh's Ted Talk "What if you were an immigrant?" provides an insight into what it's like being an immigrant to a new country. You might be able to relate to Huh's experiences, or it may provide an insight into an unfamiliar world.

(b)   Acculturation and Psychological Distress

In the previous section you were introduced to three new and important concepts: acculturation, acculturative stress and discrimination. As individuals interact with a culture that is not their primary culture their thoughts, attitudes and behaviour may change as a result. But this acculturation could lead to acculturative stress, especially if they experience discrimination. Discrimination may happen to anyone because of a number of factors, such as their race, religion, gender or sexuality. In this section, we'll narrow our focus to look at how perceived discrimination against Latinos in the US may cause acculturative stress. But the acculturation strategy of integration may help reduce the effects of discrimination.

Torres et al. (2012) conducted a correlational study on American Latinos to see if experiences of discrimination increases acculturative stress, and if this might then increase psychological distress. Earlier research has shown that around 30% of Latinos in America have experienced discrimination (Perez, Fortuna, & Alegria, 2008). As the Latino population in America is around 30% and growing steadily, the psychological effects of this discrimination is an important area of study.

A series of questionnaires were given to 669 participants to measure their levels of perceived discrimination, acculturative stress and psychological distress. They also measured their integration (in terms of language acquisition) into mainstream US culture. The participants were from a city in the Midwest region of the US and most identified as being Mexican, Mexican-American or Chicano, although there were some participants with Cuban, Puerto Rican, and South/Central American backgrounds. Around 50% were born outside of the US.

When measuring perceived discrimination they were asked questions relating to their jobs, health care, being in public and education. For example, one question in the questionnaire for students was "Teachers and students assume I am less intelligent because I am Latino." The participants had to circle a response on a Likert scale ranging from strongly disagree to strongly agree.

Their measure of acculturative stress focused particularly on stress related to language use. For example, they may be asked "It bothers me that I speak English with an accent." As with the other questions, they would circle a response from 0 ("Does not apply") to 5 ("Extremely stressful"). To assess their psychological distress, another questionnaire was used that gathered data on their feelings of depression, anxiety and physical symptoms (e.g. feeling faint or dizzy).

Analysis of the data found evidence that supported the study's original hypotheses: those participants who had higher levels of perceived discrimination also experienced higher levels of acculturative stress. The higher levels of acculturative stress also correlated with psychological distress.

Discrimination can have negative psychological effects, and the acculturation strategy that an individual adopts may influence these effects.

Discrimination is an important behaviour to know because it is a recurring theme in this chapter. Make sure you fully comprehend what it means.

Acculturation may affect behaviour through feelings of acculturative stress. Interacting with a new culture can be stressful, especially if one experiences discrimination. This could have negative effects on someone's psychological well-being.

These findings support earlier research that shows a relationship between experiencing discrimination and having high stress and psychological distress. Latinos who experience discrimination and feel like they are being discriminated against may have negative psychological outcomes, such as depression and anxiety. This is one way in which the acculturation process could influence behaviour.

Another interesting finding from the study was that those participants who had a higher Anglo behavioural orientation experienced lower levels of acculturative stress. This means that those participants who engaged more in mainstream US culture and were more fluent in English, suffered lower stress as a result of perceived discrimination. Their level of assimilation into mainstream culture was assessed based on language, and they were asked questions like "My thinking is done in the English language." It appears that the integration into mainstream culture may help to reduce the psychological effects (e.g. depression) of perceived discrimination.

Torres et al. also argue that feeling pressured to learn English and become fluent in English might make the acculturative stress that individuals experienced from their discrimination even worse.

Experiencing discrimination because of your ethnic or racial heritage is a common yet unfortunate reality for many migrants and ethnic minorities. Torres et al.'s study shows that Latinos who have higher levels of perceived discrimination also have higher levels of acculturative stress. This stress also has a higher probability of leading to negative psychological outcomes, such as depression and anxiety. While integration and developing language fluency can help reduce these effects, feeling pressured to integrate might exacerbate them.

Other examples of the effects of acculturation on individual identity, attitudes and behaviour are included in the HL extension chapter.

Guiding Question:

How can acculturation have an effect on behaviour?

Critical Thinking Extension:

Population Validity: Based on the characteristics of this sample, can you explain why the population validity of this study might be questioned? For instance, to what extent could these results be generalized across different cities in the US?

If you're interested…

Understanding prejudice and discrimination is a central theme within this chapter and you may already have some understanding of these behaviours from other subjects. The guys at Crash Course also have a history channel and a video called "Civil Rights and the 1950s." While this focuses on American culture, it will provide you some examples of extreme discrimination. You may also like to do some research to further understand any prejudice and/ or discrimination that has existed towards ethnic minorities in your own country.

Relevant Topics

- Culture and its influence on behaviour and cognition
- Acculturation
- Prejudice and Discrimination

Practice Exam Questions

- Discuss research related to prejudice and discrimination.
- Describe one study related to acculturation.
- Explain one effect of acculturation on behaviour.

Research Methods

Torres et al.'s study is a good example of a correlational study as it has two variables that co-vary (i.e. both can vary along a continuum, as opposed to being categorized). They measured the extent to which individuals felt they had been discriminated against. Their level of perceived experienced discrimination would vary from individual to individual. The other variable that is also varying is the effects of this discrimination on their psychological well-being. Using questionnaires to gather data and establish correlations enables social psychologists to draw conclusions about the correlations between variables.

Ethical Considerations

Ethical considerations in research could be applied to any aspect of the methodology, including the nature of the participants. In Torres et al.'s study they used participants who may not have been fluent in English. This makes aspects of following ethical guidelines quite difficult. For example, how reliable is their informed consent if they cannot understand it? The researchers would still need to obtain informed consent, but they would need to carefully consider how they went about this. They might, for instance, use a translator or have a document that is written in two languages. They may also need to use back translation to ensure clarity. This is when researchers translate a document back into the original language e.g. taking an informed consent form that was translated into Spanish, and then back translating it into English so the original authors can check for clarity and consistency.

3.4 Competition and Conflict
How can competition influence conflict?

(a) Competition: An Origin of Conflict

In the previous topics we focused on two particular behaviours: conformity to group norms and discrimination against ethnic minorities. In the following topics we're going to explore these behaviours further by looking at group dynamics. The term group dynamics refers to the behaviour of individuals when they are within a group, as well as how groups interact with one another.

Belonging to a group, and feeling a strong sense of identification with being a member of that group, is an important social influence that can alter our behaviour. When discussing intergroup behaviour, we refer to in-groups and out-groups. Intergroup behaviour is how different groups interact with one another. For example, how rival gangs clash in street fights or how rival schools demonstrate their loyalties in big sports matches. The in-group is the group in which someone belongs, while the out-group is the group that they don't belong to. You can probably identify at least a few of your own in-groups and out-groups. It's important to be able to use the terms in-group and out-group correctly, as it's vital for being able to clearly explain the effects of group dynamics.

One possible origin of intergroup conflict is the direct competition for resources. In the 1940s and 50s, Muzafer and Carolyn Sherif developed their ideas to explain this phenomenon. Their theory, which was later named realistic group conflict theory (RCT), attempted to explain how conflict could emerge as a result of competition between groups for resources (Sherif et al., 1961). Competition occurs when groups are opposed against one another to obtain scarce resources. This competition can easily lead to conflict. When one group can only achieve its goals through the failure of another group, this is called negative interdependence.

Competition as a result of negative interdependence is a central claim of the origins of conflict, according to RCT. As Campbell (1965) states, the very straightforward central hypothesis of RCT is that "real conflict of group interests causes conflict." Other social psychologists agree that this hypothesis is "...intuitively convincing and has received strong empirical support." (Tajfel and Turner, 1979).

One common form of conflict between groups is when opposing forces are at war with one another.

The term "resources" is rather ambiguous, but it needs to be because there are lots of different things groups might be competing for - basic needs such as food, shelter, etc. ranging all the way up to two business competing for market share in an industry. The fact that the resources are scarce is what makes the groups negatively interdependent: if there were plenty of resources the groups wouldn't need to compete with one another, and there would be no conflict. At least, this is according to RCT. In a later topic you'll learn about social identity theory, which might explain why conflict exists even when there are plenty of resources to go around.

For instance, in a sports match if there can be only one grand champion, rival sports fans might become aggressive towards one another. However, if a draw is possible, or both sides could share the championship (which is rare in sports), there may not necessarily be conflict. Negative goal interdependence can also be seen on a global scale, with countries going to war with one another over territorial disputes or other resources (e.g. oil).

To test this idea of conflict arising over competition, the Sherifs and colleagues designed a study to take place in a summer camp in Oklahoma called "Robbers Cave" in 1954 and the experiment has come to be known as the Robber's Cave Experiment. The field experiment involved two groups of twelve-year-old boys at Robber's Cave State Park, Oklahoma. The 22 boys in the study were strangers to one another, but they all shared similar characteristics in that they were white, middle-class, had both parents at home (i.e. parents weren't divorced) and they were Protestant. The boys were assigned to one of two groups using random allocation.

During the first phase of the experiment the boys were encouraged to form bonds by pursuing shared goals that required the group members to work together to achieve common aims. They chose names for their groups (The Eagles and The Rattlers) and designed flags. The groups quickly developed their own social norms within each group.

In the second phase of the experiment, the Competition Stage, the boys were made aware of the other group and the researchers specifically designed the group interactions over four to six days to cause conflict. They were put into competition with each other by playing games such as baseball and tug of war. The group that won competitions was given prizes such as pocket knives, while the losing group was awarded nothing. Hostility was demonstrated by the boys as they booed the other team and called them names during the games. One team even burned the other's flag and raids occurred between the groups' cabins.

The researchers also designed situations whereby one group gained at the expense of the other. For example, the Rattlers group was delayed getting to a camp party and when they arrived the Eagles group had eaten all the good food. The researchers had set it up so half the food looked appetizing and the other half of the food didn't look so great. The Rattlers began calling the Eagles greedy and other names, then things escalated to the point where food and even punches were thrown (Aronson et al., 2013; Sherif et al., 1954 and 1961). The groups eventually became so hostile with each other that the researchers had to physically separate them.

The experiment seemed to be successful in establishing conflict as a result of competition over resources between the groups.

It's important to regularly reflect on ethical issues regarding experiments. Can you think of any ethical issues that may arise from this study?

> **Guiding Question:**
>
> How does the Robber's Cave Experiment support the central hypothesis of RCT?

Critical Thinking Extension:

Population Validity and Controls: Sherif et al.'s field experiment could be criti-cized on the grounds of population validity (not to mention the *numerous* ethical issues). They chose boys that were white, middle-class, parents still married and had the same religion (Protestantism). But this is very different from real-life sources of inter-group conflict. For instance, there is a lot of hostility and conflict between different religious groups in the world today, and clashes between racial groups is very common. This seems to heavily influence the population validity of such a study. So why do you think they chose to have boys that were so similar?

If you're interested…

It's rather interesting to note that the novel *Lord of the Flies* by William Golding was published the same year the Sherif's published their article on the Robbers Cave Experiment. It could be worth researching which one came first, as the novel portrays a group of boys stranded on an island. They soon form two groups that end up having immense conflicts with one another. It seems very similar to what happened in the experiment, or is it just a coincidence?

(b)   Biology and Competition

Realistic group conflict theory (RCT) provides a very plausible sociocultural explanation for how competition for resources can result in intergroup conflict. But as with all behaviours, we need to look at other possible variables that might be involved. One possible biological factor that may influence competition and conflict is testosterone.

While studying criminology, you learned about how testosterone may be correlated with aggression, violence and crime. In the criminology unit, Radke et al.'s study was used to demonstrate a possible explanation for the correlation between testosterone and aggression. In this section, hopefully you were able to understand how an increase in testosterone may affect the activation of the amygdala during the perception of a social threat. The increase in the amygdala activation was higher when the participant with a testosterone injection was told to approach the angry face, instead of avoiding it. This suggests that the role of testosterone is correlated with motivation to deal with a threat and it may help prime the body physically to deal with a confrontation, because the activation of the amygdala may spark the fight/flight response and provide the physiological and emotional arousal necessary to confront a threat.

Studies have shown that testosterone is not only affected during competition that involves high levels of physical activity, it also increases in other, less physical forms of competition, like chess matches.

The term "social threat" could cover many different situations. In the Robber's Cave study, the threat could come from one group trying to take resources from the other group. When the boys in the Rattler's group arrived at the camp party, the fact that the Eagles had taken all the good food could be deemed a social threat – the presence of the other group threatens to deprive them of resources. It's clear from the descriptions of what happened that there was a lot of emotion and hostility between the two groups as well. *Perhaps* testosterone levels may have been influencing the displays of violence that occurred afterwards, as it might have primed their amygdala and triggered the physiological arousal which facilitated their high levels of emotional arousal, which would prepare them to compete with the other group. There might also be individual differences between the boys that could explain varying levels of aggression displayed. It would be unlikely to expect all boys to display identical levels of competitiveness and aggression during these interactions.

This is important to note because while Sherif was able to observe the social factors influencing behaviour, internal biological processes were ignored. Remember that when analysing explanations for behaviour, it's important to consider possible influential variables that are missing from the argument.

The effects of testosterone on social interactions and competitions is an extensive field of study. Sports are viewed as a competition for resources, because in most cases only one side can win. Taking any substance that artificially increases testosterone is widely banned across athletic competitions, as research has shown that increased levels of testosterone are an advantage for athletes as it enhances performance (Wood and Stanton, 2012).

When explaining behaviour from the perspective of one particular approach (e.g. sociocultural), you should always consider if an alternative approach (e.g. biological) might also be worth considering.

Testosterone may be influential in other types of competition as well. Wingfield et al., 1990) proposed the challenge hypothesis to explain how increased testosterone may facilitate competition in males in mating contexts. Increases in testosterone in males before competition with another male might help by increasing their aggression. An increase in testosterone in this context would facilitate the physical and mental processes required to be successful in competition.

So while RCT provides a possible explanation for intergroup conflict, it fails to recognise important biological factors that may be influencing competition and conflict.

Guiding Question:

How might an increase in an individual's testosterone levels facilitate competition for resources?

Critical Thinking Extension:

Understanding Interactions: After you are able to provide alternative explanations, you should also be thinking about how variables interact. That is to say, how two variables might be influencing one another. In this topic you've seen how group dynamics can influence competition and conflict, and how testosterone may facilitate that competition and conflict. Can you think of how testosterone may influence group dynamics and/or how group dynamics may influence testosterone?

If you're interested...

Sport Psychology was once an option in IB Psychology but due to lack of interest it was removed from the syllabus. So while there are limited avenues to explore this subject within IB Psychology, it is a field of study you could pursue after you complete the IB Diploma or even in your own time. There are numerous books and textbooks available on the subject. One example is "The Champion's Mind: How Great Athletes Think, Train and Thrive" by Jim Afremow.

Relevant Topics

- Competition and cooperation
- Origins of conflict
- Group dynamics
- The individual and the group

Practice Exam Questions

- To what extent do sociocultural factors influence group dynamics?
- Discuss research related to co-operation and/or competition.
- Contrast two origins of conflict.

Research Methods

A common method used to study group dynamics in social psychology is the field experiment. Asch's study shows us the benefits of being able to control conditions and isolate independent variables. This can be beneficial for understanding group influences on individual behaviour. But when studying the interaction of groups it's much harder to manipulate this in a laboratory setting. By creating groups in a real life situation such as a summer camp, Sherif et al. were able to see how group dynamics exist in a natural environment. It's a good example of a field experiment because the psychologists were the ones manipulating the independent variable (the stages of the experiment). This is an important characteristic of this study that distinguishes it from a naturalistic observation.

Ethical Considerations

Studies investigating the behaviour of children are particularly loaded with potential ethical concerns. If you couple this with studying the origins of conflict, you have real potential ethical issues with your research. An essential aspect of this study, therefore, would be the need to acquire parental consent. But if you were to try to explain this consideration in an exam answer, your explanation might be limited. You may be better to focus on a broader definition that simply focuses on considering the safety and psychological well-being of participants. The researchers would have had to carefully monitor the effects of their research throughout the course of the study. As participants weren't given informed consent (because they weren't aware it was an experiment), the researchers may have offered the right to withdraw to a participant during the study if they displayed any negative effects of participation. Of course, doing this could jeopardize the validity of the study.

3.5 Cooperation and Conflict
How can cooperation reduce conflict?

(a) Cooperation and the Contact Hypothesis

Realistic group conflict theory had more elements than just the idea of competition for resources explaining conflict. While Sherif et al.'s field experiment showed possible origins of conflict, it was also used to show how conflict between groups can be reduced. RCT posits that conflict cannot be reduced by simply having groups come into contact with one another. The negative goal interdependence needs to be reversed and there needs to be *positive* goal interdependence between groups to facilitate conflict resolution. This is when groups are required to work together in order to achieve a common goal, which Sherif called superordinate goals (Sherif, 1961). When groups are required to cooperate and work together to achieve superordinate goals, conflict can be *reduced*.

Making real life connections to the ideas you learn in class can help you to understand new concepts.

I've observed this frequently in sports fans. In New Zealand, rugby is a national sport and people are crazy about rugby. Fans of rival teams from different areas of the country can end up getting pretty hostile and aggressive towards each other when their teams are competing for trophies. But then the following week the All Blacks (New Zealand's national team) will be playing their arch rivals The Wallabies (Australia's national team) and those same fans from different parts of the country will be arm in arm, united against the new common enemy: the Aussies! While their respective in-groups were once in competition with one another (based on the area in the country they lived), they are now part of the same in-group (based on their nationality) and identify with one another as they compete against a new out-group. They work together by cheering for the same team to achieve a new common goal.

The effect of having new superordinate goals can be seen in sports fans, especially those who cheer for provincial and national teams.

After the competition between the groups at the Robbers Cave summer camp escalated into direct conflict, the researchers tried to see if they could reverse the effects and reduce the hostility between the Rattlers and the Eagles.

In the third stage of the experiment, after the group formation and competition stages, there was a stage of cooperation where both teams worked together and joined forces to work towards common goals. One example of this was when they had to restore a broken down truck in order to get the food supplies to the camp and they also had to work together to restore the camp's water supply. Here we can see they had the same goals: get food and water. They needed to cooperate in order to achieve these goals. The result of the cooperation, as recorded by the researchers, was reduced hostility between the boys from the different groups (Sherif, 1961).

Stereotypes can viewed as a *belief* about a group of people, prejudice as an *attitude* towards a group of people (perhaps influenced by existing stereotypes) and discrimination as an *action* towards the group (perhaps influenced by stereotypes and prejudice).

Another finding from the study was that the percentage of boys who said they had a best friend in the out-group also increased. Before the series of tasks where they had to cooperate and work, under 10% of the boys had a best friend in the out-group. After the cooperative tasks were completed, this increased to around 25% for the Eagles and around 35% for the Rattlers. It seems that by being required to cooperate with each other, members of both groups were able to reduce their prejudiced feelings about members of the out-group and even establish friendships (Sherif et al., as cited in Aronson et al., 2013).

The Robber's Cave Experiment supports the idea that conflict can emerge as a result of competition between groups, but that intergroup conflict can be reduced if the members of competing groups are required to put aside their differences to achieve a common goal.

This is similar to Allport's contact hypothesis (1954). This is another idea that emerged in the US post-World War II. At this time, social psychologists were devoted to studying the origins of prejudice within America. If origins of prejudice and inter-racial conflict could be understood, then hopefully it could also be reduced (Pettigrew and Tropp, 2000).

The contact hypothesis is similar to RCT in that it outlines some conditions that are required in order for contact between in-groups and out-groups to reduce conflict. Conflict in this context could be used as an umbrella term that includes the associated thoughts and feelings, such as prejudice and discrimination. According to the contact hypothesis, contact can reduce conflict and prejudice when four conditions are met:

1. Groups are of equal status
2. They share are a common goal
3. Their interaction (contact) is supported by social norms and there is support from an authority for the contact (e.g. it is supported by law, a teacher's expectations, an authority figure, etc.)
4. There is no competition between the groups (Pettigrew and Tropp, p94)

A lot of research has been conducted into the validity of the contact hypothesis in predicting the effectiveness of group interactions in reducing intergroup conflict. Pettigrew and Tropp (2006) conducted a meta-analysis of 515 existing studies on the contact hypothesis and found there was significant evidence to support the theory, as their findings suggest that "intergroup contact typically reduces intergroup conflict" and when intergroup contact meets the conditions of Allport's theory, there is an even greater reduction in prejudice between in-group and out-group members.

Guiding Question:

How does the Robber's Cave experiment support the contact hypothesis for reducing intergroup conflict?

Critical Thinking Extension:
Generalizability: While the Robber's Cave experiment can demonstrate the positive outcomes associated with getting conflicting groups to cooperate, the design of the experiment, including participant characteristics, may limit the generalizability of these findings. Can you think of particular groups that are in conflict with one another that these results might not be applicable to? Strong evaluations of research include explanations as well, so try to come up with good reasons why the group you have identified might not expect the same results as shown in Sherif's experiment.

Prejudice can be "broadly defined as any state of mind, feeling, or behavior that criticizes or derides others on account of a social group to which they may belong" (Allport, 1954; Brown, 2010).

Umbrella Term: a term that covers a wide range of ideas or concepts (like an umbrella covers a person). Understanding how concepts relate to umbrella terms can be valuable for analyzing the demands of exam questions and selecting appropriate responses.

If you're interested…

There is an interesting real-life application of the idea of reducing conflict through cooperation by the organisation "Seeds of Peace." This organisation designs and hosts summer camps that brings together students from areas that are in conflict with one another. You can read more about this organisation and how they aim to reduce global conflict by acting locally. Peace Child International is another such organization that you may be interested in learning more about.

(b)   Cooperative Learning: The Jigsaw Classroom

Have you been part of a jigsaw classroom activity before? What other potential benefits do you think there might be in using a jigsaw design? Can it work as well without a teacher supervising?

While RCT seems to offer plausible strategies to reduce conflict, discrimination and feelings of prejudice, can it be applied to real life situations?

One practical application of the ideas behind RCT was developed by social psychologist Elliot Aronson in the 1970s. Before you learn about the jigsaw classroom design and how it aimed to reduce conflict, prejudice and discrimination through cooperation, it's important to know a little about what was happening in many American schools at this time. As a result of the Civil Rights Movement of the 1960s, schools began to desegregate- not always by choice. Prior to this, many schools in the US, especially those in the southern states, were segregated, meaning that black kids and white kids would attend different schools. Desegregation involved these schools being combined, so suddenly classes that were once racially homogenous now had a combination of students from different racial groups. This led to numerous conflicts between members of these once separated groups, much like what happened when the Eagles and the Rattlers came into contact with each other and fought over a common goal.

During the Civil Rights Movement in the US, laws were passed with the purpose of ending segregation in schools. An example comes from Austin, Texas in 1971. Schools in this city, like all public schools across America at this time, were desegregated. This meant that Mexican, African American and white students were now attending the same schools. The early results were open conflicts, including fist fights between members of these different racial groups. The superintendent of this school district contacted Aronson to develop a strategy that might create more harmonious classroom and campus environments. The situation reminded Aronson and his colleagues of the Robber's Cave Experiment, so they designed the jigsaw classroom to try to use the concept of positive goal interdependence to achieve the goal of reducing conflict between the two groups (Aronson et al., 2013).

While a classroom might not seem like the sort of place where competition for resources might occur, if you think about the traditional classroom set-up, it's not hard to see how this competition might come about. Students are motivated to seek and understand the information so they can get the right answer. The resources may be affection and praise from the teacher or to be at the top of the class – a limited resource. While modern classrooms may aim to reduce competition, it wasn't so long ago that seemingly outdated practices encouraging academic competition were still in place. Some schools would rank students academically based on their GPA and print this on report cards. This type of practice naturally encourages competition, as not everyone can be at the top. While this is an example of *individual* competition and not *group* competition, it's plausible that members of the racial in-groups wanted to see their own members do better than members of the out-groups (an idea that will be explored in the next topic).

So in order to apply the concept of positive goal interdependence and cooperation, the jigsaw classroom involves students having to rely on one another for information in order to meet a common goal of doing well on an assessment. The process is that the necessary information needed for the assessment is divided into equal parts. Students in the classroom are also divided into equal groups. The original design involved having students in groups of six. Each student is given a different piece of information that is necessary in order to understand the big picture.

The best way to learn about the jigsaw classroom is to experience it. Perhaps you could design your own jigsaw lesson when you are studying for your next test.

So let's say you were learning about realistic group conflict theory and the Robber's Cave Experiment. In a jigsaw design your teacher would divide you into groups of six and then one student is given one piece of relevant information. That is to say, all the information you need to know about this research is broken into six equal pieces. The objective is that each student needs to read and understand their piece of information and explain it back to the other group members.

You might be thinking that this could just encourage intergroup competition within the classroom between these newly formed groups. But the jigsaw model involves another stage of cooperation between the entire class: after students are assigned their piece of information, they form "expert groups" with other students who have the same information. They form these expert groups and help each other understand the content before returning to their original group to complete the jigsaw.

Schools may be able to break down stereotypes and prejudices of students by having them work cooperatively in the classroom.

Now, instead of just relying on themselves, classmates need to rely on each other in order to get all the information to do well on the assessment. The goal (doing well on the test) requires cooperation. The aim of the jigsaw classroom was to encourage positive group interdependence and working towards superordinate goals within classrooms and to have the students of different races working together.

The jigsaw classroom is an example of a cooperative classroom strategy, also known as a cooperative learning strategy. There are a range of different types of activities and strategies that teachers can use to encourage cooperation and collaboration between students; the jigsaw classroom is just one example. Numerous studies have demonstrated the positive outcomes of cooperative learning, including increasing self-esteem, academic performance and attitudes towards school, as well as improving intergroup relations (e.g. Tsay and Brady, 2010; Slavin, 1991).

Guiding Question:

How might cooperative classroom strategies be used to reduce conflict in schools?

Critical Thinking Extension:
Methodological Limitations: Another evaluative point to consider is the generalizability and transferability of this approach. To what extent do you think the jigsaw method could be used beyond classroom and campus environments?

If you're interested…

There's an entire website devoted to the jigsaw classroom (www.jigsaw.org). You can read more about the history of the jigsaw classroom, including Aronson's original findings.

Relevant Topics

- Competition and cooperation
- Conflict resolution
- The individual and the group

Practice Exam Questions

- Discuss origins of conflict and conflict resolution.
- Outline one method used to study the individual and the group.
- Evaluate one study or theory related to competition and/or cooperation.

Research Methods

Numerous field experiments have been conducted in order to measure the effects of cooperative classroom strategies on individual outcomes. Different classrooms are assigned to practice cooperative strategies for an extended period of time while another class follows a different set of classroom practices. The field experiment is valuable in trialing the real-life applications of models designed from psychological theory. As the jigsaw classroom, for instance, was especially designed to be used in the classroom (a real life setting) it is natural that researchers would want to determine its effectiveness in such an environment by conducting a field experiment. The manipulation of the IV in the field condition is important because it provides the researchers a means of comparison.

Ethical Considerations

Once again we see the issues surrounding studying children. There are other important considerations when researchers are trialing possible beneficial treatments or models. One group of students (at least) is going to miss out on receiving classroom experiences that may be beneficial. This is similar to the use of other studies that require placebos: if a researcher has a treatment that they believe will work, how can they decide ethically who would miss out on receiving that treatment?

3.6 Social Identity Theory
How can belonging to a group affect our behaviour?

(a) Social Categorization

Realistic group conflict theory (RCT) provides a plausible explanation for origins of conflict between groups. One criticism of RCT is that is overlooks what is happening at the level of the individual – how belonging to a particular group can influence an individual, and how this might influence group dynamics. In this topic we're going to explore in more depth how belonging to a group can affect our thinking, which may affect our behaviour.

Tajfel and Turner devised social identity theory (SIT) (1979) to supplement RCT, which was developed between the 1940s and 1960s. Both of these theories attempt to explain intergroup behaviour, and in particular they focus on explaining group dynamics and conflict between groups. Developing a deeper understanding of the origins of intergroup conflict is important because it can lead to the development of more effective policies and practices to effect positive social change.

Put simply, SIT is a theory that explains how belonging to an in-group can affect our thinking and behaviour. According to SIT, when we belong to an in-group we naturally categorize people as belonging to our in-group or to out-groups (social categorization) and we compare these groups (social comparison). Moreover, our belonging to an in-group can affect the way we see ourselves (social identity). The self-esteem hypothesis aspect of SIT explains why these cognitive processes occur: we want to enhance our self-esteem and iden-

Social Categorization is the cognitive process that involves thinking about people as belonging to particular groups (e.g. the in-group or another out-group). It's one way belonging to a group can influence our thinking.

tifying with our in-group is one way of doing that. This is why behaviours such as in-group bias, stereotypes, discrimination and prejudice might occur. This summary of SIT has a lot of new terms and concepts, so do not panic if this all doesn't make complete sense right away. Throughout this topic we'll explore each of these concepts individually.

As you know, one of the main claims of RCT is that conflict between groups exists when there is direct competition for resources. Social identity theory does not challenge this claim, but goes further to explain how conflict can exist even *when there*

If you tried to learn all the components of a complex theory like SIT in one lesson, it would be very difficult. This book is designed to "drip-feed" you the core concepts. This will make it easier to learn, but it also means your revision and reflection is very important.

Our blog has lots more resources designed to help you understand RCT and SIT.

is no direct competition for resources. SIT explains how conflict can occur because the groups simply exist in the first place. SIT also explains how an individual's identification with the in-group to which they belong can influence behaviours such as conformity, stereotyping, prejudice and discrimination. How this can occur will be the subject of this topic.

We often define things as much by what they're *not* as by what they *are.* It might be difficult to feel a strong sense of identity with an in-group if there was no out-group against which to define your in-group. If your school had no rivals or no other schools to use for comparison, it might be harder to feel a strong sense of identity and loyalty to your school. According to SIT, one important cognitive process involved in intergroup behaviour is the simple act of distinguishing between in-groups and out-groups. This is known as social categorization and is one of the key components of SIT. If people didn't think about in-groups and out-groups, the effect of belonging to a group might be minimal or perhaps even non-existent. Moreover, SIT attempts to explain intergroup behaviour, and it's impossible to explain intergroup behaviour (e.g. conflict, prejudice, discrimination, etc.) without there being groups to interact with in the first place.

There are multiple facets of social identity theory, and from this introduction to the theory it's hoped that you understand the notion of in-groups and out-groups, social categorization, and how the theory sought to expand RCT's explanations of group dynamics.

Guiding Question:

Why is social categorization an important process to consider when studying intergroup behaviour?

Critical Thinking Extension:

Hypothesizing: By the end of this topic it's hoped you can apply SIT to explain a range of cognitive processes and behaviours, including stereotypes, prejudice and discrimination. Can you propose possible hypotheses for how social categorization might influence these intergroup behaviours? Stereotypes, prejudice and discrimination are highly similar and interrelated. Make sure you think carefully about what each of these terms mean and how they are related to one another.

If you're interested...

The team at Crash Course have an interesting video called "Social Cognition." This video includes a range of different examples of relationships between social influences and cognition that psychologists study. Understanding how social influences affect the way we *think* is often an important component in explaining how social influences can affect the way we *act.*

(b)   *Social Comparison*

Distinguishing between in-groups (us) and out-groups (them) through social categorization is just one aspect of Tajfel and Turner's social identity theory. Two additional important components of this theory to understand are social comparison and positive distinctiveness.

If social *categorization* is the cognitive process of thinking about groups as being separate and different from one another, social *comparison* is the very similar and highly related process of actually *making* direct comparisons between the groups. The best way to understand these processes is to relate it to your life. Think about a group you belong to, and a relevant out-group. What are some of the comparisons you could make about the two groups? Students often find this difficult to think of an in-group and out-group, often because they are not thinking about groups that are in conflict with one another. Remember that SIT was developed to explain intergroup conflict, so it is best applied to groups that are actually in conflict with one another.

Let me provide you with my example: I'm a New Zealander currently living in Japan, so I could think about New Zealanders as my "in-group" and Japanese people as an "out-group" because I'm not Japanese. When thinking about these two groups of people, I could make comparisons based on different attitudes. For example, I would describe Japanese people as being generally quite polite, but not always very friendly. On the other hand, I think New Zealand people are often the opposite: they are often very friendly but not always overly polite.

It's easy to see from my example, which I've tried to make as inoffensive as possible, that this process of distinguishing in-groups and out-groups and then comparing them could easily lead to behaviours like prejudice and discrimination. Prejudice often exists between different racial or ethnic groups in multicultural societies. To be prejudiced means you have a preconceived idea about what someone will be like, without getting to know them and without any good reason to think that way. In other words, you pre-judge someone in a negative way. Often, this judgement might have been made by stereotyping the out-group which they belong to. Social categorization, i.e. thinking about groups as "us" and "them", may lead to prejudicial feelings against the "them", the out-group.

To discriminate means you treat someone differently, and again this is often based on the out-group they belong to. Discrimination is closely related to prejudice, and could be defined as the actions that often accompany and are associated with prejudicial thoughts. For example, if someone is prejudiced towards homosexuals, there's a very good chance they will treat them differently because of their thoughts about that group of people. A wedding cake shop, for instance, might refuse to make a wedding cake to celebrate a gay

If you're a sports player, you may be able to think of ways that SIT can be applied to sports teams. Have you made social comparisons between your team (in-group) and other teams (out-groups)?

Positive distinctiveness is a potential goal for members of an in-group. They want to make themselves different and better from the out-groups.

If you understand social identity theory, you can apply this theory and its core concepts to explain a range of behaviours. This could also reduce a lot of the content you need to revise for exams. Work smarter, not harder.

marriage. Their prejudicial thoughts and feelings about homosexuality has led them to act in a discriminatory manner.

Racial and ethnic minority groups often feel discriminated against in many societies because while they make up small numbers of the population, they often make up the majority of the prison population. They feel that police officers and the judicial system discriminate against them because of prejudicial beliefs about their ethnicity (i.e. their ethnic group).

There are multiple reasons why individuals may make comparisons between their own group and the other group, and some of these will be explored in the following sections. But one of these explanations has to do with a concept within SIT known as positive distinctiveness. To be distinct, means to be obviously different from something else. In the context of explaining inter-group behaviour and conflict, positive distinctiveness has to do with one group trying to make themselves better (positive) and different (distinct) from out-groups. This could easily lead to competition as being victorious and defeating an out-group in some way could increase positive distinctiveness.

The goal of positive distinctiveness might influence actions, but could also be a motivating factor behind thought processes, too. By making comparisons between one's in-group with an out-group that make the in-group seem better, and thus make other out-groups seem negative in some way, positive distinctiveness could be increased. For example, having negative prejudicial thoughts and feelings about out-groups and discriminating against them, may help members of the in-group think of their own group as being better than them. SIT offers additional explanations for why individuals may want to compare social groups to increase positive distinctiveness, and this will be explored in following sections.

Guiding Question:

How might social comparison influence intergroup behaviour?

Critical Thinking Extension:
Alternative Explanations: There are many possible explanations for the origins of prejudice and discrimination; SIT explanations are only one possibility. Can you think of any other possible explanations for the origins of prejudice and discrimination? Are there biological factors that could be influential?

If you're interested…

Once again the helpful team at Crash Course have a video called "Prejudice and Discrimination." This video introduces multiple theories to explain these phenomena and explains some interesting studies that are not covered in this text.

(c)   Self-Esteem and Minimal Group Studies

In the previous section you learned about how the process of social comparison might lead to prejudicial thoughts and discriminatory actions as groups want to make themselves appear better than other out-groups. But why would we want to view other groups negatively just to make our own seem better?

Tajfel and Turner's original theory claimed that positive distinctiveness is a result of a natural human desire to increase our self-esteem. This is another key aspect of the theory called the self-esteem hypothesis. Tajfel and Turner suggest that "individuals will strive to achieve or maintain their positive social identity," and we can base our positive social identity by favorably comparing our in-group with out-groups (Tajfel and Turner, 1979). Our "identity" is a term that generally means how we view ourselves, so our social identity simply refers to how people view themselves based on their belonging to a particular group. Once again, try to relate this abstract concept to your own experiences to understand it better. Who are you? How do you see yourself? What is your identity? What factors influence your feeling of identity?

The self-esteem hypothesis posits that individual behaviour will be motivated by a desire to increase our self-esteem. This desire can influence group dynamics and intergroup interactions.

It seems logical that we would want to have a positive social identity and self-image. Generally speaking humans like to view themselves in a positive way. SIT suggests that it is our belonging to particular groups and our identification with those particular groups we belong to, which can enhance our self-image and enable us to have a positive social identity. Similarly, the process of social comparison can help to boost our self-esteem, especially if we view and treat our own in-group favourably at the expense of out-groups. This bias of thinking and acting towards one's in-group is called in-group bias.

In-group bias is related to discrimination. Whereas to discriminate means to act negatively towards an out-group, in-group bias involves acting positively towards one's in-group.

It should be evident how prejudice and discrimination could be explained through social identity and social comparison: by viewing other groups negatively and adopting prejudicial thoughts about them, we might boost our self-esteem because it makes our own group feel superior. Discriminating against out-groups might work in a similar manner.

Researchers have observed real life examples of social identity and self-esteem on college campuses. Cialdini et al. (1976) conducted a field study where they counted the number of college sweatshirts and t-shirts worn by students on campus after their football team had just won or lost a game. They found that after a victory students were more likely to wear clothing that showed their college's name. As Cialdini puts it, they were "basking in reflected glory." Similar studies by the same researchers showed that after the football team lost, college students were more likely to describe the team using the pronoun "they." When they won, on the other hand, suddenly they would say "we." For example, a fan might say something like "they just didn't work hard enough and the other team were better, which is why they lost." Or if they won they might say something like: "We've been really working hard for this and waiting for so long. We were just better than the other team."

In these studies you can see how identifying with the group (the college they attend) and taking pride in the victories, the college students are increasing their self-esteem. When the group loses, which is potentially damaging to a person's self-esteem, they distance themselves and may not identify with that particular group as strongly.

Cialdini's study can show how a desire to increase our self-esteem through social identity can influence our behaviour.

But researchers have also found that you don't even need to have any existing identification with a group for in-group to occur. Some of the earliest laboratory studies conducted by Tajfel and Turner when they were investigating group dynamics involved what has come to be known as the minimal group paradigm. Originally, they thought they would need to form groups and then gradually increase the similarity of the groups before they would observe in-group biases occurring. They were surprised to find that in-group bias could be observed in experimental situations even when the groups had *nothing* in common.

The minimal group paradigm design in an experiment involves participants being randomly assigned to a particular group. The groups are chosen completely arbitrarily, meaning there is no reason for why a participant is put in one group or the other. For example, they may be separated by simply tossing a coin and putting all the "heads" in one group and "tails" in another. The participants have nothing in common with other members of their in-group, which is where the "minimal group" phrase comes from: they are formed based on the basic definition of what it means to be a group in that they are simply grouped together. Numerous replications and variations of this paradigm have shown that participants rank their in-group members better and having worked harder than out-group members, they say they like them better and that they have more pleasant personalities. (Aronson et al., p 454).

The minimal group paradigm studies offer empirical examples of the effects of group dynamics on discrimination. Minimal group studies consistently demonstrate the effects of identifying with a group on how individuals favour their own group over the expense of others: i.e. they demonstrate in-group bias. In these studies, it has been shown that participants will even sacrifice their own rewards if it means increasing the difference between what they are awarding their in-group and the out-group. For example, in the table below from one of the studies (Tajfel et al., 1971) the participants could have awarded members from their in-group and their out-group 13 points. Or they could have given a member of their own group 12 and the other group 11, thus benefiting both groups. But many participants in this study (boys from a school in the UK) opted to give their in-group member (whom they didn't know, by the way) 7 points, meaning they gave the out-group 1.

| In-group | 19 | 18 | 17 | 16 | 15 | 14 | 13 | 12 | 11 | 10 | 9 | 8 | 7 |
| Out-group | 25 | 23 | 21 | 19 | 17 | 15 | 13 | 11 | 9 | 7 | 5 | 3 | 1 |

While it's a mild form of discrimination, it is still treating a member of an out-group unfavorably and demonstrating a bias towards one's own group, which is discrimination. And while it could be argued that the procedures in these studies are a long way from life in the real world, the alarming fact is that these are *minimal groups*. This discrimination is demonstrated when participants have little in common. In the above example, for instance, the boys were led to believe that their groups were formed based on preference for a painter (Klee or Kandinsky).

The results of such minimal group studies have been replicated numerous times with similar results. They provide empirical support for key claims of the social identity theory, and could be used to explain discrimination between groups.

It is essential that you understand how the minimal group paradigm studies relate to social identity theory: they provide evidence for how belonging to a group can lead to in-group bias. It could be used to explain intergroup conflict, such as discrimination.

Guiding Question:

How can the self-esteem hypothesis be supported by one or more studies?

Critical Thinking Extension:

Can you devise any possible evolutionary explanations for the group dynamics that SIT is explaining?

If you're interested…

The social psychologist Robert Cialdini (cited in this section for the study on social identity and self-esteem) has a fascinating book called "Persuasion." If you are interested in marketing and the psychology of persuasion, I highly recommend this book.

(d)   Stereotypes and Out-group Homogeneity

After learning about the outcomes of social comparison, social categorization and social identity, you might have already begun to see some possible explanations for how stereotypes come about. Stereotypes are cognitive processes and are examples of social cognition, as they are ways of thinking about others. After having learned about origins of inter-group conflict and how comparisons between in-groups and out-groups may serve to boost self-esteem, you can probably see how these same processes might explain negative stereotypes. When we perceive and compare our own in-group with an out-group, we aren't thinking about the individual members of that group. We are making broad generalizations about *all* members of the group. As a stereotype is by its very nature a generalization, you can see how this cognition can occur. By simply thinking of another group as just that, a group, we make generalizations about their behaviour. Thus, it's rather easy for stereotypes to occur. Moreover, negative stereotypes of an out-group and positive stereotypes for an in-group can serve to enhance positive distinctiveness and may help to boost the self-esteem of the in-group members who hold those stereotypes. This is a social cognitive explanation of how stereotypes may occur, based on the tenets of SIT.

Another possible explanation for stereotypes based on SIT has to do with one byproduct of social categorization: the out-group homogeneity effect. If a group is homogeneous it means that they are alike or at least they are viewed as alike. The out-group homogeneity effect is what happens to an in-group member's perception of the out-group: they begin to see members of the out-group as all being more alike than members of their in-group.

> The term "tenet" can be useful to use when explaining theories. It means central claim, belief or principle.

A sorority is a social organization for female college students. They often live in a shared house off campus. The male equivalent is a fraternity.

> It is important that you can provide at least one possible explanation for how stereotypes may form. You also need to be able to explain how stereotypes may affect behaviour.

As a stereotype is a widely held and fixed idea about a particular group of people, it's easy to see how the out-group homogeneity effect might explain the formation of stereotypes. By simply viewing all members of the out-group as being more similar than an in-group, a stereotype (a generalization about that group) could be formed (Ostrom and Sidekides, 1992).

There are numerous studies that demonstrate the out-group homogeneity effect. One example was conducted on 90 college females on a university campus (Park and Rothbart, 1982). They were asked to judge the similarity of the members of their own sorority (their in-group), as well as the similarities of the members of two other sororities. The results showed that they typically judged the out-group sorority members as being more similar to each other than girls in their own sorority.

This study, like many others, shows that when asked to make social comparisons between in-groups and out-groups, people tend to view out-groups as being more similar than their own in-group.

You can read a more detailed summary of Park and Rothbart's study on the blog.

Interestingly, in-group homogeneity has been shown to be affected by the presence of a competing outgroup (Rothgerber, 1997). If members of a group are competing with an out-group, they may view themselves as being more similar to other members of their group. This could serve to strengthen the bond between the group and unite them in defense against the competing group. Competition may therefore be another variable that could explain positive stereotypes for an in-group.

Guiding Question:

How can concepts related to social identity explain the formation of stereotypes?

Critical Thinking Extension:
Limitations: You need to be developing the habit of going one step past providing explanations for behaviour (e.g. stereotypes) and reflecting on the validity or your own explanation, including the evidence upon which it is based. This is what "critical thinking" means in IB Psychology. With this in mind, can you offer any critical reflections on the validity of your explanation of the formation of stereotypes?

If you're interested...

New Zealand television produced a powerful documentary provocatively named "Chinks, Coconuts and Curry-munchers." It explores stereotypes and racism in NZ's multicultural society and it's available to view online.

(e) Biology and Racial Bias

Social identity theory provides a rather plausible explanation for prejudice: we develop prejudiced attitudes towards members of out-groups because we judge them based on the group they belong to and we discriminate against them because we want to increase the status of our in-group, which is done to increase our self-esteem. While social identity theory focuses on the interaction of social factors and cognition to explain behaviour, it overlooks the role of biology.

With the help of modern technology and fMRIs, psychologists have been able to find that the amygdala might be associated with negative thoughts, feelings and behaviours towards members of an out-group.

There are many forms of prejudice, so it's important to note that in this section we are only looking at race-related prejudice. Phelps et al. (2004) conducted one study that investigated the correlation between implicit racial bias and amygdala activation when perceiving racially similar and different faces. If something is implied it means it's not visibly seen or explicit. An explicit bias would be a deliberate and conscious expression of prejudiced thoughts and actions against a person from a different race.

Studies have shown that in the US people's reports of prejudiced attitudes have decreased (Dovidio et al., 2000), but this has generated a new field of research into implicit bias; people may think and act biased towards racial outgroups unconsciously. We need to keep in mind that most of the research in this area investigates the attitudes of white Americans towards black Americans.

One issue with gathering data on people's racial biases is because of the social desirability effect they may not answer completely honestly on questionnaires. Other people may have implicit racial biases, which means they're not consciously aware that they favour their racial in-group over an out-group. The Implicit Association Test (IAT) has been designed to measure an individual's level of implicit bias. The implicit racial bias version of this test involves processing white and black faces, while also having to categorize words with positive connotations (e.g. love, honesty, triumph) and negative connotations (e.g. turmoil, despair, damage). Participants' responses are timed and the test measures the time differences between pairing face colours with word connotations. White American participants are typically faster at pairing black/bad and white/good combinations, than they are black/good and white/bad (Cunningham, Preacher and Banaji, 2000). This suggests an implicit racial bias which means there may exist negative stereotypes, thoughts, or attitudes towards black people that unconsciously affect judgement and thinking.

To determine whether or not the amygdala might be influential in out-group bias, researchers use a paradigm that involves participants in an fMRI machine and images of faces of different colours and ethnicities flash on the screen and their brain activity is recorded. Earlier research has shown that white participants' amygdalae may have higher activity when perceiving a racially different face, even when they are not consciously aware that they have seen a face at all (Williams et al., 2004).

You can take the IAT yourself online and it might be a good way to understand the methodology.

The activation of your amygdala when viewing this face may differ depending on your implicit racial bias.

Phelps et al. (2000) were interested in measuring the neural activity in the amygdala because of its role in emotional learning and the evaluation of social stimuli (e.g. determining if a social stimulus is dangerous or harmless). They conducted their study on white participants by initially placing them in an fMRI viewing a range of black and white faces that were taken from a college yearbook.

After the fMRI testing, they did tests to measure the participants' implicit racial attitudes using the IAT. They found similar results to other studies in that their white participants had a slower time for pairing face/word combinations of black/good and a faster time for white/good combinations. A second finding from the study was that a majority of the participants had higher amygdala activation when they were viewing black faces (racial out-group members). This triangulates other studies that have found similar results (e.g. Chekroud et al., 2014).

Perhaps most interesting from this study was that there was a positive correlation between the activation of the amygdala and the results of the implicit association test: participants that had a stronger implicit racial bias also displayed stronger amygdala activation.

We need to be very careful when interpreting these results and we can't jump to conclusions like "the amygdala causes racism" or "racism causes increased amygdala activation." The researchers themselves conclude that these results need to be interpreted with caution. The purpose of this section is simply to introduce the idea that there may be biological factors underlying our social cognition and social perceptions. While we can view intergroup behaviours from a social and cognitive perspective, we can't overlook the role of brain function in social interactions.

You will not need to remember all of the details included in this section; it simply provides you with a possible counter-point for social identity explanations of discrimination or prejudice.

Guiding Question:

How does Phelps et al.'s study suggest a correlation between implicit bias and amygdala activation?

Critical Thinking Extension:

Contradictory Evidence: Studies have also found that African Americans display stronger amygdala activation when viewing black faces compared with white faces (e.g. Lieberman et al., 2005). How might you explain these results?

If you're interested…

Cunningham et al. (2004) conducted a study that also investigated the role of the prefrontal cortex in this process. Their findings are directly relevant to what is covered during the PTSD unit about the role of the prefrontal cortex in modulating the response of the amygdala.

Relevant Topics

- Co-operation and competition
- Prejudice and discrimination
- Origins of conflict
- Social identity theory
- Stereotypes
- Bias in thinking and decision making

Practice Exam Questions

- Evaluate social identity theory.
- Explain one study related to social identity theory.
- Discuss research related to prejudice and discrimination.
- Explain how stereotypes are formed.
- Discuss the formation of stereotypes and how they may influence behaviour.

Research Methods

Cohen et al.'s study on individual behaviour and attitudes after college football games is an interesting example of a natural experiment. In order to correctly identify a particular research method used you must first make sure you know the characteristics of the different research methods (this will be covered in later chapters). It might be natural to think that this study is a field experiment. But you need to ask, "did the researchers manipulate the IV?" In this case, the IV was naturally occurring. And if the "IV" could vary along a continuum, and this is what the researchers measured, it's more probably a correlational study. In this case the IV that was expected to affect the behaviour was whether or not the team won. This cannot vary: it's yes or no. It's also not a naturalistic observation, even though they gathered observational data in a natural environment, because the study clearly had an independent variable (win/loss) that the researchers believed was influencing the dependent variable (their attitudes towards the group).

The purpose of my explanation here is to show you how careful you need to be when identifying and describing research methods. And of course if you were asked about research methods related to a particular topic and Cohen et al.'s study was relevant, you would need to go further and be able to explain why it was helpful in that particular context to focus on a naturally occurring variable.

Ethical Considerations

Protecting participants' self-esteem and their psychological well-being is at the heart of the ethical guidelines that associations use to govern psychological research. In many studies related to an individual's attitudes or behaviour in social situations, there is the chance for participants to feel embarrassment or even shame at their responses. For example, when uncovering implicit racial biases or stereotypes, participants may experience some distress or anxiety over having their attitudes revealed to them. This is important to consider when following protocols like debriefing.

3.7 Schema Theory
How do we simplify this complex world we live in?

(a)   Schema Theory: An Introduction

Social identity theory provides possible explanations for how social factors (like belonging to a group) can influence our thinking and behaviour. A product of the cognitive processes involved in social identity, including the out-group homogeneity effect and implicit bias, are very closely related to another cognitive concept called schema. Schema is an incredibly abstract but important concept to understand. A schema is a cluster of related pieces of information in our mind. Their technical description is a cognitive framework, or a system of cognitively organizing and storing information, knowledge and memories. It's not expected that you'll be able to grasp the concept of schema just from reading this definition; you will need to be actively processing and reflecting on this concept throughout the following sections.

> Schema: a cognitive framework that helps to cluster related pieces of information, knowledge or memories.

One of the functions of schema is that they save our cognitive energy by enabling us to make generalizations. Stereotypes are also examples of social schema because they are ways we make generalizations about members of other social groups. It's easier to make a generalization about someone based on a group they belong to, rather than thinking about everyone individually. Making such generalizations can help to save our cognitive energy.

In this course it is important that you know about schema theory. Unlike theories such as SIT and RCT that can be attributed to a particular group of theorists, schema theory has had many contributions from a range of psychologists over the past 80 years. By the end of this topic it's hoped that you know the following about schema theory:

- The definition of schema
- Characteristics and functions of schema
- How they might influence our mental processes and our behaviour

As with SIT, we will cover these concepts gradually over the next few sections.

Schemas (plural is also known as schemata) are mental clusters of related ideas and memories

The metaphor I like to use to explain schemas is that of a filing cabinet, or to modernize the metaphor, a filing system on a computer. Our schemas are the files and individual units of information are what make up the files. The world is such a complex place, and we're constantly being exposed to new information. Schema theorists propose that one way of organizing information and saving our cognitive energy is to bunch and group our knowledge together. As we encounter new information, it connects to our existing schema so we can make sense of it more easily and our schemas for certain areas of knowledge build over time.

The key claims of schema theory are spread out through the following sections. This makes it easier for you to gradually learn about this tricky concept. For easy revision of schema theory, see our revision materials at www.themantic-education.com.

Pirate: what springs to mind? Johnny Depp or a hacker? Schemas are a product of your experiences and individuals will have different schema depending on their unique experiences.

Let's take a classic riddle that I think illustrates the concept of schema:

A father and his son are in a tragic car accident. The father dies instantly and the boy is rushed to hospital. The doctor rushes into the operating room, pulls back the blanket and exclaims, "I can't operate on this boy, because he's my son." How can this be?

This "riddle" is simple, right? But it stumps many people and they come up with elaborate, completely implausible explanations for how the boy could be the doctor's son, when the father died in the crash. But the obvious answer, the doctor is his mother, escapes many people because they have a very fixed schema of the word "doctor." If you couldn't get this riddle very easily, it may be because when you hear the word doctor, you think of a man in a white coat with a stethoscope around his neck. You have a bunch of associated images, thoughts and memories about the word "doctor." In other words, you have a gender-biased schema of the occupation. People who can solve the riddle very easily, and for who it's not even a riddle, probably have a more gender-balanced schema.

When you hear a word or see an image and a bunch of related thoughts, feelings and ideas pop into your mind, we call that having your schema activated.

Hopefully your "psychology" schema is also slowly growing. On your first day, if you heard the word "psychology", it might have made you think about the ability to read minds. Many people who don't know much about psychology think that this is what psychology is about. But now after a bit of study in this subject when you hear the word psychology, hopefully a bunch of associated terms and ideas from your psychology schema jump into your mind, like variables, behaviour, cognition, processing, hormones, ethics, experiments, etc. The activation of schema can affect our memory and this will be investigated in the following sections.

As schema theory can be difficult at first to comprehend, it's important as you work through this topic that you are keeping notes on the key claims of schema theory, including definitions, characteristics, functions, and how they can influence our cognition and behaviour.

Guiding Question:

How might social schema save our cognitive energy?

Critical Thinking Extension:

Application: This textbook has been structured very deliberately based on some of the principles of schema theory. Learning is about making connections and gradually enhancing understanding of concepts. Can you see how this text applies concepts related to schema? Could you apply similar concepts in your own writing? (Hint: think about the purpose of introductions and signposts in writing essays.)

If you're interested…

There are a number of videos on our blog that attempt to help students understand the abstract concept of schema. If this concept doesn't make much sense right now, you may want to check out these videos and additional written explanations. You can also read a full summary of schema theory.

(b)   Schematic Processing

According to schema theory, one function of schemas is to enable us to make generalizations and predictions. For instance, we can have generalized ideas about people, places, and events. Our cognitive frameworks (schema) serve a valuable function by helping us to simplify the amount of information we constantly receive from our environment. One effect of this can be that we make generalizations about groups of people. This can result in stereotypes, which is why stereotypes are an example of social schema: they are ways we think about groups of people.

This seems to make sense; there are just simply too many people in the world for us to consider everyone on an individual basis, so schema serve to save our cognitive energy by allowing us to simplify the world and to think of individuals based on the groups that they belong to. This way of thinking may affect our interpretation of new information.

Schematic processing is another important concept in schema theory and refers to how we process new information based on our existing schema. In a social setting, this may influence our perception of others.

Cohen (1981) showed that when we think someone belongs to a particular group, we tend to remember schema consistent information. Our schematic processing leads us to focus on the information and details that are consistent with our schema. In one of her experiments, Cohen had 96 undergraduate college students watch a video of a woman with her husband having dinner and then an informal birthday celebration. The video they watched was designed so that the woman displayed equal numbers of characteristics that there consistent with a stereotype of a waitress or a librarian. For example, she liked to listen to pop music (waitress consistent) and she received a book as a present for her birthday from her husband (librarian consistent). The independent variable in the study was what the participants were told about her occupation. Half were told she was a waitress and the other half she was a librarian. The results showed that participants were more likely to remember schema consistent information better than inconsistent information. That is to say, if they were told she was a librarian, they tended to remember information that was more consistent with a stereotype of a librarian (e.g. she spent the day reading and she was drinking wine). If they were told she was a waitress, they may have remembered other details from the film (e.g. she was drinking a beer and eating a hamburger).

In this study we can see that the participants' memory may have been influenced by schematic processes. The fact that they remembered schema consistent information better than schema inconsistent information suggests that their schema may have been affecting their processing of information. It's easier to comprehend information that is consistent with our existing beliefs, and so it's probably more likely to be remembered.

It's important to note that this study doesn't demonstrate the formation of stereotypes, but it could help explain how stereotypes may affect our behaviour and how they may be reinforced. If we are provided with some information about someone that activates a particular schema (e.g. a stereotype), we may focus more on the information that is consistent with our stereotype and ignore contradictory information that

A word of warning: If you are asked about the formation or origin of stereotypes, be careful when using schema theory as it might not help you explain where the stereotypes originated from in the first place. The out-group homogeneity effect provides a better explanation for possible origins of stereotypes. This section also shows how stereotypes may affect behaviour.

Cohen's study shows how existing schema may bias our memory.

A stereotype is a type of schema; it is a social schema (a group of related ideas and memories about a group of people). Activating different stereotypes influenced the participants' memory of the video in Cohen's study.

There is another term for the tendency for people to focus on schema consistent information- confirmation bias. This will be explored in the following sections.

could challenge it. While this may save our cognitive energy, it could lead to the reinforcement of stereotypes.

To summarize, schema theory suggests that schemas serve valuable functions to save our cognitive energy and to allow us to make generalizations about people, places and events. Stereotypes may be a type of social schema, in that we categorize and make generalizations about groups of people to save our cognitive energy. This may affect our processing of new information as schematic processing may affect memory in a way that biases our memory towards remembering schema consistent information.

Guiding Question:

How might schematic processing reinforce stereotypes?

Critical Thinking Extension:

Limitation: Cohen didn't measure schema. How could you design a study that would counter this limitation? In the following section you'll see an experiment that tests when schema activation may be most influential. This section suggests that the schema affected the processing of the information; can you think of other ways it might have influenced memory?

If you're interested...

If you're curious to see if you have implicit biases towards particular racial groups, you can take an "implicit association test" through Harvard's website.

(c) Confirmation Bias

In the previous section you were introduced to the concept of schematic processing, how this might affect memory and explain how stereotypes are reinforced. The idea of schema activation was also explained, and it will be further demonstrated in this section.

Schema theory suggests that our existing schema can save our cognitive energy by making it simpler to process and comprehend new information. Cohen's study showed that if we have a particular schema activated before we encounter new information, this could affect our memory. This is one way that stereotypes may affect our behaviour, in that they could lead to confirmation bias. This bias in attention and memory could reinforce existing stereotypes.

Confirmation bias is an example of a cognitive bias that involves focusing on information and details that confirm and are consistent with our pre-existing beliefs. It's a bias in our thinking that may be a product of our desire to simplify information processing: it's cognitively easier to focus on information that is consistent with our existing schema, than it is to consider conflicting facts or details. It's another example of how schematic processing may affect our thinking.

In Cohen's study, it's likely that because of the participants' pre-existing ideas about waitresses and librarians (i.e. their stereotypical views of people who work in these professions), the information that confirmed their beliefs was more easily comprehended and able to be remembered. Their processing of information was biased towards focusing on details that were consistent with existing schema. This would also explain why their memory of these details was better than schema inconsistent information.

Another interesting example of this was demonstrated in a study that investigated common stereotypes in American culture regarding athletes. There appears to be a common view in the US that black athletes are naturally gifted athletes whereas white athletes are more "clinical." When addressing an academic conference on the issue of racism in sports, professional golfer Tiger Woods noted "We have this stereotype that black players are gifted and white players are heady" (Stanford University News, 1995).

Stone et al. (2010) conducted a study where participants were told the name of a male basketball player and shown a photo of the player before listening to a recording of a basketball game. After listening to the game, the participants had to rank the player based on his athletic ability, individual performance, and contribution to the team's performance. The independent variable in this study was the race of the man in the picture. Half of the participants were shown a photo of a black athlete, and the other half a white athlete. The results showed that when participants believed the player was black they ranked him as having "significantly more athletic

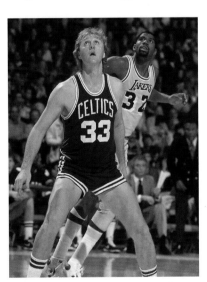

Confirmation bias is a natural tendency to focus on and remember information that is consistent with existing beliefs or opinions. According to Stone's research, when watching Larry Bird a fan might tend to remember his smart plays. On the other hand, they may be more likely to remember athletic plays made by Magic Johnson. (Image credit: Nick Antonini, Flickr.com).

Confirmation bias is a concept that could be used to address topics related to the cognitive and/or sociocultural approach.

In an exam, if you are asked about biases in thinking and decision making you can explain how confirmation bias may distort our memory.

ability and having played a better game" than those participants who thought he was white. On the other hand, the participants who thought the player was white were more likely to rate the player as "exhibiting significantly more basketball intelligence and hustle" (Stone et al., 2010).

By activating a schema of the race of a particular athlete, the participants' interpretation of their performance on the basketball court was affected. The effect of schematic processing can be seen in this study, as their schema of particular athletes was influencing their interpretation of their performance in the game. They were perhaps imagining a different style of player on the court as they listened to the recording based on the player's race and their existing stereotypes. This study seems to confirm the existence of a stereotype about athletes in the US: black basketball players are seen as being more athletic than white players, whom are thought to have higher "basketball IQ." This study also shows another example of how existing social schema affects our processing of new information and may lead to confirmation bias.

While this study doesn't explain how the social schema of race and sporting ability developed, it does show support of one key idea of schema theory - processing information based on existing schema can influence our interpretation and memory of new information.

Guiding Question:

How does the basketball player study demonstrate the effects of confirmation bias?

Critical Thinking Extension:

Evaluating Theories: Remember that one important step in evaluating a psychological theory involves determining the extent to which it can be demonstrated in studies. So far you've seen two studies that demonstrate the effect of schematic processing on memory and thinking. What aspects of schema theory have not been demonstrated in these studies?

You should also be learning to challenge the evidence you are presented with independently: after you comprehend the initial conclusions that can be drawn from a study, you should be independently raising questions regarding its validity.

If you're interested...

Quite unrelated to psychology, one of my favourite comedians, Bill Burr, has a three-minute segment on race in sports in America. This can be viewed online, but listener discretion is advised as there is coarse language.

(d) *Information Processing & Comprehension*

While one example of schema are stereotypes, which are a social schema, there are many types of different schema. Another type of schema are called scripts. These are schema related to procedures and events. Script schemas also enable us to make predictions and they can guide our behaviour in particular situations. For example, when we walk into a restaurant we've never been to before, we still know what to expect and how to behave in the situation because we have a script schema for what happens in restaurants.

Three types of schema are social, script and self.

Studies on schemas have shown that another one of their functions may be to facilitate our information processing and comprehension: how easily and effectively we can understand and remember new information. The following study uses a script schema of sorts, but it's important to note that it doesn't necessarily demonstrate the effect of script schemas on being able to make predictions of how to behave. What the following study does show is that activating particular schemas can improve the effectiveness of our processing, comprehension and recall of new information.

If we have well-developed schemas for the material we are reading we will find it easier to comprehend.

In Bransford and Johnson's classic experiment (1972) they relied on a script schema of doing laundry to test the idea that schema activation can improve comprehension and memory recall of new information. Participants in this study were read a passage that sounded rather vague and ambiguous. Here's how the passage begins:

The procedure is actually quite simple. First you arrange things into different groups. Of course, one pile may be sufficient depending on how much there is to do. If you have to go somewhere else due to lack of facilities that is the next step, otherwise you are pretty well set. It is important not to overdo things....(from Bransford and Johnson, 1972).

You can access the full passage online.

The title of the passage was "Doing Laundry", but not all of the participants were aware of this before they listened to the passage being read to them. The three conditions were:

- Group One were told the title of the passage *before*
- Group Two were told the title of the passage *after*
- Group Three were not told the title of the passage at all

The participants listened to the passage being read and then afterwards they were asked to rate their comprehension of the material and recall as much of the story as they possible could. The results were that on average the members in each condition remembered the following amount of details from the passage (out of a possible maximum of 18):

- Title before: 5.8 details
- Title after: 2.6 details
- No title: 2.8 details

The title before group also gave a self-reported higher rate of comprehension than the other two groups (4.5 out of 7, compared with 2.1 and 2.2) Being able to process the new information in relation to existing schema improved their comprehension and recollection of the passage.

When the participants were told the title of the story, "Doing Laundry" they had their schema activated. Because of this they were able to imagine the process of doing laundry and so when they heard vague details like "you have to go somewhere else due to lack of facilities" they would be able to connect this to the idea of going to

Without associated images and ideas of doing laundry in one's mind, the ambiguous passage is harder to comprehend. Schemas enable grouping of ideas so comprehension of related information is made easier.

Bransford and Johnson's study is a popular one to replicate for internal assessments.

a laundromat if they didn't have their own washing machine. By relating the new information from the passage to what they already knew about doing laundry (i.e. their "laundry schema") they were able to process information more efficiently as shown by their increased ability to recall details of the passage and a higher self-report of comprehension of the passage.

As the above study shows, one function of schemas is that they enable us to process information more efficiently and they can improve comprehension of new information. The participants who had their laundry schema activated may have been able to comprehend the new information better because they could relate the new information to their existing knowledge (i.e. their schema). It should be easy to see how understanding the role of schema in comprehension has significant applications in education. If we can understand how schema processing might influence reading comprehension, for instance, we can develop more effective strategies to try to improve literacy rates and reading comprehension skills.

By this stage in your study of schema theory, it's hoped that you can provide an accurate and concise definition of schema. You should also be able to state different types of schema (scripts and social), outline their functions and use research to explain how they may influence our cognitive processes. If you can't quite do all this just yet, keep working hard and you'll have more opportunities in the next topic as we will further explore the influence of schematic processing on memory.

Guiding Question:

How might schematic processing influence comprehension of new information?

Critical Thinking Extension:

Applications: One of the ways to evaluate a theory is to determine the extent to which it has practical applicability. As mentioned in this section, schema theory is often applied in the field of education, in particular in regards to reading comprehension. Most of what you are taught about effective writing strategies is relevant to understanding schematic processing and communication of information. How could you use what you've learned about schema theory, including schema processing, to improve the clarity of your written communication?

If you're interested...

Visit our blog through www.themantic-education.com to gain access to online summaries of key theories like schema theory, as well as see videos, mini tutorials and other resources that will help you in this course. You can find a link to Bransford and Johnson's original article as well. This could be a good internal assessment experiment to replicate.

Relevant Topics

- Schema theory
- Cognitive processes
- Stereotypes
- Bias in thinking and decision making

Practice Exam Questions

- Outline one study related to bias in thinking and decision making.
- Discuss schema theory.
- Discuss the use of one research method used to study cognitive processes.
- Explain how stereotypes may influence behaviour.

Research Methods

Many studies investigating cognitive processes use the laboratory experiment method as they manipulate the independent variable in controlled conditions and measure the effects on a dependent variable. In research related to schema and memory processes this is useful because it can enable researchers to draw conclusions about how one cognitive process (or framework) may influence another. For example, by changing when participants received schema relevant information, Bransford and Johnson were able to conclude that having one's schema activated *prior* to processing information can increase the comprehension and memory of new information. This experiment has helped to reveal further information about the role of schemas in cognitive processing.

Ethical Considerations

As we've discussed in earlier topics, ethics is very important in research involving sensitive behaviours. Stereotypes are an extremely sensitive area of study. In Stone et al.'s study, for instance, participants may not even be aware that they have stereotypical attitudes towards players from different races. During the debriefing stage of the study the researchers need to be mindful of this and they need to reveal the full nature and results of the study to the participants delicately.

3.8 Reconstructive Memory
Can we trust our memory?

(a)   Rationalization

To provide a quick summary of schema theory so far, you've hopefully learned that schemas are clusters of related pieces of memory, information and knowledge and are also known as cognitive frameworks. Schemas help us to comprehend new information more efficiently, as shown in the laundry schema study.   They also enable us to make generalizations and create expectations of events, groups and people. Activation of a particular schema may lead to changes in memory due to the effects it has on schematic processing. This could lead to stereotypes being consolidated through confirmation bias. From these examples we can see that the way we think may be influenced by external variables and social influences.

Frederic Bartlett (1932) was one of the first psychologists to study schema and schema processing. His research was conducted in the early 1900s and his focus was on how culturally acquired schema may influence the interpretation of stories. According to Bartlett's theories of schema, our memory is affected by the information we receive and our own prior knowledge and experiences, i.e. our schemas. So far we've been looking at how schemas function to process *new* information – now we're going to look at how they can influence our recollection of *old* information.

Bartlett's studies, and many others, have shown that our memory does not work like a video camera, accurately recording everything we encounter in order to be accurately recalled later when we need it. On the contrary, our memories are actively reconstructed, which means we consciously rebuild our memories each time we try to recall something. What can happen during that rebuilding or reconstruction of our memory is that distortion can occur and our memories may not be accurate reflections of reality. This early research by Bartlett further illustrates the effect that schematic processing can have on memory, but unlike earlier studies we looked at in this example the influence in this case is during memory recall, not during encoding.

Bartlett conducted a series of tests that included English participants hearing stories and then having to repeat them later by writing them down. He called this repeated reproduction as participants were repeatedly reproducing the stories they heard. One such story was a Native American folk tale called "The War of the Ghosts." The participants would listen to this story twice. After a fifteen minute delay they would then re-write the story. This story was chosen because its details and structure are rather peculiar for English participants. For instance, there is no clear conflict or rising tension and there doesn't seem to be an apparent moral or message behind this short story which one might expect if they were used to hearing fables or other short folk stories common in British culture.

Bartlett found that when there were details that didn't make sense participants tended to leave out these details when reproducing the story, or they changed the details so they would make more sense. Bartlett referred to this as rationalization, which means to adapt or omit information so that what we recall is consistent with our existing schema.

This topic is a good example of how some topics in this course heavily overlap. Finding these overlaps and making the most of them can enhance your understanding of psychology and reduce your workload.

Recall means to remember information, whereas encoding refers to the process of creating the memory in the first place during the initial processing of the information.

Bartlett's study is much like Phineas Gage: it's a classic but there are probably better studies to use in exam situations.

One example of how the story was changed reported in Bartlett (1932) was that it became shorter and the supernatural element of the ghosts in the story disappeared (Bartlett, p.118 – 124). One participant recalled the story after 15 minutes and then again after a delay of 20 hours (p.67). Two details that were changed as noted by Bartlett were that he changed "canoes" to "boat" and "seal hunting" to "fishing." The participant himself recalls that "I wrote out the story mainly by following my own (mental) images." The participant describes how he pictured the story occurring but then admits that after reproductions "the images of the last part were confused." (p.68). The reproductions of the story suggest that the participant had changed the structure of the story and omitted certain details so that it fit the story pattern that is more familiar for English participants.

The War of the Ghosts story has a peculiar pattern that is different to a typical fable or short story that English participants would be familiar with. They tended to rationalize the information in order for it to have a better fit with their existing schema.

Bartlett's English participants may have rationalized the story (by leaving out certain details and changing others) so they would fit with their schematic understanding of a typical storyline. Because of this reconstruction of the story during the process of trying to remember it, errors and distortions occurred.

Bartlett's study is a classic in cognitive psychology, although it's not without fault. His methodology seemed to be rather haphazard and in one example he seems to conduct an experiment on a participant just as he happens to run into them in the university courtyard. Nevertheless, for our purposes it serves as a good starting point for investigating the reconstructive nature of memory

Rationalization is the process of changing or omitting details that are not consistent with existing schema.

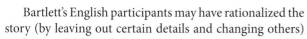

Guiding Question:

How might schema influence rationalization?

Critical Thinking Extension:

Areas of Uncertainty: The verb "suggests" is quite accurate when drawing conclusions about Bartlett's research and its relationship to schema because of the methodology that he used in his experiments. What is one reason why we cannot say definitively that Bartlett's study "proves" schema influences rationalization?

If you're interested…

Visit our blog to find the full version of the "War of the Ghosts" story. You may even be able to find Bartlett's full original 1932 publication online and read a series of reproductions of the story for yourself.

(b) Leading Questions

In the previous section you were introduced to the idea that our memory might not be reliable and it is susceptible to distortions and inaccuracies. Bartlett provided one explanation for this distortion based on the role of schema and rationalization. The extent to which we can trust our memory is an important field of research and has been the subject of numerous experimental studies.

An eye-witness is someone who sees a crime. Testimony is evidence given in court about a particular incident. Eye-witness testimony, therefore, refers to evidence a witness provides in court about a particular incident they saw.

The findings from these studies have significant applications and implications, especially when it comes to court cases and eye-witness testimony. Elizabeth Loftus is a prominent psychologist in this field and she has been called into high profile court cases to question and challenge eye-witness accounts. It's natural to assume that if someone says they saw and remember a particular detail from a crime scene then this would make pretty good evidence. For example, if a person identified the accused criminal from a line-up of suspects, or they remember the colour of a van leaving a crime scene, one might think this would be solid evidence to be used in a trial. However, Loftus has gathered substantial empirical evidence that suggests our memory may be unreliable and is susceptible to being manipulated. This casts doubts on the validity of eye-witness testimony.

One of her most famous studies showed how the wording of a question could lead to distortions in memory about a car accident. If you like to watch legal dramas you may be familiar with the term leading question. You often hear lawyers on TV shout, "Objection, Your Honour. Leading the witness." What this is referring to is how the question leads the respondent to answer in a particular way. An example of a leading question is: "How much do you like psychology?" This is suggesting that you do like psychology and is simply asking how much; it's leading you towards acknowledging you like this subject. A more neutral version of this question might be, "What are your feelings about psychology?"

Loftus and Palmer's experiment shows that leading questions may influence the memory of a particular event.

Loftus and Palmer (1974) tested the effects of the leading question in one of their earliest studies. This study demonstrates the role of leading questions on memory. In their first experiment they had 45 student participants in groups of various sizes watch several films of car accidents. The films were about 5 to 30 seconds long and afterwards the participants were asked a series of questions. In the list of questions there was one critical question that was different for individual participants. The question was "About how fast were the cars going when they (*smashed/collided/bumped/hit/contacted*) each other?" The verb used to describe the collision between the cars was different for five groups. Loftus and Palmer hypothesized that by changing the nature of the verb (e.g. smashed or hit) they could influence speed estimates of the participants. The five verbs and the mean speed estimates of the participants in this study were as follows:

(a) Smashed 40.5mph
(b) Collided 39.3 mph
(c) Bumped 38.1 mph
(d) Hit 34.0 mph
(e) Contacted 31.8 mph

These results show about a 30% higher speed estimate when the verb was "smashed" compared with "contacted." The researchers provided two possible explanations for these results. The first explanation is that the participants might not have been sure about the speed and the verb simply led them towards a particular answer. If they were not sure of the speed and thought it was around 30 to 40mph, the verb would have biased their answer in a particular direction. This doesn't tell us much about the reconstructive nature of memory and is more a possible limitation in the research methodology, if anything.

However, they also hypothesized that perhaps the verb "smashed" caused the participants to remember the crash differently. During the process of imagining the crash in order to remember the details and answer the questions, the verb may have affected the memory itself. The participants might have actually been imagining a more severe crash and a faster speed than was really portrayed in the video because of the leading question; when remembering the incident and playing it over in their minds, the verb "smashed" might have led to an actual change in the memory of the video.

But this data doesn't provide strong support for this hypothesis so they conducted a second experiment, which will be explained in the next section.

This study does not provide strong evidence for the misinformation effect; that evidence will be explained in the next section. It's included here to help build your schematic understanding of the core concepts related to the reconstructive nature of memory.

Guiding Question:

How might leading questions influence memory?

Critical Thinking Extension:

Population Validity: Loftus and Palmer's study was conducted on students in 1974. Can you think of any plausible reason why this may affect the population validity of the study? How might using an older sample lead to different results?

If you're interested…

Loftus has a TED Talk called "How reliable is your memory?" She describes many of her studies in this talk.

(c) The Misinformation Effect

The misinformation effect refers to the phenomenon of having incorrect information become part of someone's memory of an event.

Loftus and Palmer's first experiment showed that the verb in a question can influence memory. They provided two possible explanations for this. One explanation is that the verb actually distorts participants' memories of the crash, leading them to remembering the crash as being more severe and the speed of the car as being faster than it really was. This phenomenon of having erroneous external information distort memories is known as the misinformation effect. During the reconstruction of our memories of past events we may be vulnerable to remembering details that never happened. Misinformation is an incorrect or inaccurate detail of the memory that was implanted by a researcher.

Loftus and Palmer hypothesized that this might have been happening in their 1974 study so they conducted a second experiment with a modified design. In this second experiment they had 150 students watch one film of a car accident and then answer a series of questions. There were two different verbs used in these critical questions: smashed or hit. A third group of 50 students were not asked any questions about the speed of the cars. The results showed again that when the verb "smashed" was in the question this resulted in higher speed estimates than "hit." But there was another variable in this study: after one week participants were asked a different series of ten questions and the critical question in this list was "Did you see any broken glass?" Loftus and Palmer wanted to see if the verb that would suggest a stronger impact could implant a false memory of broken glass, since there was no broken glass in the original video.

The results showed that 32% of participants in the smashed condition circled "yes," they did in fact remember seeing broken glass. This is compared to 14% in the hit condition, and 12% in the control condition. These results provide some evidence for the explanation that the misinformation effect was occurring. Perhaps the verb "smashed" was influencing people's recollections of the crash and they were remembering it as being more severe than it really was, which is why they could remember seeing broken glass even when there wasn't any in the original video.

This second experiment was published in the same article as the first experiment and provides stronger evidence for the effects leading questions can have on memory.

Loftus and Palmer argue that two types of information are influential in making up someone's memory. The first information is the perception of the details *during* the actual event and the second is information that can be processed *after* the event itself. In this case, information from our environment might impact our memory processes, which could lead to distortions. They argue that the verb "smashed" provides additional external information because it shows that the cars did actually *smash* into each other. The verb that has connotations of a stronger and more severe impact than hit or collided could result in a memory of the incident that never happened, like remembering broken glass when there was none. Remember that the second question was asked an entire week after the original videos were viewed and the leading questions asked. The participants are reconstructing their memories after one week and the difference between the scores is quite significant.

The second experiment in Loftus and Palmer's 1974 series is an important one because it provides stronger evidence for the misinformation effect.

The fact that our memories may be distorted through information we process *after* the incident or a particular thing we're trying to remember has significant implications in many fields. But we could argue that these results may lack ecological validity if they are being applied to something serious like a murder trial. High levels of emotion might affect the accuracy of memories. When studying PTSD you'll learn how emotion and our physiology could actually improve our memory of emotional information. Perhaps participants weren't worried about the accuracy of their memories because the consequences of accuracy weren't as high as in a real life situation, such as a court trial. These are important questions to ask when assessing the extent to which we can generalize these findings.

Nevertheless, Loftus and Palmer's second experiment does provide some evidence for the fact that information received after an event may affect our memory. This will be explored in more detail in the final section on this topic.

Guiding Question:

How does the misinformation effect demonstrate the reconstructive nature of memory?

Critical Thinking Extension:

Alternative Explanations: It's always important to analyze both sides of the evidence. After you present one possible explanation for these results, reflect on these results and see if there are other explanations or possible limitations in the conclusions. In this study for example, why might it be important to reflect on the fact that 14% in the hit condition remembered broken glass? What are the possible implications of this result?

If you're interested…

RadioLab have a fascinating podcast called "Reasonable Doubt." It's based on a TV series called "Making a Murderer." I don't want this to sound like a clickbait title, but the twists in the story told in this podcast are (almost) unbelievable.

(d) Confabulation (False Memories)

So far in this topic about reconstructive memory you've learned about concepts like rationalization, leading questions and the misinformation effect. These variables may all have an impact on our memory. Loftus has made this her life's work, and since her first studies in the 1970s she has continued to investigate the effects of misinformation on distorting memory.

A particular type of distortion of memory is known as confabulation, which means having a false memory or a memory of something that never happened. It's a phenomenon whereby a person recollects something, or a detail of something, that never actually occurred. If the participants actually "remember" seeing broken glass when it never happened, this is an example of confabulation.

After these early studies Loftus conducted many others on the process of confabulation, i.e. implanting false memories. In one famous example she implanted a false memory in about 20% of participants that they had been lost in a shopping mall as a young child (as cited in Loftus et al., 2002). She has also conducted studies that can have participants remember something impossible - shaking hands with Bugs Bunny at Disneyland.

These studies follow a similar design in that the misinformation is indirectly introduced to the participants. Loftus' research has shown that the misinformation effect has a higher chance of resulting in a false memory if the information is indirectly introduced, as opposed to being directly implanted (Loftus, 1978).

The effects of confabulation and inaccurate eye-witness testimony can be incredibly damaging. Over 300 people in the United States alone have been wrongfully convicted and sent to jail for crimes they didn't commit. DNA evidence has been used to overturn their cases and set some of these innocent people free. In over 70% of these cases, incorrect eye-witness testimony was a factor in their conviction. One such example involves the rape of a young college woman, Jennifer Thompson-Cannino. She identified Ronald Cotton as her rapist from a police line-up and Cotton served 11 years in prison as a result of his conviction. However, DNA evidence exonerated Cotton and the real rapist was charged with the crime. Cotton and Cannino actually became friends and work together on the Innocence Project to help other people who have been wrongfully accused (Klobuchar et al., 2006). The Innocence Project is an organization with the objective of using DNA evidence to exonerate wrongly convicted criminals. They also try to use research to improve the procedures used in the justice system.

Memory research in the field of eye-witness testimony is incredibly important in this field because it can help improve the procedures that police use to increase accuracy and reliability of the identification of a criminal. In the traditional procedure, which you may have seen on TV, a line-up of suspects are put in a room and the witness has to identify the perpetrator. In this procedure, the administrator of the line-up typically knows who the suspect is and the suspect is usually in the line-up.

From the studies you've seen earlier in this section, you may be able to see how it's possible that this very procedure could produce the misinformation effect. By being led to believe that one of the suspects in the line-up was the perpetrator, this may be external information that could influence the recall of the event. Details of the person they've seen in the line-up and identified as the guilty person could become part of their memory of the event, so that their memory is distorted in a way that they now recall that individual as being part of the event.

This section has been included mainly because it's so interesting. You have more than enough material in the previous sections to discuss the reconstructive nature of memory. However, offering real life applications of findings may be useful in essay answers.

Not surprisingly, studies have shown that the accuracy of correct identification can go up if the witness is simply told, "the suspect may or may not be present" (Klobuchar et al., 2006). Simply casting a doubt as to whether or not the suspect is in the line-up can increase the accuracy of the identification and may reduce the chances of the misinformation effect causing false memories. There are many other applications of research into increasing the reliability of eye-witness testimony,

Amazingly, Jennifer Thompson-Cannino and Ronald Cotton are now friends and work together to help others who have been wrongly accused by faulty eye-witness testimony. (Image credit: PopTech, Flickr.com)

On the blog you can read about a new study by Shaw and Porter (2015) that shows how they were able to lead 70% of participants into confessing they committed a crime that never happened.

including having computer-based identification trials so the person conducting the observation cannot indirectly impose any bias.

Research into eye-witness testimony provides a good example of how psychological research can have valuable practical applications for social benefits.

Guiding Question:

How might research on memory be applied to improve the justice system?

Critical Thinking Extension:

Contradictory Evidence: Remember that it's important that after you make the obvious conclusion when analyzing studies, you then reflect on this conclusion and scrutinize the data a little more closely. Loftus' studies do not show that 100% of participants experience confabulation. This is important to consider. What other factors besides receiving misinformation might affect an individual's likelihood of developing a false memory? Consider individual differences that might exist between those participants that do experience confabulation, and those that might be resistant to it.

If you're interested…

At time of writing, the documentary "Making A Murderer" was available on Netflix. This documentary is about a man who was wrongly accused based on eye-witness testimony and what happened as a result. You may also be interested in learning about "The Innocence Project" which aims at freeing people who have been imprisoned wrongly through false accusations.

Relevant Topics

- Cognitive processing
- Schema theory
- Reliability of cognitive processes
- Reconstructive memory

Practice Exam Questions

- Discuss one or more studies related to reconstructive memory.
- To what extent is one cognitive process reliable?
- Evaluate one research method used to study cognitive processing.
- Discuss schema theory.

Research Methods

Loftus' research provides many examples of laboratory experiments and furthers our understanding of how this method can be used in cognitive research. Much of Loftus' research has been based on the role of misinformation on memory. In order to gather strong evidence that external sources of misleading information can affect the reliability of memory, an experiment is a valuable method to use. This is because all other possible variables can be controlled for and a cause-effect relationship can be drawn.

Ethical Considerations

In her Ted Talk, Loftus discusses the possible ethical implications of her research. Her studies in false memories and confabulation provide an interesting example of how ethics is rarely a black-and-white matter. Sometimes researchers need, and are allowed to, induce psychological harm or suffering if there is sufficient justification for the research. By implanting false memories and showing how this can happen, Loftus' research has helped promote programmes that seek to release innocent people from prison. The benefits of her research, it appears, outweigh the costs of inflicting mild psychological stress in participants. But this also highlights the need for ethical review committees who have the separation from the research and the experience to make such a decision. Researchers themselves are too involved in their research to make a neutral judgement, and so seeking approval from an external committee serves an important role in maintaining ethical standards in modern psychological research.

3.9 Bystanderism
Why don't people help those in need?

(a) The Smoky Room Study

The concept of eye-witness testimony and the implications of memory research on the justice system leads us into our new topic: bystanderism. In the introduction to this chapter you were briefly told the story of Catherine "Kitty" Genovese, whose murder inspired a plethora of research into the phenomenon of bystanderism. To be a bystander means you are standing by; you are observing or not acting while something is happening. Bystanderism is the term used to describe the phenomena of not helping in a situation that requires action.

Earlier in this chapter you learned about normative social influence – the influence of social pressure on an individual's behaviour, whereby they adapt their behavior to fit the social norms because they are afraid to stand out from the group. Early research into bystanderism suggests that another type of social influence may affect an individual's behaviour when they're surrounded by others: informational social influence. Informational social influence is when an individual's behavior changes because they look to other people for guidance on what is the "right" way to behave in a particular situation. This might happen in situations involving some sort of ambiguity, where the appropriate behaviour might not be clear. Someone might not have enough information to make a judgement for themselves on how they should act, so they look towards others in order to be "right." (as opposed to normative social influence, where people may look to others to see how they should act in order to be "liked").

An early study by Darley and Latane (1968) demonstrates the effect that informational social influence can have on bystanderism. In their experimental design, participants were put in a room and after a few minutes of filling out a questionnaire the room slowly began to fill with smoke. The dependent variable in this experiment is the % of participants who leave the room and tell someone about the room filling with smoke. In the control condition the participants are alone in the room. In another condition there are two passive confederates (actors who were told not to react to the smoke and continue filling out the questionnaire as if there's nothing wrong).

If you were in a room that slowly started to fill with smoke, would you go and tell someone? Interestingly, even when alone 25% of Darley and Latane's participants didn't.

When alone in the room, within two minutes of the smoke filling the room 50% of the participants in this condition went and sought help, and after six minutes 75% of participants had gone and told someone about the smoke. In the presence of two passive confederates, only 10% of the participants went and sought help within six minutes of the smoke filling the room.

The term bystanderism is not commonly used in social psychology. It appears to have been invented for the purposes of the IB Psychology course. The more common term is "bystander effect."

Informational social influence (also known as social proof) may affect an individual's behaviour, particularly in ambiguous situations.

A possible explanation for the increase in bystanderism in the smoky room study is the effect of informational social influence. The fire suggests that there might be an emergency, but the situation is ambiguous – it's not clear if there really is a fire or not.

Participants may be looking to the others in the room for guidance on how to act; they would be seeking to get information about the situation from their actions. Because they were passive, this may have influenced their thinking and they may have concluded that there's no need to tell anyone about the smoke (Darley and Latane, 1968).

Guiding Question:

How does the smoky room study demonstrate the effects of normative social influence?

Critical Thinking Extension:

Alternative Explanation: The results of the above study could also be explained as a result of the effects of normative social influence. How might have normative social influence played a role in the behaviour of the participants in the smoky room study?

If you're interested…

You can view demonstrations of Darley and Latane's smoky room experiment on YouTube, as well as interviews with the researchers. There are a number of bystanderism studies that we do not have time to explore in this course, unfortunately. You may wish to explore these on your own. You can find links and more information on the blog.

(b)   *Diffusion of Responsibility*

In Darley and Latane's early study on bystanderism we can see that the behaviour of others in an ambiguous situation may influence our own feelings of obligation to act. It can also demonstrate the effects of informational social influence, as we look to others for information regarding an appropriate course of action.

However, an alternative explanation for the smoky room study might be that the reduced rate of seeking help in the passive confederate condition could be a result of normative social influence. Asch's studies showed that when people are in a minority they can be influenced by the norms of the group. In the situation where other people are not acting, it's very plausible that a social norm has been established: there's no emergency and we don't need to act. The participant might even feel that they would be seen as "uncool" if they were to worry about the smoke coming in the room while the others didn't seem to mind.

But what if the other people in the room were not actors? What if there were three naïve participants in the room, none of who knew that the smoke was just part of the experiment? Do you think that having more people in the room would increase the % of people who went for help, or decrease it?

It seems logical that the more people there are around to help the more likely it would be that at least *one* person in the group would seek help. Interestingly, this is not what the results of their experiment (and many others) have shown.

When there were three naïve participants in the room, only 12% of participants sought help after two minutes and 38% after six. While this is higher than the condition involving passive confederates, it's still much less than when participants are alone.

Darley and Latane explain this result as an effect of diffusion of responsibility. To diffuse something means to spread it out or reduce its influence, so diffusion of responsibility is when people don't feel as obligated to take responsibility to help because there are other people around. They might think something like, "I don't need to help as someone else will do it." None of the group members in this condition were actors, and there could have been a real emergency for all they knew. But by simply having other people around, their feelings of obligation to take responsibility and to act may have decreased because there were more people around to diffuse the feeling that they should go and tell someone about the smoke.

Would you ask if this person was OK? Do you think it would make a difference if they were in a crowded town square or a quiet country lane?

Some researchers have taken this idea of diffusion of responsibility to field studies conducted in locations with varying population density. Would you expect people to be more helpful in a quiet, country town or a bustling, busy city?

Diffusion of responsibility is when an individual's feeling of obligation to act is reduced because there are others around. If someone is alone and observes a situation that needs attention they are probably more likely to act because they feel a responsibility to do so; this may be reduced in large crowds.

Numerous studies have been conducted to test the hypotheses that country people are more helpful than city people. These are typically field experiments where a confederate will do something in a public place and need help. A common test is dropping a postcard with a stamp and address on it (with the researcher's address) and then seeing how many people post the card (as measured by how many turn up at the researcher's address). Other examples include a confederate doing something like dropping a pen or a key and seeing how many people tell them about it.

Steblay (1987) conducted a meta-analysis of 65 studies that compared helping rates in rural (country) and urban (city) areas and concluded from these studies that there was evidence to suggest that there was lower helping behaviour in cities with more people. Also, the helping rate begins to decline at populations of 300,000 (Levine, 2001). Perhaps where people in cities observe a situation requiring action, they feel less obligated to take responsibility because there are other people around that might be able to help, and it's easier for them to think that someone else might do it.

From the experiment and the meta-analysis of studies measuring rates of helping others, it seems that the more people there are around to witness a situation requiring action, the less likely they are to act. This correlation could be explained through the occurrence of a diffusion of responsibility.

Guiding Question:

How might diffusion of responsibility influence bystanderism?

Critical Thinking Extension:
Generalizability – Ecological Validity: It's always important to remember that understanding human behaviour means to think about the real world contexts that we're attempt to generalize our results to. To what extent do you think these results are applicable to possible real life emergency situations?

If you're interested...

The effects of bystanderism are popular and there have been many replications done for TV shows. You can see numerous examples of replications of studies that manipulate variables to see what conditions will influence helping behaviour. In one video (available online), the film makers time the difference it takes for people to help a man when he is dressed in a suit, compared to when he's dressed as a homeless person. Remember: TV shows and YouTube clips are not credible sources of empirical evidence, and so they should not be treated as such (e.g. in your academic writing).

Relevant Topics

- The individual and the group
- Bystanderism
- Prosocial behaviour

Practice Exam Questions

- Discuss one or more factors that may influence bystanderism.
- Evaluate one or more studies related to bystanderism.

Research Methods

Darley and Latane's laboratory experiments investigating factors influencing bystanderism are good examples of how social psychologists can use the manipulation of an independent variable in a controlled environment in order to draw conclusions about relationships between variables and behaviour. In this context a laboratory is a suitable environment to conduct such studies because the researchers can have control over variables like the amount of people in the room. Some psychologists (e.g. Piliavin, 1969) have conducted field experiments on bystanderism in real life situations to see if they obtain similar results. There are pros and cons to the use of both methods when studying a behaviour like bystanderism.

Ethical Considerations

Whenever a researcher uses deception in a study they need to carefully consider how and why they are using deception. In the smoky room study deception is used in the form of the smoke filling the room; the participants do not know that this is just part of an experiment (for obvious validity reasons). This deception may have caused some mild (or even severe) anxiety or stress for participants. Being put in the room with passive confederates may have heightened their stress. When participants are subjected to such deception and potential stress, debriefing the full nature and aims of the study is essential. Remember that one guiding principle of ethical guidelines is that participants should not experience any long-lasting negative effects as a result of the study. Debriefing can help meet this aim.

3.10 Prosocial Behaviour
Why are some people likely to help more than others?

(a)   Culture and Prosocial Behaviour

When learning about factors that may influence bystanderism you were introduced to the concept of diffusion of responsibility and the irony that has been demonstrated in research: if there are more people to help it might actually decrease the chances of receiving help. Bystanderism is closely related to another important concept: prosocial behaviour. The term prosocial behaviour is a broad term that describes any action that has been done for the benefit of another individual or group. It refers to acting in a way that benefits other people.

As you've already learnt, studies have been conducted to test the extent to which some cultures may be more helpful than others. Similar to studies analysed in Steblay's meta-analysis on helping behaviour, Levine conducted two major cross-cultural studies to investigate differences in rates of prosocial behaviour across cultures. In one study, the rates of helping a stranger (i.e. prosocial behaviour) was measured across 36 cities in the United States. They tested the rate of helping by using similar methods as described earlier. For instance, in one measure "experimenters, dressed in dark glasses and carrying white canes, acted the role of a blind person needing help crossing a street" (Levine, 1994).

The strongest correlation found in this study was a negative correlation between population density and helping, while population size was also negatively correlated with helping the confederate. Population size is the total number of people living in a city, while population density is the average amount of people living per square mile/ kilometre. Population density refers to how many people are "squeezed in" to a city. These results could be explained through Darley and Latane's diffusion of responsibility hypothesis – the more people there are around to help, the less personal responsibility someone might feel to act.

Another possible explanation for these findings is Milgram's sensory overload hypothesis. According to Milgram people who live in cities are constantly having their senses bombarded. Horns are blaring, sirens going off, people are crowding the footpath. According to Milgram's theory, because of this overload people tend to screen out stimuli that is not directly and personally relevant. If something doesn't immediately help an individual satisfy their wants or needs, it's ignored. This provides another possible reason why cities that have a higher population density are less likely to help (Milgram, as cited in Levine, 1994).

But Levine's study and Milgram's theory are based on populations within the United States. While they enable some comparisons about city size and density to be made, their value in establishing cross-cultural differences is limited. In a later study, Levine and colleagues replicated the same types of procedures (e.g. a blind person needing help, dropping a pen and seeing if someone would pick it up and a person in a leg brace needing help picking up magazines) in a study across 23 different countries (Levine et al., 2001). In each country they chose the biggest city to control for the variable of population density and size: they were not interested in this variable for this study as they had already studied this.

Studies on prosocial behaviour might also be used in discussions of concepts and research related to bystanderism. A study that can help explain factors that may lead someone to help, can also be used to explain other factors that might lead people to not helping.

People in cities may not help because they are constantly bombarded with stimuli. What other factors do you think could explain why people in the city may be less likely to help than those in the countryside?

Two variables they were interested in were economic productivity and cultural values. They measured the economic productivity of the countries by comparing their gross domestic products (GDPs). Earlier research had suggested that countries where people suffered poor economic health and low productivity (e.g. not enough money, poor living conditions, etc.) had lower rates of helping than countries that were more economically sound. They also compared cultural values using measures of Hofstede's individualism and collectivism scale.

The results showed that the strongest correlation found was a *negative* correlation between economic productivity and helping. Countries with high economic productivity like the USA, Singapore and the Netherlands tended to have lower levels of helping than others such as Malawi, El Salvador and Brazil. One possible explanation offered for this correlation is that there may be a correlation between low economic productivity and traditional value systems. These traditional values may focus on helping others over obtaining wealth. Similarly, it could be that in order to develop strong economies, individuals within these cultures might have to develop attitudes that focus on their own interests at the expense of acting for the benefit of others.

According to Levine's study, people living in richer countries (like Singapore) may be less likely to help. There are a number of possible explanations for this. Can you think of some?

Another finding, although not statistically significant, was a weak relationship between cultural values and helping behaviour. Some collectivist cultures had higher rates of helping than individualistic cultures, but there were often times when the opposite was true. For example, people in the major cities in Singapore, Taiwan and Thailand (towards the collectivism end of the continuum) were less helpful on average than those in Austria, Spain and Denmark (towards the individualistic end of the continuum).

From this research we can see that while diffusion of responsibility as a result of high population density *may* account for rates of bystanderism (and conversely, prosocial behaviour), there may be other economic and cultural factors involved as well.

It is important that you accurately describe any research you use – there is a weak relationship found in this study and it's important that you do not rationalize this information to make it fit with your schema!

Guiding Question:

How might socioeconomic factors influence prosocial behaviour?

Critical Thinking Extension:
Alternative Explanations: You were provided with one possible explanation for the correlation between economic productivity and helping behaviour. Part of developing your thinking skills is being able to come up with these explanations for yourself – can you think of any possible alternative explanations for this correlation? Also, there has been (deliberately) no possible explanations offered for the correlation between cultural values and helping behaviour. Could you offer any possible explanations for why people with collectivist values may be more likely to help than those with individualistic values?

If you're interested...

Organisational Psychologist Adam Grant delivers a TED Talk called "Are you a giver or a taker?" In this talk, he discusses the idea of doing things for others and the effects it can have. It's pretty interesting to hear about "givers" and "takers." Are you an agreeable taker/giver, or a disagreeable taker/giver?

(b)   The Empathy-Altruism Hypothesis

Altruism is a type of prosocial behaviour. To act altruistically means you are doing something for someone else without any hope of reward or benefit to yourself. There have been numerous theories developed to explain altruism, as it seems to be a behaviour that is counter-adaptive in terms of evolution. If you think about it, why would someone want to help others if it in no way benefited themselves? Some people even risk their own life to help others, which really seems to go against the notion of natural selection and survival of the fittest.

One theory to explain why humans may act altruistically towards other people is Batson's empathy-altruism hypothesis. This theory predicts that when people can experience empathy for someone else, they are more likely to act altruistically towards that person and to help them out. In order to understand this theory, it is first important that you understand the term empathy. One way to think about empathy is to compare it with a closely related emotion, sympathy. To feel sympathy for someone means you feel sorry for them. You may even pity them. While empathy is closely related to sympathy, it has more to do with being able to *understand* how another person may feel given their situation.

The empathy-altruism hypothesis could be used to explain why some people are less likely to help. Piliavin (1969) showed that people were less likely to help someone who collapsed on a train if they appeared drunk. Batson's empathy-altruism hypothesis might be used to explain this.

Batson et al. (1981) designed an experiment to test this theory. It involved having participants (44 females from the University of Kansas) observe a video of a young woman named Elaine receiving electric shocks. Of course, Elaine wasn't really receiving electric shocks - she was a confederate who "turned up late" to take part in the experiment. The participant and Elaine draw cards to see who would be the "observer" and who would be the "worker." Naturally, this was rigged so Elaine was always the worker and the participant the observer. The participants were deceived in believing that the experiment was testing how people worked under unpleasant circumstances. Part way through observing Elaine receive shocks, the participants were given a chance to take her place. To make it seem believable, the experimenter and Elaine discussed how Elaine had been thrown off a horse and onto an electric fence when she was younger and she had suffered some trauma. The experimenter pretends to get an idea to ask if the participant would want to change places for the remainder of the experiment. The researchers measured altruism by seeing how many people would volunteer to take Elaine's place in the experiment and to be the "worker" receiving the shocks.

Would you swap places with Elaine?

Batson's theory posits that we are more likely to help those we feel empathetic towards. We are also more likely to feel empathy with people we are similar to, possibly because it is easier to put ourselves in their situation (a key part of empathy). Empathy may influence bystanderism and prosocial behaviour.

But how did they manipulate the emotion of empathy? There's some evidence to suggest that individuals may feel more empathy for people whom they identify with. Before the experiment began all participants filled out a personality questionnaire. Half of the participants were lead to believe that Elaine was very similar to them (high empathy) while the other half were lead to believe that she was quite different (low empathy).

Remember that altruism means to act with no benefit to yourself. One potential benefit of swapping with Elaine would be that it would reduce feelings of discomfort and guilt that participants might be feeling if they were given the chance to swap or not. To control for this variable, the researchers had an ease-of-escape condition. They manipulated the experiment so some participants were led to believe that if they didn't take Elaine's place, they wouldn't have to watch her get any more shocks. In the difficult-escape condition they were led to believe that if they didn't swap they would have to watch her get shocked eight more times.

To summarise, there are four conditions with the percentages of those people in each condition who agreed to swap with Elaine:

- High Empathy / Ease of Escape (91%)
- Low Empathy / Ease of Escape (18%)
- High Empathy / Difficult Escape (82%)
- Low Empathy / Difficult Escape (62%)

It's natural to predict that the difficult escape people would swap, because they would want to reduce their own feelings of guilt and unpleasantness at watching Elaine get shocked. The results confirmed this.

If they had an easy escape and they were in the low empathy (dissimilar) condition, only 18% of people agreed to swap with Elaine. This is compared to 91% of participants who also had an easy escape, but were lead to believe that Elaine was similar to them (i.e. high empathy condition).

Even when they had an easy escape, participants who had high empathy (high similarity) with Elaine were the most likely to offer to take her place. These results offer empirical support for the hypotheses that feelings of empathy will increase the chances of acting altruistically.

Guiding Question:

How do the results of this study support the empathy-altruism hypothesis?

Critical Thinking Extension:

Construct Validity: Construct validity is similar to internal validity. It refers to the accuracy of the measurement of a variable in a study. Do you think the researchers' manipulation of empathy was a valid way of measuring the effects of this emotion? Also, consider how these findings might be related to the study of bystanderism? How might empathy influence an individual's propensity to help someone else in need?

If you're interested…

The idea that we are more inclined to feel empathy towards people who are similar to us also provides a conceptual connection with in-group and out-group behaviour. It goes beyond the requirements of the course at this stage to discuss in-group and out-group differences in altruism, but it could be an area to explore further if you are interested.

Relevant Topics

- Bystanderism
- Prosocial behaviour
- The individual and the group
- Social responsibility

Practice Exam Questions

- Discuss ethical considerations related to research on social responsibility.
- Discuss prosocial behaviour.
- To what extent do sociocultural factors influence social responsibility?

Research Methods

Batson's laboratory experiment is another good example of the manipulation of an independent variable (empathy) in a controlled environment with the aim of determining a cause-effect relationship. Researchers often use experiments when they are testing a theory or hypothesis. In order to isolate the empathy as the variable influencing the altruism, we see that Batson had to carefully design the study by controlling for the potential extraneous variable (ease of escape). Being able to create complex experimental designs can enable researchers to isolate the IV as the only variable that is influencing the DV. This is what can allow cause-effect relationships to be drawn.

Ethical Considerations

Batson's study uses some potentially stress-inducing deception by having participants believe that Elaine is being electrocuted. As with other studies involving deception, debriefing the procedures at the end of the study would be important. And as we've seen in other examples this chapter, this debriefing would need to carefully consider how the participants may react to reflecting on their own behaviour. Imagine being a participant that didn't offer to change places with Elaine; how might this make you feel? Perhaps the researchers could alleviate the guilt or shame that this might cause by explaining that they are not alone and that others did the same. Having said that, if you were one of the 9% in the high empathy condition that didn't help, how might you feel?

Remember that explaining ethical considerations does not need to involve making black and white judgements. You simply need to show you understand a variety of factors that researchers must *consider* (i.e. think about) when designing and carrying out studies.

3.11 Promoting Prosocial Behaviour

How can we encourage people to help others?

(a) Obedience

An important goal of social psychology is to undercover the origins of behaviour in order to develop practical solutions for making society a better place. In the previous topic you saw how social, economic and cultural variables may affect prosocial behaviour.

The jigsaw classroom and adopting cooperative classroom strategies are ways that schools could help promote prosocial behaviour. Studies have also found that using the jigsaw classroom strategy can help develop empathy. As you saw in the previous topic, experiencing empathy can encourage prosocial behaviour. Bridgeman (1981) studied 120 fifth graders in an American school. Half of the students had spent two months in cooperative classrooms using the jigsaw model while the other half had been in "traditional" classrooms. After two months the students participated in a series of tests designed to measure perspective taking: were they able to see a situation from someone else's point of view. The results showed that those kids in the jigsaw classrooms were more adept at being able to see someone else's perspective. If a student can see the world through someone else's eyes, they have an essential skillset necessary to experience empathy. Here we can see that adopting cooperative learning strategies in schools could be one way of promoting prosocial behaviour.

There is another strategy that could promote prosocial behaviour and one that is far more direct: tell people to do good things. Humans appear to have a natural propensity towards following orders. This has been demonstrated in a series of some of the most famous social experiments carried out in psychology: the Milgram Experiments. After the atrocities of the holocaust during WWII, people naturally asked the question of how Nazi officers could carry out such heinous crimes against fellow humans. Stanley Milgram suggested that the behaviour of Nazi officials could be explained by the role of obedience to authority. In his experiments, Milgram discovered that a high % of subjects were willing to administer high voltage electric shocks to other participants. Subsequent adaptations of the experiment found that if the researcher giving the instructions was wearing a white lab coat, participants were even more likely to comply with the researcher and obey directions to continue with the experiment.

You might not use Milgram's study in an exam. It's included here because it's a good introduction to the concept of obedience and prosocial behaviour. It's also classic and students find it interesting.

Following these studies into the roots of extremely *antisocial* behaviour, other social psychologists conducted experiments whose findings could be applied for the *benefit* of society. Bickman (1974) conducted a field experiment where subjects where stopped in the street by a confederate who was dressed as either a guard, a milkman or a civilian. The subject was asked to do something like pick up a piece of garbage (a paper bag), give 10 cents to a stranger or to move away from a bus stop. The results showed that the subjects were more likely to comply with the directions given by someone wearing a guard's uniform, as opposed to a civilian or a milkman.

Have you observed any ways that authority is used to promote prosocial behaviour?

Another similar study was carried out by Bushman (1988): a female confederate dressed in either a uniform, professional attire or sloppy clothing. The confederate instructed passersby to give change to someone who was standing by an expired parking meter. The results showed that when wearing a uniform, people were more likely to comply with her request.

We seem to have a natural tendency to obey commands from people in positions of authority. This power could be manipulated with positive and negative outcomes.

Obedience to authority could be explained from a socio-evolutionary perspective. Human societies are typically hierarchically structured, with individuals knowing their place within the hierarchy. Maintaining structure and order within society is essential for ensuring a functional society and so complying with requests from people in positions of authority is one way of ensuring the structure of society is maintained. Without complying with requests and following instructions by those in positions of power, a social group may break down and reduce the chances of survival for the entire group.

From these studies we can see that manipulating our apparent natural inclination towards obeying people in positions of authority could lead people to act in prosocial ways. There are significant limitations in adopting these strategies, including those related to ethics. It might not always be feasible to have someone standing in uniform telling people to be good. In the following section we'll look at some more practical ways we can improve society by promoting compliance and conformity.

Guiding Question:

How could obedience to authority be applied to encourage prosocial behaviour?

Critical Thinking Extension:
Milgram's research has been introduced here because I would feel remiss if I wrote a whole chapter on social influences on behaviour and did not include this famous study. His study could also be applied to understanding prejudice and discrimination. How could you use Milgram's study to explain origins of prejudice and/or discrimination?

If you're interested…

The story of Milgram's experiment has been turned into a Hollywood film called "Experimenter."

(b)   Compliance

Understanding how we can manipulate social influence for the benefit of society is an entire field of study for some social psychologists. The art and science of persuasion is a fascinating field of study. Robert Cialdini is a psychologist who studies persuasion and he has devised six principles of persuasion. In the previous section you saw one of these: authority. While a straightforward solution to encouraging prosocial behaviour might be to simply have individuals in positions of authority tell people to do good things, this has severe practical limitations. In this section we'll see how another principle, consensus, has been employed to encourage prosocial behaviour.

If you've stayed in a hotel recently you may remember seeing a card on your pillow or in the bathroom about reusing towels. Hotels use vast amounts of water and detergents every day in order to keep laundry clean. If hotel guests could be encouraged to reuse towels, it could have a positive impact on the environment by saving thousands of litres of water (not to mention potentially saving the hotel time and money in laundry services). Cialdini has studied the language used in the hotel cards that attempt to encourage guests to reuse their towels and he has found that slight variations of the language could have significant effects through the use of the principle of consensus and the manipulation of social influence.

Most hotels focus on the environmental benefits when trying to encourage guests to reuse towels by explaining the positive environmental benefits. This is noble, but is less effective than using descriptive social norms. A descriptive social norm is a typical pattern of behaviour: what everyone else is doing. If hotels rephrase the language of their cards they can increase guest compliance with the request to reuse towels (and save the environment at the same time).

Cialdini et al. (2008) conducted an experiment in a hotel in Arizona, USA, over an 80 day period. They randomly put one of two different cards in hotel rooms asking guests to reuse their towel. The cards were slightly different, however, in their use of language. One card had written "Help save the environment" and explained to guests how reusing towels would have a positive impact on the environment and tried to encourage them to reuse their towels in this way; 38% of guests reused their towels if this card was placed in their room. A second type of card didn't focus on the environmental benefits, but instead tried to influence behaviour through social influence by making descriptive social norms obvious. The card read "Join your fellow guests in helping to save the environment." The card goes on to say that "Almost 75% of guests who are asked to participate in our new resource savings program do help by using their towels more than once. You can join your fellow guests in this program to help save the environment by reusing your towels during your stay." In this condition the rate of reusing towels significantly increased to 48%.

What is interesting to note here, Cialdini argues, is that this increase isn't the result of trial and error on the behalf of hotels: it can be the result of applying findings from research in social psychology.

Consensus can be used to obtain compliance that might have benefits for society, like saving water and electricity by re-using towels.

Consensus is one of Cialdini's principles of persuasion. It refers to the idea that people are in agreement with the "right" way to think and/or act. In other words, we're more likely to comply if we know others have also acted in a similar way.

Cialdini's book "Persuasion: The Psychology of Influence" is a highly recommended read.

From this chapter it's hoped that you understand how at least three different strategies might be employed to promote prosocial behaviour. One might be to use cooperative learning strategies in the classroom with the intention of developing empathy. If people can feel empathy they may be more likely to help others. A second strategy could be to use the principle of authority in order to generate compliance to requests for prosocial behaviour. While this seems straightforward, it might have limited applications. The final strategy as seen in this section involves using the principle of consensus and the power of social influence by making people aware of social norms. If people are made aware of how others are following social norms that are beneficial for society (e.g. good for the environment) they may be more likely to comply with requests to act in such a prosocial manner.

Guiding Question:

How might compliance techniques be used to promote prosocial behaviour?

Critical Thinking Extension:

Applications: As Cialdini points out, understanding principles of social psychology can be beneficial because of the potential practical applications. Can you think of other possible fields beyond hotels that the principle of consensus could be applied to? How might social influence be used in other ways to affect prosocial behaviour? Could these results be explained by the effects of normative social influence, do you think?

If you're interested...

You can watch a brief (11 minute) video of Cialdini explaining his 6 principles of persuasion on YouTube. There are also other studies that investigate the effects of compliance techniques to encourage prosocial behaviour that you may want to read about (e.g. Freedom and Fraser, 1966 – Foot-in-the-door).

Relevant Topics

- Prosocial behaviour
- Promoting prosocial behaviour
- Social responsibility

Practice Exam Questions

- Discuss research related to promoting prosocial behaviour.
- Evaluate one or more strategies used to promote prosocial behaviour.
- Contrast two ethical considerations related to social responsibility.

Research Methods

Cialdini's field experiment demonstrates similar benefits of this research method as does those using cooperative learning strategies. By finding a real life environment (a hotel) to manipulate the independent variable (the type of card in the room), Cialdini was able to show how understanding the role of social norms and how descriptive social norms can influence behaviour can be practically applied in real-life settings.

Ethical Considerations

The psychology of persuasion is a fascinating field, but it's also wrought with ethical concerns. Most of these post-topic boxes focus on the ethical considerations related to methodology and what a researcher does *during* the research. It's important to also be aware of how applications of findings from studies can have ethical concerns. The psychology of marketing relies on doing what Cialdini has done: applying findings from social psychology in real life situations to influence behaviour. In this context he has applied it for some good: helping the environment. But what if findings from research could be applied in other ways, like encouraging kids to consume sugary foods? It might largely be out of their control, but researchers should consider how their findings may be applied by others.

Conclusion

Throughout this chapter we've investigated a range of interrelated cognitive processes and behaviours. There have been some common themes running throughout the chapter, such as the influence of social and cultural variables on thinking and behaviour. In order to prepare you for Paper Two and the Human Relationships questions, there has been a particular focus on group dynamics and social responsibility.

During the unit on criminology it was hoped that you would be able to understand potential origins of violent behavior so that you could develop your understanding and raise questions about the best methods of reducing violence. This chapter is similar - if we can understand the underlying origins of antisocial behaviours such as prejudice, discrimination and stereotypes, perhaps more effective strategies could be developed to reduce and resolve these societal problems.

There is one particular study that I regretfully cannot fit into this chapter. Along with Milgram's experiments, Zimbardo's Stanford Prison Experiment is a classic in social psychology and can be used to understand possible explanations of group dynamics, among other topics. Zimbardo's research has shown the power situational influences can have on behaviour and may be applied to topics like understanding origins of discrimination.

In your exams you may be asked to discuss research on a number of concepts that are highly related and very similar. It's essential that you can distinguish these and apply research in an appropriate manner. For instance, co-operation, conflict resolution, competition, conflict, stereotypes, prejudice and discrimination are all interrelated and many of the studies in this chapter could be applied to a number of these topics. During your revision and preparation for the exam it is essential to think carefully about how you may address questions related to these topics because as with other chapters in this book, there is more than enough information covered to address a range of possible exam questions.

You will need to revise carefully, using the topics and supporting exam materials to guide you. It is unrealistic for you to expect to remember every specific detail of every study that has been mentioned in this chapter. What is hoped is that you would have developed broader conceptual understandings of how particular variables may influence a particular set of mental processes and behaviours. If you can understand these big ideas as well as comprehend the key terminology used within this chapter, your revision will be much more effective.

Like Phineas Gage in criminology, some studies have been included here as stepping stones to help you understand more complex problems. Be careful when choosing studies and concepts to apply to particular topics in exams as some students make the mistake of focusing on the subject matter that is easiest. This might not lead to the best exam answers. Besides helping you prepare for your exams, I also hope you've enjoyed this introduction to social psychology.

Chapter 4
Post-Traumatic Stress Disorder

Introduction

During the Vietnam War a platoon of American soldiers raided the village of My Lai and killed many innocent men, women and children. Many gave the excuse that they were simply following orders, while others disobeyed orders and refused to kill. The lasting effects of this horrific event are unimaginable, for the Vietnamese civilians and for the soldiers. While the My Lai Massacre could be used as the basis of an investigation into the *origins* of extreme examples of violence, it's not introduced here as we're going to investigate the possible *effects* of being involved in such a traumatic event.

This example is just one of the countless acts of violence that have occurred during times of war. It's no surprise then that one of the most common causes of Post-Traumatic Stress Disorder (PTSD) is being exposed to situations of war. PTSD is the name given to the psychological disorder that occurs as a result of exposure to something extremely stressful. Individuals who develop symptoms of PTSD respond to the stressor (the traumatic event) with a feeling of fear, helplessness or horror. Many soldiers and civilians exposed to the horrors of war suffer from PTSD and early reports of this disorder came from soldiers fighting in World War One, when it was called "shell shock."

Experiences as a result of war make up just some of the common traumatic stressors that can cause the development of PTSD symptoms. Other examples include losing a loved one, experiences in natural or manmade disasters, car accidents, sexual abuse, physical assaults, or being diagnosed with a life-threatening illness. PTSD involves many symptoms, but individual symptomatologies can be different.

Generally speaking, the symptoms are grouped into three broad categories:

- Re-experiencing the traumatic event
- Avoidance and emotional numbing
- Increased anxiety and emotional arousal

There are many possible symptoms of PTSD and even more potential causes. In our limited time we can only skim the surface, so we'll focus primarily on symptoms related to memory and emotion. With this in mind, this chapter begins by explaining theories of how memories are formed. By first looking at these theories and the biological factors that influence memory, we will be able to develop a better understanding of how experiencing traumatic events might affect symptoms related to memory and emotion.

By understanding possible *causes* of PTSD, we can also investigate potential *treatments*. These will be explored later in the unit. But the study of psychological disorders raises numerous questions about ethics and diagnosis. How can we accurately diagnosis someone with PTSD? And do symptoms vary across cultures? What is the potential impact of diagnosing someone with such a disorder? These are some of the big questions we'll attempt to tackle towards the end of this unit

4.1 The Multi-Store Model
How are memories made?

(a) The Multi-Store Model of Memory (MSM)

Before we begin looking at the effects of PTSD on memory, it's important to explore just how memories are formed in the first place. The multi-store model of memory (MSM) is one of many ideas that came about during the cognitive revolution in psychology of the 1950s. Before this new wave of research into cognition, psychology was dominated by behaviourism. As the name suggests, this movement focused on observable behaviours as it was believed that internal mental processes could not be studied scientifically, so they shouldn't be the focus of psychological research. However, a new wave of research into cognitive processes began in the 1950s and the MSM is one product of this.

Like the dual process model of decision making attempts to explain how processing affects decision making, the multi-store model of memory attempts to illustrate how memories are formed through the interaction of memory stores and control processes.

Multi-Store Model of Memory

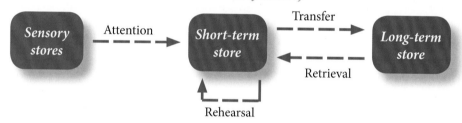

As the name suggests, Atkinson and Shiffrin's (1968) version of the multi-store model of memory posits that there are distinct "stores" for memory: sensory stores, a short-term store and the long-term store.

According to the MSM, information is first perceived and enters the sensory stores. These are modality specific stores, which means there are different stores for different modes of information. For instance, sounds would have an auditory store, and visual information a visual store (Eysenck and Keane, 2010).

The information is transferred through the stores by the control processes: attention, rehearsal and retrieval. For instance, information is transferred to the short-term store if we pay attention to it. This seems to make sense, as there's little chance we'd remember something if we weren't paying attention to it. If we rehearse information it will be transferred to our long-term store, where we can retrieve it and bring it back into our conscious memory when we need it.

The model also explains that there is a positive correlation between the amount of rehearsal of something and the strength of the memory trace created. If you only rehearse something a little, you might be able to retrieve it after a few minutes. After a couple of days it might be a faint memory. Whereas if you rehearse something

Control Process: a cognitive process that controls the flow of information from one store to another.

Decay: information may be lost through the short-term store if it's not rehearsed. This is called decay.

206

continually, you might be able to remember it for much longer because the memory trace is stronger.

Let's take a hypothetical example from a psychology class. Your teacher is explaining what normative social influence means and they say it's going to be on the test, so you pay attention. The information from their explanation goes into your sensory stores as you see the explanation on the board and listen to your teacher's voice. By paying attention to the information, it is transferred to your short-term store. You then write down the information in your notes, which is your rehearsal – you are going over the information again. About 20 minutes later in the lesson you are doing an activity and you have to help a classmate understand what the term means, so you retrieve the information from your long-term store and bring it back into your conscious memory, your short-term store. By explaining it you are rehearsing the information again. The more times you repeat this retrieval-rehearsal process, the stronger your memory trace will be, and the better you will remember the information.

The multi-store model of memory has significant empirical evidence to support the idea that our memory is made up of different stores and information flows between these stores through control processes. By this stage in your learning of the MSM you should be able to describe the model, including the different stores and the control processes.

Learning about the role of rehearsal and creating memory traces will help you to see the value in regular revision.

Memory Trace: a memory trace is a change in the brain's structure that facilitates memory storage. Neurons change their structure as a result of new learning (see NOVA's video "Memory Hackers" for this phenomenon being filmed).

> ### Guiding Question:
> How do control processes influence transfer of memory between the stores in the multi-store model of memory?

Critical Thinking Extension:

An Area of Uncertainty: To some extent the MSM seems to treat all information the same. It fails to address the role of emotion in memory. This will be explored more in later sections, but can you think how emotion might influence the control processes? Do you think all information, regardless of how emotional it is, would be rehearsed and/or retrieved in the same way, with similar effects? Can you provide examples?

If you're interested...

Crash Course has an introductory video to memory called: "How we make memories." The first half of this video is relevant for understanding the MSM, while the second half goes into details on working memory, which is the subject of the next topic.

(b)   Duration and Capacity

As well as describing the existence of the three stores and explaining how memory travels between them through the control processes, another key aspect of the multi-store model of memory is the difference outlined between the three stores as they are different in terms of their duration and capacity.

Method	Duration	Capacity
Sensory Stores	A few seconds	Unlimited
Short-Term Store	About 20 seconds	7 units, plus or minus 2
Long-Term Store	Unlimited	Unlimited

The capacity refers to the amount of information that can be held in the store. According to the MSM, the sensory store has unlimited capacity, as does the long-term store. The short-term store, on the other hand, has a limited capacity. The magic number that researchers have deduced is seven units of information, plus or minus two. This basically means that a person can hold around five to nine pieces of information in their sensory stores. If people try to keep more than this in their sensory store they will make errors or forget parts.

The duration refers to how long information can stay in the store for. The sensory stores have a very short duration, with studies suggesting information can only last in our sensory store for a few seconds before it's lost. Interestingly, iconic memory (visual sensory details) seems to have a shorter duration in the sensory store than echoic memory (memory of sounds). The long-term store, not surprisingly, has a *potentially* unlimited duration as people may be able to remember things throughout their entire lives. But the short-term store has a duration of around 20 seconds (Eysenck and Keane, 2010).

Peterson and Peterson (1959) found that unrehearsed short-term memory almost completely disappears after 18 seconds. They measured the duration of the short-term store by having participants remember trigrams - meaningless consonant triplets (e.g. XTB, MPT, PTR, etc.). Participants would be given one of these to remember but then they would be asked to count backwards in threes out loud as a form of distraction. For instance, a participant might be asked to remember TRM and then given the number 340. They would then have to say "337, 334, 331, 328…" After six seconds the ability to remember the three-letter stimuli (in the correct order) had about a 50% accuracy rate. When the time counting backwards was extended to 18 seconds, there was almost zero recollection of details.

By not giving participants a chance to rehearse the three-letter stimuli and giving them something distracting to do for various lengths of time, Peterson and Peterson could measure how long the information was able to be accurately held in the short-term store. (The lack of rehearsal prevents the information from being transferred to the long-term store.) By increasing the time counting backwards until there is 0% recollection of the stimuli, the researchers can provide approximations as to the duration of the short-term store.

Peterson and Peterson's work is another example of how studies can be used to demonstrate particular aspects of a theory. In this case their study using trigrams

Miller's 1956 article called "The Magical Number Seven, Plus or Minus Two" was instrumental in the cognitive revolution of the 1950s. It is also one of many pieces of research that led to the development of the multi-store model of memory.

If you are asked in an exam to explain a study that is "related to" a particular theory or model, you need to make it clear how the study is related. In many cases it will not demonstrate the complete theory but one particular aspect.

can demonstrate the duration of the short-term memory store. It might be important to note that this experiment was conducted in 1959, *before* Atkinson and Shiffrin proposed their multi-store model of memory. Studies like Peterson and Peterson's were part of a body of research that lead to the development of the MSM.

Cognitive psychologists use true experiments to test the effects of variables on memory. Peterson and Peterson manipulated the length of the time delay before recall in order to measure short-term memory duration.

Guiding Question:

How can Peterson and Peterson's experimental results demonstrate the duration of the short-term store?

Critical Thinking Extension:

Mundane realism: Peterson and Peterson deliberately chose meaningless consonant triplets so participants would not be able to connect them to existing schema. Do you think this poses a problem in terms of the study's design? Could we generalize these findings to other situations, like learning something important? (I.e. think about mundane realism). What other factors may limit the extent to which this study can be used to demonstrate the MSM?

If you're interested...

Joshua Foer has a really interesting TED Talk about "Feats of memory anyone can do." In this video Foer describes memory competitions and his experiences in participating in one. You will be able to see some people with seemingly endless capacity for memory.

(c) Biological Evidence of the MSM

A theory is only as strong as the evidence it has to support it. Therefore, when discussing and evaluating psychological theories and models it is important to examine their supporting evidence. In the previous section we looked at how one experiment can demonstrate the duration of the short-term store. This study has been critiqued, however, as the use of the same letters in multiple tests might have caused interference (Nairne et al., 1999).

Another way to investigate the validity of cognitive theories is to examine biological evidence that support their claims. There seems to be evidence to suggest that aspects of the MSM are biologically based. If the stores and control processes are different from one another (and memory is not just one big store in our brain), people who have damage to one aspect of memory may not experience problems with others. Case studies on patients with such abnormalities have shown just this and can be used as support for the MSM.

Perhaps the most famous example of a patient with memory problems is that of Henry Molaison, known as HM while he was alive. He suffered from epilepsy, a disorder involving uncontrollable seizures and when he was 29 his seizures were becoming so bad that he and his family decided that he should have an operation. The operation proposed was radical and involved removing a part of his brain thought to be responsible for the seizures: his hippocampus. MRI scans carried out on HM much later (in the 90s) showed that other parts of his temporal lobe were also removed (Corkin et al., 1997). HM was first studied in the 1950s by Milner and Scoville (1957) after HM's doctor noticed that he suffered numerous problems with his memory as a result of the operation.

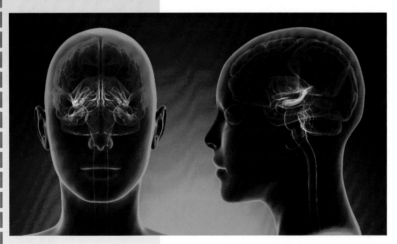

The hippocampus is in yellow in the above image. People who suffer from memory problems often have abnormalities in their hippocampi. It's also one of the first areas of the brain to be affected by Alzheimer's disease.

In one respect, the surgery was successful in that it resulted in HM suffering from fewer seizures. However, as a result of the surgery he was also suffering from anterograde amnesia: the inability to form new memories after the time of an accident. So while his memory of events from before the surgery was largely unchanged (i.e. his long term store was fine), he could not form new memories. An example described in the original article shows how his family moved houses after his surgery. Even though they only moved a few blocks from the previous address, HM could not remember the new house, and would walk to the old one instead. Milner also reports that he ate lunch in front of them, but 30 minutes later he could not remember eating. All other aspects of his character and personality remained perfectly unchanged. It was just that his ability to transfer information from his short-term store to his long-term store was damaged.

Milner tested HM's short-term memory by giving him information to remember and then testing him on it later. In one example he was given a three digit number to remember for 15 minutes. If he continually focused on this number and kept paying attention to it, he was able to successfully remember the number. However, if he was

A model in psychology is a proposed illustration of how something occurs. While a theory attempts to explain relationships between variables and behaviour, a model attempts to represent the processes of a particular phenomenon.

When evaluating models in essays you need to be able to describe the model in full and then explain how studies support (or contradict) particular aspects of the model.

There's more information about HM available on our blog. You can also try an online version of a star tracing task.

distracted he would forget it and the memory would not transfer to his long-term memory (Milner and Scoville, 1957; Squire and Wixted, 2011).

HM's short-term memory seemed to be fine provided that he was rehearsing the information and this rehearsal process seemed unaffected. And his long-term memory was mostly unaffected by the operation, meaning his long-term store was intact. However, the results suggest that there are biological components that influence the transfer of short-term memory to long-term memory. If our memory was just one big store with all the information in the same place and there was no *transfer* from store to store, patients like HM wouldn't experience such distinct abnormalities in their memory formation. Here we can see that case studies like HM's provide some evidence for the biological basis of different control processes that facilitate the transfer of information.

However, one task carried out by Milner on HM suggests that not all types of memories were affected by the operation. Our long-term memory can be broadly categorized into two different types: declarative (explicit) memory and procedural (implicit) memory. HM's memory problems mainly affected his declarative memory, as he couldn't remember new events or remember new facts. His procedural memory, on the other hand, appeared to be fine. Milner tested HM's procedural memory by asking him to trace a star in a reflection. This is very challenging without practice and HM was slow and clumsy to begin with. But over successive trials he became more fluent, even though he couldn't remember having done the task before. The results of this star-tracing task show how the hippocampus may not be required for the formation of new procedural memories.

While HM's study can show that the hippocampus may be responsible for the transfer of some types of memory from the short-term to long-term store, providing biological evidence for the control processes in the MSM, it may not play a role in the formation of procedural memory. One major critique of the MSM is that it may not apply to procedural (implicit) memory.

Guiding Question:

How does research on HM support claims of the MSM?

Critical Thinking Extension:

Contradictory Evidence: HM's study suggests that the hippocampus plays a role in the transfer of short-term memory to long-term memory. Throughout his life there weren't reports of improvements in these aspect of his cognition. Based on what you've learned about the brain, why might this be surprising? Does this lack of learning challenge other concepts you've learned about in this course? (Hint: neuroplasticity).

If you're interested…

You can see interviews with another amnesia patient in the UK called Clive Wearing. His wife, Deborah Wearing, wrote a book about Mr. Wearing's experiences called *Forever Today*. In the documentary "The Brain: Our Universe Within" you can also see how a promising young lawyer turned to an occupation of furniture making after a brain injury. Like HM, he lost his ability to form new long-term declarative memories, except his procedural memory was intact.

HM's study is another related to localization of brain function because it demonstrates the role of the hippocampus in the control process of transferring information from the short-term store to the long-term store.

Declarative memory is also known as explicit memory. It includes memories of facts, events and experiences. Declarative memory can also be further divided into other types of memory, including semantic memory (facts and details) and episodic memory (events).

Procedural memory is also known as implicit memory. It includes the ability to perform skills and tasks.

Relevant Topics

- Models of Memory
- Localization of Brain Function
- Techniques used to study the brain
- Cognitive processes
- Reliability of cognitive processes
- The brain and behaviour

Practice Exam Questions

- Explain one method used to investigate the reliability of cognitive processes.
- Evaluate the multi-store model of memory.
- Describe the multi-store model of memory.
- Outline one study related to one model of memory.
- Outline how one study demonstrates localization of brain function.

Research Methods

When investigating cognitive processes the true experiment (e.g. Peterson and Peterson) can be a valuable research method. Gathering empirical evidence is essential when testing theories of cognition. Early theories of cognitive processes relied on introspection, which involved psychologists reflecting on their own internal mental processes and using these to draw conclusions. Wilhelm Wundt, often credited as the father of Psychology, used introspection as a means of gathering evidence to test theories of cognition. This has obvious limitations in terms of objectivity and replicability – Wundt once claimed that studying the mind through introspection was like turning a light switch to try and study the darkness. By designing experiments that can test certain aspects of theories, researchers can describe their procedures in a way that would enable others to replicate their experiment and see if there is test-retest reliability. Case studies like HM's also allow researchers to study relationships between areas of the brain and behaviour.

Ethical Considerations

Case studies on patients with brain abnormalities come with many particular ethical considerations. HM agreed to donate his brain to science. After his death in 2008 his brain was sliced in 2,401 pieces to be preserved for study. Obviously, obtaining consent for such a procedure to take place is extremely important. However, HM's case isn't quite as simple as obtaining consent and comes with other interesting ethical dilemmas to consider. For example, can he really be said to have given consent if he would not be able to remember agreeing to the procedure? In this case, should family be consulted? In fact, there were questions raised over studies and procedures carried out on HM. You can read more about these in the NY Times article, "The Brain That Couldn't Remember."

4.2 The Working Memory Model
How do we use our short-term memory?

(a) An Introduction to Working Memory

After Atkinson and Shiffrin's multi-store model was introduced in cognitive psychology, the concept of the short-term store became the focus of numerous theories and studies. Baddeley and Hitch (1974) took the short-term store from the MSM and elaborated it in their working memory model (WMM).

In the previous lesson you learned how HM's memory was fine in terms of being able to hold information in his short-term store – his working memory was undamaged. Working memory is a term used to describe the process of consciously keeping information in your mind and retrieving information from your long-term memory into your short-term working memory.

To demonstrate working memory, ask your friend to give you the following problems to calculate in your head: *Take two and double it, and then add ten, and then subtract 5, and double that number.* You should be able to notice yourself making a calculation by keeping information in your mind and then consciously relating it to the other numbers that you're also consciously holding in your mind: this is what is known as working memory, and it's another name for the short-term store.

Working memory is the term used to describe the information we can process and hold in our conscious attention. Our working memory includes our attention to information in our environment and what we're consciously thinking about. It also includes that internal rehearsal of information that might enable us to transfer memory. We do not constantly have all our living memories running through our minds. If we did, we might go crazy and it'd be impossible to focus on any one task. The WMM attempts to explain the internal structures and processes involved in short-term memory.

In Baddeley and Hitch's working memory model there are a number of key components. The two that will be explored in this section are the phonological loop and visuo-spatial sketchpad.

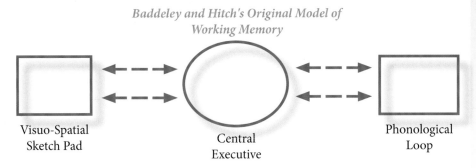

Baddeley and Hitch's Original Model of Working Memory

Visuo-Spatial Sketch Pad

Central Executive

Phonological Loop

The phonological loop is responsible for auditory information – sounds. It's a temporary storage and rehearsal system for auditory information. Imagine a friend

Working Memory: this is the term used to describe information that is temporarily stored in our consciousness and can be manipulated by moving in and out of our short-term memory. Working memory is another name for short-term memory.

213

or family member's voice right now. Can you "hear" their voice in your mind? The phonological loop is the part of your working memory that is enabling you to hear the voice. Try hearing a favourite song in your mind. Again, your ability to "hear" this song is the role of the phonological loop.

The phonological loop was later divided into two components: the phonological store (the inner ear) and the articulatory process (the inner voice) (Baddeley, 1986). The inner-ear is the storage aspect of the phonological loop, while the inner-voice is the rehearsal.

Subsequent research by Baddeley lead him to conclude that one major function of the phonological loop is to enable humans to learn new vocabulary. It might also serve as a "back-up" system for comprehending speech during "taxing conditions" (Baddeley, 1992). For instance, if you were in a difficult situation and were unable to give complete attention to what others are saying, you may be able to store the information briefly in the phonological store and then rehearse it later using the articulatory process when you had the cognitive capacity to try to comprehend what someone was saying. Imagine a solider taking heavy fire, for instance, and having an officer yell orders at them. They might not be able to process the information immediately but they might be able to recall it shortly when they were able to focus on the new information and deal with it accordingly.

Or let's say you're studying for a test at home and someone yells out to you from the kitchen. You're stressed and you're about to figure out the answer to a problem so you devote all your attention to the problem, while still hearing the voice yelling out a question. Your phonological store retains the information while you finish the problem. Once you're ready to shift your attention you can replay in your inner ear through the articulatory process what was yelled at you from downstairs and process the information accordingly. This is a valuable adaptive function.

While the phonological loop deals with auditory information, the visuo-spatial sketchpad deals with visual information. Picture a cluster of bananas, your best friend, or the inside of your room. The visuo-spatial sketchpad is the aspect of your working memory that enables you to "see" memory. It's also known as your inner-eye.

One approach to evaluating a psychological theory is to include an explanation of how it has contributed to a particular field of research. While the multi-store model may be critiqued for its focus on structure over processes, it has contributed to developments of other theories such as Baddeley and Hitch's working memory model. As we'll see in the following sections, this model also has important applications.

Cognitive capacity is a general term that refers to our ability to perform cognitive processes. An example of cognitive capacity is our working memory capacity: how much information we can hold in our working memory. This will be explored in later sections.

Drawing diagrams of models of memory is a good way to remember them. You can also use diagrams in exam answers as long as they accompany your written descriptions.

Guiding Question:

How does the WMM elaborate on components of the MSM?

Critical Thinking Extension:

Evaluation: Evaluating psychological theories is a very difficult task, but it is something you should be prepared to do for Paper One. Your general structure should include an introduction, a detailed description of the theory and an explanation of supporting evidence. This will constitute a majority of your answer. In order to get top marks, you need to be prepared to offer another possible strength, and one or two limitations of the theory. From what you've learned so far about the MSM and the WMM, could you suggest possible strengths and limitations of the MSM?

If you're interested…

In Peter Doolittle's TED Talk "How your 'working memory' makes sense of the world" you can follow along with Doolittle as he gives you a test of your working memory capacity. One way of testing your working memory capacity is to take a test of your digit span and you can find links to a range of tests on our blog.

You need to be able to describe the working memory model. It is important that you can understand major components, like the phonological loop and the visuo-spatial sketchpad. Try your best to remember the minor details as well, such as the articulatory process and the phonological store.

(b) The Central Executive and The Episodic Buffer

The working memory model can seem quite daunting at first because of the new terminology. As with all learning, the best way to comprehend the working memory model is to try to understand it in relation to your own experiences. Understanding the concept of working memory can have many practical applications, including deepening understanding of your own thought processes. A good definition of the function of working memory is that it "…allows us to actively maintain and manipulate mental information for short periods of time" (Fougnie and Marois, 2009). The ability to maintain mental information and to manipulate it for a number of reasons is a central skill in performing many cognitive tasks, like solving a complex problem or understanding something difficult.

Slave systems: the phonological loop and the visuo-spatial sketchpad.

The previous section introduced two of the slave systems of the working memory model, the phonological loop and the visuo-spatial sketchpad. These are known as slave systems because they are controlled by the central executive, which is like a controlling system that controls the flow of information between the other systems. In the original model, the central executive was "…assumed to be capable of attentional focus, storage and decision making" (Baddeley, 2011). Baddeley himself described it as "…a little man in the head…" that was capable of completing tasks involving working memory that were unable to be performed by the original slave systems: the phonological loop and visuo-spatial sketchpad.

Central Executive: the "boss" who controls the workings of the slave systems. The term executive functions refers to the processes of the central executive, like focusing our attention on different things.

For example, if you're remembering a song and you can hear the words in your mind, you're using the phonological loop. You might shift your focus to begin thinking about the music video for that song. The shift in focus of your attention is a function of the central executive.

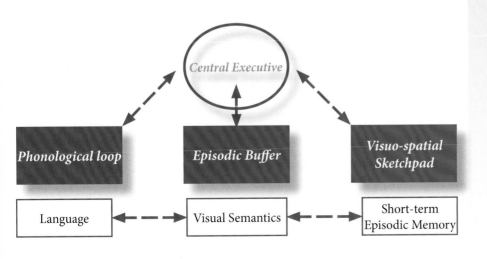

Learning theories in one big chunk is difficult, which is why this text spreads out the details over different sections. You can revise the theories using the blog, your notes and the revision textbook.

The original WMM consisted of only the three components: the central executive, the phonological loop and the visuo-spatial sketchpad. A third system was introduced in a later version of the model: the episodic buffer. The episodic buffer is a store within the short-term store that can hold chunks of information until it is needed. It also serves to connect the components of working memory with sensory perception and long-term memory (Baddeley, 2011).

As with other psychological theories, it is important that you can comprehend individual components of the theory. The WMM is slightly more complex than the MSM, so you will need to work hard to ensure you can comprehend and summarize the central executive and the three supporting systems.

Guiding Question:

How is the central executive related to the other systems in the working memory model?

Critical Thinking Extension:

Applications: Understanding psychological theories becomes far more interesting if you can apply them. Can you think of ways that understanding working memory could be applied to your own life? When do you use your working memory on a daily basis? Or perhaps you might be able to devise some hypotheses about correlations between working memory capacity and the ability to perform other tasks.

If you're interested…

You can listen to a brief interview with Baddeley on YouTube where he describes the model himself on gocognitive's channel. If you're *really* interested you can hear a 40 minute lecture on theories of memory by Baddeley as well.

(c) Evidence for the Working Memory Model

To recap, Baddeley and Hitch's original 1974 working memory model elaborated on the short-term store of the multi-store model of memory. Their original model consisted of the central executive, which was like a controlling function of the short-term store. This controlled two slave systems: the phonological loop and the visuo-spatial sketchpad. A later slave system, the episodic buffer, was also introduced to explain how working memory can be connected to perception and long-term memory.

As the WMM is complex with many component parts, there are a number of possible ways of testing these various components. One line of research has focused on determining the existence of two different slave systems that process different modalities (i.e. visual or verbal information).

A common experimental procedure is the dual-task paradigm. This requires participants to process visual and/or verbal information simultaneously. If recollection of visual information is unaffected by verbal interference, it provides some evidence for two different systems processing these different modalities (types of information).

Robbins et al. (1996) tested this using 20 male chess players from Cambridge, UK. The players ranged in ability from casual chess players to grand champions. The researchers wanted to see if memory recall would be affected by processing interfering information. For example, would having to process extra visuo-spatial information interfere with working memory capacity? The participants were asked to view an arrangement of pieces on one chess board for ten seconds. This board was on their left as they sat down facing forward. After this ten seconds they then had to try to recreate the arrangement they had just seen on a different chess board on their right. This involved them having to recreate the arrangement using their working memory.

The independent variable in this experiment was the type of distracting information they had to process while they were completing this task. In one condition, the participants' phonological loop was interfered with as they had to repeat the word "the" every second to the rhythm of a metronome. They were required to repeat the word during the ten seconds watching the board and learning the arrangement (using their phonological loop), as well as the time it took them to recreate the arrangement on the new board. In another condition, their visuo-spatial sketchpad was interfered with as they had to type into a keyboard that was out of sight under a table. They were required to type with one hand in a particular order, while they were arranging the pieces with another hand. This would have required them using their visuo-spatial sketchpad.

The results showed that there was a far greater reduction in scores of accurate recall of chess positions when the participants' visuo-spatial processing was interfered with during the keyboard task. Their average score for memory of the chess pieces was around 4/25 in this condition, compared to around 16/25 for the phonological interference.

These results provide evidence for the existence of separate slave systems that process different information during working memory tasks. The

Robbins et al.'s study suggests that visuo-spatial interference affects our visuo-spatial sketchpad. This is one of many reasons why you should never text and drive.

In memory studies modality refers to the type of sensory information, e.g. visual or auditory. So the modality of interference in this case is whether or not they were being distracted by interfering visual or auditory information.

memory of the chess pieces and the ability to arrange them in the correct order again requires visuo-spatial memory. If there was one system of working memory, there would be the same influence of scores on the memory of the chessboard regardless of the modality of interference. The fact that visuo-spatial interference had a far greater detrimental effect on visuo-spatial memory of the chessboard suggests that there are different systems for processing different information.

This study is one of many that has employed the dual task paradigm to investigate the existence of different components within short-term memory, namely the phonological loop and the visuospatial sketchpad. Differing effects on cognition based on modality provides some evidence for Baddeley and Hitch's claim that our sensory store is comprised of different components that process different types of information.

Guiding Question:

How does Robbins et al.'s dual task experiment on chess playing provide support for the working memory model?

Critical Thinking Extension:

Population Validity: When evaluating studies an important aspect to look at is the nature of the sample. In this study chess players were used because of the nature of the task. Can you think of any reasons why chess players may not provide representative results related to working memory?

If you're interested…

It was a long-standing belief that computers would never be able to beat humans in chess because they lacked intuition. However, in 1997 IBM's computer "Deep Blue" beat grandmaster champion Garry Kasparov. This was the subject of a documentary called "Man vs Machine." This was a significant event in the history of the development of Artificial Intelligence (AI) and you can read a lot more about this event in many online articles and videos.

(d)   Working Memory and Attention (ADHD)

In the previous lessons you've learned that because the function of our brain and our mental processes are so closely related, neurological evidence can be valuable when discussing the validity of models of cognitive processes. For example, HM's hippocampal damage affected his transfer of information from the STS to the LTS and this suggests that the control processes have biological bases.

One of the major strengths of the working memory model is that it has inspired research that has extended our understanding of memory, attention and other cognitive processes. Working memory capacity is also a common field of study as it has numerous applications, including in understanding PTSD. For example, people diagnosed with PTSD have reduced working memory capacity, possibly as a result of their intrusive thoughts and memories related to their trauma (Veltmeyer et al., 2009). As our working memory can only hold so many pieces of information at any one time, if someone constantly has unpleasant thoughts intruding on their thinking, they may find it difficult to focus and concentrate on other tasks.

Other research has also found correlations between working memory capacity and reading comprehension (e.g. Daneman and Carptenter, 1980). At least one study suggests that poor working memory capacity is correlated with the ability to maintain focus and concentration, especially during difficult tasks (Kane et al., 2007). Being able to maintain focus and control your attention is also an important cognitive skill. Have you ever found yourself daydreaming when the teacher's explaining something? Or at times when reading this book and you find yourself half way down the page but you've got no recollection of what you've just been reading?

A commonly diagnosed behavioural disorder is attention deficit hyperactivity disorder (ADHD) and working memory deficits have been suggested to play a role in ADHD (Barkley, 1997). Children with attentional problems experience a number of negative effects, such as poor grades and impaired social skills. Some of these effects may continue into adulthood as well. These are some of the reasons why understanding working memory problems is an important area of study for developmental and educational psychologists.

Kids who have problems with their working memory struggle to focus and pay attention. This is correlated with numerous negative outcomes, including poor grades and getting in trouble at school.

Torkel Klingberg is one psychologist working on developing programmes and tools to improve working memory and executive cognitive function in children. In one study Klingberg et al. (2005) investigated the effects of computer-based training on working memory and executive functioning, 42 children with ADHD were randomly assigned to one of two conditions for a five week trial. In the treatment condition the children played a computerized game designed to improve their working memory. There were 90 working memory tasks to be completed at least five times per week and each session lasted around 40 minutes. The tasks were also designed to increase in difficulty as the children's working memory improved. In the control condition the same computerized game was played, but the difficulty did not increase with the child's progress, so it was also easy for them to complete.

After the five weeks the children performed a range of tasks to measure the effects of the training. The results revealed significant improvements in working memory capacity, reasoning abilities and decreased displays of ADHD-related behaviours.

One aim of providing a guiding question for each lesson in this textbook is to provide you with the guidance to increase your working memory capacity and reading comprehension: by processing new information and relating it to what you know already in order to be able to answer the question, it's hoped that this continual practice will improve your cognitive capabilities (and your understanding of psychology).

Executive cognitive function: the central executive's ability to control slave systems and focus our attention.

Response inhibition is a measure of cognitive control and refers to the ability to suppress actions that are inappropriate. In the Stroop Test, this might refer to the ability to suppress a wrong answer and think more carefully to provide the right answer.

There was also a significant improvement in response inhibition as measured by performance on the Stroop Test.

These findings are consistent with other research that shows targeted practice for particular cognitive tasks can improve our mental processing and reasoning skills. By providing the original ideas, Baddeley and Hitch's research has allowed psychologists to explore the possible applications of understanding working memory processes and how these might be related to other cognitive functions, such as attention. Also, by designing specific training mechanisms, psychologists can help treat mental disorders and deficiencies, such as ADHD. This can have significant positive effects for individuals and for society.

Klingberg and others also conducted research into the neurological effects of working memory training. Findings from these studies suggest that there are neurological benefits involved in practicing strategies to improve working memory (Klingberg, 2010). You will be able to see how similar principles can be applied to understanding PTSD in the following topics.

Guiding Question:

How might working memory training improve attention?

Critical Thinking Extension:

Application: Based on what you know about PTSD and its symptoms already, can you think of ways that cognitive training and/or working memory processes may be related to the treatment and/or causes of PTSD? Hint: intrusive memories.

If you're interested…

Torkel Klingberg has a TED Talk called "Improving working memory capacity." In this talk he provides a demonstration of the types of tasks involved in the computerized training programme used for working memory training. You can also play online games to test your working memory capacity (look for tests on digit span).

Relevant Topics

- Models of memory
- Cognitive processes
- HL: The effects of technology on cognition

Practice Exam Questions

- Discuss the working memory model of memory.
- Evaluate the use of one research method in the study of cognitive processes.
- Contrast the working memory model with the multi-store model of memory.

Research Methods

The value of the true experiment in investigating aspects of cognitive theories is demonstrated in Robbins et al.'s study on chess players. They were able to manipulate the independent variable and measure the effects on the dependent variable, which was a cognitive process. This comparison in a controlled environment allows the researchers to test the validity of particular claims of models. In this instance, they were able to manipulate the type of interfering information that was being processed (auditory or visuo-spatial). The results of the different types of interference were compared. By seeing that similar information led to a far greater reduction of working memory capacity, the researchers are able to conclude that the phonological loop and visuo-spatial sketchpad are two different slave systems that process different information. The manipulation of the IV and measuring the effects on the DV in a controlled environment is the defining characteristic of a true experiment and its value in studying cognitive processes can be seen in this study.

Ethical Considerations

When explaining how and/or why particular ethical guidelines are important to consider in fields of research, identifying potential areas of sensitivity can be a good starting point. Working memory capacity has been correlated with general intelligence (Conway et al., 2003), which may be a sensitive area. The studies on ADHD also focus on a sensitive area as they are dealing with children and a psychological disorder. When the behaviours being studied may be sensitive to participants, informed consent and debriefing are important considerations. The researchers need to provide enough information about the study so the participants won't feel any undue stress or anxiety during the procedures. However, they may not be able to reveal all of the information because of concerns as to how this may influence the validity of the study. When some information is withheld (e.g. if they were in a treatment or control group), participants should be debriefed. There might also be some ethical issues associated with assigning kids who might benefit from training into a control group.

4.3 Emotion and Cognition
How can our emotions affect our thinking?

(a)   Fear Conditioning

One limitation of the multi-store and working memory models is that they don't consider the effects of emotion on memory processes. There is a lot of research that shows the effects emotion can have on cognitive processing, including how high levels of stress can affect memory. This is an important factor for us to consider, as many of the symptoms of PTSD are related to the negative effects of emotion on memory. In this section we'll begin looking at this by studying fear conditioning.

Learning to respond to a stimulus based on your experiences of that stimulus is called conditioning. A conditioned response is when you have learned to respond to a particular stimulus in a certain way. So fear conditioning is the process of learning to respond with fear when encountering a particular stimulus.

Fear conditioning was first studied by Watson and Rayner (1920) in their experiments on a baby called Albert in what is now a classic study in psychology. In these experiments, Watson and Rayner attempted to condition a fear of particular animals and objects that Albert had previously shown no reaction of fear towards.

The process of fear conditioning first involves a neutral stimulus. This is something that the learner has not previously been afraid of. In the Baby Albert experiments, Watson and Rayner used a range of neutral stimuli, including a white rat. Albert showed no signs of fear towards the rat initially. In the fear conditioning paradigm, in order to condition a fear response, a neutral stimulus needs to be paired with an aversive stimulus. An aversive stimulus is something that is unwanted, unpleasant or disliked. To show that fear could be learned, Watson and Rayner had someone smack a steel bar with a hammer so it made a loud and frightening noise.

Early tests on Albert showed that this noise would make him cry. So after first being able to touch and see the white rat (neutral stimulus), Albert was introduced to this same stimulus but now it was paired with the aversive stimulus (the metal bar being struck). The result of this was that after a few of these trials Albert showed fear and aversion towards the rat when it was presented to him even after the aversive stimulus was removed. He had been conditioned to feel fear in response to seeing the rat. Watson and Rayner hypothesized that this fear would be transferred to other similar stimuli as well (e.g. a white rabbit). To quote the original study, when Albert was shown the rabbit after conditioning "the experimenter … took hold of his left hand and laid it on the rabbit's back. Albert immediately withdrew his hand and began to suck his thumb. Again the rabbit was laid in his lap. He began to cry, covering his face with both hands…" (Watson and Rayner, 1920).

The rat and the rabbit have become conditioned stimuli. Albert has been conditioned to be afraid of this stimuli. Fear conditioning is an example of what is called classical conditioning in psychology. It is also known as associative learning: learning how to associate one thing with another.

Fear conditioning: developing a fear response to particular stimuli after repeated exposure to the stimuli coupled with aversive outcomes.

Understanding fear conditioning has important applications in the study of PTSD.

Conditioned stimulus: something that someone has been conditioned to feel fear towards. (Stimuli is plural of stimulus.)

The Baby Albert experiment is just one of many that show how we may learn to be afraid of particular stimuli. It also shows that emotion can affect cognition. In this case, the emotion is generated from the negative reactions towards the aversive stimulus and results in learning to be afraid of the particular stimulus. The negative emotion leads to the creation of an association between the aversive stimulus and the neutral/conditioned stimulus.

John Watson was the leading figure in the behaviourist movement, which came before the cognitive revolution.

For some types of traumatic events, you might be able to see how fear conditioning is relevant. Veterans in a war might become conditioned to fear certain sounds, like an airplane flying overhead or sudden explosions like fireworks. When they encounter similar stimuli when they return to civilian life it might trigger symptoms related to re-experiencing the trauma, such as flashbacks or emotions related to the traumatic experience. Many soldiers talk about not being able to stand near windows, as in combat situations this could put someone's life at risk.

Fear conditioning may explain symptoms of PTSD. From my own experience after an incident with a train crash, the sight of fire triggered flashbacks for weeks afterwards. Even if the fire was something harmless, like a BBQ or a campfire, it would trigger memories and images of the event.

Post-traumatic stress disorder may be the result of conditioned fears that have not been overcome. There are numerous biological factors involved in fear conditioning, and these will be explored in the following sections.

On our blog you can read more about my experiences with symptoms of PTSD after I tried (and failed) to pull a man from a burning car after a train accident. Learning about real life examples can help make the ideas in this chapter less abstract and more concrete.

Guiding Question:

How does the Baby Albert experiment demonstrate the process of fear conditioning?

Critical Thinking Extension:

Ethics: The Baby Albert experiment has been criticized for the ethical issues surrounding conditioning a baby to fear particular stimuli. Interestingly, when you read the original reports you can see that the researchers often considered the well-being of Albert during the study. What are the ethical issues you can identify in this study? You may want to read the original article after considering your answer.

If you're interested…

There's a website called Classics in the History of Psychology and the complete Baby Albert experiment can be found there (psychclassics.yorku. ca). You can also see original footage of the Baby Albert experiment online, including on our blog.

(b)   The Amygdala and Fear Conditioning

Watson and Rayner showed with Albert that by pairing an aversive stimulus with an object, one could learn to experience fear through association. Fear conditioning, as it has become known, has been the subject of numerous studies.

It's natural to demonstrate an instinctive fear to dangerous stimuli such as extreme heights, dangerous animals, and other common dangers in the natural world. This helps us to survive. But something else that helps us to survive is our ability to *learn* to be afraid. We may not be born with an instinctual fear for *every* possible source of danger, so learning from experience can help us to avoid potentially dangerous situations. This is the evolutionary advantage of fear conditioning.

The role of cortisol in consolidating emotional memory would have served an important survival function. For example, it would have helped our ancestors to remember the places to avoid because of potential dangers.

Because of the ethical implications involved in fear conditioning experiments, animals are commonly used for testing fear conditioning. These experiments follow similar procedures: animals are put in a particular environment, such as a special cage with the neutral stimulus usually being a bell or some other similar sound. As the bell sounds, the animal receives the aversive stimulus, like an electric shock. After a number of trials, the bell has become the conditioned stimulus because the animals demonstrate a fearful reaction towards the sound without the presence of the aversive stimulus. The effects of the conditioning might be measured in a number of ways, including changes in heart rate, skin temperature, breathing, or hormone levels.

As emotion involves physiological arousal as well as thoughts and feelings, when studying the role of emotion on cognition in fear conditioning, one cannot ignore the role of biological factors. You may not be surprised to learn that the amygdala plays an important role in fear conditioning. If you remember from SM's case study, earlier research on her showed that she had an impairment in fear conditioning (Bechara et al., 1995). This suggests that the amygdala plays a role in associating stimuli with an aversive outcome. Similarly, studies using fMRI show that the amygdala is activated when the conditioned stimulus is presented (e.g. LaBar et al., 1998). For example, if someone is conditioned to fear a particular sound, when they are in the fMRI and that sound is played their amygdala activates.

There has been considerable research into how the amygdala might influence our memory. One possible explanation is based on the role of cortisol, a stress hormone released during the stress response as a result of activation of the amygdala. Because learning to be afraid of something might serve an evolutionary advantage, it would make sense that activation of the amygdala might facilitate the development of memory that would help us to avoid fearful stimuli in the future. In earlier chapters you learned about how the activation of the amygdala during emotional experiences can trigger other physiological responses, such as the release of adrenaline. During the stress response, the hypothalamus regulates the adrenal gland's release of cortisol (Ressler, 2010). An important part of the stress response is the Hypothalamic-Pituitary-Adrenal (HPA) axis. This is the name given to the neural network that connects these three important glands in the endocrine system that release hormones and neurotransmitters in response to stress signals. Cortisol is released when the amygdala activates the HPA axis (Smith and Vale, 2006).

While parts of the brain perform particular functions, it's important to remember that most parts perform various functions and have complex networks with other areas of the brain.

The stress response is another name for the fight/flight response.

Cortisol is associated with stress and is released as part of the stress response (a.k.a. the fight/flight response). While the stress response might seem like a negative thing, it can actually serve important survival functions by helping to consolidate emotional memory. Consolidation of memory refers to the transfer from short-term to long-term memory. Buchanan and Lovallo (2001) tested the idea that cortisol can enhance our consolidation of emotionally significant information. They had two groups of participants and one group was administered 20mg of cortisol and the other group was given a placebo. After this treatment they were shown a variety of pictures. Some were emotionally arousing while others were neutral. After one week they were given a test of their memory of the pictures. The results showed that increased levels of cortisol resulted in improved memory of the emotional pictures, compared with the neutral ones.

This study suggests that the amygdala's interaction with the hypothalamus and the resulting release of the stress hormone cortisol may play an important role in the consolidation of emotional memory. The activation of the amygdala in response to a potentially threatening stimulus plays an important role in activating the stress response. The subsequent activation of the HPA axis can release cortisol, strengthening the memory formation. This will also lead to other physiological responses that will help an individual deal with the emotional stimulus, such as an increase in adrenaline which would help facilitate a fight or flight response. In this sense, developing an autonomic fear response towards things that we have learned to be afraid of is an important survival adaptation as it helps us to deal with threats.

The amygdala is also known as the emotional centre of the brain, so its role in emotion cannot be overlooked. When explaining the effect that emotion can have on cognition, the autonomic activation of the amygdala in response to a conditioned fear is an important part to consider.

Consolidating Memory: transferring memory from the short-term store to the long-term store.

Autonomic fear response: when your autonomic nervous system (including the amygdala) unconsciously triggers physiological responses (e.g. hormone release) when a threatening stimulus is perceived.

Guiding Question:

How can activation of the amygdala affect memory formation?

Critical Thinking Extension:

Hypotheses: Based on what you know about PTSD, emotion and fear conditioning, can you hypothesize any patterns of abnormal function you might expect to find in people diagnosed with PTSD?

If you're interested…

Joseph LeDoux is one of the most prominent psychologists who study the amygdala. He has a video on the Big Think YouTube channel called "The Amygdala in Five Minutes" that provides a very good summary of this important part of the brain. PBS NOVA also has an interesting documentary called "Memory Hackers." This documentary includes a lot of information that will really deepen your understanding of biology and memory.

(c)   The Hippocampus and Emotional Memory

Affective stimulus: affective means "relating to emotion" and a stimulus is anything that generates a response. So an affective stimulus is something that generates an emotional response. The school bell is an affective stimulus for many students (and teachers).

When talking about people who suffer from psychological disorders, the common practice is to phrase it in a way so that the individual is put before the disorder. For instance, "people with PTSD" or "patients suffering from depression ..." etc. This is a minor detail, but helps to ensure that diagnosis of a disorder doesn't become an individual's primary identity.

In the previous sections you saw how fear conditioning might affect cognition. By triggering the amygdala during the perception of affective stimuli, the stress response is activated through the amygdala's communication with the HPA axis. This results in the release of hormones, including adrenaline and cortisol. The increase in cortisol might help with memory consolidation for the emotional memory. The activation of the stress response during perception of emotional stimuli is important, as the release of adrenaline might help us to deal with the dangerous situation. However, abnormalities in key parts of the brain associated with fear conditioning may lead to undesirable symptoms; this could be at the heart of the development and expression of PTSD symptoms.

Brain scans on patients with PTSD have revealed two common physiological correlates: reduced volume in the hippocampus and a hyper-responsive amygdala (Shin and Liberzon, 2009). A hyper-responsive amygdala means that the amygdala activates in response to stimuli more frequently and at a higher rate than normal. This could explain the symptom of increased startle responses, which means people are "jumpy" when taken by surprise. One veteran tells the story of how his son ran up behind him and covered his eyes to play peek-a-boo. The father was startled and before he knew what he'd done he had violently thrown his son to the ground. Having a hyper-responsive amygdala could result in people being constantly and unconsciously on "red alert."

As you learned previously, the amygdala communicates with the hypothalamus when we're presented with the aversive stimulus and this triggers the release of cortisol. Studies have shown an inverted-U response to this release of cortisol: too little or too much cortisol might not have a significant effect on memory consolidation (McIntyre and Roozendaal, 2007).

But what happens if we're constantly stressed and we experienced prolonged levels of cortisol secretion? Patients with hyper-responsive amygdalae may experience high levels of emotion and increased irritability. This has been labelled amygdala hijack and there are numerous possible effects of having a hyper-responsive amygdala, including elevated levels of cortisol in response to emotional stimuli.

Elzinga et al. (2003) showed that after exposure to trauma-related stimuli, women who had PTSD as a result of childhood abuse showed increases in cortisol levels. In this study, after reading scripts that were designed to remind the participants of the trauma they had experienced, they had cortisol levels that were 122% higher than non-PTSD controls.

Low volume in the hippocampus may be a symptom of PTSD, but it also might be an etiology.

These regular spikes in cortisol levels may explain why numerous MRI studies have shown that people with PTSD have reduced hippocampal volume. The hippocampus is one of the most plastic parts of the brain and is vulnerable to stress and damage. While neuroplasticity can refer to growth and positive changes in the brain, it can also refer to atrophy and other negative effects of experience. Early animal research used rats and guinea pigs to investigate the effects of elevated cortisol levels and these studies found that increased cortisol levels can damage the hippocampus.

Sapolsky et al. (1990) wanted to determine if these findings could be generalized to non-human primates. In this study the researchers implanted pellets containing cortisol in the hippocampi of four vervet monkeys. As a control, they implanted cholesterol pellets into the hippocampi of four different vervet monkeys. The monkeys were kept in normal laboratory conditions and after one year they were euthanised so their brains could be autopsied and the effects of the pellets measured. The results showed that the monkeys with the cortisol implants had significant damage to their neurons in the hippocampus, including dendritic atrophy (the shrinking and decay of dendrites). These findings support other research that shows prolonged exposure to high levels of cortisol can decrease the length and branching of dendrites, inhibit neurogenesis, and cause neurons in the hippocampus to die (McEwen, 1999; Sapolsky, 2000).

If cortisol can negatively affect the neurons in the hippocampus of monkeys, could this be the same in humans? And how might this affect memory? Bremner et al. (1995) used studies like Sapolsky et al.'s as a basis for their research on combat veterans of the Vietnam War who had PTSD. They used MRI scans to measure the structure of the brains of the veterans and compared them with 22 healthy controls. The results showed that the right hippocampus was 8% smaller in the patients with PTSD, compared with the controls.

Vervet monkeys like these ones were used to test the effects of prolonged releases of cortisol on the hippocampus.

It is well-documented that war veterans also suffer from many symptoms associated with memory, including flashbacks, night-mares, intrusive memories and amnesia for particular war-time experiences (Sutker et al., 1991). Soldiers in combat experience high levels of extreme stress for prolonged periods of time. This high level of emotional impact may cause elevated levels of cortisol, which may damage their hippocampi.

HM's study (and many others) have shown that the hippocampus plays a role in long-term declarative memory formation. Damage to this area could explain why patients with PTSD display cognitive problems, including reduced memory capabilities (Quereshi et al., 2011). The hippocampus also plays a role in memory retrieval, which could explain a common symptom of amnesia regarding details of the traumatic event itself (Eldridge et al., 2000). For example, people who were in a car accident may not be able to remember details of the accident.

One study has found a correlation between teacher burnout and student cortisol levels. How could this correlation be explained? (Oberle & Schonert-Reichl, 2016)

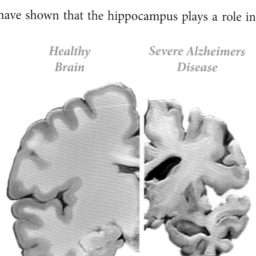

Healthy Brain *Severe Alzheimers Disease*

Diseases like Alzheimer's result in heavy atrophy of the brain. This explains the gradual decline in cognitive capabilities.

From the research in this topic we can see that emotion (fear and stress) could have positive and negative effects on cognition. On the one hand, the association of aversive stimuli and the conditioned fear along with the corresponding activation of the amygdala could facilitate the release of cortisol that helps consolidate emotional memory. This might serve an important survival function in that it enables us to develop memories that will help us to avoid danger.

Our ability to forget details of trauma could be another evolutionary adaptation. Imagine being able to remember every bad thing that's ever happened to you?

However, prolonged stress might have detrimental effects on memory as the elevated cortisol levels over long periods of time may reduce the functioning capabilities of the hippocampus. This could explain some of the common cognitive symptoms of PTSD, including impaired memory abilities and the inability to remember particular details about the traumatic event.

Guiding Question:

How might a hyper-responsive amygdala affect cognitive symptoms of PTSD?

Critical Thinking Extension:

Alternative Evidence: The above explanations provide some plausible explanations for correlations found in PTSD patients. But you must always challenge the evidence and search for alternative explanations. It would seem logical to conclude, for instance, that PTSD patients would have higher than normal levels of cortisol. Actually, there is a strong body of research that shows the opposite correlation: PTSD patients often have lower than normal levels of cortisol. How could this be explained?

If you're interested…

Daniel Goleman coined the term amygdala hijack in his book *Emotional Intelligence: Why it can matter more than IQ*. You may be interested in reading this work.

Research Methods

Elzinga et al.'s (2003) study demonstrates the use of another type of research method used in psychology that Coolican calls a group difference study. This is commonly confused with quasi-experimental designs. A group difference study compares two different groups, but the difference may have existed for so long that there are far too many confounding variables to determine cause-effect relationships. There are many examples of group difference studies being used in this chapter on PTSD. The reason why this method is common is because many studies compare results for participants with and without PTSD. If a study is investigating a significant difference between the groups, but the study is not measuring the effects of a "treatment," it could be labelled a group difference study. The value in the case of this study is that the difference in effects of cortisol secretion levels of two groups of participants can be compared. This has enabled the researchers to draw conclusions about correlations between cortisol levels and PTSD. One conclusion from this study could be that the elevated levels of cortisol may explain other symptoms of PTSD, such as low hippocampal volume. However, as there are many extraneous variables that cannot be controlled for, the conclusions are tentative and correlational.

Ethical Considerations

There are many areas of ethical concern when studying patients with PTSD that researchers need to consider. In Elzinga et al.'s study they exposed patients to stimuli that were intended to remind them of a traumatic past event. As evidenced by the 122% spike in cortisol, this clearly had some emotional effects and was potentially harmful for participants. Providing information about the procedures of the study and what participants would expect might be an important aspect of the informed consent for the researchers to consider.

4.4 Etiologies of PTSD
How might biology and cognition interact in PTSD?

(a)   Genetics

In the previous topic you learned about how the amygdala plays an important role in fear conditioning. You also saw how prolonged experience of elevated levels of cortisol may have detrimental effects on the brain, including the hippocampus. While this topic is called "Etiologies of PTSD," the previous topic also gave you plenty of possible explanations for PTSD symptoms, including amnesia and memory impairments.

When discussing origins and explanations of disorders in psychology, the term etiology is often used. Investigating the cause or origin of symptoms (their etiology) is at the heart of studying psychiatric disorders such as PTSD. One reason for this is because if we can discover underlying causes, we can develop better treatments.

You've already been introduced to some of the commonly cited biological etiologies of PTSD, including hippocampal atrophy and a hyper-responsive amygdala. But there's a question that needs to be asked of these studies that investigate the correlations between the brain and psychiatric disorders: are the brain abnormalities an *etiology* of the disorder, or are they a *symptom*? Bremner et al. (1995), for instance, showed that Veterans with PTSD had an 8% smaller hippocampus than the control group. But is this reduction a symptom of their experience in war, or was it a precondition that increased their likelihood of developing PTSD as a result of their experiences? It's a chicken-or-the-egg sort of dilemma.

It's difficult to determine if the brain abnormalities in PTSD patients are a cause or effect of the experience of trauma because patients only have their brain scans *after* they are exposed to trauma and are diagnosed with PTSD. This means there is often no data for before-and-after comparisons to be made. One way to overcome this would be to gather lots of data on people before a trauma and then compare this with what happened afterwards, but the practical limitation of this is that most people are not aware of when (or even if) they will experience trauma in the first place; it would also be expensive and time consuming.

As with genetics and violence, twin studies can elucidate the role of genetic factors on the development of PTSD. They can also provide an insight as to whether or not the difference in brain structure is a risk factor for PTSD, or a *symptom*. One way of overcoming the chicken-egg problem with PTSD symptoms is through the use of a case-control design, which can be done using identical twins.

In a case-control design the researchers gather two types of twins. The following is going to get rather tricky, so take your time to try to figure out how this design can determine if a biological variable like low hippocampus volume is likely to exist *before* trauma and increase the likelihood of developing PTSD, or *after* a traumatic event and is more likely a symptom of the PTSD.

Gilbertson et al. (2002) conducted a case-control study on 34 sets of identical (monozygotic) twins. The design might seem complicated at first, but it is based on

Etiology: the cause or set of causes of a disease or disorder.

You may be able to use the genetic origins of PTSD in Paper One or Paper Two.

some sound logic. Firstly, remember that monozygotic twins (MZT) have 100% of their DNA in common. If they've been raised in the same household they've probably had similar experiences. To use war veterans as an example, we can assume that before going off to war they had similar experiences and identical genes, so we could reasonably assume that their hippocampi would be the same in terms of structure and function.

Gilbertson and colleagues used two different types of identical twins. One set of twins has one twin who has gone to war and developed PTSD (a trauma exposed twin), and the other twin who hasn't been to war and doesn't have PTSD (trauma unexposed). These twins are compared with a second set of twins. The second is the same as the first, except the twin that went away to war (trauma exposed) did not develop PTSD. The results of the study were that trauma unexposed twins of veterans with PTSD had smaller hippocampal volumes compared to unexposed twins of veterans without PTSD.

The important comparison to make here is between the two twins who didn't go away to war (trauma unexposed). The fact that the co-twin of the PTSD patient had a smaller hippocampi compared to the co-twin of the non-PTSD veteran, suggests that the low hippocampal volume is a factor that increases the vulnerability to developing PTSD. Therefore, the low hippocampal volume may be an existing factor in an individual that might increase their vulnerability to developing PTSD as a result of exposure to trauma.

A simplified diagram of how the case-control design works to see if a smaller hippocampus is a symptom or cause of PTSD.

Other MRI results from the study corroborate earlier studies that show the correlation between PTSD in veterans and hippocampal volume. Veterans with PTSD had an average hippocampal volume of 10% less than veterans without PTSD. There was also a negative correlation found between symptom severity and hippocampal volume: the lower the volume of the hippocampus the more severe the PTSD symptoms were.

This is further evidence that suggests genetics *and* hippocampal abnormality are possible etiologies and biological explanations of PTSD symptoms related to memory.

Critical Thinking Extension:
Population Validity: This sample deals with war veterans who are suffering from PTSD. The experiences of war are quite different to other traumatic experiences that could lead to the development of PTSD. In what way might war be different to other traumatic experiences, and how might this affect the validity of this study?

If you're interested…

If you're interested in the effects of stress on the brain and/or body I would highly recommend Sapolsky's *Why Zebras Don't Get Ulcers*. He also has a series of interesting documentaries that you may be interested in watching, including one called "Stress: Portrait of a Killer."

(b)   Top-Down Processing and the PFC

So far in this chapter we've looked at two of the major potential biological etiologies of PTSD: a hyper-responsive amygdala and low volume in the hippocampus. You should be able to see how these areas of the brain may interact with our environment and cognitive processes to explain the possible development of some PTSD symptoms. There's one other important part of the brain that we haven't addressed yet: the prefrontal cortex (PFC). As you have already learned, the PFC plays a vital role in performing many cognitive processes, including processing and executive functions.

Numerous studies using MRI scans have shown that people with PTSD show decreased volumes in their prefrontal cortex. It's not only the structure that is affected, it might also be the function, as lower than normal activation of the prefrontal cortex can be seen in fMRI scans when people who have suffered from a traumatic experience are shown images related to their trauma (Shin et al., 2006). This reduced functioning of the PFC may play a role in an individual's ability to perform particular cognitive processes that may regulate emotional reactions. This could provide biological and cognitive explanations for some symptoms, including intrusive memories, increased arousal, emotional reactions and angry outbursts.

Bottom-up processing of emotion means that emotions are generated from a physiological response to environmental stimuli. Top-down processing of emotion means that emotions may begin with thoughts (originating in the prefrontal cortex) and these thoughts may affect other parts of the brain, including the amygdala, which activates the stress response. It has been a long-standing debate whether or not the experience of emotion is a bottom-up or top-down process. Research now suggests that both processes may play a role in the generation of emotion (Ochsner et al., 2010).

The PFC may affect PTSD symptoms through its role in top-down processing. You've seen extensive examples of how our amygdala receives input from our sensory organs, which is bottom-up processing, so let's now turn our attention to the relationship between top-down processing and symptoms of PTSD.

Top-down processing means thoughts and ideas can originate in our mind and

It's interesting to note that high levels of cortisol are not commonly found in people with PTSD. In fact, they tend to have slightly lower than normal levels of PTSD. This has also been a surprising finding for psychologists.

In criminology we focused on bottom-up processing. Now it's time to see how it can work both ways.

that can influence other areas of the brain responsible for processing sensory information, like our amygdala. In other words, instead of our stress response affecting our thoughts (bottom-up), our thoughts can influence our stress response (top-down). This means that negative emotions and the activation of the HPA axis may be generated from our negative thoughts (Taylor et al., 2010). As the PFC functions in executive cognitive control, including controlling our working memory, poor function in this area may explain such symptoms of PTSD, including intrusive memories: if we cannot control the regulation of sensory information in our short-term memory, we may experience unwanted (intrusive) memories that we can't "shake." These intrusive memories are one symptom of PTSD. This may lead to other symptoms, like depression and prolonged negative emotional states: if we can't get rid of our negative thoughts this is likely to get us down and keep us down, so to speak

How you think can influence your emotion. This is a powerful lesson to learn and has many implications for the study of disorders related to emotion.

Numerous studies have shown that the ability to regulate our emotions using top-down processing is an important function of the vmPFC (e.g. Koenigs and Grafman, 2009). Top-down processing by the ventromedial prefrontal cortex (vmPFC) also means that when our amygdala autonomically activates and triggers our stress response, a properly functioning vmPFC helps to regulate this reaction by enabling us to have cognitive control of our thoughts, feelings and emotions. It also results in a decrease in activation of the amygdala.

So while in the previous topic you saw how emotion might affect our cognition, the relationship also works in the other direction: our cognition can affect our emotion. Understanding the role of the vmPFC in top-down regulation of emotion will be important to fully understand how we might be able to treat PTSD, which is something we'll investigate later in this chapter.

You may be able to apply what you've learned in this topic to other topics in this course, such as the origins of violent crime.

Guiding Question:

How might reduced function in the vmPFC explain some symptoms of PTSD?

Critical Thinking Extension:

Making Connections: Think back to the Stanford Marshmallow Experiments. These studies showed that children who were able to exercise an ability to resist the temptation of one marshmallow and wait until they were given two, grew up to be more successful in other areas of life, such as in academics. Knowing what you do about the brain and behaviour, could you hypothesize why demonstrating an ability to perform cognitive control as a young child might lead to success later in life? Another question to consider is could top-down processing also be applied to the study of criminology?

If you're interested…

Psychology Today's online magazine has an article that discusses the debate between the processing of emotion called "Emotional Control: Top-Down or Bottom-Up?"

(c) Cognitive Reappraisal

In the previous section your understanding of the generation of emotions was enhanced by the introduction of a new idea: top-down processing. Our emotions aren't just a product of perception of environmental stimuli, they may also be generated from our thought processes. Understanding this process is important in order to fully comprehend etiologies and treatments of disorders such as PTSD.

The ability to diminish our fear through cognitive reappraisal and top-down processing is a cognitive ability that may be diminished in PTSD patients. Cognitive reappraisal is a strategy used to reduce emotional reactivity by considering the source of the emotion and thinking about it in a different way; the source of the emotion is reappraised, or re-evaluated. It's a type of top-down processing that involves our thought patterns reducing our emotional reaction generated in the amygdala. Understanding the role of cognition and thought patterns in etiologies and treatments of PTSD is just as important as understanding biological bases. In fact, it's hoped that you will be able to see how they're interrelated and can influence one another.

To test the role of the vmPFC in cognitive reappraisal, researchers use an experimental paradigm that involves participants being exposed to emotional stimuli while in an fMRI. They are then instructed to try to alter their emotional response to the stimuli through cognitive reappraisal. Urry et al. (2006) investigated the correlation between the vmPFC and the amygdala during a cognitive reappraisal task using fMRI scanners. In this study, 19 participants were exposed to a range of images while they were in the fMRI. The images were selected carefully so they ranged in ratings of emotional unpleasantness. The aim of the study was to expose participants to images that would induce an emotional response and then record their brain activity as they cognitively reappraised the images.

The reappraisal was manipulated as participants were flashed the images they were told to "increase," "decrease" or "attend." The participants received training in cognitive reappraisal, so they were able to follow the instructions. The strategies they were taught are included in the boxes below.

Increase	• Imagine someone you love experiencing the situation in the image (e.g. a car crash) • Imagine a more intense version of the scene shown in the image (e.g. a vicious dog on a leash is shown in the image, and the participant imagines it breaking free)
Decrease	• Think about the situation as being fake or unreal • Imagine the situation has a better outcome than the one shown (e.g. imagining that the people shown in a horrific car crash all survived and were fine)
Attend	• Maintain focus on the stimuli (control condition)

While the participants were performing these cognitive reappraisals, their brain activity was measured. The results showed that higher activation of the vmPFC during cognitive reappraisal to decrease the emotional effect of the stimuli led to greater reduction of the activity of the amygdala. This supports other similar studies that also demonstrate the role of the vmPFC in cognitive reappraisal and how this can reduce the activation of the amygdala during the processing of emotional stimuli (e.g. Delgado et al., 2008).

Yet again we see the importance of understanding environmental, biological, cognitive and emotional factors contributing to behaviour. If a patient has abnormalities in their prefrontal cortex, they may not be able to perform cognitive reappraisal of affective (emotional) stimuli. This means that their emotional arousal generated in the amygdala and the accompanying negative thoughts will persist, keeping their stressful and emotional state high. An elevated sense of arousal and emotional affect (experiences of negative emotion) are symptoms of PTSD. This could explain some of the other emotional symptoms, such as increased startle responses and angry outbursts.

The research in this section provides you with another demonstration of the concept of localization of brain function.

Cognitive reappraisal also applies to thinking differently about the traumatic event itself. If someone experiences intrusive thoughts or memories about their trauma, they may use cognitive reappraisal strategies they learn in therapy to reduce the emotional impact of these thoughts.

On the other hand, if they have developed thought patterns and constantly make negative appraisals of stimuli, they may be activating their stress response through top-down processes. For instance, someone who is experiencing nightmares or intrusive memories may be thinking, "I can't cope" or "I'll never recover." These thought patterns could be making the anxiety and stress response worse. Thus, cognitive *and* biological factors may explain the development and/or expression of symptoms of PTSD.

One category of symptoms in people with PTSD is also related to the avoidance of people, places and events that might remind them of the trauma. Perhaps through their conditioned fear of stimuli and their inability to regulate their emotional reaction because of their hypo-responsive vmPFC, patients with PTSD may find it easier to simply stay away from places that might trigger emotional reactions that they can't control. This may lead to feelings of isolation and depression.

From what you've learned in the unit on meditation and mindfulness and their effects on the prefrontal cortex volume, and top-down control of the amygdala during

Hypo-responsive is the opposite of hyper-responsive. If something is hyper it means it's overactive. A hypo-responsive area of the brain means it *lacks* reactivity to stimuli.

processing of emotional stimuli, you might be getting an idea of how treatments could be developed so that cognitive practice might lead to long-term structural changes in the brain. These treatments are the basis of a topic covered later in this chapter.

Guiding Question:

How might a hypo-responsive vmPFC influence emotional reactions to stimuli?

Critical Thinking Extension:

Alternative Explanations: So far we've looked at biological and cognitive etiologies of PTSD. Can you think of how cultural and/or sociocultural factors may be influential in the development of symptoms of PTSD? Think about what you've learned already about the environment and brain development.

If you're interested…

It helps to make learning about psychological disorders concrete by hearing real life stories about how people cope with this disorder. Devin Mitchell is a photographer who has produced a series of photos of people coping with PTSD and how they see themselves. The images are quite powerful and can provide some insights into the psychological effects of this disorder.

Relevant Topics

- Explanations for Disorders
- Etiology of Abnormal Psychology
- Cognitive Processing
- Emotion and Cognition

Practice Exam Questions

- Discuss two explanations for one or more disorders.
- To what extent can disorders be explained from the biological approach?
- Outline one study related to emotion and cognition.
- Discuss one ethical consideration relevant to the study of etiologies of abnormal psychology.

Research Methods

Urry et al.'s 2006 study is another example of the use of the true experiment when researching explanations of disorders. In this study, the researchers control the environment and extraneous variables. They also manipulate the independent variable, which is the type of cognitive appraisal of the stimuli that the participants are to perform. The dependent variable is the measure of the brain function during this particular task. Through the use of the experimental design you might think that researchers can draw a cause-and-effect relationship between the type of cognitive appraisal being practiced and the part of the area of the brain that is functioning. However, when using fMRIs and measuring brain activity, researchers need to be wary about drawing such cause-and-effect relationships. For example, do we know it's the cognitive appraisal that is causing the brain to function, or the function of the brain that is enabling the cognitive appraisal? This ambiguity means we can often only draw correlational conclusions when using fMRIs.

Ethical Considerations

Many of the studies you have seen involve exposing participants to stimuli that are designed to provoke an emotional reaction of some kind. This has obvious ethical implications. Informed consent would be important to ensure that the participants are not surprised by what they are asked to do while in such an experiment. The right to withdraw would also be important if the task became too stressful. This would be an especially important consideration if you were exposing victims of trauma to trauma-related stimuli.

4.5 Prevalence of PTSD

Are some people more prone to PTSD than others?

(a) Gender Differences

When discussing psychological disorders, prevalence refers to the frequency of diagnosis for a particular disorder. A prevalence rate is the percentage of a population that are diagnosed with that disorder. It's important to investigate differences in prevalence rates across different groups of people, as this might help identify certain individuals or groups who are at-risk for developing particular disorders. In this topic we are going to look at three factors that may influence prevalence rates of PTSD: gender, socioeconomic status and developmental influences during childhood.

One of the most commonly cited differences in the prevalence of PTSD is related to gender. Some studies have shown that females may be twice as likely to develop PTSD, despite reduced exposure to traumatic events (Irish et al., 2011). The aim of this section is to provide you with a possible explanation for this increased likelihood for females to develop symptoms of PTSD. Specifically, we'll look at how gender differences in cognitive appraisal and thought patterns might explain the difference in prevalence rates for men and women.

Before we look at the role of gender, let's first recap how negative appraisal may influence PTSD symptoms, as numerous studies have shown that negative appraisals of traumatic events increases the likelihood of developing PTSD (e.g. Nixon et al., 2005). A negative appraisal means making a negative evaluation or assessment about the stressor and/or one's ability to cope with it. These negative appraisals may have an effect on our physiology through the top-down activation of the stress response. If we have continual negative thought patterns this may increase our stress response and lead to increased activation of biological patterns of stress, such as prolonged activity of the HPA axis. This top-down effect of negative appraisal may explain negative emotions, such as distress, panic, and fearful reactions to environmental stimuli. This could explain symptoms of PTSD related to anxiety and arousal, such as hypervigilance, exaggerated startle responses, irritability and/or angry outbursts.

In order to compare gender differences in post-traumatic vulnerability after a series of terrorist attacks in Israel in the early 2000s, Solomon et al. (2005) gathered data from over 500 men and women. They used questionnaires to gather a representative sample of the adult Israeli population and the questionnaires gathered data on a range of factors related to cognitive appraisals of the attacks, such as self-efficacy and sense of threat. The sense of threat in this context refers to the extent to which an individual feels that the stressor is threatening and dangerous, while self-efficacy refers to how likely an individual will feel confident in being able to deal with the stressor and its emotional impact. If someone has high self-efficacy it means that they believe that they will be able to cope with threat, including its effects.

The results showed that men were significantly more likely to be exposed to traumatic events than females, yet females reported higher levels of trauma and stress-related symptoms than men. PTSD was also six times more common in women. While it's natural to assume that more exposure to stressful and potentially traumatic

---

A lifetime prevalence rate refers to the percentage of a population that are diagnosed with a particular disorder at some point in their lifetime.

It's important to note that prevalence rates vary across cultures.

Negative appraisal: When talking about PTSD, this means making a negative assessment or judgement about a stressor. For example, an Israeli may have thought that they couldn't cope with the attacks and that they were probably going to die. This is a negative appraisal.

Self-efficacy: the extent to which you are confident in your ability to complete a task or achieve something. In the context of PTSD, it refers to one's belief in their ability to cope with the stressor and its effects.

events would increase the likelihood of developing PTSD, these results suggest that exposure alone cannot explain the difference in prevalence rates of PTSD.

The difference may be explained through the different cognitive appraisals of the situations made by men and women. The researchers found that males were generally more positive about the future and they displayed higher levels of self-efficacy - they had greater confidence in their ability to cope with attacks and terror related events. This difference in thought processes may explain the difference in the prevalence of the trauma related symptoms shown in the studies. If someone feels like they are unable to cope with traumatic events and that circumstances are beyond their control, this is a negative appraisal and may activate stress related emotions and physiological symptoms. However, if someone feels in control and can positively appraise stressors, they may reduce their likelihood of developing symptoms of PTSD like a persistent negative emotional state.

Having confidence and high self-efficacy can reduce the chances of a traumatic experience leading to PTSD. If you think that you can overcome something, this will have positive physiological effects.

Similarly, females in the study were also more likely to report a higher sense of threat from the attacks and were more afraid for their own safety and for the safety of family members. This gender difference in the cognitive appraisal of the situation being more threatening corroborates other research that suggests females may rate negative life experiences as being more negative and less controllable than men (e.g. Matud, 2004).

In summary, while the increase in prevalence for PTSD in females might seem easily attributable to an increase in exposure to traumatic events, research suggests that even though males are exposed to more trauma, they are less likely to develop PTSD. This could be because of differences in cognitive appraisals and thought patterns, which might lead to different emotional responses to the stressor. It's important to remember, however, that there are multiple factors in PTSD that are not accounted for by these cognitive differences between males and females.

One symptom of PTSD is a persistent negative emotional state. This means that an individual feels a negative emotion (e.g. fear, horror, guilt, shame, etc.) for an extended period of time.

It's interesting to note that gender differences have also been found in the function of the amygdala in response to emotional stimuli. This might explain gender differences in the development of PTSD and responses to emotional events.

Guiding Question:
Why might females be more likely to develop PTSD than males?

Critical Thinking Extension:
Population Validity: Solomon et al.'s study was carried out on Israeli participants and was related to a very particular type of traumatic event. Could you think of plausible reasons why these results may not be generalizable to another specific culture and/or type of traumatic event?

If you're interested…

The full article of Solomon et al.'s 2005 study is available online and is written in a language that is accessible to most IB students. In their discussion they offer interesting explanations for possible cultural factors related to Israeli culture that may affect the differences in gender responses to trauma. They also discuss how gender roles may change during times of war, which could help explain the difference in prevalence of PSTD.

(b)　Race and Socioeconomic Status

Both explanations in this section could be grouped under the term social status, which refers to things like employment and level of wealth and education.

An important sociocultural explanation for the development of PTSD is the likelihood that one is going to be exposed to a traumatic event. In Solomon et al.'s study about Israeli's experiences of terrorist attacks, it might be natural to assume that as a whole Israelis during this period of time would have a higher incidence of PTSD compared with many populations, as they are exposed to far more acts of terror than other areas.

Similarly, one's occupation could also increase chances of developing PTSD as it may increase exposure to trauma, thus increasing chances of developing aversive reactions to this exposure. For instance, serving in the military and experiencing combat would increase the exposure to traumatic events and explain the increased prevalence rate of PTSD in veterans compared with non-veterans. PTSD has a lifetime prevalence rate of 8% in the general population but it's as high as 30% in war veterans who have seen active combat (Kessler et al., 1995, 2005; Koenen et al., 2008). This difference in prevalence could be easily explained due to the fact that if you're constantly exposed to traumatic events, you are likely to experience high levels of stress for a prolonged period of time.

Interestingly, significant differences have been found in US soldiers of different races who fought in the Vietnam War. Numerous studies have shown that the prevalence of PTSD tends to be highest in Hispanic and black veterans, with the lowest prevalence in white veterans. There have been many possible explanations put forward to explain this difference in prevalence, including the fact that ethnic minorities may be exposed to more direct combat and more stress during their service (Green et al., 1990). If racial minorities had higher exposure to extreme stress and direct combat during their service, as studies have indicated, this may explain their higher prevalence rate of PTSD diagnosis.

Socioeconomic factors may influence cognitive appraisals of devastating events, like the 2011 tsunami in Japan.

Another contributing factor may be the amount of stress *after* the war experience. If you know about the historical context of the Vietnam War, during this time back home in the United States the Civil Rights Movement was in full swing. Many blacks, Hispanics and other minority groups were fighting for equal rights and upon their return, soldiers from these minority groups may have experienced more aversive events than their white comrades. Perhaps this may contribute to the difference in the prevalence rates of PTSD among Vietnam War veterans (Schlenger & Fairbank, 1996).

This provides us with one example of racial differences in the prevalence of PTSD symptoms with some possible explanations. Let's move away from war and look at how race and socioeconomic status might be related to the development of PTSD after exposure to a different type of traumatic event: a natural disaster.

If we experience a natural disaster, like a hurricane that destroys our property, our ability to deal with this disaster will have significant effects on our cognitive appraisals. If we lose everything but we've got plenty of money and resources to cope, our thought patterns may be more focused on how to deal with the stressor and overcome the effects. However, if we have low socioeconomic status and we lose our homes and/or other valuable possessions in a natural disaster, our cognitive appraisals of the event may be far more negative. We may have anxious or negative thoughts about the impacts of the disaster and how we're going to cope financially.

This may explain differences in the prevalence of PTSD in Florida after Hurricane Andrew. Garrison et al. (1995) investigated the cross-cultural differences in PTSD symptoms after Hurricane Andrew. They studied around 350 black, Hispanic and Caucasian teenaged participants six months after the hurricane. The researchers used a structured interview and focused on such things as "disaster experiences and emotional reaction, disaster-related losses, lifetime exposure to violent or traumatic events, recent stressful experiences, and psychiatric symptomatology." The results showed approximately 9% of females and 3% of males across the sample met the criteria for PTSD. This is similar to previous research that we've than shows a gender difference in prevalence rates. In terms of racial differences, the rates were highest amongst blacks and Hispanics (8.3% and 6.1% respectively) and increased with age.

The number of stressful events that were experienced after the disaster had a stronger correlation with PTSD symptoms than the severity of the experience *during* the actual hurricane. These events could be related to the ability to cope with the damage of the hurricane. One possible explanation for the increased prevalence rates could be economic disparity that exists between racial groups. Income statistics suggest there is a large disparity between the levels of wealth based on race in the USA, with whites (non-Hispanics) having an average net worth of around seven times more than non-whites (pewresearch.org). When a natural disaster strikes there is significant material damage. If a family struggles to find the economic resources to deal with the aftermath of such an event, this may increase the stress and anxiety caused by the disaster. That is to say, socioeconomic status might affect an individual or a family's ability to cope with a situation that threatens their livelihood. This additional stress could increase negative cognitive appraisals of the traumatic event, which could lead to a higher rate of PTSD symptoms when compared to other ethnic groups that are more economically secure.

This explanation is consistent with other studies investigating PTSD rates that have also demonstrated a negative correlation between income and the development of PTSD symptoms following a traumatic event (Irish et al., 2011).

In summary, an obvious sociocultural factor that could explain differences in prevalence rates is an individual's occupation and/or likelihood to be exposed to trauma. However, studies on the effects of natural disasters have also revealed racial differences in the development of PTSD. This could be explained through the interaction of socioeconomic status and cognitive appraisals.

Socioeconomic status refers to one's social and economic standing in society.

Psychiatric symptomatology: A group of symptoms related to a psychiatric disorder, in this case symptoms related to PTSD.

Net worth: a measure of wealth and socioeconomic status that involves adding the total value of one's assets and subtracting liabilities.

Here we can see another example of how social variables may influence cognition, which could explain behaviour. Understanding these relationships is essential for deep understanding.

Critical Thinking Extension:

Alternative Explanations: Can you think of any alternative explanations that might exist for differences in prevalence rates of PTSD in Garrison et al's study? You may also want to consider the sample of this study: the sample studied teenagers. How might this offer a potential limitation in the explanation provided?

If you're interested…

Richard Wilkinson discusses global economic inequalities in his TED Talk "How economic inequality harms societies." This is an interesting example of how subjects like economics and psychology can overlap. It's also a good video to watch to understand the practice and value of using correlational analyses to draw conclusions.

(c)   *Developmental Influences*

So far in this topic we've explored three differences in prevalence rates based on:

- Gender
- Occupation
- Social (and socioeconomic) status

The final factor that will be explored in this topic relates to developmental influences and how our experiences when we're young may influence probabilities of developing PTSD later in life. Numerous studies have shown that experiencing traumatic experiences as a child may increase the chances of developing PTSD as a result of experiencing a traumatic event later in life (e.g. Breslau et al., 1999). There are numerous possible explanations for this and in this section we'll explore just a few.

You may be asked about the influence of biological, cognitive and/or sociocultural factors' influence on the prevalence of PTSD, so as with all topics the more you understand from this topic the better prepared you will be.

As you may remember from the unit on criminology, there have numerous studies into the effects of childhood experiences on brain development. This may provide an alternative explanation for differences based on socioeconomic status to that offered in the previous topic. Another study by Luby et al. (2014) conducted a longitudinal study that gathered data over five to ten years from kids beginning from age three to six. The findings from their studies corroborate other evidence that shows correlations between poverty and brain development. In this study, children raised in poverty were more likely to have lower volume in their amygdala and their hippocampus. Remember the twin study earlier that showed low hippocampal volume may be a risk factor for PTSD? While genetics may explain lower volume in the hippocampus, it may also be a result of experiencing poverty as a child. Perhaps experiencing poverty and deprived environments as a child leads to the development of the neurological abnormalities that are potential risk factors for developing PTSD.

Another interesting finding from Luby et al.'s study was the relationship between parenting and hippocampal development. In one of the assessment procedures, the researchers used a procedural paradigm that is often used to measure parenting. They put the child and their parent (or caregiver) in a room with a brightly coloured gift within arm's reach of the child. Similar to the marshmallow studies, they tell the child that they are not allowed to open the gift until their parent completes all the questionnaires. This is done to put some stress on the child-parent relationship as the child will presumably be impatient to open the gift, and the parent will feel some pressure to

Parenting styles can have significant influences on a child, including their brain development.

complete the questionnaires. Trained observers measure the interactions between the parent and the child. They measure supportive versus hostile strategies used by the parent towards the child. A supportive strategy might be praising the child for waiting while a hostile strategy might involve threatening them with punishments if they don't follow the rules or sit still and "stop nagging!"

Could the caregiver-child relationship be influenced by socioeconomic variables?

The HL Extension lessons on the TPH-2 gene might also be relevant to the concepts discussed in this section.

The results from this study support other studies that show a positive correlation between supportive parenting and hippocampal development. The more positive and supportive parenting strategies that were used, the more likely the child was to have higher volume in their hippocampus. This corroborates other findings that measure correlations between neurocognitive development and more extreme forms of neglect and abuse than the one described above (e.g. Gould et al., 2013).

As you can see, there are a number of possible interacting factors that could be contributing to the development of neurological risk factors that could explain the development of PTSD later in life. Growing up in an emotionally, physically or psychologically deprived environment could lead to a lack of development in important areas of the brain, such as the hippocampus. Even more moderate parent-child interactions and relationships could influence physical and psychological development.

Guiding Question:

How might childhood experiences increase the development of risk factors associated with PTSD?

Critical Thinking Extension:

Making Connections and Hypotheses: There are some possible connections between the various possible factors that may influence prevalence that have deliberately not been explained. For instance, Chiu et al.'s 2011 study is one of many that has found an association between socioeconomic status and PTSD. How might parent-child relationships interact with socioeconomic status to explain these findings?

If you're interested…

Nadine Burke has an excellent TED Talk on the effects of childhood trauma, "How childhood trauma affects health across a lifetime." You may also be interested in learning more about the longitudinal Adverse Childhood Experiences (ACE) study she references. This study tracks individuals throughout their lifetime and draws correlations between childhood experiences and later outcomes.

- Etiologies of abnormal psychology
- Explanations for disorders
- Prevalence rates and disorders
- Neuroplasticity
- The brain and behaviour

Practice Exam Questions

- Discuss one or more etiologies of abnormal psychology.
- Contrast two explanations for one disorder.
- Discuss the prevalence rates of one disorder.
- Evaluate research related to etiologies of abnormal psychology.
- Outline one study related to neuroplasticity.

Research Methods

Luby et al.'s (2014) study is a good example of the value of a correlational study as both variables can co-vary. The researchers used observations to gather data on the rate of supporting and/or hostile strategies used by the parent to motivate the child to wait to open the gift. This data can then be correlated with the volume of the hippocampus in the children, which is another variable that can vary between participants. This highlights one of the values of the correlational study in that it can provide insights into possible relationships between variables (like parenting) and developmental factors (like brain development). However, the correlational study is inherently limited by the fact that it can only draw correlations and one must be extremely careful when drawing conclusions (and applying them) from correlational data. There might be other variables involved as well, such as socio-economic status. As we saw, poverty is correlated with low hippocampal volume. Poverty might also be a source of stress and anxiety; it's possible that parents from lower socioeconomic backgrounds may be dealing with more stress than other parents and this affects their patience and their parenting. This is one example of how it's important to consider multiple factors when drawing conclusions from correlational data.

Ethical Considerations

We've seen in other studies, ethical concerns are abound when studying children. They're compounded when parenting and brain development are involved. In Luby et al.'s study parental/caregiver consent would be a must as the kids would have been required to undergo MRI scanning in order to measure their hippocampal volume. The researchers would not have been able to provide full disclosure as to the nature of the research and its aims *before* it was conducted, as this may have led to social desirability effects: caregivers would want to be seen as good parents in the eyes of the researcher. Some deception was therefore necessary. Like other studies involving deception, debriefing would be important. Ensuring anonymity would have also been imperative in this study, as the caregivers would not want sensitive information about their parenting styles shared.

4.6 Biological Treatment

How can we use drugs to treat the symptoms of PTSD?

(a)   Drug Therapy and SSRIs

Now that we've thoroughly explored etiologies of PTSD, it's time to turn our attention to treatments. Determining how to treat people suffering from psychological disorders is an ancient debate and the history of psychiatry is fascinating, but often very troubling. A common historical practice has been to put people suffering from mental illness in psychiatric hospitals, which were often called "mad houses" or "looney bins." Thankfully our understanding of psychological disorders is far better now, but best approaches to treatment still remains highly debated.

Treating disorders is an ancient practice with early methods including trephining, which involved cutting a hole in someone's head. Ancient cultures perhaps realized that the source of psychological disorders lay in the activity of the brain. In order to relieve the tension and stress in the brain, or to allow evil spirits to escape, individuals' brains had holes drilled into them. Skulls have been found with new growth of the skull around the hole, suggesting individuals lived through this treatment.

During the 1940s another technique was developed to alter the structure and functioning of the brain: the frontal lobotomy. This was a gruesome treatment that involves hammering an icepick into the frontal lobes of patients and disconnecting the frontal lobe from the rest of the brain. From what you've learned about the role of the frontal lobe in complex cognitive processing, you may be able to imagine some of the effects of this treatment: patients' emotions were blunted, and their intellect, self-awareness and thinking ability were impaired. The developer of the frontal lobotomy shared the Nobel Prize for medicine in 1949, although this is not without controversy.

Psychiatry is the study and treatment of mental illness.

You can find many interesting documentaries online about the history of psychiatry and psychiatric hospitals, including BBC's "Mental: A history of the madhouse."

Trephining and the **frontal lobotomy** are included here for purposes of interest. In exams, you're better to focus on SSRIs and modern treatments.

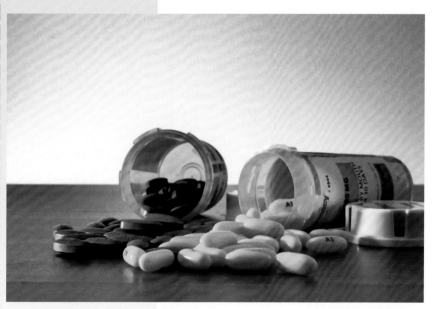

Like other biological treatments, pharmacotherapy (drug therapy) is based on the assumption that the cause of symptoms is physiological.

The frontal lobotomy was practiced throughout the USA and other Western countries through the 1940s and 1950s. However, the development of drug therapy led to the demise of the use of the lobotomy as a psychiatric treatment. Drug therapy is the common practice of treating disorders with pills and medications. It's a desirable form of treatment because it's relative easy, cheap, can be self-administered, and the effects are experienced in a short period of time (within a couple of weeks). This may be why around 50% of European adults use prescription medication (Eurostat online).

Drugs alter brain function through their effect on neurotransmission. For example, people lose their impulse control after drinking because the alcohol is influencing neurotransmission and inhibiting activity in their prefrontal cortex. Drugs used to treat disorders are no different. Their effects are a result of increasing or decreasing circulating neurotransmitter levels in areas of the brain.

If you remember from the earlier chapter on criminology, neurons communicate with each other by sending messages. Drugs can influence neurotransmission by increasing or decreasing the amount of specific neurotransmitters that are involved in this communication process. This will impact the functioning of neural pathways in areas of the brain where the drugs are having an effect. Neurotransmitters like serotonin are fired from the pre-synaptic neuron into the synapse. When they are in the synapse they bind to receptor cites on the post-synaptic neuron. This binding on the post-synaptic neuron is how the pre-synaptic neuron sends messages to the post-synaptic neuron.

Neurotransmitters can be inhibitory or excitatory. An excitatory neurotransmitter stimulates neural activity, while an inhibitory one inhibits it.

The only prescribed drugs for PTSD approved by the FDA in the USA are selective serotonin reuptake inhibitors (SSRIs). You may know some SSRIs by other names such as Zoloft, Prozac and Paroxetine. SSRIs are known as selective because they appear to primarily affect serotonin, not other neurotransmitters. A common finding in people who suffer from depression and anxiety related disorders (e.g. PTSD) is that there is dysfunction in their serotonin systems (e.g. Murrough et al., 2011). SSRIs might help by improving the effectiveness of serotonin transmission in the brains of people with these disorders.

There is currently no way to measure serotonin levels in the brains of living people. Serotonin levels have to be measured using other means, such as taking samples of blood and spinal fluids.

SSRIs work by blocking the reuptake of serotonin. After neurotransmitters are fired into the synapse they bind with the receptor sites of the post-synaptic neuron. After this binding and sending of their signal, they are released back into the synapse. They are then either broken down in the synapse by enzymes, or they are reabsorbed into the pre-synaptic neuron. This process of reabsorption is called reuptake. By blocking the receptors responsible for the reuptake of serotonin, the SSRIs increase the available serotonin in the synapse, resulting in increased stimulation of the receptor sites of the post-synaptic neuron. This process continues throughout neural pathways in the brain. So by increasing serotonin in the synapse, SSRIs increase the likelihood that serotonin will bind with receptor cites and send signals between neurons.

SSRIs have been shown to be an effective biological treatment for PTSD.

SSRIs are recommended as a first line of treatment for PTSD as there is robust evidence that shows that they are effective in treating PTSD symptoms (Stein et al., 2000). For example, MacNamara et al. (2015) treated 17 US war veterans for 12 weeks with SSRIs and found that 12 of the 17 veterans had at least a 50% reduction in symptoms.

From this section it's hope you can see how SSRIs might work and you have some evidence to show that they are helpful in treating PTSD. In the next section we'll use further details from MacNamara's study to explore just *how* SSRIs might be effective in treating symptoms (and etiologies) of PTSD.

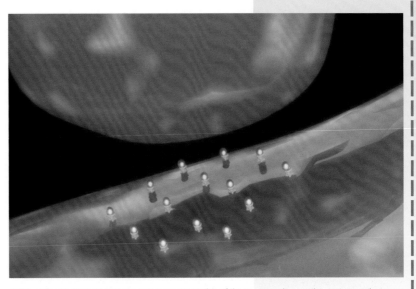

In this close-up diagram you can see a representation of the receptor sites on the post-synaptic neuron being stimulated by neurotransmitters.

Guiding Question:

How do SSRIs influence neurotransmission?

Critical Thinking Extension:

Hypotheses: From what you know about the possible etiologies of PTSD, can you hypothesize what areas of the brain SSRIs might influence in order to treat PTSD?

If you're interested…

There's an online "game" you can play called 'Mouse Party' (learn.genetics. utah). You select cartoon mice that are on different drugs and drop them into a chair to see what's going on inside their brains as a result of the drugs. You can also find numerous videos on our blog that show how SSRIs work.

(b)   *Effectiveness of SSRIs*

Selective serotonin reuptake inhibitors (SSRIs) are a common treatment for several disorders, including PTSD. People suffering from depression are often prescribed SSRIs such as Prozac, and one reason this may work is that depression has been correlated with dysfunction in serotonergic mechanisms. By increasing the levels of serotonin in the synapse, an individual may be able to have a more stable mood, as mood regulation is one role of serotonin. In this section we're going to explore in a little more depth the effectiveness of SSRIs in treating PTSD.

Serotonergic mechanisms refers to the receptor sites and other parts of neurons involved in the transmission of serotonin.

If you remember from criminology, serotonin can influence the functioning of the prefrontal cortex, especially when we're perceiving emotional stimuli. Passamonti et al.'s study (2012) showed that when serotonin levels were reduced after drinking a substance that lacked tryptophan, participants showed reduced connectivity between their amygdala and their prefrontal cortex when viewing angry faces, but not when viewing neutral or happy ones. With reduced PFC activity, an individual may be less able to perform cognitive reappraisals and reduce the activity in their amygdala.

This can be further seen in the MacNamara et al. (2015) study using war veterans and cognitive reappraisal tasks. In this study there were 34 male veterans of Operation Iraqi Freedom (OIF) and Operation Enduring Freedom (OEF); 17 were diagnosed with PTSD and 17 without PSTD. They all underwent an fMRI scan while they were doing an emotional regulation task that required top-down processing and cognitive reappraisal of emotional stimuli. This is similar to studies described earlier in this chapter where participants saw unpleasant images and had to "maintain" or "reappraise." In the maintain condition they experienced the images naturally, while in the reappraise condition they used strategies to try to reduce the negative affect of the unpleasant images.

> Making connections across topics and units in this course will help deepen your understanding of important concepts, like how transmission of serotonin may influence PTSD symptoms.

After this first set of gathering data, there was a 12 week break before they were tested again with the same task. However, within the 12 weeks the participants with PTSD were treated with an SSRI called paroxetine. After the 12 weeks of treatment all participants did the same emotional reappraisal task in the fMRI. The results showed that the paroxetine was effective in reducing the symptoms of the PTSD. After the 12 weeks of treatment, 70% of the PTSD group (12/17) showed at least a 50% reduction in their PTSD symptoms. This result alone suggests that the SSRI paroxetine is effective in treating PTSD.

In this image of an fMRI scan you can see the area of the sensory motor area (SMA). The anterior cingulate cortex (ACC) is a part of the vmPFC and will be the subject of a study later in this chapter.

The results also corroborated other evidence that shows SSRIs can increase function in areas within the prefrontal cortex during cognitive reappraisal. There was an increase in activation in the dorsolateral prefrontal cortex, an area of the brain associated with the maintenance of emotional regulation. The results also showed increased activation in the supplementary motor area (SMA), an area of the brain near the PFC. This is another area of the brain that has been correlated with top-down processing and down-regulation of the amygdala (ibid).

> The study in this section can show us how SSRIs might work to treat PTSD.

From this study and others like it that show similar results, we can get a clearer understanding of how SSRIs might treat the symptoms of PTSD. By increasing the levels of serotonin available in particular areas of the brain, such as the PFC and the SMA, these areas of the brain may be able to have improved function. Improved function in these areas of the brain will enable an individual suffering from PTSD to perform important cognitive tasks that may help reduce their anxiety and stressful reactions to emotional stimuli, including cognitive reappraisal of emotional stimuli.

While this is surely beneficial, the use of drug therapy may be limited in addressing the underlying biological correlates of psychological disorders, such as decreased volume in the PFC. Also, this treatment was only over a three month period and what might happen if a person stopped taking their medication? In the next topic we'll look at treatments that address the cognitive side of PTSD and that may be able to effect long-term neurological change.

Guiding Question:

How might SSRIs reduce symptoms of PTSD?

Critical Thinking Extension:

Treating Symptoms or Etiologies: We can see from this evidence that SSRIs might be pretty good at reducing the symptoms of PTSD. But is this really effective in treating PTSD? The aim of therapy for disorders should be to alleviate symptoms, but also to address root causes. Can you think of some potential etiologies of PTSD that SSRIs may not be able to address?

If you're interested...

The National Centre for Biotechnology Information (NCBI) is an excellent source of original journal articles. Many of the studies cited in this text come from this source. If you're interested in learning about how we can increase serotonin without drugs, you can read a full original article on this cite called "How to increase serotonin in the human brain without drugs." Not surprisingly, diet, exercise and getting outdoors are three factors explained in this article.

- Treatment of Disorders
- Biological Treatment
- Assessing the effectiveness of treatment
- The brain and behaviour
- Techniques used to study the brain in relation to behaviour
- Neuroplasticity
- Neurotransmitters and their effect on behaviour

Practice Exam Questions

- Explain how one neurotransmitter may have an effect on human behaviour.
- Discuss one technique used to study the brain in relation to behaviour.
- Evaluate the effectiveness of one biological treatment for one or more disorders.
- To what extent is one biological treatment effective in treating psychological disorders?

Research Methods

A common experimental paradigm for testing the effectiveness of drug therapy is to conduct a tightly controlled clinical drug trial using the true experiment method. In these designs, participants are randomly allocated to a treatment (drug) or control (placebo) group. The participants take the drugs over a period of time and its effectiveness is measured. No such study has been included in this section, as they often do not tell us much about *how* the drug works to treat the disorder. For this reason, MacNamara et al.'s study was used. There were many aspects of this study that were excluded from the description, because they are not immediately relevant to the effects of SSRIs that were are focusing on. The full methodology of this study highlights the difficulty in classifying studies onto black-and-white categories of research methods. A good challenge would be to find the original article (the full article is available online) and determine what research method you think this best suits. The research methods for treatments will also be explained after the next topic.

Ethical Considerations

Studies using ingestion would require informed consent to be gathered from participants as there are ethical issues with asking people to consume substances without their knowledge of what the effects might be. In MacNamara et al.'s study researchers would need to carefully consider just how much information to reveal to the participants. On the one hand, if they told them they were receiving SSRIs that might help their symptoms the patients may experience better recovery due to the combined effects of the medication and the placebo effect. However, they were interested in investigating the effects of the SSRIs on brain function, so they would want to try to isolate this variable; this may lead the researchers to decide to withhold some information until the debriefing process.

4.7 Psychological Treatments
How can we address the etiologies of PTSD?

(a) Exposure Therapies (ET)

There are many positives in using drug therapy to treat disorders: it's easy, can be self-administered, works relatively quickly, and is cheaper than individual therapy sessions. But there are a few downsides, too. SSRIs are selective, but this doesn't mean that they are selective in the particular neural networks that they influence. This could explain why there are often unwanted side-effects of taking medication: an increase in serotonin in the PFC may be beneficial, but increasing serotonin in other areas of the brain may cause other unwanted effects.

Another limitation of drug therapy is that it might treat the symptoms of a disorder (e.g. depression or feelings of anxiety), but it may not address the underlying cognitive etiologies. We saw earlier that paroxetine can increase function in the PFC and the SMA, although it may not help patients who can't effectively reappraise emotional stimuli in the first place. It also might not help the structural abnormalities that are so commonly observed in patients with PTSD, such as hippocampal volume.

Before the invention of drug therapy, people have sought the help of psychiatrists to help them overcome their mental health problems. Cognitive Behavioural Therapy (CBT) is an umbrella term that includes many types of treatment that seek to align behaviour, emotion, and thinking. Whereas drug therapy is based on the assumption that disorders are caused by chemical imbalances in the brain, CBT is based on the assumption that disorders are a product of a disruption in thinking, behaviour and emotion. A particular type of CBT is exposure therapy (ET), which is another

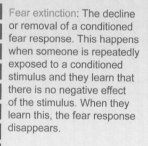

Treatments that only aim to alleviate symptoms and not treat causes are often called palliative treatments.

Fear extinction: The decline or removal of a conditioned fear response. This happens when someone is repeatedly exposed to a conditioned stimulus and they learn that there is no negative effect of the stimulus. When they learn this, the fear response disappears.

Using virtual reality technology can help with the fear extinction process. This is also used to treat anxiety disorders like phobias.

broad term that covers multiple different types of psychological treatments. Types of ET include virtual reality exposure therapy (VRET), systematic desensitization and flooding. ET attempts to treat PTSD and other anxiety disorders by using fear extinction. As you've learned, fear conditioning is the process of associating particular stimuli with aversive and unpleasant reactions. This is a form of learning and it's at the core of understanding PTSD. Fear extinction occurs when the conditioned stimulus is repeatedly presented to someone with no aversive stimulus. This results in new learning; i.e. the stimulus isn't harmful. ET is often used in other anxiety disorders as well, such as phobias. By exposing patients to emotionally arousing stimuli in any number of different ways, ET aims to treat the aversive associations individuals make with particular stimuli.

The amygdala and the ventromedial prefrontal cortex (vmPFC) have been shown to play a role in fear extinction, which could also explain why abnormal functions in these areas of the brain may be correlated with PTSD. Individuals with healthy functioning in these areas may find it easier to able to extinguish their conditioned or instinctual fear response to stressors or reminders of the stressor. Without the proper functioning in these areas of the brain, the conditioned fear may remain. We'll see in the next section how exposure therapy can improve function in these areas.

Systematic desensitization involves gradually exposing someone to increasingly arousing stimuli. An example of using systematic desensitization could be when treating phobias. If someone was afraid of snakes they might see a picture of a snake, or lots of pictures. They would slowly look through the pictures until they could manage to control their responses. They may then hold a toy snake, gradually increasing this to a more life-like rubber snake and then eventually they may be able to hold a real snake. The end goal is similar to flooding, but the process is done more gradually.

Another type of exposure therapy is imagination therapy. Just as it sounds, this requires participants to use their imagination in order to expose themselves to their stressor. One obvious limitation of this form of treatment, however, is the fact that some people may be better at using their imagination than others. The clinician also can't see what the person's thinking, so it may be difficult for them to manage the sessions.

One new form of treatment for PTSD that is growing in popularity is virtual reality exposure therapy (VRET). Like other forms of exposure therapy, there are many variations of VRET but they essentially use the same paradigm: participants use virtual reality technology to re-experience events and situations that have been designed to reflect their stressor. For example, a war veteran may be put in a simulated battlefield and asked to relive his or her experiences. Or perhaps someone who experienced a car crash and gets flashbacks every time they try to drive would be put in a virtual world where they can experience driving a car again.

The idea behind VRET is that it uses the principles of fear extinction to treat the symptoms of PTSD. Patients would probably experience startle responses, autonomic physiological arousal and hyper-responsiveness while experiencing the virtual world. But because they know they are in a safe place (the clinician's room) and the stimuli is not real, they may be able to learn to change their emotional appraisals of stimuli. Knowing that the stimuli is harmless and doesn't pose a threat would help shift their cognitive appraisals and patterns, and help extinguish conditioned fears.

In summary, the fear extinction paradigm involves repeated exposure to the conditioned stimulus without the presence of an aversive stimulus. This is not a case of unlearning the fear response, but is actually a new form of learning whereby the person learns that the stimulus is non-threatening. The prolonged exposure in the comforting

Flooding may be used as a treatment of anxiety disorders and attempts to treat the fear of particular stimuli by immersing the patient in exposure to the stimuli. For example, if someone had a phobia of cats they may be put in a room filled with cats. An obvious downside to this treatment is that it has obvious ethical considerations associated with it.

Virtual Reality Exposure Therapy can help people to remove their conditioned fear responses through exposure to stimuli without aversive consequences.

and supportive atmosphere of a caring environment can help the extinction training reduce the effects of perceptions of conditioned stimuli. Through regular exposure to trauma-related stimuli during the virtual reality sessions, patients experiencing PTSD symptoms may be able to extinguish their conditioned fears.

Guiding Question:

How can fear extinction be accomplished with exposure therapy?

Critical Thinking Extension:

Limitations: In this section you've seen how psychological therapies such as exposure therapy can help to treat cognitive etiologies of PTSD. Can you think of any possible limitations in using this form of treatment?

If you're interested...

Dr. Brenda Wiederhold's TED Talk, "Can Virtual Reality Ease Post-traumatic Stress Disorder" provides some personal insights into the treatment of PTSD. Hearing personal stories about PTSD and its treatment can take what we're learning from the page and make it feel more "real." ABCNews has another good short video about the use of VRET, including an interview with a leading researcher in this field, Albert "Skip" Rizzo.

(b) Effectiveness of Psychological Treatments

Earlier in the chapter we looked at fear conditioning, which is when someone is conditioned to feel fear. One of the possible reasons why individuals may develop PTSD is because they have dysfunction or abnormalities in the brain that may enhance fear conditioning and/or make fear extinction more difficult. For example, increased amygdala activity has been shown in people with PTSD during fear conditioning tasks (Bremner et al., 2005). A hyper-responsive amygdala might enhance acquisition of learned fear responses. It might also increase emotional and physiological reaction to stimuli after the traumatic experience and with repeated exposure to stimuli that remind the person of the stressor.

The ventromedial prefrontal cortex (vmPFC) also plays a role in fear extinction which may help to explain why a hypo-responsive vmPFC is often correlated with PTSD symptoms: after developing the conditioned fear to stimuli, reduced function in the vmPFC may make the extinction of the conditioned fear response more difficult. If therapy could address these potential underlying etiologies, they may be able to effect greater long-term improvements in individuals with PTSD, and other disorders (Milad et al., 2007).

The ventromedial prefrontal cortex is a good example of how particular areas of the brain can be involved in multiple different functions.

If you remember from studying criminology, meditation and mindfulness practice have been shown to have positive effects on brain structure and function. For instance, Buddhist monks who practice meditation tend to have increased volume in their prefrontal cortices. Desbordes et al. (2012) also showed that mindfulness practice may reduce the activation of the amygdala when viewing negative emotional stimuli. This research is further evidence of neuroplasticity: the brain's ability to change throughout our lives as a result of experiences. Using mindfulness to improve thought processes and improve brain function and structure is a growing area of research in treatment for psychological disorders. Some studies have used mindfulness to treat PTSD and show signs of success (e.g. Kearney et al., 2011).

Drug therapy and cognitive therapy may both improve the functioning of important areas of the brain.

Neurological effects: changes in the brain.

Felmingham et al. (2007) tested the neurological effects of imagination therapy (a form of exposure therapy) and cognitive restructuring. These forms of cognitive behavioural therapy would help people with PTSD to alter their appraisals of the stressor and other emotional stimuli. Cognitive restructuring requires the same cognitive mechanisms of mindfulness: being able to exercise executive control of one's thoughts. The therapist tries to help the patient change their thinking from being maladaptive and irrational, to more healthy and positive. For example, some people who survive a traumatic event have survivor's guilt: they feel guilty for surviving while friends or family died. This negative thought pattern could be restructured so they no longer feel guilty, but instead they feel fortunate and lucky to be alive.

The study gathered results on five females and three males who were experiencing PTSD as a result of car accidents or assault. They gathered data on the effectiveness of the therapies using a Clinically Administered PTSD Scale (CAPS) questionnaire. After the eight weeks of sessions, all participants revealed at least a 30% reduction in their CAPS scores. This data alone suggests positive effects of exposure and cognitive therapy.

While exposure therapy could be difficult for patients, it can have positive outcomes.

You can see a video of cognitive restructuring in action on our blog.

The Clinically Administered PTSD Scale (CAPs) is a structured interview used to assess the severity of PTSD symptoms.

Psychotherapy: a course of treatment that aims to treat disorders with psychological methods, rather than medical ones.

The participants' brain function was also measured before and after the treatments. They were asked to view a range of fearful and neutral facial expressions while in the brain scanner. The results showed a positive correlation between CAPS scores and amygdala activation. That is to say, as CAPS scores decreased so did the activation of the amygdala. This suggests that the exposure therapy and cognitive restructuring was not only able to reduce symptoms, but it might also have been having an effect on the function of the amygdala. As you'll know by now, reduced activity of the amygdala in response to emotional stimuli could be very beneficial for treating the symptoms of PTSD associated with emotional arousal and anxiety.

The results also showed a negative correlation between CAPS scores and functioning in a specific area within the vmPFC called the anterior cingulate cortex (ACC). This means that as the activity in the ACC increased, the patients demonstrated fewer symptoms of PTSD. Many neuroimaging studies on people with PTSD have found reduced vmPFC activity and this is an important area of the brain involved in the process of fear extinction (e.g. Lanius et al., 2001; Shin et al., 2005). The vmPFC also enables top-down regulatory control over the amygdala during fear processes (e.g. emotional response to perceived threatening stimuli) so improving the function of the vmPFC would be a good step towards addressing possible etiologies of PTSD. This is because it would help with the fear extinction process and exercising executive cognitive control of thought patterns – negative and intrusive thoughts and memories could be ignored and positive ones could be focused on.

While drug therapy may work more immediately and is often cheaper than psychotherapies, there may be benefits to using a combined approach. Both therapies have been shown to improve the function of important areas of the brain when processing and perceiving emotional stimuli. However, drug therapy is limited in that it might not address the underlying cognitive etiologies of the disorder. Psychotherapy could be beneficial because it enables patients to improve their cognitive functioning and thought processes. This could have more significant long-term effects as patients may be able to monitor their own thought processes and alter their patterns of cognitive appraisals. This would reduce the need to be dependent on drug therapy in the long-term.

Guiding Question:

How might psychotherapy address cognitive and/or biological etiologies of PTSD?

Critical Thinking Extension:
Population Validity: The above study (Felmingham et al., 2007) uses a very small sample size (n = 8) and from two particular types of trauma (abuse and car accidents). Could you explain why these results might not be able to be generalized to other populations? Think about rape victims or war veterans, for instance. Could you hypothesize possible reasons *why* we may not be able to expect the same results in these populations of people with PTSD?

If you're interested…

Rebecca Brachman's Ted Talk "Could a drug prevent depression and PTSD?" provides an insight into the world of psychiatry and drug therapy. In this talk you can get an idea of how researchers can test the effectiveness of drugs using animal studies. She also discusses interesting overlaps between PTSD and depression and how they may be related.

Relevant Topics

- Etiology of abnormal psychology
- Explanations for disorders
- Treatment of disorders
- Psychological treatments
- Assessing the effectiveness of treatment(s)
- Neuroplasticity
- The brain and behaviour
- Techniques used to study the brain and behaviour

Practice Exam Questions

- Evaluate psychological treatments for one or more disorders.
- Discuss the effectiveness of one treatment for treating disorders.
- Contrast two explanations for one disorder.
- Discuss one effect neuroplasticity can have on human behaviour.
- Explain the use of one technique used to study the brain and behaviour.

Research Methods

As with many studies using brain imaging technology, Felmingham et al.'s (2007) study is a good example of the benefits of a correlational study. This is a correlational study and not an experiment because there is no independent variable in the study; all participants received the cognitive training, so there was no other group to compare them to. The two co-varying variables were the Clinically Administered PTSD Scale (CAPs scores) and the function in the ACC. This is an interesting correlational study in the sense that the correlation is between two effects of one treatment: the therapy. From this correlational study we are able to determine the relationship between PTSD symptoms (as measured by CAPs scores) and brain function.

Ethical Considerations

Any study involving patients who are experiencing the symptoms of a mental illness is fraught with potential ethical concerns. Extreme sensitivity would be required when debriefing patients on the results of their CAPs scores. It's not hard to imagine that if a patient did not have an improvement in their CAPs scores (i.e. a reduction in symptoms) they may take this news quite poorly. Their self-esteem also might be affected by receiving news of the results of their brain scans if showed minimal or no improvements.

4.8 Culture and Treatment
How can cultural values influence the treatment of psychological disorders?

A reductionist view is one that considers only one approach to understanding behaviour (e.g. biology causes behaviour). A holistic view is one that considers numerous approaches to understanding human behaviour, including biological, cognitive, social and cultural.

(a) Cultural Attitudes to Medication

It's hoped by this stage in the chapter you can see how drug therapy and psychotherapy can be invaluable in the approach to treating psychological disorders such as PTSD. Understanding the origins of psychological disorders is important when trying to make an informed decision about the best approaches to treatment. For instance, if someone had the reductionist view that that disorders were merely the result of chemical imbalances in the brain, they'd probably be content with just taking medication. But this would limit their treatment because it might not address underlying etiologies. Or if someone else believed that disorders stemmed from maladaptive or irrational thought processes, they would probably seek help to redress this issue, but they might ignore the short-term benefits of taking medication, which again could influence their treatment.

In this topic we will look at the role of culture in treatment. More specifically, we'll look at how cultural beliefs may affect one's view towards the best sources of treatment. An individual's culture might even influence whether or not they seek help for treatment in the first place. For this reason, it's important that psychiatrists and other professionals involved in the field of mental health recognize and understand different cultural perspectives when it comes to approaches to treating disorders.

An example can be seen in Horne et al.'s study (2004) that investigated cultural differences in attitudes towards using medication. They gathered data from 500 undergraduate students in the UK who identified as being either from an Asian cultural background or from a European cultural background. They found that the Asian students were more likely to have negative attitudes towards using medication and they were more likely to perceive them as intrinsically harmful and addictive substances. If someone has these attitudes towards medication, there's a good chance they'd be less likely to follow a prescribed course of drug therapy.

Are some cultures over-reliant on drug therapy?

From this study we can see that a clinician would have to consider a patient's cultural background when prescribing a particular course of treatment. If they were to prescribe a course of drug therapy, for instance, they may need to consider the cultural values and beliefs of their patient because this might influence whether or not they would actually follow through with the treatment.

Cultural attitudes towards different treatments could influence the treatment of psychological disorders. What works in one culture might not work in another. Whereas Western cultures have a high reliance on medication, traditional and natural therapies may be preferred in other cultures.

This understanding of differing cultural contexts in the delivery of therapy is known as cultural competency and it is an important issue in psychiatry, especially in multi-cultural societies. A therapist needs to be competent in understanding the diverse cultural backgrounds of their patients and continually learning about how people from different cultures may feel about certain approaches to treatment.

In summary, some treatments, like drug therapy, have been developed in particular cultural contexts, which might influence how applicable, acceptable or even how effective they might be for people that are from a different cultural context.

Guiding Question:

Why is cultural competency important in the treatment of disorders?

Critical Thinking Extension:

Culture and Treatment: Drug therapy attempts to treat psychological disorders by altering neurochemistry in the synapse. Our thought processes can also influence this process, as you've seen already in this chapter. This could explain the placebo effect: if people believe a drug will be effective, it is more likely to be effective. Could understanding placebo effects apply to a discussion of the role of understanding cultural attitudes towards drug therapy?

If you're interested…

There's a fascinating (and gruesome) video extract of a documentary about brain surgery in Africa. You can see a "witch doctor" perform open-skull surgery on a patient. Be warned: it's not for the faint hearted.

There are many different ways people may be involved in the field of mental health. When describing such a person you could use one or more of the following terms: clinician, psychologist, psychiatrist, mental health professional.

The primary difference between a psychiatrist and a psychologist is that a psychiatrist can prescribe medication. In order to become a psychiatrist you would need to attend medical school. The term clinician can be a good one to use as it describes anyone treating a person with a disorder.

The term "non-Latino whites" means "white people." One needs to be mindful of terminology when categorizing individuals by race, so if you prefer you could also say "Caucasians" or "European Americans."

(b)   Cultural Attitudes to Etiologies

In the previous section we explored one of the roles of culture in treatment: people from different cultural backgrounds may have different beliefs about the effectiveness and value of particular treatments, which needs to be considered by those prescribing treatments. Cultural attitudes towards types of treatment may influence the treatment process and this is something that mental health professionals need to bear in mind.

Different cultural beliefs may also influence individual attitudes towards the underlying etiologies of disorders. If cultures have different attitudes towards the origins of disorders, this could explain why there are different rates of seeking help and access to treatment across different groups of people. In multicultural societies clinicians need to be aware of cultural attitudes towards disorders if they want to provide effective mental health services.

For example, in the United States there are significant disparities in rates of access to mental health services across different ethnic groups. This could be attributed to different cultural beliefs about the origins of psychological disorders, as "...different cultural beliefs about mental illness may influence the type of treatment that is sought and how mental illness is addressed and managed" (Jimenez et al., 2012). Racial minorities (e.g. African-Americans, Latinos and Asian-Americans) are under-served in the mental health field and they have higher drop-out rates of treatment when compared to white Americans. They might also receive a lower quality of care (Hwang et al., 2008; Nelson, 2003). This results in minority groups having to endure prolonged psychological suffering because they cannot undergo the treatment and the care they need. This is a significant issue in understanding the role of culture in the treatment of disorders and highlights the need for cultural competency in clinicians offering treatment.

One reason why minority groups may have higher rates of dropping out of treatment is because of their beliefs about the origins of their illness. For instance, if someone doesn't think their mental illness has anything to do with neurochemistry, they might be unlikely to follow a full course of pharmacotherapy.

To investigate different cultural attitudes towards etiologies and treatments, Hwang et al. (2012) used questionnaires to gather data on attitudes towards mental health of over 2,000 US participants aged over 65 years old. They were grouped by ethnicity: non-Latino whites, African-Americans, Asian-Americans and Latinos. The researchers hypothesized that the minority groups' attitudes towards the origins of mental health problems would be different to non-Latino whites.

One of the questions the participants were asked was: "*What do you think causes depression?*" The results revealed different attitudes towards causes of depression. African-Americans were more likely to believe that it resulted from stress or worry, when compared to other groups. When asked what they think would help them get better, they were also more likely to say they would seek spiritual advice. Latinos, on the other hand, were more likely to opt for medication.

When it came to speaking to someone about their mental health problem, African-Americans were more likely to want to speak to a family member or someone living with them, and non-Latino whites were more likely to seek help from a psychiatrist. Asian-Americans were less likely to speak to anyone and were more likely to desire that their treatment provider belonged to the same racial group as them.

The results supported the researchers' original hypotheses by showing that there were significant differences between racial groups when it came to causes of disorders, preferences for treatments and treatment providers. These cultural differences in attitudes towards psychological disorders could explain why ethnic minorities have lower rates of seeking help and higher drop-out rates of treatment. For example, if someone is more likely to seek spiritual help, mainstream psychiatric facilities may be ineffective in offering services for that person. Or if there is not someone of the same racial group to offer treatment, this might result in someone not seeking help at all, or ending their course of psychotherapy sessions early.

Mental health professionals and organizations need to be aware of these cultural differences and how they may impact treatment. In this instance we can see how culture may affect the treatment of disorders because different cultural attitudes towards disorders might influence how people seek help for treatment and their willingness to follow through with treatment.

In your exams you may be asked about the "role of culture" in treatment. The role of culture that has been explained in this topic is the effect cultural values and beliefs may have on the treatment of disorders. Understanding how cultural backgrounds could influence courses of treatment is an important consideration for mental health professionals.

Guiding Question:

What is one role of culture in approaches to the treatment of psychological disorders?

Critical Thinking Extension:

Application: The above explanation about how cultural beliefs may influence approaches to treatment is quite broad and general. Can you relate this to your own cultural background or understanding of cultural differences to provide some specific examples? Can you also think of some contradictory results in Hwang et al.'s study? The Latinos were more likely to use medication. Is this consistent with the other findings?

If you're interested...

One of my favourite novels and films is "One Flew Over the Cuckoo's Nest." While this isn't related to culture and treatment, it does provide an interesting insight into the world of psychiatric hospitals in the US 50 years go. A more modern look at life in a psychiatric ward can found in the novel and book "It's kind of a funny story."

Relevant Topics

- The role of culture in treatment
- Cultural influences on identity, attitudes and behaviour
- Culture and its influence on cognition and behaviour
- Assessing the effectiveness of treatment
- Treatment of disorders

Practice Exam Questions

- To what extent does culture play a role in treatment of one or more disorders?
- Discuss the role of culture in disorders.
- Outline one study related to cultural influences on attitudes or behaviour.
- Discuss cultural influences on behaviour.

Research Methods

Once again in this topic we can see the value of using questionnaires when gathering data across large sample sizes. When making generalizations across entire races of people it's important to gather large data sets in order to ensure the results are valid and reliable. As there are many individual variables that might influence attitudes and perceptions, having a large sample size across people of the same racial, ethnic or cultural background (depending on the aim of the study) can reduce participant variability and provide a more accurate measure of cultural influences on the variable being measured. The use of a questionnaire in this context is extremely useful because it can enable researchers to gather this data more quickly and easily than with other methods. It also allows them to quantify behaviours, which is important for conducting statistical analyses.

Ethical Considerations

An important issue to consider in cross-cultural research that is related to ethics and hasn't been discussed before is cultural sensitivity. This is a very broad term that refers to the need to be aware of, and sensitive towards, different cultural beliefs. If researchers are conducting research and using questionnaires with participants who are from a culture that they are not personally knowledgeable about, they run the risk of asking culturally insensitive questions. For instance, it might be a taboo in some cultures to discuss issues of mental health or to ask personal opinions about people's attitudes towards topics related to mental health. Seeking advice and guidance from a peer or colleague who has knowledge of a particular cultural group could be one way to ensure the procedures and apparatuses used in the research are culturally sensitive.

4.9 Diagnosing Disorders
What are some of the issues associated with diagnosing disorders?

(a)   Culture and Diagnosis

In the previous topic we explored the role of culture in treatment. One conclusion from Hwang et al.'s study was that people from different ethnic backgrounds may have different views towards etiologies and possible treatment options for disorders. This is closely related to the subject of this topic: diagnosis.

In order to provide an accurate diagnosis of a disorder it's essential to first identify the symptoms. In the next section we'll look at one of the tools that professionals can use to facilitate making an accurate diagnosis.

Another important consideration in the diagnosis and treatment of psychological disorders is understanding how symptoms may vary across cultures. Throughout this course you've seen a number of examples of how cultural values may influence our cognition, biology and behaviour. With this in mind, it's not surprising to find that people from different cultural backgrounds may have varying symptomatology.

> Symptomatology is the set of symptoms that are characteristic of a disorder.

A common finding is that people from Asian cultures tend to experience more physical symptoms of depression when compared with Western patients. For example, one study compared patients from two different cultures who had been diagnosed with depression. They found that the Japanese patients tended to display more somatic (physical) symptoms, such as headaches, stomach cramps and neck pain, when compared with Americans who had also been diagnosed with depression (Waza et al., 1999). If a patient is from a cultural background that is different to the professional making the diagnosis, they may not be familiar with a culturally specific symptomatology. This could lead to an inaccuracy in diagnosis. It might also influence the course of treatment that could be recommended for a particular patient. This would be important to recognize if you were trying to make an accurate diagnosis.

> Knowledge and understanding of cultural differences in symptomatology can influence the validity and reliability of diagnosis.

This is similar to the idea of a culture-bound syndrome, which is a disorder found in one particular culture. Hikikomori is one example of a culture-bound syndrome. This is a disorder found in Japan that is characterized by social isolation, anxiety and school absenteeism.

> Culture-bound syndrome: a psychological disorder that is particular to one culture.

A second important cultural consideration in diagnosis is understanding the effects diagnosis and seeking treatment might have on an individual. Different cultures have different attitudes towards mental health issues. For this reason, in some cultures there is more of a stigma attached to diagnosis of mental health issues. A stigma is a negative

The symptoms of disorders may vary across cultures. There may also be differences in how frequently people seek help, which could explain why Japan has relatively low rates of reported depression but high rates of suicide.

People offering treatment should be aware of the possible negative psychological effects that receiving treatment might have, including being stigmatized.

label or a "mark of disgrace or discredit that sets someone apart from others" (Murphy, 2014). If someone is diagnosed with a particular disorder others may look at them differently or perceive them differently because of their diagnosis.

This could be another cultural variable that influences approaches to treatment as some people may not seek treatment or help if they are worried about being stigmatized. An example of potential stigma can be seen Turvey et al.'s study (2012) that compared attitudes towards depression in Russian, South Korean and American participants over the age of 60. Only 6% of the American participants viewed depression as a sign of weakness. On the other hand, Russian and Korean participants were fare more likely to label those with depression as a sign of being weak (61% and 78%, respectively). With this attitude attached to depression in some cultures, individuals may be less likely to seek help for fear that they may be labelled as weak.

This is another important consideration in diagnosis, as health care professionals need to be aware of the potential detrimental effects a diagnosis of a disorder may have on an individual. Existing attitudes might also influence how openly someone may discuss their symptoms, which could also affect the validity of diagnosis. In cultures where men are discouraged to share their feelings as it's a sign of weakness or femininity, for instance, it may be difficult for professionals to make an accurate diagnosis because they have not had the full set of symptoms revealed to them.

In order to receive appropriate treatment, accurate diagnoses are required. However, there are many cultural factors that might influence a mental health professional's ability to make an accurate diagnosis. Being aware of such cultural variables and developing cultural competency is important for psychologists dealing with people with mental health issues.

Guiding Question:

How can culture influence approaches to the diagnosis of disorders?

Critical Thinking Extension:
Applications: The issue of stigma and differences in symptomatology across cultures could be applied to a range of topics. Can you think how you could use this research in a discussion of: the role of culture in treatment, assessing the effectiveness of treatment, and/or the validity and reliability of diagnosis?

If you're interested…

You could do some research to learn about possible culture-bound syndromes that exist in your home culture.

(b)   *Diagnosis and the DSM*

By this stage in our study of PTSD you should have a firm understanding of its symptoms, etiologies and possible treatments. In the previous section we began to look at diagnosis and how culture may influence the diagnosis of disorders. In abnormal psychology diagnosis refers to being able to determine whether or not someone is suffering from a recognizable psychological disorder, and what particular disorder/s they are experiencing.

The Diagnostic and Statistical Manual of Mental Disorders is the most commonly used classification system in Western psychiatry. (Image credit: F.RdeC, wikicommons.com)

As with other disorders, diagnosing PTSD can be extremely difficult. Humans have evolved the potential to develop conditioned fear; it's a healthy adaptation that can help us to survive. So where do we draw the line between having a healthy fear of something, and suffering from a "psychological disorder?"

The issue of defining normality and abnormality and distinguishing the two is a long-standing debate. The reason why psychologists and psychiatrists attempt to distinguish abnormality from normality is because it can facilitate accurate diagnosis. As we've already discussed, an accurate diagnosis of disorders is important so patients can receive appropriate help and treatment.

One way that psychiatrists attempt to clearly distinguish normality from abnormality is with the use of classification systems. A classification system is a detailed description of a range of psychological disorders that are categorized (or classified) and accompanied by detailed descriptions of symptoms. The specific disorders are classified by their defining characteristics. For example, eating disorders include bulimia and anorexia nervosa and binge eating disorder. These are all grouped, or classified, based on similar symptoms.

The most common classification system used in Western psychiatry is the Diagnostic and Statistical Manual of Mental Disorders (DSM). The DSM is an extensive manual (print and online) and is currently in its fifth edition as it is regularly reviewed and updated to keep up with developments in our collective understanding of psychological disorders. When someone seeks professional help and counseling, the DSM can be used to determine whether or not they are suffering from a particular disorder and if so, what disorder they might be diagnosed with.

The DSM identifies diagnostic criteria that attempt to help clinicians make accurate diagnoses. For PTSD, some of these criteria are grouped into the following categories:

- Being exposed to a traumatic stressor.
- Symptoms related to intrusive memories (e.g. unwanted thoughts and memories of the stressor, flashbacks, nightmares, aversive reactions to internal or environmental cues that remind the person of the stressor).
- Avoidance of stimuli that may be associated with the traumatic event(s) (e.g.

What is "normal?" Try to come up with a definition of what you think "normal" means. Can you think of healthy people that wouldn't fit your definition?

The full DSM V is available online and it would be worth reading the section on PTSD, if you haven't done so already.

avoiding places or environments that may remind the person of the stressor).

• Negative changes in thought patterns and mood after experiencing the traumatic event(s) (e.g. memory loss regarding the trauma; negative appraisals of the causes or consequences of the trauma, such as blaming themselves; persistent negative emotional states).

• Changes in levels of arousal (e.g. hypervigilance, problems with concentration, exaggerated startle responses, irritability and/or angry outbursts).

Psychiatrists and psychologists who are in a position to offer a diagnosis of PTSD can use the classifications within the DSM to facilitate their diagnosis, i.e. they use this tool to help them determine normality from abnormality. They can draw a conclusion regarding if the person has experienced a "healthy" and natural reaction to the experience of a traumatic event (or events), or if they have demonstrated sufficient evidence (i.e. symptoms) to warrant the diagnosis of an abnormal response and corresponding psychological disorder.

In summary, making an accurate diagnosis is just as important in psychiatry as it is medicine. A misdiagnosis or not offering any diagnosis at all could have negative consequences for patients. But the line between what is normal and abnormal is highly subjective and often difficult to determine. Using classification systems such as the DSM can facilitate the process of diagnosing disorders by providing clear descriptors of symptoms.

Guiding Question:

How can classification systems help with distinguishing normality from abnormality?

Critical Thinking Extension:
What are the limitations in using a classification system like the DSM to make a diagnosis of a disorder? Possible limitations could be related to cultural bias, clinical bias and/or subjectivity of the criteria.

If you're interested…

You can access the entire DSM online and can read the descriptions of symptoms of other disorders you may be interested in.

(c) *Validity and Reliability of Diagnosis*

In the previous section we looked at one way that mental health professionals attempt to determine the difference between abnormality and normality: classification systems. The use of a tool like the DSM-5 can facilitate valid and reliable diagnoses of disorders as it provides a full description of the types of symptoms and examples of specific symptoms of disorders. If a patient's symptoms accurately match those in the provided classification, a diagnosis can be made. In this section we'll look at how even when using a very detailed classification system like the DSM-5, there may be issues related to the validity or reliability of diagnosis. Similar to its use in research, the term validity in diagnosis refers to accuracy: has the "right" diagnosis been made? Reliability refers to the extent to which more than one professional agrees with the diagnosis (similar to test-retest reliability or inter-rater reliability in research).

Diagnosing a disorder is rarely a simple process as each individual's symptoms are different and even determining between two different disorders can be very difficult as people often experience comorbidity: two or more disorders at the same time. For example, in the DSM-5 depressive, anxiety and substance-related disorders are in a different category to trauma and stressor related disorders. But people who experience traumatic events often experience comorbidity as they are diagnosed with one or more additional disorders related to anxiety, depression and/or substance abuse. The problem is that "…PTSD can unfortunately mimic virtually any condition in psychiatry" (Shay, 1994). This makes it incredibly difficult to make an accurate diagnosis.

> **Comorbidity:** the presence of one (or more) additional disorders to the primary diagnosis. E.g. being diagnosed with PTSD *and* depression.

The criteria can also be open to interpretation. For example, the DSM-5 states that the symptoms are present for at least one month after the traumatic event(s). Does this mean that if you sought help after three weeks a diagnosis of PTSD could not be made? How strict would a professional follow this criterion? This would be used as a guideline only and demonstrates the difficulty in quantifying diagnostic criteria.

Clinical bias is when the existing beliefs, values or attitudes of a clinician influence the diagnosis of a disorder.

For this reason, the symptoms outlined in the DSM-5 are mostly qualitative and descriptive, so they're open to interpretation. The term "persistent," for instance, is used frequently in the descriptions of the symptoms. But how frequently must they occur in order for them to be "persistent?" Other words such as "prolonged" or "intense" may also have differing interpretations based on the professional providing the diagnosis.

The fact that there is an element of subjectivity in the interpretation of the descriptors in the DSM-5 invites the possibility of clinical bias; the bias of the clinician making the diagnosis. Clinical bias in the interpretation of a patient's symptoms and the subsequent diagnosis could influence the validity and/or reliability of diagnosis.

A particular form of clinical bias may be confirmation bias. In the context of psychiatry, confirmation bias could influence the diagnosis in one of two ways:

(a)   By affecting the interpretation of the patient's symptoms
(b)   By influencing the clinician's search for new information to test their original diagnosis (Mendel et al., 2011)

Perhaps the most famous study investigating the validity of diagnosis and the influence of confirmation bias was carried out by Rosenhan in 1973; this will be explored in the next section.

Guiding Question:

How might clinical bias influence the validity of diagnosis?

Critical Thinking Extension:
Quantifying Symptoms: A possible alternative to using qualitative descriptions of symptoms would be to offer quantitative ones. What issues could you foresee with trying to quantify symptoms of PTSD and/or other disorders?

If you're interested…

Ben Shephard's book "A War of Nerves: Soldiers and Psychiatrists in the Twentieth Century" is a historical account of psychiatry and war. If you have found the subject of PTSD and veterans particularly interesting, you may want to read this book.

(d)   Confirmation Bias

So far in this topic we've looked at a range of issues related to factors that may influence diagnosis, including clinical bias and cultural competency. But as with all topics in IB Psychology, we also need to be considering the evidence. In this topic we'll explore one major study that can be used in discussions of factors influencing diagnosis.

In the 1970s the field of psychiatry came under heavy scrutiny and criticism as a result of a covert observational study by David Rosenhan and his colleagues (Rosenhan, 1973). In this paper, called "On being sane in insane places," Rosenhan described his own experiences and those of his colleagues after being admitted to a variety of psychiatric hospitals across the United States.

The study investigates the difficulties in defining normality and abnormality, and the inherent repercussions for valid and reliable diagnoses of psychological disorders. Prior to this study, some researchers had conducted participant observations of psychiatric hospitals, but this was often for a short time and the hospital staff knew of their presence. Rosenhan wanted to take this research one step further – he conducted a participant, naturalistic, covert observation. He was interested in investigating whether the eight pseudopatients would be diagnosed based on their objective symptoms and behaviours, or if the nature of the environment would influence the interpretation of their behaviours by the professionals providing the diagnosis. Perhaps his aim can be best summarized by the question he poses in the opening to his article: "if sanity and insanity exist, how shall we know them?"

Rosenhan was one of the pseudopatients, along with 7 others. They sought admission into 12 different hospitals on the East and West coasts of the United States. The only symptom they gave the hospitals was that they had been hearing a stranger's voice in their head. The voices were unclear, but they told the doctors that they thought they said "thud", "empty" and "hollow". One reason why these words were chosen was because there is a suggestion that they are signaling some sort of crisis in the individual's life, such as their life is "empty" or "hollow." After they were granted admission into the hospital, all the other details about their lives and their personal histories that they told the hospital staff were true and they were also told to act normally.

Of the 12 admissions to the hospitals, 11 were diagnosed with schizophrenia and one was diagnosed with manic-depressive psychosis. They remained in the hospitals for a range of 7 to 52 days, with an average of 19 days. After the pseudopatients were admitted to the hospital, they carried on behaving normally and told the staff their symptoms had stopped. They took notes and made other observations, at first hiding this in case the staff found out. But after they realized the staff weren't paying attention to them, they took notes freely. This resulted in other patients in the hospital raising questions about the authenticity of the pseudopatients' illnesses. In fact, during the first 3 admissions to hospitals, 35 of 118 patients expressed some concern regarding whether or not the pseudopatients were really ill. This raises an interesting question: why could the diagnosed "mentally insane" recognize sanity, while the trained professionals could not?

> Rosenhan's study can be applied to multiple topics related to abnormal psychology. You might need to think carefully about how you could apply this research.

> Pseudopatient: someone who is pretending to be a patient.

> There are many forms of schizophrenia. Generally speaking it's regarded as a breakdown between thoughts, feelings and behaviours. Some types of schizophrenia involve the inability to determine what's real and imagined.

A lot of psychiatric hospitals like the ones Rosenhan's pseudopatients were admitted to are no longer in use. Some people argue that prisons have become the new "insane asylums" as many criminals also have psychological disorders.

269

While they were on the hospital wards, the pseudopatients made notes about their experiences. In his article Rosenhan details the dehumanization that was experienced by the pseudopatients while they were in the care of the hospital staff. He believes that it is the power of the label (in this case schizophrenia) that influences the way the clinicians interpret their behaviour: "Once a person is diagnosed abnormal, all of his other behaviours are colored by that label" (Rosenhan, 1973). This is how confirmation bias (a form of clinical bias in this context) could influence the validity of diagnosis – arguably, the psychiatrists could have been able to recognize their error in diagnosis and been able to identify the fact that patients were normal and healthy individuals. However, their bias may have impaired their ability to accurately judge their behaviour once they were within the walls of the hospital.

For example, Rosenhan describes how a perfectly normal description of one of the pseudopatient's relationships with family members was interpreted by the clinician in a way that was consistent with his diagnosis of schizophrenia. Their behaviour of writing notes, which was viewed accurately by many patients as a sign that they might be journalists or someone conducting research, was also labelled as abnormal behaviour by the psychiatrists. In many cases they were released with diagnoses of "schizophrenia in remission," which Rosenhan argues is very different to a diagnosis of being "sane."

After this original study was conducted, one hospital heard of the findings and challenged Rosenhan to send pseudopatients to their hospital with the belief that they would be able to spot the fakes from the genuine patients. Over a three month period, 193 patients were admitted for treatment and received a judgement based on the staffs' beliefs if they were an actual patient or not. Of these 193, 41 were judged with high confidence by at least one member of the staff to be a pseudopatient, while 19 were suspected as being a pseudopatient by a psychiatrist and at least one other member of the staff. In fact, Rosenhan had not sent any pseudopatients during this time (Rosenhan, 1973).

Rosenhan's classic study can be used to demonstrate a range of issues associated with diagnosing disorders, including the value of classification systems, what constitutes normality and abnormality, issues in validity and reliability of diagnosis and how clinical bias may influence diagnosis.

> **Dehumanization:** the process of making an individual or a group of people feel like they are less than humans, like they don't possess the positive qualities of being an individual person.

> **Clinical bias** is a bias in judgement made by a clinician. The bias may influence the diagnosis or treatment of a patient.

Guiding Question:

How does Rosenhan's study demonstrate the effects of clinical bias in diagnosis?

Critical Thinking Extension:
Limitation of the Methodology: Rosenhan's methodology has been criticized. Do you think it's fair to criticize the psychiatrists for providing a misdiagnosis of schizophrenia? You may also want to consider how Rosenhan's study could be applied to discussions of a range of topics, including normality versus abnormality, the importance of classification systems, and the validity and reliability of diagnosis.

If you're interested…

You can see interviews with Rosenhan where he describes his study and the issues he investigated. His original article is also available online and the language is accessible for high school students.

Relevant Topics

- Factors influencing diagnosis
- Normality versus abnormality
- The role of clinical bias in diagnosis
- Validity and reliability of diagnosis
- Biases in thinking and decision making

Practice Exam Questions

- Discuss research related to validity and reliability of diagnosis.
- Discuss the use of one or more classification systems in diagnosis.
- Discuss the role of clinical bias in diagnosis.

Research Methods

Rosenhan's study used a naturalistic observation. Unlike most of the research explored in this course, this is an example of a qualitative study. The data Rosenhan gathered was descriptive; it wasn't based on numbers and figures. In this particular context the use of a naturalistic observation is valuable because Rosenhan wanted to investigate psychiatric hospitals and how people were treated once they were admitted. By being able to observe this natural environment as it actually exists, the data gathered could potentially be a more accurate reflection of what these hospitals were really like. However, an issue with qualitative data is that it might be subject to researcher bias, especially in the analysis stage. Rosenhan's pre-existing ideas and beliefs about psychiatric hospitals may have influenced his own confirmation bias as he focused on and emphasized details of his researchers' notes that confirmed his existing views.

Ethical Considerations

There are also ethical implications with conducting covert observations, as those being observed are not aware of it. One way to counter this is by obtaining retrospective consent. This means asking for the subjects' permission to use notes and data gathered on them, but you ask *after* the research has been conducted (i.e. retrospectively). Obtaining retrospective consent may have been important to maintain high ethical standards in Rosenhan's research. However, what if the hospitals refused? There is a good chance that the hospitals would not provide consent for the data to be used because it might be embarrassing or they may believe it could damage the credibility of the field of psychiatry. If they refused the use of their data, then Rosenhan's time, money and effort would have been wasted. There might be a cost-benefit analysis that would need to be taken into consideration: can we publish findings without retrospective consent in order to effect important change in psychiatric practice? Once again we see that ethics is rarely black and white.

Conclusion

The world of mental illness is a fascinating and important field of study. Throughout this chapter you've seen how there may be multiple factors interrelated in the origins, symptoms and treatments of a disorder like PTSD. It is also hoped that you may be able to apply what you've learned in this unit to your own experiences. For instance, if you're now aware of how our thinking can influence our stress response, this may have implications for how you manage your own stress in the future. Perhaps understanding the pros and cons of taking medication might influence your own personal choices regarding this form of treatment.

It's also quite valuable to understand how memories are formed and the concept of working memory. Learning is about remembering, so being aware of factors that can influence your memory, including your own thought processes (e.g. rehearsal), can have valuable practical applications. Understanding working memory may also aide in your ability to practice being meta-cognitive – aware of your own thinking. Being aware of the positive effects of a practice like mindfulness is also beneficial knowledge as this is an easy exercise you can perform almost anywhere and at any time.

The structure of this chapter is similar to the others: origins of behaviour are explored first for the deliberate purpose of setting up the investigation of the effectiveness of particular treatments. This has hopefully provided you with a deeper understanding that will facilitate your ability to critically assess the effectiveness of treatments.

In terms of exam preparation, the topics covered in this chapter can be used in multiple parts of the course. In fact, this chapter covers almost the entire biological approach. The only biological approach topic that isn't covered in this chapter is the effect of pheromones on behaviour (covered in Love and Marriage). This provides you with multiple options for approaching exam questions. If you weren't confident in the concepts in the Criminology chapter, for instance, you could use material from this chapter instead.

It's important to note that you've been given more than enough information in this chapter to approach multiple exam questions. When you're revising for the exams, you may need to critically select the particular studies and concepts that you want to use for particular topics. For example, there are too many possible explanations for PTSD included in this chapter to include them all in an exam answer. When revising this particular topic, you might want to narrow your focus on one biological, one cognitive and one sociocultural explanation. Where possible, try to exploit overlaps during your revision.

As with all the topics in this course, we've only had time to skim the surface of abnormal psychology and the world of mental illness. I hope there's something in this chapter that has sparked your interest for further study.

Successful preparation for Paper Two questions about Abnormal Psychology will take careful revision. Be sure to check out our blog for resources that can help.

Chapter 5
Love & Marriage

Introduction

They met on the set of a Hollywood film, although he was still married at the time and she had kids from a previous marriage. Nevertheless, they got married, adopted 3 children and had three more of their own. In all, they shared their love and their lives with six children and were married for ten years. And then it was over.

We're not going to analyze Brangelina. I introduce their relationship here because it contains many elements that we *are* going to look at in this chapter on love and marriage.

Firstly, Brad Pitt is widely regarded as an incredibly attractive man, and has been for the past 30 years. What makes him so attractive? Perhaps Pitt's facial features and physique signify that he has good genes and this is why he is attractive. Angelina Jolie is rather beautiful as well, and although we won't have time to investigate the feminine characteristics that males typically find attractive, it does make for interesting extended research if you're interested.

Sadly, like many married couples, Brangelina's love did not last. The significant increases in divorce rates in the US and many other countries has prompted extensive research into marriages in order to understand why some succeed and others fail. We are going to investigate some of this research to get an insight as to why some marriages might end in divorce, while others last a lifetime. As with other units, one of the important concepts we are investigating is the fact that if we can understand underlying origins, perhaps we can implement better treatment and prevention strategies.

But attraction and the prevalence of divorce are different from culture to culture. Would Bollywood experience rates of divorce as high as Hollywood? Also in this chapter we'll be looking at how cultural values might be relevant in the study of the formation and dissolution of marriages.

Romantic relationships are fundamental to the human experience and so they're worth exploring. In this chapter you'll be exposed to a tiny selection of possible answers to some important questions surrounding love and marriage. As always, it's important that you are basing your psychological understanding on the empirical evidence provided, and that you are thinking critically about your own understanding based on that evidence.

The role of attraction in relationships is just one topic we're going to explore in this chapter. (Image credit: Georges Biard, wikicommons.com)

5.1 Evolution of Attraction
Why are we attracted to some people more than others?

(a) Evolution and Behaviour

To procreate is a biological way of saying to have babies.

The *biological* purpose of life is to procreate. In other words, living organisms need to produce offspring so genetic material can be passed on from generation to generation. If you think about it, if organisms didn't reproduce then their species would become extinct. This biological *purpose* in life is not to be confused with the *meaning* of life; these are separate concepts altogether.

In the study of criminology we focused on understanding the biological factors that influence aggression and how these might be explained from an evolutionary point of view. That is to say, those biological factors increase our chances of survival, which increases our chances of being able to procreate, so these biological traits are more likely to be passed on. When small mutations in our genes result in behavioural changes that increase our chances of procreation they increase the likelihood of the new (mutated) genes being passed on to offspring. Over thousands of years these small mutations add up to significant developments. Thus, the process of evolution takes hundreds of generations as biological changes are a result of slight mutations in genetic material that compound over time.

An evolutionary explanation of behaviour is one that explains how a particular behaviour can help us to survive and/or pass on our genes. A deeper explanation would include how the biological traits that are likely to be passed on facilitate a behaviour that enables survival and/or procreation.

Much like other biological aspects in our psychology course, evolution is another one we have to skim over. To recap from earlier topics, the key concept for you to understand is that *genes will be passed on if they affect our biology in a way that influences our behaviour and increases our chances of survival.*

In terms of evolutionary explanations of behaviour we need to identify a particular behaviour that we can examine from an evolutionary standpoint. That is to say, we need to be able to explain how and why one particular behaviour could increase our chances of survival (i.e. passing on our genes). The fact that this behaviour has enabled survival is why it would be observable today. You could do this with many behaviours, but what's important in psychology is that you have the research to support your explanation.

Fear, fear conditioning and aggression are three such behaviours that could be explained from an evolutionary standpoint. The behaviour we are going to focus on in this section is attraction, and more specifically, physical attraction.

"Masculine" facial features include a square jawline and a low brow.

Attraction to particular facial characteristics might increase our chances of having strong and healthy babies because they signal who has "good" genetic material. It's important to remember that in human procreation, 50% of the genetic material comes from either parent, so we want to make sure we select our mate carefully. There's an evolutionary advantage in procreating with someone who is going to increase the likelihood of producing healthy offspring. This is the key to attraction: we may find ourselves *physically* attracted to someone who shows particular characteristics that suggest they would be a good person to have babies with. Attraction to particular individuals may be a result of biological processes influencing our perception and judgement of characteristics that signify a beneficial mate who has the genes we want for our offspring.

Sex hormones like testosterone can influence physical development and appearance and in the next section we're going to investigate female attraction to facial characteristics that signify varying levels of testosterone.

A mate in a human biological sense is someone we want to procreate with.

Guiding Question:

How might evolutionary processes influence attraction?

Critical Thinking Extension:

Hypothesizing Missing Links: Many students make the mistake of trying to say how evolution can explain the behaviour without first explaining how evolution could explain the existence of the biological factor that is influencing behaviour. By this stage in the course you should have a sound understanding of how biological factors can influence our behaviour. So the chain of effect is that if we behave in a way that increases chances of survival, the biological factor that facilitates that behaviour will be passed on through our genes. And then the biological factor that was passed on will increase the likelihood of offspring behaving in the same way, and so on. This is quite complex to understand, but could you apply this explanation to one particular behaviour and its biological correlates?

If you're interested...

The BBC released a four episode series called "Human Instinct." Episode 2/4 is called "Deepest Desires" and includes an exploration of sexual attraction and behaviours.

(b) Testosterone and Attraction

Testosterone is a sex hormone that is produced primarily in the testes of men, which is why it's considered the male sex hormone. It is responsible for the physical changes during puberty that help a boy become a man. Some of the effects of testosterone are the growth of body hair, broadening of the shoulders, deepening of the voice, and lowering of the brow and squaring of the jaw – essentially, the development of "masculine" features.

As you can see in the criminology chapter, high levels of testosterone may influence aggression, particularly in response to social threat. A male with high levels of testosterone may be more physically capable of maintaining social status by facilitating aggressive actions and being competitive. A female might be attracted to high levels of testosterone as they signal an ability to protect and provide for her and her offspring. If a male can maintain high social status he will have access to more resources, which would be able to support the female as she carries and raises the babies. Remember, we are talking from an evolutionary point of view, so we have to think about what "social status" might mean over the past centuries.

Other studies also correlate secondary sex characteristics with good health and strong immune systems. A secondary sex characteristic is a visible physical trait that enables gender differences between males and females to be identified, without being directly related to sexual reproduction. Masculine facial features and other signs of masculinity that begin to occur at puberty are examples of secondary sex characteristics. One explanation for why masculine features signify good health is that they require high levels of testosterone. One explanation for this is that high levels of testosterone suppress the function of the immune system, so only healthy males with strong immune systems would be able to cope with the release of high levels of testosterone that would be needed to develop strong secondary sex characteristics, like a masculine face (Little et al., 2011).

There is a lot of research investigating attraction. Specific research focuses on comparing how a female's menstrual cycle may influence what she finds attractive. Several different studies have all shown that females tend to have a stronger preference for masculine faces around the time of ovulation, when they are most likely to become pregnant. Johnston et al. (2001) tested this by gathering 42 female participants from New Mexico State University in the lab and asking them to view male and female faces on a computer. The researchers created computer images that could be manipulated by the participants, so they could drag a cursor and make the faces more masculine or feminine. The researchers asked the participants to choose different faces that met different "targets." For example, one of these targets was "an attractive male face," so participants were asked to manipulate the face until it best met that description.

The results showed that when females were at the stage in their menstrual cycle with the highest chance of conception, they had a stronger preference for masculine faces. Of all the different targets (e.g. attractive female face, healthy looking male/female face, etc.) the stage of their cycle only significantly changed their opinion on the "attractive male face." This suggests that the attraction to a masculine face was higher around ovulation and less at other times, and it was the only preference that was affected by the changes in hormones that occur during the menstrual cycle.

These results corroborate other similar findings that suggest hormones play a key role in attraction in two ways. Levels of testosterone can influence a male's attractiveness by signifying his suitability as a mate. Also, the hormonal changes in a female during the menstrual cycle may also affect what type of male face she is more attracted

You may be bored with testosterone and if you want a different hormone to study, make sure you study the role of cortisol in the stress response and its effect on memory and the hippocampus in the PTSD chapter.

As an alternative to testosterone, you could do some research on how estrogen may influence female characteristics and the effect this has on attraction in males. There is considerable research in this area.

Women are most fertile at the ovulation stage of their menstrual cycle.

to, and might increase the chances that during the fertile stage of her cycle she will be more attracted to signs of good genes for procreation.

Testosterone was chosen for this section as it has good connections other topics, including pheromones that you'll learn about later in this chapter.

Guiding Question:

How might hormones influence attraction?

Critical Thinking Extension:

Gender Bias: What do *males* find attractive? While this study deliberately has a limited gender perspective because it's focusing on what females find attractive, it nevertheless limits our understanding of attraction in *all* humans by focusing on only one gender. It's not a methodological limitation of the study because the aim of the study was specifically to focus on females, but it is a limitation of the applications of the study in understanding attraction across humans. One way of demonstrating abstract thinking skills is to raise these kinds of questions in your answers. Moreover, you could do some additional research into studies that investigate the types of faces that males find attractive.

If you're interested…

The US Documentary Channel released a 45 minute documentary called "The Science of Sex Appeal." In this video you can see an interview with Lisa Debruine discussing studies similar to the one above. She is one of the researchers who worked with Jones in the above study and has conducted a lot of research in this field. This is one of many resources that explore the plethora of factors involved in attraction and sexual behaviour.

(c)   *Evolution and Attraction*

Johnston et al.'s study from the previous section may be criticized on the grounds that it was conducted in one particular culture. Just because these results were obtained in New Mexico, USA, does this mean they would be consistent across cultures?

While David Buss' study (1989) doesn't investigate the same specific variables as Johnston et al., it does provide some insight into cross-cultural similarities in attraction. By gathering data from 10,047 participants across 37 cultures, Buss was able to see if men and women around the world desired the same qualities in a mate.

He also hypothesized that gender consistency in attraction to particular characteristics across cultures would suggest an evolutionary explanation for this attraction. This is because if humans from many different parts of the world value the same traits in a mate of the opposite gender, it suggests that this attraction is not being influenced by cultural factors. It is far more probable that this attraction is operating at a biological level.

If behaviour is consistent across cultures it may suggest a biological basis for that behaviour, as humans are biologically similar around the world.

Buss' study did find a cross-cultural similarity in gender preferences when it comes to age

One of the first aims of the study was to compare the differences in preferences between men and women. Buss hypothesized that due to evolutionary pressures, males and females would prefer different traits and that this would be consistent across cultures. That is to say, males from all cultures would desire similar characteristics.

Social status is important for many reasons. It's important that you can understand how social status might be important for survival, including across different cultures and time periods.

One of his hypotheses was that males would prefer a female who was younger. The results showed that this was the case and across all 37 cultures males preferred mates who were younger. This can be explained from an evolutionary perspective as females are most fertile in their early 20s, and fertility decreases after this age (Buss, ibid). From an evolutionary standpoint, males wouldn't want to exert effort and resources into trying to procreate with a female who lacked fertility. The health risks of carrying a baby to full-term also increase with age, so from a male's point of view it would be an advantage to have a youthful mate who has a higher probability of being able to take care of the offspring and ensure the successful passing on of genes.

Even though Buss didn't specifically predict it, the results also showed that across all culture females preferred a mate who was older. This could also be explained from an evolutionary perspective: having a higher social status would enable a male to provide better protection and resources for a female and her offspring. As there is a lot of physical investment in carrying a baby to full-term and raising a baby, a female would be at an advantage if she had a male who could provide and support her and her baby. An older male would have a higher probability of being higher in social status and rank, which might explain why females showed preference for older males.

There were some other interesting cross-cultural differences that were found in the study, and these will explored in the next topic. However, you may want to try to apply an evolutionary explanation to the following results:

- Females placed higher value on financial prospects than males
- Males placed a higher emphasis on "good looks"
- Males from 23 of the 37 cultures placed higher emphasis on chastity than females

Guiding Question:

How does Buss' study suggest that evolution can explain attraction?

Critical Thinking Extension:

Area of Uncertainty/Alternative Explanation: While Buss' study does provide some evidence to suggest that there is an evolutionary basis for mate preference and attraction, are there other possible factors that could explain these gender differences in preferences?

If you're interested…

The complete study of Buss' is available online and the language is accessible for most IB students.

Buss' study provides more evidence for the role of evolution in attraction.

Attraction is often a key factor in forming a romantic relationship. But is this the same across cultures? We'll explore this idea later in the chapter.

Relevant Topics

- Evolution and behaviour
- Hormones and behaviour
- Formation of relationships

Practice Exam Questions

- Discuss one or more evolutionary explanations of behaviour.
- Explain how one hormone may affect one behaviour.
- Discuss the formation of personal relationships.
- Discuss research related to the formation of personal relationships.

Research Methods

Johnston et al.'s study could be classed as a quasi-experiment as the variable that is having an effect is the female's time of the menstrual cycle. The assumption is that physiological changes during this time influence what the women find attractive. While the effects of this variable are investigated, the participants cannot be randomly allocated to conditions and it is not the researcher who is manipulating the IV. This is why this study could be considered a quasi-experiment. This type of study can be useful in understanding the correlation between menstrual cycle and attraction to masculine faces as it can provide valuable data that supports evolutionary explanations of behaviour.

Ethical Considerations

Anonymity would be an important characteristic in any study where an individual is offering information about preferences to something as personal as what they find attractive. Imagine if they had a partner who was opposite to what they rated as being attractive. This could cause harm to an existing relationship.

Confidentiality (e.g. not telling people who participated in the study) might also be important as those in existing relationships may become jealous at knowing their partner was participating in a study about attraction.

5.2 Pheromones and Behaviour
How might pheromones influence attraction?

(a)   Pheromones: An Introduction

We have looked at numerous examples of how chemical messengers may affect our behaviour. Hormones like adrenaline and testosterone are transmitted through our blood while neurotransmitters like serotonin are transmitted through the process of neurotransmission. There is also evidence to suggest that there is another type of chemical messenger that is transported in a different way.

A pheromone is a type of chemical messenger that is transmitted from one individual to another through the air and is detected through the sense of smell in the receiving individual. Their technical definition is: "substances which are secreted to the outside by an individual and received by a second individual of the same species, in which they release a specific reaction, for example, a definite behavior or a developmental process…" (Verhaeghe et al., 2013).

Pheromones have been studied extensively in animal research and there is considerable evidence to suggest that they do influence *animal* behaviour. But there is much debate as to whether or not they affect *human* behaviour.

Animals have a specific part of their olfactory system that detects most pheromones and this is called the vomeronasal organ. Part of the reason why there is much debate as to whether or not pheromones influence human behaviour is that there is no evidence that the vomeronasal organ functions in the human olfactory system. We have this tissue in our bodies up until birth, but most of the evidence suggests it doesn't function after birth. However, many animals detect pheromones through their sense of smell, so it is possible that humans may still detect pheromones through smell (Verhaeghe, ibid).

The olfactory system is the name given to the parts of our sensory system that enables us to smell things.

During mating season many animals give off signals that try to increase the likelihood of procreation. Stags "roar" and spread their scent to attract females.

There is evidence that suggests pheromones may play a role in the mating process of animals. For instance, studies as far back as the 1960s show that presenting a female pig with the scent of a boar (male pig) will result in the female adopting a mating readiness stance (Cutler, 1999). The specific pheromone that might have this effect has been identified as androstenone.

To see if vomeronasal organ tissue was required to detect androstenone, Dorries et al. (1997) blocked the vomeronasal organ in one group of domestic pigs. They administered androstenone to this group, as well as to another group of control pigs. The results showed that there was no difference in the behaviours of the two groups of pigs as a result. This provides some evidence for the fact that the vomeronasal organ is not needed to detect pheromones. If this is the case, it could mean that pheromones might be able to be detected by humans through their regular sense of smell. Remember that humans and animals have very similar biological processes, which is why animals are often used in psychological research.

This section is designed to give you a general overview of what pheromones are and how they might work. The following sections provide you with more detailed information about how another pheromone, androstadienone, might work alongside secondary sex characteristics to signify good quality genes.

Even though humans' vomeronasal organ apparently doesn't function anymore, we may still detect pheromones through our sense of smell.

Guiding Question:

How does the study on domestic pigs suggest pheromones may be capable of affecting human behaviour?

Critical Thinking Extension:

Hypothesizing: You have probably learned by now that detailed explanations of variables and behaviour include providing explanations of *how* the variable influences the behaviour. Can you hypothesize *how* the detection of pheromones through the olfactory system may result in an observable action?

If you're interested…

If you like newts, livescience.com has an interesting article called "Newt Pheromones Put Females into Mating Frenzy."

(b) *Androstadienone*

In the previous section you were introduced to a new kind of chemical messenger that is only recently being studied in some detail in regard to its effect on human behaviour. While the study on female boars might suggest that the pheromone androstenone may affect behaviour, it didn't provide much insight into how it may affect behaviour in humans. The following study introduces a new putative pheromone that has been studied in humans and provides some insight into its role in the sexual behaviour of humans.

Androstadienone is found in male sweat and may help females in the process of selecting a suitable mate. Whereas testosterone may influence mate selection by providing *visual* signs of health and fertility, androstadienone may send signals through the sense of smell.

Studies have tested the relationship between smell and attraction by having males wear a t-shirt for a few days and then place them in a bag for females to smell. The results of this research suggest that humans may give off signals through smell that suggest if one is a good match to procreate with (e.g. Wedekind, 1995). But studies like this only show that smell might facilitate attraction and appropriate mate selection and they don't necessarily investigate *pheromones*. I mention this study here because it simply provides some evidence that smell can affect attraction by providing a signal of good quality genes.

Androstadienone is released under the arms of men and has the strongest impact on females.

One study that *did* investigate androstadienone specifically was by Saxton et al. (2008) who conducted a study using androstadienone during speed dating tests. The researchers placed cotton wool under the nose of female participants. There were three conditions as the cotton wool either contained androstadienone mixed with 1% clove oil, 1% clove oil only, or just water. The clove oil was used to make the control and the pheromone smell the same. This was hoped to isolate the chemical reaction as the factor affecting the behaviour, not the pleasantness or unpleasantness of the smell of the pheromone.

The results of two out of three of the studies showed that the females who were exposed to the androstadienone rated males as being more attractive than those that had just water or clove oil. This suggests that the pheromone androstadienone that is given off in male sweat may act as a chemical messenger to increase feelings of attraction in a female.

But yet again we are faced with the issue that we've seen before: this research doesn't fully explain how pheromones may affect our behaviour. In the next section you will see how androstadienone may work together with visual signals to send signals that facilitate mate preference.

Putative pheromone: When writing about the influence of pheromones on human behaviour, they are commonly referred to as putative pheromones. Putative is an adjective used to describe something that is generally considered or reputed to be something. So androstadienone is referred to as a *putative* pheromone because while it is generally considered to be acting as a pheromone, there is still a lot of debate about whether or not this is true.

Even though humans' vomeronasal organ apparently doesn't function anymore, we may still detect pheromones through our sense of smell.

Guiding Question:

How does the above evidence suggest that pheromones may influence human behaviour?

Critical Thinking Extension:
Hypothesizing: From an evolutionary stand-point, could you provide plausible reasons why a sense of smell might be important for attraction? Hint: electricity.

If you're interested…

The New York Times has an article that explores the sweaty t-shirt study further called "Studies Explore Love and the Sweaty T-shirt." While this study isn't about pheromones, it could still be used in other parts of the course, including the formation of relationships, the role of genetics in behaviour and evolutionary explanations of behaviour.

(c) Androstadienone and Attraction

Mate quality is another scientific term used to describe how suitable someone might be to mate with. Remember that "quality" refers to the suitability in being able to produce healthy babies that are likely to survive and be able to keep passing on genetic material.

In the previous section you were introduced to the idea that attraction might be influenced by smell. Being attracted to particular smells might help us choose a quality mate. Androstadienone may affect the attraction of females through their role of signaling mate quality. This male pheromone has been shown to have a stronger effect than androstenone on female vomeronasal organs (Jennings-White, 1995 as cited in Cornwell). It also activates different parts of the hypothalamus in men and women (Savic, 2001), which could affect gender responses to this androstadienone.

Cornwell et al. (2004) exposed participants to male and female pheromones, including androstadienone, and compared the results. Their participants were 56 male and 56 female participants between the ages of 17 – 26 who were recruited from the University of St. Andrews, Scotland. While the study also measured male preferences in females, to be consistent, we will only focus on the female side of this study.

Participants were shown faces from a range of ethnicities and the faces ranged in appearance from 50% feminized to 50% masculinized. The women were asked to rate which face they would prefer for a short-term or long-term relationship. After they were shown the photos, they were asked to smell five different vials. In these were androstadienone, androstenone, a female pheromone, and two control oils (one was clove oil and the other was oil of cade).

The results showed that there was a positive correlation between the female's preference of masculine facial characteristics and their preference for the smell of the androstadienone (the masculine pheromone). This suggests that preference for masculine facial characteristics corresponds with a greater liking for masculine smells.

The researchers conclude that pheromones and facial characteristics might work together by revealing an individuals mate quality. For instance, if a male has high concentrations of androstadienone and a masculine face it could provide two indicators for a female that he has high testosterone levels. This could be an indicator of dominance and/or good overall health (Cornwell et al., op cit.).

From this study, we start to get a better understanding of *how* androstadienone might influence attraction. It could work like other signs of mate quality in that it shows potential female mates that the male giving off the scent of the androstadienone would make for a good mate because he has desirable genetic material (e.g. high levels of testosterone). So while facial characteristics can send a visual signal, pheromones may work by sending signals through the sense of smell.

It is important to note that there are numerous factors that influence attraction and we are only looking at a very select sample. Also, there are many individual differences in preference between males and females in attraction. We've looked at this from a biological view, but haven't properly considered how other variables like cognition and culture may affect relationships. This will be the subject of the next topic.

Dominance in this context is another way of saying the ability to maintain a high social status. It's closely connected with aggression and competitiveness, which are also correlated with testosterone. For instance, the ability to display aggression might help maintain dominance.

Guiding Question:

How might androstadienone influence behaviour?

Critical Thinking Extension:

Ethics: Men and women have dreamed for centuries of a "love potion." What are the possible practical and ethical implications of the findings from studies like Cornwell et al.'s?

If you're interested…

These sections have addressed how pheromones may increase feelings of attractiveness. One study measured male responses to the smell of female tears. You can find a summary of the article online. It's called "Woman's tears contain chemical cues."

Relevant Topics

- Pheromones and behaviour
- Hormones and behaviour

Practice Exam Questions

- Discuss evolutionary explanations of behaviour.
- Explain one study related to pheromones and behaviour.
- To what extent do genetics influence behaviour?
- Explain how one pheromone may influence human behaviour.

Research Methods

Cornwell et al.'s study is a good example of a field experiment. A speed-dating situation is a naturally occurring event and the researchers manipulated the variable of detecting pheromones during participation in this event. By showing that pheromones might affect attraction in a real life setting, the study can add to the growing body of evidence that suggests pheromones affect human behaviour.

Ethical Considerations

When conducting field experiments debriefing becomes incredibly important. The speed-dating study is a great one for discussing the role of debriefing. On the one hand, if a female's perception of a male was altered because of the pheromone it might be beneficial to inform her of this. However, in doing so a potential future relationship might be jeopardized as she may disregard initial feelings of attraction as just being a result of the pheromones. Would it be more ethical to inform the participants which group they were in, or simply say there were three different groups?

5.3 Culture and Attraction
How might cultural values affect attraction?

(a) Cultural Values

The previous topics were designed to show you how biological factors may influence attraction. But only looking at personal relationships from a biological perspective is reductionist. Here you'll see how cultural values may influence attraction and this section is designed to recap the concept of cultural values and Hofstede's descriptions of cultural dimensions. What we think is important might be affected by our cultural environment.

In the previous section we examined biological origins of attraction and how hormones, face shape and genetics could influence attraction. But it is important that we don't overlook the role of attraction in deciding to ask someone on a date, because after all, the formation of a romantic relationship most probably begins with the first stages of attraction. It makes sense if you think about it, but this is not always the case, like in cultures that have arranged marriages and we'll look at those later.

Let's first look at romantic relationships where people *do* get to choose whom they take on a date. It probably begins with attraction. When you hear the word attraction you might be thinking about physical attraction. But attraction is more than just physical. Have you ever been *physically* attracted to someone you've just met and then after getting to know them you thought that you would never want to date them… ever? Or has the opposite happened? You thought, "well *they're* not much to look at…" … but then you become good friends and you start hanging out and then you realise, "Hey, I think I'm in love."

Again we are seeing in psychology and in relationships that it's not just biology; getting to know someone could also affect our desire to form a romantic relationship with them. As we've seen in previous sections an influential factor in our thought processes can be our cultural background. Depending on the culture we're from we may have different values and these values may affect our judgement. We're going to look again at *how* cultural values could affect the way we think about a potential mate.

To recap, according to Hofstede's descriptions of cultural dimensions there is a tendency in individualistic cultures to place higher value on independence and stress the importance of individuals taking care of themselves and their immediate family (e.g. husband, wife, kids, and parents). Having the power and the right to be an individual and to make your own decisions (individual autonomy) and self-expression are also highly valued.

On the other hand, in collectivist cultures people may be defined by their relationships and their obligations more than by their personal achievements. Individual autonomy and self-expression are not encouraged and group harmony is more important than individual achievement. Individuals in collectivist cultures can expect their relatives or in-group members to look after them in exchange for loyalty to the group. Basically, a society's point on this continuum is reflected in what has more emphasis – "I" or "We".

A cultural dimension is a term used to describe two opposing sets of cultural values. Cultures may vary along the continuum of which set of values they most embody.

We can see in this section another example of how psychology is about understanding relationships: how we think may be affected by our cultural background, and this might affect our behaviour.

When you use the term group harmony, make sure you think carefully about what you mean. What group are you referring to? What does "harmony" look like in that group? Many students love to use this term, without fully considering what it means.

I can't stress enough how important it is to remember that these are very broad generalizations and you need to remember that when describing these cultures and cultural values. Think about which cultural dimension you most identify with and how would you feel if someone said, "You're from a collectivist culture so you don't value self-expression", or, "You're from an individualistic culture so you don't think about keeping harmonious relationships in your family." We can and do make generalizations in psychology – but we always have to make sure we remember they are in fact generalizations.

Guiding Question:

How might cultural values influence attraction?

Critical Thinking Extension:

Economics and Culture: Part of understanding psychology is also connected to understanding other subjects. Economic factors can affect cultural values. Can you think about how and why economic factors may affect cultural values?

If you're interested…

You can view interviews with Hofstede on YouTube or visit his website at geert-hofstede.com to learn more about cultural dimensions.

(b) Mate Preference

In this topic we are going to revisit a concept closely associated with attraction, mate preference. In biological terms to "mate" means to procreate and so a "mate" in that sense means a person you would like to have babies with. In Buss' study he investigated mate preference by gathering data on what types of characteristics were preferred when choosing a mate. From this study you were shown the cross-cultural *similarities* in mate preference, which provide evidence for evolutionary explanations for the gender *differences* in mate preference. However, Buss also gathered data on cross-cultural differences.

Buss measured mate preference by having participants fill out a questionnaire asking participants questions about how desirable particular traits were (such a good looks, chastity, ambition, social status, financial prospects, etc.) They also gave them a list of certain characteristics and they asked the participants to rank them in order of how important they are when considering whom to marry. Examples of these characteristics were attractiveness, good earning capacity, and ambition. The data were analyzed and correlations between cultural dimensions and mate preference identified. One of the correlations found was that females from collectivist cultures placed a higher value on traits like social status and ambition, when compared with females from individualistic cultures (Buss, 1989).

There are multiple possible explanations for the correlations Buss found and I will provide you with only *one* and do so on the proviso that you remember that this is just one interpretation. You are encouraged to challenge, disregard or elaborate on it. The key is that you understand from these results just *how* cultural values may affect the *formation* of relationships.

When identifying research methods there are often grey areas. For example, is Buss' study an example of a correlational study or a natural experiment?

Our cultural values may influence how we think. This could affect how we view potential mates.

One possible explanation for the fact that females from collectivist cultures might place a higher value on social status and ambition could be based on the increased value placed on the thoughts, feelings and opinions of members of the extended family, which is valued more in collectivist societies. Because in modern society social status is obtained by wealth, in order to bring pride to the extended family it might be important to raise social status. For this reason if a man already has social status it might make him more attractive. Similarly, if he has ambition it might not matter if he doesn't have status and wealth *now*, the ambition will increase the chances he will have in the future. Through being successful in terms of status and wealth a man may have a higher chance of bringing pride to the female's family and/or raising the status of the entire family if a union is formed, thus making him more desirable. This would be considered important to the wider family. So this isn't to say that status and ambition are not valued in individualistic cultures (remember that females *across* cultures valued these traits), but that it's one possible reason why it's *more* valued in collectivist cultures.

But this was only one explanation of one of the results. Could you come up with your own explanation of the results? And there were other results as well. The table below shows other results from the study.

Males	*Females*
Males from individualistic cultures tended to place less emphasis on domestic skills.	Females from individualistic cultures tended to place less emphasis on ambition and financial prospects.
You'll notice that these results can be examined from either viewpoint. That is to say, you could begin by thinking "Why might collectivist values place higher emphasis on social status." Or, "why might individualistic cultures place less emphasis on social status?" An excellent explanation is one that could do both!	

Guiding Question:

How might cultural values influence mate preference?

Critical Thinking Extension:

Tolerating Uncertainty: Many students want to make concrete statements and generalizations. Critical thinkers realize that the world is not black and white and that explanations of correlations are not always definitive answers. What are some reasons why we cannot make definitive claims about cultural values and mate preference based on Buss' study alone?

If you're interested...

Buss' whole article is available online for free ("Sex Differences in Human Mate Preferences") and the language is mostly accessible for DP students.

(c)   *For Love or …?*

As you saw in the previous section, cultural values may affect the way we think about prospective partners for mating and marrying. Another important factor that culture may affect is how we think about the role of love in a relationship. Before we explore this idea, it might be worth taking some time to think about your own interpretation of the word "love."

Throughout history and in many modern societies marriage is not about the love between two individuals, it's about the union of whole families. Will you consider marrying someone you don't love, but who is chosen for you by your family?

In this section we're going to continue our investigation into the extent to which cultural values may influence the formation of a marriage. We're going to look at the varying importance placed on love by some cultures over others. This also becomes important when we try to understand why marriages might be more likely in some cultures to dissolve (e.g. end in separation or divorce).

Would you marry someone who had everything you wanted in a mate, but you didn't love?

In cultures like Pakistan and India, divorce rates are incredibly low when compared to places like the United States. There are multiple possible reasons for the differences in these divorce rates and once again it's important to remember that we are only looking at a very limited scope of possible explanations.

Levine et al. (1995) conducted a cross-cultural study on college students from eleven different cultures that compared the importance people from different cultures placed on love when deciding whom to marry. The researchers measured attitudes towards the importance of love in a marriage by asking the following question:

- "If a person had all the qualities you desired, would you marry them if you weren't in love with them?"

The participants answered "Yes", "No" or "Neutral" and the data were analyzed. This question is assessing the extent to which love is a key ingredient in the decision to choose a marriage partner. What would your answer be? If you could "build" your dream life-partner that had everything, but for whatever reason you didn't *love* them, would you marry them?

Levine et al. hypothesized that attitudes towards the importance of love in getting married would be different in collectivist and individualistic cultures. The results did in fact find that participants from India, Pakistan and Thailand were the most likely to answer "Yes", they would marry someone they didn't love if they had all the right qualities. They also found a very strong correlation for love being a pre-requisite for marriage in individualistic countries like the USA, the UK and Australia. That is to say, participants from these countries were more likely to require being in love with someone in order to marry them. These results suggest that there is a correlation

A common saying is that in individualistic countries people marry the person they love, in collectivist countries people love the person they marry.

between the culture someone comes from and the value they place on love when getting married.

One possible explanation for these results is based on earlier work by Triandis (2001), who has investigated Hofstede's cultural dimensions. He proposes that in collectivist cultures, social norms and duty are more important than personal pleasure (Triandis, as cited in Levine et al.). This might explain why love is not as important to forming a marriage in cultures such as India and Pakistan: in these collectivist cultures other factors need to be taken into consideration when deciding whom to marry. Social norms such as the practice of arranged marriages and having parents and extended family members heavily involved in the match-making process mean that the *individual's* choice in their partner is limited. They also might feel that it's their duty to follow their parents' wishes and agree to marry the person who has been chosen for them. And since love is a really about individual choice, we can see that love might not be such a factor when forming marriages in these cultures.

From this section it's hoped that you have been able to see how cultural factors might also affect feelings of attraction and the formation of a marriage. These same variables will become important later in this chapter when we think about cultural factors that add to explanations of why marriages might end in divorce.

Guiding Question:

How might cultural values influence the formation of a marriage?

Critical Thinking Extension:

Population Validity: Like many other studies, Levine et al.'s 1985 study compared the preferences of college students. Could you explain why the results from this demographic might not be generalizable to older age groups? What variables might influence a change in perception as people get older?

If you're interested...

The issue of arranged marriages is an important and often controversial one. There are many documentaries available online about this practice that you may be interested in watching. For example, there are at least two TED Talks that deal with this topic. One is for the case of arranged marriages ("Ira Travedi: The Case for Arranged Marriages") and the other is opposed ("Sabitina James: My Flight From an Arranged Marriage".)

Relevant Topics

- Culture and behaviour
- The formation of relationships
- Interpersonal relationships

Practice Exam Questions

- To what extent do sociocultural factors affect the formation of relationships?
- Discuss one or more influences of culture on behaviour.
- To what extent do cultural dimensions affect one behaviour?

Research Methods

As with Buss' research, Levine et al.'s study is another example of the value of using correlational studies when investigating behaviour across cultures. It's impossible to isolate cultural values as an independent variable to be manipulated in the laboratory, so correlational methods must be used. By gathering data across cultures and using questionnaires to quantify behaviour, the researchers can draw conclusions about cultural differences in approaches to relationships.

Ethical Considerations

An important part of informed consent is providing participants with the knowledge that their results will be anonymous and their participation confidential. This is important from a methodological validity viewpoint, as it will increase the probability that participants will give honest answers. Participants from cultures that practice arranged marriages, for instance, may not feel comfortable expressing opinions that may go against this practice (e.g. in a study like Levine et al.'s). Assuring them *before* the study that their results will be anonymous and their participation confidential will improve the validity of the data and will reduce their psychological stress during the study.

5.4 Communication and Relationships

Why are some couples happier than others?

(a)   Positive Communication

Have you ever seen an elderly couple walking and holding hands? It's just one of the sweetest things to see. Perhaps this is because a long-lasting marriage seems to becoming rarer, especially in developed countries with very high divorce rates. But what makes the difference between a happy and successful marriage and an unsuccessful one?

Dr. John Gottman has been researching married couples for over thirty years trying to understand patterns of communication between couples and the effect this has on marriages. In his research he has tried to uncover correlations that might explain how and why some couples remain happily married, while others end their marriage in divorce. How does a couple go from the happiest day of their life (presumably) on their wedding day and being madly in love, to sitting across from one another in the divorce-lawyer's round table office arguing over who gets the TV/kids/dog?

He summarizes his findings as follows:

"In great relationships people seem to have the motto: 'Baby, when you're upset, the world stops and I listen.'

In unhappy relationships the motto seems to be: 'I don't want to be with you when you're so *negative*. Go away.'"

From this idea we can see that communication is vitally important in a marriage. This is what the research suggests: the difference between happy marriages and unhappy ones is how couples communicate. Interestingly, Gottman suggests that it's not the frequency or the intensity of arguments in a relationship that dictate marital satisfaction - it's the patterns of communication (Gottman, 1985).

Gottman's studies and others have shown that positive communication can increase the happiness in a marriage.

Marital satisfaction refers to how happy someone is in their marriage. Low marriage satisfaction is a strong indicator of future divorce.

Gottman's research began in the 1970s and he has been conducting longitudinal research on married couples for decades since. This means that over many years the same couples are interviewed and data is gathered to see how their marriage is going.

Much of this research has been conducted through observations in what Gottman calls "The Love Lab". This is an apartment that is designed to be as realistic as possible, and just like a normal apartment. Couples are invited to spend a weekend in the "lab" and there are cameras situated throughout the apartment that record the couple's discussions, body language and general behaviour. They also measure things like their blood pressure and heart rate, to see the physiological effects of their interactions. For obvious reasons they don't, however, film them in the bathroom (Gottman and Silver, 1999).

One of these studies took place between 1983 and 1987 and followed 73 couples over this four year period (Gottman and Levenson, 1992). The mean ages of the participants were 30 years old (husbands) and 28 years old (wives). This was one of Gottman's earliest studies where coding strategies were used to observe patterns of communication between married couples. They originally gathered data on 200 couples but narrowed this down to 73 based on results from initial questionnaires: they wanted to get couples that had a range in marital satisfaction from not very satisfied to very satisfied.

Gottman and Levenson observed the couples in their lab for short periods of time. The procedure involved the couples coming to the lab and engaging in discussions while being filmed. The couples had not spoken to each other for at least eight hours that day (e.g. they would have been interviewed after both couples had been at work) and they were asked to discuss three topics:

(a)　What they did during that day
(b)　A source of conflict in the marriage
(c)　A mutually agreed "pleasant" topic

The couples were observed and their patterns of behaviour and communication were analyzed. One coding technique used by Gottman and Levenson was the Rapid Couples Interaction Scoring System (RCISS). This helped quantify interactions between the couples. From the observation data they categorized the couples into one of two groups: regulated and non-regulated couples. A regulated couple was defined as a couple whose ratio of positive to negative interactions gradually increased throughout the observed discussions. There were 42 regulated and 31 non-regulated couples identified in this study. We'll discuss the outcomes of the non-regulated couples in the next section.

> Regulated and non-regulated was an operational definition used by Gottman and Levenson.

One correlation found was that the regulated couples reported higher marital satisfaction, more positive ratings of their interactions and more positive emotional expressions towards each other. The ratio of positive to negative communication in the regulated couples was 5:1, which means there were 5 positive interactions to every one negative interaction. Examples of "interactions" include what was said, how it was said and other non-verbal body language gestures. From this early research Gottman and Levenson proposed that a stable marriage requires positive communication to regulate the interactions of the couples. If the ratio is at least 5:1, then the couple will experience increased marital satisfaction.

Gottman candidly refers to the regulated couples as "the masters." In the next section, we'll look at "the disasters."

Guiding Question:

How might positive communication increase marital satisfaction?

Critical Thinking Extension:

Generalizability: There are two obvious characteristics of this study that require scrutiny in terms of its validity: the time and culture. This study was conducted in Indiana, in the US. What cultural factors may limit the extent to which these results could be generalized to marriages across cultures? The second factor is the year in which this was conducted. This study was conducted over 30 years ago. What might have changed since then that could limit the validity of applying these results to modern marriages?

If you're interested…

Because of the immense importance and popularity of his subject of research, Gottman has become rather famous. There are numerous interviews with him that you can watch online. In one of these (with Anderson Cooper on Youtube) he discusses what he calls "The Four Horsemen of the Marriage Apocalypse." These are four patterns of communication that he believes can predict divorce.

(b)   *Negative Communication*

In the previous section you were introduced to the role that positive communication can play in a marriage. Gottman and Levenson found that if couples are arguing over something but are able to gradually focus on the positives and have positive verbal and non-verbal interactions, they will have higher levels of marital satisfaction and will be less likely to consider marriage dissolution (i.e. separation or divorce).

These results can help us explain one of the roles of communication in a marriage. But it can also help explain why a marriage might end. Gottman has stated that he can predict divorce with over 90% accuracy using mathematical models that he has devised after decades of research. He can do this within five minutes of observing a couple discussing a point of conflict in a marriage (Gottman, 1994).

There is a large body of research that draws a similar conclusion: negative patterns of communication in a marriage can decrease marriage satisfaction and may lead to divorce.

Over the four year period of Gottman's original study, 36 out of the 73 couples contemplated ending their marriage (49%). When comparing the regulated and non-regulated couples, 7% of the regulated couples divorced during the four year period and 19% of the non-regulated couples did. This shows that increased negative to positive ratios of communication may increase the chances of divorce. The researchers also concluded that non-regulated couples were: "…more conflict engaging, more defensive, more stubborn, more angry, more whining, more withdrawn as listeners, less affectionate, less interested in their partners, and less joyful than regulated couples" (Gottman and Levenson, 1992). This is pretty strong evidence that a high negative to positive ratio of communication may affect a marriage.

Another phenomenon in marriage research is something called the demand/withdraw communication pattern (Holley et al., 2013). This is also known as *wife* demand/ *husband* withdraw pattern because studies have shown there is a typical pattern of behaviour associated with each gender. This pattern involves a wife placing demands on her husband to discuss or deal with a particular issue, but to avoid conflict the husband withdraws from the situation and avoids discussing the matter. The effect of this is an increased desire from the wife to deal with the issue, placing more demands on the husband, but the husband still doesn't want to discuss the matter so withdraws even further. The conflict is never resolved and the end result is marriage dissatisfaction and a desire from both parties to terminate the marriage (Bradbury,

A large body of research says that negative communication patterns in a relationship can have damaging effects. The man here is stonewalling.

In your exam you may be asked about why relationships change or end. Change could mean an increase or decrease in marital satisfaction and divorce could be the end.

2000). Gottman calls the withdrawal or shutting down of communication stonewalling and it is one of the patterns of communication that he uses to predict divorce.

Other researchers have also found that the demand/withdraw pattern of communication is one of the strongest predictors of divorce and this pattern has been observed in studies since the 1970s (Holley et al., 2013). There's a strong body of research that suggests this pattern of communication will lead to marital dissatisfaction and will have negative consequences for a marriage.

This could help explain Gottman's regulated vs. non-regulated couples findings. If one partner has an issue that they want to discuss and the other is open and receptive to the idea, they can engage in communication about it and perhaps resolve the issue. This may explain the increased positive to negative ratio found in happy couples. However, if there is avoidance and withdrawal this might only increase the negative communication from one partner which could make the communication pattern increasingly negative, which may explain the correlation between non-regulated couples and marital dissatisfaction.

Gottman and Krokoff (1989) also found a negative correlation between husband withdrawal and a decline in marital satisfaction, which provides further evidence for the negative effects stonewalling and the demand/withdrawal communication pattern can have on a relationship. Interestingly, their three year longitudinal study also found that disagreement and having angry arguments was a sign of unhappiness in the marriage. Surprisingly, however, they were also a good predictor that in the long-run the marriage would get better and marital satisfaction would increase. This suggests that it's not the nature of arguing that matters. Instead, arguing and dealing with problems could be beneficial for the long-term health of a marriage.

From these studies we can conclude that if couples argue and fight it might not necessarily be a bad thing, provided they can work and communicate to overcome their sources of conflict. What is worse than arguing and fighting, it appears, is one partner withdrawing from the conflict and the issue never being resolved.

In the next section, we'll look at possible physiological explanations for the gender differences in stonewalling behaviour.

Imagine a wall made of stone: it's cold, doesn't move and doesn't respond when you shout at it. This is why Gottman uses this metaphor to describe someone avoiding communication by shutting themselves down and blocking their partner out.

The demand/withdraw communication pattern might be applied to either spouse (husband or wife). However, Gottman claims that over 80% of stonewallers are males.

Guiding Question:

How might negative communication patterns affect a marriage?

Critical Thinking Extension:

Applications: In the exam you may be asked about the role of communication in marriages or explanations for why marriages may change or end. The research in this topic provides you with material to address both of these questions. How could you apply research into the demand/withdraw pattern of communication to address both topics?

If you're interested…

John Gottman co-authored a very popular book called *The Seven Principles of Making Marriage Work*. One of the reasons researchers investigate why relationships end is so they can develop more effective marriage therapy interventions. Gottman's book provides seven strategies that help couples make their marriage work.

(c)   Biology and Communication

In the previous two sections you've seen the importance of having healthy communication strategies in a relationship. If couples don't have enough positive communication or one partner withdraws from dealing with problem areas in the relationship then the research shows that their marriage will suffer as a result. On the other hand, dealing with problems head on and maintaining a high ratio of positive to negative communication strategies can be the key to maintaining a happy relationship.

But what are the physiological factors involved in communication and its effect on a marriage? A lot of research has been conducted on the physiological correlates of the demand/withdraw pattern of behaviour.

Emotion is an important aspect of relationships for many reasons. This is why Gottman and other researchers measure the physiological effects of communication on couples and Gottman and Levenson have conducted other studies that have correlated the long-term effects of physiological arousal on marital satisfaction.

In one study of 21 couples over a three year period they found a strong correlation between high levels of physiological arousal and a decline in marital satisfaction. There was also a very strong correlation (0.91) between the husband's heart rate (a measure of physiological arousal) and the decline in marital satisfaction. Their research has also shown that during arguments, husbands demonstrate higher levels of physiological arousal than females and it takes males longer to reduce their arousal (Gottman and Levenson, 1985).

This might explain why males tend to be the ones who withdraw from communication and stonewall: they experience higher levels of physiological arousal and so their withdrawal and stonewalling is an attempt to reduce their high levels of emotion. So the stonewalling and withdrawal might be a strategy employed by males to reduce their high levels of arousal and emotion. But the problem still exists because it doesn't lead to resolving the conflict that generated the high level of emotion in the first place. The withdrawal might be a behaviour by the husband to reduce his feelings of emotion.

There could be a bidirectional relationship between the physiological arousal and the communication. The demands from the wife to deal with a problem might increase a husband's physiological arousal. This leads to stonewalling and/or withdrawal to decrease their emotional state. But this increases the wife's frustration and anger, increasing her negative emotion and demands of the husband. And so the cycle may continue until both couples agree that it's best if they dissolve the relationship.

> **Guiding Question:**
>
> How might physiological arousal and communication have a bidirectional relationship?

Critical Thinking Extension:

Making Connections: Based on research you investigated in the chapter on criminology, can you provide an explanation as to why husbands may demonstrate higher levels of physiological arousal? You may also be able to connect what you learn in this chapter to cognitive appraisals and reappraisals, if you study PTSD as well.

Researchers often measure levels of emotion in individuals by obtaining measures of physiological responses, such as heart rate and skin temperature. This may be triangulated with self-reported feelings of emotion.

In correlational studies, the strongest positive correlation is 1.0. The closer the correlation gets to 1.0, the stronger the correlation.

If you're interested…

Jenna McCarthy has an interesting and very light-hearted TED Talk called "What you don't know about marriage." In this talk she summarizes a wide range of interesting findings from research on factors that affect marital satisfaction, including the perils of winning an Oscar for best actress.

Relevant Topics

- Personal relationships
- The role of communication in personal relationships
- Explanations for why relationships may change or end

Practice Exam Questions

- To what extent do biological factors explain why relationships may change or end?
- Evaluate one or more studies related to personal relationships.
- Discuss the role of communication in personal relationships.

Research Methods

Gottman's "Love Lab" is another example of how differentiating between research methods can often be a grey area. On the one hand, it could be classed as a naturalistic observation because in Gottman's new lab in Seattle, Washington, every attempt is made to make it like a real-life retreat to allow couples to interact naturally. On the other hand, it is a controlled environment where they measure behaviour carefully. Regardless, it does highlight the benefits of observations over self-report data forms. As Raush (1974) puts it, "Studying what people say about themselves is no substitute for studying how they behave…. Questionnaires and scales of marital satisfaction and dissatisfaction have yielded very little. We need to look at what people do with one another" (as cited in Bradbudy et al., 2000).

Ethical Considerations

Ethical considerations abound in research investigating such a personal issue like marriage. One major consideration would be informed consent. Many studies on married couples involve asking them to discuss something that may lead to conflict and arguing. The participants would need to be told that this would be part of the study, as couples whose relationship is fragile and unstable may not be willing to put themselves through the psychological stress of arguing in front of cameras and researchers.

5.5 Culture and Relationships
How can cultural factors influence divorce?

(a)   Culture and Relationships

In the previous topic we investigated the effects that various types of communication strategies can have on a marriage. We also looked at how biological factors may influence, and be influenced by, patterns of communication in a relationship.

In this topic we're going to further our understanding of how cultural factors may influence the formation of a relationship, and how these same cultural factors may affect the probability of a divorce. It seems plausible that communication might affect marital satisfaction and this could be consistent across cultures. But would this necessarily lead to the ending of a marriage? This topic is designed to provide possible cultural explanations for differences in divorce rates across cultures.

Research like Gottman's that looks into communication and marriage is based very much in the US. Could these results be generalized? One study compared 50 US couples with 52 Pakistani couples to see if the correlations between communication and marital satisfaction would be consistent across these two cultures. They also compared these groups with a third group of 48 Pakistani immigrant couples living in the United States. They did find in fact that similar correlations existed across the culture groups - couples who had more positive communication had higher levels of marital satisfaction. However, the correlation was stronger in the US group than the Pakistani group (and to a lesser extent the immigrant group) (Rehman and Holtzworth-Munro, 2007).

What this suggests is that communication can affect a marriage across different cultures, but it may be more influential in Western cultures.

Communication might not have the same effect across cultures. The outcome of negative communication might not be the same, either.

Levine et al.'s study (1995) had another aim that wasn't shared earlier. The results showed a positive correlation between divorce rates and the importance of love in marriages. That is to say, those cultures that placed a higher importance on love also had higher rates of divorce. This is where cultural values and the reasons for getting married in the first place might influence divorce rates. If a marriage was formed on the basis of love then this is an individual choice. No-one can tell you whom to love and so in individualistic cultures where personal autonomy is valued, the freedom to marry whomever you like may make it easier to also dissolve that marriage.

Moreover, individualistic values including freedom of individual choice over family relationships and obligations may result in divorce, as divorce might be a more commonly accepted practice (i.e. it's a social norm). For example, it would be much easier to get divorced if you didn't have to worry about offending families or keeping the family together and could make your own decision to dissolve the marriage. If you were faced with the fear of being a social outcast because divorce was not a social norm, this might also affect an individual's decision to stay married.

People may not feel the same pressures to stay married if they are no longer in love with the person. On the other hand, if the marriage was formed with many factors taken into consideration and the impact of the extended family on the marriage was considered, and/or extended families were involved in the process of forming the marriage, this may increase the personal responsibility of keeping the marriage together. It might also influence the ease in which the marriage could be dissolved.

The correlation found in Levine et al.'s research between the value of love in relationships and the divorce rates could help us understand the role of culture in explaining why some marriages are more likely to end in divorce compared to others. This could add to the already discussed communication and biological factors that might have negative effects on a relationship and help explain why a marriage may decrease in satisfaction, but not necessarily end.

> It's important that you think carefully about how this research might be applied to explanations for why relationships may change or end. This may be more difficult than you first think.

Guiding Question:

How might cultural values explain differences in divorce rates across cultures?

Critical Thinking Extension:

Could there be other factors that may explain some countries like India and Pakistan's low divorce rate? For instance, Levine's study also investigated economic factors. One possible way of exploring this topic further is to hypothesize how economic factors may influence attitudes towards divorce and conduct some research to test your hypotheses.

If you're interested…

Alex Gendler has an interested animated TED Ed video called "The history of marriage." The history of same-sex and arranged marriages are also explained in this brief yet very interesting video.

Cultural factors may affect attitudes towards divorce. This could be a factor in explaining why some cultures have much lower divorce rates than others.

(b) *Attitudes Towards Divorce*

What we can see from looking at studies on cross-cultural differences in attitudes towards love is that they provide plausible explanations for the role that cultural values may play in explaining why relationships might end. That is to say, in a culture that considers multiple factors in forming a relationship, a divorce might not be an easy option. Just because negative communication patterns emerge and a couple is unhappy, it doesn't mean that there is an equal probability across cultures that divorce will result.

But these explanations are, as Levine and his colleagues suggest, speculative. This means we can't know for sure and we need to be wary of making speculations that aren't based on really solid empirical evidence.

A more direct correlational relationship between cultural values and divorce rates could be explained through an investigation into attitudes towards *divorce* and what happens when the love leaves a relationship. This was a further element in Levine's investigation that wasn't mentioned earlier, but will be explored here.

Along with the question stated earlier about marrying for love, the researchers also asked participants to consider these statements….

- *If love has completely disappeared from a marriage, I think it's probably best for the couple to make a clean break.*
- *In my opinion, the disappearance of love from a marriage is not a sufficient reason for ending a marriage and should be viewed as such.*

The participants were asked to circle "Agree", "Disagree" or "Neutral". In these questions the researchers are directly investigating the relationships between attitudes about love and marriage and how this might affect divorce rates in those cultures. The results showed a positive correlation between divorce rates in countries where participants felt that when love has disappeared from a marriage making a break is the best option (e.g. Brazil, UK). Participants from the Philippines and Pakistan, on the other hand, were most likely to *disagree* that an absence of love was reason for ending a marriage.

Other studies have also found similar results that suggest a correlation between individualistic and collectivist values and attitudes towards divorce, meaning that individualistic cultures were more open to the idea of divorce. Other studies have shown that even within the United States there are correlations between divorce rates and individualist/collectivist attitudes. That is to say, states that have more individualistic attitudes (e.g. states in the Mountain West and Great Plains) have higher divorce rates than those with more collectivist attitudes (states in the Deep South) (Toth and Kemmelmeier, 2009).

This aspect of Levine et al.'s research simply provides more evidence for the role that cultural variables may play in explaining why marriage might be more common in some places over others. While communication may have an adverse effect on a relationship and could lead to the disappearance of love from a marriage, not everyone will feel that this is grounds to get a divorce.

Guiding Question:

How might cultural factors explain why relationships may change or end?

Critical Thinking Extension:

Reflecting on Generalizations: It is important that you are always careful when making generalizations. Many students draw conclusions from this data to say "Collectivist cultures will have less divorce because they don't value love." You have to remember that these results are statistical averages from around 1,000 participants across countries – to make such a claim shows that you haven't thought about individual differences or how individuals within cultures may have different values. It's essential that you reflect on your thinking because it is this self-reflection about your own knowledge and understanding of the world that will enable you to be a more informed citizen.

If you're interested…

Levine et al. (1985) is available online and the language is accessible for most DP students if you wanted to read the entire report.

Relevant Topics

- Personal Relationships
- Role of communication in a relationship
- Explanations for why relationships may change or end

Practice Exam Questions

- To what extent can sociocultural factors explain why relationships may change or end?
- Discuss sociocultural factors relevant to personal relationships.
- Evaluate one study related to personal relationships.

Research Methods

Levine et al.'s study highlights the benefits of the use of questionnaires in cross-cultural studies that investigate correlations between variables. By using questionnaires a lot of data can be gathered and behaviours can be quantified. Making cross-cultural comparisons and comparing correlations enables researchers to draw conclusions about cultural variables and their influence on behaviour.

Ethical Considerations

Cultural sensitivity needs to be considered and demonstrated when conducting cross-cultural research, especially if instruments used to gather data are created in one culture. For instance, questions about attitudes towards personal matters like relationships might be acceptable in some cultures but inappropriate to others. Researchers need to carefully consider the effects of their procedures when conducting cross-cultural research.

Conclusion

Early in the chapter we saw how attraction could be the result of primal instincts as we're driven by thousands of years of evolution and physiological forces. We might find ourselves drawn to someone because of the sound of their voice, the structure of their face or even how they smell. But as with all behaviours, we can't overlook the role of culture and cognition. While humans are animals, we're not always animalistic. To focus solely on the biology of attraction and the formation of relationships would limit our understanding. Our cultural environment affects our values, too, and this can influence our thoughts and actions, including whom we want to choose and keep as a marriage partner.

What we can learn from the research about healthy marriages is similar to other units: we seek to understand origins of behaviour so we can implement effective treatments. If we know why people are likely to get divorced, we can develop strategies to stop the problem before it begins. Failing that, we may be able to develop better marriage counselling strategies that seek to restore a couples' sense of commitment and marital satisfaction.

This chapter aimed to spark an interest in the study of interpersonal human relationships, as it's a popular area of study and one that has many applications.

As with other units, this chapter has provided you with more than enough material to prepare you for exam success. For the biological approach, for instance, you now have more choices of topics to apply to questions regarding evolution, hormones, and pheromones. In the socio-cultural approach, you could use the research in this chapter to address questions about cultural dimensions and cultural origins of behaviour. This is in addition to the obvious connections to the interpersonal relationships section of the Human Relationships option.

As with all units in this textbook, the hardest part was leaving out all the fascinating research that we could investigate. There's a plethora of research on the factors that influence human attraction, including the role of the female sex hormone estrogen. This could make for an interesting additional research project, if time in the course permits. Similarly, Gottman's popularized notion of the "Four Horsemen of the Apocalypse" proved too difficult to manage with the existing content, but it makes for an interesting extra investigation.

Becoming an expert in Interpersonal Relationships (i.e. Love and Marriage) could be a good strategy to prepare for Human Relationships questions in Paper Two, as you will get one essay question from this topic.

Human interaction and relationships are an integral part of the human experience. Knowing how to develop and maintain healthy ones, therefore, is a pretty relevant topic to study. Learning about how communication between people can affect relationships is valuable knowledge and maybe you'll even can start to consider some of the concepts we've explored in this chapter in your own relationships, both platonic and romantic.

Chapter 6
Quantitative Methods

Introduction

Understanding how and why psychologists use particular methods and techniques when conducting research is at the heart of the IB Psychology course. There may be a lot of new terms and ideas that will be introduced in this chapter, so it's recommended that this material is approached after you have a solid grounding in the subject and knowledge of a range of different studies. If you have been reading the summaries of research methods and ethics at the end of each topic, this chapter will help consolidate your learning and prepare you to apply what you've learned in your own explanations and evaluations of research.

Research in psychology can be roughly categorized into two broad categories: quantitative and qualitative. Quantitative research deals with numbers and statistical analyses. It enables researchers to draw conclusions about relationships between variables by turning behaviour into measurable quantities. Qualitative research, on the other hand, gathers data that is descriptive and cannot be analyzed using statistical tests. Qualitative methods and related concepts will be addressed in chapter nine.

One of the aims of this course is to help you develop an understanding of the range of possible options psychologists have when designing and carrying out research. It's recommended that all IB Psychology students learn about the quantitative methods in this chapter as understanding these methods will provide you with a range of possible options for addressing exam questions - you may be asked about the use of research methods in any of the topics in the core and the options. This chapter is also designed to help you understand core concepts involved in conducting your own experimental research for your Internal Assessment.

Another aim of this chapter is to encourage you to reflect on the nature of the three different approaches to understanding human behaviour that are integral to the IB Psychology course. These are the biological, cognitive and sociocultural approaches. In order to help encourage reflection on these different approaches, each quantitative method in the first topic is explained in relation to one of these approaches. For example, there's a particular focus on how and why laboratory experiments are used in the cognitive approach, and why correlational studies are used in cross-cultural research in the sociocultural approach. This is not to say that these methods are not used in other areas of study. This has been done to provide you with guidance on how to relate research methods with particular topics.

By the end of this chapter it is hoped you will be able to independently analyze and discuss the use of research methods in relation to different areas of study in psychology. You will also be ready to carry out your own experiment for the Internal Assessment.

6.1 Quantitative Methods

How and why do researchers use quantitative methods in psychology?

(a) True Experiments

Manipulate: Control, handle, manage. In experiments, the researchers manipulate the IV by managing it carefully to create different conditions for comparison. It's best to understand this term by looking at examples of IVs in experiments.

The term experimental method encompasses a range of types of experiments that measure relationships between independent and dependent variables, including natural experiments, quasi-experiments and field experiments (which will be explained later in this topic). In psychology the term experiment has a rather precise definition, whereas in mainstream media the term is often used to describe a study that wasn't an experiment at all.

A true experiment (also known as a laboratory experiment) is a type of experimental method that involves the manipulation of an independent variable (IV) and a measurement of the effect of this on a dependent variable (DV). The conditions created by the manipulation of the variable happens in a controlled environment so cause and effect relationships can be investigated. The true experiment is a common method across all areas of psychology. In this section we'll explore how and why it's used in the cognitive approach to understanding behaviour.

True Experiment: a quantitative research method that involves the manipulation of an independent variable in order to measure the effects on the dependent variable. The aim of an experiment is to isolate extraneous variables and investigate cause and effect relationships.

An integral part of the cognitive approach is understanding how variables can influence our cognitive processes. In order to measure this, researchers design experiments that involve the manipulation of an IV that is hypothesized to have an effect on a particular cognitive process. Here we can see that one way laboratory experiments are used in the cognitive approach is to have a cognitive process as the dependent variable. For example, in studies related to stereotypes and memory, the independent variable is the information given to the participants prior to processing and interpreting a piece of information. They are then given a recall test and the effects of this information on memory are measured. For example, in Stone et al.'s (2010) experiment the IV was the race of the basketball player in the photo they showed the participants. The DV was how they perceived and remembered the player's performance.

Bransford and Johnson's (1972) experiment is another example of how an independent variable (prior knowledge) is manipulated in order to test the effects on cognition. In their case the dependent variables were comprehension and recall. By manipulating an IV and creating different conditions, the researchers can measure the effects of this and compare the results to draw conclusions about the effects of variables on particular cognitive processes.

Loftus and Palmer's (1974) experiments on the misinformation effect provide further examples of how experimental designs can be used to measure the effects of external variables on cognitive processes. In these experiments the independent variable was the wording of the leading question and the dependent variable is memory. By manipulating the presence of misinformation (e.g. in the form of a leading question) the researchers were able to compare the results of the groups and draw conclusions about the effects of leading questions and misinformation on memory.

While experiments at the cognitive level of analysis might have the cognitive process as the dependent variable, they also include studies that measure the *effect* of cognition. In this way, the cognitive approach involves experiments that include cognition as the independent variable. Many studies that investigate neuroplasticity fall in this category. In these studies, participants are required to perform different cognitive processes while the effects on physiology (e.g. brain structure and/or function) are measured. For example, Desbordes et al.'s (2012) study involved the manipulation of an independent variable (the type of cognitive practice) and measured the effects this had on a dependent variable (the brain function during processing of emotional stimuli).

This experiment is an interesting example of how the term 'laboratory experiment' might be misleading. While many laboratory experiments do take place in laboratories, others may not. The goal of a true experiment is to investigate cause and effect relationships between the IV and the DV. In order to do this, all other extraneous variables must be controlled for as much as possible. Having an experiment take place in a controlled environment (e.g. a laboratory) is just one way that researchers can isolate the independent variable as the only factor influencing the dependent variable. How researchers design experiments to control for extraneous variables will be explained in the next section.

> An extraneous variable (also called a nuisance variable) is any variable other than the IV that may affect the DV.

Examples of True Experiments in the Approaches			
Approach	Study	Independent Variable	Dependent Variable
Biological	Radke et al. (2012)	Testosterone levels	Brain activity while perceiving faces with different emotion
Cognitive	Cohen (1981)	Information provided about the "women's" job (waitress or librarian)	Memory: the amount of stereotype consistent information remembered
Sociocultural	Asch's Experiments	Group size (is just one variable he manipulated)	Rate of conformity

In summary, key characteristics of a true experiment include:

- Manipulation of the independent variable and measures the effect/s on a dependent variable.
- Extraneous variables are controlled for as much as possible.
- The aim is to investigate cause and effect relationships between variables.

Guiding Question:

How and why are experiments used in the cognitive approach to understanding human behaviour?

Critical Thinking Extension:
Limitations: What do you think are the limitations of conducting research on humans using laboratory experiments? See if you can come up with some examples to support your evaluation. You also may want to try to practice on your own the ability to identify the use of a laboratory experiment and explain why it was used. Another way of extending yourself is to choose another topic and explain how and why laboratory experiments are used in that topic.

One of the most famous experiments in social psychology is Zimbardo's Stanford Prison Experiment. You can see Zimbardo's Ted Talk called "The Psychology of Evil." As you're watching this video, you may want to be asking yourself, "is this *really* an experiment?"

(b)   Experimental Designs and Controls

As you've seen in the previous section, the primary aim of a true experiment is to investigate a cause and effect relationship. The validity of the conclusions from experiments regarding cause and effect relationships can be enhanced by controlling for extraneous variables. This can be achieved through the use of experimental designs and controls. As you will be conducting an experiment for your internal assessment, you need to know and be aware of these concepts when designing an experiment.

To begin with, there are three main experimental designs: independent samples (aka independent groups), repeated measures and matched pairs. These terms refer to how participants experience the conditions of the experiment. In an experiment subjects may be randomly allocated to the treatment condition or the control condition (also known as the treatment and control *groups*). When participants experience different conditions, the research design is an independent samples design. For example, in Desbordes et al.'s (2012) study on the effects of meditation on the brain there was one treatment group who received mindfulness training, another group who received another form of cognitive training and a control group. These groups are independent and provide different samples of data, hence this experimental design is called independent samples. The researchers randomly allocated the participants to one of the conditions.

By being able to use random allocation to assign participants to the conditions, researchers can control for extraneous variables like the participant expectancy effect or order effects and increase the likelihood that their results are from the effects of the independent variable, not these other variables. For example, if Loftus and Palmer's participants experienced both conditions (e.g. reading "smashed" on one day and then "hit" on another), they may have guessed the aim of the experiment, which may cause the participant expectancy effect.

Sometimes it might not be desirable to use independent samples, as participant variability may confound your results. Participant variability refers to the differences in your participants that could influence the results. For example, in Bandura's Bobo Doll study, he might have ended up with more naturally aggressive children in one of the groups if he used random allocation. This could distort the results. One way of avoiding this is to have large sample sizes to decrease the chances of this happening. Bandura had around 50 kids for four conditions and to control for participant variability he used a matched pairs design. This is where participants are matched on some relevant criteria and then they are allocated to different conditions. Bandura had the kids' levels of natural aggressiveness rated (by teachers and daycare supervisors) and then he split them according to their ratings. Other experiments often match participants based on characteristics such as age, gender or occupation.

A third design possibility is called repeated measures. This is when all participants experience all conditions of the experiment. For instance, in Passamonti et al.'s (2012) study on the effects of tryptophan depletion (i.e. low serotonin) on the functioning of

---

Participant expectancy effect is when the participant suspects a particular result in the experiment, and so their behaviour changes, which affects the validity of the data.

See the glossary for definitions of these key terms.

The **order effect** is when the order of the task asked to do in a repeated measures experiment may influence the results.

A **confounding variable** is any variable other than the IV that has influenced the DV.

the brain they had participants come into the lab on two different days. On one day they drank a placebo and on the other they drank the tryptophan depleting drink. The researchers used counterbalancing to control for order effects, which means randomizing in what order the participants drank the treatment/placebo (e.g. half would drink placebo first and then tryptophan depletion drink, and the other half would do it in the opposite order).

They also used a double-blind design, which is when neither the researchers nor the participants know who is experiencing which condition of the experiment. A single-blind design is when only the participant doesn't know which group they belong to. The use of blind designs can help to control for researcher bias. Researchers may unconsciously interpret results differently if they have a particular hypothesis, or they may give off subconscious cues towards the participants about how to act during the experimental procedures that may also affect the results.

To summarize, there are a number of controls that researchers can use when designing experiments. These controls help to reduce the influence of confounding variables such as order effects, participant variability, participant expectancy effects, and researcher bias. The use of blind designs, counterbalancing and research designs (e.g. MP, RM, IS) can help control for extraneous variables and improve the internal validity of an experiment.

When you are designing your own experiment for your IA, you will need to apply your understanding of some of these key concepts in your own work. Understanding the experimental design and the use of controls can also enhance your ability to evaluate experiments that you may use in other parts of the course.

Clinical drug trials need to employ a variety of controls to ensure the validity of the conclusions regarding the effects of new drugs.

If you're evaluating research in an essay, remember that part of an evaluation includes *strengths*. If you know that a study employed particular controls, you could include these in your evaluation and explain how they help to increase the validity of the experiment's conclusion.

Internal Validity: the extent to which the experiment accurately investigates a particular relationship.

Guiding Question:

Why are controls used in experimental research?

Critical Thinking Extension:

In the following sections you will learn about other research methods. Can you think of any subjects of study where allocation into different conditions is impossible? (Hint: think about studies investigating brain function). You can also extend yourself by revising some key studies you have learned about. Can you identify possible extraneous variables that might influence the results? How could the researchers control for these?

You may want to be referring back to the terms and definitions in this section when you are conducting your IA.

If you're interested...

One of the guys from the Crash Course channel also hosts a video on the SciShow channel called "Human Experimentation: The Good, The Bad, & the Ugly." Do you think Jenner's "experiments" were really "experiments?"

(c) Field Experiments

Field Experiment: an experiment (with the manipulation of an IV and effects on DV measured) conducted in a naturalistic setting.

The primary benefit of conducting a laboratory experiment is that extraneous variables can be controlled for and the independent variable can be isolated as the only variable that is operating on the dependent variable, which allows conclusions to be drawn regarding cause-effect relationships. But an obvious critique of the laboratory experiment is that this might not reflect what happens in real life, and psychologists are interested in understanding real life human behaviour, not only what happens in a laboratory.

This is why conducting a field experiment is often a valuable type of experiment to conduct because behaviour in real-life environments (the "field") can be studied. A field experiment is when there is a manipulation of the independent variable by the researcher, but this happens in a naturalistic environment. Field experiments are often used to investigate social influences on behaviour.

SL and HL students need to be able to explain the use of research methods when studying particular topics for the core and the options (Paper One and Two).

A classic example of a field experiment was conducted on a university campus in Florida by Clark and Hatfield (1989). In this study the researchers wanted to investigate the differences in responses to sexual offers by men and women. The researchers had a range of confederates approach students on campus and ask a question along the lines of, 'would you like to go to bed with me tonight?' 0% of females agreed to this request by males, whereas around 70% of males agreed to go to bed with an unknown female. This is an example of a field experiment as the independent variable (the gender pairing of the proposer/receiver of the offer) is being manipulated by the researchers as they have chosen the confederates and given them the instructions to approach attractive subjects of the opposite gender. It also happens in a naturalistic environment, which is in a central outdoor area in a large college campus. The dependent variable is the rate of acceptance of the offer.

Perhaps a better example of a field experiment being used in social psychology is Sherif et al.'s classic experiment at the Robber's Cave Summer Camp. In this experiment we can see the benefits of manipulating the independent variable (e.g. conditions of competition and cooperation) in a real-life setting. The researchers deliberately chose participants that were quite similar in characteristics to control for participant variability. By manipulating the conditions within the summer camp, they were able to test the hypotheses about factors that influence levels of conflict (i.e. competition and cooperation).

Studies on bystanderism also use field experiments. A famous study by Piliavin et al. (1969) involved a confederate collapsing on a train. One independent variable in this experiment was the appearance of the confederate. In one condition he held a cane for the purposes of appearing injured. In another condition he held a bottle and smelled of alcohol. The researchers found that people were more likely to help an injured person over a drunk one. Another variable they tested was the race of the person in need: on some trials the confederate was a black man, and in others a white man. This research furthered our understanding of bystanderism in real life situations.

Field experiments take place in naturalistic settings, like a busy train station.

In order to determine the particular research method used, you need to know the definition of the method and methodology of the study in question. You may need to write down on paper the definition and the method and make sure they match. For example, I may think that Cialdini's experiment on re-using hotel towels is a field experiment because this happens in a naturalistic setting (i.e. a real hotel). It meets one of the criteria, but I need to ensure that it's an experiment as well or else I might get caught out. I can make sure it's a field experiment by asking myself, "What was the independent variable and was it manipulated by the researchers?" In this case, the IV was the wording of the card asking people to re-use their towels. There was a clear IV, and it was manipulated by the researchers as they wrote the different cards and randomly assigned them to various rooms.

By following the above thought processes, I can make sure that I have a clear explanation of *how* a field experiment was used in a particular study. I now need to make sure that I can clearly explain *why* it was used in relation to a topic. Cialdini's field experiment is relevant to "Social Responsibility" (Human Relationships) and "The individual and the group" (Sociocultural level of analysis). The explanation of why a particular method was used needs to include the characteristics of the method and why they were useful in relation to the particular topic. In the case of field experiments, this involves focusing on why a naturalistic setting for the experiment was valuable, and why it was beneficial to manipulate the independent variable. In both cases, my explanation would focus on the benefits of being able to manipulate the level of perceived social influence. By comparing the effects of differing levels of social influence the researchers can draw conclusions about the effects this might have on behaviour. By conducting this experiment in a naturalistic setting, it allows stronger evidence for the applicability of using such compliance techniques to encourage people to act in a socially responsible manner in real life situations.

If I was applying this to "Social Responsibility," I would focus on this aspect of the research in my explanation. For instance, I might conclude that Cialdini's field experiment helped support the argument that social influence can be used in real life situations to promote prosocial behaviour and to encourage people to act in a socially responsible manner.

On the other hand, when applying it to "The individual and the group," I would focus on this concept in my explanation and how the field experiment relates to this idea. I might say, for instance, that the use of a field experiment design in Cialdini's study enables the researchers to show that individual behaviour can be influenced by the group (e.g. social influence).

While both explanations would be very similar, the application to the particular question and topic would be slightly tweaked. Application is an essential part of an excellent explanation because it shows your understanding. By practicing your ability to apply studies to demonstrate a range of concepts you will develop a deeper understanding of core concepts in psychology, like how and why certain research methods are valuable in particular areas of study.

To summarize, the key characteristics of a field experiment are:

- There is an independent variable and a dependent variable.
- The IV and DV have been manipulated in a naturalistic setting.
- Because of the environment it's harder to control for extraneous variables.

Be careful when identifying research methods and examples of studies: make sure your example fits the characteristics of the method you are explaining.

Guiding Question:

How and why are field experiments used to study social influences on human cognition and behaviour?

Critical Thinking Extension:

As with the previous section, there are two key ways that you need to try to extend your thinking when studying research methods. The first is to think of potential limitations of using the particular method in that field of study. Can you think of (and explain) any limitations in using field experiments to study social influences on behaviour? Can you think of any other field experiments you are familiar with and apply an explanation of how and why this method was used in that particular context?

If you're interested…

Field experiments tend to be interesting in their design as it's easy to imagine what we might do if we were in a similar situation. Aron and Dutton's (1974) "shaky bridge study" is a classic in the field of attribution and arousal. You can find a summary of this study on our blog. Have a read and see if you think this is an example of a "field experiment."

(d)   Quasi-Experiments

In a true experiment researchers can randomly allocate participants to different conditions, which may help to control extraneous variables and help to establish cause and effect relationships. Being able to randomly allocate participants can help control for participant variability and increases the chances of the measures of the dependent variable being a result of the manipulation of the independent variable. The ability to randomly assign participants to a condition of the experiment is one of the defining characteristics of a true experiment. While the true experiment is valuable in psychological research, it does have some limitations.

When studying human behaviour, there are often times when a variable might be influencing behaviour but participants cannot be randomly allocated to a condition. Sometimes there is clearly a situation when a particular variable is influencing behaviour and comparisons can be made. This is where a quasi-experiment is used. A quasi-experiment is when a study meets some of the criteria of a true experiment, but not all of the criteria can be met. For example, there might be an investigation into the effects of one variable on another, but the participants cannot be randomly allocated to a particular condition.

Numerous studies that investigate neuroplasticity by measuring and comparing the effects of practice on brain structure use a quasi-experimental design. These studies are investigating the effects of a particular treatment or experience on the brain, but participants cannot always be randomly allocated to a particular condition in the study. For example, in Lazar et al.'s 2005 study mentioned in the Criminology chapter, the effects of meditation were investigated. This study had one group of experienced meditators who were being compared with novices. In this example, it was not the researchers who were able to randomly assign participants to a condition, experienced or novice, yet they were clearly investigating the effects of an IV (meditation) on a DV (grey matter in the brain). This is a good example of a quasi-experiment.

A quasi-experiment might investigate relationships between IVs and DVs, but other conditions of a true experiment cannot be met (e.g. participants cannot be randomly allocated to a treatment or control group.)

Another quasi-experiment that investigated the effects of experience on brain development was carried out by Elizabeth Maguire (Maguire, 2006). This study compared the brain structures of London taxi drivers and bus drivers. In order to become a taxi driver you have to train for years and memorize all the street maps of London. An earlier study by Maguire had found that there were significant differences in the structure of the hippocampus when taxi drivers were compared with a control group. However, there were multiple possible explanations for this difference, so Maguire conducted this follow-up study to control for those variables. By comparing taxi and bus drivers, variables like driving experience, job experiences, age and education could be controlled for. The experience of training to become a taxi driver and doing this for a job is the variable that Maguire wanted to investigate the effects of. While other variables could be controlled and a cause-effect relationship is being studied, the participants cannot be randomly allocated to either condition. For these reasons this study could be considered a quasi-experiment.

From these and other examples we can see the value of quasi-experiments in the biological approach. It enables researchers to investigate relationships between variables, even when participants cannot be randomly allocated to conditions in the experiment.

In summary, key characteristics of quasi-experiment include:

- The presence of an IV and a DV (there is typically some sort of "treatment" being studied).
- The IV is not manipulated by researchers (i.e. it's pre-existing) so extraneous variables cannot always be controlled.
- Participants cannot be randomly allocated to a treatment or control condition.

A quasi-experiment still involves some type of "treatment" or experimental condition (e.g. yoga therapy) but one or more characteristics of a true experiment can't be met (e.g. random allocation to a condition).

Identifying grey areas in distinguishing methods and studies would make for valuable "critical thinking" in essays.

Guiding Question:

How and why are quasi-experiments used in the biological approach to understand human behaviour?

Critical Thinking Extension:
Applications: When a study investigates the relationship between biology and cognition, it's possible to apply this study to multiple possible questions from different topics. How could you use the same study to explain how and why a quasi-experimental design is used in two different topics? E.g. one from biological approach and one from the cognitive?

If you're interested…

Research methodologies is not every student's favourite aspect of the IB Psychology course. However, if this area of the subject does interest you I higly recommend Hugh Coolican's informative book, *Research Methods and Statistics in Psychology*.

(e)   *Natural Experiments*

As we saw in the previous lesson, sometimes there are interesting variables that have occurred naturally that may be of interest to the researchers. The term quasi-experiment was created to explain an experimental study that does not meet all the criteria of a "true" experiment, but there is an effect of some kind of treatment. Similar to the quasi-experiment is the natural experiment.

When identifying a study as a natural experiment be sure you identify clearly the independent variable that is naturally occurring.

A natural experiment is when a researcher investigates the effects of an independent variable that is occurring naturally. The independent variable in a natural experiment is usually an environmental factor. For example, Becker et al. (2002) conducted a natural experiment in Fiji after the introduction of television. In 1995 TV was introduced for the first time on one of Fiji's islands. The researchers wanted to investigate the effects this might have on eating disorders and attitudes in young women on the island. In this case, the naturally occurring independent variable (the introduction of TV) was of interest to the researchers as they could investigate the effect this had on eating behaviours and attitudes of the Fijian girls. This research can help develop our understanding of how media influences may play a role in eating disorders.

Because natural experiments often include the introduction of a variable in the environment, they are often used to study the effects of social influences on behaviour. The introduction of TV (and other media) is a social variable influencing behaviour. The effects of media on behaviour is a common variable in natural experiments and can be compared with Bandura's experimental research from the 1960s. The benefits of laboratory experiments in this area of study is that extraneous variables can be controlled and the study is quite straightforward. But could these results be applied to naturalistic settings?

An example of a natural experiment investigating a causal relationship between media and violence was carried out by Dahl and DellaVigna in 2009. In their natural experiment they measured the effects of the release of violent blockbuster movies on acts of violence. They found that on the days that a violent movie is released, violent crime is actually reduced between 6pm and midnight (by a small margin – just over 1%) and further reduced between midnight and 6am. There explanation for this is that people who are prone to committing acts of violence are in the movie theatres and are preoccupied with this, so they are not in a place to commit an act of violence. Being in a movie theatre also reduces alcohol consumption, which could further reduce violent acts. By studying the naturally occurring variable of the release of block-buster movies, these researchers were able to investigate relationships between media and violence.

Cialdini et al.'s 1976 study on the effects of the football team's success is another example of a natural experiment. In this case the independent variable

The introduction of TV in Fiji is an example of a naturally occuring independent variable that researchers wanted to investigate.

was whether or not the college football team won. This is a variable that is naturally occurring, but still might influence behaviour (wearing the clothing with the name of the college). This variable's influence on behaviours related to social identity could not be manipulated in a laboratory, so the researchers make the most of naturally occurring environmental variables.

It's important to note that the difference between a quasi- and natural experiment is very slight and it's not always possible to make a black-and-white distinction. In fact, natural experiments are considered a type of quasi-experiment. The definition of quasi-experiment has also become much broader than its original definition. To make matters even more confusing, field experiments might also be considered a quasi- experiment. It's very easy to get confused and frustrated at trying to categorize studies and label them as using a particular method. If you are unsure if a study is a natural experiment or a quasi-experiment, you can identify it as a quasi-experiment (since a natural experiment is a type of quasi-experiment). When identifying the use of a quasi-experiment you can keep it simple and see if the study:

- Is investigating a causal relationship between an IV and a DV, and...
- Lacks one or more characteristics of a true experiment (e.g. participants cannot be randomly allocated to conditions).

If the study meets these criteria, it can be accurately labelled a quasi-experiment. But don't get too hung up on categorization - the key concept for you to understand about research methods is that there are multiple possible ways for researchers to study human behaviour, and each method has its own strengths and limitations.

In summary, key characteristics of a natural experiment include:

- The presence of an IV and a DV.
- The IV is a naturally occurring variable in the environment.
- The IV is not manipulated by researchers (i.e. it's naturally occurring) so extraneous variables cannot always be controlled.

When explaining natural experiments in relation to a particular topic make sure your explanation is clearly focused on *why* the study of a naturally occurring variable is useful in that particular context.

Guiding Question:

How and why are natural experiments used in the sociocultural approach to understand human behaviour?

Critical Thinking Extension:

Areas of Uncertainty: Categorizing studies and labelling them as using one method or another can be a difficult and often an impossible task. Can you think of studies that could fit the description of a field, natural and quasi experiment?

If you're interested...

An interesting natural experiment was carried out on the small island of St. Helena. TV was introduced in the 1990s and the researchers wanted to see if this would have an effect on the level of violence displayed by the school kids on the island. You can read more about this study on our blog.

(f) *Correlational Studies*

Remember that studies may be relevant to the biological, cognitive and/or sociocultural approach. There aren't always clear distinctions between these three approaches.

In previous sections you've seen how laboratory experiments are carefully designed in order to control for extraneous variables and isolate the independent variable as being the only variable that is operating on the dependent variable. If this can be successfully achieved, a cause and effect relationship may be established. But it's not always possible to manipulate important variables that are of interest to researchers. For example, the introduction of TV, treatments or particular experiences are naturally occurring variables that psychologists want to investigate. This is where quasi experimental methods can be valuable.

In this section we'll explore a non-experimental quantitative research method, the correlational study. Correlational studies do not have IVs and DVs as such. They have two (or more) variables that can co-vary, which means they can both vary along a scale. For this reason, they are not investigating the effect one variable has on another. Instead, they are measuring the strength of a relationship between the variables.

Correlation coefficient: a number that denotes the strength of the correlation between variables.

Data is gathered in a correlational study using different techniques, such as questionnaires, interviews, observations or brain imaging technology. Statistical tests are applied to the data to determine the correlations between the variables. A perfect positive correlation has a correlation coefficient 1.0 and a perfect negative correlation is -1.0. The closer the scores are to 1.0 or -1.0 the stronger the correlation. For example, a positive correlation of 0.24 is not as strong as a correlation of 0.76. A correlation coefficient of 0 in the statistical analysis means there is no correlation. When assessing the strength of correlations in research it can be beneficial to know the value of the correlation coefficient.

Because they may not be able to control for all extraneous variables, quasi experiments may only provide insight into correlational relationships, not causal ones. For this reason, correlational studies are very closely related to quasi experiments and often their distinction is blurred. There is one way that may help you to distinguish a quasi experiment from a correlational study. A correlational study doesn't necessarily have an independent and a dependent variable. The relationship between the two does not work in one particular direction and there may be a bidirectional relationship. This is why it's considered a non-experimental method.

Research on cultural influences on cognition and behaviour provide good examples of the use of the correlational study. In these studies both variables can exist along a range of values. Cultures are not 100% individualistic or collectivist - their scores on this scale can vary along a range. The other variable (the behaviour) in these studies can also vary. For example, in Levine's research on prosocial behaviour he gathered data to determine the extent to which cultures were on the individualism/collectivism scale. This variable could range along the continuum of Hofstede's scale with 120 at one end and 0 at the other. The extent to which people from different cultures helped also varies. So while the cultural values of the participants is a naturally occurring variable, because it can vary along a continuum

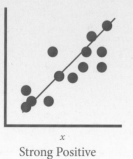

Strong Positive
Correlation

Strong Negative
Correlation

Weak Positive
Correlation

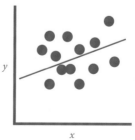

A positive correlation is when as one variable increases, so does the other. A negative correlation is when as one variable increases, the other decreases.

and so can the other variable it's related to, it's a better example of a correlational study than a natural or quasi experiment.

Correlational studies are often used in the biological approach as well. A biological factor is one variable and the other is behaviour. Data is gathered from participants using various methods and then the statistical tests are conducted to determine the strength of the relationship between the two variables. For instance, when studying what might cause a disorder like PTSD, correlations between particular aspects of the brain (e.g. function in a particular area) and symptoms are determined.

In summary, correlational studies are of particular value when both variables can vary along a range. By gathering data and conducting statistical tests to determine the existence and strength of correlations between variables, researchers can provide possible explanations for the existence of the relationship. Correlational studies might also inspire further research in a particular area and experimental methods may be used to further understand the nature of the relationship between variables. For example, numerous studies have revealed a negative correlation between hippocampus volume and PTSD symptom severity. This inspired a twin-study that sought to determine if this brain abnormality in people with PTSD was a cause or a symptom. The results suggested that low volume in the hippocampus is a pre-existing risk factor that may increase the likelihood of developing PTSD after being exposed to trauma. Early studies that deduced the correlation led to research that developed our understanding of the relationship between the hippocampus and PTSD.

To summarize, the characteristics of a correlational study are:

- There is not an IV or a DV as such, but two variables that can co-vary.
- Statistical analysis is conducted in order to determine the correlation coefficient (the strength of the correlation between variables).
- Questionnaires, technology and other tools are used to gather data in order to measure correlations.

Guiding Question:

How does a correlational study differ from an experiment?

Critical Thinking Extension:

Areas of Uncertainty: As you've seen, it's not always easy to classify experiments. For example, would you call Desbordes et al.'s study on mindfulness a laboratory experiment, field experiment or a correlational study? Could you describe this study in a way that shows that it's one method, or another? Or all?

If you're interested…

Correlation definitely does not mean causation. Tyler Vigen demonstrates this concept to the extreme on his website (and in his book) where he explores spurious correlations, like the amount of deaths by drowning in a pool per year correlating with the number of films that Nicolas Cage appears in. (tylervigen.com)

Surveys and questionnaires are used in correlational studies. You can read more about these methods on ThemEd's IB Psychology blog.

Visit our blog for examples of exam answers and other resources that address research methods (http://ibpsych.themantic-education.com)

Check out our blog for more detailed explanations of how and why correlational studies are used in different areas of study.

(g)   Case Studies

In the previous sections you've been introduced to the idea that categorizing research methods is not a black-and-white process and there is often not a clear distinction between methods. It's hoped that instead of finding this frustrating you can appreciate the deeper conceptual understanding that this course is trying to help you to develop: researchers have a range of research techniques and methods at their disposal and their choice will depend on their aims and the context of their research.

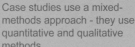

Case studies use a mixed-methods approach - they use quantitative and qualitative methods.

The research method in this section, the case study, is an interesting one in that it combines qualitative and quantitative methods. The definition of a case study is an in-depth investigation of an individual, small group or organization. Case studies use quantitative and qualitative methods to gather data and draw conclusions and may also be carried out over a long period of time.

In this text we explore two important case studies: SM and HM. The use of a case study on patients with brain damage was especially useful before the invention of modern brain imaging technology, such as fMRIs and MRIs. With fMRIs we can now see what areas of the brain are functioning when particular tasks are being performed. Case studies like HM's (covered in the PTSD chapter) existed before this technology, which is why they were particularly valuable. Having said that, Corkin et al. (1997) used MRIs to measure the extent of HM's brain damage. This later research still contributed to the case study of HM and developed our understanding of the relationships between neurology and cognition.

Feinstein et al.'s case study on SM was the first that investigated the role of the amygdala in the induction of fear. SM's bilateral amygdala damage was rare because it was isolated to the amygdala and other parts of her brain were unaffected. Because of the unique damage to her amygdala, she has become a valuable case to study. If researchers were to use brain scanners in an experimental design, they would only be able to correlate the amygdala function with perception of frightening stimuli. By gathering observation data in field studies like taking her to a haunted house or exotic pet store, the researchers could actually observe her behaviour. The self-report quantitative surveys they used also helped to triangulate their observational findings. In order to actually measure fear responses, behavioural observations may be of more value in this case than brain imaging.

SM's study is also a good example of how researchers apply a range of data gathering techniques to draw conclusions from case studies. She filled out quantitative questionnaires that had questions based on how much fear she experienced during the pet store visit and the haunted house. The researchers also gathered observational and interview data. This use of methodological triangulation is often a key feature of case studies in psychology and is part of what makes them an *in-depth* investigation.

Brenda Milner was one of the cognitive psychologists who studied HM for decades. (Image credit: Eva Blue, wikicommons.com)

SM's case study was carried out *after* the development of brain imaging technology but is still an example of how case studies on patients with abnormalities in the brain can provide an insight into the functions of the human brain. One reason for this is because "whereas functional imaging typically reveals activity in distributed brain regions that are *involved* in a task, lesion studies can define which of these brain regions are *necessary* for a cognitive process" (Muller and Knight, 2006).

It is important to note that case studies are used in many areas of psychology, not just on patients who have brain abnormalities. It just so happens that in this text two of the prime examples of case studies happen to be about such patients.

To summarize, the key characteristics of a case study are:

- They're an in-depth investigation of an individual, small group or organization.
- Multiple methods are used to gather data.
- Quantitative and qualitative data is gathered and analyzed.

The purpose of this topic is to provide you with a chance to reflect on how and why particular quantitative methods are used. As you continue to learn about new studies, you can be reflecting on their methodology and thinking about the choices behind using such methods.

Guiding Question:

How and why are case studies used when investigating the brain and behaviour?

Critical Thinking Extension:

Limitations: One of the major critiques of case studies is that because of their small sample sizes, the findings may not be able to be generalized to a wider population. As you'll know by now, this evaluation is limited and needs explanation, including reasons and/or examples. Can you think of specific reasons why HM's and/or SM's results might not be generalizable?

If you're interested...

The British Psychological Society has an online article called "Psychology's 10 Greatest Case Studies – Digested." This list includes Phineas Gage and HM, as well as some others that might be new for you as they're not included in this text. If you're interested in the psychology of childhood development, you may be interested in learning about the case of a girl named "Genie." Do be warned, the details of Genie's story and why she was studied may be distressing.

Relevant Topics

- All topics in core and options

Practice Exam Questions

- Describe how one research method is used to study cognitive processes.
- Explain the use of one research method in investigating the individual and the group.
- Evaluate the use of one or more research methods involved in the study of cultural origins of behaviour.
- Discuss the use of one or more research methods used to study prosocial behaviour.

6.2 Techniques to Study the Brain
How and why is technology used to study the brain?

(a) Magnetic Resonance Imaging (MRI)

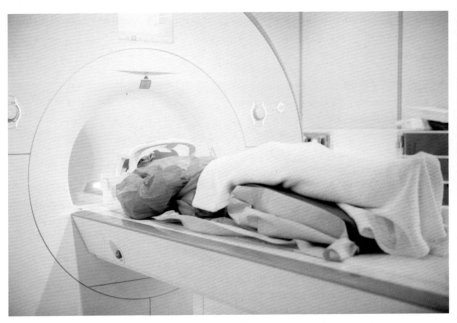

MRIs and fMRIs are big machines where participants lay down and have their brain activity measured. You can probably see why the right to withdraw is a key ethical consideration.

With modern brain imaging technology (e.g. MRIs, fMRIs, etc.) psychologists can investigate correlations between the brain and behaviour using a range of new technological techniques that don't involve harming animals. Case studies and animal studies are useful for some purposes, but brain scanning devices allow researchers to actually see the structure and activity of the brain. These machines perform slightly different functions and produce different types of images of the brain, so it's important to know in particular the key difference between what a magnetic resonance imaging (MRI) scan shows compared with a functional magnetic resonance imaging (fMRI) scan. It's also essential that you can explain how and why these technologies are used to study the brain and behaviour, using examples of research to support your answer.

An MRI scanner is used to take images of the *structure* of the brain. If you've had an injury you might have been in an MRI yourself; they are also used to look at muscle damage when people have injuries. You don't have to know how an MRI *works*, but you do need to know how and why MRI is *used* in psychological research.

Some of the studies we've looked at that used an MRI scan were:

- Vietnam Head Injury Study (Grafman et al., 1996).
- Neglected Children and Brain Development (Perry and Pollard, 1997).
- SM's Case Study (Feinstein et al., 2012).
- The Iowa Gambling Task (Bechara et al., 2000).

- Meditating Monks (Lazar et al., 2005).
- Studies on poverty and neglect in children (Luby et al., 2013).

MRI's are useful in a few general areas of the biological and cognitive approaches to understanding behaviour because they enable conclusions to be drawn about relationships between brain structure and behaviour. In many studies, the MRI is used to identify and determine differences in brain structure that may be correlated with changes in behaviour. The damage to a particular area of the brain is hypothesized to be a cause of difference and participants are grouped by this characteristic (with the help of the MRI). For instance, in the Iowa Gambling Task and the Vietnam Head Injury Study, MRIs can be used to find people with damage to the areas of the brain that are relevant for the study by helping to identify the exact location and extent of damage. Those participants are then asked to perform certain tasks (e.g., participate in the gambling game, complete questionnaires that measure aggressiveness, etc.). From their performance on the tasks and comparisons with control groups who have healthy, undamaged brains (as shown in MRI scans) conclusions can be made about the role of different parts of the brain in particular behaviours. The MRI scan facilitates the investigation of the role of particular areas of the brain in behaviour.

On the other hand, MRIs can also measure the *effects* of behaviour on brain structure in experimental research. This can be seen in studies that use MRIs in the investigation of neuroplasticity. The studies investigating poverty and neglect on the brain structures of children are examples of how MRIs can help researchers study relationships between naturally occurring variables and the development of the brain. These are examples of how MRIs are very useful when conducting quasi experiments and correlational studies.

MRIs can also be used in true experiments. One interesting study that also demonstrates neuroplasticity compared the brains of people who couldn't juggle. Half the participants trained for three months at juggling and the other half didn't. Before the study their brains were similar, but after three months of learning how to juggle they found a difference in the brain structures (using MRI) between the two groups. In particular, the juggling group had a change in the structure (increased grey matter) in parts of the brain involved in processing and storing complex visual motion (Draganski et al., 2004).

Researchers can also use MRIs in correlational studies. This can be seen in criminology studies that take groups of particular types of criminals and scan their brains to see if there are similarities. They can also compare the scans to healthy controls. Raine was part of such a study that correlated childhood aggressiveness and early psychopathic traits with smaller amygdala volume (Pardini et al., 2014). The use of MRI scans in studies like these enable researchers to identify particular behaviours (e.g. aggressiveness) and see if there are correlations with the structure of particular areas of

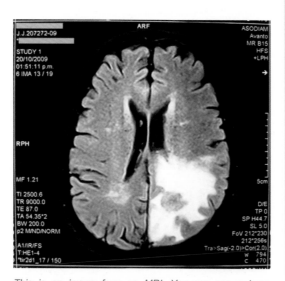

This is an image from an MRI. You can see a large tumour by the white space on the bottom right. MRIs show the structure of the brain. (Image credit: Bobjgalindo, wikicommons.com)

There are numerous ways you can explain how and why MRIs are useful to study the brain and behaviour. It's important that you try to develop your own understanding and find the right studies to support your argument.

the brain. By finding out that the amygdala volume is different in the participants in the above study, researchers can conclude that the amygdala may play a role in behaviours like aggressiveness, violence and psychopathic traits. This is of interest in and of itself, and may also spark further research into this relationship.

In summary, MRIs can play integral roles in experimental and non-experimental methods in two key ways. One involves using the MRI to measure *existing* damage or structural abnormalities in the brain. Behavioural measures are recorded and so correlations can be deduced about relationships between particular parts of the brain and behaviour. Another way that MRIs might be used is to measure the changes in the brain as a result of particular experiences, as shown in studies investigating neuroplasticity.

Guiding Question:

Why are MRIs useful when studying the brain and behaviour?

Critical Thinking Extension:

Evaluation: MRIs can only show static images of the brain; they cannot display ongoing brain activity like fMRIs and PET scans. This limits the use of MRIs to particular types of studies. What particular areas of study is the MRI not very useful for investigating? Another limitation of brain imaging is that they often only explain correlations. Can you use one of the studies above to explain how the study can only show correlation and not causation?

If you're interested...

Can we measure all behaviours in a brain scanner? In his TED talk, "What if we could really read the brain?" Matt Wall explains some existing uses of MRI and other brain imaging technologies, but more importantly he provides an insight into the possible future of brain imaging technology. In 50 years' time when you're very old and needing a brain scan, MRIs and fMRIs will be thought of as ancient devices.

(b) Functional MRI (fMRI)

While MRIs measure the *structure* of the brain, fMRIs enable researchers to investigate the function of the brain. The MRI shows a still image, whereas fMRI machines enable us to see which areas of the brain are activated when performing certain tasks. As with MRIs, fMRIs can investigate brain function as a potential influence on behaviour, as well as measuring the effects behaviour can have on the brain.

In fMRI scans, images are produced of the parts of the brain that are activated at any one time while the participant is in the machine. When neurons in a particular part of the brain are firing, more blood is sent to that area of the brain. The fMRI detects this change in blood flow, allowing correlations between areas of the brain that are active and the particular tasks being investigated. The areas that are activated can be seen onscreen, so researchers can measure areas of the brain that are functioning during particular behaviours and cognitive tasks.

Here are some of the studies that have used fMRI scans:

- Phobias and the amygdala activation (fMRI) (Ahs et al., 2009).
- Brain activation on perception of emotional stimuli, e.g. serotonin and testosterone studies (Passamonti et al., 2012; Radke et al., 2015).
- Mindfulness and meditation (Desbordes et al., 2012).
- There are numerous studies in the PTSD chapter that also use fMRIs.

fMRI has been used extensively in studies investigating the perception and processing of emotional stimuli. Many studies throughout the chapters on Criminology and PTSD, for instance, use the similar methodology whereby a participant is placed in an fMRI machine and they are exposed to emotional stimuli.

fMRI scans can be useful in experimental studies that measure the effects of changes in biochemistry on brain function. For example, Passamonti et al.'s (2012) experiment manipulated the levels of serotonin in participants and used fMRI to measure the effects this had on the function of the prefrontal cortex during the perception of emotional stimuli. Radke et al.'s (2015) experiment on testosterone did something similar, although they manipulated testosterone through injections. Both of these experiments manipulated the participants' biochemistry and then used the fMRI scans to measure the effects this had on the functions of particular areas of the brain during perception of different faces. In these examples we can see how the brain function is the dependent variable and the fMRI enables researchers to record changes in brain function as a result of the manipulation of an independent variable. The use of fMRIs in this experimental procedure can help further our understanding of the possible role biological factors (e.g. serotonin and testosterone) may play in behaviours such as aggression and violence, because we can see how they impact brain function during particular tasks. In this way they further our understanding of relationships between the brain and behaviour.

Another use of fMRIs in criminology is to detect abnormalities in brain function during particular tasks in people prone to aggressiveness or violence. Kiehl et al. (2001) conducted one such study where they compared the brain function of criminal psychopaths with criminal non-psychopaths and non-criminal controls. In this study they asked participants to perform a memory task involving remembering emotional words (e.g. hate) and non-emotional words (e.g. chair). They found that there was reduced activity in the limbic system (amygdala, hippocampus, etc.) of the psychopaths compared to the other groups. The use of fMRI in this study allowed the researchers to measure cognitive processing and its relationship with particular areas

Whereas MRIs measure structure, fMRIs measure function and activity.

Another common brain imaging technology is PETs. These work in a similar way to fMRIs. Raine (1997) used a PET to compare brain function in criminals with controls.

of the brain (including the hippocampus and the amygdala). The fact that psychopaths had reduced functioning in these areas could help explain why psychopaths tend to have reduced emotional reactions: they lack the proper functioning in the parts of the brain responsible for emotional reactions to stimuli.

In experimental research the effects of variables on brain function can also be measured using fMRIs. As with MRIs that can measure structural changes as a result of treatment or repeated practice of something, fMRIs can measure changes in the function of particular areas of the brain as a result of treatment. Desborde et al.'s (2012) study on the neurological effects of meditation and mindfulness is an example of how fMRIs can be used in experimental procedures to gather before and after data on brain function and determine the effects of particular tasks on the brain. When studying PTSD you will see many examples of how fMRIs are used to measure the effects of treatment on brain function.

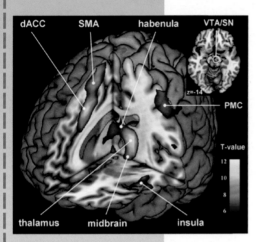

Here you can see how an fMRI image enables the function of particular areas of the brain to be shown. Included in this image is the ACC and the SMA, which are relevant to the studies in PTSD. (Image credit: F.RdeC, wikicommons.com)

To summarize, while the MRI can allow correlations to be studied between brain *structure* and behavior, the use of fMRI facilitates the study of correlations between brain *function* and behaviour.

It is important to note that if you are asked in exams about the use of "techniques" to study the brain and behaviour, you should focus on technological techniques such as MRI and fMRI scans. If you are asked about "methods," you should focus on the quantitative methods that use these techniques (e.g. quasi experiments, laboratory experiments, correlational studies, etc.)

Guiding Question:

Why are fMRIs useful when studying the brain and behaviour?

Critical Thinking Extension:

Evaluation: While technology can be useful, there are significant limitations. What are the limitations of using brain imaging technology to investigate particular areas of behaviour? Are brain imaging studies fundamentally limited by a lack of ecological validity?

If you're interested...

Another type of technology used to study the brain is called SPECT. Dr. Daniel Amen uses this type of technology extensively in his research and he delivers an interesting TED talk that summarises his findings called "Change your brain, change your life."

- Techniques used to study the brain and behaviour
- Ethics and research methods

Practice Exam Questions

- Describe one technique used to study the brain and behaviour.
- Contrast two techniques used to study the brain and behaviour.

Research Methods

Technology can be used as part of correlational studies and laboratory experiments, as well as case studies. The type of research design they are applied to depends on the aims of the research.

Ethical Considerations

The right to withdraw is an important consideration when using technology because of the nature of the machines.

Debriefing is also important because participants would naturally be very curious about what the researchers found out about their brains. In some studies where the aims are not obvious (e.g. viewing angry/sad/happy faces) the participants would naturally be curious about the research and the results and so it would be important to debrief them so they could leave the study without any possibility of anxiety or stress as to why they were being studied in the first place. Anonymity is also important to consider because participants may not want others to know about their brain structure or function, especially if they have abnormalities.

6.3 Sampling Methods
How do we gather participants for quantitative studies?

(a) Random Sampling

Sample

Target Population

When you carry out your internal assessment you will also need to gather participants for your sample and so you'll need to think carefully about what sampling method you'll use and why.

When designing and carrying out research, psychologists need to consider multiple factors. One of these includes who will actually participate in the study and how these participants will be found. The term used to describe the group of participants in a study is a sample. The sampling method refers to how those participants are gathered. In this topic you'll be introduced to the sampling methods that are commonly used in quantitative research. This topic is most relevant to your internal assessment.

One of the most commonly misused terms by IB psychology students is random sampling. A random sample is when every member of the target population has an equal chance of being asked to participate in the study. The reason why students misuse the term random sampling is because they do not think of random in a mathematical sense. A common inaccurate description of random sampling in student experiments is something along the lines of, "we walked into the classroom and randomly asked who was there to participate in our study." As the following explanation should show you, this is not random sampling.

The target population refers to the wider group to which the researchers are expecting their results can be generalized to. The sample is a small selection of that larger population. For example, after the September 11th terrorist attacks in the United States in 2001, researchers conducted studies on US citizens to investigate the psychological effects of the attacks. One study (Schuster et al., 2001) used phone interviews to gather their data. In this case the target population was adult-aged American citizens. There are around 400 million US citizens which would make it impossible to ask each and every one to participate, which is why a sample is collected in with the intention that the sample represents the target population and the results can be generalized. This particular study used a telephone interview and random-digit dialing to gather a sample of 560 adults. This is an example of random sampling, as every phone number in the US would have an equal chance of being called and so all members of the target population would have an equal chance of participating. The use of technology or a random number generator is one way to ensure that the sample is statistically random, and not just haphazard.

Generalize: in psychological research to generalize findings means you can take the results from your sample and presume the same would apply to a larger group.

The primary benefit of using a random sample is that it has a high probability of being a representative sample. When conducting psychological research, one major aim is to ensure that your sample is an accurate representation of the wider group you are studying (i.e. the target population) so you can accurately generalize findings. The larger the sample size the more probable it is that the results will be generalizable as a large sample size will minimize the effects of participant variability.

Random sampling may also reduce the chances of researcher bias. Researcher bias is when the attitudes, values or beliefs of the researcher may interfere with the research process. If a researcher has a particular hypothesis, they may unconsciously wish to gather results that will support their hypothesis. This could lead to obtaining a sample that might be more likely to produce the desired results, as opposed to producing representative results. The use of random sampling can reduce the possibility of researcher bias influencing the results because they will not select the participants, their random generator will.

When conducting psychological research, one must also consider the practical elements as well. Gathering a true random sample can be rather difficult as it means getting the contact details of every member of your target population so that they can be included in the random sample generator. There are alternative methods for sampling, and these will be explained in the following sections.

In summary, characteristics of a random sample include:

- Every member of the target population has an equal chance of being asked to participate.
- The aim is to obtain a sample that is representative of the target population.
- It might have practical limitations, such as gathering the contact details of all members of the population.

A large sample reduces the chances of sampling bias, which is when the sample is not an accurate reflection of the wider population to which the conclusions will be generalized.

HL students will also need to be aware of sampling methods for Paper Three.

Guiding Question:

How might a random sample increase the possibility of generalizability?

Critical Thinking Extension:

Area of Uncertainty: What is a target population? Defining a target population can be troublesome. It also raises the question, why bother defining it at all? Is the purpose of psychological research not to understand *all* human behaviour? Can you think of a study that you've learned about that might have a particular target population?

If you're interested…

Be sure to regularly check our blog for new "Two Minute Tutorials." These aim to provide you some guidance on a range of concepts, including random sampling.

(b) Self-selected/Volunteer Sampling

As you learned in the previous section random sampling can be an effective means of gathering a representative sample. The major limitation though is that it can be time consuming. It might also be difficult to get all the contact details of members of the target population in order to ensure that each of them has an equal chance of being able to participate in the study.

Random sampling involves generating a list of possible participants and then approaching them to ask to participate in the study. Another way of gathering a sample is to reverse this: have people approach you and volunteer to participate in the study. This is called self-selected sampling, or volunteer sampling.

Self-selected sampling naturally relies on the use of some form marketing or advertising in order to let people know that there is a study that they could participate in. Posting a flyer on a noticeboard, advertising in a magazine or sending out a message via social media are all possible methods of attracting volunteers to your study.

Using a notice board to advertise for a study is a common way of gathering a self-selected/volunteer sample.

Sampling bias: when some members of the target population are less (or more) likely to be included in the sample.

Self-selected sampling is commonly used when the course of the study might take some time. For example, studies investigating how changes in female hormone levels may influence attraction to particular facial characteristics (as discussed in the chapter on Love and Marriage) often require gathering data at several different points. Self-selected sampling may be beneficial in studies like these that require a lot more involvement than something simple like filling out a questionnaire or a one day commitment. Because participants have to give up more time, one would expect less people to be willing to participate. If a random sample was used, researchers might waste a lot of time asking lots of people who would say no, or who may sign-up and then drop out later. Asking for volunteers ensures that people are willing to commit to the time involved in the study and that they actually want to participate in the research in the first place. If there are particular participant characteristics that the researchers are looking for, they can list these in their marketing.

But this particular method is not without its downsides. By having participants decide who participates there is the chance of sampling bias. People may only volunteer if they have particular beliefs or opinions relating to the subject being studied. For example, if volunteers were asked to participate in a study relating to issues of gender and identity, it might attract people that felt strongly about this particular topic. This might not provide a representative sample and so it could affect the validity of the results.

Depending on the specifics of the study, it might also be that only extroverted people who have a lot of confidence might sign-up, as it could be outside a lot of people's comfort zones to agree to participate in a study.

As you can start to see, there are a number of factors that researchers need to consider when planning their research. It often involves doing a cost-benefit analysis that includes issues of validity as well as practicality. You will need to go through these same planning and thought processes as you design your experimental research for your IA.

If you decide to use volunteer sampling it is essential that you carefully describe how your sampling method falls into this category. Many students make the mistake of oversimplifying their description by saying something like: "we used a volunteer sampling method because all participants volunteered to be in our study." While this isn't *incorrect*, it doesn't provide sufficient context for how this is a volunteer/self-selected sample because *all* participants in IB Psychology experiments will be volunteers regardless of the sampling method – for ethical reasons you cannot research on someone against their will or without their knowledge. Be sure to describe your procedure carefully, including *how* participants self-selected themselves to participate in your study.

To summarize, characteristics of a self-selected/volunteer sample include:

- Participants are the ones that approach the researchers as volunteers to participate in the study.
- There is typically some form of advertising by the researchers that calls for participants.
- The sample may not be representative as sampling bias may occur.
- Participants may have more commitment to the study, especially those requiring multiple data points.

Guiding Question:

How does a self-selected/volunteer sample differ from a random sample?

Critical Thinking Extension:

Areas of Uncertainty: Distinguishing between different sampling methods can be very difficult. Read the description of a "purposive sample" in the Qualitative Methods chapter and see if you can clearly identify a difference between self-selected sampling and purposive sampling.

If you're interested…

You could design an experiment to test the effectiveness of self-selected sampling. You could try using two different mediums of advertising (e.g. Facebook versus bulletin board sign-up) or maybe try two different types of studies in the same place. Do you get the same or different people signing up? Could this be an issue in research?

(c)   *Opportunity/Convenience Sampling*

Before we look at another common sampling method in quantitative research, remember that you do not need to discuss sampling methods in Paper One or Two. For Paper Three (HL students only) you need to be able to identify the sampling method used in an example study and state at least two characteristics of the sampling method. All students need to use one particular sampling method when conducting your experimental research for the IA, and you need to be able to describe and explain the method you have chosen.

Finding a whole class that is available at a convenient time to run an experiment is a common way of gathering a sample for IB Psychology IA experiments.

You've probably noticed already in this course that a vast majority of psychological studies take place using college participants. The reason for this is a simple one: convenience. College campuses are often where the studies happen and researchers are primarily psychology professors working on college campuses where there are thousands of potential participants, many of whom would be willing to give up their time for a few dollars or even simply for the experience of being in a study.

It's not surprising, therefore, that opportunity sampling is a very common technique used to gain a sample. This is when a researcher gathers their participants by simply asking people who are available at the time that is convenient for the participant and researcher. For this reason it's also known as convenience sampling.

Opportunity sampling is the most common sampling method used in IAs.

Opportunity sampling is also the most common form of sampling method for IB Psychology students' internal assessments. This is primarily because of practical reasons: you have a limited amount of time to conduct your research and you want to gather a suitable amount of participants as conveniently as possible. The primary advantage of using an opportunity sample, therefore, is that it's far more convenient than random sampling and ensures you can gather a sufficient sample. Also, with self-selected sampling if you post a sign-up or send out a message on social media announcing the time and place of your experiment, you may end up with a sample that is too small. These are the practical factors you need to take into consideration when planning your study. Using an opportunity sample may be a way to overcome these problems.

A common form of opportunity sampling is when people stand in a busy area with lots of foot traffic and stop people and ask if they would spare a few minutes to fill out a questionnaire. The participants just happen to be walking by and the time is convenient for them. It's obviously an opportune time for the researcher as well, because they're standing there with the clipboard with the sole purpose of gathering data.

Levine's study on prosocial behaviour is another example of an opportunity sample. If you'll remember, Levine's confederates were in public places and required the help of strangers. They would do things like pretending to be blind and needing help crossing the street. The participants in this case are not aware that they are in fact the subjects of experimental research, they just happen to be in the area at the time of the study. Thus, they're part of an opportunity sample.

A potential limitation in using an opportunity sample is that there could be an increased chance of researcher bias. If a researcher is gathering data on individual participants, they may only ask participants whom they think will provide data that is consistent with their hypotheses. For example, if a study was investigating attitudes towards college spending on sports versus academics, a researcher might believe that the college is spending too much on sports and ignoring investment in other areas of the school. If they were conducting a survey on campus they may (consciously or unconsciously) approach students whom they think would be likely to provide the data consistent with their views and avoid those that might think otherwise.

In summary, an opportunity sample:

- Gathers participants who happen to be available at a given time.
- Is based on convenience, both for the participant and the researcher.
- Depending on the nature of the study, there may be a chance of researcher and/or sampling bias.

These sampling methods are commonly used in studies that gather quantitative data. They tend to have large sample sizes and aim to gather representative data with the goal of generalizing findings to a wider population beyond the sample. Like other elements of research design, decisions have to be made by weighing up issues of validity and practicality. While it's probable that you will use one of the above sampling methods for your IA, you may want to read about purposive sampling (in Qualitative Methods) as well, especially if you are in a small school.

Guiding Question:

Why do you think IB Psychology students tend to use opportunity sampling?

Critical Thinking Extension:

Area of Uncertainty: Blurred Boundaries: What if you approach a classroom filled with students that you think would be valuable for your study? Is this purposive or opportunity? For example, if a researcher investigating alcoholism went to an Alcoholics Anonymous (AA) meeting and gave out questionnaires to AA members in a meeting, would this be purposive or opportunity? This is a grey area and highlights the importance of description. How could you describe this sampling method in one way to show that it was purposive, and in another to show that it was opportunity?

If you're interested…

A fun way to learn about different sampling methods is to use skittles or M&Ms. Have a bowl of about 100 multi-coloured lollies (candy) and the bowl represents your target population. How would you gather a sample of 20 from the bowl using the different methods? The fun part about this exercise is you get to eat your participants afterwards. Not many ethics review boards let you do that (credit to Joseph Sparks from tutor2u for this idea).

6.4 Ethical Considerations
Why are ethics important in psychological research?

(a) Ethics in the Approaches

You're hopefully starting to get an idea of how psychologists must consider multiple factors when planning, designing and conducting studies. Practical issues, such as the research design and sampling methods, must be considered in relation to validity. As well as these issues, at the heart of psychological research are ethical considerations. An ethical consideration can be broadly defined as any aspect of research that must be considered in relation to appropriate conduct and procedures, especially relating to the psychological and physical health and well-being of others. This includes thinking about those immediately affected by the research (participants) and the potential for others to be affected in the long-term as a result of publication, interpretation and/or application of the findings.

Another important ethical consideration relates to researcher integrity. In other words, researchers must be honest in their recording and reporting of results, with absolutely no fabrication or misleading data. This particular consideration provides less room for discussion in our course than others, so others have been the focus.

Ethical considerations are closely associated with ethical guidelines and you can read more about these in the introduction. This section provides you with the opportunity to reflect on some of the major ethical considerations that you can observe in particular areas of study through the core and the options.

The following ethical guidelines are quite common across various psychological associations around the world:

- Informed consent
- The right to withdraw (including withdrawing data)
- Debriefing
- Considerations regarding deception
- Anonymity
- Appropriate justification (for any harm or potential harm caused)
- Researcher integrity
- Review and approval by ethics review committees

As with all topics in psychology, to demonstrate your understanding of ethical considerations you need to have accurate descriptions and clear explanations. This requires being able to clearly define the ethical guideline or consideration that is relevant to a particular topic, as well as being able to provide a general description of common methodological procedures relevant to a particular topic. This accurate and detailed description will enable you to provide a clear explanation of the relationship between the ethical consideration and the topic. This is what will be required for short answer responses.

Ethics refers to guiding principles of behaving in a way that is considered "right" or "appropriate." Researchers follow ethical guidelines to ensure their research is ethically appropriate.

For Paper One and Two it would be beneficial to become an expert in two or three ethical considerations so you can discuss them in-depth across a range of topics.

To consider ethics means to think about how research may impact others and make decisions based on an understanding of these potential effects. This includes thinking about the effects of research on animals.

For example, a common procedure used to study the brain and behaviour is the use of technology such as MRIs and fMRIs. Because of the nature of these machines the right to withdraw is an important consideration because they're noisy, uncomfortable, require being still for long periods of time, and people may become claustrophobic. Here we can see a clear relationship between the methodology used in this area of study and the ethical consideration. However, this might not be a great example to explain because finding a particular study that demonstrates this might be difficult because it could end up with a rather generic explanation that can make little use of evidence (i.e. a study) to support your explanation.

Perhaps a better example would be to discuss the consideration of anonymity when using brain imaging technology. This provides us with a better opportunity to relate the methodology, the consideration, and the desire to reduce psychological harm. It's natural to assume that people would be sensitive about information regarding their brain being published and having others aware of such personally relevant information. Keeping their data anonymous, and their participation in the study confidential, would be an important consideration for researchers. Here we see again the relationship is explained between the consideration, the methodology and the topic. I can now go further to explain this in relation to a range of possible studies that gather information about brain function. For example, in Bechara et al.'s study using the Iowa Gambling Paradigm, participants who have lesions in the vmPFC may not wish others to know about their tendency to act on impulse. In extreme circumstances this could lead to individuals being manipulated. Another important consideration in this study would be debriefing. The researchers would need to be very mindful of the participants' feelings as they revealed the results of the research. It might be quite unnerving to find out that one's brain injury could have such an effect on behaviour. But it might be important to reveal this information so the participants can be aware of this and how it might affect them.

As you can see, it's essential that you are connecting the ethical consideration to the methodology of the study. Another example would be relating to Loftus' research on false memory. There are particular ethical implications of implanting false memories in participants of potentially traumatic events. Debriefing would be important to consider in studies on the misinformation effect and false memories because part of the ethics of psychological research is that participants should finish a study in the same (or improved) psychological and/or physical health as they were in when they began the study. It would be important in these designs that debriefing occurred so that participants would understand what happened and that the memory is false. This might help ensure that they wouldn't have any undue future suffering from memories of traumatic incidents.

It's important to remember that you are not required to make a definitive judgement about whether or not a study is ethical. This is a common misconception that many students have. You need to demonstrate your understanding of ethics and research in relation to particular topics; you are not required (and are not advised to) make definitive judgements about how ethical a study was. You are to explain possible ethical considerations and/or guidelines that are relevant to particular topics based on common methodologies used in those topics of study.

It is not expected that from this one section you can explain ethics across all topics. It is hoped that as you are reading and analyzing studies throughout the course you can bear in mind relevant ethical issues associated with these studies.

Remember you can use ThemEd's IB Psychology Facebook page for students to post any questions you have about the IB Psychology course.

Remember that the approaches are merely a general theme of research and studies could be applied to more than one approach.

Loftus explains the ethics issue in one of her Ted Talks, "Eyewitness Testimony." In this talk you can see how ethics is not a black-and-white judgement. Often the benefits of the research might outweigh the short-term ethical dilemmas. This is one role of an ethics review committee: to weigh these pros and cons and to make a decision to approve or deny the research proposal accordingly.

How can you demonstrate understanding of an ethical consideration related to a particular topic in the core approaches to understanding behaviour?

Critical Thinking Extension:

Other Ethical Considerations: The term "ethical considerations" is often used synonymously with "ethical guidelines" in IB Psychology. Can you think of something that researchers might need to consider in relation to ethics that is not related to one of the considerations stated in this section? Alternatively, can you think how following ethical guidelines might influence the validity of a study?

If you're interested…

The International Union of Psychological Science has published four guiding principles for conducting research of the highest ethical standards. You can view these principles online at www.iupsys.net.

(b) Ethics in the Options

There is little difference in the nature of ethical considerations in the options as there are in the approaches. When considering which ethical considerations are relevant to a particular topic, try to find common characteristics of the methodologies used in the research, including the procedures and the participants. For instance, in studies investigating PTSD the participants are those who are experiencing symptoms of a disorder. These characteristics could be relevant to particular ethical considerations, especially when considered in relation to the procedures. As well as procedures and participants, the findings and conclusions of studies are another aspect that could be considered in relation to ethical considerations.

Preparing for essay questions addressing the options (i.e. in Paper Two) requires a general understanding of the interaction of biological, cognitive and/or sociocultural factors. Therefore, if you're careful enough you can also identify studies that overlap the approaches and the options. In order to maximize the effectiveness of your exam preparation, it would be advisable to focus on studies and their relevant methods and ethical considerations that can be applied to the core topics and the options topics. Finding these overlaps is one valuable way of managing your workload when it comes to revision time.

Let me give you an example that may make more sense after you've studied the PTSD chapter. Understanding the etiologies (origins) of PTSD involves careful examination of the interaction of biological, cognitive and environmental factors. To provide some context first, it might be useful to know that research has shown that the ventromedial prefrontal cortex (vmPFC) can influence the function of the amygdala: a healthy functioning vmPFC may reduce the activation of the amygdala in response to fear-inducing stimuli. This is because the vmPFC allows people to perform a cognitive process called cognitive reappraisal, which means reassessing the potential harm of a particular stimulus. If someone can reappraise their initial emotional response (using their vmPFC), the activation of their amygdala can be reduced, resulting in a reduction in the stress response.

Ethical considerations in research are similar across topics in the core and the options.

Studies that investigate the role of the vmPFC in cognitive reappraisal and their connection to PTSD can be used to discuss ethical considerations and/or research methods relevant to the following topics:

- The brain and behaviour (Biological approach)
- Cognitive processing (Cognitive approach)
- Emotion and cognition (Cognitive approach)
- Etiology of disorders (Abnormal Psychology)
- Treatment of disorders (Abnormal Psychology)

For example, Felmingham et al. (2007) investigated the effects on the functioning of the vmPFC as a result of therapy involving cognitive restructuring (learning how to change thought patterns). They found that cognitive therapy could increase the activation of a specific area within the vmPFC. You could potentially use this study to demonstrate your understanding of important ethical considerations in psychological research across a range of topics. This would require careful description and very clear explanation that involved application to the particular topic. For example, applying an explanation to the topic of the brain and behaviour might focus on the anonymity aspect as participants may not want information about their brain function shared, including changes as a result of treatment. On the other hand, you might choose to emphasize the debriefing element when discussing treatment as some people may not have experienced the same level of improvement as others and this may be disconcerting, especially for people already suffering from PTSD. That is to say, sensitivity during the debriefing process and care for the potential impact of the debriefing on participants would be important to consider. Similarly, if applying this study to the topic of emotion on cognition the emphasis should be placed on how the ethical consideration relates to the influence of emotion on cognition. For example, researchers may have an ethical obligation to debrief their participants at the end of the research (if they didn't inform them at the beginning) that the cognitive training might be able to reduce their cognitive symptoms of PTSD relating to memory problems and improve their general cognitive functioning through reducing the impact of their emotional reaction to stimuli. The patients may not have been aware of this and it might be ethically questionable to withhold this information from the participants, even after the study has concluded.

In summary, the nature of explanations and discussions of ethical considerations is similar across the options and the approaches. What is important is that you can clearly apply your explanations to the relevant topic you are addressing.

Excellent explanations of ethical considerations involve relating the particular consideration/s to the common characteristics of research methodologies (e.g. participants, equipment and procedures) for a certain topic.

Guiding Question:

How can one study be used to highlight one or more ethical considerations related to topics in the core and options?

Critical Thinking Extension:

Limitations: Using the study you have chosen to answer the guiding question, can you suggest possible limitations of following this ethical consideration? For instance, how might this affect the validity or reliability of the study? When discussing ethics in research, explaining how following ethical guidelines may impact validity of research is an excellent way to demonstrate critical thinking.

(c)   Discussing Ethics

It's most likely that you will be asked to "Discuss" ethical considerations in essay questions.

If you are asked to write an essay on ethical considerations in relation to a particular topic in the core (Paper One, Part B) or the options (Paper Two) it is important that you can go beyond explanation and demonstrate "critical thinking." Essay questions will use one of four command terms (discuss, contrast, evaluate or to what extent) and these all require you to critically reflect on your own explanation, including the evidence upon which your explanation is based. Many students make the mistake of critically evaluating studies based on validity in essay questions that ask students about ethical considerations. This section provides you with some ideas on how you can go beyond explanation of ethical considerations and demonstrate critical thinking in essays.

Regardless of the topic in question, you're likely to be explaining why particular ethical guidelines are important to consider in relation to a particular topic. It's advisable to focus on why following those guidelines would be an important consideration in order to maintain the ethical standards of psychological research. As essays require you to go beyond explanation, one way of doing this is to reflect on how following particular guidelines might have an impact on the validity of the study.

For example, when providing informed consent researchers would need to consider just how much information to reveal to the participants. They need to strike a balance between making sure that participants are comfortable and confident in the methodology of the study, while ensuring that they haven't revealed so much information that the participant expectancy effect may influence their results. If researchers reveal too much information, participants may alter their behaviour and damage the validity of the conclusions.

Similarly, in conformity studies such as Asch's, if the participants were fully informed about the nature of the study and told that the rest of the group were confederates, the entire validity of the study would be jeopardized as the effects of normative social influence would be nullified. In this case, deceiving participants in believing that the confederates are genuine participants is quite necessary.

Another potential confounding variable relevant to informed consent is known as the social desirability effect. People have a natural tendency to want to be liked and to be viewed favourably by others,

Following some ethical guidelines could impact the validity of research. How much these psychologists reveal to the participant before the study needs to be carefully considered.

so if researchers reveal too much about the aim of the study the participants might alter their behaviour so they're seen as a good person. For example, in the minimal group paradigm studies if the researchers told the full aims of the study and how they wanted to see if participants were going to award points based on fairness or if they were going to demonstrate in-group bias, this information may lead the participants towards awarding points based on fairness, as this is seen as a more socially acceptable behaviour.

In any experiment involving a placebo or control group, an element of deception may also be necessary. An initial explanation of ethics involved in studies using placebos could focus on how this necessitates adequate debriefing. To go further might include explaining a possible downside involved in debriefing after studies using placebos, especially those focused on treatments of psychological disorders. For example, if a researcher hypothesizes that a particular course of treatment might help (e.g. SSRIs, cognitive restructuring or exposure therapy) to treat a disorder, some participants will miss out on this actual treatment and will be unknowingly allocated to a control group that is hypothesized to have no effect on treatment. During debriefing this might be made clear to participants and it's possible that researchers might experience some emotional backlash from participants because they may feel they were "duped." One possible way of avoiding this is to inform participants in the beginning that the conditions of the experiment are randomized and they may be in a control or the treatment condition. Then again, this information might affect the way participants engage with the treatment throughout the study and could also influence the results as they may continually try to figure out what group they're in.

If you are asked to "contrast" ethical considerations, you need to think carefully about significant ways in which the guidelines differ. One way to do this would be to focus on the different ways in which a particular guideline attempts to reduce or minimize psychological harm. For example, informed consent may aim to reduce the stress of a participant *during* the course of the research and enable them to participate knowing that their psychological well-being is not in fear of being damaged. Debriefing, on the other hand, attempts to reduce the chances that there will be any enduring effects *after* the study is completed.

For Paper One and Two it's enough to be able to explain and discuss ethical considerations related to the methodology of the studies used. For Paper Three, HL students will also need to understand how these guidelines may be relevant to the reporting of results and the application of findings, which will be explained in the chapter on qualitative methods.

Deception is purposefully leading someone to believe something is true when it isn't.

Remember that withholding information and deception are two different things. Just because a researcher doesn't provide all the information regarding the aims of the study, doesn't necessarily make it deceitful.

Guiding Question:

How might following ethical guidelines influence the validity of a study?

Critical Thinking Extension:

Independent Application: It would be impossible for this textbook to provide you with every possible way of explaining ethical considerations or research methods relevant to particular topics. All I can do is provide you with the information and the guidelines – it is up to you to be able to independently apply your understanding to a range of possible questions. With this in mind, can you apply what you've learned from this section to a study you've learned about? For instance, can you explain how following a particular ethical consideration in one study might jeopardize its validity?

If you're interested…

The UK comedy "Freshers" has an episode where university students sign up for a clinical drug trial. Things go awry when the temptation to find out if they're in the placebo or treatment group becomes too much to bear. While this is a fictional comedy, it does actually provide a glimpse into the possible mentality of people in a clinical trial.

Relevant Topics

- All topics in core and options

Practice Exam Questions

- Describe one ethical consideration relevant to the study of cognitive processes.
- Outline one ethical consideration relevant to the study of genetics and behaviour.
- Discuss one or more ethical considerations related to the study of cultural origins of behaviour.

6.5 Evaluating Studies
How do we evaluate studies in psychology?

(a) *External Validity*

One of the major aims of the IB Psychology course is to develop your ability to independently analyze and critically evaluate evidence. This is why all your exam answers require you to use evidence to support your arguments and explanations. Evidence in psychology comes from research, which means studies and/or theories.

It's essential that you can use studies and theories to demonstrate relationships between:

- Variables and behaviour.
- Ethical considerations and research methodology.
- Research methods and areas of study (i.e. "topics").

By now in the course you should have a sound grasp of the study of psychology, including its structure and general patterns. It's important that you are working towards being able to regularly move past knowing and understanding and that you can critically reflect upon your own understanding, including evaluating the evidence upon which you've based your understanding. This is an essential transferable skill and a key goal for this course.

With this in mind, it's important to revisit one of the key concepts related to critically evaluating studies in psychology: external validity. One major goal of the Critical Thinking Extensions is to be able to push you beyond explanation of relationships and to consider the extent to which these can be applied to a different context. This idea is the crux of external validity: to what extent can the findings be applied beyond the immediate context of the study? The purpose of conducting quantitative research is to generalize findings. Therefore, going beyond explanation requires determining the extent to which the findings can be generalized. As with ethical considerations, it's important to focus on specific details of the methodology used in studies during critical evaluation. In this section, you'll see how three key concepts can relate to critically evaluating methodology based on procedures and participant characteristics.

Earlier in this chapter you were introduced to the idea of representative sampling: gathering a sample that is representative of a wider population. One way of evaluating a study is to analyze the characteristics of the participants. The extent to which the characteristics of the sample will enable the conclusions to be applied beyond the context of the study is known as population validity. When revising studies, it might help to make a note of one or two key characteristics of the participants, including age, gender, nationality or ethnicity. This can help demonstrate your knowledge of the study, and might also be useful for a critical reflection. For instance, many studies related to PTSD that have been used in this book use war veterans as participants. You could ask questions or even explain possible characteristics of war veterans that might limit the extent to which these findings could be generalized to people who suffer from PTSD as a result of *other* traumatic stressors. Or if the mean age was quite young in a particular sample, is there a reason to suspect these findings might not apply to an

Don't forget that evaluation includes strengths, so you can explain the strengths of a study based on its designs. It's likely that you will be able to explain strengths of a study in relation to internal validity and offer one or more critiques based on generalizability.

Generalizability: the extent to which findings can be applied beyond the context of the study.

older population? Or consider culture. Most studies happen in the US and a critical reflection of population validity might take into consideration possible factors that might limit the ability to generalize the findings from one particular culture to another.

Another way to determine the external validity of a study's results and conclusions is to consider its ecological validity. To assess ecological validity, you must consider the extent to which the environment of the study reflects other situations. The most common error students make when discussing ecological validity is to make an over-simplified claim such as: "this study was carried out in a laboratory and so it lacks ecological validity." Your critical reflections and counter points in essays still require *description* and *explanation*. The above statement shows knowledge of a key term, but does not suggest that a student knows how to *apply it*.

You need to make it clear in your description what about the environment was unnatural and explain how that might not reflect a particular real life environment that you're trying to generalize the conclusions to. For example, you might argue that the results from Bandura's Bobo Doll experiment *might* lack ecological validity because of the fact that young kids were in a controlled environment with a set amount of toys. In their own homes they may have a larger array of toys to choose from and more distractions. These distractions could reduce the chances that they'd opt to play with the doll that they've just observed the researcher play with. This could reduce the chances of the behaviour being reinforced so quickly. Similarly, if using the study to show how violence might be learned from TV, it could be argued that children don't always have a really obvious target (e.g. the big inflatable doll) that matches perfectly what they've just seen modelled on the television. Often the violence seen on TV isn't immediately and directly practicable. For instance, a child may see a cartoon where one character drops a large anvil on another (a classic weapon in old cartoons), but they probably wouldn't have a big anvil around that they could use to replicate this behaviour. As you can see, an effective assessment of ecological validity still requires explanation – you are showing how the methodology of the study might not relate to a particular "real life" environment.

Similar to ecological validity is the concept of mundane realism, which refers to the extent to which the task that participants are asked to perform is representative of a real life situation. Like population and ecological validity, explaining possible limitations of a study based on mundane realism requires you to first fully understand the relationship that the study is demonstrating and how it might be applied in the *immediate* context first.

Studies like Radke et al.'s that use fMRIs might be critiqued based on the mundane realism of their procedures. Observing images on a screen as we lay motionless in a small space within a massive machine is not an everyday activity. A good critique needs to go further than this and relate the task to the particular applications of the study. For example, if you are using this study on testosterone and its influence on the amygdala to explain the correlation between violent crime and testosterone, you should try to provide a clear explanation of how observing angry faces might not reflect a real life situation that could

When explaining generalizability, you need to ask questions related to the relationship between the methods of the study and the context the results are being generalized to. For example, you should go further than simply saying, "brain imaging machines are an unnatural environment so they affect ecological validity."

Do not be fooled – providing a strong explanation of ecological validity is very difficult.

Critical thinking requires in-depth knowledge and understanding.

Make sure you understand first, before trying to evaluate.

lead to a violent crime being committed. Or if you're looking at fMRIs and PTSD studies and the activity in the amygdala you need to think about how viewing these unpleasant stimuli might be different to viewing unpleasant stimuli in real life and how this might affect the possibility of generalizing the findings beyond the laboratory. You may be able to see that ecological validity and mundane realism are closely related, but whereas ecological validity refers to the environment, mundane realism refers to the task.

You can see that evaluation requires high levels of abstract thinking. If you can't explain how it's applicable to one context, there's little chance you'll be able to critique a study based on its external validity. This is why it's essential to understand first before you try to go beyond and evaluate studies. For example, if you don't understand how Radke et al.'s study can be used to explain the correlation between testosterone and aggression, you will not be able to critique the mundane realism of the procedures effectively.

As you develop your confidence in evaluating psychological studies based on external validity, it might help to focus on the general concept of generalizability first before trying to apply specific terms such as ecological and population validity and mundane realism. If you cannot fully explain how a study may lack generalizability, simply asking questions relating to generalizability can also be a good way to show critical thinking.

When critiquing a study, bear in mind any aspects that may influence generalizability.

Guiding Question:

Why is it important to *understand* a study before you try to *evaluate* it?

Critical Thinking Extension:

Independent Practice: Can you find one study that you have learned about so far and try to evaluate it based on concepts related to external validity?

If you're interested...

You can read further explanations of how to explain limitations related to generalizability on ThemEd's IB Psychology blog. These explanations include more examples as well

(b)   *Internal Validity*

The previous section provided you with a general outline of how to critique psychological studies based on their generalizability. If a study's methodology is such that the results might not be applicable to different people, situations or scenarios, the validity of the results and/or conclusions might be questioned.

There are a few important things to remember, though. First of all, you may not need to critically evaluate *any* study based on validity in your exams. You need to apply your critical thinking to the demands of the question and some questions can be answered without an in-depth explanation of issues related to validity. For example, if you were asked to discuss ethical considerations in relation to a particular topic, the validity of the study's findings would be largely irrelevant to this question. Similarly, if you were asked to evaluate the use of research methods used in relation to a particular topic, your evaluation should focus on the characteristics of the method – not necessarily on the validity of the conclusions of the study you're explaining.

When questions ask something along the lines of "to what extent does one variable influence a particular behaviour?" you may also be able to write excellent answers without evaluating the validity of the evidence you have used. Your reflection on your explanation might include explaining evidence that suggests there's a completely different variable that might affect the same behaviour. For example, if you were asked "To what extent does one hormone influence one behaviour?" you could explain how testosterone might influence aggression and support your explanation with evidence. While you could evaluate the study, a more relevant way to address the question might be to explain that testosterone alone may not explain aggressive behaviour and other variables like serotonin and cultural values (e.g. culture of honour) may also be influential. Many students make the mistake of trying to evaluate all studies in essays, regardless of their relevance to the question. This is not an advisable strategy because your answer needs to be focused on the question.

Having said that, understanding external validity and its related concepts is an important part of being able to critically evaluate studies. Whereas external validity refers to the extent to which the findings can be generalized beyond the immediate context to new situations, people or scenarios, internal validity refers to the extent to which the results of the study were actually because of the manipulation of the independent variable. In a true experiment, for example, internal validity of the results can be assessed by determining to what extent the researchers successfully controlled for extraneous variables and isolated the relationship between the IV and the DV. If the methods they used allowed some chance that extraneous variables confounded the results, the internal validity of the results may be questioned.

The practical reality of this course is that we do not always have sufficient time to devote to the scrutiny of the methodology of studies in order to assess internal validity. Also, quantitative studies cited in this text employed numerous controls and have been published in peer-reviewed journals; it might be difficult to independently critique a study based on internal validity. But don't forget that an

The more you understand the higher the probability you'll be able to demonstrate critical thinking in response to the wide range of potential exam questions that may be asked.

Asking you to independently and critically evaluate the internal validity of a peer-reviewed study's results would be like asking you to evaluate Shakespeare's use of iambic pentameter.

Mistakes made during the design or conducting of an experiment could be a threat to the internal validity of the results.

evaluation includes strengths as well as limitations. In order to be able to explain the strengths of a particular study, it is necessary to know a few details about its methodology, especially any controls that were employed. If you know a study used one of the following controls, you could explain *how* this might enhance the validity of the results in the context of the area of study:

- Triangulation (data, researcher, methodological)
- Experimental design (e.g. independent samples, repeated measures, matched pairs)
- Random allocation
- Counterbalancing
- Blind designs

For example, Bandura used a matched pairs design for his experiments. This reduced the possibility of participant variability and helped to isolate the effect of the observation of the model that was causing the observed aggressive behaviour.

Another example would be Passamonti et al.'s study on tryptophan and serotonin, which used a repeated measures design and counterbalancing. The repeated measures would control for participant variability in terms of brain function and the counterbalancing would have controlled for order effects. If all participants began with the same condition this may have affected the results because their first trial might have been their first time in an fMRI. They may have been more comfortable during the second trial and their results could have reflected this. By counterbalancing the researchers could control this potential confounding variable.

While critiquing the internal validity of an existing study's results may be difficult and unnecessary, you will need to be able to offer a thorough evaluation of the strengths and limitations of your own experiment. This can include factors related to external and/or internal validity. With that in mind, it is hoped that what you've learned throughout this chapter will be valuable in helping you to thoroughly plan, design, conduct and analyze your own experimental research.

> You can find detailed descriptions of key studies on our blog. These descriptions may include more details of methodology.

> Another concept similar to internal validity is construct validity. This refers to how close the variables in a study resemble what they're actually measuring. For example, is defining "social threat" as an angry face on a screen similar to social threat in real life?

Guiding Question:

How does internal validity differ to external validity?

Critical Thinking Extension:
Independent Practice: Can you find one study that you have learned about so far and try to evaluate it based on concepts related to internal validity?

If you're interested…

A "study" that I like to use when introducing the concept of internal validity comes from a commercial for a type of chewing gum. Identical twins were paired in an art gallery and participants made ratings of the twins, but one was chewing gum and the other wasn't. See if you can explain all the factors that make the internal validity of this study highly dubitable.

Conclusion

Our knowledge and understanding in psychology is based on evidence. In other words, how we know what we know comes from research. In the beginning of this course you were introduced to some basic concepts of research in psychology. The aim of this chapter was to explore concepts related to quantitative methodology in a little more detail.

As with all the content in this book, the ultimate goal is that you can transfer what you've learned in this chapter beyond the classroom. Understanding research methodology, for instance, could be relevant in numerous ways. Whether or not you continue studying psychology beyond IB, there's a high probability that at some point in your life you will have to gather data and draw conclusions based on that data. You'll be forced to make decisions on how best to carry out your research so you can draw reliable conclusions. This practice also transcends a range of academic disciplines.

With that in mind, alongside any research is a necessity to consider the ethics and possible implications your actions may have on others. It is hoped that an ability to identify ethical considerations in existing research will prepare you to carry out your own ethically sound experiments for your IA, as well as strengthen your ability to consider the effects particular actions may have on others.

Psychology is an inherently interesting subject because much of what we learn is immediately and directly relevant because understanding how and why we think and act the way we do can enhance our lives. But it's equally crucial that we know upon what evidence we're basing our understanding. Being able to critically evaluate research is another essential transferable skill that is hoped you will have acquired if not by now, at least by the end of the course. This is not an easy skill and will require a lot of practice. Remember that it's far less important for you to know the strengths and limitations of the individual studies used in this text, as it is for you to be able to independently scrutinize and critique evidence for yourself. This is why the studies have not been evaluated for you, but rather the Critical Thinking Extensions provide you with regular prompts to guide your critical thinking practice and this chapter has provided additional practice at performing this challenging task.

When revising and preparing for your exams, I recommend selecting key studies that can be used across a range of topics in the course to support an explanation of a variety of concepts. You may find around 10 or 15 key studies that could be used in multiple topics, including research methods and ethics. Focusing on a smaller number of studies that can be used as evidence to support a range of arguments can increase the effectiveness of your revision. It will also give you the time to practice performing your own thorough independent evaluations of these studies based on their internal and external validity.

As you read and apply future studies, it is hoped that you will start to independently apply your critical thinking skills to the evidence and begin challenging assumptions and raising questions on your own. Practicing this independently will help you further develop your skills as a psychologist.

Chapter 7
The Internal Assessment

Introduction

Now that you've become familiar with psychological research and the experimental method, it's time for you to try your hand at conducting your own true experiment. The IB Psychology Internal Assessment (IA) is designed for you to get first-hand experience of planning, designing, conducting and reporting on a psychological experiment. You are being assessed on your knowledge and understanding of core concepts relating to the experimental method, including your ability to apply these concepts in your own procedures and reporting. This chapter is designed to guide you through the process of completing this assignment.

Many students get excited when they hear that they get to conduct an "experiment" and they begin planning all sorts of elaborate, borderline-evil plans. So before you begin and get carried away, cackling like a mad professor, it's important to go over a few very important rules that you need to follow for your IA.

Collaboration: It is mandatory to work as part of a group of two to four students to complete your IA. The initial stages of your IA will be a collaborative process. After you have your data, the remainder of the assignment should be completed independently.

Ethical Considerations: You are not allowed to conduct any experiment that use:
- Placebos
- Ingestion (e.g. effects of drinking coffee) or inhalation (e.g. drugs or smoking)
- Deprivation (e.g. effects of sleep deprivation)
- Conformity
- Obedience
- Children under 12
- Non-human animals
- Stress, anxiety, or any form of harm (physical or psychological)

Experimental Method: You need to ensure that as the researcher, you are the one who is manipulating the independent variable in your study and you have only one individual variable (with two conditions). This means that using a natural or quasi-experimental design is not allowed. For instance, you cannot investigate differences between age, culture, or gender. You also need to ensure that you're conducting an experiment, not a correlational study. Because of the difficulty in conducting statistical analysis on complex experiments, it's strongly recommended that you use a simple experimental design, which involves manipulating one independent variable and having only two conditions.

Your final report will be approximately 1,800 – 2,200 words and will consist of four general sections:

I. Introduction
II. Exploration
III. Analysis
IV. Evaluation

More explanation of the writing of the final report is included later in this chapter.

7.1 Planning

How do you plan your experiment?

(a) Choosing a Study

The first step in carrying out your experiment is to decide what topic you're going to investigate. You are allowed to choose a topic that comes from any area of psychology, but it's important that the study that you are replicating is based on one that has been published in a peer-reviewed publication. It is advisable to do a replication or a partial replication of a well-known study that is clearly related to a particular theory or phenomenon. The best chances of success are to keep it simple. For this reason, and the fact that biological and social experiments tend to break the "rules" of an IA, it's recommended you choose an experiment from the cognitive approach to understanding behaviour.

This list is not exhaustive and you can conduct experiments not included here, as long as they are approved by your teacher.

Here are some examples:

Bransford and Johnson (1972): Comprehension and Background Knowledge: This study investigates the effects of background knowledge on comprehension.

Loftus and Palmer (1974): Leading Questions: You can replicate this study by using different verbs in a leading question and measuring their effects. It's advised to only have two verbs, not all five.

Craik and Tulving (1975): Levels of Processing (LOP): This is a model of memory that is not included in this textbook, but might be interesting for your IA. The LOP model suggests that the deeper we process information the more likely we are to remember it.

It's essential you make sure your chosen experiment is in line with the IB's rules about what is acceptable. You run the risk of having your IA score a zero if it is deemed inappropriate. Animal studies are definitely out of the question.

Mueller and Oppenheimer (2014): Hand-writing vs Typing: If you are a fan of taking notes on your laptop, this study might interest you. Related to the idea of levels of processing, this study investigated the effects on learning of different note-taking strategies (hand-writing or typing).

Rauscher et al. (1993): The Mozart Effect: This study produced surprising (and highly debated) findings that listening to Mozart can increase spatial reasoning skills.

Music and Cognition: There are a range of studies that investigate the effects of listening to different types of music on cognitive performance. You may like to do some research and find a suitable study to replicate (e.g. Shih, Huang and Chiang, 2012).

Peterson and Peterson (1959): Short Term Store Duration: Conducting your experiment can be a good chance to revisit an experiment that could be used in other areas of the course, such as Peterson and Peterson's experiment related to the multi-store model of memory.

Chartrand and Bargh (1999): The Chameleon Effect: This effect refers to unconscious mimicry of the actions of others. To conduct this experiment you would need to do careful research and consider your IVs and DVs *very* carefully.

Dijkstra and Pieterse (2008): Effects of Indoor Plants on Stress: You might not replicate this particular study, but it could serve as a beginning point for your research into the effects of plants on human behaviour. This study found that indoor plants in a hospital waiting room had stress reducing benefits. Before you choose such a study, it's important to consider the practicalities involved and to seek approval from your teacher first.

Kaplan (1995): Restorative Environments: If you are interested in the effects of nature on cognition, apa.com has a good article called "Green is good for you." Stephen Kaplan is a leading researcher in this area and his 1995 article ("The restorative benefits of nature") may also be a good starting point. This might help start your research into a suitable theory, model or study upon which to base your IA.

Stroop (1935): The Stroop Test: In this classic experiment J Ridley Stroop studied the effects of interfering stimuli on perception. It investigates the effects of incongruent and congruent colour words on speed of perception (e.g. red/ green/blue/blue).

Kleinke, Peterson and Rutledge (1998): Facial Expressions and Mood: "Fake it 'til you make it" is a common saying and there may be some element of truth to it. This study investigates the effect that mimicking facial expressions may have on mood.

The Mere Exposure Effect: There are a number of studies investigating the phenomenon known as the "mere exposure effect," which is a tendency for increased exposure to positively affect preference.

Sparrow, Liu and Wegner (2011): Google Effects on Memory: With the widespread reliance on google to find information, researchers have investigated the effects this may have on memory. If people believe that they will have future access to information their memory of the information may be impaired, and instead of remembering the information they will remember where to find it again. The study suggests that the internet may act as a type of external memory system.

Dual Task Paradigms and the Working Memory Model: According to the working memory model, we use different short term processes when we learn new information: visual and auditory. The dual task paradigm requires participants to experience some form of interference (visual or verbal) that may affect their recollection of information (e.g. Robbins et al., 1996).

For ease of conducting the inferential statistical analyses on your data later in the process of the IA, it is advisable that you conduct a simple experiment. This requires modifying any experiment that has more than two conditions or more than two independent variables. For example, for Loftus and Palmer's experiment it would be a good idea to use only two different verbs, not all five. While it might be tempting to have elaborate designs, you will have more chances of being successful in this assignment if you keep it simple!

Be sure to refer to the guidelines in the introduction as you are choosing an appropriate study, especially regarding ethics.

We'll continue to keep updating this list on our blog, so be sure to check it out for more information.

All choices should be discussed with, and approved by, your teacher.

(b)   Background Research

After you've chosen a relevant study and this has been approved by your teacher, you need to do some research and background reading. You should try to find the original published article of your study and read it in its entirety, taking note on the context, aims, methods, results and conclusions. I would recommend first making sure that you fully comprehend the procedures used in the study and ensure that it would be acceptable for you to use for your experiment. Remember that you can make small modifications to the original study's procedures to suit the purpose of this assignment.

It's also important that you understand the original context of the study you are replicating, including any particular theory, model or phenomenon upon which it's based. Reading original journal articles will also help to give you an idea of the general style, structure and content of experimental reports. The "Introduction" section of published articles is especially important to read and review, as this provides the context for the study by summarizing relevant previous research on that topic.

In order to get full marks for the introduction in your IA you need to make sure that "...the theory or model upon which (your) investigation is based is described." This should guide your background research. An example of a study being based on a theory or model would be studies investigating an aspect of schema theory and effects on memory processes. If you were conducting a study related to schema theory, you would need to be able to describe this theory. The same applies for other theories or models, such as levels of processing, the multi-store model or the working memory model. It's essential that you understand the context (background information) relevant to the study you are replicating.

> In order to ensure academic honesty and avoid being accused of academic malpractice, take careful notes of your sources. Your final report will include these references.

The IA takes hard work, grit and determination to do well. There's a lot to do in a short amount of time, so you have to be prepared to work hard if you want to do well. This begins with conducting careful background research on your study.

Depending on the nature of your research, the description of the theory or model that you're basing your experiment on might be quite brief. The full context could be provided through a detailed description of one or more studies that are related to the theory on which yours is based. For example, the dual processing model of decision making could be summarized in a couple of sentences and then a more thorough description of the study you are replicating could be described and explained in relation to the model.

After you have understood the theoretical background of the study that you are replicating, it's important that you can explain how your study is related to the theory or model.

As you're reading you should be continually thinking about your own experimental design, including what your independent and dependent variables will be.

Your background research should result in having the following information:

1. A detailed description of the original study you are replicating.
2. The context of the original study, including previous research.
3. An explanation of how the original study is related to a model, theory or phenomenon.
4. The relevance of the original study, e.g. possible applications.

While the above list is written in order of importance, you will need all this information if you are aiming to achieve high marks.

(c)   The Aim and Variables

After you've conducted your background research and you understand the context of the original study, you can begin the planning stages of your own experimental replication. Before you begin designing materials and procedures, there are two essential elements of your experiment that you need to be able to state clearly:

(a)   Aim
(b)   Independent and dependent variables

Aim

Remember that the purpose of conducting a true experiment is to investigate a cause-effect relationship between variables. For this reason, a clear statement of an aim should include the independent and dependent variable and the relationship between them that you are investigating.

Another important aspect you will need to include in your final report is an explanation of the relevance of the aim of the study. This could include explaining possible applications of understanding the relationship between the variables you are investigating. Its relevance might also be based on its relationship to an existing theory. For example, if an experiment can test claims of a theory or model, this could be one way that it's relevant.

Relevance: in this context could mean many things. One way to think about the relevance of the study is in its possible applications in other fields. It could also mean its relevance in terms of an existing theory or model.

Independent and Dependent Variables

As you are conducting an experiment it is essential that you are manipulating an IV and measuring the effect this has on a DV. As mentioned earlier, it's advisable to stick to a simple experiment where you have two conditions (one IV) and one measure of a DV.

You will also need to operationalize your IV and DV. An operational definition of a variable is a specific definition of how the variable exists in your particular study. For example, the term "memory" is very broad and could be interpreted (and measured) in many different ways. One of the aims of publishing psychological research is to enable others to replicate your study to determine its test-retest reliability. While you are not going to be publishing your findings for others in such a manner, it's still valuable to understand why you're doing things like operationalizing variables.

Operationalized: when a variable is defined in a way that makes it objectively measurable or observable

It is important that a researcher knows exactly what their independent and dependent variables are. Thus, they need to have an operational definition. Operational definitions are useful when the DV is quite subjective.

For example, stress, attention, perception, IQ, memory, attraction, violence and conformity are all behaviours that are not easily quantifiable and their definitions can be subjective (open to different interpretations). This is why experiments must use operational definitions.

If I was conducting an experiment on the effects of my patented drug Rememberol on memory, for instance, I would need to clearly define how I was measuring memory. It might be something like, "scores on a memory test" or "ability to remember details from a written test."

By this stage in your planning, you should have your aim clearly stated and operational definitions of your IV and your DV.

(d) Research and Null Hypotheses

After you've conducted your background research and constructed your aim, IV and DV, you need to think about your hypotheses. A hypothesis is a tentative and testable prediction of what you think will happen. Your research hypothesis (also known as an experimental hypothesis) is a statement of the predicted effect of the IV on the DV. This prediction should be based on the background research and existing evidence that you've gathered in preparation for carrying out your own study. That is to say, this prediction should be consistent with the results of other studies that you have researched.

The reason why you need to operationalize your variables is that these should be present in your research hypothesis in order to get full marks for your introduction.

Statistical Significance: the results have had statistical tests applied to them and the results of these tests provide strong evidence to show that the results of the experiment are not due to chance or luck, but are in fact a result of the manipulation of the IV.

One potential problem with proposing a hypothesis is that it could lend itself to researcher bias. Many students are disappointed when their research doesn't "work" and produces contradictory results to the original study. This provides a valuable learning experience regarding the dangers of researcher bias.

One way to reduce the possibility of researcher bias influencing the experiment is to devise a null hypothesis. A null hypothesis states that no significant difference is expected to be found between the groups on the measure of the dependent variable. A common practice in scientific research is to refer to the null hypothesis when interpreting tests of statistical significance (this will be explained later). You are not conducting your experiment with the intent of "proving" your research hypothesis, but rather to test the validity of your null hypothesis. This is a slight, but significant difference in thinking.

Your research hypotheses are about making a prediction of what you think will happen. But instead of using tarot cards and crystal balls, you will be using scientific research that has been published in peer-reviewed articles.

You should be making some mention of significance in your hypotheses, as statistical significance is a key concept in psychological research (it may help to skip ahead to the section on inferential statistics if you're not sure what this means).

Null Hypothesis: a statement that predicts there will be no significant effect of the manipulation of the IV, or that there will be no significant difference between the conditions in the experiment.

Rememberol Example
Research Hypothesis (H₁): The group taking Rememberol before studying will have a significantly higher average score on the memory test than the group taking a placebo.

Null Hypothesis (H₀): There will be no difference in scores on the memory test for the Rememberol and Placebo groups.

Research Hypothesis (aka Experimental Hypothesis): a statement that shows your prediction about what will happen to the dependant variable as a result of the manipulation of the independent variable.

More than any other assignment in IB Psychology, the internal assessment requires very careful use of language. You need to take the time to be very careful and deliberate with how you write things like your aim, variables and hypotheses. These statements are packed with important information but should be very concise, so your word choice and phrasing are really important. Your first attempt probably won't be good enough, so make sure you are writing and re-writing, tweaking and editing until you're really happy with how accurately you are conveying your intended meaning.

(e)   *Design*

Now that you know your hypotheses, it's time to begin figuring out how you're actually going to test these. A very important consideration is the experimental design. Will you use a repeated measures, independent samples (a.k.a. independent groups) or matched pairs design?

Making decisions about how best to carry out experimental research involves weighing up pros and cons. There will be benefits and disadvantages in using any of the possible experimental designs; you need to work with your group members to determine the best choice for the context of your study. Your choice will be based on issues relating to practicality and validity.

For your exploration you need to *explain* your research design. This explanation will include a statement of the design you've chosen and a clear description of your methodology so that it's clear that you've identified the correct design. For instance, if you are using repeated measures you need to provide an outline of how your study was carried out so that the examiner can see that you did in fact use repeated measures, and not independent samples.

You also need to go further and provide an explanation of your design, which would include one or more reasons justifying this choice. This justification could be based on practical reasons, such as the size of the available sample at your school. But ideally it would include an explanation that shows how this design helped to control for possible confounding variables, such as order effects, participant variability or participant expectancy effects. Similarly, you may wish to explain how these variables may *not* be a consideration, enabling you to choose the design you have.

Try to identify particular potential confounding variables that you are aiming to control for through your experimental design choices.

If you are using an independent samples design, you'll need to include a brief statement about how your participants were allocated to either group. For instance, if you are using random allocation you can provide a brief outline of how this allocation was achieved. Make sure that you are taking careful notes as you are working through these steps.

> The more detailed your notes are as you work through this task, the easier the writing of the first draft will be.

> Control: an aspect of research methodology that helps with the isolation of the independent variable as the only variable influencing the dependent variable.

> Random allocation: assigning participants to either condition in your experiment using a randomized procedure (e.g. pulling names out of a "hat" or using an online group generator).

(f)   Sampling and Participants

You are almost ready to start creating your materials and planning your full procedures but before this you need to consider who is actually going to participate in your study.

As with your design, your choice of participants and your sampling method needs to be explained. Once again this requires stating the characteristics of the participants and sampling method, describing how they were gathered and then providing a reason for your choice. Your explanation could be related to issues of practicality and/or validity.

Remember that your sample cannot involve children under 12 years of age, and if you are using children between the ages of 12 and 16 you need to use a parental consent form and obtain parental consent for these participants (this can be part of your informed consent – explained in the next topic).

You'll need to think carefully about how you can find 15 to 20 people to participate in your study. You could co-ordinate with other groups who are conducting different experiments to make the process easier.

Experimental research involves carefully describing the characteristics of your participants, including factors such as age, gender, language fluency and nationality. You need to consider the context of your research carefully and think about possible characteristics that are relevant for your study. For instance, if your procedure will involve lots of reading, then literacy levels (i.e. reading comprehension skill) will be an important factor. Or if you're conducting the Stroop Test you would need to ensure that no participants are colour blind.

The explanation of your choice of participants will include a description of their relevant characteristics and reasons why you felt these were appropriate for your study. You may want to start by writing down a list of characteristics related to participant variability that may be potentially confounding variables in your study. Then think about how you could gather a sample that would control for these variables.

You need to also plan the sampling method you are going to use, including how you will get your sample. You will need to explain your choice, so be sure to consider this carefully. As with all other considerations, your reasoning can be based on considerations of practicality and/or validity. A sample size of around 15 to 20 participants is sufficient for this assessment.

You need to think carefully about your sampling method, because there may be elements of convenience in a volunteer sample, and all samples require volunteers. You may have to select for some criteria, which is part of purposive sampling. You will need to decide which sampling method term best matches your proposed sampling procedure.

Practicality versus validity: to focus on the practicality of something means to think about how feasible or realistic it is to do given the circumstances. Using convenience sampling is an example of a practical consideration trumping concerns about validity and representative sampling.

You will use one of the following sampling methods:

- Random
- Opportunity/Convenience
- Self-selected/Volunteer
- Purposive*
- Snowball*

At some point during the planning and preparation process, you will need to decide when and how to actually find your participants. Be sure to make note of their relevant characteristics (e.g. age, language, ethnicity, gender, etc.) as these will need to be described and explained in your report.

Many students want to obtain a random sample because they want their experiment to be "perfect." If you begin trying to plan for a random sampling you will soon learn the practical difficulties involved. It's perfectly fine to use convenience sampling (or other methods) because of these practical realities. There are multiple ways you can obtain your sample as well, including asking your teacher for help finding a class that is scheduled at the same time as your Psychology class that might be willing to take part in your study.

Many students make the mistake of oversimplifying their descriptions. For instance, a student might explain how they chose a volunteer sample by saying "we used volunteer sampling as all our participants were volunteers and chose to be in our study." This is far too brief and doesn't clearly show how your method is best labelled a self-selected/volunteer sample as *all* IA participants have to volunteer – you can't test people against their will.

*The last two sampling methods are typically used in qualitative studies. One reason for this is that there is a probability that they will not be a representative sample. However, there are some instances when using such a sampling method would be highly appropriate and justifiable. If you are to choose one of these methods, you need to ensure that you clearly describe how your sampling method is an example of one of these methods, and you need to ensure that you've provide a suitable justification for using this method.

7.2 Preparing
What should you do before starting the experiment?

(a)   Ethical Considerations

It is essential that your experiment maintains high ethical standards. You should have checked and double-checked the criteria in the introduction to ensure that your study meets these standards before moving forward with your planning.

This may be an appropriate time to do some research into the specific ethical guidelines of the psychological association of your country, which can probably be found online.

The IB also has strict ethical guidelines that you must follow, including:

- Gathering explicit consent from all participants in the form of a signed document. A blank copy of this needs to be included in your appendices.
- Informing all participants of the aims and objectives of the experiment. This can be done during the debriefing stage of the study, if revealing this *before* the study is conducted might interfere with your results.
  - o The IB guide states that partial deception is allowed if providing full information would affect the outcome of the study. In this instance, debriefing is even more important.
- Explicitly offering the right to withdraw to all participants. This can be included in the informed consent form.
- Guaranteeing anonymity to participants and maintaining this through all documentation. Again, this can be included in the informed consent.
- Debriefing all participants after the study is conducted, including revealing the full extent of the study (aims, hypotheses, results, etc.) This is especially important if some information was withheld from participants in the beginning. At this time participants should be given the right to withdraw their data for any reason.

Make sure you meet all these requirements and keeping track of your documentation as you work through the assignment.

Deception is often confused with withholding information. These are two different concepts, although sometimes the line between them is a grey area. To deceive someone means to lead them to believe something that isn't true. For example, in Asch's study the participants were deceived because they were led to believe that the actors in the group were all naïve participants. Withholding information means that you are not revealing all of the information to participants. For example, if you were conducting a study related to the multi-store model of memory, you might tell participants "…this is a study relating to memory." You have not deceived them, because this is true. But you have withheld some information, like *how* it's related to the multi-store model of memory. Withholding information can be an acceptable practice if it's not expected to cause any undue harm or suffering. And even *partial* deception is "…permissible provided (the researchers) do no harm and participants are fully debriefed at the end" (Psychology Guide, p.59).

Deception: when someone is led to believe something that isn't true.

As you've seen throughout this course already, juggling ethics and validity of research is often a grey area. Where you are confronted with such grey areas, you should *always* consult your teacher.

(b)   Planning Procedures

It's now time to begin planning how you are actually going to conduct the experiment and gather the relevant data. This is also a good opportunity to discuss with your group the possible confounding variables that you haven't already thought about, because as part of your report you will need to explain the controls that you have used. Your experimental design, allocation method, participants, sampling and how you handle ethical considerations may already be controlling for particular variables. There may also be other considerations as well, like time of day, location, noise, etc.

How closely you are replicating the original study will also influence how much original thinking will need to go into your planning. For example, if you are conducting a study like Bransford and Johnson's study on comprehension, you may decide to use their original materials and follow their procedures. If you are designing a study based on the effects of plants and mood, you may need to put more effort into planning and designing the procedures, including finding and creating the materials required.

If you have been working through each section of this chapter, you should already have many elements of your procedure covered.

At this stage of the process it's also advisable for you to figure out what materials you are going to need. You can create a list of the materials and begin thinking about ways you can ensure that these will be appropriate for your aims. In your final report you will need to explain your choice of materials. This doesn't mean giving reasons for using materials like pens and paper. It refers to other materials that are particularly relevant to the manipulation of the independent variable and/or the measure of the dependent variable. For example, if you are using word lists you might want to explain how you created the word list and why you created it this way. If you are using slides, videos or images, you will also need to describe how you created and/or chose these particular materials and explain your reasoning.

Proposing your experiment to an ethics review committee (group of classmates) could be a fun way of making sure you have met all the ethical guidelines put forward by the IB.

You might want to set up ethics review committees in your own class so you can pitch your research proposals to the committee to see if they meet the ethical standards put forward by the IB.

(c)   Producing Materials

You will need to produce a range of materials for carrying out your study, regardless of your procedures. Most importantly you need to have your consent forms with all the relevant information on them ready. It is advisable to produce a set of standardized instructions that you will read to all participants to ensure that there is consistency of conditions across treatments.

Another important factor to consider will be how you are going to collect your data. Your final report will require a table of your raw data to be included in the appendices, so one important tool that you'll need is a method of clearly and reliability collating the data from your participants.

You need to explain your choice of materials in your final report. This should focus primarily on the material/s designed particularly for the manipulation of the IV and the gathering of the data for the DV. If your test includes a list of words to be recalled, for example, you would need to describe how you created the list and explain why you created it this way for your study. If you have modified the original study and used different materials for any reason, you might want to provide some justification for this as well.

After you have your materials produced and your procedures planned, you should be ready to conduct a pilot study.

You can find sample consent forms and other examples of IA related work on our blog.

(d)   Pilot Study

It's best to do things right the first time! Students often make the mistake of thinking that they've got everything ready for their experiment and then when they have a room full of participants eagerly awaiting the experiment to begin they realize they've forgotten something. Conducting a pilot study is an effective way to spot any potential errors before you begin gathering your sample and conducting your experiment on your actual participants.

Conducting a pilot study and getting feedback from your classmates is a really good way of making sure that you are not going to make any easily avoidable errors.

An important part of carrying out your experimental investigation is that it provides you with the opportunity to practice being professional. For this reason it's imperative that you take the procedure seriously and you maintain a high level of professional conduct, even when carrying out the pilot study. After the IA is complete, many students lament the fact that they cannot do it again and do it better.

You will want your participants to take your experiment seriously. In order for this to happen, you need to be conducting the experiment in a professional and academic manner; your participants will only take your experiment as seriously as you do. It's normal to feel nervous during this process, especially if you are standing in front of a room full of people. Practicing giving your instructions, just like you would any other presentation, can help reduce these nerves and will reduce the likelihood of you "getting the giggles" during the research process.

(e)   *Experimenting*

It is hoped by this stage of the IA process that you have completed all the planning and preparation and you're ready to start conducting your tests and gathering your data.

As you are conducting your experiment it is important to keep note of important aspects of the procedures that might be influencing the results. As part of the evaluation of your experiment you need to include explanations of strengths and limitations of the procedures, materials, design, etc. If there were circumstances beyond your control that might have affected your results it's important to note these, as they may be useful for your evaluation.

Remember that you will not be rewarded if you explain numerous avoidable errors in your experimental procedures that may have affected your results. The IB guide explicitly states that, "human error or accidents and omissions that could easily have been avoided with a little foresight and planning are not acceptable as limitations." (p.53). This is one reason why it's really important that you are well-prepared before beginning to gather your sample and conduct your experiment.

Good luck and have fun.

7.3 Analyzing
How do you analyze your data?

(a) Descriptive Statistics

Was it fun? Do you wish you could do it over? I hope everything went well and you have gathered sufficient data. It's now time to do some statistical analysis of your results in order to draw conclusions about the relationship you were studying. Remember you have carried out an experiment with the aim of determining the effect of one variable on another. The statistical analysis needs to be carried out to see if there really was an effect and the descriptive statistics will help you to demonstrate your findings. At this point in the IA process, your collaboration with your group members should finish and the remainder of the assignment is completed individually.

Central Tendency: the average. This descriptive statistic provides a general idea of the average results for both conditions.

Descriptive statistics describe the data: they offer a general summary and enable general conclusions to be made about the nature of the findings. When someone is reading your report, the descriptive statistics provide them with an overview of your results. You will need to apply descriptive statistics that highlight the central tendency (also known as the average) and the dispersion of the data (also known as the spread or variability).

By far the most common measurement of central tendency in psychological research is the mean. If you have no outliers, a mean is probably a suitable descriptive statistic to use for variability and the standard deviation would be the measure of the variability, as this is used with measurements of a mean. However, if you had outliers that may have skewed your results, you may want to use a different measurement of central tendency, such as the median, mode or percentages. If you use one of these measurements, you may also need to use a different measurement of the spread of the data, such as the range, quartiles or the interquartile range.

Dispersion (a.k.a. spread or variability): a measure of the dispersion of your data. This measures how spread out your data are.

Just like with other parts of your experiment, there are lots of choices when it comes to statistics and analyzing your data. You need to make your decisions carefully.

It is important that you think carefully about the descriptive statistics you choose to apply to your data as they need to be appropriate to your aim and research hypothesis. You could also apply more than one measurement if this was relevant, but it's not required.

Your choice of descriptive statistics may also be influenced by the type of data you gathered for your dependent variable. If you replicated Loftus and Palmer's experiment about remembering broken glass, it would be redundant to calculate the mean, median or mode – percentages would be the only relevant calculation of an average you could use. It's important that you are careful in your selection of the descriptive statistics that you will apply to your data as they need to be consistent with your hypothesis.

The standard procedure in presenting psychological research is to present your descriptive statistics in a table as well as a written summary. Creating a table of your results would help with the presentation of your findings in the final report and it might also make creating a graph easier as well. All raw data should be included in your appendices and only calculated statistics should appear in the body of the report. A common mistake that students make is having poorly labelled tables that are not clear. Communicating information clearly is an important skill you are practicing during this process.

Remember that you are writing your summary of the descriptive statistics so your reader can get a general understanding of your findings. You do not need to explain the significance of the results in relation to existing research, as that happens in your evaluation. You should, however, be making it clear what your results were.

You do not need to include a justification of your choice of descriptive statistics. However, you will score low marks if the choice is not suitable for your hypothesis. It's a good idea to refer to the original study you are replicating and take note of how they have presented their results in words and table form. While you're probably not going to be copying what they have done exactly, it is a good way to get an idea of how to present findings in psychological research.

The best way to understand the requirements of the IA is to read examples of existing research. While these are often in more detail than is required of you, they will give you an idea of the nature and purpose of different sections of a psychology report.

(b) Graphing Data

After you have calculated your descriptive statistics you need to present these visually for your readers. Your graph needs to address the research hypothesis, which means that it should clearly display the data so the relevance of your findings in relation to the hypothesis can be clearly seen. The results from the two conditions of your experiment and the results of the manipulation of the IV should be clearly presented. Your graph should primarily represent your measure of central tendency. It might be relevant and appropriate to include the dispersion in some way, like using error bars.

A good way to see if your graph is clear and consistent with your hypothesis is to show it to someone who is not working in your group and see if they can determine the aim of your experiment just from looking at your well-labelled, clear and accurate graph.

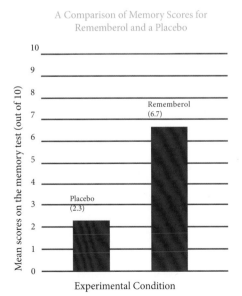

A Comparison of Memory Scores for Rememberol and a Placebo

In my fictional experiment, the treatment condition (Rememberol) resulted in scores almost triple (6.7) that of the placebo condition (2.3).

There are multiple different types of graphs that you could construct, including a pie chart, bar graph, or line graph. The choice will depend on the context of your research, especially your aim and research hypothesis: you need to be presenting the findings in a way that makes sense in terms of your hypothesis.

As an example, let's imagine I was conducting my Rememberol experiment and my hypothesis was that taking Rememberol before studying would increase the memory as measured by the memory test. A pie chart representing the proportion of remembered details given by participants in either condition would be a rather ineffective way of showing my findings. A line graph with the participants along the x axis and memory scores along the y axis would also be rather redundant because the order of the participants is irrelevant to my hypothesis. With only two conditions, a simple bar graph comparing the average scores would be effective in presenting the results of my research and the manipulation of the IV. Once again, it's a good idea to refer to the original study to see how a graph has been used to present the findings from the study.

It's essential that your graph is correctly presented, which means it's accurate and does not try to mislead your readers by presenting the data in a distorted fashion. For instance, if you were doing a memory test and the maximum score was 15, you would probably want to have your y-axis go all the way to 15. If the mean scores were 2.9 and 2.5, some students might be tempted to have a graph that only shows up to 4 with increments of 0.1 to exaggerate the differences between the scores. This would not be a correct way to present the data because it has been done with the intent of exaggerating findings. As with all graphs you also need to make sure it's clearly labelled and has a clear title.

You do not need to include a justification of your choice of graph, but you should provide a summary of what the graph is representing in a caption. You might score low marks in this section if the choice is not suitable for your hypothesis.

(c) Inferential Statistics

Statistical Significance: this is a conclusion based on the results of inferential statistics tests. If results are statistically significantly at the given probability value (e.g. 0.05) it means that they were an effect of the manipulation of the IV – *not* simply due to chance.

Descriptive statistics are valuable because they can allow readers to get an overview of your findings and they make the results visible. However, they are limited in the depth of information they can provide. Psychological research is typically only published if its results have statistical significance. This means that statistical tests have been applied to the data and the tests show that there is a very low probability that the results were simply a result of luck or chance. Inferential statistics are used to determine if the results are from the effect of the manipulation of the independent variable. If the results of an experiment have statistical significance, it means that the differences observed between the conditions in the experiment were a result of the manipulation of the independent variable. If the results do not have statistical significance, such a conclusion cannot be drawn and the results may be simply due to luck or chance.

In psychology we set the probability value at ≤ 0.05 (5%). This means that we're conducting tests to make sure there is a less than a 5% chance that our results were simply due to luck or chance and that there's a 95% chance (or higher) that the results were in fact a result of the manipulation of the independent variable. The inferential statistics tests that we apply to our data can tell us if our results are significant or not. If the results are statistically *significant*, we can reject the null hypothesis and accept the research hypothesis.

If we only looked at the results in the table on the left, we would probably draw the conclusion that Rememberol can increase our test scores, because the mean is 18.6 compared with only 15. But if we look a little more closely at the data we can see that in the placebo condition there were actually three out of the seven matched pairs that had a higher test score than their partner in the Rememberol condition. In one of these the difference was quite large (18 versus 10). From this

Test Scores After Taking Rememberol	Test Scores after Taking a Placebo
23	12
24	26
19	15
10	13
15	9
29	10
10	18
Mean = 18.6	Mean = 15

data, would you be confident in saying that Rememberol can increase test scores? Imagine if these were the results to test the benefits of an actual drug. Would you be willing to try a new drug that had a 3/7 (43%) chance of having no effect at all or making your symptoms worse?

There are a number of different tests of statistical significance and you need to choose the appropriate test based on two criteria:

a)   Your experimental design (and type of data)
b)   The level of measurement of your data

Determining your experimental design will be straightforward: did you use repeated measures, matched pairs or independent samples? Repeated measures and matched pairs gather related data. Independent samples gathers unrelated data. The choice of tests differs depending on if your data is related or unrelated.

Figuring out your level of data may be slightly more difficult. There are three levels of data that are relevant to determining an inferential statistical test: nominal, ordinal, and interval data.

Nominal Data: This is when data is categorized into different groups. The important aspect of nominal data is that there is no order among the responses; they can only be categorized. For example, there is not a "highest to lowest" order. Answer "yes" or "no" to the question about seeing broken glass in Loftus and Palmer's experiment would be an example of nominal data because the data is grouped into categories.

Inferential statistics are conducted to make sure that your results were really due to the manipulation of the IV, and not just because of luck.

Ordinal Data: The main feature of ordinal data is that it can be put into ranks, or "ordered'; this is the primary difference of ordinal data from nominal data. Ranking something on a scale, as used in Likert scales are commonly considered ordinal data if they have been invented for the purposes of the test and have not been reliably tested (Coolican, p.339). For example, if you had participants rank their mood on a scale of 1 – 10 after being in a room with or without plants, this could be considered ordinal data.

Interval Data: Unlike ordinal data, interval data has a consistent scale throughout so the difference from one data point to the next is measured on a consistent scale. Using a questionnaire that has been professionally designed and tested for reliability is considered interval data. Memory and test scores are considered interval (or ratio) data. Time taken to complete a task is another example of interval data.

Determining the level of measurement of different types of data is not always a black-and-white process. There could be differing opinions on what level of measurement different types of data are. With help from your teacher, you should try your best to identify what type of data you have collected. The two most important things for you to learn during this process of conducting inferential statistics are:

a)   How to choose the right test.
b)   Why we conduct inferential statistical tests in psychology.

On our blog you can read an important articled called "Why we rarely (if ever) use the word prove in psychology." Before you use the word "prove" in your IA, make sure to read this article.

Related and unrelated data: refers to whether or not individual scores in different conditions can be directly comparable. Matched pairs and repeated measures designs gather related data. As independent samples come from different people that aren't matched, the data is unrelated.

Vassarstats.net is a good online calculator to use for inferential statistics. You can find more detailed instructions on how to conduct these tests on our blog.

There is a fourth level of measurement: ratio. It's only necessary to determine if your data is at least ordinal when choosing the right inferential statistical test to apply.

You can find out more information on conducting inferential statistical tests on our blog.

Critical Value: this is the number you use to compare the result of your inferential test in order to determine whether or not your results are statistically significant. The critical value can be found using a table from a credible online source, or from a statistics textbook.
Significance level: the significance level, also denoted as α, is a value set for an inferential statistics test. It is usually set at 0.05 (5%), which means for the results to be significant there needs to be less than a 5% likelihood the results were due to chance.

Socscistatistics.com is another useful website with online calculators.

Once you know your experimental design and the level of data you have gathered, you can select your inferential statistical test. There are a number of online calculators that you can use to conduct your tests. If you use one of these be sure to get a screen shot of the calculations so you can put them in the appendices of your final report.

As most IAs gather data that is at least ordinal, you are most likely going to use a Mann-Whitney U test or a Wilcoxon Signed Ranks test. If you have nominal data, you will need to use a Chi-squared test. A very basic summary of these tests has been provided for you below. It is not necessary to carry out the calculations by hand, although your teacher may decide that this is a valuable experience. It is enough for the purposes of the IA to use an online calculator, input your data and obtain your results from the calculations using these tests. However, it is essential that you understand *what* you are doing and *why*. It is a missed learning opportunity, and you are prone to making costly errors, if you just input your data and report the results without understanding what these results actually represent.

Mann-Whitney U Test

You will use this test if you have unrelated data and your data is at least ordinal. Calculate the value of U (using an online calculator or by hand) then find the critical value based on your sample size and ≤0.05 significance level by using a relevant table (which can be found online or in a statistics book). If your U value is equal to or less than the critical value, your results are significant and you can reject the null hypothesis.

When you write your results of the Mann-Whitney test you should include the critical value based on the group sizes (Na, Nb) the p value, the U value and whether or not based on your results you accept or reject the null hypothesis.

Wilcoxon Signed Ranks Test

Use this test if you have related data and your data is at least ordinal. Calculate the value of W (using an online calculator or by hand). Then, find the critical value based on your sample size and 0.05 significance level by using a relevant table. If your W value is equal to or less than the corresponding critical value (based on N), your results are significant and you can reject the null hypothesis.

When you state your results of the Wilcoxon test you should include the critical value based on your sample (N) and the p value, the W value, a statement of significance of the data, and whether or not based on your results you accept or reject the null hypothesis.

Chi-square Test

You will use a chi-square test if your data is nominal (i.e. participants results are assigned to categories) and you have unrelated data (e.g. independent samples). If you have two conditions you will be using a 2x2 table to input your data and your degrees of freedom (df) value is 1. Remember that you are inputting the number of participants in each category, not descriptive statistics such as percentages. This test will help you calculate the value of chi-square. Your results are significant if the calculated value of chi-square is equal to or larger than the critical value (corresponding with the df).

Once you have crunched the numbers you will be able to determine if your results are statistically significant. You can then reject or accept your null hypothesis accordingly.

Results in the 'Wrong Direction'

It might so happen that your descriptive statistics are inconsistent with your research hypothesis. For instance, if I conducted an experiment on Rememberol I may have found higher test scores in the placebo group. If this happens in your experiment you still need to see if your results are "significant" as it's a requirement of the assignment. Learning how and why inferential statistical tests are applied in psychological experiments is a key learning outcome in this course.

t-tests

Students often ask about the use of t-tests. In the past, IB Psychology students have been encouraged to use non-parametric tests (e.g. Mann-Whitney, Wilcoxon, Chi-square) and discouraged from using t-tests because the data gathered usually does not fit the assumptions necessary for a t-test. However, this point is debatable as there are different schools of thought and the use of the t-test could be acceptable. As with all steps of the IA, your choice of inferential statistical test should be made in consultation with your teacher.

One-Tailed versus Two-Tailed Tests

You will need to determine whether or not you are doing a one-tailed or a two-tailed test. A one-tailed test is often conducted when there's a one-tailed (directional) hypothesis. A one-tailed hypothesis is a prediction that variable (a) will have an effect on variable (b) in one direction. For example, if I hypothesized that taking Rememberol would increase test scores, this is a one-directional hypothesis and so I would conduct a one-tailed test.

A two-tailed hypothesis is when there is a prediction of an effect, but the effect could go in either direction. For example, if I hypothesized that Rememberol would have an effect on test scores, but I wasn't sure if this would increase or decrease the scores, this is a two-tailed hypothesis and so I would conduct a two-tailed test.

There are many components to the IA and there isn't enough space in this book to provide full explanations for all requirements. Be sure to use our blog to check for additional materials that will be helpful for you during this process.

The use of one- or two-tailed tests is a potentially contentious issue, with different schools of thought on the topic. As always, trust the guidance of your teacher with such issues.

N = sample

The p value is the calculated value of probability. If your p value is less than 0.05 your results are statistically significant. Not all online calculators will provide the p value, so if it's not included do not worry - just make sure to screen shot your results and include them in the appendices.

Most IB Psychology IAs have one-tailed research hypotheses as they are predicting a manipulation of the IV increasing a DV.

7.4 Presenting
How do you write an experimental research report?

(a) Introduction

Once you've conducted your experiment and crunched the numbers, it's time to construct the first draft of your report. You will only be allowed to submit the first draft of this assignment and get feedback from your teacher *once* during this process. The second draft will be your final submission, so if you want to do well on this assessment you must strive to make your first draft as complete, thorough, and accurate as possible. The more detailed your notes have been as you've been working through this task, the easier the writing of the first draft will be.

It might make more sense to start writing your analysis section before your introduction, as your results should be fresh in your mind after having just conducted your tests.

Your entire report will be approximately 1800 – 2200 words and you have four sections of similar value. This should provide a general guide for how much to write in each section (i.e. around 400 to 600 words per section).

The introduction is worth 6/22 marks and you can see the description of how to get full marks in the box below.

> - The theory or model upon which the student's investigation is based is described and the link to the student's investigation is explained.
> - The aim of the investigation is stated and its relevance is explained.
> - The Independent and Dependent Variables are stated and operationalized in the null or research hypotheses.

The theory or model upon which the student's investigation is based is described and the link to the student's investigation is explained.

The purpose of any introduction is to provide the reader with context. In psychology reports introductions tend to begin with a broad overview of the topic being studied. They then offer some review of existing research, including relevant theories or studies. You should aim to do something similar in your introduction, although yours will be very brief.

To find the full rubric for the IA and plenty of other resources visit our website at www. themantic-education.com.

If your experiment is related to an existing theory or model, such as schema theory, the working memory model or the multi-store model, the description should be rather straightforward. Be sure to include references and follow a consistent referencing format throughout your work (e.g. MLA or APA).

It might also be useful to describe any relevant phenomena that your study is based on and/or investigating. For example, Loftus and Palmer (1974) has been used to demonstrate the influence of schematic processing on memory. It might also be relevant to explain the misinformation effect in this study, as this is a relevant phenomenon that might help put a replication in context. There aren't rigid rules for writing an introduction, as it depends on the context of your experiment. How you write about the context of your research will vary from topic to topic.

After you have summarized the relevant background information related to your experiment, including describing prior research, you then need to explain your replication. Remember that explaining means showing how things are related, so it's imperative that you can explain how your research is relevant to the existing research that you have described.

For example, I might conduct an experiment on the effects of Rememberol. But if in an original (fictional) study they measured the effects of the drug by using reading comprehension, I might replicate the experiment to see if the same effect could be found for math tests. This link to existing research would be even stronger if in my introduction I had described previous research that suggests studying for English and Math uses different parts of the brain; my experiment is seeing if the drug can be used across subjects, not just one. In this way, I am explaining *how* my replication is linked to the original research.

A good introduction is a bit like a map: it shows where others have been and where you plan on going.

A common visual metaphor used to describe introductions is that of an upside-down triangle: start broad and then narrow to the specifics. After providing some context for your research you should be narrowing towards the specifics of your experiment, including describing the operationally defined variables and clearly stating the aim of the experiment.

The aim of the investigation is stated and its relevance is explained.

You also need to make sure that you clearly state the aim of your experiment. The aim of any experiment is to investigate a cause-effect relationship between variables. This should be reflected in the statement of your aim.

To gain full marks you need to explain the relevance of the aim of your experiment and why it's being carried out. The reason behind carrying out your experiment needs to go beyond something superficial like, "I'm conducting this experiment because it's part of my IA." If you are using a very similar design to the original, think about the possible applications of the research. If you have modified an experiment or designed your own based on existing research, you should explain how your modifications are relevant to this area of investigation.

This criterion is requiring you to demonstrate your understanding of the significance of the research you are replicating.

The Independent and Dependent Variables are stated and operationalized in the null or research hypotheses.

Following the inverted triangle approach to writing an introduction, it should finish with a clear statement of your research (experimental) and null hypotheses. It should be clear from the statement of the hypotheses what your independent and dependent variables are.

In research reporting, H_1 denotes the experimental hypothesis, while H_0 denotes the null hypothesis.

For example, let's say my Rememberol experiment is testing memory. I would need a more operationally defined dependent variable than "memory" because this is too vague and general. I might operationalize it as, "scores on a reading comprehension test" or maybe something like "test scores on remembering country capitals." In this case my IV would not need much operationalizing because it would involve the type of drug taken (Rememberol or placebo).

So my hypotheses might look something like:

H_1 = *Participants who take Rememberol before studying will achieve significantly higher scores on the reading comprehension test compared to participants who take a placebo.*

H_0 = *There will be no significant difference in scores on the reading comprehension test for groups in the Rememberol or placebo condition. Any differences observed will be due to chance.*

Notice how in the first hypothesis both conditions of the experiment are included and the extra detail "before studying" helps to operationalize the IV. The DV is operationalized in a concise manner with the phrase "scores on a reading comprehension test." It's not necessary to operationalize this further, as the details of the test will be included in other areas of the report.

(b) Exploration

The primary purpose of the introduction is to put your experiment into context. You describe the related research, explain how and why yours is relevant and provide some indication of the aim and hypotheses you are making based on this existing research. After you have done this effectively, the purpose of your exploration is to show the design choices you made for your experiment.

This section is worth 4/22 marks and you can see the description of how to get full marks in the box below.

> - The research design is explained.
> - The sampling technique is explained.
> - The choice of participants is explained.
> - Controlled variables are explained.
> - The choice of materials is explained.

As you can see from the rubric you need to *explain* all your choices. The IB definition of explain works well in this context: "provide a detailed summary, including *reasons*." A good explanation will include accurate, concise and relevant description (summary), so be sure to include this as well.

One reason for describing elements of your research, such as your sampling technique and research design, is that it enables you to provide the evidence that you do know these concepts and that you have applied them properly. If you only provide reasons, there's no way that your teacher (or an IA examiner) can make an accurate judgement on your level of understanding.

You can find a checklist for self-editing of your IA on our blog.

When you are providing reasons and justifications for your choices, your reasoning should demonstrate your understanding of experimental design and how issues related to ethics, practicality, and validity all need to be considered in psychological research. Do note, however, that you do not need to include all of these for every point: only include the most relevant points for each explanation.

The points in your exploration can be included in any order and do not need to follow the order in the rubric.

The research design is explained.

Make sure you state the research design you have used (independent samples, matched pairs or repeated measures). It is a good idea to include a brief description of your procedures so that it's clear *how* you applied this research design in your particular experiment. For example, if you were using independent samples you can describe both conditions and how participants were allocated to either condition. After you have provided this context, go further and provide at least one reason why this design was suitable for your experiment.

The sampling technique is explained.

As with the research design, I recommend clearly stating the sampling method that you have used and briefly describing *how* you obtained your sample. After this information is provided, go further and explain why this sample was chosen for your particular experiment. It might be that your choice was based on issues of practicality, and this is a valid factor to include in your explanation.

The choice of participants is explained.

Before you can explain your choice of participants you need to outline the relevant characteristics, such as age, gender, ethnicity, etc. These should be summaries (e.g. the mean age, a total of male or female, etc.) and you do not need to state the characteristics of individual participants. You should aim to find at least one characteristic that is relevant to your experiment that you can explain. For example, if you are conducting an experiment that requires reading comprehension skills, you would have considered this in your sampling and this is where you explain those decisions. You might, for example, explain how you wanted a minimum age of participants and/or those of a similar age to control for variability in reading skills. You might have excluded EAL students for the same reason, so you would include the fact that your participants were native speakers.

Your explanations need to be relevant to your study.

The choice of materials is explained.

You do not need to explain basic materials such as pens and paper or rooms used. It might help to think of the materials that you need to explain as the tools or the instruments you used. It's likely that you had to create and/or source particular materials to carry out your experiment. For example, if your participants watched a video of some kind, you need to describe the video and then explain why it was chosen. If you are conducting an experiment using word lists you have created you can describe the nature of the word list and provide one (or more) reasons for why you made it this way.

The state→describe→explain format should provide some guidance for how to write this section of the report.

Controlled variables are explained.

As you were planning your experiment you would have been discussing with your group the multiple extraneous variables that needed to be controlled for. This is where you can explain how you attempted to control those extraneous variables in the design of your experiment. It's possible that you have already explained how other design choices have controlled for particular variables. In this case, you do not need to include them again.

Remember that you're writing your report so someone else can understand what it was you did and why. Your writing should be clear and accurate so someone who didn't see your experiment could comprehend your procedures.

The variables could be things like time of day, interfering noises, or characteristics of participants (e.g. age, gender). It is hoped that you have already controlled for common confounding variables, such as order effects, participant variability or researcher bias.

It is natural to ask "how much do I need to explain?" This is a very difficult question to answer and the best I can provide is: it depends. One approach I recommend is to explain at least two points for each design element (e.g. sampling, design, methods, etc.) in your rough draft. After you have completed the entire rough draft, you will know where you are in terms of word count and how much you need to remove. How many words you need to trim will influence your editing choices.

From your explanations in your exploration your reader should be able to comprehend the procedures of your experiment. You should make sure that you reference all of your materials in the appendices, including things like informed consent, standardized instructions, materials/instruments used, etc.

(c) Analysis

In the exploration you have explained your choices made during your experimentation process. The third section of your report is based on the reporting of your findings, including your statistics. If you have followed instructions and your teacher's guidance carefully, it should be rather straightforward to get top marks in this section.

This section is worth 6/22 marks and you can see the description of how to get full marks in the box below.

> - Descriptive and inferential statistics are appropriately and accurately applied.
> - The graph is correctly presented and addresses the hypothesis.
> - The statistical findings are interpreted with regard to the data and linked to the hypothesis.

Descriptive and inferential statistics are appropriately and accurately applied.

Your descriptive statistics should be presented neatly in a clear table that is well-labelled and easy to comprehend. Results should be presented visually and in writing to make it easy for the reader to comprehend your findings; this is why you need to make sure you have clear labels and your results are clearly presented. You do not need to include your inferential statistics in a table, only descriptive statistics.

Your inferential statistics test needs to be the correct choice based on your data and design. While it's not a requirement to justify your chosen test, this can be done in one sentence and may be worthwhile to include in this section. For example, it could be stated as easily as "Our experiment used repeated measures and our data was at least ordinal, so we used a Wilcoxon Signed Ranks test to test for statistical significance." It is then important to outline the results of the inferential test and state whether or not you accept the null hypothesis.

While it's important that you know *why* you chose to use a particular inferential test, you do not need to include this justification in your report. This might be useful to note if your word count is on the high side. To show the examiner your reasoning, you could always include this in the appendices along with the calculations.

The graph is correctly presented and addresses the hypothesis.

The graph should present your findings after you have analyzed the data. As with descriptive statistics, you do not need to explain your choice of graph, but it is essential that an appropriate graph has been chosen. You are also not required to include more than one graph.

Do not present a graphed version of raw data as this will be difficult to follow and won't be related to your research hypotheses.

The statistical findings are interpreted with regard to the data and linked to the hypothesis.

Along with presenting your descriptive statistics in a table, you should also provide a written summary of the results. You need to analyze your descriptive statistics in terms of the average/s and variance and summarize these findings in a few sentences and this should be linked to your hypothesis. If there are any interesting findings in the data you can comment on these as well.

You also need to make a statement of the significance of your results as indicated by the inferential statistics that you applied. Make sure that you include relevant details, such as the probability value, the significance level (≤ 0.05), sample or group sizes, the critical value and the relevant calculated value (e.g. U, W, chi, etc.) You should state whether or not your results were significant and if you are subsequently accepting or rejecting the null hypothesis.

Attention to detail is key when reporting findings in the analysis section of the IA. Many students make simple and avoidable errors in their first and final drafts simply because they are careless. The analysis section is arguably easier than the exploration and it's worth more marks, so it's essential that you take great care in completing this section of the written report.

Remember that there should be no raw data included in the body of the report and all raw data tables and calculations should be included in the appendices.

Visit the blog for examples of how to write summaries of descriptive and inferential statistics.

(d)   Evaluation

This final section in a psychological report is often called the "discussion." This is where you explain the significance of the results you have found in comparison with the existing research and where you provide an evaluation of your experiment, including suggested modifications for further research.

This final section is worth 6/22 marks and you can see the description of how to get full marks in the box below.

> - The findings of the student's investigation are discussed with reference to the background theory or model.
> - Strengths and limitations of the design, sample and procedure are stated and explained and relevant to the investigation.
> - Modifications are explicitly linked to the limitations of the student's investigation and fully justified.

The findings of the student's investigation are discussed with reference to the background theory or model.

The opening paragraph of your evaluation should provide an explanation of how your results relate to the study you have replicated. The significance of this in terms of the model or theory they are based on should also be explained. This includes comparing your results to that of the study you are replicating and explaining similarities and/or differences found. Conclusions regarding your study and what it demonstrates should also be made.

Strengths and limitations of the design, sample and procedure are stated and explained and relevant to the investigation.

You need to include an explanation of strengths and limitations of your design, sample and procedure. This requires careful examination and scrutiny of your methodology. If possible, try to explain strengths that you haven't previously explained in your exploration. You have already shown in your exploration your understanding of how to employ controls to isolate the independent variable, so it might be unnecessary to re-explain them in this section.

Having said that, if you have planned your experimental investigation carefully you were probably aware of the strengths before even conducting the experiment. In this case, you might use this section to explain strengths of your methodology that were *not* included in the exploration.

It would be enough to explain a couple of strengths and focus primarily on limitations. There are a few reasons for this. Firstly, as it's been mentioned you've already demonstrated your understanding of the strengths of the research in earlier sections. Also, in the IB Psychology guide it states that the evaluation of the experiment "should focus on: the limitations of the method" and "suggestions for improving the method." There is no mention of the strengths in this explanation. It is also not a common practice in psychology articles to explain strengths – the focus is on possible limitations and suggestions for modification. This being said, the rubric states that strengths *and* limitations are required so you should be sure to include both.

Remember that you cannot include limitations that were a result of *easily* avoidable errors on the behalf of the researchers. You will need to identify possible extraneous variables that may have influenced the results that you could not have planned for and this will require careful scrutiny of your methodology. For instance, saying that you laughed and mumbled during your instructions so participants couldn't hear properly would not be a legitimate detail to evaluate as this could have been easily avoided. However, after conducting your experiment you may realize that some of your materials could have been designed more effectively. For instance, it might be noticeable by the responses you got from multiple participants that they didn't understand a particular critical question in

You need to scrutinize your methodology in order to explain strengths and limitations of your experiment. This part of the process should be completed independently.

one of your tests. Even though this was technically avoidable, if it's a genuine error and clearly could have influenced the results it's a valid limitation to explain.

Your evaluation could be based on issues related to internal and/or external validity. It is important to remember, however, that evaluation still requires explanation. For instance, making an empty statement like "our sample size was small so population validity may be questioned" does not demonstrate an understanding of research methodology. All IB Psychology IAs will have rather small sample sizes, so this by itself is a limited critique. You need to provide reasons why characteristics of your experiment influence the validity of the results.

Do your best to include explanation of strengths and/or limitations relating to all three aspects of methodology: design type, sampling and procedures.

Modifications are explicitly linked to the limitations of the student's investigation and fully justified.

After explaining the limitations you need to provide suggestions for modifications based on these limitations. For example, if I explained how the results suggest that participant variability may have been influential in my Rememberol experiment, I would then need to explain how I could modify the design of my experiment so I could reduce the chance of this happening again.

While the IB Psychology guide suggests that your modifications may be "… proposed on the basis of a fresh consideration of the experimental design," the rubric states that your modifications must be explicitly linked to the limitations of the investigation. I would recommend focusing on modifications linked to your limitations first, and only including other modifications if time and the word limit allow.

(e)   Presentation

Along with the body of your report that is made up of the four major sections, there are also some other elements you will need to include in your final report.

Title Page

Your title page should consist of:

- The title of your investigation
- Your IB candidate code
- The IB candidate code for all group members
- Date, month, and year of submission
- Word count

Contents Page

After your title page it would be a good idea to have a table of contents that clearly indicates the contents of your report.

References

Your work needs to meet the high standards of academic honesty required by the IB. You should use a standard method of referencing, including in-text citations (e.g. APA or MLA) and a list of references. While your references are not assessed, if your work is deemed to be an example of academic malpractice (because you have not included references) the IB guide clearly states that "you will not be awarded a grade for this subject."

Appendices

The appendices are included at the end of your report, after your evaluation. Materials in your appendices are not included in your word count.

Your appendices should include:

- Raw data (ideally collated in a table or other format that fits on one page).
- Calculations used for statistics (e.g. screen shots from online calculators, printouts or hand-written calculations).
- Standardized instructions.
- Any supplementary materials used for the experiment (e.g. word lists, screen shot of video, sample slides from presentation, etc.)
  - o Do use common sense when including materials in your appendices. For example, if you have a slideshow with twenty images you do not need to include twenty pages of images. Either collate them on one page or select a few as a sample.
- Documentation of ethical guidelines being followed:
  - o One copy of an unsigned consent form.
  - o Debriefing materials (e.g. a copy of the email/script used for debriefing).

Word Count

Only the body of your work will be counted towards the final word count. This means references and material in the appendices does not count towards the word count.

IA submissions should be anonymous, so do not put your name or candidate number on your report. If your name or other identifiable details appear in your report (e.g. your school's logo or name on an informed consent form) you can black these out before submitting.

The word count only includes the four sections of the body of your report (Introduction, Exploration, Analysis and Evaluation). Appendices, references and other details are not included in the word count.

This report is a formally presented academic paper and so the language, style and structure of your report should reflect this. Similarly, you should be writing in an academic font sized 11 or 12. You should have clear headings for the four major sections of your report as well (Introduction, Exploration, Analysis and Evaluation). It's a personal preference if you would like to include sub-headings under these categories (e.g. dividing "Exploration" into sampling, participants, design, etc.).

Take the time to make your report look professional. You've spent hours on this assignment and it would be a shame to submit something that on the surface doesn't reflect the depth of preparation and work that has gone in to the final product. Think of it this way: you wouldn't spend weeks trying to get into shape for a big date and then show up in your Sunday sweats.

Conclusion

We learn by doing and it's hoped that by going through the process of conducting your own experiment your understanding of the research process in psychology has been developed even further.

Many students find out first-hand what it's like to experience the very real threat of research bias influencing their results. They talk of their disappointment when their experiment didn't "work" and how they felt if they just had a few more participants maybe they could have got the results they *wanted*. Or if they could just leave out a few of the participants' data their results would be perfect! The reflection process brings about genuine understanding of the threats of bias to the research process.

It's easy to think about psychological studies in the abstract – to think about them as being things that just exist and forgetting that they were constructed by humans and so are prone to human error. Due to the nature of this course there simply isn't the time to deconstruct the studies we're exploring in any great detail. This is why the internal assessment process is such a valuable one in IB Psychology.

You can also apply what you have learned from this project in other areas of the course. For example, you may be able to identify potential confounding variables in examples of studies and explain how these may have influenced the results. Or you might be able to explain how the use of controls in a study could have helped to increase the validity of the findings. This might be applied to a relevant essay question in Paper One and/or Two, or possibly for Higher Level students in Paper Three.

I hope you enjoyed the experience of conducting a psychological experiment and learning about some new concepts like inferential statistics along the way. Research findings are everywhere in the media and learning how to interpret these with an analytical eye is an important life skill. Whether or not you are pursuing a career in psychology in your future, what you have learned during this project will be valuable.

After completing your IA and finishing your final draft to the best of your ability, you should be able to congratulate yourself on a job well done and take a well-earned break.

Chapter 8
HL Extensions

Introduction

As a Higher Level IB Psychology student, you get the opportunity to explore some really interesting extra topics. The topics, concepts and research used in this chapter are designed to build on your existing learning from the other units.

Animal Studies: This topic is designed to reinforce and build on learning from the criminology unit. Throughout these lessons you'll explore how studies on animals have deepened our understanding of the relationships between biological variables and human behaviour. However, the ethical considerations and other limitations are also important to consider.

The theme of this topic is the value of using animal models to provide insight into the role of genetics, hormones, and brain function in human behaviour.

Globalization and Behaviour: Globalization is a term that describes the increased interaction of people from different parts of the world. We are no longer living in isolated tribes, but participating in a "global village." This process is helped by immigration and advances in technology. In this topic, themes from the social influence unit are integrated in an in-depth exploration of the relationships between globalization, immigration, acculturation, marginalization, discrimination, religious extremism and conflict.

The major theme of this topic is how individuals may be influenced by changes occurring in the physical and cultural environment as a result of globalization.

Technology and Cognition: It seems to be a fact of life that one generation will always criticize the next. When pen and paper was introduced to classrooms some people worried that kids wouldn't learn how to write with chalk. But it can't be denied that the prevalence of modern technology means it's important to study the potential effects this might have. In this topic you will explore multiple types of technology and their effects on cognition. These topics are not as themantically connected as the others, but are written more as a series of individual lessons. This has been done to give you and your teacher the freedom to approach these based on best timing, interest and relevance. They would be best approached after learning about working memory in PTSD, so I would recommend these as the last topics to study.

The major theme of this topic is the positive and negative effects of technology on cognitive processes and their reliability.

Instead of adding more unrelated content to the course, these HL topics have been carefully chosen to deepen your understanding and appreciation of concepts covered in other chapters.

This course can be taught in any order. While this textbook has been written with a particular order in mind, your teacher could find a better way.

The HL extensions also provide opportunities to conduct individual investigations in areas of interest.

8.1 Animal Studies and Behaviour
Should animals be used to study humans?

(a) Animal Studies on the Brain and Behaviour

While you might find this topic unsettling if you are an animal lover, as psychologists we cannot overlook the importance of animal research in understanding human behaviour. One benefit of using animals in experiments is that they can provide us with valuable information about the functions of various parts of the brain. By damaging specific areas of the brain and then observing the changes in behaviour, psychologists have been able to draw conclusions about the role of individual parts of the brain in behaviour.

The general procedure is to observe the animals' ordinary behaviour before performing an operation that lesions (damages) or ablates (removes) an area of the brain. After this operation the experimenter records changes in the animals' behaviour. These effects are compared with control groups who might have no surgery, a sham surgery, or surgery on different areas of the brain.

Examples of this experimental procedure can be seen in studies on the amygdala and emotion that were explored in the criminology chapter. Early studies on rhesus monkeys were carried out as far back as the late 1800s (Brown and Schafer, 1888, as cited in Amaral and Adolphs, 2016). These studies involved ablating entire temporal lobes and noting the changes in behaviour. This research showed that after ablation, the monkeys were surprisingly tame and were less fearful of humans. They also demonstrated emotional blunting, which means they showed a lack of observable emotional reactions. This early research provided early evidence that the temporal lobe must have something to do with the emotion of fear.

Sham surgery: a fake, placebo surgery. This is performed to make sure that it's not the process of experiencing a surgery that is causing observable changes in behaviour.

Lesioning is damaging parts of the brain while **ablating** is removing whole areas.

Emotional blunting: displaying reduced signs of emotion (also called blunted affect).

In the 1950s, similar experiments involving bilateral amygdala lesions were carried out on rhesus monkeys. Weiskrantz (1956) experimented on rhesus monkeys to see if the amygdala was a specific part of the temporal lobe associated with fear. In this experiment, the behaviour of the monkeys was observed before and after the lesioning surgery. Weiskrantz wanted to quantify the behavioural changes so he carefully measured how fearful the monkeys were before and after the surgery. To see if it was the damage to the amygdala specifically that changed the monkeys' behaviour, a control group was needed for comparison. This control group had a different part of their temporal lobe lesioned - the inferotemporal cortex (IT).

Early monkey studies showed that the amygdala plays a role in the fear response by ablating this part of the brain. The results showed that when the monkeys' amygdalae were removed, their fear towards humans was reduced.

The results showed that the monkeys who had their amygdalae lesioned were quite tame and had apparently lost their fearful reactions to the humans. They would even approach the researchers, who were able to pat them. The control group, on the other hand, continued to display the same pre-surgery levels of fear towards the human researchers.

This was the first study to show that damage to the amygdala specifically would bring about the same observable tameness and lack of fear as damage to the entire temporal lobe. By comparing behavioural changes before and after surgery, and being able to compare across two different groups of monkeys who had different areas of the temporal lobe lesioned, Weiskrantz's experiment furthered our understanding of the role of the amygdala in emotion.

With MRIs and brain imaging technology, patients with damage to particular areas of the brain (like SM's damage to her amygdalae) are able to be identified for study. However, such technology wasn't available to these early researchers, so they needed to rely on lesioning and ablating animals' brains. This early research has provided a strong foundation of evidence that still today helps to corroborate findings of human studies, including those on case studies such as SM.

And while some people with brain damage (like SM and HM) appear from time to time to make for valuable case studies, they are also incredibly rare. So even though they can be used in modern research on the brain, it might not be possible for many studies to be conducted because there are far more researchers wanting to carry out case studies than there are suitable cases. Animals, on the other hand, can be bred in captivity for the purposes of experimentation, making it easier to find experimental subjects.

In summary, one of the primary advantages of using animals in experiments is that it enables neuroscientists to conduct carefully controlled experiments on the relationship between brain function and behaviour. These were particularly valuable before the development of brain imaging techniques.

Bilateral refers to both sides, so a bilateral amygdala lesion means damaging both amygdalae (one on each side of the brain). SM had bilateral amygdala damage.

The temporal lobe includes numerous parts of the brain, including the amygdala and the hippocampus.

Neuroscientist: a psychologist who specifically studies complex relationships between the brain and behaviour.

Guiding Question:

How are animal studies used in experiments on brain function and behaviour?

Critical Thinking Extension:
Limitations: A good discussion of research methods first involves describing how that method is used in a particular context (in this case, the brain and behaviour). The next step is to explain *why* they are useful. This will be practiced in later sections, but you can get a head start now by adding an explanation of *why* to your description of *how*.

If you're interested…

New Scientist's YouTube channel has a short video about animals that can have their amygdalae activated by lasers ("Mice made to kill using mind control lasers"). The effect of "turning on" the amygdala is really quite interesting. This is similar to studies using animals and lasers that are shown towards the end of the NOVA documentary "Memory Hackers."

(b)   Animal Models and Hormones

In the previous section, we looked at how animal experimentation can be valuable in understanding relationships between brain function and behaviour. By conducting carefully controlled experiments involving lesioning or ablating specific areas of the brain and measuring the behavioural effects, neuropsychologists are able to draw conclusions about the relationship between brain function and behaviour.

Humans and animals share similar biological characteristics, including brain structure. This is why studies using animal models can provide psychologists with an insight into relationships between brain function and behaviour. But humans also share other physiological similarities with animals. For example, we have the same hormones and these send chemical messages in much the same way in humans as they do in animals. So the use of animal models in research can also reveal potential relationships between hormones and behaviour.

As with experiments on brain function, animals are useful in endocrinology experiments because psychologists can alter levels of hormones and measure changes in behaviour. The ability to conduct well-controlled experiments that isolate the manipulation of the hormone level as the only variable influencing behaviour enables cause-and-effect relationships to be determined.

One of the most widely studied hormone-behaviour pairings is testosterone and aggression. By being able to conduct experiments on animals and manipulate hormone levels, researchers can study the effects of elevated levels of testosterone on behaviour. Albert et al.'s (1986) experiment on alpha male rats and testosterone levels is a good example of the value of using animal models in psychological research. The aim of this experiment was to see what happens when levels of testosterone were changed in alpha male rats. This carefully controlled experiment manipulated testosterone levels by castrating the rats. The researchers also controlled for social status by choosing to study only alpha males from different populations (i.e. cages). By keeping social variables constant and having control conditions for comparison, the researchers could compare the results of the manipulation of the testosterone on aggressive behaviour. For example, the castration group was compared with the castration and testosterone replacement group.

By being able to place rats in different cages with one another, the researchers were also able to draw conclusions about the role of testosterone in facilitating behaviour associated with social dominance (e.g. behaving aggressively in order to be the dominant rat). For example, when a subordinate rat (lower rank) is put in the same cage as a castrated alpha, the subordinate rat overtakes the castrated alpha rat as being the dominant male. Similar experimental procedures would be difficult (if not impossible) to replicate on humans.

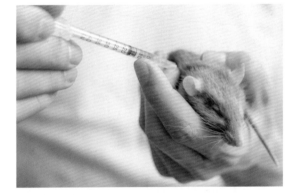

Animal models of the effects of physiological changes on behaviour can provide insight into how hormonal changes may affect human behaviour. Injecting hormones is one way that physiology is manipulated in animal experiments.

Animal model: can be defined as the demonstration of a phenomenon in a non-human animal.

Endocrinology: the study of hormones.

Insight: to get an insight means you can understand something that was previously unclear or unknown. Animal studies provide insights into human behaviour because they can reveal relationships between biological variables and behaviour that we're not sure of and might be difficult to study in humans.

You can read the full description of Albert et al.'s experiment in the criminology topic 2.4.

Rat studies like Albert et al.'s have provided valuable insight into relationships between testosterone and aggression. This has inspired further research on humans, like that of Radke et al. (2015) that can now use fMRI technology to find correlations between testosterone levels and brain function. But while experiments on humans in controlled environments can investigate cause-and-effect relationships between hormone levels and brain function, they often can't measure the effects on behaviour. For example, just because participants have increased amygdala activation when they're motivated to approach a threat (as shown in Radke et al., 2015), it doesn't necessarily mean they will behave aggressively. This is where our understanding of the relationships between variables and behaviours can be enhanced by the *combination* of studies on humans and other animals: the animal model shows the connection between the hormone and behaviour, while the fMRI study can fill in the missing pieces and show *how* the hormone may affect behaviour through its influence on brain function.

The use of animal models also allows researchers to measure the effects of the manipulation of hormone levels in a way that would be extremely unethical to do to humans. Sapolsky's research on vervet monkeys (in the PTSD chapter), for example, shows the effects of prolonged exposure to increased cortisol levels on the hippocampus. Small capsules containing cortisol (and cholesterol in the control condition) were inserted in the brains of the monkeys to measure the effects this would have on the structure of the neurons in the hippocampus. The results showed that the cortisol damaged the neurons in the monkeys. This study helped to provide an insight into the effects that prolonged stress can have on the brain (as cortisol is released as a result of the amygdala's activation of the HPA axis during times of stress). It would be unethical to perform such an experiment on human subjects and, to be honest, I doubt there'd be many volunteers.

From the above examples we can see more examples of the benefits of using animal models in experimental research: the experiment can happen in a tightly controlled environment, enabling cause-and-effect conclusions to be drawn. It also enables the manipulation of variables in ways that would be unethical and impractical to perform on humans.

Aggression is difficult to define and there are many possible definitions. One way to think about it is as any behaviour that has the intent of threatening or harming another being. That harm may be physical or psychological.

The effects of cortisol on genetics will be explored later in this chapter, as will ethical issues related to this type of animal research.

Sapolsky's experiment using vervet monkeys and cortisol secretion can be used to demonstrate the value of animal models in research on the brain and behaviour *and* hormones.

Guiding Question:

How does one study on hormones demonstrate the value of using animal models in Psychology?

Critical Thinking Extension:

Limitations: One of the limitations of using animal models is that they are reductionist – they focus only on biological variables. Can you think of cultural or environmental variables that limit the extent to which we can generalize findings from Albert et al.'s or Sapolsky's research?

If you're interested...

Robert Sapolsky has an excellent TED Talk called "The biology of our best and worst selves" in which he summarizes most of what we learned during criminology.

(c)   Animal Models of Neuroplasticity

In the previous sections we've looked at how animal research has played a significant role in understanding correlations between biological processes and behaviour. These types of experiments are the backbone of biological psychology.

But you might be thinking, '*These are mice and monkeys. How can they give us an insight into human behaviour?*' Actually, when it comes to studying biology and behaviour, humans are very similar to other primates: we have about 99% of our DNA in common with chimps and about 93% in common with rhesus monkeys. Our brains also have very similar structures and even our neurotransmission processes are similar to other animals.

In fact, animals as different to humans as sea slugs (Aplysia) have been invaluable sources of information used to understand human neurology. Eric Kandel has won the Nobel Prize for his work over the past 50 years studying the neurons of Aplysia. Whereas humans have about 100 billion neurons, these sea slugs have about 20,000. They make for excellent laboratory animals because their neurons are abnormally large and it's easy to locate particular types of neurons. This means that individual neurons can be removed from the slug and studied. But despite their simple neurological structures, Aplysia can "learn" basic things. By training them in various learning and memory-related tasks, Kandel and other neuroscientists have been able to observe the neuronal changes that occur as a result of learning (Kandel et al., 2014).

Kandel's early work on Aplysia involved a process of learning and memory called fear conditioning (learning to fear something). If you touch an Aplysia in its syphon (water spout) it will retract its gill slightly to defend itself. But if you touch the syphon and also give it a mild electric shock, the gill will retract even further. The sea slugs are trained to "fear" the touching of the syphon because they learn that when their syphon is touched there is also a strong shock. Over time, the same gill-withdraw reflex can be observed by just touching the syphon, without having to give the shock. In other words, the sea slug has learned to fully defend itself when it feels its syphon being touched. The fear conditioning of the gill-withdraw reflex became the focus of Kandel's studies on how memories are stored in the brain.

In order for the Aplysia to withdraw their gills in response to the touching of the syphon, their sensory neurons have to communicate with their motor neurons. The sensory neurons detect the touch and the motor neurons withdraw the gill. In an early study, Kandel and Tauc (1965) were able to observe the physical changes that were occurring in the neuron as a result of learning. Because of their large neurons that are easy to find, Kandel and Tauc were able to remove individual neurons from the slugs and study their processes under a microscope. In fact, they could actually recreate the conditioning process by stimulating the neurons while they were removed from the sea slug. The neuronal changes could then be observed under a microscope. The results showed that the neurons actually changed their anatomical structure and grew new synaptic connections between sensory and motor neurons. The stronger the learning,

This is the syphon.

This is an Aplysia Californica, like Kandel uses in his research.

The sea slug's biological name is Aplysia. Its gill-withdraw reflex is a way of defending itself against threats.

We have over 200 types of neurons. Sensory neurons detect sensory information and motor neurons send signals to our muscles so we can move.

the stronger the connections. This incredible discovery was the first evidence that our brain physically changes when we learn and remember something.

While the case study on HM (as discussed in the PTSD chapter) has been extremely important in the field of cognitive neuroscience, animal models have also been valuable. HM's case was one of the first pieces of evidence that memory has a biological base, but with the help of the abnormally large neurons of the Aplysia, Kandel and others have been able to demonstrate how memory produces changes at a cellular level. This finding has been corroborated by more modern research using fMRI and MRI that shows the neurological changes resulting from learning and experiences (e.g. in studies on the effects of juggling, meditation, watching TV, etc.). By removing and studying Aplysia neurons under the microscope, neuroscientists can see how the brain changes through neuroplastic changes in individual neurons.

Kandel's research provides us with another excellent example of the value of animal models in studying the brain and behaviour. Even an animal as physically different to a human as a sea slug still possesses similar physiological characteristics and similar neuronal functions. The ability to remove individual neurons and study them under a microscope has allowed neuroscientists to provide valuable insight into the biological basis of memory storage. While in the previous examples we saw how it is the biological variable that is manipulated to study the effects on behaviour, in this case we can see how it is the behaviour (learning) that is having an effect on biology.

The next topic will explore how *genetic* similarities between humans and animals can be beneficial for research purposes.

Guiding Question:

How can studying Aplysia help psychologists understand human memory?

Critical Thinking Extension:
In this section you've seen how studies using sea slugs are valuable because their neurons are similar to humans. But how do you think this similarity in neuronal structure was discovered in the first place? What types of studies would have been carried out before we could know about our own neurons?

If you're interested…

You can see video representations of Kandel's work, including the extraction of a neuron from an Aplysia, in the NOVA documentary "Memory Hackers." There is a shorter video on the PBS YouTube channel that shows the same process, called "A Memorable Snail."

Synaptic connections: the connection of dendrites and axon terminals. Neurons communicate with each other by sending neurotransmitters across the synapse.

Cognitive neuroscience: the study of relationships between cognition and the brain.

(d)   Selective Breeding and Aggression

In the previous topic we started to look at some of the benefits of conducting laboratory experiments on animals. To recap, these experiments allow psychologists to determine how variables such as brain function and hormones can influence behaviour. They can also show the influence of behaviour on brain structure (e.g. Kandel's studies on Aplysia). To conduct similar experiments on humans would be unethical, and often practically impossible. The ability to manipulate variables like hormone levels and brain function in animal experiments has had a tremendous impact in developing our understanding of biological processes involved in human behaviour.

Animal modeling is also used in the study of genetic influences on human behaviour. We inherit our genes from our parents and these genes influence our physical and psychological development. One way that animal models can be used to study the relationship between genes and behaviour is through selective breeding. This is when animals that demonstrate particular traits are selected to mate with one another and have babies that will share their genes. Mice are commonly used for this purpose as multiple generations of mice can be bred over a relatively short period of time. Mice can begin reproducing after they are about two months old, so a few generations of mice can be bred in about one year. This means that the effects of genetic inheritance over multiple generations can be studied in a relatively short period of time. This is one reason why they are valuable in genetics research.

Selective breeding has been used to study genetic influences on aggression in mice. This is done by selectively breeding on a criterion known as attack latency. The attack latency in a mouse is measured by seeing how long it takes a mouse who is used to living in a particular cage (a resident mouse) to attack another mouse that is put in this same cage (the intruder mouse). Mice are then determined to have a long attack latency if they wait for a few minutes before attacking, or don't attack the intruder at all. On the other hand, a short attack latency means they are quick to attack and so they're considered the most aggressive. This commonly used experimental paradigm for measuring aggression in mice is known as the resident-intruder paradigm.

Researchers investigating the link between genetics and aggression selectively breed mice based on their attack latency. They can separate mice based on their latencies and then develop different strains (groups) of mice. This allows comparisons to be made between a short-attack latency strain (more aggressive) and a long attack latency strain (less aggressive).

For example, Van Oortmerssen and Bakker (1981) selectively bred mice from a group of wild mice that were found in a barn. They tested this first group of wild mice using the resident-intruder paradigm and selected those animals with the shortest latency attack scores (most aggressive) to produce offspring and create one strain of aggressive mice. They also selected the mice with the longest latency attack scores (least aggressive) and had these mice produce offspring in order to create a different strain of mice to compare. This resulted in two different types of mice to compare over generations of selective breeding.

The latency scores were compared over 11 generations of the mice from this selective breeding programme. Their results showed that the latency scores gradually decreased with each generation in the short latency group (aggressive strain of mice). This group of mice were quicker to respond with aggression towards an intruder that was put in their cage. What this suggests is that with each generation the mice were becoming increasingly aggressive. Because all other variables were controlled in the laboratory, this increase in aggression over generations can be attributed to genetic

---

Animal modeling: The use of animals to study and demonstrate biological processes and phenomena. Animal modeling shows what could be expected to happen in humans as we share similar physiological characteristics.

Selective breeding: In psychology, this is the laboratory equivalent of natural selection: instead of nature determining who passes on the most genetic material, it is the researcher. Animals are selected to breed with one another to produce offspring with particular characteristics.

Genes: these are made up of DNA and are found in our cells. They store and communicate information that can influence our physical development.

In genetics research, a strain is a sub-type of a particular species. In mice studies, it means a group of mice share similar genetic material that is different from other mice.

inheritance. The results also corroborated earlier findings by demonstrating a heritability of 0.30 for aggressive behaviour.

By creating different strains of mice and comparing them in the resident-intruder paradigm, the researchers are able to study the extent to which differences in aggressive behaviour are due to genetic influences. This is because all other variables are kept constant in the laboratory and it's only the selective breeding based on demonstrations of aggression that separates the groups. Therefore, the differences can be assumed to be a product of genetic inheritance. This type of selective breeding was particularly helpful before the development of more advanced methods of studying the role of genes on behaviour. These more advanced techniques will be the subject of the following sections.

Selective breeding involves choosing animals to breed with one another based on particular characteristics. The resident-intruder paradigm can be used to identify the characteristic of higher or lower levels of aggression. This test involves putting a stranger mouse (the intruder) in another mouse's cage (the resident).

Heritability: the extent to which variations in behaviour can be attributed to genetics. In this case, the variation in levels of aggression (as measured by attack latency scores) was calculated to be 30% genetics and 70% other factors.

Guiding Question:

How can selective breeding be used to study genetic influences on aggression?

Critical Thinking Extension:

Applications: The concept of selective breeding of animals has been used in many fields. Can you think of other ways selective breeding is used? Hint: do you have any pets?

If you're interested…

The US National Library of Medicine has a video that explains how to carry out the intruder-resident test. You can find a link on our blog. You can also see videos of tests in action and this is a good way of making learning from this topic visible and concrete. I like to get my students to recreate the test using toy rats in my laboratory (i.e. classroom).

(e)   Genetics and Neurotransmission

We've already seen how experiments that damage areas of the brain were particularly valuable to neuropsychologists before the invention of modern brain imaging techniques. Similarly, before more advanced methods were developed to study genetics, selective breeding strategies used to create different strains of mice were an important way of investigating the genetic influences in aggression. In this section, we're going to look at modern and more sophisticated methods used to study the influence of individual genes on behaviour.

Selective breeding has been used in recent studies where specific genes are identified and mice are selectively bred based on the identification of a particular gene. In fact, researchers can actually delete an individual gene from an animal and then observe the effects this has on behaviour. By deleting a gene to create a strain of genetically modified mice and comparing the behavioural effects with another strain, the influence of that specific gene on behaviour can be determined. This experimental process of gene ablating is similar in concept to brain ablation shown in other experiments.

The example we're going to look at in this section is related to a gene that influences serotonin. In the criminology chapter, we looked at how serotonin is a neurotransmitter that has been associated with impulsive and aggressive behaviour. The explanation for this could lie in the relationship between serotonin and the function of the prefrontal cortex (PFC): low serotonin levels reduces activity in the PFC, which could interfere with an ability to inhibit aggressive reactions. Animal studies using ablating and lesioning techniques have shown that even in rats, damage to the prefrontal cortex can increase aggression and that disrupting serotonin in the PFC can also increase aggressive behaviour (Takahashi and Miczek, 2014). The role of genetics in this relationship between serotonin, the brain, and behaviour, is what we'll focus on in these lessons.

Serotonin (also called 5-hydroxy-tryptamine, or 5-HT) is made from an amino acid called tryptophan. The TPH-2 gene (Tryptophan Hydroxylase-2), plays a role in this conversion of tryptophan into serotonin: the TPH-2 gene sends information from the nucleus in a cell to begin the process of converting tryptophan into serotonin. If this gene is ablated, it will affect the ability to convert tryptophan to serotonin, thus resulting in reduced levels of serotonin in the brain.

One way of studying the influence of individual genes like TPH-2 is to use genetically modified animals. These animals have undergone gene ablating surgery and are called knockouts. Researchers produce knockout mice by deleting genetic material in the laboratory and artificially impregnating female mice with embryos containing the modified genes. The mice fertilized with the modified genes will produce offspring and some of these offspring will be able to breed and produce even more offspring with the gene knocked out. Through this genetic modification and selective breeding, a particular strain of knockouts can be created.

Genetic ablating: another way of saying having genes deleted or knocked out; the sequence of DNA that makes up the gene is deleted. This means the information from that gene cannot be sent from the nucleus. In the case of TPH-2, the gene cannot send the information needed to synthesize serotonin from tryptophan.

Humans have about 20,000 genes. A person's entire collection of genes is their genome.

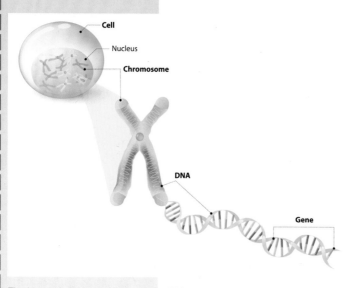

The human body is made up of cells. Within each cell is a nucleus, which contains chromosomes. Within the chromosomes, are our strands of DNA. A gene is a segment of DNA. Knocking out a gene means to delete or "silence" a particular sequence of DNA so it becomes ineffectual. Isn't biology fascinating?!

Humans also have the TPH-2 gene, which has been studied in people with disorders related to serotonin dysfunction.

For example, Mosienko et al. (2012) ablated TPH-2 genes in order to create a group of TPH-2 knockout mice. In this study, the researchers compared their genetically modified mice with a control group. A number of tests were conducted to study the effects of the knocking out of the TPH-2 gene and one of these tests was the resident-intruder test we learned about in the previous section.

The results of this test were that the TPH-2 knockout mice attacked six times faster than the control group. The total number of attacks and the total time attacked was also seven times more than the control group of mice. The resident-intruder test lasts for a total of ten minutes, but 100% of the TPH-2 knockout mice attacked within five minutes of the test beginning, compared to 22% of the control group. These results show that knocking out the TPH-2 gene caused a significant increase in aggressive behaviour.

The experiment could also explain how serotonergic dysfunction could be the result of the TPH-2 gene being turned off, and this could help psychologists understand how genes, behaviour, the brain, and neurotransmission are connected. Animal studies like this enable researchers to investigate the role of specific genes on behaviour. In the experimental procedures, the function of the TPH-2 gene is the variable that is being manipulated and all other variables can be controlled, so cause-and-effect relationships can be established between the function of the gene and aggressive behaviour.

As with other types of variables in animal studies, the manipulation of genetics by researchers in a controlled environment could not be replicated on humans. However, studies like Mosienko et al.'s can still help psychologists to understand the role of genetics in human behaviour as we also have TPH-2 genes.

In summary, through the use of knockout animals, individual genes can be correlated with changes in behaviour. This helps to further our understanding of how genetic variations could explain phenomena such as increased aggression in some individuals. However, the role of the environment can also influence our genes, and this is something that will be explored in the next section.

TPH-2 knockout mice: mice that have been bred in the laboratory to have the genes responsible for producing TPH-2 ablated (deleted).

In case you're confused - the test doesn't put the TPH-2 knockouts in the same cage as the control group and see who attacks first. They use a third group of mice as the "intruders."

Serotonergic dysfunction: abnormalities in the process of serotonin transmission. One part of this process is synthesizing serotonin from tryptophan.

This study also provides evidence for the effects of reduced serotonin on aggressive behaviour.

Guiding Question:

Why are knockout mice useful when studying genes and behaviour?

Critical Thinking Extension:

Areas of Uncertainty: In human subjects we can explain serotonin and violence by saying that humans can think through long-term consequences and use system two processing. Can we say this about animal models? What are the cognitive differences that may exist between humans and non-human animals that may limit generalizability?

If you're interested…

You can read more about how knockout mice are made at learn.genetics. utah.edu. The UC Davis Mouse Biology Program also has a video on YouTube about making knockout mice called, "Mice Tales."

(f) *Epigenetics: Genes x Environment*

As we've seen in numerous examples already, laboratory experiments on animals enable psychologists to conduct experiments that isolate individual biological variables and measure the effects this has on behaviour. In the previous section we saw how modern genetics testing can allow researchers to delete genes in animals, which can provide further insight into the influence of *specific* genes on behaviour. If humans didn't possess similar genetic material to animals, these studies would be of limited value.

But what's the value of knowing how a knocked-out gene influences behaviour? In humans we can't (ethically) delete genes so it might seem strange to use this experimental paradigm with animals. While genes aren't naturally deleted in humans, their activity can be influenced by a combination of biological and environmental factors. This means that it might be our environment that is doing the knocking out. This influence of the environment on genetics is called epigenetics.

In this section, we're going to look at how animal studies have helped psychologists understand how prolonged stress early in life can affect the gene expression of the TPH-2 gene. Investigating this relationship can further our understanding of how genes interact with environmental variables.

Early stressful events and the effect this has on behaviour has been the subject of a lot of research, both on humans and animals. In the criminology chapter, we touched on a study by Caspi et al. (2002) that showed correlations between MAOA gene variation, early life stress, and antisocial behaviours in adulthood. It seems that it's not only the variation of the MAOA gene that predicts aggressive behaviour, but it is the combination with stress and trauma when we're young.

Researchers can understand the epigenetics involved in this relationship by using animal models. This is done by exposing animals to stress when they're young and then measuring the effects on gene expression. Before we look at an example, it's important to know that one factor that influences the expression of the TPH-2 gene is the hormone cortisol. Cortisol is released during times of stress and this secretion of cortisol activates TPH-2 expression (Chen and Miller, 2012). But prolonged stress can alter the brain's response and studies have shown that adults who were exposed to prolonged trauma early in life (e.g. childhood sexual and physical abuse) have *lower* levels of cortisol later in life (Trickett, et al., 2010). The resulting reduction in cortisol could reduce the expression of the TPH-2 gene.

Gardner et al. (2009) investigated the effects of prolonged early life stress on the expression of the TPH-2 gene in rats. The stressful experience in this study involved the rats being separated from their mothers and being handled by the researchers for fifteen minutes a day for the first two weeks of their life. The pups get used to the handling as this

Removing a baby rat from its litter for 15 minutes every day would be stressful for the pup. The evidence suggests that this continual early-life stress can affect gene expression. You have probably started to see the numerous ethical issues involved in animal studies.

Epigenetics: the effect of environmental factors on gene expression.

You can read more about Caspi et al.'s research on our blog.

Gene expression: the sending of information by a gene. Genes send information from the cell to other parts of the body in order to start processes, such as synthesizing serotonin from tryptophan..

Cortisol: a stress hormone that is released during the stress response (the fight-flight response).

condition of the experiment was aimed to replicate decreased stress sensitivity as a result of constant early-life stress. That is to say, the rats become accustomed to the stress and with each handing their body reacts with reduced sensitivity.

The results showed that when the rats became adults, they had a 55% reduction in the expression of their TPH-2 gene compared with a control group. This could be due to the fact that the levels of cortisol being released in the brain were reduced as a result of the prolonged stress. In other words, the repeated stress early in life reduced cortisol levels later in life as a result of the brain adapting to the stress. Because cortisol activates the gene, reduced cortisol would explain the reduction in activity of the TPH-2 gene. While the cortisol isn't silencing the TPH-2 gene, it seems to be doing a good job of keeping it quiet. This could have significant effects on the serotonin levels and brain function, and provides more possible explanations for results of studies like those shown in the study by Caspi and colleagues.

By using animal models in this experiment, the researchers can isolate the variable of early life stress and directly measure the effects on gene expression of a specific gene. When this is combined with other research on genes and behaviour, we can get a deeper understanding of epigenetic processes. For example, early life abuse in humans is often correlated with antisocial behaviour as an adult. While this could be a result of social learning, it might also be the result of alterations in genetics in response to environmental stressors. But this study fails to look at how stress in adult life could influence gene expression. People usually don't just commit acts of violence or aggression without first being provoked. In the next section we'll look at how genetics, early life stress *and* adult stress may be related in antisocial behaviour.

Epigenetic processes: effects of the environment on gene expression.

Guiding Question:

How can early life stress influence gene expression?

Critical Thinking Extension:

Areas of Uncertainty: Earlier in this chapter we looked at Sapolsky's research that showed increased levels of cortisol over time damages hippocampal neurons. How does the aim of Sapolsky's experiment seem to be inconsistent with the research in this section? In other words, what is Sapolsky hypothesizing about stress that is inconsistent with Trickett et al.?

If you're interested…

MinuteEarth has a really good cartoon demonstration of epigenetic processes, called "Epigenetics: Why Inheritance is Weirder Than We Thought." This video also shows how epigenetics can influence traits that are inherited by our offspring.

(g) Epigenetics and Adult Stress

In the previous section you were introduced to the concept of epigenetics (Gene x Environment interactions). Genes are turned on and off by a number of factors and one of these factors is the release of hormones. Cortisol is released by the HPA axis during times of stress. This activates the expression of the TPH-2 gene (i.e. it turns it on). Alterations in cortisol secretion as a result of experiencing stress early in our lives could influence gene expression and have an effect on serotonin in the brain: if the TPH-2 gene's function is inhibited, serotonin levels will be disrupted because the body won't receive the information needed to convert tryptophan into serotonin. The resulting reduction in cerebral serotonin could have many negative outcomes, including increased aggression. Animal experiments like these can provide insight into results of longitudinal studies on humans that show correlations between early life experiences and antisocial behaviour in adulthood.

One important component in this relationship is the neuroplasticity of the stress response. This reaction to stress in our environment is the result of different neural networks communicating with one another, including those in the amygdala and the HPA axis. As you've seen when studying criminology (and PTSD), these neural networks can change over time as a result of experiences. Experiencing high levels of stress for long amounts of time as a child, may actually alter the brain's neural networks. This could explain why numerous studies have shown reduced levels of cortisol in people who were abused as children compared with controls - their brains may have adapted in response to the stress (e.g. Carpenter et al., 2009). Similarly, a common finding in people with PTSD is reduced levels of cortisol, which could also be the result of the brain's adaptation to prolonged stress. This adaptation of the release of cortisol in response to stress as a child could impact gene expression in response to a stress as an adult.

To test the effects of social stress in adult life, Gardner et al. (2009) used the same test rats that had been conditioned to stress from a young age. To recap, these rats were removed from their mums and handled for 15 minutes a day for the first two weeks of their life. In another aspect of their study, the researchers manipulated experiences of adult social stress by using a test that's similar to the resident-intruder paradigm we looked at earlier. This test is designed to measure the physiological effects of social defeat. In this design, the test rat is the intruder and the other rat is the resident. To ensure stress, the resident is always heavier than the test rat. This means that the odds are stacked against the poor, little intruder/test rat and it will always be defeated by the resident. This would be a highly stressful situation.

In this experiment, all test rats were defeated by the resident rat. After this social defeat, the effects on the gene expression were measured and the results showed that the test rats had 44% less expression of the TPH-2 gene when compared with a control group.

This suggests that experiencing prolonged stress at a young age could impact the gene expression in response to stress as an adult. This effect may be a result of reduced cortisol levels being secreted in response to the stressful event. In other words, the brain has adapted to stress as a result of early life stressful experiences, and this change alters the release of cortisol when we experience stress as an adult. Without a healthy activation of the stress response and cortisol secretion when we're stressed, the TPH-2 gene won't be activated by the cortisol, resulting in reduced serotonin in the brain.

Gardner's study provides some clues as to how early life stress may alter our physiological response to stress in adult life. If someone experiences high levels of stress

The term "antisocial" is often used as an umbrella term in psychological research because it includes any action that causes harm to others. Violence, aggression and crime are examples.

Some genes are turned on and off all the time. For example, TPH-2 activation fluctuates on a daily cycle.

It's important to note that the rats in Gardner et al.'s study *aren't* knockouts – they are having their TPH-2 gene expression influenced by stress responses.

over long periods of time, the neuroplastic changes that happen in the brain as a result might affect the release of cortisol when they experience stress as an adult. This alteration in the secretion of cortisol has a flow on effect in that it would reduce the activation of the TPH-2 gene, which would reduce available serotonin in important areas of the brain, like the prefrontal cortex. A violent attack in the name of revenge is just one behaviour that might be explained by this potent cocktail of epigenetic processes. Low serotonin is also correlated with other disorders, such as depression. Perhaps epigenetics can explain how different people react emotionally to being "defeated" in social situations.

Animal models of epigenetics could provide insight into correlations between early life stress and antisocial behaviour later in life - the early stress alters the brain's response to stress as an adult, resulting in reduced cortisol secretion during stress, which reduces TPH-2 gene expression, which reduces available serotonin in the brain, which could affect function of the PFC. Why is this important to understand? Because if we understand causes, we can have a better chance of reducing effects.

Once more we see how behaviour is the product of complex interactions between our environment and internal processes. Animal experiments allow psychologists to study epigenetic processes by isolating individual genetic and environmental variables in carefully controlled experiments. While they cannot provide definitive answers, they do give us important pieces of the puzzle.

Gene expression is measured by analyzing the level of mRNA in the cell.

The interaction of variables in this section is rather complex, but when understood completely it can be used to show the benefits of using animal models to study:

- The brain (serotonin and neuroplasticity).
- Hormones (cortisol and the stress response).
- Genes (TPH-2 gene).

Guiding Question:

How might early life experiences influence responses to stress in adulthood?

Critical Thinking Extension:
Hypothesizing: Based on its role in producing serotonin, can you propose any hypotheses about how the TPH-2 gene might be studied in humans? If you have time and are interested, you could do some research to see how this gene is studied in humans. This might give you more research to discuss in relation to other topics in the course.

If you're interested…

SciShow has a really good video called "Epigenetics". This video goes into detail about how epigenetic changes can actually influence how genes are passed on from generation to generation.

(h) Ethics I: Suffering and Welfare

I know you've been bursting for an opportunity to discuss the ethical implications of using animals in psychological experimentation. There's no escaping the fact that while animals can be useful in psychological research for many reasons, there are important questions that must be asked regarding the ethics of these procedures.

The first of these considerations we'll look at are related to animal suffering and welfare. As with human research, psychology organizations (e.g. German Psychological Society, National Psychology Association of India, etc.) put forward guidelines for animal research. Within these guidelines there are specific things to consider when using animals. The nature of these guidelines might differ slightly from one country or organization to the next, but they are based on similar principles.

A common research guideline for the use of animals is that animal welfare must be a priority. Unless it's part of the experiment, all animals should also have adequate food, water and comfortable living environments. For example, even though Rosenzweig and Bennet were studying the effects of environmental deprivation on brain development, they still ensured that the mice in the control condition had adequate food and water. Just because the animals might suffer as a result of experimental procedures, it doesn't mean their living conditions can be ignored.

But there's often an unavoidable element of harm that is inflicted on animals during psychological experimentation. A common ethical guideline is that no unnecessary suffering should occur during the experiment. For example, if an ablating surgery is to be performed, animals should be anaesthetized so they don't suffer during the surgery. This also applies for experiments involving surgeries performed in order to alter hormone levels.

If it is clear that an animal is experiencing distress or is suffering seriously as a result of experimental procedures, researchers should consider euthanizing the animals to put an end to their suffering. Similarly, when animals need to be killed for the purposes of the research, they should be euthanized with as little suffering as possible. For example, in Sapolsky's research the monkeys had to be killed in order to measure the effects of the cortisol secretion on the hippocampus. When post-mortem operations are required, the animals should be killed in a way that is humane and results in minimal pain. Studies involving measuring gene expression in the brain often require post-mortem operations, so all animal used should be euthanized when this is necessary.

Most of the animal experiments we've looked at in this chapter involve changing the animal's physiology in a way that is irreversible. This might be a change in genetics, brain function, or levels of hormones. In human studies, the general guideline is that participants should finish a study in the same physical and psychological health (or improved health) as they began the experiment. The reason animals are used in studies is often because to manipulate biological variables on humans would result in long-lasting and irreversible physical or psychological damage: this is why we experiment on animals, not humans. But is it ethical to make an animal experience something we wouldn't want to do to a human? This is one question at the heart of the debate over the use of animals in psychology experiments.

There's no escaping the fact that results of experimental procedures could be that animals experience suffering. For example, while it might seem that Weiskrantz's experiment on the bilateral amygdala ablation in the rhesus monkeys had a positive outcome because they were tame and approached the researchers to be touched, there

---

Animal welfare: taking care of the animals.

To euthanize means to kill an animal (or person) in a humane (painless) way. A lethal injection is a common way that animals are euthanized.

Post-mortem operation: carrying out a surgery or dissection *after* the subject is dead. Post-mortem studies were how researchers first learned about the human body and brain.

Is it right to perform experiments on animals instead of humans? This is a subjective question without a definitive answer.

were also other side-effects of the surgery. One of these was that the monkeys began to eat their own feces. Brain ablations in experiments like this one are irreversible. Researchers need to think carefully about what steps to take to limit animal suffering due to unexpected results in experiments.

In summary, even though the experimental procedures might result in the animals experiencing distress or suffering, this should not happen unnecessarily. All steps should be taken to ensure that animal welfare is a top priority and the animals have proper food, water, and living conditions. However, an element of suffering may be an unavoidable result of irreversible experimental procedures. If animals are experiencing severe trauma or pain, researchers need to consider euthanizing them to minimize suffering. Similarly, in post-mortem studies the animals should be killed in a humane way.

Is it "right" to keep animals in laboratories just so we can better understand ourselves? This is one of the questions at the heart of the debate about the ethics of animal studies in psychology.

We'll explore the issue of suffering in animal research in more depth in the next section.

Guiding Question:

How can psychologists consider animal welfare during experimental studies?

Critical Thinking Extension:
Limitations: In human research, deception is sometimes necessary to ensure the validity of the findings. Providing too much information could cause confounding variables, like the expectancy effect. Can you think of any limitations involved in following ethical guidelines related to animal studies? For example, why might it be a difficult decision to euthanize an animal before the experiment has ended and all data is gathered?

If you're interested…

In the 1960s, Harry Harlow conducted a series of experiments on rhesus monkeys with the intent of understanding attachment and bonding between mothers and their children. You can find numerous videos of these experiments online and they provide a stark look at the downside of using animals as experimental subjects. Similarly, the case of Edward Taub and the "Silver Spring Monkeys" makes for an interesting exploration into the discussion of animal studies and ethics.

(i)   Ethics II: Suffering vs. Justification

In the previous section we began discussing the ethics involved in animal research. The term ethics is quite difficult to define, but at its core it refers to the *consideration of the impact of our actions on others*. In animal research, we need to consider the impact the research might have on the animals, but also for those who might benefit from the research. Consider the following series of questions:

- Would you kill an ant to find a cure for cancer?
- Would you kill 1,000 ants to cure cancer?
- Would you kill a chimpanzee to cure cancer? What about a human?
- Would you kill a dog to cure AIDs?
- Would you kill your pet dog to cure AIDs?
- Would you make 1,000 animals suffer for an entire year in order to cure cancer and AIDs? Would the type of animal make a difference?

> Justification: in animal experimentation this means there's a valid reason for carrying out the experiment. In other words, if animals are going to suffer, it should be worth it.

The above series of questions are designed to get you thinking about the role of justification in animal experimentation. While animal suffering is often unavoidable, this consideration has to be coupled with the justification of the research. For example, there wouldn't be much justification for conducting an experiment that lesioned the amygdalae of rhesus monkeys to measure the effect on the fear response. There is already enough existing evidence and understanding of the role of the amygdala, that to cause suffering on an animal for this purpose would be unjustified.

That's not to say that researchers have stopped lesioning the amygdalae of monkeys. What this means is that in order for an experiment to be approved by an ethics review board, there needs to be a clear justification for the experiment. In modern lesioning studies, this means taking existing research further and testing new hypotheses that might be of value to the psychological community.

> Can using animals for testing make-up be compared with using animals in psychological research? How does justification play a role in this debate?

Let's consider the experimental procedures used in rat studies. The resident-in-truder paradigm and the similar social defeat test require putting rats in stressful and potentially harmful situations. Similarly, Gardner and her colleagues took baby rats away from their mums and handled them in a way that would stress them out. Is it right to subject animals to this kind of treatment? Perhaps it depends on the possible applications of the findings. For example, by discovering how early life stress could affect gene expression in response to stress as an adult, psychologists could understand why many people who are abused as kids grow up to become violent adults. By understanding the underlying causes of violent and criminal behaviour, as a society we could devise better strategies for prevention and even break the cycle of violence that is so prevalent in many communities. Is this worth the suffering of rats? This is a highly subjective debate (and a fun one to have in class).

This same issue also applies to studies investigating the role of hormones on behaviour. The many animal studies linking testosterone with aggression have furthered our understanding of the role of this hormone in human behaviour. As testosterone is often correlated with violent crime in humans, understanding

Would you euthanize a chimpanzee if it meant curing a disease like cancer or Alzheimer's? What if the animal was a sea slug? Truly understanding ethical considerations in psychological research means being able to consider multiple perspectives.

this link could help us reduce violent crime in society. Similarly, understanding the detrimental effects of increased cortisol on the brain has had numerous applications and benefits for humans. One example is that it can help us to understand the underlying origins and effects of stress-related disorders, such as PTSD. As with much of psychology, if we can understand causes maybe we can develop better preventions and treatments.

Let's also consider Kandel's research on Aplysia. The discovery of the biological basis of memory has had tremendous benefits, including in understanding memory disorders. Research continues to explore the underlying biological origins of Alzheimer's disease, a degenerative disease that ruins the quality of life for many elderly people in their old age. This modern research may have been impossible without early work on Aplysia that uncovered the role of neurons in memory storage. Is it justifiable to breed Aplysia in a laboratory for the sole purpose of sacrificing them to advance our own understanding of the human brain? Can we justify the killing of animals to reduce suffering and improve the lives of humans?

Perhaps part of the debate includes the animal in question. Can we consider sea slugs and chimpanzees in the same way? One has far more complex social networks and is able to perform more cognitive processes. This means they are able to experience more "emotion" than other animals, so does the way we consider animal research depend on the animal model we're using?

Whether studying the brain, hormones or genetics, the ethical considerations involved in animal research are pretty much the same. One of the central debates at the heart of animal research in psychology is whether or not it's acceptable to harm animals for the sake of science.

What's my opinion on the matter? Do I think it's right to use animals in experimentation? Well…it depends.

Guiding Question:

Why is justifying animal experimentation an important ethical consideration?

Critical Thinking Extension:

Areas of Uncertainty: During the Holocaust, Nazi doctors performed many experiments on Jewish and other prisoners. Obviously, there has been a shunning of these studies and thankfully they have not been allowed to contribute to scientific understanding. If animal research has been carried out under unethical circumstances, but the findings could have significant applications, should we be able to use that research? This could have implications for our use of historical research that was conducted before ethical guidelines were published.

If you're interested…

Lesli Bisgould is an animal rights lawyer who is working to change the status of animals from property to legal person. Her TED Talk, "It's time to re-evaluate our relationship with other animals," she brings up some of the ideas we've covered in this section, including suffering and justification.

(j)   Other Limitations

In the previous sections we've touched on one of the key limitations in animal research – ethical issues. Whether or not it's right to harm animals in experimentation is a subjective debate. In this section we're going to take some time to reflect on other possible limitations of the use of animals in research. But first, here's a quick recap of the primary benefits of using animal models to understand human behaviour:

- Variables can be manipulated in a way that would be unethical (or impractical) to do on human participants (e.g. damaging brains, removing genes, and altering hormones).
- Researchers can control extraneous variables in experiments to determine cause-and-effect relationships (e.g. consistent living conditions and social status).

Animals are selected for study because they share similar physiological characteristics as humans, and it is the physiological processes and their relationship with behaviour that psychologists are studying. But by its very nature animal modeling is a reductionist approach: studies using animals only focus on the biological variables involved in behaviour. The complex interactions of culture, society, and cognition with biological variables has to be overlooked.

For example, Kandel focused only on the effects of implicit fear conditioning on neuronal structures, Gardner and colleagues studied the role of stress on a very specific gene, and Sapolsky studied the effects of one hormone on a specific area of the brain. All of these experiments investigate relationships between one very isolated variable and a narrow definition of a dependent variable. This raises the question, how accurately can animal models reflect human behaviour, when our behaviour is subject to so many other interacting variables?

What all of these studies fail to consider are the complex social, cognitive, and cultural processes that can influence human behaviour. But don't get me wrong, this is not to say animal studies are a waste of time. Far from it. But it does mean that we have to be very careful when trying to apply these results to explain human behaviour. For example, just because a pellet of cortisol in the brain of a monkey damages its hippocampal neurons, doesn't necessarily mean stress will damage a human's. One reason is because our culture and the society we are raised in will influence our early life experiences, which could alter the stress response and the release of cortisol later in life.

Similarly, the behaviours in animal studies often have to be overly simplified in order to be operationalized. The extent to which we can say these behaviours are similar to human behaviour in real life situations might also be questioned. For example, the resident-intruder paradigm is used as a measure of

> **Reductionist approach:** investigating a phenomenon through the study of only one type of variable (e.g. biology).

Can we really predict similar effects in humans as we see in animals? While human physiology is similar to other animals, our social, cultural and cognitive systems are far more complex. To what extent do you think this might influence the generalizability of animal studies?

aggression in rats. But when was the last time you lived in a cage for 12 weeks and then were asked to interact with a stranger? Similarly, could handling a baby mouse for two weeks for fifteen minutes a day be compared to severe physical or sexual abuse of a child? Here we can see that another factor to consider when using animal models is the extent to which the operational definitions of variables are applicable to human settings.

In summary, animal studies only provide individual pieces of the puzzle. While these pieces can provide *insight* into the bigger picture, by themselves they can never fully *explain* it.

Guiding Question:

What are the difficulties in applying animal models to humans?

Critical Thinking Extension:

Application: An important part of explaining limitations of animal studies is being able to provide specific examples of how findings may not apply to human settings. Can you take one finding from an animal study and explain one or more reasons why it might not apply to humans? You could focus on the effects of stress on TPH-2 gene expression, testosterone on aggression, or lesioning of the amygdala.

If you're interested…

Eric Kandel has an interview on the BigThink channel called "Learning and Memory in the Brain: How Science Cracked the Brain's Code." In this interview he discusses how and why he took a reductionist approach to understanding the biology of memory storage.

8.2 Globalization and Behaviour
How can the changing world affect the individual?

(a) Cultural Values and Happiness

Globalization has many definitions and it is a process that involves social, economic, cultural, political and technological factors. At its core, globalization refers to the increasing interaction between countries, cultures and individuals as a result of global forces. As Arnett (2002) puts it, globalization is "a process by which cultures influence one another and become more alike through trade, immigration, and the exchange of information and ideas." One effect of globalization is that cultural values might change as a result of this bidirectional influence.

But is the influence *really* bidirectional? How many American TV shows and films do you watch? The chances are, even if you're not American, you will be exposed to American pop-culture. You may even have a favourite American band, actress or singer. Or perhaps the influence is from Europe, maybe Britain or France. The point to consider here is that globalization is not always a two-way process. In fact, it's often referred to as Westernization as media spreads Western beliefs and values through the internet, TV shows, films, books, and music.

How might this Western media be influencing other cultures? In this section, we'll focus on how the spread of individualistic values might be having a negative effect on the happiness of individuals in collectivist cultures.

To recap, individualist cultures place emphasis on the "I" and encourage competition. This can have positive effects, in that people are more socially mobile, which means they can rise in their social status. But the competition could also have negative effects – it might hurt their interpersonal relationships. In order to counter the negative impact of competition, individuals in these cultures learn the interpersonal skills needed to actively seek friendships and relationships. This would help to reduce the negative effects of being an individual and competing with one another (Ogihara and Uchida, 2014).

But what happens when individualistic values are adopted by people in cultures that haven't adopted the strategies to combat the effects of competition? Globalization could be influencing Japan and other collectivist cultures, as individualistic values and beliefs are adopted by members of these societies. But this might cause a problem, because while the value of individualism may become internalized, the accompaning strategies of making friends and seeking out relationships have not been taught. That is to say, the competitiveness and the desire to place emphasis on the individual could become part of an individual's values, but this might not come with the additional strategies to protect against the isolation that this might cause. As humans have an innate desire to belong and to feel connected with one another, this could have negative effects on happiness and general life satisfaction.

To investigate the effects of individualism in a collectivist context, Ogihara and Uchida (2014) investigated how a change in values might be influencing the subjective well-being of young Japanese students. In their study, they gathered data from

Let's flip this if you are American – how many foreign TV shows and films do you watch?

Subjective well-being: an umbrella term that includes measures of happiness, life satisfaction and general feelings about life.

114 students from two universities – one in Kyoto, Japan and the other in Wisconsin, USA. They first asked participants to complete questionnaires in order to measure their level of individualism or collectivism. An example of a question asked to assess individualism is: "Doing better than others gives me a sense of self-respect," and an example of a question from the collectivism questionnaire is "I can't respect myself if I break relationship harmony within my group." Participants answered using Likert scales (1 – strongly agree, 7 strongly disagree). The researchers also found out how many close friends the participants had, and they used a range of questionnaires to measure their happiness, life satisfaction and their physical and psychological emotional states.

The results from the statistical analyses showed a negative correlation for individualism in Japanese students and their overall subjective well-being. That is to say, the more individualistic they were, the less happy and content they were. In addition, the number of close friends a Japanese student had was a mediating variable - the inability to make friends is *why* the individualistic values led to being less happy and content with life.

While globalization might be changing values in some cultures, this change could have detrimental effects. For instance, if a person adopts the competitive values of an individualistic culture but hasn't been enculturated with the right skill-set to seek interpersonal relationships, they might end up without friends and being unhappy.

This study highlights a possible negative effect of globalization – as Western ideas pervade foreign countries it can bring a change in values and beliefs, especially amongst young people. As people adopt these new ideas and values, they may find themselves at odds with their home culture. In Ogihara and Uchida's study we can see that the competitive and individualistic students in Japan found it harder to make friends. The sense of belonging to a group and making close interpersonal friends is an essential part of being human, so being deprived of this could have consequences for our happiness.

But why did the individualism not affect the American students? People who grow up in individualistic cultures may have learned the strategies required to develop close friendships, while still maintaining their individualism and competitiveness. Students in countries dominated by collectivist values, like Japan, might not know how to do this and so making friends would be much harder.

Mediating variable: a variable that explains the relationship between one variable and another. In this case, the number of close friends explains why individualism in Japanese students results in less overall happiness, so the number of friends is a mediating variable.

In the next section, we'll look at a specific example of Western TV influencing the attitudes of young people in a collectivist culture.

Guiding Question:

Why does individualism affect happiness in Japanese students, and not American students?

Critical Thinking Extension:
Population Validity: As with most studies, this one uses university aged participants. Would you expect these same results to apply to younger or older people in Japan? Can you think of reasons for this? What about other collectivist cultures? Would you expect these same results in another culture that is high on the colectivism scale? Can you explain why?

If you're interested…

Are you curious to know if you're more individualistic or collectivist? Visit our blog to find links to a bunch of tests you can take to measure this.

(b)   TV & Attitudes

Globalization has also been called Westernization. It's often seen as less of an inter-action of cultures than a one-directional influence from the West, outwards towards other countries. One global process that facilitates this globalization/Westernization is the spread of technology to new parts of the world. As developing countries adopt new technology, they can become influenced by the ideas that are transmitted through mass media. This new introduction of technology and exposure to mainly Western media as a result of globalization can have profound effects. In this lesson we'll look at a study by Becker et al. (2002) that used the introduction of TV on an island in Fiji as an opportunity to investigate the effects this would have on the eating attitudes and behaviours of teenaged girls.

Before we look at the research, let's first discuss the relationship between the media and eating disorders as the effect of TV and other media on eating disorders is a popular field of study. One reason why exposure to TV could influence eating disorders is that the characters and people we see in commercials and in shows could influence the transmission of values and attitudes about eating. They do this through portraying thin, attractive and glamorous people living the lives we wish we had. In other words, TV portrays idealized images of people and those watching may adopt a desire to be like who they see on TV. Young girls are especially at risk for being influenced by the media in such a way, because the media places more emphasis on body image for girls than it does for boys.

In Fiji, by contrast, the traditional values have placed value on "robust" body-types and before the introduction of TV eating disorders were incredibly rare, with only one reported case of anorexia in the 1990s (Becker et al., 2002). The difference between the cultural values transmitted through television and the existing values within Fijian society made for an ideal set of circumstances on which to investigate the effects of globalization on eating attitudes in young girls from a media naïve population.

If young girls want to be like the thin and glamorous models and characters they see on TV, this may affect their attitudes and behaviours towards eating. For example, it could encourage dieting and other negative eating-related behaviours, which could lead to developing eating disorders. To investigate the effects of the introduction of TV on eating attitudes and behaviours, Becker et al. (2002) used a mixed-methods approach, combining quantitative and qualitative methods. Their first collection of data was in 1995, one month after the introduction of TV. They compared with a second set of data in 1998. The sample of the study were Indigenous Fijian teenaged girls from two different schools (average age 17).

In order to quantify the changes in eating attitudes and behaviour, the researchers used a questionnaire that is widely used in eating disorder studies called an Eating Attitudes Test (EAT). As the name suggests, this asks a series of questions about attitudes towards eating. For example, participants select a score on a range from strongly agree to strongly disagree in response to statements like, "I like my stomach to be empty," "I have the impulse to vomit after meals," "I engage in dieting behaviour," etc.

The results of the EAT tests showed that the Fijian girls attitudes towards eating had changed. In 1995, only 13% of the girls had an EAT score over 20. By 1998, after only three years of the introduction of TV, this had risen to 29%. More evidence to suggest that it was exposure to TV that was the significant factor

---

An attitude is a way of thinking about something. In this context, we're looking at how people think about their body image and eating.

Etiologies of disorders: Becker et al.'s study could help explain etiologies of eating disorders and why eating disorders may be less prevalent in developing nations.

Media naïve population: a group of people who have not been previously exposed to media.

A score at or above 20 on the EAT test signifies that there is a need for concern about the individual's eating, so data was compared at this point on the test in Becker et al.'s study.

One aspect of globalization is the spread of ideas through tech-nology. The introduction of TV on the island of Vanua Levu in Fiji made for an opportune time to study the effects of TV on body-image and eating attitudes in young girls.

comes from the fact that the girls with TVs in their homes were more than three times as likely to have an EAT score over 20, when compared with girls without a TV.

As we can see, according to the Eating Attitudes Test scores the introduction of TV clearly had a negative influence on girls' attitudes towards eating. But what about the behaviour? In 1995, 0% of the girls reported vomiting after eating, which is a strong warning sign of disordered eating behaviours as it's one of the major symptoms of bulimia nervosa. This number increased to 11% by 1998. Similarly, while before the introduction of TV in 1995 dieting was quite rate, 69% of the girls reported engaging in dieting behaviour three years later. Body image was also affected as 74% said they felt too big or fat.

The qualitative data gathered in semi-structured interviews corroborated these quantitative findings and provides more insight into the change in thinking that may be underlying these changes in eating attitudes and behaviours. A common theme emerging from the interviews was an admiration for the characters the girls were seeing on TV and a desire to emulate them. Some girls also reported in interviews that they believed it was the introduction of TV that was influencing their body image.

This study provides some strong evidence to suggest that the introduction of TV in naïve populations could alter eating attitudes and behaviours. Researchers hypothesize this is because when people watch the idealized portrayals of characters and people on TV, they want to become like these people they admire. As the characters are often thin, this could alter the way people think and feel about eating and dieting.

An important process in globalization is the spread of ideas through the media. The current emphasis placed on attractiveness and an idealization of thinness in Western media could change the attitudes and behaviours of people in cultures for whom this is new.

This study could be used in support of social learning theory, as well as a demonstration of how acculturation may influence behaviour.

Body image: how we think about our bodies.

Could the introduction of TV be influencing the girls' sense of identity as well?

Guiding Question:

How can globalization influence attitudes towards eating?

Critical Thinking Extension:

Contradictory Evidence: It seems that there's some contradictory evidence within the reported results. Can you see it? Take the fact that there was one reported case of anorexia nervosa before the study was conducted and compare this with their 1995 measures on the EAT test. Do you see anything peculiar?

If you're interested...

You can take the EAT online to get an idea of what this test looks like and the kinds of attitudes and behaviours it measures. Time magazine also has an interesting article online called "How Social Media is a Toxic Mirror." This article provides some counter-arguments to the positive effects of Facebook on self-esteem that we'll look at in the cognitive extensions.

(c)   Immigration and Extremism

While globalization can occur through processes related to economics, technology and the media, another component is the increased movement of *individuals* between countries. While migration is not a new phenomenon, it has rapidly increased over the past century due to developments in transportation that have made it increasingly easy to move from one country to the next. Immigration is an important topic in today's societies, as many countries welcome refugees and immigrants from countries around the world. When someone migrates from one country to another, they need to adjust to the change in culture. How they adjust to this change is an important field of study.

One particular group that has been studied are Muslims immigrants. The interaction of forces related to immigration, Islam, extremism, and terrorism are of particular importance in today's society and so in this section we'll explore the links between acculturation and religious extremism in Muslim immigrants and their home communities.

In the social influence chapter, we learned about acculturation: the process of change that occurs through interaction of cultures (Berry, 2002 & 2005). Acculturation is also commonly defined as the change that can occur in an *individual* as a result of interaction with a new culture. Berry outlines two distinct ways that acculturation might occur. On the one hand, a migrant moving to a new country might become a part of their new culture and be included. They may, however, be excluded or exclude themselves from their new culture.

The acculturation strategy that we're going to focus on in this section is marginalization. In the context of acculturation strategies, marginalization is when someone has no desire to participate in the new culture they have moved to, and they do not wish to maintain the cultural heritage from their home culture (Berry et al., 2002; Berry, 2005). In a sense they become "culturally homeless." One negative outcome of marginalization is that it could lead to an individual adopting radical and extremist beliefs. With the issues we currently face as a global community, this is an important phenomenon to investigate.

Lyons-Padilla et al. (2015) conducted the first known empirical study on the relationships between acculturation strategies, identity and extremism. They hypothesized that adopting the acculturation strategy of marginalization could lead to Muslim Americans feeling like they don't belong anywhere, that they've lost a sense of identity and may lack a sense of purpose or meaning in their life. They call this feeling of a lack of purpose and self-worth, significance loss. They also hypothesize that feeling significance loss could lead immigrants to become more sympathetic with extremist interpretations of Islam.

To test their hypotheses, the researchers surveyed 200 first and second generation Muslim immigrants across the United States. In order to measure the extent of the acculturation process of marginalization adopted by the immigrants, they asked participants to respond to statements like, "I do not wish to maintain my heritage culture values or adopt American values as I feel uncomfortable with both types of values." They then correlated this with their support for a radical interpretation of Islam. Once more using Likert scale, participants responded to statements such as "It is important to give to Islamic charities, even if their ideological beliefs may be extreme at times" and "Combative jihad is the only way to conduct jihad."

Their results showed a highly significant relationship between the extent of marginalization and feelings of significance loss ($p < 0.001$). In other words, the more

---

Religious Extremism: this is an attitude towards a particular religion (or religious text) that is not held by the majority of people who belong to that religion. Religious extremism exists in Christianity, Islam and other religions.

Acculturation results in changes in beliefs, values, attitudes, language and behaviour.

Significance loss: a term used by Lyons-Padilla and her colleagues to describe a general loss of purpose and meaning in one's life. This could be the result of a lack of cultural identity and belonging.

the Muslim Americans adopted an acculturation strategy of losing their cultural identity from their heritage culture *and* didn't integrate into mainstream American society, the more they felt a sense of significance loss. This feeling of significance loss was also strongly correlated with adopting a more radical interpretation of Islam.

What these results *suggest* is that how an individual adapts and adjusts to a secondary culture as a result of immigration could affect their sense of identity and purpose. If they marginalize themselves by rejecting their home culture and excluding themselves from participating in the larger society of their new culture (in this case, the United States), they may experience a loss of personal and/or cultural identity. They may also have a reduced sense of purpose in their life.

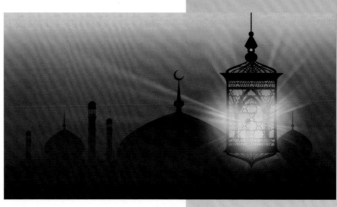

Immigration is one component of globalization, as people spread ideas and beliefs by moving from one country to another. How an individual adapts to their new country (i.e. the acculturation strategy they adopt) can influence their thinking, attitudes and behaviour. In these sections we look at Muslim immigrants, marginalization and radicalization.

By itself it's easy to imagine how this would have negative effects on marginalized immigrants. But what is of even more significance in this research is the correlation of significance loss with radical interpretations of Islam. As Islamic extremist groups like ISIS are responsible for many terrorist attacks, adopting a radical view of Islam could be a step towards joining one of these groups.

This concept and the possible behavioural effects of marginalization, significance loss and radical interpretations of Islam will be discussed in the next section.

Guiding Question:

How might marginalization influence religious beliefs?

Critical Thinking Extension:

Applications: Explain one (or more) reasons why Jim-Bob is wrong when he interprets these results by saying, "If Muslims don't join our society then they're going to become terrorists."

If you're interested…

You can read Lyons-Padilla's full article online and it's written in a language that is accessible to IB DP students. You can find a link to it on our blog. I recommend taking the time to study the diagram included, as it's a useful visual representation of how multiple variables may interact to effect extremism.

(d)   Marginalization and Radicalization

In the previous section we saw research on Muslim immigrants in the US that found significant correlations between marginalization, significance loss and Islamic extremism. In this section, we'll explore in a little more detail how marginalization is important to understand in the context of radicalization, religious extremism and terrorism.

Understanding why people might join radical terrorist organizations like ISIS is extremely important for obvious reasons. If an individual develops extremist religious attitudes and joins a terrorist group, the dangers for innocent people are significant. Many ISIS recruits actually come from America and countries in Europe and are recruited to carry out terrorist attacks in these foreign countries (Baker, 2015). If as a global community we can understand what might be drawing these young people to extremist groups, we might be able to end the attacks that are killing innocent people.

Individuals who are separated from mainstream society and have lost their cultural heritage, may find themselves more prone to joining fundamentalist religious groups. The research suggests that it's not their beliefs that push them to these groups, but their desire for belonging to a group that encourages them to adopt extremist beliefs.

While it might seem plausible to assume that people in extremist groups like ISIS are religious fanatics, research on the characteristics of violent extremists suggests this is not the case. Some people see these violent groups as offering something that they are missing from their lives (Lyons-Padilla et al., 2015). In other words, it's not their beliefs that draw them to the group, it is actually their desire to join a group that leads them to change their beliefs.

Lyons-Padilla et al.'s study was introduced in the previous section, but not all of their findings were discussed. They also measured correlations between marginalization, significance loss and support for a fundamentalist group. They used quantitative questionnaires to measure the extent to which an individual was sympathetic towards a fundamentalist group. A description of a fictional extremist group who "…were clearly against American maltreatment of Muslims," and promised belonging, commitment and loyalty was given to participants. To reduce the chances of the social desirability effect influencing the results, the researchers didn't ask how the participants directly felt about joining the group. Instead, they asked questions about how they thought their friends might feel towards the group.

Their results showed that feelings of significance loss could be used to predict support for the fundamentalist Islamic group. That is to say, the more significance loss someone felt, the more likely they were to support a fundamentalist Islamic group. Interestingly, there was not a significant correlation between marginalization and support for the fundamentalist group. This suggests that it's only if marginalization leads to a sense of significance loss that people may become sympathetic towards a fundamentalist group.

This provides more evidence for the researchers' hypothesis that it's when people lose meaning and importance that they might be drawn to these groups in the first place. Extremist and terrorist groups might "offer a sense of belonging, purpose, and the promise of recognition and status to anyone who works on their behalf"

(Lyons-Padilla, p.2). This is similar to social identity theory – humans have an innate desire to belong to a group and this belonging can affect the way we think and act. If people are marginalized and experience a sense of loss, a group that has a strong ideology and purpose can offer them something that they're missing in their lives. Extremist religious groups are especially attractive to people who may lack of a strong sense of identity (i.e. marginalized and culturally homeless people). The rules, beliefs and purpose offered by an extremist group might help fill the void that is missing in a marginalized individual's life. The distinction between the in-group ("us") and the out-groups ("them") can also provide a sense of social identity that was missing before (Hogg et al., 2010).

The ideas in this section are closely related with the concepts involved in social identity theory.

To summarize what we've seen so far in the research, it seems that immigration (a product of globalization) requires an individual to adopt a particular acculturation strategy. They might opt to integrate with the larger society or they may opt to exclude themselves. The acculturation strategy of marginalization is when an individual both rejects their home culture and excludes themselves from their new culture. This could lead to a loss of identity and purpose, a concept named significance loss. Individuals who experience significance loss might be more inclined to adopt extremist views because they represent the values of an extremist group that has a strong sense of purpose. The desire to join such a group could be the result of a desire to fill their lost purpose and feel like they belong somewhere.

While marginalization can refer to an acculturation strategy adopted by an individual, it can also refer to the exclusion of individuals by the larger cultural group. This exclusion could be one origin of religious extremism.

It's important to remember that in 2015 this was the first known empirical study on the above effects of globalization and marginalization. These results need to be interpreted carefully. Nevertheless, understanding these interactions is a valuable field of study and the possible applications of these findings will be discussed in the next lesson.

Guiding Question:

Why might marginalized individuals be more likely to join an extremist group?

Critical Thinking Extension:

Construct Validity: This term refers to the accuracy of a tool in measuring a construct (i.e. a behaviour or variable). Could you identify any reasons why construct validity might be questioned in this study?

If you're interested...

In his TED Talk, British man and former radical, Manwar Ali, gives us an excellent look "Inside the mind of a former radical jihadist." As with all studies in psychology, learning about real-life examples will give you a better understanding of the concepts and behaviours you're studying. His desire to "give doubt its rightful place" is a lesson that is widely applicable in psychology. The film "Colors" can also provide a fictional look at the role of significance loss in gang culture in LA in the 1980s.

(e)   Defenses Against Extremism

In the previous sections we've looked at some pretty complex interactions between globalization, immigration, marginalization, religious extremism, social identity and fundamentalist groups. But why learn about this? Like most aspects of psychology, if we know the origins of behaviours we can develop strategies to encourage prosocial behaviours, and discourage antisocial ones. In this section we'll look at the importance of reducing discrimination and encouraging inclusion as two important ways we can combat extremism and terrorism.

Another finding from the study carried out by Lydons-Padilla and colleagues is that experiences of discrimination moderated (i.e. made worse) the effects of marginalization on significance loss. Moreover, discrimination had a highly significant effect on feelings of significance loss. Simply put, if someone reported more discrimination they were more likely to feel like they lost purpose and meaning in their life. Discrimination, therefore, is a moderating variable that can increase the likelihood of marginalization leading to significance loss, religious extremism and support for radical religious groups.

But researchers didn't just assess marginalization. They assessed participants on all four of Berry's acculturation strategies: assimilation, integration, separation and marginalization (Berry, 1980). In this section we'll focus specifically on integration: being a part of the new culture and keep aspects of the home culture, too. In the context of a Pakistani Muslim immigrating to America, for instance, integration might include observing daily prayers and celebrating Ramadan, while learning English and making non-Muslim friends. Research suggests that integrating into the new culture can reduce the effects of perceived discrimination and reduce the negative effects this might have on depression and other negative outcomes.

An important finding from Lydon-Padilla et al.'s study was that integration had a strong negative relationship with significance loss. This means that the more inclined a person was towards integration, the less significance loss they felt. This is consistent with other research that suggests immigrants who are integrated experience the healthiest and happiest adjustment to life in a new country (Berry, 1997). For example, when looking at discrimination and mental health in Latinos in the social influence chapter, we saw that integration could explain the effects of perceived discrimination on acculturative stress and mental health (Torres et al., 2012).

What we can see is that there's an interaction between the individual and the group. On the one hand, how a person chooses to acculturate in society can have an effect. Similarly, the way society treats an individual can exacerbate the effects of their acculturation.

The point I'm drawing your attention to here is that it's not just the actions and attitudes of the individual that we need to consider. While marginalization is used to describe how an individual acculturates after immigration, it is also a term used to describe social exclusion by members of the larger society (Berry et al., 2002; Berry, 2005). By not giving people a chance to join and integrate into society, individuals can become marginalized. By reducing prejudice and discrimination and encouraging inclusion in society, we can effect change on an individual and a societal level.

Moderating variable: a variable that can alter the strength of influence of one variable on another.

The research and concepts discussed in this extension are highly relevant to the study of group dynamics.

Ramadan: a celebration in Islamic faith that lasts for a month and is characterized by day-time fasting and evening celebrations.

Sarah Lyons-Padilla and her colleagues' study suggests that integration can moderate the effects of marginalization on religious extremism and sympathy towards fundamentalist groups. In other words, by accepting and integrating immigrants into society, both the individual immigrant and the larger society will be much better off.

If we include immigrants and minorities in society and fight to reduce prejudice and discrimination, we can reduce the feeling of losing one's identity and sense of self, while promoting harmony and reducing the chances that people will join terrorist organizations. While the policies of some governments is to fight terrorism by excluding Muslims from society and to marginalize them, what the research suggests is that this is actually adding fuel to the fire. Therefore it is not through mass exclusion and marginalization of people based on the actions of a few extremist individuals that we will end extremism and terrorism; if we want peace, we must promote and practice inclusion and integration.

It's important to remember that these findings have not been replicated in other studies, so their conclusions need to be interpreted and applied with caution. They perhaps provide insight into possible relationships, but definitely do not *prove* anything.

Guiding Question:

How might making an effort to include Muslim immigrants in society reduce religious extremism?

Critical Thinking Extension:

Applications and Hypotheses: The "interaction of local and global influences" in globalization and behaviour has not been explicitly addressed in this topic. This is a topic best studied in your own local context. Can you hypothesize how globalizing factors might be influencing your local, social or cultural environments? This would make for an excellent additional topic to explore.

If you're interested...

In her TED Talk, Dalia Mogahed provides us with a powerful talk about being a Muslim in America ("What it's like to be Muslim in America"). I highly recommend watching this talk, as she discusses many of the ideas we've explored in this topic, including radicalization, extremism, tolerance, integration and acceptance. She sums up why many people need to change their opinions of Islam when she says "ISIS has as much to do with Islam as the Ku-Klux Klan has to do with Christianity."

(f)   Globalization and Methods

When studying animals in a laboratory it's relatively easy to isolate individual biological variables to study. This is why the experimental procedures can be valuable. Even when studying the effects of technology on cognition, experimental procedures can isolate individual variables and allocate participants to different conditions to measure the effects of the technology on our thinking.

But how would one go about manipulating the variables that we've looked at in this topic? Could you imagine conducting an experiment with the independent variable being globalization and acculturation strategy or experiences of discrimination? The practical and ethical considerations in such an experiment mean that other methods have to be used.

Becker et al.'s (2002) study on eating attitudes in Fiji provides us with a good example of the benefits of using a natural experiment in social psychology. Sometimes there are naturally occurring environmental variables that researchers hypothesize will have an effect on behaviour. By gathering data before the variable is introduced and comparing it with what happens after, the researchers can make conclusions based on the effect of the natural introduction of a variable. In this case, studies on the effects of the introduction of TV are of relevance to studies on the effects of globalization as TV and other media are a key factor involved in the ever-increasing interaction of cultures.

When it comes to studies on acculturation, an experimental method could have serious limitations. The independent variable in a study like Lyons-Padilla (2015) would have to be the acculturation strategy (e.g. marginalization versus integration). But what would an integration "treatment" look like? Cultural transmission and the process of acculturation is a process that involves language, interacting with other people, religion, media, and a whole bunch of other variables. It makes it practically impossible to devise an experiment where acculturation could be studied in a controlled environment.

When such practical limitations exist, but researchers want to study possible relationships between variables, using statistical methods of correlational analysis is a good option. In studies related to cultural processes, one variable is related to culture. In the acculturation studies on Muslim immigrants, for example, one variable was their response to a range of questions about their acculturation strategy. They can then compare this with other variables, such as how much they've felt discriminated against.

The benefit of running correlational analysis tests on data is that researchers can see if variables are related. They can also see how strongly the variables are related by calculating correlational coefficients, which can provide even stronger evidence to support particular hypotheses. They can also find out what variables *aren't* related to one another. For example, in the Muslim immigrant study they found that the acculturation strategy of assimilation had no significant effect on significance loss or extremist attitudes.

Becker et al.'s study could also be considered a mixed-methods approach, as it combines quantitative and qualitative methods.

The diagram in Lyons-Padilla et al.'s original study (available online) is excellent for showing the correlations between variables.

Becker et al.'s study in Fiji shows the benefits of a natural experiment in studying the effects of globalization on attitudes and behaviour. Similarly, when studying cultural influences on behaviour, correlational studies are often important because cultural origins of behaviour involve many factors and so they're difficult to manipulate in an experimental design.

Using quantitative data and questionnaires is also an integral part of the process of correlational studies. Without reducing these complex behaviours down to quantifiable measurements, there would be no way of conducting the analysis. However, this raises concerns regarding construct validity – how accurately are the questionnaires measuring the intended variables? Can a vulnerability towards joining an extremist group really be measured by asking someone how their friends would feel about such a group?

While experimental methods are valuable in some fields of study in psychology, those involving complex cultural processes require other methods. As variables between relationships might still be studied, the use of correlational statistical analysis tests is invaluable.

Construct validity: This concept is closely related to internal validity. Strictly speaking, internal validity only applies to experimental methods. Construct validity refers to how well the tool measures what it intended to (e.g. how well does a questionnaire measure sympathy towards religious extremism?)

Can we really measure individualism or happiness through a questionnaire?

Guiding Question:

Why are correlational studies commonly used in studies on globalization?

Critical Thinking Extension:

Application: Can you use Ogihara and Uchida's study to explain why correlational analysis methods are beneficial in studies on globalization and behaviour?

If you're interested…

By this stage in the course it's hoped you have learned to deal with correlations and causations very carefully. In her TED Talk, "The danger of mixing up causality and correlation," Ionica Smeets explains some really interesting examples of bidirectional ambiguity in correlational studies.

8.3 Technology and Cognition
Can technology change the way we think?

(a) Computer Games and Working Memory

Atkinson and Shiffron's multi-store model of memory combined existing ideas of memory.

When cognitive models (e.g. dual processing model of thinking, multi-store model and the working memory model) are developed in psychology, they enable researchers to conduct studies and test hypotheses based on the model. When enough empirical evidence is gathered in support of the model, cognitive psychologists can expand on the research and use the model and the related concepts to discuss cognitive processes. This is how cognitive models can contribute to our understanding of behaviour and cognition in psychology.

For example, while the MSM has numerous limitations and is often critiqued for being overly simplistic, its role in developing our understanding of memory cannot be overlooked. It could be compared to Kandel's reductionist model of memory storage using Aplysia: the early research showed that synapses grow as a result of learning. This was really influential in our study of how the brain stores memory, but if we stopped there we'd have a limited understanding of this phenomenon. Similarly, the MSM can be a good starting point for understanding memory processes, and it has inspired further research that has clarified distinctions between short and long-term memory and the function of control processes.

The central executive is the part of working memory that controls the flow of information from the long-term to the episodic buffer, as well as from one slave system to the other.

An example of how the MSM furthered our understanding of memory processes is the development of the working memory model (WMM) by Baddeley and Hitch. While the MSM focuses on storage, the WMM looks at storage *and* processing of information. This model has also provided more ideas about short-term memory and has inspired research on short-term memory processes. For example, tests have been created to measure aspects of working memory. Brain imaging research has also been carried out to see if particular areas of the brain play a central role in working memory processes like the central executive.

Another example of the contribution the WMM has made to cognitive research is that it gives cognitive psychologists the language and framework to study other related cognitive processes, such as attention. In this section we're going to review the research on the use of brain training games on working memory and attention.

One example is Klingberg et al.'s (2002) experiment on children with ADHD aimed to measure the effects of computer-based training on working memory and executive function in children aged 7 to 12. To recap, 42 kids who had been diagnosed with attentional disorders were randomly allocated to one of two conditions. The treatment condition involved playing a computer game that was created to improve their working

The creation of computer games to enhance working memory capacity and other executive functions is a relatively new field in cognitive science and highlights the potential positive effects of the use of technology on cognition.

memory. The game was designed so the tasks became increasingly harder as the kids' scores improved. In the control condition, the kids played the same game but it was not designed to increase in difficulty. The kids were expected to play the games for around 40 minutes a day, for five days a week.

The kids were tested after five weeks of treatment and again after three months. The results showed that the kids in the treatment group had a significant improvement in their working memory skills. The parents also reported reduced symptoms of inattention and hyperactivity. Here we can see one positive benefit of cognitive training on working memory and attention using computer games.

To test their working memory, the researchers used a task called the span-board task. In this task, there is a group of items laid out on a table. The researcher points to a series of the objects and the child needs to remember the order the researcher pointed to them. They then need to copy the researcher and point to the objects in the same order. In other words, after watching the researcher they need to hold the pattern in their episodic buffer until they need to repeat the process. Repeating the process would require replaying the information through the visuospatial sketchpad so they could repeat this in the right order.

Other studies have shown that there are neurological changes that occur as a result of working memory training. This is not surprising, since we know that how we use our mind can change our brain. In one study, Klingberg and his colleagues (Klingsberg et al., 2004) tested the neurological effects of five weeks of working memory training on adults. They found the training had significant effects on activity in the prefrontal cortex and an area in the parietal lobe that is associated with interpreting sensory information. This suggests that working memory training might actually cause neuroplastic changes that facilitates working memory and behavioural improvements.

ADHD is a very common disorder in many countries. But there is a debate about whether or not it's an epidemic, or if it's just over-diagnosed. One reason for concern is that kids are prescribed medication to treat their ADHD. This is why brain training games are so alluring – they could be improving cognitive functions and reducing unwanted impulsive behaviours without the need for medication. This has sparked a massive industry with multi-million dollar companies that design, create and sell these games. One estimate states that in 2014, people spent over $750 million dollars on computer-based brain training games (Yong, 2016).

But the actual effects of these games is under serious scrutiny. A comprehensive review was carried out by Simons et al. (2016) to assess the research and the effectiveness of these sorts of games. The study was an international collaboration of 133 scientists and practitioners, so you can get a sense that this is a "hot topic" in cognitive psychology. What they concluded from their review was that the games can help performance on closely related tasks. However, they found that the tasks had limited transfer to other related or general cognitive tasks. What this means, for example, is that the games might improve the kids' scores on the span-board task. But if they improved on this task, it doesn't mean it can be transferred to other cognitive skills, like reading comprehension, the ability to inhibit impulsive thoughts and actions, or improving long-term memory. They also found numerous flaws in many of the studies that claimed to demonstrate the positive effects of these programmes.

This is an important finding because many companies that have been created to design these products are selling them by telling people that they can improve their general cognitive skills. In fact, one of the major companies was sued and needed to pay $2 million dollars because they made false claims about their products (Yong, 2016).

Working memory: One aspect of working memory is our ability to retrieve information from our long-term memory and hold it in our short-term memory. Another component of working memory is being able to control the flow of thoughts in and out of our consciousness.

The prefrontal cortex plays a role in tasks requiring executive function. It is the most widely studied part of the brain in working memory studies.

The ability to concentrate and focus attention is one role of working memory and the central executive.

So while brain training games have shown some positive effects in studies, they serve as a good reminder that we should always scrutinize the counter-evidence before we can say we "know" anything.

Guiding Question:

How can computer-based training improve working memory?

Critical Thinking Extension:

Ethical Issues: Considering the impact of the applications of results on others is an important aspect related to ethics in psychological research. This includes thinking about how the use of findings beyond the study might impact others. What are the ethical considerations related to the application of findings in this study? For instance, think about how using these findings to sell games could have a negative impact on others.

If you're interested...

Ed Yong has an article about the criticism of brain training games in his article on theatlantic.com. The article is called "The Weak Evidence Behind Brain Training Games" and includes more detailed results from Simons et al.'s study.

(b) Virtual Reality and Fear Extinction

Virtual Reality Exposure Therapy (VRET) is a type of exposure therapy that operates on the assumptions of fear extinction. In this section we're going to continue our investigation into how VRET uses fear extinction to reduce symptoms related to PTSD and phobias. Before we look at this process, let's first recap the process of fear conditioning that is explained in chapter four.

Fear conditioning is a type of classical conditioning and is the result of learning to associate a neutral, unconditioned stimulus (US) with an aversive stimulus (AS). Simply put, we learn to fear something because that signifies a bad thing is about to happen. It's important to note that the learning that results after fear conditioning is not necessarily a conscious process. The stimulus might not bring the memories of the event into the working memory: the learning is happening at a subconscious, biological level and the stress response that occurs after a stimuli is perceived by the amygdala is involuntary. So when a veteran hears fireworks go off, they don't consciously think, "fireworks means explosions so I need to take cover." Instead, the perception of the conditioned stimulus (fireworks) triggers an unconscious, conditioned fear response through the activation of the nervous and endocrine systems.

One useful detail to note is that people with PTSD also show increased generalization of fear conditioning (Mahan and Ressler, 2012). An increase of generalized fear conditioning means that the conditioned stimulus is more likely to be experienced in response to other similar stimuli. For example, fireworks going off aren't identical to a bomb exploding, but it might cause the same fear response. The conditioned stimulus (bomb dropping) has been generalized to a new setting (fireworks). People with PTSD don't necessarily have to encounter an identical stimulus to the one that occurred during their trauma – the conditioned fear generalizes to new conditions.

Let's now look at how the many different forms of VRET might help to extinguish conditioned fears. VRET involves having participants experience a "virtual reality," as computer technology immerses people in virtual worlds that mimic real life. As the technology gets better, it will become increasingly realistic. VRET aims to reduce anxiety and fear-related symptoms by repeatedly exposing the client to the conditioned stimulus without the aversive stimulus. This process is aimed at extinguishing the fear response and causing new learning. The benefit of VRET over imagination therapy is that the technology is so life-like that it's better at "tricking" the brain and causing new learning.

While it might appear peaceful and serene to us, being in an environment like this might trigger a conditioned fear response in a war veteran, as this would be a highly dangerous place to be during combat because you're so exposed. VRET allows clients to re-experience being in such environments and could help extinguish their conditioned fear by helping the individual (and their brain) learn that there's nothing to be afraid of anymore.

War veterans, for instance, may use VRET to re-experience the conditions on a battlefield. Someone with arachnophobia may be put in a world where they can walk in a room that has spiders and people with a fear of flying could also use VRET to simulate being in a plane.

To test the effectiveness of VRET in treating PTSD symptoms, Rothbaum et al. (2001) used the treatment with 8 Vietnam War veterans. During the virtual reality treatment they were exposed to two different environments. In one they were in a Huey Helicopter (the type used to transport troops in Vietnam) flying over a landscape that looked like Vietnam. In the other virtual world they were in a field surrounded by jungle. For the second environment, it's easy to imagine how this would bring about a

Fear extinction: removing (or extinguishing) a conditioned fear. Fear conditioning and fear extinction are types of learning.

Classical conditioning was first observed by a biologist in Russia, Ivan Pavlov, who was studying the digestive systems in dogs.

Generalization of a conditioned fear is when the conditioned fear occurs in response to similar stimuli.

In modern psychiatry, the term "client" is sometimes preferred over "patient." Either term is acceptable and is more appropriate than "participant" or "subject" when talking about people involved in some form of therapy, even if it is part of a study.

The cognitive process influenced by VRET could be identified as learning or memory, as these are interrelated concepts.

An effect size is a statistical measurement of the strength of the effect of the independent variable on the dependent variable. 0.2 is a weak effect size, 0.4 is medium and 0.8 is considered strong. In this context, a strong effect size (>0.8) suggests that VRET has a strong effect on reducing PTSD symptoms.

fear response: being surrounded by jungle means the enemy could hide and if you were in an open field you would be exposed. Veterans of combat in the Vietnam War would have a conditioned fear to being in such an environment because when this happened during the war it meant their life was in danger. Veterans of wars in the Middle East have a similar conditioned fear of standing near open windows (due to experiences related to sniper attacks).

Using the Clinically Administered PTSD Scale (CAPs), the results showed that all clients had a reduction of symptoms when they had a check-up six months after the treatment. The reduction in symptoms ranged from 15% to 67%. These results suggest that VRET can be effective in treating the PTSD.

Similarly, a meta-analysis conducted by Parsons and Rizzo (2008) found a significant effect in using VRET to treat a range of anxiety-related disorders, including PTSD and phobias. Their results showed an effect size of 0.87 for PTSD and 0.92 for arachnophobia when comparing VRET with other treatments.

VRET can influence the cognitive process of conditioned fear by repeatedly exposing the client to their fear-inducing stimulus without an aversive stimulus. It can also do this by using realistic computer technology, without exposing the person to any real harm as they know they're in a safe environment. This process may actually be erasing the memory of the conditioned fear, or it might be causing new learning. Whether or not fear extinction erases memory or forms new memory is a source of debate.

But how could VRET be influencing fear extinction? It may actually be influencing the learning process by improving the function of another part of the brain, the ventromedial prefrontal cortex (vmPFC). In one study, LeDoux et al. (2004) found that before treatment a group of 10 patients, like many others with PTSD, had hyper-responsive amygdalae and hypo-responsive vmPFC. The results of the study showed that VRET helped to increase the vmPFC function and reduce amygdala activation when exposed to emotional images. As the vmPFC has been shown to play a role in fear extinction, VRET may facilitate this learning process by actually changing the neural circuitry of the brain.

In summary, the digital technology used in VRET may have positive effects for people with PTSD. The technology can facilitate fear extinction, which is a type of learning. It may also be having neurological effects, which could explain the changes in cognition.

Guiding Question:

How might VRET have a positive influence on cognitive processes?

Critical Thinking Extension:

Limitation: We cannot call Rothbaum et al.'s study an experiment. Why not? How might their methodology affect the validity of their conclusions?

If you're interested…

In the NOVA documentary "Memory Hackers," there's a fascinating segment about how drugs are being used to erase conditioned fear in a process known as reconsolidation. You can see a man with arachnophobia erase his fear overnight. This works by operating on another fascinating neurotransmitter that we haven't had a chance to explore in this text, noradrenaline.

(c) Facebook, Self-Image and Self-Esteem

In this section, we're going to look at how using Facebook can affect self-esteem. As with other examples of digital technology, social media sites like Facebook have been the subject of scrutiny regarding their effects, particularly on young people.

Research has shown that Facebook can enhance social self-esteem, which can be defined as someone's perceptions of themselves in relation to other people, including how they think about their attractiveness, relationships and their physical appearance. Facebook may also provide people with low self-esteem the chance to experience social interactions, without the anxiety that comes with face-to-face interactions.

On the other hand, Facebook may reduce self-esteem because it makes people aware of themselves. When our own selves becomes the subject of our conscious attention, it could have positive and negative outcomes. One reason it could have a negative outcome is that we might judge ourselves based on social norms. This could decrease self-esteem because "most people fall short of social standards when self-awareness is heightened." This social comparison and self-evaluation can have negative effects on self-esteem (Gonzales and Hancock, 2011).

In one study, reported in an article called "Mirror, Mirror on my Facebook Wall," Gonzales and Hancock (2011) conducted an experiment to see if using Facebook would have a positive or negative influence on self-esteem. They hypothesized that Facebook would enhance self-esteem through a process of selective self-presentation. Social media sites allow people to select the aspects of themselves they want to share with others. For example, people using dating apps choose the best pictures to portray themselves. When updating your Facebook profile picture, or writing something on your wall, you'd probably put something that shows the best side of you. What happens as a result of these selected presentations of ourselves is that they can influence our self-image. The way we've presented ourselves to the world becomes the way we think about ourselves and results in an identity shift, which means our thinking about who we are has changed. This ability to select what we portray to the world and the subsequent impact it can have on our self-identity, could boost self-esteem (Gonzales and Hancock, 2011).

In order to test this hypothesis, the researchers conducted an experiment that required one group of participants to log-in to their Facebook. The researcher left the room for three minutes and the participant was free to use their Facebook account, and they received no specific instructions from the experimenter. After the three minutes, the experimenter returned and gave them a few questionnaires to complete, including one used to rate their feelings of self-esteem. They also asked if they made any changes to their Facebook wall during the three minutes.

The participants' scores on the self-esteem test were compared with the control groups in the experiment who didn't access their Facebook accounts and showed that the Facebook groups reported higher feelings of self-esteem. There was also further support for the selective self-presentation hypothesis because participants who made changes to their Facebook wall reported higher self-esteem than people who didn't make any changes.

It appears from the study that selecting and editing the information we portray to the world can actually boost our self-esteem. This could be because how we present ourselves on social media could alter our self-image and cause an identity shift.

Self-esteem: confidence in our abilities. Our self-image can influence our self-esteem.

Selective self-presentation: deliberately and carefully choosing which aspects of ourselves we wish to portray to the world.

Self-image: our perceptions of ourselves. Your self-image focuses on considering the answer to the question, "who is (insert your name here)?" Self-image is a cognitive process.

While self-esteem is a way of thinking, an IB examiner may question whether or not this is technically a "cognitive process." For that reason, it might be best to write about another topic in exams. This topic has been included here for interest more than exam preparation.

Using social media might help increase self-esteem because it enables people to select what they portray to the world. This positive image they portray becomes internalized and part of their self-image, which might increase their self-esteem. But be careful – it comes with risks.

But before you go off telling your parents, "I told you so - social media can boost my self-esteem," it's important to consider for a moment some other factors. I will only briefly mention here a whole field of research that has investigated social media and addiction. This research focuses on the role of a fascinating neurotransmitter that we haven't had a chance to explore in other aspects of this course – dopamine. Dopamine is a neurotransmitter that is called the "pleasure chemical" because its release is associated with feelings of pleasure. When you're expectantly awaiting something great to happen, dopamine is released. Like when you take a great photo and post it on Instagram and you're anxiously checking your likes. Dopamine is also released when you receive a reward, like a flurry of nice comments after a post on your Facebook wall.

While this all seems lovely, there is a dark side to dopamine as these same neural circuits involved in experiencing pleasure are those involved in addiction. The release of dopamine in response to expecting reward is what motivates us to get stuff done. In fact, if there's uncertainty thrown in there our dopamine centre (the nucleus accumbens) goes into overdrive. So if we post something and we're not sure what the response will be, we experience high levels of dopamine. This process has been used as the basis of numerous studies into addiction to the internet and social media. It's mentioned here because it's a fascinating topic and you should be aware of how the use of social media might not only be influencing your thinking, but it could also be changing your brain.

Guiding Question:

How might Facebook affect our self-image?

Critical Thinking Extension:

Methodology: Construct Validity: How accurate do you think the researchers' measure of self-esteem was? Do you think that the evidence presented here is strong enough to conclude that Facebook is a positive influence? Which other factors related to using social media do you think could influence self-esteem?

If you're interested...

The full article by Gonzales and can be found online and is accessible for IBDP students. You can watch a video on our blog of Sapolsky explaining the dopamine research, as well as AsapSCIENCE's video about how social media is changing our brains ("Five crazy ways social media is changing your brain right now").

(d)   The Internet and Memory

Smartphones have taken the fun out of arguing. You're probably too young to even know what it was like to have an argument with someone last for weeks or even years because both of you are too lazy to actually do the research and find the answer. But now if we hear a song and we wonder who sings it, we can Shazam it. If we're wondering who's that girl in that TV show and 'what have I seen her in before?' We can IMDB it. And let's not forget, if we have a question about *anything*, we can always Google it!

But does this easy access to unlimited information affect our memory? If we know we can always find out the capital of Mongolia with the touch of a button, or how to get from Steve's house over to Nathan's with an app, why would we waste cognitive energy converting this information into long-term memory?

Sparrow et al. (2001) conducted a series of experiments to study the effects of external information storage systems (e.g. the internet) on memory. In one of their experiments they wanted to see how knowing we would have access to information at a later date would affect our long-term memory of that information. In their design, they had participants read a selection of trivial pieces of information and then type these into a computer. An example piece of trivia from the study is "An ostrich's eye is bigger than its brain." Half of the participants were told that the information they typed in the computer would be saved, while the other half were told it would be deleted.

Having a world of information at our fingertips seems to be having an impact on our memory. But is this impact positive, negative, or is it just a change?

The results showed that those participants in the saved-condition remembered less information than those in the erased-condition. In other words, if the participants knew they could access the information again later, they were worse at remembering it.

This experiment was designed to imitate our daily use of external storages of memory and search engines like Google. Sparrow et al. argue that the internet has become like an external memory storage system and so we do not need to transfer information to our long-term memory because we can just search it on our phones or Google it on our tablet. In this same series of experiments, the researchers also showed that participants were better at remembering where to find saved information, than they were at remembering the information itself. They conclude that our memory processes may be adapting to the ubiquitous use of computer technology in our daily lives: because we can store information in external systems, we don't need to remember it for ourselves, but we do need to remember where to find it again.

Another way computers may be affecting our memory is in how well we create memories in the first place. There are a number of studies that suggest handwriting is better for learning and remembering than typing (e.g. Kiefer et al., 2015). This may be good to know before you go off to University. Many students think that because they can type faster than they write, they can take "better" notes on their laptops. However, typing what a teacher says without processing the information and making sense of it might result in more notes, but it will not enhance memory. Actually, it might even have a detrimental effect on learning (Mueller and Oppenheimer, 2014).

Encode: the encoding of memory refers to the process of creating a new memory.

Typing versus handwriting is related to another model of memory called levels of processing.

Digital technology brings with it many advantages and benefits in our lives. But we should never forget that the most complex machine in the known universe is the human brain. When it comes to memory and your brain, the old saying is true: use it or lose it!

Guiding Question:

How might the internet influence memory?

Critical Thinking Extension:

Area of Uncertainty: Are the effects of the internet on memory that we've explored in this section a negative or a positive effect? Or is it a bit of both, or neutral? Are these changes in the way we remember information just natural adaptations to living in a digital age?

If you're interested...

Adam Thierer has an interesting article in Forbes' online magazine called "10 Things Our Kids Will Never Worry About Thanks to the Information Revolution." Could you guess what those ten things are?

(e)   TV and Executive Functions

Before the invention of the smartphone, parents worried about how much time their kids were spending in front of the TV. This is one reason why Bandura's Bobo doll experiments in the 1960s measured the behavioural effects of watching violent television. If you can recall, kids who watched cartoon violence were more likely than a control group to imitate the violent behaviours they saw on TV. One of the major limitations of this study, however, is that the *cognitive* effects of watching the TV are overlooked. We don't actually know what was happening in the minds of the children and we can only make assumptions based on their observable behaviour.

Executive functions: this is another umbrella term that includes working memory, attention, and the ability to delay gratification.

So how can watching TV affect our thinking? Numerous studies have investigated the effects of watching television on working memory and executive functions. Having a large working memory capacity is important for learning as the ability to hold information in our conscious attention and to make sense of it is crucial. Why, even now as you're reading this explanation you need to be thinking about the complex vocabulary that's being used and how it relates to what you're trying to understand in this lesson. Without the ability to process and consider this information, your comprehension of these ideas and what you're reading would be severely limited.

Christakis et al. (2004) conducted a longitudinal study on over 1,000 American children with the aim of seeing if watching TV as a young child (one and three) would increase the chances of having attentional problems when they got older (at age seven). After conducting their correlational analyses, the results showed that the main predictor for attentional problems at age seven, was hours spent watching TV at ages one and three. One finding from the study was that for every hour on average they watched at age three, they were 10% more likely to have attentional problems at age seven.

Attention is closely related to working memory in that it is the role of the central executive to maintain our concentration on particular tasks. One reason why TV might affect attention is that it requires very little cognitive effort. Images appear and disappear, and we can sit on the sofa with a bowl of chips and turn off our brain. But could this depend on the type of TV we watch? If we're watching educational documentaries or foreign films that require careful concentration, maybe these could be beneficial. However, watching TV that has lots of quick-cuts and things happening so quickly that we don't really have to think very carefully about what we're watching, could have negative effects.

Research suggests that it's not just how much TV kids watch that is the issue, it's also what type of TV they watch. With kids having increasing amounts of control over the media they consume, this is an important issue to study.

To study the effects of different types of TV watching on executive function and working memory, Lillard and Peterson (2011) conducted a clever experiment on four year olds. In order to isolate the type of TV being watched as the variable influencing working memory and executive functioning, the researchers randomly allocated 60 four year olds to one of three conditions. In the fast-paced TV condition the kids watched SpongeBob Square Pants. This show has an average scene length of 11 seconds, which means on average every 11 seconds it cuts to a different scene. The slow-paced TV condition watched another cartoon, Caillou. The difference in this cartoon is that the scenes are longer and only change on average every 34 seconds. A third group watched no TV and did drawing activities instead. The kids watched TV (or drew) for nine minutes before completing a range of tests on their working memory.

A common test for measuring working memory capacity is the digit-span task. This task measures memory span, which is the amount of numbers a person can accurately recall after being shown a set of numbers. The digit-span task involves showing numbers (digits) to participants and asking them to remember the digits in the right order. In this study, they used a backwards digit span task, which means they told the kids a series of numbers and the kids had to repeat them backwards. For example, they would say, (3…7…8…" and the kid would have to repeat "8…7…3…" The test got gradually harder as the number of digits to remember increased all the way up until a possible 15 numbers, but the kids were asked to stop once they got three wrong. This is one of four such tests that were used to measure the effects of watching different types of TV on executive function.

The digits-span task is a common measurement of working memory. You can find numerous tests online so you can find out your own working memory capacity by measuring your memory span.

The results showed that the kids who watched nine minutes of SpongeBob (fast paced) scored significantly less on the digit-span and other tests of executive function than the group in the drawing and slow-paced TV conditions. It seems that it's not just about how much TV a child watches, but the type of TV could have different effects, too.

The researchers also tested the kids on their ability to delay gratification using a procedure similar to the marshmallow paradigm.

Could there be biological effects? If what we watch is continually changing how we think, it's not hard to imagine that extensive TV watching will be having a neurological effect. Interestingly, research in Japan has shown a negative correlation between TV watching and grey matter in our old friend, the prefrontal cortex (Takeuchi et al., 2013). Perhaps this could also explain the results of Christiakis et al.'s study.

Critical Thinking Extension:

Correlation vs. Causation: Whenever you are discussing the results of correlational research, it's always important to consider whether or not the association could be explained in a different way. For example, it's tempting to say that Christakis' et al.'s study shows that watching TV caused the attentional problems. However, there are many confounding variables. Can you think of other explanations for this relationship? For example, could the relationship be explained in the other direction?

If you're interested…

In Dimitri Christakis' TED Talk, "Media and Children" he summarizes his study and studies similar to Lillard and Peterson's. He also talks about neural pruning, which is a fascinating phenomenon that we haven't explored elsewhere in this text, so it's well worth a watch.

(f)   Cell Phones and Inattentional Blindness

Just as kids being glued to the TV sparked decades of research into the effects of watching TV on behaviour and psychological development, the smartphone glued into the palm of young kids has also inspired heaps of research into the possible effects this may have. In this section, we'll look at how cell phone use can cause something called inattentional blindness. If you drive a car, or are going to start soon, this topic is highly relevant.

Teaching your teenaged child to drive is a parenting fear I'm dreading. And while many people these days have a fear of dying in a plane crash, a terrorist attack or being eaten by a shark, we really should be more afraid of driving. Young (and old) drivers glued to their cell phones and unable to wait five minutes or pull over to send a text or make a call are causing more and more accidents. As you may have already started driving, or will soon start taking driving lessons, it's pretty important that you learn why using your phone and driving is a pretty stupid idea.

Inattentional blindness is a perceptual phenomenon that occurs when people are distracted and fail to see something that is clearly visible to them. This was most famously studied by Simons and Chabris (1999) using an experimental procedure that went viral. In the procedure, the participants watched a video that has two teams of people standing in a circle passing basketballs back and forth. One team has black shirts and the other team has white shirts. The participants are asked to count how many passes go from one black shirt-wearing player to another. The video gets pretty messy, so it takes really careful attention to count the passes. The problem is, that this careful attention to one task causes about half of the people to miss the fact that there's a person in a gorilla suit that walks right into the middle of the game, stops and does a little dance, and then keeps walking out of the video.

Inattentional blindness: our inability to see things even when they are right in front of us because our attention is focused on something else.

The gorilla experiment went viral on the internet. I have to admit, the first time I took this experiment I didn't see the gorilla, either.

People who don't see the gorilla are demonstrating inattentional blindness: a failure to see something really obvious in our immediate visual field, because we're too busy concentrating on something else. In this case, we're so busy counting basketball passes that we don't see a gorilla dancing in front of our eyes.

Can you see where this is going with texting and driving? Some people are stupid enough to actually look at their phones in their lap and take their eyes off the road while driving. This is obviously dangerous as you can't break for a stopped car if you're not even looking at the road. But the phenomenon of inattentional blindness occurs even if you are "looking" at the road. Even if you were so skilled at texting that you could do it without looking, you still wouldn't be able to "see" objects in the road because your attention is elsewhere.

The limited capacity of our working memory means that we cannot focus on too many things at once. Because of this, texting or talking on the phone while driving can cause inattentional blindness.

Strayer and Johnston (2002) provide some evidence for this effect in a dual-task study that required participants from the University of Utah (average age 21) to perform various tasks while performing tasks on a computer that were meant to simulate reactions to traffic. In two conditions, participants listened to books on tape or the radio and their ability to detect traffic signals and their reaction times to unexpected events (like a car braking in front of them) were recorded. The results showed that talking aloud, or listening to a book or the radio did not affect their reaction or their perception. However, when participants were asked to engage in conversations on a cell-phone, they were twice as likely to miss traffic signs and their reaction speeds were slower.

In 2015, 3,477 people were killed in traffic accidents because of distracted driving (nhtsa.gov).

Similarly, in a second experiment the same conditions were used by a more realistic driving simulator. After comparing reaction times, the experiment showed that the cell-phone condition participants were significantly slower to react to unexpected events while driving. In fact, three of the participants in the cell-phone conversation condition got into accidents. This occurs even when the conversation happens using a hands-free device.

This negative effect on the reliability of our perception could be explained through inattentional blindness: if you're driving while trying to send a text or have a conversation, this requires thought and is cognitively taxing, and takes attention away from the road. This means that even when things happen in front of you, you might not be able to perceive them, or at least your perception will be slower.

Remember that your working memory is limited, and new research suggests you can only hold about three or four pieces of information in your working memory (not the magic 7 plus or minus 2 originally hypothesized by Miller in the 1950s). If those mental resources are going into other, less important tasks like sending a Snapchat, your reaction time to someone in front of you or a kid running into the road will be reduced.

Don't become a statistic: ignore the dopamine in your brain that's urging you to check your buzzing phone and listen to your prefrontal cortex telling you to make them wait. It's better than the alternative.

Critical Thinking Extension:

Hypothesize: Could using your phone at other times have a similar effect? Or think about if these results could be generalized to other multi-tasking situations based on what you now know about working memory capacity and attention. What would you predict regarding an experiment into the effects of listening to a lyrical song while studying, compared with listening to instrumental music?

If you're interested…

You can watch the gorilla experiment online. This experiment has multiple conditions, so you could replicate this for your internal assessment. However, even in the original study some of the data had to be thrown out because the participants already knew of the experimental procedures – if you know to expect the gorilla, you're likely to see the gorilla.

(g)   True Experiments

Through the previous topics we've been learning about the various positive and negative effects of modern technology on cognitive processes. If we review some of the studies that were carried out to measure these effects, we can see that many of these were true experiments. Let's look at the following studies:

- ADHD kids and computer-based training (Klingsberg et al., 2002).
  - o   *Positive effects on working memory and executive functions.*
- Fast- vs. slow-paced TV watching (Lillard and Peterson, 2011).
  - o   *Negative effects on working memory and executive functions.*
- The internet and memory storage (Sparrow et al., 2001).
  - o   *Negative effects on the reliability of memory.*
- The effects of cellphones on inattentional blindness (Strayer and Johnston, 2002)
  - o   *Negative effects on the reliability of perception.*
- Facebook and self-esteem (Gonzales and Hancock, 2011).
  - o   *Positive effects of Facebook on self-image and self-esteem.*

All of these experiments involve the manipulation of an independent variable and a measure of the effects on a dependent variable. In all cases, the independent variable is an element of digital technology, whether it's using Facebook, cellphones, the internet, TV or computer games. It's no surprise that this is a common research method when studying the effects of technology on cognitive processes because the true experiment is the most reliable method to use when investigating cause-and-effect relationships between variables. In this case, the researchers want to see if technology actually does *cause* changes in cognition.

Another characteristic that these experiments have in common is that participants were randomly allocated to either treatment or control conditions. This is one of the defining characteristics of true experiments. The ability to randomly allocate participants can reduce the chances for participant variability having an influence on the

You can use studies from the higher level extension to discuss ethical considerations and research methods related to the core topics as well.

Random allocation is a defining characteristic of the true experiment. However, a true experiment could use repeated measures, in which case random allocation is irrelevant.

results. In other words, it reduces the chances that participants in one condition would share a particular characteristic that might confound the results. When measuring the effects of technology on cognitive processes, this strengthens the validity of the conclusions regarding the technology as the cause of change in the cognitive processes.

Along with manipulating an independent variable and random allocation, another defining characteristic of the true experiment is the control of confounding variables. The only experiment in the list above that *didn't* take place in a controlled environment was the kids and the computer training. This is because this particular experiment involved the kids having to go through a five week training course. By conducting the other experiments in controlled environments and having control conditions for comparisons, the researchers can strengthen their conclusions regarding the influence of technology on cognition. For example, by having a drawing group and a slow-paced TV group in the TV and executive function experiment, the researchers could determine the extent to which fast-paced TV caused effects on working memory skills (and not just TV in general).

Perhaps one of the reasons why the true experiment is so popular in studies on the influence of technology on cognition is because this is an issue that affects nearly everyone in the developed world. By conducting well-controlled experiments, stronger conclusions regarding cause-and-effect relationships can be determined. This can provide valuable knowledge not only for the psychological community, but also for the general public. When longitudinal studies are conducted, on the other hand, it is harder to make causal conclusions. This type of study will be the subject of the next section.

> Remember that the terms "true experiment" and "laboratory experiment" can be used interchangeably and refer to the same research method. Perhaps the term laboratory experiment is best used when the experiment actually took place in a lab (e.g. the Facebook and TV studies) and true experiment when it didn't (e.g. the computer training studies).

Guiding Question:

Why are true experiments used to study the effects of technology on cognition?

Critical Thinking Extension:

Application: The answer to this section's guiding question should be pretty straight forward. However, it's important that you can support your answer with an explanation of a specific example. Could you use one of the experiments listed in this section to demonstrate the benefits of using a true experiment?

If you're interested…

Larry Rosen has a really interesting talk on Wisdom 2.0's YouTube channel, called "Technology and the Brain, the Latest Research and Findings." In this talk he summarizes a plethora of fascinating research.

(h)   *Longitudinal Studies*

In the previous section we saw how the true experiment is common when studying the effects of digital technology on cognitive processes. One reason for this is because they enable researchers to isolate the digital technology as the variable that is *causing* a change in cognition. However, one critique of many of these studies could be that they only measure short-term effects. For example, in the Facebook study they were on their Facebook wall for three minutes, and they only watched nine minutes of a fast-paced TV show in the other experiment. The average 2 year old in America, by comparison, watches over two hours of TV a day! Can conducting a test by using such short exposure time really provide us with any relevant insight into the "real" effects of the use of technology on cognitive processes?

This is one benefit of using longitudinal studies that measure correlations between the use of technology and measures of cognitive performances. The reason why longitudinal studies are useful is that they can measure the long-term effects of the use of, and exposure to, digital technology. Whereas the experimental studies often measure effects of short-term exposure, the longitudinal studies enable correlational analyses to be applied to the data to determine the long-term effects of use of technology.

For example, in Christakis et al.'s (2004) study they compared data from when the children were one, three and seven years old. By finding correlations between the hours spent watching TV as a toddler and attentional difficulties as a seven year old, conclusions can be drawn about the long-term negative effects of infants' extended exposure to TV. While it could be argued that these studies can only show correlation and not causation, the statistical tests that are applied to data in these studies can test for effects of known confounding variables, which allows tentative cause-and-effect conclusions to be made.

While experiments may be beneficial for showing short-term effects of technology on cognition, longitudinal studies are valuable for showing long-term effects.

But when does a study become longitudinal? The five week training programme by Klingsberg and colleagues on computer-based training and working memory might be too short to be considered longitudinal. Or is it? A similar study by Toril et al. (2016) was carried out over eight weeks and the researchers labelled this a longitudinal study. The participants in this study also used a computer-based training programme from the company that was sued for false advertising. This was one of the studies that found significant positive effects of the training sessions on measures of working memory capacity and long-term memory.

In summary, studies that use experimental procedures and involve engaging in tasks over a long period of time demonstrate the same benefits as studies like those on TV watching from a young age – they measure the effects of long-term exposure to digital media.

We can see that while an experiment is an effective way to investigate short-term changes in cognition caused by the use of technology, longitudinal studies can help determine effects of long-term use of technology. As with all research, the choice of methodology will be influenced by the aims and the context of the study.

Longitudinal study: a study that is carried out over a long period of time. It allows researchers to measure changes and compare results at different time periods.

Guiding Question:

Why are longitudinal studies useful for studying the effects of digital technology?

Critical Thinking Extension:

Limitations: In this section you've seen the advantages of using longitudinal studies when investigating the effects of technology on cognition. Could you think of any disadvantages of such an approach?

If you're interested…

In his TED Talk, "What makes a good life? Lessons from the longest study on happiness," Robert Waldinger talks about the longest study ever conducted. It is run by Harvard University and began way back in 1938. The study began following over 700 young men from two different areas: Harvard University, and the poor areas in Boston. The study now includes over 2,000 of the kids and grandkids from the participants in this study. While this isn't about technology and cognition, learning the conclusions they've discovered about what makes people happy is well worth the watch.

Conclusion

There will be at least one essay question in Paper One, Part B that asks about one of these topics in the HL extensions.

You may have one, two or all three exam questions in Paper One, Part B that ask about the HL extensions.

The concepts discussed in these HL extension topics are intellectually demanding. This has been deliberate because as an HL student, it's important you're suitably extended and challenged. I still hope they've been enriching, interesting and furthered your skills as a psychologist.

Instead of adding more unrelated content to the course, these HL topics were carefully chosen to deepen your understanding and appreciation of other concepts you've already studied. As with every topic in this book, the materials in this chapter have provided you with more than you need for the IB Psychology exam. Remember that the exams are a random sample of your knowledge, understanding, thinking and communication skills. They don't require you to dump everything in an answer, but rather to demonstrate your abilities. Be critical in selecting the materials in order to prepare to showcase what an expert psychologist you have become.

But besides helping you to ace your exams, it's hoped that what you've learned in these topics will help serve a bigger purpose:

- By having an in-depth comprehension of the immense value animals can provide in explaining and predicting human behaviour, while still being able to consider the ethical implications of such research, you will now be able to make informed judgements about these issues in the sciences.
- Technology will not go away; instead of blindly condemning or consuming it, hopefully you've become more critical of your engagement with technology, and you'll be able to think about the pros and cons of its use and applications.
- Perhaps most importantly, as the world seems to be becoming increasingly divided along superficial differences between groups, it's hoped that you can see how practicing tolerance, acceptance, and inclusion can be an effective weapon in fighting for peace.

What we know about learning and schema is that details of memory fade over time, but the ideas remain. In twenty, ten or even two years' time you might not remember about the TPH-2 gene, but hopefully you'll remember why we need to prevent the abuse of innocent children. You might not remember the details of the gorilla study, but I hope you'll think twice about checking that text while you're driving. And while you might not remember the term "significance loss," you'll hopefully know why tolerance and understanding will always trump discrimination.

As a psychologist and a future citizen who will help to lead the shaping of our global society, you can use these ideas to effect change - both on an individual level, and a societal one.

Chapter 9
Qualitative Methods (HL)

Introduction

Psychology first emerged as a subject when philosophers began questioning the operating of the mind and asking questions about the human psyche. But one obvious problem with trying to study the mind is we can't see what people are thinking. And if we can't see it, how can we study it?

There was a perception that psychology wasn't a real science because the scientific method couldn't be applied to the human mind: how can you test hypotheses about the way we think if it can't be observed? A desire for psychology to be considered a real science led to the popularity of the experimental method because it helped to give credibility to psychological research. By conducting experiments, researchers could gather empirical evidence to test theories. But then the limitations of applying the experimental method to human research required a variety of other research methods to be applied, including case studies, quasi-experiments and correlational studies.

Phenomenon: something that can be observed.

Such quantitative research involves studying the relationship between variables and these variables are quantified. But can human behaviour always be understood by using numbers? Can we really measure the effects of migration on an individual by giving them questionnaires and reducing their human experience to numbers and statistics? Would this really give us an understanding of an individual's subjective experience of being uprooted from one country and moving to another?

Such questions and inherent limitations in quantitative research have led to the increased use of *qualitative* methods in psychological research. Whereas quantitative data refers to numbers and statistics, qualitative data is descriptive. An underlying assumption behind qualitative research is that human behaviour and mental processes are too complex to be understood by using only numbers and statistics; gathering descriptive data can be of value as well because it can provide more detailed insight into human experiences of particular phenomena.

This chapter includes examples of studies that investigate experiences of phenomena such as losing a child, gang-related behaviour, and being diagnosed with a psychological disorder.

Qualitative studies explore individual's experiences of phenomena through a range of methods. In this chapter we'll focus on how and why particular observation and interview methods are used in qualitative research, bearing in mind that case studies (a mixed-methods approach) have already been addressed in chapter six.

Gathering qualitative data and analyzing it to understand human behaviour has its own set of issues, especially those related to researcher bias and objectivity. We naturally interpret information based on our existing knowledge, values and beliefs. There are multiple ways in which researcher bias may influence qualitative research - from the design, gathering and analyzing data all the way to writing the report. These issues will also be explored later in the chapter, with the aim of furthering your understanding of research methods in psychology.

9.1 Qualitative Methods

How and why do researchers use qualitative methods in psychology?

(a) *Naturalistic Observations*

Empirical evidence refers to any evidence gathered through sensory experience, including observation. We've seen how observational data has been gathered in some experimental studies, such as Bandura's true experiment using the Bobo Doll and Sherif et al.'s field experiment at the Robber's Cave Summer Camp.

Whereas these studies involved quantifying the variables they were measuring during their observations, naturalistic observations in qualitative research collate qualitative data. Observations in qualitative research are inherently naturalistic because observations carried out in controlled environments are typically part of experimental studies. During a naturalistic observation the researchers gather their data using field notes.

One of the most famous examples of a qualitative study that used a naturalistic observation is Rosenhan's study that was reported in his article, "On being sane in insane places." In this study his pseudopatients were admitted to psychiatric hospitals after reporting symptoms of hearing voices in their heads. After being admitted to the hospitals they began taking their field notes. The pseudopatients (i.e. the researchers) were observing the behaviour of the hospital staff and patients in their natural environment of the hospital, and making general observational notes on the experience of being a patient in a psychiatric hospital.

Rosenhan's study demonstrates another important aspect of naturalistic observations, which is that they may be overt or covert. An overt observation is when the subjects are aware that they are being observed as part of a study. Rosenhan's study was a covert observation, as the hospital staff and patients were *unaware* that they were being observed as part of a psychological study.

Another characteristic of naturalistic observations is that they may be a participant or a non-participant observation. A participant observation is when the researcher becomes a member of the group they're observing in order to get an insider's perspective on the phenomenon under investigation. A famous example of a covert, participant, naturalistic observation was carried out by Leon Festinger and his colleagues called "When Prophecy Fails." These researchers joined members of a cult group who believed the earth was going to end. They were interested in observing the reactions of the members of the group when the date passed for the end of the world and their prophecy had failed. The researchers pretended to be believers in order to become a part of this group and make their observations of their reactions. There are obviously some ethical considerations involved in covert observations and these will be explored in the next topic.

An example of an overt naturalistic observation was carried out by Sudhir Venkatesh, a social scientist who was originally studying gangs in Chicago as a researcher's assistant. He was collecting data by going around South Chicago and asking gang members questions. After being held hostage because one group thought

Field notes: descriptive observational notes that a researcher takes while in the field.

Examples of qualitative studies are cited throughout this chapter. However, these are for illustrative purposes only: you do not need to remember these for Paper Three. What is needed is an understanding of key terms and an ability to apply them to an example study.

he was a spy for a rival gang, they convinced Venkatesh that he could not understand their experiences by asking them silly questions from surveys; he had to live their life and see the world through their eyes (Venkatesh, 2008).

Venkatesh published a book about his experiences called, "Gang Leader for a Day."

This final example demonstrates what we've seen in quantitative studies: sometimes the distinctions between methods are not black-and-white. One could argue that Venkatesh's was a participant observation, because Venkatesh tried to immerse himself in the gang culture in order to gain a better perspective of what their life was like. However, the extent to which he became a member of the gang could be disputed. Nevertheless, it provides a good example of one benefit of the participant observation in qualitative research – it enables researchers to be able to experience particular phenomena (in this case life as a gang member and the perspectives of community members towards the gangs) from the perspective of the subjects of the observation.

The experiences of individuals you've seen in these three examples, including life as a gang member, belonging to a cult and living in psychiatric hospital, might be difficult to quantify and measure using experimental or correlational methods. These examples demonstrate one benefit of qualitative research – descriptive data can be gathered to provide an insight into the subjective experiences of subjects in naturalistic environments.

These are the "projects" in Southside Chicago where Venkatesh conducted his research.

In summary, naturalistic observations involve researchers taking field notes and gathering data on subjects' real life behaviour in naturalistic settings. The key characteristics of a naturalistic observation are:

- Subjects' naturally occurring behaviour is observed in their natural environment.
- Field notes and other data gathering techniques (e.g. videos) may be used.
- The observation may be covert or overt, participant or non-participant.
- Observations are sometimes followed by interviews with subjects.

Guiding Question:

Why might a naturalistic observation be used in a qualitative study?

Critical Thinking Extension:

Later in this chapter we will explore issues related to researcher bias in qualitative research. Can you think of how researcher bias could potentially influence naturalistic observational studies?

If you're interested...

You can watch an interview on YouTube with Venkatesh in which he describes his research on gang culture. He has also written a book about the experience called "Gang Leader for a Day." You can read more about Festinger's study online as well and Wikipedia has a summary of the events of the night when the world was supposed to end.

(b) Unstructured Interviews

In the previous section you were introduced to a common method in qualitative studies, naturalistic observations. Interviews are another common method used to gather data in qualitative studies. In psychological research they involve a researcher asking questions of participants while recording and then analyzing the responses. In the following sections we'll explore three different types of interviews: unstructured, semi-structured and focus group interviews.

Unstructured Interview: a style of interview that has topics to cover, but allows flexibility in the order and content of the questions.

The first type of interview method we'll look at is the unstructured interview, which arose from studies in sociology and anthropology. It resembles a conversation more than a formal Q&A style interview. Do not be fooled by the name – all interviews have at least some type of structure. Even in an unstructured interview "the researcher has a number of topics to cover" (Breakwell et al., 2001, p.240). The difference is that the "…precise questions and their order are not fixed" (ibid). In this method the interview evolves as a result of the interactions and discussions between the interviewer and the interviewee. Whereas structured interviews have prescribed and closed questions, unstructured interviews use open-ended questions that allow the interviewee to say as much or as little as they choose.

They may also form an extension of a naturalistic observation as the researchers triangulate their observational data with interview data (Patton, 2002). Unstructured interviews may be focused, which means the interviewer would be aware of any time the interviewee is deviating from the subject matter of interest. If this happened they might try to use their interviewing skills to guide the interviewee back towards the topic of interest.

On the other hand, an unstructured interview might not require focus on a particular topic. It may instead have the general aim of gathering in-depth information. In this instance, a researcher may not have any pre-planned set of questions and would be happy to let the conversation evolve naturally. This latter technique may be valuable when gathering information in an area that the researcher knows little about. (Jamshed, 2014). As with other research methods, the nature and style of the interview would depend on the aims and context of the study

Unstructured interviews allow a lot of flexibility for the researcher when asking questions, and even greater flexibility for the participant when providing answers.

An example of a social scientist using unstructured interviews can be seen in Prowse's (2012) use of unstructured interviews when studying street gangs. In order to understand the world of street gangs, a range of people were interviewed. These interviewees had different connections to the gangs, such as being members, informants, victims, associates or investigators. The general topics for the interview were chosen based on the characteristics of the participants being interviewed. This study also highlights another benefit of using interviews as well as other methods, such as observations; Prowse reports that the interviews enabled areas of uncertainty or perceived contradictions that had been observed in field studies to be followed-up with and clarified in interviews. The interviews themselves also became "thematic" as particular topics arose as the focus during the evolution of the discussion.

In qualitative research the goal isn't necessarily to investigate relationships between variables and behaviour. Often the goal is to uncover and understand participants' experiences of particular phenomena, such as belonging to a street gang. Being able to ask open-ended questions and have natural discussions with participants allows researchers to gain an insight into the perspectives and experiences of the participants that would be impossible with other methods like a quantitative questionnaire.

To summarize, the key characteristics of an unstructured interview are:

- The interviewer has topics to cover, but the precise questions and order is flexible and not fixed.
- The interview evolves as a result of the social interaction of the researcher and the participant.
- It involves asking open-ended questions.
- It is likely to resemble a conversation more than a formal interview.

Characteristics are summarized because the first question in Paper Three will require you to identify the method used in the stimulus study and outline two characteristics of the method. The study could be quantitative, qualitative or mixed-methods, so it is important that you can remember at least two of the key characteristics of each of the methods and you can identify them from the summary provided. It is a good idea to remember three characteristics, so you're safe if you forget one on exam day.

The terms interviewee, participant and subject can be used interchangeably in the context of discussing qualitative interviews.

Guiding Question:

Why might an unstructured interview be used in qualitative research?

Critical Thinking Extension:

Triangulation: An important concept in qualitative research is triangulation. One type of triangulation is methodological triangulation: using more than one method to gather data. Why might it be beneficial to conduct an unstructured interview alongside naturalistic observations? You may want to think about Venkatesh's, Festinger's or Rosenhan's research to help you with this question.

If you're interested...

Yale University's YouTube channel has a series of videos explaining qualitative research methods, including the use of interviews. These are informative, more than they are interesting.

(c)   Semi-Structured Interviews

We saw in the previous lesson how interviews can be used to provide additional information to clarify questions that arise from naturalistic observations. An unstructured interview resembles a discussion and is often referred to as a guided discussion. As the name suggests, there is less structure in an unstructured interview than a structured one. This might be useful for a number of reasons, including allowing subjects to freely communicate their experiences and ideas.

But if a researcher had a very specific set of issues or topics that they would like to discuss, an unstructured interview may not be suitable. Similarly, if they wanted to compare responses to particular questions across a range of participants, the unstructured interview method may not be the best method. They may instead use a semi-structured interview. The structure in this interview method comes in the form of the interview schedule that is planned beforehand. This guide includes the general themes or topics that the researcher wants to cover in the actual interview, and perhaps loosely formed questions or general areas of discussion. The interview will consist of a range of questions, including open-ended questions that allow for the interviewees to provide detailed responses, as well as more directed and closed questions for gathering specific information.

In a semi-structured interview, the researcher asks a combination of open and closed questions, and they are free to prompt the interviewee and go in to more depth depending on the responses provided by the participants. This flexibility is what allows for a lot of valuable data to be collected. As with an unstructured interview, it also results in the interview resembling more of an informal conversation and a discussion, rather than a formal interview.

An example of the use of a semi-structured interview used in a qualitative study was Kistin et al.'s (2014) study on parenting. Individual, semi-structured interviews were carried out on 30 traumatized, low-income mothers to gather data on their experiences of parenting. One aim of the study was to gain an understanding of how stressors in the mothers' lives may influence their approach to disciplining their children, as harsh disciplining is a risk factor for maltreatment of kids. The interview schedule consisted of general and open-ended questions that were followed by probing questions. An example of an open-ended question the interviewers asked was "Can you describe a typical day for me?" This was then followed by probing questions that were designed to elicit data about the parent's relationship with their child, their interactions, and how they coped as parents. For example, one probing question was "Can you think of a time with your child when you felt like you were going to lose it?" Further probes were written in the interview schedule, and these included questions based on getting more information about

Experiences of parenting and motherhood is a common subject of qualitative studies.

Semi-structured interview: this has more structure than an unstructured interview as there is a series of topics and questions to be addressed in the interview. There still exists flexibility to explore areas of interest as they arise in the course of the interview.

Interview schedule: the series of questions to be asked and topics to be covered that is prepared before the interview takes place.

settings, feelings and thoughts (about the incident revealed from the initial question). The use of the interview schedule means that similar topics were discussed with all participants, which enables comparisons of responses and general themes regarding these topics to be deduced.

The researchers were also interested in understanding the experiences of these mothers as they had experienced trauma in their past. Perhaps for ethical considerations, the interview guide did not prompt the interviewers to ask questions related to trauma. However, if this was brought up organically in the course of the interview they asked the participant to elaborate. This is a good example of the benefit of having an interview schedule: ensuring particular questions are asked will enable comparisons to be made across participants, but having the freedom to ask follow-up questions based on responses can help to elicit information that wasn't expected and may not have been revealed in a structured interview.

This study provides a good example of the value of qualitative research and semi-structured interviews as parenting is a highly subjective and personal experience. The researchers in this case had particular areas of interest that they wanted to explore and they had the aim of making comparisons and general conclusions across participants. This may have been why they chose a semi-structured interview, as opposed to an unstructured one.

To recap, the key characteristics of the semi-structured interview are:

- It follows a general interview schedule that has been pre-prepared.
  o This ensures similar topics are addressed in each interview, allowing for comparisons to be made across participants.
- It asks a combination of open and closed questions.
- The interviewer has freedom to ask additional questions and/or provide prompts.
- It resembles a conversation.

Guiding Question:

Why might a semi-structured interview be used in a qualitative study?

Critical Thinking Extension:

There are a number of factors that could influence an interviewee's responses during an interview. Data in qualitative interviews is reliant on interviewees giving open and honest responses that can provide detailed information for the researchers. Can you think of any factors that may influence the responses of participants during an interview? Imagine you were one of the mothers in the study above: what might influence how detailed, open and/or honest you were in your responses?

If you're interested…

Kistin et al.'s full study can be found online. It's called "A Qualitative Study of Parenting Stress, Coping, and Discipline Approaches Among Low-Income Traumatized Mothers." Reading examples of qualitative studies can help make abstract ideas a little more concrete. You can also see some of their materials they used, including a sample of their interview schedule.

(d)   Focus Group Interviews

The term rich is often used to describe qualitative data. It refers to the detail, relevance and value of the information gathered. Rich data allows in-depth analysis.

A focus group interview is an interview conducted in a small group, usually around 6 to 10 people.

Interviews are a valuable method for researchers to gather data on individuals' experiences of phenomena. When conducted by a well-trained and skilled interviewer, they can provide rich data. One of the possible limitations of conducting individual interviews, however, is that participants may be reluctant to share their experiences in a one-on-one setting. This is one reason why a focus group interview method might be beneficial. A focus group interview is an interview that occurs with a small group of participants. The interviewer in these interviews acts as a facilitator of the group discussion.

Focus groups can be valuable in qualitative research because they promote group interaction and this may encourage participants to reveal information in a way that might not happen in a one-on-one interview. For example, if someone is quite shy and may not want to express an opinion about a certain topic, they may be encouraged by hearing someone else discuss it first. This could give them more confidence to share their own thoughts. Perhaps by hearing the views and opinions of others, participants may be prompted to reflect on their own experiences as well. They may think of something to share because of what someone else has said. This type of social facilitation of a discussion may not happen in an individual interview. How the group members share opinions and discuss perspectives can also provide valuable insight for the researchers.

An example of focus group interviews in use can be seen in North et al.'s (2014) qualitative study on the experiences of New York workers during and after the 9/11 attacks. In order to gather a broader perspective on the range of effects this event might have had on people working at ground zero and other places around New York City, the researchers conducted a series of 21 focus group interviews with a total of 141 different participants. They formed their focus groups based on the location of the company where the participants worked. That is to say, there were focus groups made up of people that were working in companies at ground zero and in the tower at the time of the attack. Other focus groups were made up of people working in companies located a couple of blocks away from the towers. The sample was a volunteer sample, as people offered to participate after hearing about the study from their companies. There was one interviewer who ran all 21 focus groups in a "nondirective fashion" and "groups were given initial introduction on the purpose of the groups, and broad instructions were provided to elicit spontaneous discussion of members' thoughts, perceptions, feelings, responses, and concerns related to their experience of the 9/11 terrorist attacks" (ibid). The focus groups lasted for about an hour and they were recorded. As with all qualitative methods, after the focus group interviews were conducted the data was analyzed to find recurring themes.

Focus groups are facilitated by an interviewer, but rely on the interactions of group members to produce rich data.

In the context of this research it might be easy to see how a focus group might encourage participants to share their experiences. The 9/11 attacks were traumatic for many people and some may be reluctant to share their full experiences with a researcher in an individual setting. By being supported by others in the room who have been through something similar, they may have more confidence to share experiences. On the other hand, it might also be that some people may be less inclined to talk in front of others.

Another example of focus groups in qualitative research was carried out by Kim et al. (2016) who conducted a study with the aim of gaining a deeper insight into the relationship between playing free social gambling games on social media sites and migrating to real online gambling. You may have seen in your own social media use how online gambling companies create gambling apps and games that can be played for free. The hope of these games is to hook users into the gambling experience and encourage them to migrate to real online gambling games. In this study, three focus groups on a total of 30 participants were carried out in order to understand this phenomenon from the users' perspectives. The groups consisted of a mix of young college males and females from two Canadian universities, all of whom had not played the "real" online gambling. The focus groups were conducted and recorded and afterwards the data was analyzed in order to find recurring themes and draw conclusions.

One of the these themes was the fact there was a "great deal of resentment expressed over how Facebook now charges money to players for certain games in order to prolong their play and thus be more competitive" (ibid). While it's not described in the study, this could be the sort of idea that is raised by one member of a focus group. One member of the group may raise this concern and then others may agree and this prompts a discussion in this particular area. The extent to which others in the group agree with the statement and share similar views could lead researchers to make the interpretation of there being a "great deal" of resentment.

In summary, focus group interviews rely on group processes and interactions to help elicit rich data from participants based on their experiences of a phenomenon. The key characteristics of a focus group are:

- They are an interview that consists of a group of interviewees (usually around 6 to 10 people).
- They rely on group processes and the interaction of the individuals within the group to help reveal information that might not be shared in individual interviews.
- The interviewer acts as a moderator of the interview and it resembles an informal group discussion. An interview schedule would still be used in a focus group interview.

> Remember that you do not need to remember these studies for Paper Three. They are described to help you understand qualitative methodology.

Guiding Question:

Why might a focus group interview be a valuable method in a qualitative study?

Critical Thinking Extension:

Later in this chapter we'll look at ways to evaluate qualitative research. As the data is quite different to quantitative studies, our approach to evaluation needs to be different as well. In an experiment, one way to measure validity is to assess the extent that extraneous variables may have influenced the results. How do you think "validity" might be assessed in qualitative studies?

If you're interested...

TEDEd has an informative video called "How Focus Groups Work." It provides some interesting history of the focus group interview, including the researchers who pioneered the approach in post-WWII studies. It also explains their use in market research, which is a common way focus groups are used. If you watch "The Simpsons", the episode where Poochy joins the Itchy and Scratchy show also demonstrates the use of a focus group in market research.

9.2 Sampling Methods
How do we gather participants for qualitative studies?

(a)   Snowball Sampling

Snowball sampling is a type of non-probability, convenience sampling. Seeds are used to identify possible participants.

Probability sampling: using sampling methods where all members of the population have an equal chance of participating in the study. Random sampling is an example of probability sampling. Opportunity sampling is a non-probability sampling method.

Seed: a person encouraged by researchers to find other participants to join the study.

In the previous topic we explored a range of observation and interview methods that are commonly used in qualitative studies. As with quantitative research, we need participants from whom to gather our data. In this topic we'll explore two sampling methods that are common in qualitative studies: snowball sampling and purposive sampling.

The goal of gathering data from a sample in quantitative studies is to draw conclusions that can be generalized beyond the sample. To achieve this aim, researchers may use probability sampling methods to ensure that their sample is representative of the target population. However, the aim of qualitative research isn't necessarily to generalize findings from the study to a wider population. For this reason, different sampling methods may be used.

A common sampling method used in qualitative studies is snowball sampling. If we say something is "snowballing," it means it's gradually getting bigger, like a cartoon image of a snowball rolling down a snowy mountain and gradually increasing in size. This is how a snowball sample works: the sample size gradually increases as a small group of initial participants invite others to take part in the study. These initial participants who ask others to join the study are called seeds. When new participants are found, they are also encouraged to recommend others to participate. This continues until the desired sample size is reached.

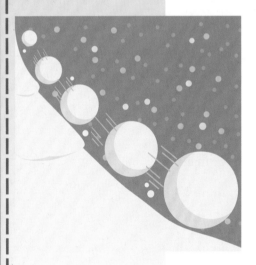

The snowball metaphor that gives this sampling method its name can be seen in this image.

This method can be a useful way for researchers to gather participants, especially if the participants are from environments or situations that make them difficult for researchers to get to agree to participate in a study. For example, if a researcher was conducting a study related to participation in illegal activities (e.g. drug addiction or prostitution) participants may not be willing to come forward to participate. By having people known to potential participants approach them and encourage them to participate, researchers can gather participants from hidden populations (Faugier and Sargeant, 1997).

Snowball sampling may be valuable for studying hidden populations for other reasons as well. In order to conduct a random sample, the researchers need to have a list of all potential participants. With some groups, such as homeless people or illegal immigrants, this list would be impossible to obtain. Self-selected/volunteer sampling might not work either, as there might be a stigma attached to the characteristic of interest to the researchers. For instance, if a researcher wanted to study males suffering from depression or the use of banned substances by ex-professional athletes, potential participants may not feel comfortable volunteering to talk to a complete stranger to about their issues and experiences. However, having a friend or someone they know tell them about the study might encourage them to come forward and share their experiences.

Another limitation in a self-selected sample could be that it might be difficult to reach the intended participants with the advertising materials needed for a volunteer sample. For instance, if a researcher was interested in studying homeless people, a volunteer sample might not work because they may struggle to contact the researcher even if they could see the information about the study.

Another example that employed a snowball sample was Sulaiman-Hill and Thompson's (2011) study on refugees in Australia and New Zealand. In their mixed-methods approach they used qualitative interviews and quantitative questionnaires to study "socially invisible refugee groups" of Afghan and Kurdish origin in Australia and NZ. In order to make comparisons between the groups, quantitative question-naires were used. Qualitative interviews were used to understand their experiences of adjusting and settling into their new homes. These researchers opted for a snowball sample because "former refugee communities may be socially invisible and wary of outsiders" (Ibid). To make sure that their sample was as representative as possible, the researchers used a range of seeds so that a wide range of participants could be approached to make up the sample.

As with other elements of research design, decisions made regarding how to obtain a suitable sample will depend on the nature of the study being conducted. While it may be limited in terms of representativeness, and could be prone to sampling bias, snowball sampling provides researchers with a viable option of finding participants that may be hard for them to contact.

The key characteristics of a snowball sample are:

- A small group of initial participants (called seeds) invite others whom they think would be suitable participants.
- Participants continue to invite others, until the desired sample size has been reached.
- It is particularly useful for studying hidden populations and other groups of people that may be hard to reach.
- It is based more on convenience and may be susceptible to sampling bias.

While snowball sampling is common in qualitative studies with small groups, it's important to note that it may also be used in quantitative research. As you first come to understand qualitative and quantitative research, it can be useful to see the distinctions between these two approaches, including methods common to either approach. However, it's also important to explore the overlaps between the approaches and methods and to realize that studies do not necessarily fall into one category or another. For instance, researchers may adopt a mixed-methods approach, which means combining qualitative *and* quantitative methods.

Hidden Population: a group of people that are hard to contact or reach. They remain socially "out of sight." Examples include minority immigrant populations or those engaging in underground and/or illegal activities, like drug dealing or gang-related activities.

Guiding Question:

Why might a researcher use snowball sampling in a qualitative study?

Critical Thinking Extension:

There are pros and cons to using different methods in research. In this lesson we've focused on the benefits of a snowball sampling method. Can you think of potential limitations in using a snowball sample? If we think about the above study on refugees, how might the nature of this sampling method influence the accuracy of the researchers findings based on experiences of immigrants to these countries?

Snowball sampling is similar in a way to word-of-mouth marketing and the phenomenon of things "going viral" in our digital world. Kevin Allocca is a professional YouTube watcher (yes, that's a real job!) and he explains why things go viral and why this matters in his brief TED Talk, "Why videos go viral." This is loosely related to qualitative research, but it's interesting nonetheless.

(b) Purposive Sampling

Purposive Sampling: when the researcher recruits participants that have a particular set of characteristics that are relevant for the study.

In the previous section you were introduced to a non-representative sampling method, snowball sampling. As with other choices to make when designing and carrying out studies, researchers need to consider multiple factors in their decisions. Snowball sampling can be a convenient means of gathering participants from hidden or hard to reach populations. One of the limitations of relying on snowball sampling, however, is that the researchers give up an element of control over who participates in the study. This may be an issue if researchers desire participants who have a particular set of characteristics. In such a study a purposive sample may be a more suitable means of gathering participants.

If something is purposive it means it's done with a purpose, so when purposive sampling the researchers deliberately (and purposefully) select and recruit participants for their study because they possess particular characteristics that are of interest to the researchers. This recruitment may happen through contacting participants directly, through advertising, or perhaps by having possible participants referred. And in fact, a purposive sample may have an element of snowballing: researchers may use seeds that have particular characteristics and instruct them to ask others who share those same characteristics.

An example can be seen in Sutan and Miskam's study (2012) that used a purposive sample in their qualitative study on Muslim mothers who had experienced perinatal loss (the death a baby either before or just after birth). The study investigated the psychological and social impacts of this loss through qualitative interviews. The researchers wanted to gather a sample that included a range of ages and previous experience with perinatal loss, so they recruited participants after selecting them from a list provided by the hospital. In this instance, we can see that sometimes researchers may want to choose their participants because of particular characteristics that would make them suitable for their study. In this case it was based on getting a range of ages and experiences. Purposive sampling may also prove beneficial if the characteristics of interest are rare in a general population.

A purposive sample can also be gathered by relying on referrals by others. This can be seen in studies that investigate the psychological effects of disasters on children (e.g. Norris, 2006). In these studies samples may be quite large and the children may be asked by researchers to participate in their study by a number of different methods. For example, the researchers may contact the school counsellors or psychologists in a particular district that has experienced a natural disaster. They would inform them of the intended study, including its aims and requirements. In this instance, school

Purposive sampling is used when researchers want to gather participants who have particular experiences that the researchers want to learn about. People who have experienced a natural disaster may be part of a purposive sample.

counsellors would be able to identify potential participants in the research and could inform the children and their parents about the study. If they were interested, their details may be given to the researchers who would contact them about participating.

Purposive sampling may also be used in case studies. For example, SM was selected because of the unique damage to her amygdalae. Another example is Hoagwood et al's study on a ten year old boy after experiencing the loss of his uncle in the September 11th attacks in the USA (2007). The experiences of this particular boy were recorded and reported to provide clinicians and child psychiatrists with an understanding of the typical experiences for a child going through emotional trauma in the aftermath of the attacks. Because he had common characteristics and experiences, he was chosen by the clinicians to represent a typical case.

These are just some examples of information rich cases that researchers might seek to participate in a study. Purposive sampling is mainly used in qualitative and mixed-methods approaches because of the obvious risk of researcher bias. Whereas the aim in a quantitative study is to ensure generalizability of results, qualitative studies typically seek a depth of understanding of subjective experiences of phenomena (e.g. experiencing a particular trauma). For this reason, sometimes it is necessary to recruit and select participants that have the best opportunity for providing valuable data in which to conduct the investigation.

In summary, the key characteristics of a purposive sample are:

- Participants are asked to participate by the researchers because they share characteristics that are of interest to the study, such as knowledge or experience of particular phenomena.
- They may be recruited through a range of methods, such as advertising, direct contact or by being referred by someone else (e.g. school counsellor, hospital, or social worker).
- It may use snowballing.
- It is a non-representative sample and there is a chance of researcher bias.

> If a case is information rich it means it has the potential to provide the researchers with detailed information relevant to the aims of their study.

Guiding Question:

Why might purposive sampling be used in qualitative research?

Critical Thinking Extension:
Application: Because of the risk of researcher bias and the aim of generalizability, experimental methods rarely use purposive sampling methods. However, in some schools when students are conducting an internal assessment there may be circumstances that result in a purposive sample being the most appropriate choice. Can you think of when a purposive sample in an IA experiment might be more appropriate than other methods?

If you're interested...

You can find a full article explaining purposive sampling methods on PubMed Central called "Purposeful sampling for qualitative data collection and analysis in mixed method implementation research." I realize this may not interest most students, but you never know.

9.3 Ethical Considerations

How are ethics relevant to qualitative and quantitative studies?

(a) Carrying Out the Study

See the Exam Preparation chapter for the Paper Three questions that will be relevant to ethics and research.

Research methods and ethical considerations are recurring themes throughout this course. Understanding multiple possible ways in which to consider ethics in research is also essential for Higher Level students as this will form the basis of the second question in your Paper Three exam. The primary purpose of this topic, therefore, is not so much to introduce new information but to further your understanding of the multiple ways in which ethical considerations may be relevant to psychological studies.

Along with informed consent and the right to withdraw, having a study approved by an ethics review committee and debriefing participants are common practice in all studies. It is hoped that you have been thinking about the relevance of these ethical considerations throughout the course and practicing explaining their relevance to examples of research. Along with these considerations, anonymity and parental consent are common to many studies.

Retrospective consent: getting permission from participants to analyze and report findings after the data has been gathered.

However, the nature of the methods used in the study may alter how ethical guidelines are applied. With some qualitative methods, it may not be appropriate to obtain informed consent. For instance, if a researcher is conducting a covert observation it would defeat the purpose entirely if they sought informed consent. This is one instance where retrospective consent may be more relevant. To be retrospective means to look at something after it has happened (your perspective is looking back on the thing that just happened). This is a consideration particular to covert observations because in a covert observation it is not practical or even feasible to get informed consent from participants before or during the observation because then their "cover" would be blown and the covert observation would no longer be covert. So researchers might seek retrospective consent, which means the participants are informed of the study *after* it has taken place and agree to the data being analyzed and published.

Ethics in psychology is about understanding and considering how research may impact others. How would you feel if you were being observed during class without knowing about it?

As with quantitative studies, in qualitative studies participants are given the right to withdraw from the study. This could mean that they refuse to participate any more. It might also mean that they withdraw their data after the study has been conducted. Researchers can also share their interpretations and conclusions with interviewees and give them the right to make clarifications about what they have said. For instance, Kistin et al.'s (2014) study on parenting, trauma and coping strategies may have involved a follow-up interview where the researcher summarized the interview, asked for points of clarification and revealed their analyses of the parent's experiences. This process ensures accuracy of the research and offers participants the right to withdraw data or responses from the final report.

As you can see, most of the ethical guidelines that are recommended by psychological organizations could be applied to an explanation of ethics related to carrying out any study.

Guiding Question:

What ethical considerations are relevant to carrying out any study?

Critical Thinking Extension:

In order to achieve top marks in Paper Three it is important that you can apply your knowledge to the study presented in the stimulus material. You may also be asked about ethical considerations in relation to topics in the core and/or options. Therefore, a good way to prepare for all three papers is to use key studies that you're already familiar with as practice stimulus material for Paper Three. Find one such study and see if you could explain how particular considerations would be relevant to that study.

If you're interested…

Milgram's study on obedience to authority is a classic when discussing the debate between ethics and contributing to our body of knowledge in psychology. Apa.org has an interesting article about the replications of Milgram's experiments called, "Replicating Milgram."

(b)   Reporting Findings

In the previous section we reviewed a range of relevant ethical considerations that may be relevant to carrying out a study. Considering the possible impact of research is at the heart of understanding the role of ethics in psychology. When studying quantitative methods, our focus has been mostly on the impact this may have during the data gathering and analysis stages of the report. However, research may also have an impact during the reporting and/or the application of findings from a study.

In this section we'll examine ethics regarding reporting the results of a study. There are different ways researchers may report results of their study: we will focus on the most obvious one, which is through the actual article that is written about the study and published in a psychological journal. You should be familiar with what these articles look like, especially if you've already conducted your IA.

The most obvious consideration in reporting results is anonymity, which may be defined as the state of having names and identifiable characteristics removed (or changed) from data and all reporting documentation. This is to ensure that the person/s involved cannot be identified. When reporting results, participants should remain anonymous, like HM, SM and KF. Another example could be seen in Hoagwood et al.'s study on the ten year old boy's experiences after September 11th. In this case anonymity would be necessary to protect the well-being of the child. For example, he may become the subject of bullying if other kids his age found out about his psychological troubles.

Reporting findings can be done in psychological journal articles, in media interviews or in other mediums. For example, some psychologists may report their findings of evidence to support treatments they have developed.

Along with anonymity, debriefing is also an essential consideration related to reporting the results as it occurs after a study has happened and involves the researchers informing the participants about the full aims and results of the study. During the debriefing process the researchers would need to consider how much and what type of information they reveal to the participants. In order to gather valid and accurate results, some information may have been withheld from participants, or they may have been deceived. Participants should be debriefed in full, which includes explaining how, why and where the researchers intend to report the findings.

Psychologists report their findings when they publish their articles in journals. You would have read at least one of these journals when researching for your IA.

On the other hand, participants may be informed of how researchers intend to report findings before the study commences when giving informed consent. For example, if a study is being conducted as part of a larger parent study or part of a longitudinal study, researchers would need to consider the implications of revealing this information to participants before the study takes place. It may be that the researchers have the intention of keeping data on record for an extended period of time for later reports, which should be revealed to participants. For example, in studies such as the Vietnam Head Injury Study, the data becomes part of an on-going collection of data to be used in future studies. Keeping information on file to be used for future reports has particular ethical issues. This may also apply for methods such as interviews and observations where recording devices are used. If material is to be kept on file for future use, participants should ideally be informed before the study begins.

Confidentiality: being kept secret or private. Confidentiality may refer to various aspects of a study, including participation or information revealed during the study.

Confidentiality is another ethical consideration that goes hand-in-hand with debriefing and informed consent when reporting results. Researchers obviously cannot keep all data confidential or else they'd have nothing to report. However, it may be the case in some studies that participants have revealed information to the researchers that they do not want shared with anyone else. For example, a drug addict might reveal in an interview particular experiences with the researcher. A relationship of trust may have been established and information was provided simply to give the researcher a deeper insight into an underground and private world. The participant may, however, request this information be kept confidential and that it is not to be shared with others, including in the final report.

If confidentiality has been promised to participants, researchers need to honour this when they are reporting results. Confidentiality also applies to the participation of the study: some participants may not want others to know that they are taking part in a study and so this could be a factor for the researchers to consider.

Similarly, the right to withdraw data is also a relevant consideration in reporting results from studies. If participants have been offered the right to withdraw their data from the study, this right must be honored. They may, for instance, wish to have removed responses or information that was uncovered through the course of the study. For example, in Sutan and Miskam's study (2012) on Muslim women and their experiences of perinatal loss the mothers may have revealed experiences in their interviews that they later thought were too personal. If they have asked to withdraw their responses from the data, the researchers have an ethical obligation to uphold their promise to withdraw data from the final report. Regardless of the effects on the research process, these assurances offered to participants must be upheld.

As well as agreeing not to publish information that has been requested to be withdrawn or kept confidential, researchers must also report all results that have been included for final analysis, even those that weren't of significance or were outliers to the original hypotheses. It may be tempting for researches to "fudge the numbers" or to ignore data that are inconsistent with their hypotheses or beliefs. However, when reporting results researchers need to maintain their integrity by including all suitable data for analysis.

Perhaps researcher triangulation could help with maintaining researcher integrity throughout the process. If researchers are unsure of their conclusions, having another researcher analyze the data can strengthen the validity and credibility of the conclusions. It would be more ethical to submit a report for publication that has been reviewed by multiple researchers in this way.

Another interesting ethical consideration that we haven't explored before is the fact that in their report researchers should disclose potential conflicts of interests in the study. A conflict of interest in this context might be when a researcher has two potential goals that may be in competition with one another. For example, if a drug trial has been funded by a pharmaceutical company, it may be ethically questionable to not disclose this information to the public. The researcher has conflicting interests: on the one hand they want to maintain scientific rigour in their study. On the other, they may be conscious of having funding cut off, affecting their ability to carry out further research. If a study has received funding from any institution this information should be disclosed.

It could be argued that researchers have ethical considerations regarding integrity when they are reporting their findings in other media, not just published articles. Popular media has a tendency to sensationalize and dramatize psychological research. If a psychologist was seeking fame and wanted to make a name for themselves, they could potentially use this to their advantage when reporting findings to the popular media. Keeping academic integrity to avoid wrongfully informing people of research through mass media is an important academic and ethical consideration. Do note, however, that this final point is mentioned here more for interest than for exam preparation.

Integrity: the quality of being honest and having good character.

Researcher triangulation: having more than one researcher collect, analyze or review data and conclusions.

To disclose means to reveal or make something known. A conflict of interest is when someone has two goals that are in opposition with one another.

There is some evidence to suggest that research sponsored by a drug company is more likely to have outcomes that are favourable to the drug company (Lexchin, 2003).

Guiding Question:

How can ethical guidelines be applied when reporting results?

Critical Thinking Extension:

In order to practice applying knowledge of ethical considerations to existing studies, think of a study you are familiar with from the course and try explaining why they should consider one of these ethical guidelines when reporting the findings of their results. Some examples could include Rosenhan's study on psychiatric institutions, Zimbardo's Stanford Prison Experiment, or MacNamara et al.'s study on the effectiveness of SSRIs to treat PTSD.

If you're interested...

There is another type of bias that can influence our collective knowledge and understanding in psychology: reporting bias (a.k.a. publication bias). If research fails to achieve results that are statistically significant, they probably won't be published. But if a variable *doesn't* influence a behaviour, isn't that just as valuable to know? An interesting article on the subject can be found at nature.com, called "Social sciences suffer from severe publication bias."

(c)   Applying Findings

The previous section aimed to show you how a range of possible considerations may be relevant for the reporting of results. Of those discussed earlier, anonymity, debriefing, keeping promises of confidentiality and withdrawing data are probably the most likely to be relevant to consider when reporting findings.

Do remember, however, that an *ethical consideration* doesn't necessarily have to be considering how an ethical *guideline* will be applied in a study. There may be ethical considerations that do not have a particular guideline associated with them. You may be able to simply describe what a researcher may need to consider in order to ensure their reporting is modelling appropriate ethical conduct in psychological research. For example, in a study related to different ethnic groups there may be labels assigned to describe different groups of people. The researcher would need to consider the most appropriate and inoffensive label to use. They may consult members of different groups for advice and guidance. For example, would they report "whites" and "blacks?" Or, "Caucasians" and "African Americans?" This is a relevant ethical consideration, although it doesn't necessarily fit with a specific guideline. While this point isn't directly relevant to reporting findings, perhaps, it does illustrate the fact that ethical *considerations* can go beyond just ethical *guidelines*.

There are also some generic ethical guidelines that are relevant to applying findings from studies. For instance, if the researchers are conducting a study with the aim of applying their findings in a particular way, they would need to consider including this in the consent form they use when obtaining informed consent. For example, if a twin study was being conducted to see if hippocampal volume was a symptom or etiology of PTSD in order to screen future military recruits, this information should be disclosed to participants as they may not want to contribute to a research with this purpose. However, it might not always be feasible to disclose such information before a study. In the natural experiment on the Fiji islands with the introduction of TV, for instance, if the researchers revealed the aims of the study to the participants it may affect their thinking and the validity of the results.

While the nature of the extent of disclosure in the informed consent form may be considered before the study begins, this may only be relevant if the researchers already know how they intend to apply findings. As a researcher may hypothesize but cannot fully predict their results, it might be that debriefing is more relevant to applying findings from research. If a study reveals a particular set of results that may be applied in a particular way, researchers may wish to consider revealing this information to participants during debriefing.

For example, there have been studies conducted to improve the eye-witness testimony procedures. If the aims of these studies were told beforehand it may confound the results by causing partici-pant expectancy effects. However, if such a study was conducted with the intent of trialing the effectiveness of a procedure that was going to be practically applied in the justice system, as in the case of

To apply findings means that they are used in some way. For example, Gottman has applied the findings from his studies to develop marriage training seminars. Research on neuroplasticity and the benefits of yoga have been applied to improve the life of prisoners in jail and to reduce recidivism.

Ethical guidelines and ethical considerations can be treated synonymously. However, you may be able to think of an ethical issue relevant to a particular study that is not related to a particular guideline.

The field of genetics research is filled with ethical considerations regarding the application of findings from research. Once again, it is about the possible effects the application of findings may have on others that needs to be considered.

eye-witness identification computer programmes, participants should have this revealed to them during the debriefing.

Keeping with the same example, if one study on improving the procedures of eye-witness testimony had impressive and significant results, would it be advisable to then overturn all existing procedures and create laws to be passed implementing this new procedure? Such an application of findings from one study could have ethical implications, especially if the validity of the results could be questioned. This is where once again we see the overlap of the concepts of validity, reliability and ethics. Ensuring test-retest reliability and validity of results may be important to consider. Disregarding such considerations could have a negative impact on those affected by the application of findings that have not been sufficiently tested and whose results are questionable.

Similarly, cultural considerations are also relevant to the application of findings from studies. Those applying findings from research in a different cultural context would need to consider the potential impact this might have on others. For example, the jigsaw classroom and research in cooperative classrooms has had an impact on practices in Western education. But would it be appropriate to apply this to other cultures? As you saw when studying enculturation, some cultures value compliance and obedience over intuition and innovation. Perhaps the same could be said for having student-centered classrooms where the responsibility is put on the students to take charge of learning. A student-centered classroom might be endorsing and encouraging values that are conflicting with a different culture.

It is hoped that this topic has given you some time to reflect on important ethical considerations in qualitative and quantitative research. Knowing the key terms related to common ethical guidelines can give you some confidence and sound knowledge to approach the exams. However, you will need to use your critical thinking to select and apply the considerations most relevant to the stimulus study and explain how they're relevant. You may also find that you can explain interesting ethical considerations in the stimulus study that you have not thought of before. Having a balance of existing knowledge and an open mind to thinking critically is a sound approach to Paper Three.

As ethics is related to the concept of being mindful of the well-being of others, the application of research might have significant effects on other people. Being aware of these effects is at the core of understanding the ethics involved in the application of research.

The focus on the effects that research may have on others is at the heart of understanding ethics in psychological research.

Guiding Question:

How are ethics relevant to the application of findings in research?

Critical Thinking Extension:

Explaining potential ethical considerations related to applying the findings of a study is probably the most difficult question related to ethics in Paper Three. Practice, therefore, is essential. Think of studies that you are familiar with and try to explain how an ethical guideline may be relevant to the application of findings. You can also practice by trying to think of a relevant general ethical consideration, not necessarily one that is related to a guideline.

If you're interested…

Genetics research is filled with ethical considerations regarding the applications of the findings. In this TED Talk Paul Knoepfler discusses "The ethical dilemma of designer babies." Nature.com also has an interesting article about genetics and ethics called "Ethics: Taboo Genetics."

9.4 Evaluating Studies
How do we evaluate qualitative studies?

(a)   Generalizability

Generalizability refers to the extent to which findings from one study can be applied to people, places or situations beyond the context of the original study.

Quantitative research is conducted with the intent of being able to make conclusions about relationships between variables that would be applicable to other people, places and situations beyond the context of the study. For example, experiments that assess the effectiveness of treatments for depression are conducted with the hope that the findings and conclusions could be beneficial for other people suffering from depression, not just the sample. The study is designed in a way to increase the likelihood that the same results could be expected for people other than those in the sample, i.e. we would expect that the same relationship between the treatment and the outcome would apply to the relevant wider population. As you've learned in other chapters, one approach to evaluating results from quantitative studies like experiments or correlational studies is to assess generalizability.

Similarly, field experiments such as the Robber's Cave Experiment are conducted with the goal of understanding how social and environmental variables may influence intergroup behaviour. In this case, the researchers were trying to understand relationships between variables that could be applicable to groups beyond the 22 boys in the experiment. This ability to apply findings and conclusions beyond the context of the original study is an essential consideration when determining the validity of a quantitative study.

A good starting point for assessing generalizability is to look at the sampling method and the characteristics of the participants. Random sampling is the best way to ensure generalizability, but in this chapter we've seen how non-probability sampling methods might be used in qualitative studies. Providing plausible explanations for how the nature of the sample may influence the applicability of the results beyond the research context is key in discussing generalizability.

Most psychology research may suffer from a Western bias as this is where most of the research is conducted and published. Could findings from studies be applicable to other groups, like this Amazonian tribe?

For example, in Sulaiman-Hill and Thompson's study on refugees in Australia and New Zealand, a snowball sample was used with multiple seeds. The fact that numerous seeds were used and a large sample was gathered can increase the likelihood that these results could be generalized to other refugees in these places. However, the sample was only of refugees in Australia and New Zealand, so perhaps the same findings might not be applicable to other countries where Afghan and Kurdish refugees have migrated.

In summary, an important aspect of methodology to examine when assessing generalizability is the sampling method. The goal of representative sampling methods (e.g. random sampling) is to obtain a sample that is representative of a wider population, thus increasing the probability that the findings are generalizable. However, this is not always a practical means to gather participants and so issues of validity need to be balanced with practicality. This may lead to characteristics of the sample influencing the possibility of generalizability.

Guiding Question:

How can the sampling method influence the generalizability of the findings from a study?

Critical Thinking Extension:

You can prepare for Paper Three, Question Three "Discuss" questions by identifying and understanding key concepts that are relevant to the question. In this section, for instance, you know the sampling will be described in the question and this is relevant to generalizability. However, to earn full marks you also need to be able to apply this understanding to a study you've never seen before. A good study to practice explaining sampling and generalizability is Torres et al.'s study on acculturation and discrimination. What factors may influence the generalizability of findings from this study?

If you're interested…

On our ThemEd IB Psychology blog you can find a post called, "So you want to assess ecological validity?" This is one concept related to generalizability that many students struggle to apply correctly. This post explains how to properly assess ecological validity.

(b)   Transferability

In the previous section we reviewed how sampling is relevant to an investigation of the generalizability of a study. Generalizability is based on probability and statistics, so it is most applicable to quantitative studies. Generalizability implies that the study has the intention of being representative; a sample is drawn that is representative of a larger population. Qualitative methodology has been adopted in psychology because there is an understanding that there is value in studying individuals' and small groups' subjective experiences of phenomena. Studies are often conducted with the aim of getting an in-depth understanding of the experiences of a particular phenomenon and may not be carried out with the intent of investigating cause and effect relationships or even correlational ones. The nature of qualitative research means that "generalizability" may not be a suitable term to use as the sampling is not conducted with the aim of representing a wider target population.

In qualitative studies the term transferability is often used in addition to, or in place of, generalizability. Transferability refers to the extent to which the findings can "transfer" from one context to another. This is a similar concept to generalizability as the "context" may refer to a setting or participants outside the original study. One way to think about the difference between these concepts is that researchers design quantitative studies with the goal of generalizability; when referring to transferability it is the *reader* of the research who may have the goal of transferability. After a study

The concepts of transferability and generalizability are very similar. Transferability is a substitute for generalizability in qualitative research.

Phenomenon is an umbrella term in psychology that refers to "anything that can be perceived or observed" (Oxford Dictionary of Psychology, p.571). In this chapter we've looked at studies that investigated experiences of phenomena such as losing someone in a terrorist attack, coping with trauma while parenting, and being admitted to a psychiatric hospital.

is reported, other psychologists may read the study and decide to apply one or more findings from the study to a new situation or group of people.

Representative Sampling: obtaining a sample that is representative of a wider population.

As transferability primarily refers to settings and populations, it can be approached in the same way as generalizability. The change in terminology from quantitative to qualitative studies has come about because of the differences in aims and approaches in both types of research. Because generalizability is often applied to representative sampling, it is not appropriate in qualitative studies. As the two concepts are so similar and both apply to populations and settings of the study, you may assess them in the same way.

If a quantitative study is replicated and the same results are achieved, this strengthens the reliability of the findings and could increase the chances of generalizability beyond the original study. As with this concept of test-retest reliability in quantitative studies, the transferability of findings from one qualitative study to another setting or population may be increased if the findings of the study have been corroborated by similar findings in other studies. For example, if a study on Afghan refugees in the USA obtained similar results to the study in NZ and Australia, this could increase the possibility of transferring these results in an attempt to understand experiences of an immigrant population in the UK. A hypothetical example would be if naturalistic observations of life as a gang member have been carried out in more than one country and have obtained similar findings, this may increase the possibility of being able to transfer these findings to gain insight into gang culture in other countries.

Corroborated: to confirm or give support.

Another way findings may be transferred from a study is if they are used to form the basis of a new theory or inspire other research. A reader of a qualitative study may extract a relevant finding and develop a research question or theory relating to this result. A quantitative study could be designed to test the theory that has been extracted from the qualitative study. This is an example of how findings have been transferred from a qualitative study to form the basis of a theory and further quantitative research. For instance, in Kistin et al.'s study on parenting and approaches to discipline in low-income, traumatized mothers, a psychologist reading the report may develop a theory based on the relationship between a particular stressor and parenting.

For example, a common theme emerged from the interviews in the parenting study in that mothers felt: "…repetitive child behaviors are the most stressful" (ibid). A child psychologist might read this report and decide to conduct a quantitative study to investigate the possible correlations between repetitive child behaviours and parent stress levels. Or perhaps an experiment could be designed to see if it is actually parental stress that results in more repetitive behaviours, possibly as a means of getting attention. These are just some examples of how findings from a qualitative study may be transferred to a new context by the reader of a particular study's report.

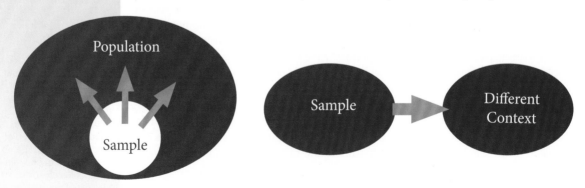

Generalizability   Transferability

As transferability is assessed by the reader, the extent to which transferability can be assessed can be influenced by the contextual description in the report, including relevant characteristics of the participants and the setting/s. Without knowing the full context, it would be difficult to compare the original context with the one that a researcher may try to transfer findings to.

If we look at a hypothetical study on gang culture, for instance, there might be a lot of contextual factors relevant to the study. These could include economic factors such as the level of wealth or poverty in the area and how the gang makes money. They might include issues related to ethnicity, like the characteristics of the members of the gangs or if they arise in communities with ethnic majority or minority populations. The underlying values or goals of the gang could also be relevant. For instance, "White Power" and "Black Power" have issues of race at their core, whereas other gangs might not. Summarizing these details in a study can be useful for readers to understand the context of the study. This may help assess transferability as readers could make informed judgements as to whether or not the results from this study would apply to a new context (e.g. a different gang in a different environment)

It is natural to feel confused when distinguishing transferability and generalizability as the two concepts are very similar and there is significant overlap between the two. It has been included in this section to provide you with a further insight into how the terminology and concepts in qualitative and quantitative research may differ based on their aims and methodologies.

Contextual Description: including details in the report of the characteristics of participants, researchers, settings and relevant background information.

Guiding Question:

How can other research influence the transferability of results from a study?

Critical Thinking Extension:

If a quantitative study is replicated with similar findings, or a qualitative study's findings are corroborated with results from another study, this may increase the generalizability/transferability of the findings. But would this always be the case? What factors might influence the extent to which other findings could influence generalizability/transferability?

If you're interested…

Brian Nosek facilitated a study called "The Reproducibility Project" (Open Science Collaboration). This involved having over 100 well-known experiments reproduced to make conclusions about the overall reliability of psychological research. Alarmingly, only 36% of the replications had significant results (compared with 96% of the originals). The failure of replications to gain similar results has come to be known in psychology as "the reproducibility crisis" (a.k.a. the replicability crisis). You can read more about this online. A good article in "The Atlantic" on the subject is called "How Reliable Are Psychology Studies?"

(c)   Credibility

In the previous lessons you saw how transferability is to qualitative research what generalizability is to quantitative research. The aims and methods of these two types of research are quite different and so the means of assessing and evaluating different types of studies need to be different as well.

Quantitative research can be assessed for its external validity (i.e. generalizability), as well as its internal validity. As you learned while studying quantitative methods and conducting your IA, internal validity is another important concept to consider when evaluating quantitative studies. The internal validity of the conclusions of a study refers to the extent to which the conclusions are based on an actual measurement of the relationship between variables. If there were extraneous variables that may have confounded the results, for instance, the findings may lack internal validity. If the Paper Three stimulus is a quantitative study, you can explain how controls may be designed in the study to ensure internal validity. These controls may be related to the experimental design (repeated measures, matched pairs, independent samples), or procedural controls such as standardization, counter-balancing and single/double-blind designs.

In qualitative research methodology the aim is not necessarily about investigating relationships between variables, so employing controls may become irrelevant to the methodological design.

When assessing the credibility of a qualitative study you may ask, "Can I trust the researchers' findings and conclusions?" Another term for credibility is trustworthiness. In qualitative studies, triangulation is often used to ensure the results are credible. There are multiple types of triangulation and three main examples will be explored in this topic. To begin with, we'll look at how researcher triangulation may help increase a study's credibility.

Researcher triangulation may ensure the results are an accurate reflection of the participants' experiences by increasing the likelihood that the researchers' observations and data are consistent with what really happened. For example, in Festinger's study on the cult that believed the world was going to end, there was more than one researcher collecting field notes on their observations. This means their notes could be compared at a later time to ensure they were consistent with each other. If observational notes are consistent, the findings will be more accurate and thus the conclusions more credible. This is similar to inter-rater reliability in quantitative observations.

Another example of researcher triangulation can be seen in Kistin et al.'s (2014) study on parenting, as the strategies for analyzing the data and drawing conclusions "…were also presented to a group of pediatric health services researchers for feedback." By seeking the assistance and feedback of outside professionals with specific expertise, the researchers in this study could help ensure that the processes they used to gather data and draw conclusions would accurately represent "truth." In doing so, they may help to ensure their results and conclusions are credible.

Credibility: the extent to which the findings and conclusions from the study are trustworthy or believable.

Researcher triangulation is when there is more than one researcher involved in the research process, either when designing the study, gathering data, analyzing results or drawing conclusions.

Inter-rater reliability: the extent to which the observational data gathered by two or more researchers are consistent with one another. Eg. Bandura had multiple observers gathering data (i.e. counting the kids' aggressive actions).

Consulting with other researchers and seeking the feedback and advice of professionals with particular expertise can increase the credibility of findings.

In summary, credibility refers to the extent to which findings accurately and truthfully represent the participants' experiences of the phenomenon being studied. By employing researcher triangulation at one or more points in the research, including the design, data collection, analysis or writing of conclusions, the researchers may help to ensure the credibility of their findings.

Guiding Question:

How can researcher triangulation help to ensure a study's credibility?

Critical Thinking Extension:

Using methodological triangulation may not necessarily ensure credibility of findings. For example, if a researcher has made particular observations and then conducts a follow-up interview, perhaps their interpretations of the observation may influence the interview process. Thus, the data may not bring the researcher any closer to understanding the "truth." Can you think of any possible limitations in using researcher triangulation to ensure credibility?

If you're interested…

The BBC has a fascinating documentary called "Science Under Attack," which is hosted by Nobel Prize winning geneticist, Sir Paul Nurse. This documentary explores why the public may not trust scientific research and is a defense of the "…importance of scientific evidence and the power of experiment, and a look at what scientists themselves need to do to earn trust in controversial areas of science in the 21st century" (from bbc.com).

(d)   Researcher Bias

Researchers have to make decisions throughout the research process with the aim of balancing validity/credibility issues with those of practicality. In the previous section you saw how test-retest reliability (corroboration of findings from other studies) and researcher triangulation are two concepts related to ensuring the validity, reliability and credibility of findings from research. In this lesson we'll look at how other forms of triangulation can be used to ensure credibility.

A threat to the validity and credibility of research is researcher bias, which is when the researcher's existing values, beliefs or opinions influence the study in some way. Researcher bias could affect quantitative or qualitative research. In an experiment, if a researcher knew if a participant was in a treatment or control group, they may interpret their behaviour differently. For example, in Bandura's Bobo Doll experiments the researchers gathering the observational data might have been more likely to count an ambiguous behaviour as aggressive if they were aware of the condition the child was in. One way to avoid bias in quantitative studies is to use blind designs.

Another possible way that researcher bias may influence quantitative studies is in the design of materials and procedures in a study. We have seen in Loftus and Palmer's research that the nature of a question can influence results. If researchers are designing questionnaires to gather data for a study, the wording of their questions may reflect

In a single-blind design the participant is not aware of which condition they are in, whereas in a double-blind design neither the participant nor the data gatherer (e.g. interviewer, observer, researcher, etc.) are aware of which condition the participant is in.

their own biases and could unconsciously result in leading questions being asked. Using existing and well-tested questionnaires that have been shown to gather reliable results is one way this bias could be avoided. For example, in studies investigating body image, the "Body-Self Relations Questionnaire" is used. When measuring symptoms of PTSD the structured interview tool the Clinically Administered PTSD Scale (CAPS) is used. Combining the use of such a tool with a blind design in experimental research could help reduce researcher bias and increase the validity of the results. By using tested methods of gathering data researchers in quantitative studies may help to avoid bias.

As qualitative studies do not employ the same controls as quantitative studies, like standardized instruments and blind designs, different methods for avoiding bias need to be considered. Moreover, there are multiple ways in which researcher bias may influence the research process in qualitative studies, including in the designing, data gathering, analysis, and reporting stages. There are multiple ways that this influence may be reduced. It might also help to note that one way of ensuring the results of a study are credible is to reduce the possibility of researcher bias having an influence. Therefore, concepts like researcher triangulation can be applied to a discussion of generalizability, credibility and researcher bias.

Like researcher triangulation, methodological triangulation may also help to ensure the researchers are gathering data that accurately reflects participants' experiences of a phenomenon, potentially increasing the study's credibility. It might also be used to reduce the chances of researcher bias influencing results. Methodological triangulation is when more than one data collection method is used in the study. For example, during a field observation a researcher might notice something that they don't quite understand. Follow-up individual or focus group interviews could enable the researcher to clarify any points they were unsure about, or to follow-up with any questions that might have arisen from their observation. By seeking such a clarification, they may reduce the chances their biases may have influenced the accuracy of their recording and/or interpretation of their observations.

For example, in Rosenhan's research they noted that doctors spent very little time interacting with patients. This was interpreted as adding to the dehumanizing experience of being in a psychiatric institution. Perhaps interviewing doctors would have uncovered more information about why this happens, leading to a more accurate portrayal of the realities of the mental health care system at the time.

Another example can be seen in SM's case study. They employed methodological triangulation by gathering observational data and by asking her to complete questionnaires based on her self-reported experiences of fear during the conditions. By using more than one method and checking the consistency of the results across the two methods, the researchers can reduce the chances of researcher bias influencing the interpretation and recording of the observational data, thus increasing the credibility of the case study.

Using a random sampling method is another way that researchers may reduce the chances of researcher bias influencing quantitative research.

Methodological triangulation is when more than one method is used to gather data.

Researcher triangulation is one of many ways that researchers can reduce the chances of bias influencing their results.

Like other forms of triangulation, methodological triangulation can increase credibility in two ways: one is by increasing the accuracy of the recorded data and thus more closely revealing the participants' thoughts, feelings and experiences. The other is by reducing the chances that researcher biases may influence the results.

Another form of triangulation is data triangulation, which requires gathering data from more than one place, point in time or group of people.

Guiding Question:

How can triangulation reduce researcher bias?

Critical Thinking Extension:
By this point in the topic you should have a sound understanding of how researchers could employ triangulation to reduce researcher bias and in the process, increase the credibility of their findings. You now need to be able to apply this to an existing study. Can you explain how triangulation could be applied to a study to reduce bias/increase credibility?

If you're interested…

You may like to read about how our expectations can influence the behaviour of others. This has been studied in experimental situations and is known by different names, including the Pygmalion Effect, the Rosenthal Effect, or the experimenter expectancy effect. Another interesting effect is the Hawthorne Effect, which is when our behaviour changes simply as a result of being observed.

(e)   Analyzing Qualitative Data

The purpose of this final lesson is to review the core concepts covered in this topic and to introduce one new idea that is an essential component of qualitative research.

When you conducted your internal assessment you applied descriptive and inferential statistics to your data in order to draw conclusions about the relationship between your independent and dependent variable. But as qualitative research doesn't gather numerical data the process for analyzing the results in order to draw conclusions is different. Conducting an inductive content analysis is one common method of analyzing data in qualitative research. This is also called a thematic analysis, a name which might provide a better insight into what the process involves.

Imagine carrying out 21 focus group interviews as North and colleagues did in their study of the experiences of workers in companies close to ground zero after the New York terrorist attacks. Each interview was about an hour long. After recording the interviews, the information would have been transcribed, which means taking it from a recorded format and typing it out in written form. These transcripts then need to be read, and re-read so the common themes can be identified. This is what a thematic analysis of qualitative data requires: reading the descriptive data, coding individual pieces of information and then identifying recurring themes.

The process of a thematic analysis is similar to identifying themes in a novel: you analyze the individual details of the novel and then find the ideas that are recurring throughout the book in order to draw conclusions about the recurring themes.

In the study on experiences of 9/11, for instance, the researchers identified five broad themes that were recurring in the responses throughout various focus groups: disaster experiences, emotional responses, workplace issues, coping, and issues of public concern. Specific ideas related to these broad themes are then reported. For example, one theme that emerged from the analysis was that members of the Ground Zero companies tended to focus on their own emotional responses to the disaster, whereas the members of companies further from the towers focused on the responses of others.

As you could imagine, when interpreting qualitative data there is a very real threat of researcher bias influencing the thematic analysis. One way of reducing this bias (and increasing credibility) is to use researcher triangulation. By having independent coders interpret the data and then check each other's work, the likelihood of individual bias influencing interpretation of the data could be reduced.

An example of this practice being implemented can be seen in Kim and colleague's study on social gaming apps and online gaming that we looked at when discussing focus groups. In this study they used two researchers who conducted the coding part of the thematic analysis independently. They reported that "the initial categories generated by the data were highly consistent between the two raters in regards to general themes and number of categories." After this initial comparison, the data was reviewed two more times to resolve any disagreements and "...category names were reached through consensus after discussion between raters" (Kim et al., 2016). This example of researcher triangulation during the thematic analysis is one way researchers could reduce the chances of researcher bias influencing the results of the study. By including this description of the process in their report they are also trying to ensure the credibility of their conclusions.

Rosenhan's naturalistic observation on psychiatric hospitals is another example of how researcher triangulation could have been used in the data analysis process to reduce researcher bias and increase the credibility of the results. It is not reported in the original article if there was just Rosenhan or if there were others involved in the analysis of the data gathered during the study. Because much of the data is descriptive, the interpretations of the information are open to researcher bias and confirmation bias. When describing a pseudopatient's experiences of telling a psychiatrist about his family history, for instance, Rosenhan reports that the "...facts of the case were unintentionally distorted by the staff to achieve consistency with a popular theory of the dynamics of a schizophrenic reaction" (Rosenhan, 1974). If it was only Rosenhan reading and drawing conclusions from the field notes of the researcher assistants gathering data in the study, there is a possibility that his bias could have influenced the analysis of the data he used to draw this conclusion. By consulting with another researcher, possibly even consulting with the original researcher who made the notes, biased interpretations during the analysis could be avoided.

As we can see, researcher bias can influence the research process at multiple stages. Employing various forms of triangulation can help reduce researcher bias and thus ensure the findings of the study are credible.

Conducting a thematic analysis is a taxing and time consuming process.

Guiding Question:

How can researcher triangulation during thematic analysis increase the credibility of a study?

Critical Thinking Extension:

Application: In the stimulus summaries in Paper Three there are not always details about potential sources of researcher bias, so you may have to think of plausible hypothetical reasons how researcher bias may influence the results and how triangulation can reduce this. Kim and colleague's study on social apps and online gaming is a good study to use to practice applying an explanation of how researcher triangulation during a thematic content analysis can influence credibility. The full study can be found online and used as practice.

If you're interested…

The process of conducting a thematic analysis of qualitative data is very similar to analysing a work of poetry to try to determine the central idea. If you wanted to practice two skills at once (qualitative methods and literature analysis), you could choose a poem you have studied in your English class and conduct a thematic analysis on that poem. Begin by identifying the individual bits of information in the poem, then find how they're connected and then finish with one or more central themes that connect the details together.

Conclusion

The inclusion of qualitative methods in the IB Psychology course enables you to develop a deeper understanding of the processes involved in conducting psychological research. It also provides you with a wider understanding of the range of methods available for psychologists to investigate human behaviour and mental processes.

Even though quantitative and qualitative methods can be roughly categorized and distinguished from one another, it's important to appreciate that there is significant overlap. In fact, many studies use a combination of methods and sometimes there are grey areas when trying to categorize particular methods. The methods employed by researchers will depend on the context of the research, including the aims, the nature of the participants and the setting.

Understanding how and why psychologists may use a variety of methods has many benefits. For one, this is the focus of your Paper Three higher level exam. You will be asked to demonstrate your knowledge of research methods and relevant ethical considerations in this paper.

Understanding research will also be valuable beyond the IB Diploma. It's likely that at some point you will want to investigate a particular topic and secondary sources of information available to you might not be sufficient in drawing a valid conclusion. This might require you to conduct your own study in order to gain a better understanding. The concepts you've learned in this course will help you to make informed decisions when conducting your own primary research. For example, perhaps you're starting a business and you want to do some market research on what types of products would sell best. You might triangulate questionnaire responses with actual product testing results. Or maybe you're organizing an event at college and you'd like to find out what would make it successful, so you email a questionnaire to get data and conduct some informal interviews. Maybe you'll ask someone else to help so your conclusions are more valid.

Being able to identify the characteristics of a study that influence the validity of the findings will help you in exams and beyond because being able to consider the merits of an argument, including the evidence upon which it is based, is an essential skill. Similarly, being able to consider the potential effects research may have on others can help you assess psychological research and will prepare you to become an adept psychologist.

In terms of exam preparation, you can prepare for Paper Three by making sure you know research methodology terms and concepts relevant to the static questions. You will then apply this knowledge and understanding to the stimulus material.

Qualitative methodologies are not always the most interesting or popular for IB Psychology students. However, it's hoped that the examples of qualitative studies provided throughout the chapter helped to make some of the abstract concepts a little more concrete, and dare I say, even interesting.

Chapter 10
Exam Preparation

Introduction

You'll only use about 5-10% of what you've learned in this course in the actual exam.

Take a moment to think about the validity of the above statement. It comes as a surprise to most students. But the IB allocates 150 hours of learning time for SL students and 240 hours of learning for HL students. The SL exams are 3 hours total, while the HL exams are 5 hours total. Just by looking at these numbers, it shouldn't take long to realise that there's no way you can communicate *all* or even *most* of your learning in the time you are given in the exam situation.

This is really important to understand, because many students underperform in exam situations by trying to show how much they *know*, and they miss out showing how much they *understand* and how well they can think *abstractly* about their under-standing. This leads to exam answers that are filled with descriptions, very little expla-nation and little critical thinking. By exam time it's hoped that you have a working understanding of the differences between knowing and understanding. Hopefully you can also grasp the concept of abstract (and critical) thinking, how to show it, and why it's important.

Many students underperform in assessments because they are not fully aware of the purpose of the assessment.

In order to do well in your exams you need to think of them like a random sample from your psychological brain. They are a snapshot of your learning. Exam writers create the exams so that a good sample of your learning can be obtained to increase the likelihood that accurate generalizations can be made about your understanding of all of the IB Psychology course based on your responses. There's no way the IB can assess your knowledge, understanding and thinking regarding every topic in the course, so they take a sample. This is why you'll only use about 5-10% of what you've learned in the course.

So why do you need to study *all* of the course if you're only going to write about some of it in the exam? Because you don't know which 5-10% you'll need to write about! If we all knew exactly what questions to expect in the exams, they would be a lot easier (and the course would be a lot more boring). You need to learn the whole course so you're ready for *any* question.

The exams are not just about how much you know: they're also about how much you understand.

You can use the materials in this chapter towards the end of the course before your exams begin as this chapter helps you with practical guidance and strategies to achieve your maximum potential in exam answers. However, it's recommended that you practice responding to exam-style questions throughout the course. It would be advisable to be continually familiarizing yourself with the content, guidelines and expectations of the exams and different styles of exam answers. Regular practice, getting feedback and implementing feedback in future practice is the best strategy for developing the skills necessary to write excellent exam responses.

Remember to strike a balance between enjoying the study of psychology because of its inherent interest and relevance, with preparing for exams. After all, the key to doing well in your exams is to become an excellent psychologist!

10.1 Intro to Examinations
Why are you doing exams?

(a) Purpose and Audience

Many students underperform in exams because they do not consider their purpose and audience.

In order to create an effective product you have to understand your product's purpose. In IB Psychology exams, your products are written answers to exam questions and so it's imperative that you understand the purpose of writing these answers in exams if you are going to produce excellent ones.

As outlined in the introduction, the purpose of IB Psychology exams is to determine the extent to which you understand psychology. Now "understanding psychology" is incredibly broad and vague so it would be impossible to see how well you understand psychology and everything about it in the limited time you have in the exams. This is why specific questions are asked that have the purpose of assessing your understanding of significant relationships. If you can understand these relationships you have developed conceptual understanding, which is a major goal of the IB course. The relationships you need to understand are between one or more of the following:

- Behaviour
- Cognitive Processes
- Variables (e.g. factors affecting and/or affected by behaviour and/or cognition)
- Research and Methodology
- Ethical Guidelines and Considerations

All of your exam questions have the purpose of assessing your knowledge and understanding of significant relationships between the above topics.

The purpose of the different exam questions may be to assess one or more of your levels of thinking regarding these concepts as well. Remember that the three levels are:

1. Knowing
2. Understanding
3. Abstracting ("Critical Thinking")

You can easily identify which level the question is asking you to reach by the command term used in the beginning of the question (e.g. describe, explain, discuss, etc). You will learn more about these command terms later in this chapter, including where to expect them and how to address them.

A common mistake students make in exams is focusing too much on *describing* when the question is asking for *explanation* or *discussion*. This results in too much time spent on showing *knowledge* and not

A well-structured, concise and well-developed answer is what your busy examiner is looking for.

enough time demonstrating *understanding* and/or *critical thinking*. Understanding the purpose of the IB Psychology exams, and the types of questions being asked in each paper is key to achieving your potential in these exams.

Considering your audience is just as important as purpose when writing effective IB Psychology exam answers. Many students write poor exam answers because they don't think carefully enough about for whom they are writing: an examiner. In this section I'll give you an examiner's perspective of exam answers so you can think about your poor, hard-working examiner as you write your answer so you can make their life easier. You want to make it as easy as possible for an examiner to award you top marks, so you need to be thinking about them as they sit at their desk just before summer vacation with a pile of exam answers to get through.

Try to maintain a formal, academic style in your exam answers.

There are many practical elements of marking exams that you should be aware of. If you can understand these factors you can write answers that will satisfy what your examiner is looking for in your answers and thus increase the chances they'll reward you with a favourable mark.

Firstly, you have to understand that examiner's get paid per paper so they don't have any motivation to spend longer than is necessary to assess your work. Unlike your teacher, they have no inherent motivation for you personally to succeed or fail; they simply want to assess your work as quickly and as accurately as possible. You will learn some tips later about how structuring your answer (including concise and relevant introductions) can help keep your examiner happy from the first moments they start reading your work.

This is the key reason why practical features of your exam answers, such as careful planning and legible (readable) handwriting may be more important than you think. Examiners do not want to spend excess time trying to decipher your handwriting if it's difficult to understand. They also won't be impressed by an answer that waffles around and doesn't make a relevant point. For this reason, being clear, focused, accurate and concise is one key to writing excellent answers.

You can find free exam materials on our blog. Visit www.themantic-education.com for more information.

Purpose and audience are inextricably linked: you are writing exam answers to show the examiner you have detailed understanding of particular relationships in psychology. The examiner is not reading your work for entertainment or pleasure, they are reading your answers because it's their job and so your answer should reflect this. In addition, your answer should maintain an academic and formal tone.

Students often ask if they can use bullet points, diagrams, headings and sub-headings, etc. Writing exam answers is no different to other forms of written communication – if it helps you to communicate your intended meaning then go for it. Bullet points and diagrams can be effective ways to show the examiner you understand complex research methodology. It also helps them to see this quickly and easily. A table or bullet points might easily show results of a study, or key points of a theory. The purpose of any writing is to communicate meaning to an intended audience so if you can use strategies to help you with that purpose, then use them. What I would suggest, however, is that all visuals (e.g. diagrams and graphs) should *accompany* the written descriptions and/or explanations that they are trying to clarify.

A common critique of exam answers is that they're too descriptive: you need to be going *beyond* description to make sure you are explaining. Show the examiner you understand significant relationships in psychology.

Imagine how many students will describe the multi-store model of memory if the exam question is "Evaluate one model of memory." Your descriptions need to be clear, concise and accurate, but they should only provide context for your explanation and evaluation. Diagraming the MSM could be a fast way to show your examiner you know the model and then they can skim read your description and get to your far more interesting explanation and evaluation.

Don't underestimate the importance of structure: your reader (the examiner) doesn't know what you've studied and what points you're going to make, so you need to structure your answer carefully so they can follow your train of thought.

In short, you want to make your examiner's job as easy as possible. That is to say, you want to make it easy for them to award you high marks. So understanding purpose, audience, the question being asked and how these are related is key to constructing strong exam answers that will earn you high marks.

Paper One and Two are straightforward to prepare for because you know pretty much exactly what the questions *might* be. What makes them difficult, however, is that there are a lot of possible questions that might be asked. This is why it's almost impossible to memorize exam answers that will score top marks – the more effective approach is to develop an *understanding* of the topics in the course so you can apply your understanding to any possible exam question.

For Paper Three you will be told *exactly* what the questions will be. This will make it easy to prepare for and to ensure you can write excellent answers.

The following sections provide you with more specific guidance on the content of each exam paper and how to revise effectively for them. At first reading, these explanations will seem very confusing, complex and abstract. This is why it's strongly advised to read these guidelines and practice writing answers throughout the course.

(b) Command Terms and Levels of Thinking

The fundamental purpose of examinations is to assess your level of achievement in IB Psychology. Your level of achievement will be assessed on the extent to which you demonstrate high achievement in each of the three levels of thinking:

1.   Knowing
2.   Understanding
3.   Abstracting (i.e. critical thinking)

See our blog for a full explanation of the three levels of thinking.

In order to achieve the best marks possible, it is important to understand what level of thinking the different exam questions are asking you to demonstrate. In order to make the expectations clear for students the IB uses specific command terms in every question. These command terms correspond with each of the three levels of thinking and they are as follows:

(1) Knowing	(2) Understanding	(3) Abstracting
Identify Outline Describe	Comment Suggest Explain	Discuss Evaluate To what extent… Contrast
Paper One Section A (SARs)		
Paper One Section B and Paper Two (Essays)		
Paper 3 Question 1		
Paper 3 Question 2		
Paper 3 Question 3		

You can see that all assessments in IB Psychology require knowledge and understanding. On our blog you can find full explanations and visual diagrams of the differences between the three levels of thinking and what these look like in exam answers.

10.2 Paper One
What will be in Paper One?

(a) Contents

Paper One is based entirely on the three approaches. Any of the following topics may be the basis of a question in Paper One.

Paper One Content		
Biological Approach	**Cognitive Approach**	**Sociocultural Approach**

1. The Brain and Behaviour
    a. Technology in Research
    b. Localization of brain function
    c. Neuroplasticity
    d. Neurotransmission
 	
2. Hormones
    a. Hormones
    b. Pheromones
 	
3. Genetics
    a. Genetics
    b. Evolution
 	
4. Animal research **HL Only**
	1. Cognitive Processes
	    a. Models/Theories of Memory
	    b. Schema Theory
	
	2. Reliability of cognitive Processes
	    a. Reconstructive Memory
	    b. Thinking and decision making
	    c. Cognitive Bias
	
	3. Emotion and Cognition
	    a. Emotion and Cognition
	
	4. Technology and Cognition **HL Only**
		1. Individual and the Group
		    a. Social Identity Theory
		    b. Social Cognitive Theory
		    c. Stereotypes
		
		2. Culture
		    a. Culture
		    b. Cultural Dimensions
		
		3. Cultural Influences on Individual Attitudes, Identity and Behaviours
		    a. Enculturation
		    b. Acculturation
		
		4. Globalization **HL Only**

Research methodology and ethical considerations relevant to the topics may also form the basis of an exam question.

These topics will have command terms placed in front of them and might have additional phrases added to make a question. For example, understanding of "Neuroplasticity" might be assessed in an exam through any one of the following questions:

- Describe one study related to neuroplasticity.
- Evaluate research related to neuroplasticity.
- Discuss ethical considerations relevant to research on the brain and behaviour.

Our revision text, *IB Psychology: A Revision Guide*, will also help you to prepare for your IB Psychology exams.

You can see from the range of possible questions that might be asked about any topic that the ability to have an in-depth *understanding* of topics and research (including methodology and ethical considerations) is the key to exam success in IB Psychology. It's essential that you can *apply* your understanding to a range of different possible exam questions. This is why memorizing things like studies, theories and terms can help to *begin* your learning and your revision, but memorizing alone has significant limitations in preparing for success in the exams.

You can also see that the same topic can have different command terms. This is because these questions might appear in different parts of the exam so they will require different depths of thinking.

By designing the course that allows for this wide-range of possible questions the IB is trying to make sure you can apply your learning in multiple ways. This is because an effective education is about being able to use what you have learned in more ways than just in the exam. If you haven't developed the ability to transfer your learning *beyond* exam day, your IB experience would have been a pretty big waste of time.

Just remember that all of the questions in Paper One will require an understanding of significant relationships between variables, behaviour, mental processes, and research (including ethics and methods).

Exam Revision Tip: At the completion of the course when you're doing your revision, try to find the overlaps in the core and options topics. For example, after studying Love and Marriage you might decide that you want to use the role of testosterone in attraction to be able to explain how hormones may influence behaviour and an evolutionary explanation of behaviour (topics from the biological approach), as well as using this to prepare for any questions about the formation of relationships (Human Relationships).

Exam questions are constructed by taking the topics and creating significant relationships between them.

(b) Paper One, Section A: Short Answer Responses (SARs)

This part of the exam consists of three questions that will use level one or two command terms: Identify, Outline, Comment, Describe, Suggest or Explain. There are three questions with one from each of the different approaches. These are called short answer questions (SAQs) and so you will write short answer *responses* (SARs). The SAQs are designed to assess your knowledge and understanding of biological, cognitive and sociocultural approaches to studying psychology, as well as relevant research methods and ethical considerations. There is no difference in requirements for SL and HL in Paper One, Section A.

The questions asked in this section will be will be based on the topics from the biological, cognitive and sociocultural approaches.

Short answer responses (SARs) require a demonstration of knowledge and understanding; essays require all three levels.

It is important that you are confident in writing explanations of significant relationships related to *all* of the relevant topics. This is because any of these topics could be the basis of an SAQ in Paper One and you have to answer *all three* questions. If you make sure to answer all of the guiding questions in each section of the textbook, you will be well-prepared for this.

You can write your own practice short answer responses (SARs) to the questions by using a suitable level one or two command term and applying it to one of these topics so that it asks a question based on important understanding of relationships in psychology. You can also find possible exam questions at the end of each section in the other chapters.

Here are some example SAQs:

- Outline one method used in a study related to stereotypes.
- Describe social cognitive theory.
- Explain one bias in thinking and decision making.
- Outline one model of memory.
- Explain one study related to schema theory.
- Outline one evolutionary explanation of behaviour.
- Explain one ethical consideration related to research on genetics and behaviour.
- Outline one study used to investigate the relationship between the brain and behaviour.

(c) Section B: Essays

This paper consists of three questions that are each based on one of the different approaches to understanding behaviour. These questions use level three command terms (To what extent, Contrast, Evaluate, Discuss) and so require you to show knowledge, understanding and critical (abstract) thinking. You choose one of the three questions to answer.

The content from the course that is being assessed in Part A and Part B is the same: they are both assessing the three approaches. What will change is the level of thinking and depth of response required. Similarly, Part B questions may be more general as you have more time to write detailed answers to these questions.

For your essay writing in Paper One, Section B you will have the choice of which question to answer. There will be one from each approach, so one revision method might be to choose one approach to become an expert in. Being able to reach the abstraction level and being prepared to write an essay about every topic in all three approaches would be incredibly difficult. Preparing for Section B by becoming an expert in one approach could be an effective way to revise and prepare for this section.

Exam Revision Tip: Try writing a practice SAR and then use the same core argument you've used in this SAR and develop it into an essay response. You can see how this can be done by looking at the example answers in this chapter.

10.3 Paper Two
What will be in Paper Two?

(a) Contents

This paper is one hour for SL students and two hours for HL students and is based on the options topics. You will have three questions per topic and like Paper One, Part B, you get to choose your response. The Paper Two questions have the same requirements as Paper One Part B questions. Thus, they will also use level three command terms. Do note, however, that they may use level one or two command terms as well.

It might be possible (and it's hopeful) that you can use some of the same relationships you've studied for Paper One in a Paper Two answer. For instance, you may be asked in Paper One about social identity theory and you could use this theory to explain origins of conflict in the Human Relationships option. Similarly, biological etiologies of PTSD could be used to answer questions in Paper One on the biological approach and/or Paper Two in Abnormal Psychology.

The style and structure of your Paper Two essay will be the same as Paper One's essay; all that changes are the potential topics.

Options Topics (SL = one option, HL = both)	
Human Relationships	*Abnormal Psychology*

1. Personal Relationships
   a. The formation of personal relationships
   b. Communication and personal relationships
   c. Why personal relationships change or end
 	
2. Group Dynamics
   a. Co-operation and competition
   b. Prejudice and discrimination
   c. Origins of conflict and conflict resolution
 	
3. Social Responsibility
   a. Bystanderism
   b. Prosocial behaviour
   c. Promoting prosocial behaviour
	1. Factors Influencing Diagnosis
	   a. Normality versus abnormality
	   b. Classifying disorders
	   c. Clinical bias in diagnosis
	   d. Validity and reliability of diagnosis
	
	2. Etiology of Abnormal Psychology
	   a. Explaining disorders
	   b. Prevalence rates
	
	3. Treatment of Disorders
	   a. Biological treatment
	   b. Psychological treatment
	   c. Culture and treatment
	   d. The effectiveness of treatment

Questions related to the above areas of study and topics may also be based on the following: • Biological, cognitive and/or sociocultural variables • Approaches to research (i.e. research methodologies) used in relevant studies • Ethical considerations in relevant research	

Don't be that one HL student every year who writes two essays from the same option! Similarly, don't be that one SL student every year who tries to write all three essays from one option!

Personally, I recommend focusing on etiology and treatment for abnormal psychology, and leaving factors influencing diagnosis as #3.

Standard Level Students – One Hour

Standard level students will write one essay in one hour based on one of the options. This is why SL students need to ensure that they are fully prepared for any possible question that might come from at least one of the options.

Revising carefully to ensure that you are well-prepared for questions from any topic is really important during your preparation for the exams.

Higher Level Students – Two Hours

Higher level students need to write two essays in response to two questions from two different options topics: Abnormal Psychology and Human Relationships.

Exam Revision Tip: After all the units in the course have been completed and it's time to review, I encourage my students to adopt a 3-2-1 approach. This involves selecting particular approaches and topics to become an expert in, while focusing less on others. For example, a student might plan on becoming an expert in the biological approach to understanding behaviour (their #1) and they'd ensure that they're fully prepared to write essays about all of these topics. They would also be prepared for any SAQ about the cognitive and sociocultural approaches, but perhaps not as ready to write full essays (e.g. they might not evaluate the evidence and explanations during their revision).

This same approach can be done for the HL extensions topics, and the topics in the options for Paper Two.

10.4 Paper Three (HL Only)
What will be in Paper Three?

(a) Contents

The structure and content of Paper Three differs from Paper One and Two primarily because it has static questions. A static question means that it doesn't change, so you know *exactly* what the questions might be. Whereas in Paper One and Two you need to remember studies and apply them in your answer, in Paper Three you are given stimulus material which means you are given a summary of a study and you have to answer the questions in response to that stimulus.

The stimulus will have a summary of a study one page long that will follow this general structure:

- Aim and general background information
- Description of the methodology of the study, including details about:
    o   Sampling
    o   Ethical considerations
    o   Procedures
- A summary of the results
- A summary of the conclusions and possible applications

There are *five* questions in total that you must answer.

Paper Three is focused on assessing your knowledge and understanding of research methods. The stimulus paper may be based on a study using qualitative *or* quantitative methodology, so you need to be equally prepared to answer questions relating to either approach.

Question 1 (actually three individual questions): (9 marks total)

You will need to answer *all* three questions in relation to the stimulus provided.

I)   Identify the method used and outline two characteristics of the method.
II)   Describe the sampling method used in the study.
III) Suggest an alternative or additional (*research*) method giving one reason for your choice.

Question 2: (6 marks)

You will be given *one* of these questions (i.e. you don't choose – only one will appear).

I)   Describe the ethical considerations that were applied in the study and explain if further ethical considerations could be applied.
II)   Describe the ethical considerations in reporting the results and explain ethical considerations that could be taken into account when applying the findings of the study.

You should be practicing writing exam-style answers throughout the course.

477

Question 3: (9 marks)

As with Question 2, you will be given *one* of the following questions:

I)   Discuss the possibility of generalizing the findings of the study.
II) Discuss how a researcher could ensure that the results of the study are credible.
III) Discuss how the researcher in the study could avoid bias.

You will be given a one-page summary of a study, so your revision needs to be based on methodology, *not* on existing studies. Having said that, an effective way to prepare for Paper Three and Paper One and/or Two at the same time is to choose a range of different studies (qualitative and quantitative) that you might use in Paper One and/or Two and practice writing Paper Three answers about those studies. For example, you could use the following studies to practice writing answers about these research methods:

Method	*Studies*
Observation	Rosenhan's study "On being sane in insane places"
Case Study	SM and/or HM
Natural Experiment	Becker et al.'s study on TV in Fiji
Laboratory Experiment	Passamonti et al.'s study on serotonin and brain function
Field Experiment	Sherif et al.'s Robbers Cave Experiment.
Correlational Study	Buss' cross-cultural study on mate preference Levine's study on cultural dimensions and attitudes towards marriage

10.5 Short Answer Responses
How can you write excellent SARs?

(a) What is a Short-Answer Response (SAR)?

An SAR is written in Paper One Section A of the IB Psychology exam. There are three short answer questions (SAQs) asked and you must write an SAR in response to each of these questions. The phrase "short-answer" is highly subjective so it's important that we define an SAR in the context of the IB Psychology exams. So in order to understand just how short an SAR should be, let's do some general calculations so you know what your examiner is realistically expecting of you.

In Paper One you have two hours to write three SARs each worth 9 marks each and one essay worth 22 marks. This means one SAR is worth 18% of Paper One so Section A in total is worth about 55%, leaving 45% for the essay.

This means how you divide your time in the exam is really important. You don't want to spend 30 minutes for each SAR and leave yourself only 25% of the time left (30 minutes) to write an essay worth 45% of the exam's mark. Thus, a general guideline is to spend approximately one hour on Section A (SARs) and one hour on Section B (essay).

This allows for approximately 20 minutes per SAR. Writing effective answers involves careful planning, so two to five minutes of the 20 should be spent planning. The average 17 year old writes about 15 – 17 words per minute (Dutton, 1992 and Mason 1991, as cited in Addy, 2004), so an SAR should be around 225 – 350 words. It would be very difficult to write three 350 + SAR answers in one hour, so it would be advisable to adjust the length and depth of your answer depending on the three questions provided. Hopefully at least one of the three SAQs will be a description of research (study or theory), which can be shorter than an explanation of a relationship. Explaining the influence of biological variables on behavior and/or cognition often takes the longest to explain.

Remember that the short answer questions may use any of the following command terms:

- Identify
- Outline
- Describe
- Comment
- Suggest
- Explain

One of these command terms will be used in reference to one or more of the following:

- Behaviour and/or cognitive processes (e.g. memory, stereotypes)
- Biological, cognitive or socio-cultural variables (e.g. hormones, group influences)
- Research (studies and theories)
- Research (methodology and ethical considerations)

I highly recommend getting plenty of practice at writing short answer responses before you try essays. The reason for this is that many of the skills of writing effective SARs can be applied to writing excellent essays, too.

The limited time you have in the exams means you need to be concise in your responses. It also means that you don't need to try to memorize as many details of studies as you can: you have to understand how to use them as evidence to support a core argument.

You can find a copy of the IB SAR rubric on our blog.

Exam Revision Tip: A common error in answers that ask students to outline, describe or explain a particular model or theory is that students only spend one or two sentences describing the model/theory, and spend a majority of the answer on describing and explaining a relevant study. When the question is something like, "Describe the (insert theory/model here)…" you should show how well you know that theory or model, and only use a study to demonstrate one or more of the claims of the theory/model after you have offered a full description.

While there are a number of possible command terms, "explain" is the most important to communicate your understanding of significant relationships as they apply to the exam question.

(b)   Command Terms in SARs

If the SAQ uses a command term other than explain, my advice is to cross it out and write explain in its place. In order to get top marks in an SAR you might need to explain but a different command term has been used. This is because you need to demonstrate knowledge and *understanding* that is "accurate and addressed the main topics/problems identified in the question."

You also need to describe research that is "explicitly linked to the question." In other words, you need to explain how research is applicable to the question being asked, which requires understanding (i.e. the explanation of relationships). If you were asked to "Outline how one study demonstrates localization of brain function" for example, you would still need to show how the results of the study show a relationship between the behaviour and the function of the brain, which requires explanation (the demonstration of a significant relationship in response to a question or problem).

Similarly, the difference in definitions between outline and describe as provided by the IB are:

Outline: give a *brief* account or summary
Describe: give a *detailed* account or summary

According to these definitions outline means that you simply provide less information than in a description. But in an SAR you are writing your response to show your examiner that you have detailed knowledge of research, so there's no point in running the risk of being too "brief" in case your examiner mistakes your knowledge of the definition of the command term (outline) with a lack of knowledge of the research. Moreover, in the rubric it explicitly states that in order to get top marks your answer needs to be "supported by appropriate research which is *described...*" (emphasis added). There's simply no reason to just outline in an SAR. Similarly, it's unlikely you'll be asked to "identify" or "suggest" in an SAQ. These are more applicable to Paper Three.

Moreover, no matter how detailed your description is, without explanation you are only showing your knowledge. The SAR rubric clearly states "knowledge and *understanding*" are required for top marks.

Sometimes you are asked to outline or describe a study related to a particular topic. For instance:
* Outline one study related to neurotransmission.
* Describe one study that demonstrates localization of brain function.
* Outline one study related to biases in thinking and decision making.

Whenever you are using a study, my advice is to go further than description and explain the relevant relationship that the study demonstrates. For example, explaining *how* the study demonstrates the effects of neurotransmission on behaviour, or *how* the study demonstrates localization of brain function, etc.

The IB definition of explain is to "give a detailed account or summary including reasons or causes." Here you can see how description is required within an explanation because a description means to give a detailed account or summary. But in an explanation you need to go further (i.e. reach level two) by showing "reasons or causes." If this definition is clear for you, that's all you need.

However, I often find that the phrase "including reasons or clauses" isn't always applicable or easily understood and so I like to use an alternative definition for an

The IB recommends that even if a level one command term is used, you should demonstrate the ability to analyse and apply. Therefore, you should always be explaining in short answer responses.

The exams have been deliberately designed to try to make it impossible to memorize answers and regurgitate these in the exam. For this reason, it's essential that you understand relationships so you can apply them to multiple possible questions.

explanation: communicating understanding of one or more significant relationships by applying them in response to a question or problem.

Our definition of explain is a little different to the IB's, but it should make the expectations more clear.

On the surface this seems far more complicated, but it is a more accurate definition of an explanation. If you think about how you use the term "explain" in an everyday sense you are trying to get someone else to understand something. In explanations in the context of school assessments you need to explain something to your examiner so they can see that you understand how one or more things are related. The ways things are related is what shows you understand their significance and what they demonstrate. This requires a lot more thinking than simply memorizing something, which is why it's level two. It requires the connection of two or more units of information in a significant manner.

Don't you just love stock photos that try to look natural but just really aren't? But seriously, effective preparation for your exams is as much about understanding the demands of the questions as it is about revising content.

Let's break down some examples:

• Explain one bias in thinking and/or decision making.

The relationship here is between bias and thinking and/or decision making. In other words, how does one particular bias affect our thinking/decision making? For instance, you could explain *how* confirmation bias may affect the way we think about others (e.g. stereotypes). Moreover, you would need to explain how results from a study demonstrate this relationship, which makes the explanation more complex but is a necessary requirement and will demonstrate a deeper understanding.

• Explain one study related to schema theory.

What this question is really asking is "Explain how one study is related to schema theory." The relationship between the study and schema theory is implied in the question, but you should make the relationship explicit through detailed explanation.

• ~~Outline~~ Explain one evolutionary explanation of behaviour.

Similar to the above, you need to explain how evolution may have influenced behaviour, and/or vice-versa. Moreover, this is not a level one question as the command term outline would suggest because as there's no mention of research in the question you have to add an explanation of how research supports your answer, which involves communicating your understanding of the significant relationship between the study and the evolutionary explanation of behaviour.

You can see that even when using a level one command term, the exam questions still require you to demonstrate understanding of a significant relationship (level two).

• ~~Outline~~ Explain one ethical consideration in research on genetics and behaviour.

This requires an explanation of the relationship between the methodology of a study on genetics and a relevant ethical consideration. What this question is really asking you to do is "Explain how one ethical consideration is relevant to a study on genetics and behaviour." This could involve an ethical consideration that was applied or that could have been applied. Either approach is fine.

It's really important to remember that all Paper One and Two questions require the use of research.

(c)   Structuring Effective SARs

In your IB psychology exam you are *writing to show the examiner you understand how psychological concepts can be demonstrated in research*. Remember that your examiner wants to know that you can use research to demonstrate a relationship, which will show your conceptual understanding. This is what the phrase "addresses the main topic/problem in the question" is referring to. The examiner is reading your work to see that you *understand* the specified topic. Because they want to mark your work as quickly and as accurately as possible, and you have limited time and words to waste in an SAR, writing clearly, concisely and staying focused on the question is a key to writing excellent SARs.

A general framework for writing effective SARs is:

- Introduction
- Point (Description → Explanation)
- Conclusion

Introduction

Like any good introduction the purpose of your opening lines is to give your reader some context: your examiner wants to know how you're going to answer the question so they can process your answer quickly and accurately. Basically, you are trying to activate their schema so they can easily process the rest of your answer. This involves outlining the relationship/s and stating the relevant research in your opening lines.

Your introductory paragraph in an SAR should:

- outline the specific relationship you are explaining (as is required by the question)
- state the specific research you will use to demonstrate the relationship

Point / Central Argument

SAQs will be phrased in a way to allow you to make one key point about a specified topic. You want to write a well-developed argument that uses research to support your answer to show you know and understand the topic. To show your *knowledge* you need detailed, relevant and accurate descriptions. In order to show your *understanding* you need clear explanations of significant relationships between topics. Here are some relationships you may need to explain and use research to support your explanation:

- Between a variable and a behaviour (e.g. a hormone and behaviour)
- Between a study and a theory (e.g. how HM's study supports the MSM)
- Between an ethical consideration and a particular area of study (e.g. why informed consent is an important consideration when studying effects of brain injuries).
- Between a research method and a particular area of study (e.g. how correlational studies are used to investigate cultural influences on behaviour).

Description

Descriptions are necessary to provide context for your explanations. In an SAR your descriptions will be based on behaviours, cognitive processes, variables, methodology, ethical considerations, studies and/or theories. Before your explanation will make sense you need to provide context by describing. Remember that description is an umbrella term that includes statements, definitions, outlines, identifications, etc. You need to critically select the relevant points to describe. You have limited time so

Many of the skills used in writing IB Psychology answers can be transferred to other subjects. For example, when writing essays about novels in English class you don't try to summarize the whole plot: you only describe enough of the plot so your analysis makes sense. The same applies in Psychology: don't try to summarize the whole study: just select those details that help you illustrate your point (i.e. help you demonstrate a significant relationship).

you will not be able to show everything you know – just enough to provide context for your explanation.

Explanation

Unless the question has asked you to outline or describe a theory, you will need to explain a significant relationship between two of the above topics (behaviour, variables, etc.). Your explanation needs to show that you understand *how* two or more things are related and that you can apply this relationship to address the question. Explanation comes after description because you need the details first before you can show how they're related.

Conclusion

You do *not* need a lengthy conclusion in your SARs. A basic restatement of your core argument is all you need. You won't be marked down if you don't have a conclusion, but a conclusion simply allows your examiner to know that you made all the points you wanted to. It also provides you with one last chance to clarify the point/s you were trying to make.

Without a conclusion your answer doesn't have closure. It's like when you're listening to someone give a speech and they don't end in a way that makes you know they've finished, so you sit and wonder when to start clapping. You don't want your examiner to feel like you ended abruptly and you didn't finish making your point. Moreover, the one sentence statement of your argument gives you one last chance to show your understanding.

The diagram below shows a general structure. However, this may vary depending on the question and/or how you intend to answer the question.

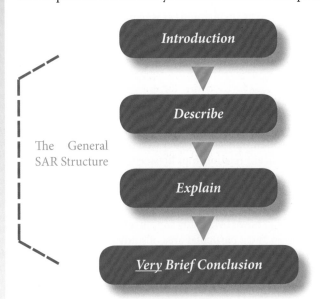

The General SAR Structure

Explain how one neurotransmitter may affect human behaviour.	*Comments*
One neurotransmitter that may affect human behaviour is serotonin, as studies have shown that it's correlated with increased violence and impulsive behaviour. This correlation might be explained by the influence of low serotonin on the prefrontal cortex. This can be demonstrated in Passamonti et al's study.	*The specific relationship between the variable and behaviour is stated, and so is the supporting research.*
Our prefrontal cortex helps us to regulate our impulsive actions, so when we do have heightened physiological arousal in response to someone threatening us, our PFC enables us to regulate our behaviour and possibly restrain from reacting violently. Passamonti et al's study shows that serotonin affects both the amygdala and the prefrontal cortex, which might explain why low levels of serotonin have been correlated with violence.	*Description of the role of the PFC provides context for the later explanation.*
In this study, a repeated measures design was used with healthy volunteer samples. On one day they consumed a drink that lacked tryptophan. Tryptophan is an important amino acid that helps to build serotonin, so it was expected that this condition would have lower levels of serotonin. In the control condition they drank a placebo. After they consumed the drinks they were put in an fMRI and were exposed to happy, angry and neutral faces while their brain function was measured.	*The relevant details of the study are described accurately and in enough detail to provide context for explanation.*
The results showed *reduced* function of the prefrontal cortex in the low-serotonin condition when they were viewing the angry faces, but not the neutral or happy ones. This suggests that serotonin plays a role in reducing PFC function when we are exposed to social threat.	*Results are stated and then their significance in relation to the role of serotonin in violence is explained.*
This may explain how serotonin can influence violent behaviour because if someone is in a situation of conflict or is threatened by an angry person, their amygdala may fire and their physiological arousal is high. This increases emotional arousal, which could lead to an aggressive reaction. But because their PFC function is low they may have a reduced ability to regulate impulsive decisions and actions, so they may react violently without thinking.	*The answer shows understanding of __how__ low serotonin might affect violent behaviour; it shows understanding of a significant relationship in response to the question.*
From this study we can see that our diet may affect our serotonin levels and this could affect our brain function when we are in threatening situations. The effect serotonin has in reducing PFC function during times of social threat may explain its correlation with impulsive behaviour and violence. (350 words)	*The two sentence conclusion restates the key argument put forward in response to the question.*

The above example is at the longer end of an SAR because of the nature of the question. In order to show *how* serotonin may affect impulsive behaviour and violence there is significant description required to give the results of the study context. You can see that often describing the study is done very briefly (around 100 words in this case). Only relevant details are included to demonstrate the significant relationship – in this case between levels of serotonin, social threat, activation of the PFC and violence. Description of the role of the prefrontal cortex and what happens physiologically are also included as these provide context for the later explanation of *how* the low serotonin might influence violence.

10.6 Essays
How can you write excellent essays?

(a) *What is an Essay?*

I advise that essays in IB Psychology should only be approached after you've had considerable practice at writing effective SARs. This is because the skill of writing responses to IB Psychology questions and using research to support your answer is a new one for all students and the skills for writing excellent SARs apply to writing excellent essays. There is only one major point of difference: offering a "counter-point" (i.e. offering a counter-argument). But much like there's no sense trying to think abstractly about relationships if you don't understand the relationship first, there's no point practicing writing counter-arguments if you can't first write a well-developed argument to begin with. You'll learn more about what a counter-point is and how to write one later in this topic.

You may find it difficult to write this many words in the time allowed; make sure that you have had plenty of exam practice before exam day so you know how much you can write. This will allow you to plan your answers so you can describe, explain and show critical thinking.

If we use our calculations regarding writing speed, we can deduce that essays in IB Psychology should be approximately 800 - 900 words long. You write essays in Paper One (in response to one of the three essay questions) and in Paper Two.

This is another example of how in your IB Psychology exams you are actually drawing on a very limited amount of your knowledge. Think of all the topics you've studied for the options and you're only going to write *one* essay on *one* topic you have studied (remember SL study one option and HL study two). But it's imperative that you are well-prepared to show your examiner an excellent snapshot of your knowledge, understanding and thinking.

The skills you need for writing effective essays are very similar to writing effective SARs. The table on the opposite page provides a quick comparison between SARs and Essays in IB Psychology.

One key to success in exams is to be prepared to apply any of your learning from the course in any of the questions. There are so many possible questions and variations of questions that it might not be possible to prepare for all of the possible ways for you to demonstrate critical thinking in your answers. You should be prepared to apply critical thinking as you plan your essay answers in the exam conditions. The exams have been designed to encourage this because this way they can assess the extent to which you can demonstrate critical thinking in response to a problem that you haven't pre-prepared.

You can write your own practice essay questions as easily as you can write your own SAQs. You simply create a significant relationship on one of the topics and add a level three command term. To use the same topics from the previous examples of Paper One, Section A, here are what three essay questions might look like:

Biological Approach: Discuss one or more effects of neurotransmission on behaviour.

Cognitive Approach: Discuss one or more ethical considerations related to research on the reliability of one cognitive process.

Sociocultural Approach: Evaluate one study related to the study of cultural dimensions and behaviour.

You will notice that sometimes the questions require depth of understanding by specifying one specific topic. For instance, the question above requires an evaluation of only one study. To write an essay evaluating one study requires an in-depth knowledge and understanding of the methodology and applications of this one study. On the other hand, questions can invite breadth or depth of knowledge and understanding to be demonstrated by giving students choice to write about "one or more" or "two" particular things, like in the neurotransmission question listed.

Quite often the question won't specify a particular number, but will be quite open-ended. For instance, the cognitive approach question above might be worded:
"Discuss ethical considerations related to research on the reliability of one cognitive process."

Where you see a question that uses a plural (e.g. considerations) you need to write about at least two, but you could write about more if you wished. My advice is that you need to reach all three levels (knowing, understanding and abstracting) in essays so if you have an in-depth understanding of the course you will find that writing about two factors is often more than enough.

To "analyze the demands of the question" means to identify the significant relationship that is being addressed and what you need to show you understand about that relationship. This is often the case in other subjects' exam responses, too.

Comparison of SARs and Essays in IB Psychology

Similarities	Differences
Both SARs and Essays… …require demonstration of knowledge and understanding, thus both require detailed description and explanation. …must use research to support arguments. …should have clear introductions that outline the key argument being made in the answer and states the research that will be used to support the answer. …should finish with a clear and concise conclusion that summarises the core argument that has been made. …should have clearly identified paragraphs and signposts. …can include a range of strategies to help the clear communication of ideas (e.g. diagrams, bullet points, headings/sub-headings, etc…) …add command terms to topics from the syllabus.	You have roughly one hour to write an essay whereas you only have around 15 – 20 minutes to write an SAR. An essay is approximately triple the length of an SAR (i.e. around 800 - 900 words) Essays require you demonstrate the ability to think abstractly about your knowledge and understanding. Essays use level three command terms whereas SARs only use level one or two. The level three command term invites the abstract thinking (discuss, evaluate, to what extent, contrast) Thus, there's no evaluation in SARs; evaluation is only relevant in essays. You are always given a choice about what essay question to choose (in Paper One Section B and Paper Two), whereas you have no choice with SARs and are expected to answer all three.

Higher Level Extension Questions: Paper One Section B

HL students may be asked to write essays in Paper One Section B about one or more of the HL extension topics. There is a chance that none, one, two or all three of the Paper One Section B questions will be based on the HL extension topics. These questions will be a combination of one of the three core concepts for each extension in combination with one of the three topics from the relevant approach. Ethics and research methods may also be combined in these HL extension questions.

Here are some example questions:

Biological Approach: To what extent are animal models valuable in research on the brain and behaviour?

Cognitive Approach: Compare positive and negative effects of modern technology on the reliability of one cognitive process.

Sociocultural Approach: Evaluate *one* method used to study the influence of globalization on cultural origins of behaviour.

You'll notice that these questions are extremely demanding, arguably more so than the core questions, which is why they are for HL students. You need to be prepared to write an essay on any of the three extension topics.

Options Topics

Here are some sample essay questions from the optional topics Human Relationships and Abnormal Psychology.

Human Relationships

- Discuss the role of communication in personal relationships.
- Compare two ethical considerations in research on prejudice and discrimination.
- Discuss the influence of biological, cognitive and/or sociocultural factors in bystanderism.

Abnormal Psychology

- Discuss the role of clinical biases in diagnosis.
- Compare biological explanations for one disorder.
- Evaluate research investigating the biological treatment of psychological disorders.

Just as with Paper One, ethics or research methodology may be the basis of questions in Paper Two. Similarly, any of the topics within each option may address biological, cognitive and/or sociocultural approaches to understanding that topic. Similarly, the questions may require depth and/or breadth of knowledge and understanding.

If you compare the IB's SAR and essay rubrics you can deduce that the only real difference is in the addition of the "Critical Thinking" criterion.

When you provide a counter-point in your essay you should try to state one of these key terms that shows which element of the critical thinking you are referring to and sign-post for your examiner that you are demonstrating "critical thinking". You can refer to the examples later in this section, the reference material in the introduction, or the Critical Thinking Extensions throughout the book for more information on what critical thinking looks like in exam answers.

If you compare the IB's SAR and essay rubrics you can deduce that the only real difference is in the addition of the "Critical Thinking" criterion.

(b) *Command Terms in Essays*

The nature of the command term (evaluate, discuss, contrast, and to what extent…) will influence the counter-point you offer.

Evaluate: your point should have included an explanation that focused on the applications (e.g. strength/s) of whatever it is you are evaluating (e.g. study, theory, explanation, etc.) Your counter-point could focus on the limitation/s of the explanation you have provided.

Contrast: If you are asked to contrast you will need to have two relationships. Your point should explain the first. Your counter point should also explain the second, but the explanation of this relationship should highlight a significant difference between the relationships.

To what extent…This command term simply means a relationship demonstrates something but invites you to provide an alternative explanation. Your counter-point should be an alternative explanation or a limitation for what you have explained in your main argument.

Discuss: This command term invites freedom. You have the freedom to offer many different counter-points to whatever it is you are being asked to discuss. Your counter-point may be related to limitations of supporting research, alternative explanations, limitations of applications and/or ethical considerations regarding applications, etc.

Without practice at example questions, these explanations are rather abstract and vague. Therefore, the best way to develop fluency in writing excellent essays is to practice and get feedback.

Here are some examples of point → counter point outlines in response to essay questions with the different command terms. The next section will go into more detail about structuring effective essay responses. While these might seem basic, well-developed explanations of these points would result in essays of at least 800 words.

The four command terms for essays invite you to go further than explanation. But they still require description and explanation as well.

Question: *Discuss one or more biases in thinking and decision making.*

Point: Confirmation bias can explain stereotypes and may be related to schema processing. This can be shown in Cohen's study using the librarian/waitress video.

Counter-point: Confirmation bias doesn't explain how the schema/stereotypes are formulated in the first place, only how they are confirmed after initial formation. Perhaps other theories like SIT could explain their formation.

Question: *Evaluate Social Identity Theory*

Point: Social identity theory can be demonstrated in minimal group paradigm studies and can explain behaviours such as prejudice, discrimination and stereotyping. It can also be applied to real-life examples such as riots at sports matches.

Counter-point: Social identity theory fails to consider biological factors in inter-group behaviour. Studies have shown there may be biological bases for out-group discrimination (e.g. autonomic activation of the amygdala) and the role of biology during inter-group conflict (e.g. testosterone, PFC, amygdala, etc.)

Question: *Contrast two origins of conflict.*

Point: *Intergroup* conflict can be explained through the *sociocultural* approach using realistic group conflict theory and social identity theory.

Counter-point: *Interpersonal* conflict can be explained through the *biological* approach and the role of the amygdala and PFC in times of social threat.

Question: *To what extent does one study demonstrate localization of brain function?*

Point: SM's case study demonstrates the role of the amygdala in the perception of emotional stimuli and being able to experience fear.

Counter-point: While they did record other emotions, such as laughter, the case study didn't explore the extent to which SM could experience *all* emotions, such as shock and sadness. Generalizability may also be questioned, as her brain damage is a result of a genetic disease and whether or not these results could apply to populations without this genetic disease is a valid question.

(c)   *Structuring Effective Essays*

Guidelines for structuring essays are very similar to structuring an SAR. You need:

I.   a clear introduction that shows your examiner *exactly* how you intend to answer the question

II.   good body paragraphs that have logical groupings of ideas and signposts so your examiner can follow the points you are making throughout your answer

III.   a logical and concise conclusion that neatly wraps up your answer.

As a general guideline for body paragraphs in essays, the description → explanation → abstraction order is generally logical to follow.

Moreover, the point → counterpoint structure is a good guideline to use in preparing for essays. The "point" is one well-developed explanation of a significant relationship. In other words, you basically have an SAR within your essay but you've got a bit more freedom to develop that explanation because you have more time. You may also be able to demonstrate abstraction by showing how that relationship can be applied to a particular area of study. For example, applying SIT to explain stereotypes, SCT to explain violence, neuroplasticity to explain PTSD treatments, etc. How you demonstrate your abstract thinking will depend on the content of the question and the command term used.

After you have made a clear and well-developed point which shows your understanding, you then offer a counter-point to show your ability to think abstractly about the relationship/s you have just explained in the first point. The nature of the counter-point will depend on the question and the command term used as well as the content of your response. Your counter-point will probably consist of one of the following:

- Explanation of one or more limitations of the research (including methodology and/or applications)
- An alternative explanation based on a different approach to understanding behaviour
  o   E.g. explaining how SCT ignores significant biological explanations of conflict and/ or how observing others might influence physiology in relation to conflict.

Suggested essay structure:

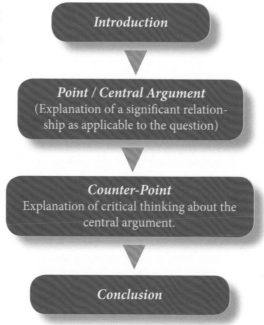

Introduction

Point / Central Argument
(Explanation of a significant relation-ship as applicable to the question)

Counter-Point
Explanation of critical thinking about the central argument.

Conclusion

The following table provides a summary of the essay structure…

Introduction	Your introduction should state the following: • the specific relationship/s you are going to explain • the counter-point you are going to offer regarding that relationship • the research you are going to use to support your answer
Point	Your "point" is an explanation of a significant relationship that has been applied to the question. This will require description and explanation, as well as the use of research to support your explanation.
Counter-point	Your counter-point should show you can think abstractly about the relationship you are explaining. It should be connected to the point and should offer a counter-claim.
Conclusion	Your conclusion should restate your point/s and counter-point/s.

You can find more sample answers and exam materials on our blog and in other exam preparation resources we have at www.themantic-education.com

Introduction

You'll notice the IB rubric has a criterion called "Focus on the Question." In the IB subject guide it states that "students must identify the problem or issue being raised by the question." You can do this by "restating the question". However, to score 2/2 you need to *explain* to show that you "understand the issue or problem".

The term "problem" in this context may be confusing for you as the questions aren't always phrased in a way so that a problem is directly obvious. I would define the "problem" or "issue" in each exam question as the specific relationship requiring explanation, as well as the abstraction involved in that relationship. In other words, you need to state your point and counter-points clearly as well as the relevant research.

As with all IB Psychology Paper One and Two exam questions the relationship requiring explanation in the question may be about variables, behaviour, cognitive processes, research (including methodology) and/or ethics. Your introduction should clearly identify the specific relationship/s between these factors that you are going to explain in order to address the question.

If you do this well, it will also help with your "Clarity and Organisation" which is another element of the IB rubric for essays.

Point / Central Argument

Explaining your main point requires similar skills in paragraph structure, signposting, description and explanation as in SARs. Activating schema through the identification of the relationship you are explaining is key to writing good body paragraphs. If you are describing a study or theory, for instance, it's important to first of all make your examiner know why you are describing the research. E.g. the point that the study is relevant to.

The accurate description of research in essays achieves two goals:
- Demonstrates knowledge
- Provides context for explanation

Just like with SARs, you need to critically select the details you include in your description. You want to show detailed knowledge but you have to balance this with allowing time to show understanding of the research through clear explanations. Many students make the mistake of thinking that the longer their descriptions of studies the more knowledge they will show and the better their answer will be. However, another key element is that your description is *relevant*. By including too much description of research you run the risk of including irrelevant details, which will reduce your marks for knowledge, reduce your time for explanation and will reduce the focus and organisation of your answer. In short, it dilutes the central point that you are making.

There are no guidelines as to length or content of body paragraphs. A paragraph is simply a group of sentences connected by one idea. Their purpose is to help your reader follow your point by making it easier for them to follow the order of ideas you are presenting. Planning the order of these ideas and the content of each paragraph in your plan is key to writing effective essays during the pressure of the exam situation. One practical tip on exam day is to leave a line between each paragraph to simply help your examiner clearly see your paragraph structures so they can follow your argument.

Having one well-developed point that clearly explains a significant relationship and applies that relationship directly to the question using research to support the answer is better than trying to make numerous under-developed points. In fact, if you have a deep understanding of the relationships you've been studying in this course you'll find that in the time available it's very difficult to make more than one well-developed point.

Counter-Point
The counter-point is where you reinforce for the examiner your depth of knowledge, understanding and your ability to think abstractly about significant relationships. The nature of your counter point will depend on two things:
(a)   If the essay question asks for one or more relationships
(b)   The command term used in the question

(a) In the options topics, questions often ask about two or more variables' influence on a specific behaviour. For example:

* Contrast two etiologies of one disorder.
* Discuss explanations for why relationships may change or end.
* Evaluate two explanations for one disorder.

Where you have questions like this, the second factor should ideally form the basis of your counter point. If you can connect the two factors like this, it will help organize your answer and will also demonstrate abstract thinking.

Where there is a plural and no number stated (e.g. "Discuss explanations...") it is my advice to select two. Writing about three or more will result in superficial explanations. It is important that if a plural is used in an exam question that you do write about at least two, because writing about only one will drastically reduce your available grades. Try to choose two that can be used in a point→counterpoint structure.

Conclusion
Your answer should end with a clear and concise conclusion that restates the core argument/s you put forward in your essay. It serves the same purpose as the concluding statement/s in your SARs. Just like with SARs, it allows you one final opportunity to re-state and, if necessary, to clarify the central point and counter-point you were making in your essay. It also shows the examiner that you have made all the points that you wanted to in your essay.

Many students make the mistake of skimming over the top of answers and they end up being too descriptive. Be sure to describe *and* explain in SARs and essays.

(d)   Example Essay

"Evaluate one study related to the effects of neurotransmission on human behaviour."

One study that demonstrates the possible effects of neurotransmission on behaviour is Passamonti et al's laboratory experiment on serotonin and its effect on the activity of the prefrontal cortex (PFC). Many studies have shown correlations with low levels of serotonin and impulsive and violent behaviour. This laboratory experiment can help explain the correlation by showing the effects of low serotonin on the activity of the PFC during times of social threat. But while this study might help elucidate the relationship between serotonin and violence, the generalizability of these findings may be questioned due to the nature of the study and the participants.

The relationship between the study and its demonstration of neurotransmission is stated. The counter-point is also stated, as is the relevant research.

Passamonti et al's research investigated the influence of serotonin levels on brain function, particularly during social threat (e.g. viewing angry faces). Violent behaviour may come about as a result of brain function, in particular the function of our amygdala and prefrontal cortex: serotonin may affect these parts of the brain and this study supports this explanation.

Context is provided with brief overview of the study and the particular area of research it's relevant to.

When we perceive an angry face or someone who is angry threatens us, our amygdala is activated and our body prepares to fight or flee. If we feel threatened when we see anger in someone else, we end up with high physiological arousal which serves the purpose to help us to defend ourselves. Our prefrontal cortex helps us to regulate our impulsive actions, so when we do have heightened physiological arousal in response to someone threatening us, our PFC enables us to regulate our behaviour and possibly restrain from reacting impulsively or violently. Studies have shown in criminals low levels of serotonin. Passamonti et al's study shows that serotonin affects the functioning of the PFC, which might explain why low levels of serotonin have been correlated with violence.

Context for explanation is provided through description of physiology and how the study is related to this.

In this study, a repeated measures design was used with healthy volunteer samples. On one day they consumed a drink that lacked tryptophan. Tryptophan is an important amino acid that helps to build serotonin, so this condition had lower levels of serotonin. In the control condition they drank a placebo. After they consumed the drinks they were put in an fMRI and were exposed to happy, angry and neutral faces while their brain function was measured.

Relevant details of the study are described.

The results showed *reduced* function of the prefrontal cortex in the low-serotonin condition when they were viewing the angry faces, but not the neutral or happy ones. This suggests that serotonin plays a role in reducing PFC function when we are exposed to social threat (e.g. an angry face).

These results can be used to explain how serotonin can influence violent behaviour because if someone is in a situation of conflict or is threatened by an angry person, their amygdala may fire and their physiological arousal is high and the serotonin reduces their PFC function which means they have a reduced ability to regulate impulsive decisions and actions, so they may react violently without thinking.

The results are stated clearly and the significance of the results in terms of demonstrating neurotransmission are explained.

Numerous studies have correlated serotonin with aggression, impulsive behaviour and violent crime, but by using a laboratory experiment and isolating

This paragraph highlights the strength of the study by reinforcing what it demonstrates.

the independent variable of low levels of serotonin on brain function during times of social threat (viewing angry faces), this study can provide a plausible explanation as to how low serotonin levels might explain impulsive behaviour and correlations with violence.

However, the study could be questioned on the grounds of ecological validity because of the research methodology used. The participants' brain activation was measured while they were laying down in an fMRI and viewing images of an angry face. This is very different to what happens in real life when someone is threatened and may respond violently (e.g. by murder or serious assault). Just by correlating brain activity with seeing an angry face doesn't necessarily mean we can generalize these findings to situations involving extremely high levels of danger and threat, such as are often involved in violent crimes. Similarly, typically when we are confronted we are not in a tiny space like an fMRI. Perhaps our brain activity might be different if we are not enclosed in a small area.

A clear explanation of ecological validity shows the student can think about the relationship in an abstract manner by questioning the extent to which the relationship it demonstrates can be applied to different context/s.

Similarly, this study only supports an explanation of violence in situations where someone is responding to emotion in someone else (the brain was activated in response to the angry face). This methodology means that there are significant limitations in using these results to explain violence when the violent person is the aggressor. i.e. they are the ones that initiate the violence, as opposed to just being the ones who respond aggressively or attacks without being provoked.

The same applies for explaining generalizability, where a clear reason is provided for why the findings might not be applicable.

We can see from this study that our diet may affect our serotonin levels and this could affect our brain function when we are in particular situations. The effect serotonin has in reducing PFC function during times of social threat may explain its correlation with violent behaviour. However, based on the nature of the methodology and the participants, the extent to which this study can be applied to explain violence in all situations and across genders can be questioned. (825 words, approximately)

The essay ends with a concise summary of the point and counterpoint.

The above essay only uses one study in the answer as the question is asking to evaluate one study. However, in order to achieve full marks it is recommended that you include at least two studies in essay answers.

Important note: The advice that I've provided on how to structure essays is for general guidance only. There are times, for example, that you might want to offer a range of arguments and evidence in response to the question. The point then counter-point structure can be used only if you have sufficient depth of knowledge to write a detailed response. In some cases you might find it better to provide a range of examples in order to achieve high marks for each of the marking criteria.

Hopefully you'll have enough practice at writing essay questions before the actual exam, so you'll be able to develop a style that works for you.

(e) Frequently Asked Questions about Essays and SARs

- Do I need to include details like how many participants in my description?

Only include *relevant* information for your description. If it's *irrelevant* to your explanation, then don't include it. If it's relevant for an evaluation for instance, then the sample number could be stated later in the answer when you get to the evaluation of the study. Again, descriptions provide context and are at most 150 words so don't waste time and words on irrelevant descriptions.

- How much do I describe?

Look at the relationship in the question. Only describe as much as needed to make your explanation make sense (don't dump on the page – select relevant details in your planning process!) Examiners don't want to read boring summaries of irrelevant details. Remember – examiners care as much about what you *understand* as well as how much you *know*!

- Do I have to remember specific numbers in results?

One thing you are being assessed on is the level of detail in your knowledge. The more detailed (and specific) your knowledge, the better. However, there are so many results for you to know that memorizing specific numbers (e.g. the %s in Asch's conformity studies) is less important than being able to explain the significance of these results. Make sure you can remember and describe the results in a *general* manner first and explain their significance. Once you can do this with *all* relevant studies, then you go back and add the details. My point here is that there's no point using valuable time and effort to memorize specific results if it means you run out of time to *understand* the significance of those results.

- Do I always need to use studies?

These are my answers to these questions. Some examiners may disagree, but this advice just uses a common sense approach.

All answers should be supported by evidence and studies are a key source of evidence in psychology, so you should be using studies (and theories) to support your core arguments and counter-arguments. However, when the question is focused on a particular theory or model, make sure that the theory or model is the focus of your answer.

- Do I need to remember names of researchers and the year of the study?

This is far, far, far down on the list of things to revise and memorise. Make sure you can first describe studies (in around 150 words or so) and *explain* how they demonstrate significant relationships. Then, and only then, begin remembering names and possibly years. You may find remembering names is useful to be able to associate the name with the study and recall details, so if this helps then go for it. Remember that the focus of your memorizing of level one details (knowing) should be on those details that help you understand significant relationships. If details like names and dates don't help you develop a further understanding, put them further down on the list to remember. They can be useful to show an examiner the specific study you are referring to, but you are given so many studies in IB Psychology that it's an unrealistic expectation to memorize all names and dates to use in exam responses.

- Can I use material from the options (e.g. abnormal psych') in Paper One?

Yes. Absolutely! And if possible you should. The examiner doesn't care where in the course your understanding of relationships in psychology comes from – they only care about your understanding of the relationship and how that can be demonstrated in research. If it's applicable – use it!

- Can I use content from one question in Paper One in another?

If it's relevant, absolutely, yes. And you should to cut down on the overlap. Identify the relationship and use the research appropriately. There are no "rules" on which studies can and/or cannot be used anywhere in the exam. If they demonstrate the relationship, use it and be sure to explain *how* it demonstrates the relationship! For example, you could use SM's case study in an SAR about localization of brain function and in an essay on ethical considerations related to research on the brain and behaviour (if these two questions were asked in an exam). You can also use studies from one approach in another, provided they are relevant to each approach (e.g. Bechara et al.'s study is relevant to thinking and decision making, as well as localization of brain function).

- Can I use diagrams?

Yes, of course. Why not? If a diagram helps you to explain a relationship, absolutely use a diagram. But it should only be used to *support* your *written* descriptions and explanations. Diagrams are often helpful to show complex studies and their results quickly and easily. It might help you to plan your diagram as well so you remember the details. For example, the IOWA gambling task is a complex study so a quick diagram might help to support a written description of the methodology and results, which will also help the examiner easily see that you comprehend the study.

- What about bullet points?

Same point as above. How you actually communicate your understanding doesn't matter – what matters is that you can!

10.7 Paper 3 Responses

How can you write excellent Paper Three responses?

(a)   What is a Paper 3 response?

While Paper One and Two are designed to primarily assess your knowledge and understanding of specific relationships between variables, behaviours and cognitive processes, Paper Three is designed entirely to assess your knowledge and understanding of research methods. Therefore, it's important that your answers demonstrate your detailed, accurate and relevant knowledge and understanding of research methodology and ethical considerations as applicable to each of the static questions.

Paper Three responses are a mix between SARs and eSARs (*extremely* short answer responses). You have five answers you need to write in one hour, so time is tight. This means you need to have a comprehensive understanding of the requirements of each individual answer to strike a balance between not wasting effort, while still addressing all demands of the question. This section aims to help you with this by explaining the requirements of each question.

You can find all the necessary information regarding the specific research methods in the other relevant chapters.

(b)   Question 1

Remember that *all* three questions from Question 1 will be asked, so you need to be prepared to answer all three. There are 9 possible marks available for Question 1 (a, b & c).

1a. Identify the method used and outline two characteristics of the method. (3 marks)

The method used in the study will be quantitative or qualitative. There is a chance that it will be a mixed-methods approach that uses a combination of both methods (e.g. a case study gathering quantitative *and* qualitative data). One (or more) of the following methods will be used in the stimulus study:

A survey uses questionnaires or interviews to gather data from a large group of people. It is unlikely that you will be asked about the use of a survey in Paper Three, but you never know.

Qualitative		Quantitative	
a.	Case Study	a.	Experiment
b.	Naturalistic Observation	b.	Field Experiment
i.	Participant or Non-participant	c.	Quasi-Experiment
ii.	Covert or Overt	d.	Natural Experiment
c.	Interview	e.	Correlational Research
i.	Unstructured or semi-structured	i.	Survey or Questionnaire
ii.	Individual or Focus Group		

It may be up to you to identify one of the methods that has been used, or the method might be stated in the stimulus, which makes identification very easy. In addition to identifying/stating the method, you need to outline two key characteristics of the method. A good revision strategy would be to revise *three* characteristics for each method, in case you get into the exam and you forget one.

You could answer this question in a few sentences:

- Statement of the method used (1 mark)
- Outline at least two characteristics (2 marks)

1b. *Describe* the sampling method used in the study. (3 marks)

The sampling method used in the study will most likely be stated in the stimulus, so all you need to do is re-state that in your answer for one mark. However, you should be prepared to identify the sampling method from the description of how the sample was obtained, if it's not stated. You get one mark for correctly stating/identifying the sampling method that was used.

One of the following sampling methods will be used:

i.   Random
ii.   Convenience/Opportunity
iii.   Volunteer/Self-selected
iv.   Purposive
v.   Snowball

The remaining two marks available are for the description so you need to include at least two relevant characteristics of the sampling method. You could state three characteristics of the sampling method to be safe.

It's advisable to describe how the method was used in the stimulus as well. This will help to show your examiner that you *understand* the sampling method and you're doing more than simply rewriting memorized answers.

For instance, if a purposive sample was used you can state one characteristic of this sampling method being that "participants are specifically chosen because they have characteristics that make them valuable sources of data for the phenomenon being investigated," and then you can provide an example of at least one of the characteristics of the participants in the sample that made them valuable sources of data. You then do the same for the second characteristic of this sampling method.

You could answer this question in a few sentences:

- Statement of the sampling method used (1 mark)
- Statement of one characteristic of the method and a statement of an example of that characteristic that can be shown in the stimulus. (1 mark)
- Statement of a second characteristic of the method and a statement of an example of that characteristic that can be shown in the stimulus. (1 mark)

1c. *Suggest* an alternative or additional (research) method giving one reason for your choice. (3 marks)

For this question you need to identify the alternative *or* additional research method. You then need to explain why that different research method could have been used rather than the one in the study. *Or*, you could explain why another method could have been used in the study as well (i.e. in addition). You should provide one general reason for your choice and then support that reason with an explanation of how it is relevant to the specific stimulus study.

You can suggest a method that comes from the same or from a different approach. For example, if a field experiment was conducted you could suggest a qualitative method (e.g. interview) or another quantitative method (e.g. questionnaire).

The key part to this question is that your reasoning for an additional/alternative method is logical and is based on the characteristics of the method you have suggested. To get three marks here you need to state and outline another method, including how it would be used. You then need to give one reason why it could be used based on specific details of the methodology.

After you make this point, while it might not be needed to get full marks, it would be a good idea to apply your explanation to the specific context of the stimulus. This final point will show your examiner that you have thought carefully about the study and its methodology and you are doing more than just writing memorized answers.

You could answer this question in a few sentences:

- A statement and definition of the alternative/additional method.
- A description of how this method could be used in the context of the study.
- An explanation of why this particular method would be useful in the context of the stimulus study.

Perhaps the best option in this question is to explain how an *additional* method could be used. This might be more straightforward than explaining how an *alternative* method could have been used.

(c)   Question 2

Remember that you will be given *one* of these questions (i.e. you don't choose – only one will appear). Having said that, the preparation for both questions is quite similar. There are six possible marks available for Question 2.

Both of these static questions require knowledge and understanding of ethical considerations relevant to psychological research. These include, but are not limited to, the considerations explained in other chapters:

- Informed (and parental) consent
- Considerations regarding deception
- The right to withdraw (and right to withdraw data)
- Debriefing
- Anonymity and confidentiality
- Approval from an ethics review committee
- Researcher integrity

2a. Describe the ethical considerations that were applied in the study and explain if further ethical considerations could be applied. (6 marks)

This question requires you to explain a minimum of six ethical considerations because your examiner will award a maximum of one mark per relevant point. You need to explain at least three considerations for each part of the question.

For the first part of the question, there should be at least three ethical considerations directly stated and/or outlined in the stimulus (e.g. they got informed consent, debriefed participants and gave them the right to withdraw). You should state these in your answer and provide a brief summary of how and/or why they were applied. For example, you could explain how debriefing may reduce the chances of psychological stress or harm as a result of a specific procedure used in the study.

For the second part of this question, I recommend instead of "explain if further ethical considerations could be applied" add "*and/or how*" to the question, so it reads "explain if *and/or how* further ethical considerations could be applied." I suggest this because it's probably easier to explain how *additional* ethical considerations could be applied to the stimulus, rather than explaining why *none* could be applied. Nevertheless, you might find that the study is ethically solid and there are good reasons why no further ethical considerations need could be applied, but this is unlikely. Even if this is the case you still need to state the consideration that doesn't need to be applied and a reason why not and this might be difficult.

It is far more probable that the exam setters (if they choose to use this question) have deliberately excluded some relevant ethical details to allow for you to explain why *additional* ethical considerations could be applied.

2b. Describe the ethical considerations in reporting the results and explain ethical considerations that could be taken into account when applying the findings of the study. (6 marks)

To answer this question you can still focus on ethical considerations the researchers applied in the course of the study (e.g. informed consent, debriefing, etc.). For example, participants need to be informed and/or debriefed on how the results may be reported and/or applied. Keeping participants' data anonymous is essential in reporting and applying findings, as well.

The same guidelines for the first ethics question also applies:

- The considerations might be stated and/or you need to identify considerations that aren't mentioned.
- Cross out "describe" and write "explain" because you have to relate the considerations to the particular methodology of the stimulus study (e.g. go beyond memorizing)
- You need to include six considerations as a minimum and three from each section.

You can read more about ethical considerations in the Introduction, Quantitative and Qualitative Methods chapters.

The stimulus should provide some details that might allude to how findings may be used, so look carefully for these details.

You might achieve marks by stating relevant ethical considerations, providing a general reason why they're important, and then doing your best to apply them to the study. A good way to prepare is to make sure you know the ethical considerations and you can explain why they're important in research in general. Combine this revision with revising ethical considerations in other studies used in the course.

Exam Revision Tip: Try to combine preparation for ethics and research methods questions in Paper One and Two with revising for Paper Three. I like to give my students a list of studies that are relevant to a particular topic (e.g. the Brain and Behaviour) and then get them to identity common research methods and ethical considerations relevant to these studies. Finding commonalities like this can enhance conceptual understanding and allows you to show deeper knowledge and understanding of research methods and ethics questions in your explanations.

(d)   Question 3

As with Question 2, you will be given *one* of the following questions:

I)   Discuss the possibility of generalizing the findings of the study.
II)   Discuss how a researcher could ensure that the results of the study are credible.
III)   Discuss how the researcher in the study could avoid bias.

You can prepare for this question by making sure that you know what the three key terms in the question mean and that you understand how they are influenced by particular methodologies in research (e.g. data collection methods, procedures and sampling).

You will have around 20 minutes to plan and answer this question, so the length will be similar to an SAR (around 250 – 350 words). You should have time to make *two* well-developed explanations. So this means you have to know methodology, explain how methodology relates to generalizability/bias/credibility and then apply that explanation to the specific context of the study.

Preparing to write answers using the following guidelines will allow you to ensure you can get at least a few marks, regardless of the stimulus material because you will be able to show knowledge and understanding of research methodology and how this relates to one of the concepts in the questions: generalizability, bias or credibility. The ability to apply your understanding to the stimulus material is what will earn you top marks. The best way to prepare for that is to write practice responses, receive feedback, improve them and then repeat this process as often as possible.

You should have time to make at least two clear points that demonstrate knowledge and understanding of research methodology and how particular details of methods relate to one of the three concepts.

I)   *Discuss the possibility of generalizing the findings of the study.*

Generalizability is a term commonly applied to quantitative studies; transferability is the similar concept that is commonly applied to qualitative studies. These two concepts are very similar in that they both refer to the process of applying findings beyond the context of the present study. However, if qualitative methodology is used you should demonstrate your understanding of the concepts of generalizability *and* transferability. If a quantitative method is used you can focus on generalizability only.

II)   *Discuss how a researcher could ensure that the results of the study are credible.*

In the question regarding generalizability you need to focus on the presented details of the study as the basis of your answer. However, these questions on credibility and bias are asking you to hypothesize what a researcher could potentially do, not necessarily what they have done already.

Triangulation is a way that could ensure a study's results are credible. Remember that credibility is a term used in qualitative research, so if the stimulus material is using quantitative research you should actually be discussing validity. While you might not be marked down for using the term credibility in relation to quantitative studies, it does pay to use the correct terminology wherever possible.

III) *Discuss how the researcher in the study could avoid bias.*

As with the other Paper Three questions, top marks will be awarded to those students who can apply their explanations to the particular context of the study. The ability to hypothesize possible ways of reducing bias and explaining them clearly is important to demonstrate to an examiner because one purpose of learning about research methodology in psychology is so that in the future when/if you design your own research studies you can apply your learning in that process. By explaining how these concepts relate to a study you've never seen before, your examiner can assess the extent to which you are well-prepared to transfer your learning from this course.

The use of triangulation to avoid bias could be applied to qualitative or quantitative research. The use of a blind procedure in an experimental study could also help to avoid bias.

The command term is "discuss", which means there should be some "critical thinking" to provide a "balanced review." If you have time, you could comment on the limitations of your explanations. This could be used in all three responses. For example, you might comment on issues of practicality related to using triangulation.

(e) *Example Stimulus Study*

The most important thing to remember with Paper Three responses is that you know exactly what the questions might be. This makes preparation easier. The difficulty is that you don't know what the research stimulus will be, so it's important that you get lots of practice at answering these questions with practice research summaries.

Remember that the research might be qualitative or quantitative. The following example answers are going to be based on SM's case study that was looked at during the study of criminology. Remember that it is expected that you would have never seen the study before in Paper 3: this is for demonstration purposes only.

Here's an example of what a stimulus study would look like:

The stimulus material below is based on a study on the role of the amygdala in experiencing fear.

The amygdala is a part of the brain that performs many functions associated with emotion. Clinical observations of patients with brain damage suggest that there is a correlation between amygdala damage and the ability to feel fear. Before this study there were no empirical investigations on this relationship. The aim of this study, therefore, was to systematically investigate the correlation between amygdala damage and experiencing fear.

This case study was conducted on SM, a woman in her 40s who has amygdala damage as a result of a genetic disorder. Patients with damage to both amygdalae (i.e. the part of the amygdala on both sides of the brain) and with only damage to this part of the brain are difficult to find. The researchers used a purposive sample of one patient who has such damage. SM was known to the researchers because she has participated in numerous studies. She gave her informed consent to participate in the study and was given the right to withdraw at any time.

To test her reaction to fearful stimuli the researchers exposed her to three different situations that would be expected to provoke a response of fear. This involved taking her to a haunted house, an exotic pet store filled with snakes and spiders, and watching clips from scary films. The researchers gathered qualitative data during overt observations of SM's behaviour and reactions in each situation. They also gathered quantitative data from self-report questionnaires.

From the observations the researchers concluded that SM showed no signs of fear to any of the stimuli presented. The self-report questionnaires also showed that she experiences fear at a much lower level than the normal population.

From the observation the researchers concluded that the amygdala plays an important role in generating an emotional response to fearful stimuli. From the questionnaires they were also able to conclude that the amygdala plays a role in the subject experience of feeling fear. The research also reported that SM has been in dangerous situations due to her lack of fear.

This case study on SM supports other research that suggests the amygdala plays an important evolutionary function in survival: having a healthy fear of dangerous stimuli can help us to avoid such stimuli and increase our chances of survival.

Feinstein, Justin S., Ralph Adolphs, Antonio Damasio, and Daniel Tranel. "The Human Amygdala and the Induction and Experience of Fear." Current Biology 21.1 (2011): 34-38. Accessed online.

(f)   *Example Answers to Questions 1*

A.   Identify the method used and outline two characteristics of the method.

This study used a case study method. A case study:

- *…is an in-depth investigation of an individual, group or organisation. In this study they did an in-depth study of an individual with rare brain damage.*
- *…might use a mixed methods approach, which means they use various methods to gather data, such as interviews, tests and observations. This case study used observations of SM and used questionnaires to gather data as well.*

B.   Describe the sampling method used in the study.

This case study used a purposive sample. A purposive sample:

- *…involves getting participants who have the characteristics that are relevant for the specific area of study. In SM's case, she was asked to be the subject of the case study because of her unique situation of having damaged amygdalae with the rest of her brain intact.*
- *…may involve snowballing. In this case there was only one participant, so snowballing wasn't needed.*

C.   Suggest an alternative or additional (research) method giving one reason for your choice.

An additional method that could have been used could be a semi-structured interview. Semi-structured interviews allow researchers to gather qualitative data on participants' experiences by using an interview schedule and asking open and closed questions. The interview could have been used to triangulate the conclusions from the observations of SM's experiences during the scary experiences, i.e. they could have helped to ensure their interpretations of their observation of her lack of fear were accurate and were a true representation of what she was feeling during these experiences.

(g)   *Example Answer to Questions 2*

Question 2: (6 marks)

Only the first ethics question has been answered here.

I)   Describe the ethical considerations that were applied in the study and explain if further ethical considerations could be applied.

It's important that you mention at least three points from each part of the question.

Anonymity was applied in this study by keeping SM's real name anonymous. Anonymity is important in research to respect participants from any negative repercussions resulting from participating in the study. This is important in SM's study because her privacy needs to be respected, especially since she suffers from unique brain damage (she may get unwanted attention because of how interesting her lack of fear is).

Informed consent was applied and this was important because it could help ensure SM would know that although the situations were scary, they wouldn't cause her physical harm and she'd be safe. Similarly, the right to withdraw was applied and this would be important in this study as SM was exposed to scary situations that might have induced psychological stress. The right to withdraw can alleviate these effects.

There was no mention of the study being approved by an ethics review committee. Studies should be approved by an ethics review committee before being carried out, especially when using potentially stress-inducing procedures like this one.

It does not mention whether or not SM was debriefed or specifically given the right to withdraw particular data from the study. These two considerations are important. It might not have been appropriate to disclose all aims of the study to SM before it took place (for reasons of validity/credibility) so she should be debriefed afterwards so she knows why she gave up her time for the study and the potential applications of the research. The researchers could have also gone through their observation notes with SM and summarized their interpretation of the observation. Giving SM the right to withdraw incorrect observational notes at this time would help to ensure that no misleading information was published in the final study.

(h) Example Answer to Questions 3

Only one question has been answered here.

I)   Discuss the possibility of generalizing the findings of the study.

Generalizability refers to the extent to which findings from one study can be applied to populations beyond those in the study. The purposive sample used in this study limits the extent to which the findings can be generalized. However, methodological triangulation might increase the possibility of generalization from SM's case study.

In qualitative research the goal isn't always to generalize findings. This is why purposive sampling is commonly used: instead of finding a sample that is representative of a wider population, researchers find participants who have particular characteristics that are of use for the study. A purposive sample therefore, might not be representative of a wider population which influences generalizability. This study used a purposive sample of SM because she has a rare case of amygdala damage that is hard to find. For this reason, she makes a valuable person to study. However, the fact that she is only one person limits the extent to which we can accurately generalize the findings to other participants. She also suffers from a genetic disease, which could be a possible influence on her experience of feeling fear which might affect generalizability: i.e. her genetic disease may be a confounding variable in this study.

Using data and/or methodological triangulation could increase the possibility of generalizing the findings from this study. The researchers could use data triangulation by getting other samples of people with amygdala damage and see if they get the same results (demonstrating test-retest reliability). Similarly, experiments using brain imaging technology on healthy participants that measure correlations between brain activity and emotional stimuli might also increase the probability of generalizability if the answers obtained were similar. For example, scary and harmless stimulus could be shown on a screen and the function of the amygdala recorded. This might increase the chances that results from SM's study could be generalized to wider populations because there would be more supporting evidence.

So while the necessary purposive sample in this study reduced probability of generalizability to other populations, triangulation could be adopted to remedy this. (340 words)

Having an in-depth understanding of the use of research methods and being able to use the relevant terminology is the key to being well-prepared for Paper Three.

Conclusion

The key to success in IB Psychology is to maintain a harmonious balance between learning about Psychology and preparing to do well in your exams. If you spend the whole course thinking and worrying about what will be on the exam and how to write perfect answers, you'll probably never develop the understanding of the course required to do well on these exams in the first place. Similarly, if you focus only on the interesting aspects of the course and those that excite your passion for the subject but you never worry about how to show your understanding in an exam response, your final results will not reflect your true capabilities as a psychologist.

It is hoped that the guidance in this chapter has also helped you to understand the why behind writing effective exam answers. If you can understand, for instance, why outlining the scope of your essay in the introduction is important and you know how to do this, there's a good chance that you will be able to use this skill in other subjects. Similarly, if you know why signposting is effective in communicating your ideas, you can use this communication skill in many areas, not just IB Psychology exam answers.

Some final pieces of wisdom I'd like to share with you have come to me from two very important women in my life, my mother and my wife.

Growing up my mother always told me that "life's about balance." It's really essential that you focus on maintaining a balance throughout the hectic exam preparation season – your brain will thank you for it. Make sure you get plenty of sleep and exercise and you eat healthily and your life is not just about revision. And as mentioned earlier, strike a balance between enjoying Psychology for the sake of it and studying to do well on exams.

My wife loves to remind me that "many a little makes a mickle!" A mickle is a large quantity, so this is essentially like the saying "slow and steady wins the race." Doing a little bit of revision regularly, throughout the course in fact, is the best way to approach your exam preparation. It's not expected that you will be able to read this chapter and then suddenly write perfect answers. It takes a lot of practice and this should be approached throughout the course. Leaving it all to the last minute is, of course, a poor approach. If you have worked hard throughout the course, you will be far better prepared than if you have waited until the last month before the exams to prepare.

I hope this chapter and this textbook will help you exceed your potential in the exams. Be sure to use our blog (https://ibpsych.themantic-education.com/) and to keep an eye out for other materials we've published that will help you prepare for the exams.

Good luck.

Chapter 11
The Extended Essay

The Extended Essay (EE) is one way the IB Diploma Programme attempts to help you develop the skills needed to pursue independent and effective research in a subject of interest. It also provides you with practice in writing an essay of considerable length (4,000 words), which is an invaluable skill for those of you heading towards further academic study.

If you are writing your EE in Psychology, you need to choose a topic that's interesting and is approved by your supervisor. After you have selected a topic, you can construct an initial research question that will get you started in the research and writing process. Your final product is an essay of around 4,000 words (maximum).

The IB recommends spending approximately three to five hours with your supervisor throughout the process. Please remember that all the advice and guidance included in this chapter is of secondary importance to the advice and guidance that you will receive from them. There are also three mandatory reflection sessions that must be completed during the course of the EE as well. Along with the essay, you will also submit a reflection form of around 500 words (maximum) and your final session will be a viva voce, which is an interview with your supervisor that is carried out with the purpose of making sure the work you have submitted is your own.

Your EE must not include primary research and you should be relying on secondary sources of information only (i.e. research published in peer-reviewed journals or other credible sources). You should not conduct your own interviews, experiments, surveys or any other form of research. In fact, if you do include primary research in your EE your essay may be flagged by the IB and you may fail the diploma. The IA is your opportunity to conduct primary research – the EE requires you to examine existing research.

The EE has the potential to be an interesting and exciting project. You have a head start towards success if you are motivated, have a topic of interest that you wish to explore, and some questions to get you started in the research process. If you take your time to choose a topic to investigate that is interesting, you'll find the EE will provide you with an exhilarating sense of academic discovery as you uncover research and formulate ideas that you never knew existed. Like any major project, one of the hardest things is getting started, so the purpose of this chapter is to help you in the initial stages of getting your EE project under way.

The EE is a compulsory requirement for diploma candidates and is optional for course candidates.

(a)　Getting Started

I want to begin by reiterating the fact that all guidance here is secondary to the guidance, support and advice you will receive from your EE supervisor. The EE process is highly personalized and there are many variables that will influence your research and writing along the way, so I can only provide very generic advice that will not be as helpful as the targeted and specific guidance you can receive during your regular meetings with your EE supervisor.

The EE is a challenging process for many reasons. For one, it demands a substantial time commitment and the IB advises that it should be the product of around 40 hours of work. Some students mistakenly think the EE in Psychology is easier than other subjects, but this is a false assumption. To research and write about a topic in Psychology is just as difficult as other subjects, so it should only be undertaken if you have a genuine interest in what you are researching and you are motivated to spend the time it takes to explore a topic in sufficient depth.

The first step in getting started with your EE is choosing a topic. It is acceptable to study a topic that is related to something that you have studied during this course. For example, when studying criminology you may have developed an interest in the origins of violent crime and you might wish to explore this further. Perhaps there was a very specific topic within this unit that you wished you had more time to study, like alternative strategies to reduce recidivism. Using a topic that has been taught in class can be a good starting point for your investigation. However, it should only be the *starting point*. To write an excellent essay, you will need to go far beyond what's included in this or any other introductory textbook.

There might be an area of psychology that you wanted to explore that is not in this book or the curriculum. For instance, you may wish to investigate an anxiety disorder, like Obsessive Compulsive Disorder, but you haven't learned about this in class. It is fine to choose a topic that has not been taught, provided this is approved by your supervisor.

It is important, however, that your topic is based on Psychology and not another subject like Sociology or Economics. For example, conducting an investigation into the social effects of the privatization of prisons in the US is more related to Economics and Sociology because this topic lacks a focus on *individual behaviour*. Remember that Psychology is the scientific study of individual behaviour and mental processes. Your choice of topic, therefore, should be an investigation into some aspect of individual human behaviour. You may wish to make it simple and choose a topic that explores the relationship between a specific variable and a specific behaviour.

Choosing a topic may begin with identifying a behaviour that you are interested in, such as depression, conformity, aggression, psychopathy, drug addiction, etc. You can then begin narrowing your focus into a particular area of study in relation to this behaviour, like causes, effects or methods of treatment.

Alternatively, you might begin by thinking of a variable that you think (or know) has an effect on human behaviour, such as the use of social media,

Many a little makes a mickle – this philosophy is the key to writing a good EE.

You need to go well beyond the information that is summarized in textbooks like this one if you want to write an excellent EE.

You probably won't come up with the best topic or question straight away. It will take some careful reading and researching.

drug use, poverty, depression, yoga, etc. You could begin with this and then begin exploring resources to craft your topic. To put it another way, you might begin with a specific IV and consider how this might affect a DV, or the other way around.

It is fine to begin with a broad topic and narrow your focus as you progress through the research process. For example, you might want to study stress. The first question your supervisor will probably ask you is, "what about stress to do you want to investigate?" This is where you will need to begin doing some wide reading and start narrowing the focus of your investigation. On the other hand, you may have a specific topic from the outset, such as how using Facebook can increase the chances of anxiety disorders in teenagers. You may even know of some studies that have been conducted on this phenomenon. The variability involved in the EE process makes providing generic advice very difficult, so again, consult regularly with your advisor.

Some students of mine in the past have come to me with questions like, "I want to know what makes people happy." This is a genuinely interesting question and it's a good place to start if one is interested in this topic, but it will need to become more focused as this is too broad. What I would tell my student in this case is, "that sounds like a fascinating question, and if it's still your question in a month's time then you haven't done enough research."

However you begin your investigation, you will ultimately need a focused topic and an effective research question. Guidance on how to achieve this is included in the following sections.

(b) Wide Reading and Narrowing Your Focus

Your EE needs to be based on a topic and a research question that can be effectively addressed in the word limit of 4,000 words. A question like, "What makes people happy?" is an example of a question that is far too broad to be addressed effectively because there are so many possible variables that may influence happiness.

You will only be able to narrow your focus if you have knowledge of the topic you are investigating. If you have already started with a focused topic like the effects of social media on anxiety in teenagers, this is probably because you are aware of research in this field already.

Perhaps you have a focused topic, like the relationship between bilingualism and academic success, but you don't know much about this relationship. You've just guessed that bilingualism is related to academic success somehow. Hypothesizing in this way could be an effective way to begin your research process, but I would offer a word of caution: if you begin with a focused topic that you don't know much about you run the risk of discovering that actually there's no relationship there, or that there is very little relevant research in this area. For this reason, if you are not sure if your topic has been studied extensively, it might be wise to keep your topic broad to begin with as you conduct your wide reading.

Throughout your reading you should be searching for ways to narrow the focus of your topic and to construct an effective research question. For example, if I wanted to know what makes people happy I would begin by reading to try to get a general

---

Sidebar notes:

Having a broad question to start with is perfectly fine, but you won't submit a very good essay if your question is still vague and general by the end of your research.

Wide reading involves consulting a range of sources of information that are related to your topic in order to get a better understanding of what it is you want to investigate.

The more you know the easier it will be to narrow your topic. If you don't know much in the beginning, you'll need to do wide reading.

idea of the existing research in this field. Because I have no specific variables identified in my topic, I would be trying to see if there are particular variables that are commonly studied in relation to happiness. In the course of my wide reading I might find that there are numerous studies on correlations between wealth and happiness. So now in the course of my wide reading I have narrowed my focus to a relationship between two variables: wealth and happiness.

The more you read and research the more focused your topic and research question will become. I advise my students that they shouldn't think of their topic or research question as being set in stone, but always open to adjusting, adapting and tweaking. This is especially true in the early stages of the research process.

The earlier you start reading and researching, the better your final essay will be.

(c)   Crafting a Research Question

Generally speaking, the process of getting started in your investigation involves first choosing a particular area of psychology that interests you. This might include a broad or specific topic. Once you have done enough initial wide reading and you have focused your topic sufficiently with help from your supervisor, you need to develop a research question.

You can read more about research questions and the EE in our blog post called, "Is this a good EE question?"

As the EE is highly individualized, the process of crafting an effective research question will also vary greatly from student to student. In an ideal world you would choose a topic, narrow that topic so it is focused and ensure that there is sufficient research to conduct a thorough investigation. You would then construct a perfectly written research question that would allow you to thoroughly investigate your topic and produce a well-written essay. However, the realities of the research process is that it's seldom the case that you will begin with the same research question that you will end up with. In fact, throughout the course of your research you won't just be using one research question, you will have many. Your overarching question should guide all these other sub-questions that you will ask throughout the process. After all, during your research you will be continually learning, and learning is about asking and finding answers to questions.

For example, let's say I chose the topic of what makes people happy. After doing some wide reading I narrow this to focus on the relationship between money and happiness. I then construct a research question, "Does money make people happy?" I now have a starting point for my investigation and I can begin looking at studies (and there are many) related to this question. Perhaps after doing quite a lot of research I find a lot of evidence to suggest that there is in fact a correlation between money and happiness. But perhaps the bulk of the evidence is focused on correlations between personal wealth and well-being. I might even find a body of research that investigates specific correlations between increasing personal wealth and personal well-being. So now my question has evolved based on this body of new research that I have discovered and I am now asking, "How does wealth affect our well-being?" The change of the phrasing from "Does" to "How" reveals the progression in my understanding of the topic based on my research: my latter question implies that wealth does affect our happiness, which is what is suggested by the many studies I have read about in my research process. But looking at my question, I don't like the word "our" because I am not really investigating you and me. So I would tweak this slightly again to read, "How does wealth affect individual well-being?" But still, I don't like the word "does" because this is definitive. Another tweaking and my new question is "How can wealth affect individual well-being?" Even still I don't like the word "individual" because it seems too clunky, so I cut it out and I now have, what I think is an effective question to continue with my research: "How can wealth affect well-being?"

In the early stages of your research process, it can be beneficial to treat your research question like an evolving and living thing.

The reason I have walked you through my thought-processes in the above paragraph is because I want to show you how it can be beneficial to think of the research question as a living thing that can evolve. You should be continually crafting and restructuring your question to ensure that it accurately represents what you are trying to explore in your investigation. Obviously, the earlier you construct a clear research question the more focused and effective your writing processes will be. This is where there is an obvious correlation between time and effort spent on the research and the quality of your final product. The more research you have gathered, read, sorted and filtered the more informed your research question will be.

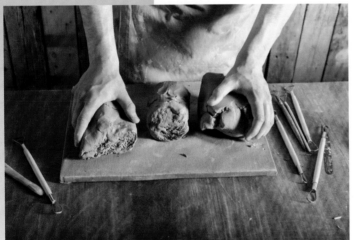

Sculpting is a good metaphor to use when thinking about your EE process: you start with a big hunk of clay (your broad topic) and you craft this into something refined and precise (your final research question). The writing of your essay will also resemble the sculpting process, from taking all your chunky research findings and crafting them into a well-written essay.

It might even help to consider the research question as more like the title of your final essay, as opposed to one concrete, immovable and unchangeable question that dictates the entire research process.

The vast majority of IB Psychology EEs begin with the phrase, 'To what extent…' This is because this question naturally encourages the critical thinking by offering the possibility of introducing one or more counter-arguments. You can write excellent essays with this type of question, but the following types of questions could also make for excellent extended essays:

- Does Facebook cause anxiety in teenagers?
- How can yoga reduce criminal recidivism?
- Does bilingualism increase intelligence?

The best advice I can offer about writing a good extended essay is pretty basic – do the research. The more research you find, the more material you have to craft an excellent question and construct a brilliant essay.

(d) Sources and Resources

Without a doubt the most common piece of advice that IBDP graduates give to new IB students regarding the EE is - *don't procrastinate*. With the multiple IAs you have to complete for your regular subjects and the regular projects and assignments that you have for your regular course work, many students put their EE off for too long and end up having to rush through the process. If you want to write an excellent essay you need to devote the time needed to conduct thorough research, write clear notes, craft your research question, and engage in productive discussions with your supervisor.

It has already been mentioned but it bears repeating that no primary research is to be conducted for your EE. This means that you definitely should not be conducting your own experiments, interviews, surveys, etc., as part of your research.

You are encouraged to consult a range of credible sources of information. Websites such as Psychology Today and the American Psychological Association are often a good place to *begin* your wide reading and focusing your topic, as are general psychology textbooks. They often summarize studies that might also provide more information about your topic. The bulk of your EE, however, should be drawing on research published in peer-reviewed journals.

One tip for finding sources of relevant information is to read the references of relevant articles that you find. If you find a peer-reviewed article that addresses your topic, this same article will also reference other studies and articles that have explored the same or a similar topic. This can help ignite a journey down a road of discovery!

When you are finding studies, reading the abstracts carefully can save you time reading entire articles. The abstracts are designed to give you an overview of the article, so you should read these carefully as you are conducting your research. For instance, while the title of the article might sound really relevant, the abstract might suggest it's irrelevant and so you can skip it and keep searching. Or, if the abstract seems to summarize what you're looking for, you can make the choice to invest the time in reading the full article. The introduction will also include a review of relevant literature, and following the articles cited in the bibliography can also help your investigation.

Remember that there's more to writing an excellent essay than simply how many studies you find. There is also no magic number of studies that you need to include. Your essay should present core arguments that you are presenting in relation to your research question. Sometimes you may need to describe a study in a lot of detail in order to contextualize your argument. Other times you may only need a one or two sentence summary. As with writing other essays, you need to critically select the evidence you include in your essay and think carefully about how you use that evidence.

Taking careful and thorough notes is especially important throughout the EE process. You will need to provide references for all your sources. It's far easier to keep notes of your sources as you are taking notes than it is to try to go back later and trace where you found your information.

There's no secret formula to writing an excellent EE – it takes hard work and thorough research. The more research you can gather, the easier the entire process will be, from crafting a clear and concise question to structuring a well-developed argument in response to that question. If 4,000 words might seem daunting to begin with, once you've conducted thorough research you'll find that the challenge won't be reaching the word limit, it will be trying to stay under it.

You will enjoy the research process a lot more if you have chosen a topic you are interested in. It's hoped that you may even experience the thrill of academic discovery as you find the answers to interesting questions you pose throughout the process.

4,000 words is about as long as this chapter. It's not that much once you do the research.

You can reference textbooks in your essay, but the bulk of your research should be coming from articles published in peer-reviewed journal articles. Many of these can be found in full online using Google Scholar. Your school may also have access to databases (e.g. Questia) that can be useful for conducting your research.

If you know what your central argument and evidence are before beginning, the final product may be easier to construct and will read more coherently.

You can find more resources for the EE on our blog, including rubrics and tips for writing the essay.

One hint for writing the final essay that might seem obvious is that you will probably find it easier to start writing *after* you've conducted your research, gathered the evidence and crafted your question. If you try to research and write the essay at the same time, you might find that you'll often get stuck and will need to delete or re-write whole sections. Be sure to consult with your supervisor regularly, and check our blog for new ideas and resources that will help you through the EE process.

If you're conscientious, hard-working and reflective, the Extended Essay project will be an exciting discovery of new ideas and concepts. Remember, many-a-little, makes a mickle!

Chapter 12
Conclusion

(a) A Brief History of Psychology

It might seem odd to include a brief history of psychology at the end of the course, but if you were introduced to the following names and ideas in the beginning it might not make much sense - you'd probably have no clue about Watson and Baby Albert, Kandel and his Aplysia or Milner and HM's hippocampus. But I would feel remiss if I didn't include at least a brief summary of the history of psychology. It's also good way to recap some of the major topics in the course.

While psychology is a relatively new science and only really began in earnest in the late 1800s, its origins can be dated back to Plato, who in 387BC proposed that the brain was the core of our mental processes. There was little advancement of the ideas of Plato and the other Ancient Greeks until the Renaissance and the Age of Enlightenment in the 1600s and 1700s, when philosophers and physicians started contributing ideas that would lay the foundation for modern psychology.

In the 1800s, things began moving more rapidly. Phineas Gage's accident in 1848 generally marks the beginning of neuroscience as his accident provided the first clues that our brain function and personality are linked. While Gage gave insight into the role of the frontal lobe, other early cases in Europe helped us to understand the brain's role in language. French physician Paul Broca conducted a case study on a man called Tan who had a speech impediment and a post-mortem operation revealed that he had damage to a particular part of the brain, an area now known as "Broca's area." While Broca and Tan provided insight into the functions of language *production*, Carl Wernicke, a German neurologist and physician, conducted similar studies and discovered that damage to a particular part of the brain can affect language *comprehension*. This came to be known as "Wernicke's area."

Tan was given this name because it was the only sound he could make.

Studies like Wernicke's and Broca's may have helped to reduce the popularity of a pseudo-science called phrenology. This was popular for the first half of the 1800s and involved making predictions about people's personalities based on lumps on their head. Phrenology was based on the idea that our behaviour was related to the size of the brain in different areas. While this concept is not complexly erroneous, the practical application of it was: phrenologists believed that different sized areas of the brain would protrude at different places in the skull, and so by measuring the bumps on a person's skull you could deduce what type of personality they had.

Phrenology is a good example of the need for empirical evidence in psychology. This demand for robust evidence is one reason why "The Father of Psychology," Wilhelm Wundt, opened the first psychology laboratory at the University of Leipzig in Germany in 1879. It was only four years later that a student of Wundt's opened the first psychology laboratory in the USA.

Wilhelm Wundt is considered the father of psychology and he opened the first psychology laboratory in 1879.

William James, another founding father of psychology, contributed to the growth of the subject in 1890 when he published his book, *Principles of Psychology*, in which he defines psychology as the science of mental life. From this publishing, the serious and scientific study of psychology flourished.

One of the most dominant figures in psychology throughout the 20th century was Sigmund Freud. In 1900, he published his book *The Interpretation of Dreams*. Freud's theories are based on the idea that our behaviour and thinking are products of deep-seeded unconscious desires and memories stemming from our childhood. One of his theories was that we could understand these unconscious thoughts by studying the content of dreams.

But in the early 1900s another school of thought about the origins of human behaviour began to emerge after John B. Watson published his articles and his infamous studies on Baby Albert. Watson's behaviorism became the most popular movement in American psychology and behaviorists believed that the mind could not be studied scientifically because it could not be seen. How could Freud claim, they argued, that our behaviour is a product of our unconscious selves when we can't observe these forces at work? Since empiricism is about gathering evidence from the senses, behaviorists like Watson argued that we need to be able to observe phenomena if we want to study them reliably and objectively. Watson's ideas inspired a whole movement of behaviorist researchers, most notably B.F Skinner who proposed training pigeons to drop bombs and developed a box to raise babies (called the "Skinner Box").

Bandura's early theories on social learning were a reaction against Freud's theories of the unconscious mind and behaviorism's reductionist approach of viewing behaviour as a trained response to environmental stimuli. He argued that human thinking cannot be overlooked when studying behaviour and that our social environment is a key force in shaping how we think and act. In order to empathize the role of cognition in learning, the theory was later renamed social cognitive theory.

It was also the behaviorist movement against which the cognitive scientists of the 1950s revolted. During the "Cognitive Revolution," cognitive scientists began arguing that the mind could be studied empirically, one just needed to use the right methodologies. Experiments on cognitive processes, including memory, flourished in this time and led to a plethora of publications about cognition. It is based on studies from this era that Atkinson and Shiffrin proposed the multi-store model of memory (1968), which later in turn inspired Baddeley and Hitch's working memory model (1974).

Behaviorism was attractive because prior cognitive research lacked empiricism. Bartlett, for example, was very haphazard in his methods and James said introspection was like flipping on a light switch to try to study the darkness.

But let's not overlook the famous case of HM's, whose case of amnesia gave Brenda Milner an opportunity in 1957 to study the biological origins of memory. Her findings contributed to the growing field of cognitive neuroscience, which was helped with Kandel's experiments on Aplysia and the biological basis of memory formation and storage.

With modern developments of technology used to study the brain, like the fMRI and MRI, cognitive neuroscience has only increased in prominence and importance in psychology. These technologies have enabled researchers to conduct studies on brain function and behaviour that would have been the stuff of dreams for early psychologists like James and Wundt. But if there's one thing we've learned from the replicability project, it's that we should make sure what we know is sound before we make bold claims or propose radical applications. While there are some really interesting studies emerging, many of which were included in this text, a healthy dose of skepticism is important.

The debate at the centre of psychology for the past 100 years is whether or not our behaviour can be explained through nature or nurture. We now know undeniably that both of these forces play a role in shaping who we are, how we think, and what we do. But perhaps the question shouldn't be about understanding the origins of our thoughts and actions, but more about how we can make them better. In other words, how can we use what we know in psychology for the benefit of humankind? This is the driving question at the heart of psychological science, and the overarching theme of this book. After completing this course, hopefully you'll be able to apply your new knowledge and understanding to improve your own life, and perhaps even the lives of others.

(b) Final Thoughts

Congratulations on getting to the end of this first ever textbook that uses the themantic model™ of teaching and learning. The themantic model is based on the neurological and cognitive evidence of how we learn, which is all about making connections. By gradually introducing new information in a relevant and related way, you had plenty of opportunities to comprehend concrete details while understanding increasingly complex and abstract concepts. As a result, you've no doubt become an excellent psychologist who comprehends complex terminology and concepts, can explain how variables influence behaviour, and use evidence to support your answers. You can also offer counter arguments and critical reflections on your own understanding, showing how behaviour is too complex to understand by a single approach and we need to have a healthy skepticism of all evidence.

Another guiding philosophy we have at ThemEd is that learning should be relevant, meaningful, interesting, and long-lasting. The topics selected in this text weren't just selected because they are the best for your exam preparation. While they certainly have provided you with more than enough material to use when acing your IB Psychology exam, it is also hoped that the concepts and topics explored in this text would be of interest and relevance for you now, and perhaps even in the future.

Our goal at ThemEd is to help teachers teach, and students learn. Because when it's done right, education has the power to sow the seeds of change, both on an individual level and a societal one. It's my sincere hope that this text has helped plant a few seeds that one day will take hold and grow into something significant.

After you complete the IB Diploma and start looking towards the future, it's hoped that the ideas you've acquired while studying psychology will stay with you for a long time.

(c)   *Acknowledgements*

First and foremost I would like to thank my wife, Satomi, for her patience and support throughout the process of writing this book and for agreeing to stick around for the next 50 years while I write plenty more.

This book wouldn't exist without the hard work and dedication of the team at Themantic Education™, either – Kim for the amazing graphic design work, Evan for learning how to publish and distribute a book so I didn't have to, Jamie for figuring out how to get it into your hands and Merrill and Tara for doing their best to correct my many mistakes.

When I first began teaching IB Psychology I leaned heavily on the existing books by other authors. I would like to thank Jennie, John, Jette, Alan, Christos and Christian for their work and always being up for a healthy debate and discussion about teaching psychology. I'm also very appreciative of Corry Blades, who gave me the confidence to begin publishing my own materials for a wider audience.

I love to help teachers teach and students learn, so I'd like to thank everyone who has given me positive feedback on my resources, especially Marjo, Anita, Paul, Jennifer, Shari, Martin and Karen. Your early words of encouragement boosted my confidence in this resource.

And last but not least I'd like to thank my students. Thanks for being a fun group of people to spend time with on a daily basis. I look forward to vacations ending more than I do them beginning, and Mondays are honestly more exciting for me than Fridays. You're the reason why.

This book was written for you and future editions will be written for future students. If you've found this book useful, or you can think of ways it could be improved for future editions, please give us feedback through the Facebook groups or our blog.

Cheers,
Travis

Glossary

You can use this margin to write notes and/or translations of the key terms.

Ablating: Surgically removing something.

Abstract idea: An idea that is not immediately observable or measurable.

Abstract thinking: To think beyond concrete terms and ideas and comprehend things beyond their immediate context.

Abstracting: To extract abstract ideas by comparing concepts, topics and examples.

Acculturation strategies: Berry outlines four acculturation strategies (assimilation, integration, separation and marginalization). These refer to how an individual adapts to a secondary culture.

Acculturation: The process of interacting with a new culture that can lead to change in an individual.

Acculturative stress: Psychological stress or other negative emotional outcomes that may result from the process of acculturation.

Activating schema: Being presented with information that stimulates particular thoughts or memories.

Adaptation: A change in an individual organism that has helped it to survive (and procreate).

Adrenaline: A hormone released during the fight-flight (stress) response. It increases heart rate, blood pressure, produces instant energy and increases alertness (US = epinephrine).

Affective stimuli: Anything that creates an emotional response.

Aggression: This can be defined in many ways. It is generally acting in a threating manner and/or demonstration of anger or hostility directed at another person.

Aim: In the context of psychological studies, it is the purpose of conducting a study, usually written as a statement of the relationship that is being investigated.

Alpha male/female: The socially dominant male/female in a group. They have the highest social status.

Altruism: Doing something for the benefit of others without expecting anything in return.

Amygdala hijack: A term used to describe a hyper-responsive amygdala that overrides activity in other areas of the brain.

Amygdala: An area of the brain that has been called our emotional centre. It is part of the limbic system, along with the hippocampus and hypothalamus.

Androstadienone: A pheromone that has been associated with physical attraction.

Anglo-behavioural orientation: In Torres et al. (2012) this was a measure of integration and was measured through their language use (Note: language can be an important part of acculturation).

Animal welfare: Taking care of animals in a way that ensures their general health.

Anonymity: In research, this means the names of participants in a study are not revealed.

Anterograde amnesia: An inability to remember details after an event or accident.

Articulatory process: In the working memory model this is a part of the phonological loop. It is the "inner voice" (what allows us to hear auditory information in our working memory).

Asch paradigm: An experimental procedure that involves judging the length of lines while in the presence of confederates.

Assimilation: One of Berry's acculturation strategies, this is when an individual separates themselves from their heritage culture and fully adopts the norms of the second culture.

Associative learning: Learning how to associate one thing with another. This is an umbrella term that covers fear conditioning, classical conditioning and other types of associative learning.

Assumption: Believing something to be true without solid evidence or facts.

Attack latency: A measure of aggression used in rodent studies. It's the length of time a resident rodent (e.g. mouse or rat) waits before attacking an intruder. The rodents can be classed as having a short attack latency (high aggression) or long attack latency (low aggression).

Attitude: A way of thinking about something. e.g. having a healthy attitude about one's body or an attitude towards religious extremism.

Autonomic fear response: When our stress response is activated by an unconscious perception of a fear-inducing stimulus.

Autopsy: Performing a surgery to study the physiology of something after it is dead.

Behaviour: Typically speaking this refers to an observable action but in the IB Psychology course it's used as an umbrella term that includes observable actions and internal mental processes.

Bias: When an individual's existing thoughts, beliefs or ideas influence their thinking or behaviour.

Bidirectional ambiguity: When the direction of a causal relationship is uncertain.

Biological correlate: A biological factor that has a relationship with a particular behaviour or cognitive process.

Blind design: When the researcher and/or participant is unaware what condition they are in during an experiment.

Body image: How we feel about and evaluate our physical appearance and our body.

Bottom-up processing: Processing information that is directly based on stimuli in our environment.

Building block: In the thematic model of curriculum™, this is defined as an individual unit of information. E.g. a key term, variable, behaviour, study, theory, etc. Knowledge is about comprehending building blocks; understanding is about relating them in order to answer a question or problem.

Bystanderism: The phenomenon of people not helping someone in need.

Case-control study: A type of study in the etiology of disorders that involves comparing people who have a disorder (the case) with those who don't (the control).

Castration: The act of removing the testicles from an animal.

Causation: When one variable is responsible for the change in another.

Central executive: An aspect of Baddeley and Hitch's working memory model that controls the flow of information from long-term to short-term memory and also controls the slave systems.

Central nervous system: The brain and spinal cord.

Child training practices: A general term used to describe techniques used to teach children during their upbringing. Parents and teachers are two examples of people who employ child training practices.

Classification system: In the diagnosis of disorders, a classification system is a way of organizing and describing psychological disorders. The DSM is an example of a classification system.

Cognition: An internal process requiring perceiving, processing, encoding and/or recalling of information. It's what happens in our "minds."

Cognitive appraisal: Making an assessment of a stimulus (cognitive reappraisal means to make a secondary assessment after the initial assessment).

Cognitive behavioural therapy (CBT): An umbrella term that refers to any psychotherapy that aims to improve the relationships between thoughts, emotions and behaviours. Exposure therapies are a type of CBT.

Cognitive capabilities: An individual's ability to perform cognitive processes with varying degrees of difficulty or complexity.

Cognitive capacity: Our ability to perform cognitive tasks.

Cognitive framework: Another name for schema. It refers to how related pieces of information and knowledge are stored in our memory.

Cognitive neuroscience: The scientific study of relationships between cognition and the brain.

Cognitive process: A form of processing, perceiving, remembering, encoding or learning information. It's something that happens in our "minds".

Cognitive restructuring: An aspect of psychotherapy that involves changing thought patterns from being harmful to healthy.

Cognitive scientist: Someone who studies the mind in a scientific manner.

Collectivism: An aspect of the individualism/collectivism cultural dimension that emphasizes the group over the individual.

Comorbidity: The presence of two (or more) diseases or disorders in an individual that exist at the same time (e.g. suffering from depression and PTSD).

Compliance: Acting in a way that is consistent with someone else's wish or command.

Comprehension: The ability to grasp the meaning of something.

Concept: An abstract idea.

Conceptual understanding: An understanding of an abstract idea. In psychology, conceptual understandings are based on relationships between variables, cognition, behaviour, ethical considerations and research methods.

Conditioned response: An unconscious reaction to a stimulus that happens as a result of experience or training. Conditioning is the process of developing a conditioned response.

Confabulation: The process of remembering something incorrectly or recalling something that never happened as if it did.

Confederate (a.k.a. a "stooge"): An actor in a study that is working for the researcher.

Confidentiality: In a study, this is when someone's participation and/or specific data are kept secret. See anonymity for comparison.

Confirmation bias: The tendency to focus on and remember information that is consistent with existing beliefs (and ignore contradictory details).

Conformity: When an individual's thoughts and/or actions are changed in a way that make them consistent with the actions or expectations of others. It's most often applied to situations involving an individual conforming with the norms of a social group.

Confounding variable: A factor in a study other than the IV that has affected the results.

Consolidation (of memory): The process of fixing information in long-term memory.

Construct validity: The extent to which a tool accurately measures a construct. Examples of constructs could include behaviours, mental processes or variables.

Contact hypothesis: A theory that outlines conditions that need to exist for the contact between groups to reduce conflict, prejudice and discrimination.

Control group (a.k.a. control condition): The group in an experiment that receive a treatment that is not expected by the researchers to have an effect.

Control: A measure taken to limit the influence of extraneous variables.

Correlation co-efficient: A measure of the strength of a relationship between two variables in a correlational study. 1.0 is a perfect positive correlation and 0 suggests there is no correlation.

Correlation: A relationship between variables, or an association of variables with one another.

Correlational study: A study that does not investigate a relationship between variables in a particular direction, but rather investigates the existence (and strength) of a relationship between co-varying variables.

Cortex (plural = cortices): The dense outer-layer of the brain.

Cortisol: A stress hormone released by the hypothalamus during times of stress. It is one of many glucocorticoids.

Covert observation: An observation that happens without the subjects' knowledge.

Critical thinking: Reflecting on the validity of one's own knowledge and understanding.

Culpability: The extent to which a person can be held accountable for their actions. If someone is culpable, it means they're to blame.

Cultural competency: In psychiatry, this involves being familiar with the norms of the patient's heritage culture. It's an important consideration in diagnosis, as well as prescribing and administering treatment.

Cultural dimension: A description of cultural values that range along a continuum.

Cultural norm: Something that is considered "normal" for a particular culture group.

Cultural transmission (a.k.a. cultural learning): The process of developing and understanding the cultural norms of a particular culture.

Cultural values: What a cultural group collectively holds to be important; a common belief.

Culture of Honor: The name given to the idea that one should defend their honor when they are challenged or threatened.

Culture-bound syndrome: A disorder that is unique to a particular culture.

Data triangulation: Getting information (data) from two difference sources.

Debriefing: Revealing details of a study to participants after the study finishes.

Deception: Leading someone to believe something that isn't true.

Decision making: Making a decision involves choosing an action, belief or strategy. Our decisions are based on our judgements.

Declarative memory (a.k.a. explicit memory): Memory of things that can be consciously recalled (semantic and episodic memories are types of declarative memories). Compare with procedural (a.k.a. implicit) memory.

Demand characteristics: An aspect of a study that might give a participant a clue about how they are expected to act. It could confound results of a study.

Demand/withdraw communication pattern: A phenomenon commonly observed in marriages whereby one partner (usually the wife) raises an issue (the demand) and the other partner (usually the husband) avoids dealing with the issue (withdraws).

Dendritic atrophy: The shrinking of dendrites on a neuron.

Dependent variable: The variable in a study that is being measured.

Deprived: Having little stimulation in the environment.

Descriptive social norm: How others are acting. Making people aware of descriptive social norms can influence behaviour. See also normative and informational social influence.

Descriptive statistics: Statistics that summarize the general findings of a study.

Diffusion of responsibility: When the feeling of responsibility to act is reduced because of the presence of other people (e.g. one may think "someone else can help.")

Digit-span task: A test of working memory capacity that involves seeing how many digits (numbers) can be kept in working memory and accurately recalled.

Discrimination: Treating others differently based on a characteristic, which is typically their belonging to a particular group based on age, race, sexuality, nationality, religion, etc.

Double blind design: When both the researcher and the participant are not aware of the experimental condition that the subject is in.

Drug therapy (a.k.a. pharmacotherapy): Taking medication to treat an illness.

Dual Processing Model of Judgement and Decision Making: A model that describes two systems of processing information. The system used in processing will influence judgement and decision making.

Dual-task paradigm: Any experimental procedure that involves having to perform two tasks at the same time.

Ecological validity: The extent to which the conditions of a study reflect a natural environment.

Effect size: A statistical measurement of the strength of an IV on a DV. Anything over 0.8 is considered a strong effect.

Emotion: A general definition would include the physiological and psychological effects of experiencing something that has a strong impact on a person.

Emotional blunting: A reduction in emotional reactivity; a lack of ability to experience emotions.

Emotional reactivity: The extent to which someone reacts emotionally to provocation or stimuli.

Emotional stimulus: Anything that generates an emotional reaction.

Empathy-altruism hypothesis: A theory that suggests feelings of empathy increases altruism.

Empirical evidence: Evidence that has been gathered from direct observation. This is in contrast to other sources of "knowledge" that rely solely on one's own thoughts or opinions.

Encoding: The initial process of creating a memory.

Enculturation: A general term that describes the process of cultural transmission and learning the cultural norms of one's home culture.

Endocrine system: The name given to the various glands throughout our body that control the release of hormones.

Enriched (environment): Having lots of sources of stimulation in the environment.

Epigenetics: The effects of environmental influences on genetics. It's also defined as the study of changes in the expression of a gene.

Episodic memory: A type of declarative (explicit) memory, episodic memory is a memory of events.

Ethical consideration: What a researcher must think about (i.e. consider) based on the real and potential effects of their research on others.

Ethical guideline: A general rule or guiding principle set forth by a psychological organization.

Etiology: An origin or cause of a disease or disorder.

Evolution: The process of gradual change through the compounding effect of mutations over time.

Executive functions: An umbrella term referring to a range of cognitive processes that require conscious processing, such as working memory, inhibition and system two processing.

Experimental method: An umbrella term that refers to studies that rely on the investigation of a relationship between an independent variable and a dependent variable.

Experimental paradigm: A common procedure used in experimental research. Examples include the Asch, marshmallow, minimal group and dual task paradigms.

Exposure Therapy: A type of CBT that involves exposing an individual to an emotional stimuli in any number of different ways (e.g. through physical contact, imagination or virtual reality).

External emotional stimuli: Something beyond ourselves that generates an emotional reaction. Emotion can be the result of external stimuli (bottom-up) and internal thought processes (top- down).

External validity: The extent to which the conclusions of the study can be applied to a context beyond the study itself. Factors to consider are place, procedures and participants.

Extraneous variable: A variable that isn't being studied.

Eye-witness testimony: Evidence given in a trial by someone who claims to have witnessed an event.

False memory: A memory of something that never happened (reporting a false memory is called confabulation).

Fear conditioning: The process of learning to be afraid of something.

Fear recognition: The ability to see that other people are afraid.

Field experiment: An experiment that takes place in a natural environment.

Fight-flight response (a.k.a. the stress response): The name given to the series of physiological changes that occur in times of stress; e.g. when a threat is perceived.

Findings: Another way of saying "results," although the term "findings" might also include the conclusions drawn from the study.

Focus group interview: An interview of a small group of people (around 6 to 10 people).

Food accumulation (high and low): The extent to which a culture can store food for the long term. Farming and agricultural societies are high food accumulating, while hunter-gatherer societies are low food accumulating.

Functional Magnetic Resonance Imaging (fMRI): A development of the MRI, this machine enables researchers to measure the brain as it's actually functioning. It allows researchers to measure various levels of activity in different areas of the brain.

Fundamentalist Group: A group based on extremist interpretations of a particular religious belief. ISIS and the KuKlux Klan are examples of fundamentalist groups.

Gene expression: The process of a gene sending information from the cell to influence physiological processes. E.g. Expression of the TPH-2 gene means sending information to start the process of converting tryptophan to serotonin (TPH-2 gene) and expression of the MAOA gene means sending information to start the production of the enzyme monoamine oxidase (MAOA).

Generalizability: The extent to which conclusions from a study can be applied to (generalized) contexts beyond the study itself.

Genes: Segments of DNA found on chromosomes within cells. We have about 20,000 genes.

Genetics: The study of genes and their effects.

Genome: A complete set of genes in an organism. A genotype refers to an organism's genome.

Global neglect: An operational definition of neglect in Perry and Pllard's study that involves ignoring many aspects of care for a child for extended periods of time, such as emotional, social, cognitive and physical neglect.

Grey matter: Areas of the brain made up of mostly cell bodies, which is mostly grey in colour (as opposed to white matter, which is mainly axons).

Group difference study: The term Coolican (2014) uses to describe a study that compares two groups, but there are too many confounds to deduce a causal relationship.

Group dynamics: A general term used to refer to how groups interact and/or how individual behaviour can be affected by influences from the group.

Hawthorne effect: A phenomenon that has been observed to occur that refers to how an individual's behaviour changes simply because they are aware they are being watched.

Heritability: The extent to which variability between organisms can be explained by genetics.

Hidden population: A group of people that are difficult to find. Purposive sampling can be useful when studying hidden populations.

Hippocampus: A part of the brain in the limbic system that plays important functions in memory processing.

Hormones: Chemical messengers that are released by glands in the endocrine system and can spark changes throughout our brain and body.

Human Genome Project: An international collaboration by scientists to map human DNA.

Hyper-responsive: When an area of the brain demonstrates increased reaction to stimuli.

Hypo-responsive: When an area of the brain demonstrates reduced reaction to stimuli.

Hypothalamic-Pituitary-Adrenal Axis (HPA Axis): The name given to the neural network that connects these three glands in the endocrine system.

Hypothalamus: A part of the brain in the limbic system that affects many of our body's physiological processes.

Hypothesis: A prediction of what might happen.

Identity shift: A change in the way we think about who we are.

Identity: Our sense of who we are.

Imagination therapy: A form of exposure therapy that involves having participants recollect and re-experience emotional situations (through imagination).

Implicit memory: see procedural memory.

Implicit racial bias: Having a racial bias that we are not consciously aware of.

Independent samples: When an experiment involves different groups experiencing different conditions.

Independent variable: The variable in an experiment or study that is being manipulated by the researcher. It is the "cause" in a cause-and-effect relationship.

Individual autonomy: A trait that is valued in individualistic cultures that refers to an individual's right and responsibility to make their own decisions without interference from others.

Individualism: An aspect of the individualism/collectivism cultural dimension that places individual factors over group processes.

Induction of fear: The ability to have fear induced in oneself; to be made to feel afraid.

Inductive (thematic) content analysis: A method used to draw conclusions from qualitative data that involves identifying broad (superordinate) themes and sub-themes (subordinate themes).

Inferential statistics: Statistics tests designed to measure statistical significance of data.

Informational social influence: When someone's behaviour is changed as a result of looking towards others for information on how to act in an ambiguous situation.

Informed consent: Providing participants with information about a study and gaining their permission before making them the subject of study.

In-group bias: Behaving in a way that favours one's own group over other out-groups.

Initiative: Being able to think and act independently, especially in a creative manner.

Innovative: Being able to create something new.

Integration: The healthiest of Berry's four acculturation strategies, this involves maintaining elements of the heritage culture and adapting to the new culture.

Intergroup behaviour: The interaction of groups. Intergroup conflict is an example of intergroup behaviour.

Internal validity: The extent to which the measure of the dependent variable was a result of the manipulation of the independent variable. Technically, it only applies to experimental methods. See also construct validity.

Inter-rater reliability: When two (or more) researchers' data gathering or analysis is consistent with each other's.

Interview schedule: An interview plan that includes the specific topics and/or questions that a researcher aims to address in the course of the interview.

Interview: Gathering data by verbally asking questions and recording responses.

Iowa Card Game (a.k.a. Iowa Gambling Task): A paradigm used in studies that involves four decks of cards that have two distinct reward probabilities – high risk, high reward and low risk, low reward.

Isolate: To make separate. In experiments, researchers isolate the IV in the sense that they make it separate from the other variables affecting the DV and try to make sure it's the only one.

Judgement: Making a judgement involves making an assessment based on the information available. Judgment follows processing as the judgment is a result of the processing that has taken place.

Justification: In psychological studies, this refers to having a valid reason for inducing psychological and/or physical harm on research subjects.

Knockout Animal: An animal that has had a specific gene silenced so it is no longer to be expressed.

Knowing: Themantic Education's definition of "knowing" refers to building blocks: it's the ability to recall individual units of information.

Laboratory experiment (a.k.a. true experiment): When an independent variable is manipulated, extraneous variables are controlled for to isolate the IV and participants are randomly allocated to either a treatment or control condition.

Leading question: A question that is phrased in a way so that it directs the respondent towards providing a particular answer.

Lesion: Damaging or scarring to the neurons in a particular part of the brain.

Likert scale: A commonly used quantitative measure that requires participants to circle a response to a particular statement. E.g. "I love psychology." 0 – Strongly Disagree, 1 – Disagree, 2 – Agree, 3 – Strongly Agree.

Localization of brain function: The term used to describe the fact that particular areas of the brain have particular functions.

Longitudinal study: A study carried out over an extended period of time.

Magnetic Resonance Imaging (MRI): a machine that enables researchers to see the physical structure of the brain in 2D and 3D images.

MAOA Gene (a.k.a. the "Warrior Gene"): This is the monoamine oxidase A gene, which is a particular gene that affects neurotransmitters. Variants are collectively known as MAOA-L genes, and it is these variations of the gene that are correlated with violence.

Marginalization: In terms of Berry's acculturation strategies, this is when an individual separates themselves from their new culture and loses their heritage culture as well. Marginalization can also be a process that involves members of the larger society excluding other members of society (e.g. discriminating against minority immigrants).

Marital satisfaction: Being happy and satisfied with one's marriage.

Marriage dissolution: Ending a marriage, either by separation or divorce.

Matched pairs: An experimental design whereby participants are matched based on a particular characteristic and assigned to different conditions from one another.

Mate preference: Who we would prefer to marry and/or procreate with.

Mate quality: How suitable someone is to procreate with in terms of their ability to provide our offspring with healthy genetic material.

Mediating variable: A variable that explains the relationship between one variable and another.

Memory trace: A physiological change that happens at the neuronal level as a result of learning.

Menstrual cycle: The monthly cycle of hormones and other physiological changes that happen in females and facilitate reproduction.

Meta-analysis: A type of study that involves gathering the results from a collection of other studies and drawing overall conclusions based on the collection of results.

Metacognition: Reflecting on and being aware of one's thinking and cognition.

Methodological triangulation: Getting data from more than one method. For example, observing someone and asking them to fill out a questionnaire.

Methodology: The methods used to gather data, test hypotheses and draw conclusions.

Mindfulness: A form of meditation where concentration is devoted to becoming aware (or mindful) of one's thoughts. It is often practiced as a strategy for stress reduction and relaxation.

Minimal group paradigm: An experimental procedure that involves putting people who have little or nothing in common into groups and the seeing if their identification with the group affects their behaviour.

Misinformation effect: The phenomenon of having a false memory implanted by exposing participants to misleading information.

Moderating variable: A variable that influences the strength of one variable's effect on another variable.

Mundane realism: The extent to which what a participant is required to do in experimental procedures reflects what would happen in real life.

Mutation: An alteration of a gene that can be passed on to subsequent generations.

Natural experiment: A study that uses a naturally occurring independent variable, while still having suitable controls so plausible cause-effect relationships can be drawn.

Naturalistic observation: An observation of subjects in a natural environment.

Negative appraisal: Assessing an emotional stimulus as being potentially harmful or threatening.

Negative correlation: A relationship between two variables whereby as one increases the other decreases.

Negative interdependence: In group dynamics, this is when for one group to achieve a goal they require another group to fail.

Neglect: Ignoring someone or a part of their well-being for extended periods of time. Types of neglect of children studied by Perry were social, emotional and physical.

Neural pathway: A system of neurons that are connected and send messages during the performance of particular cognitive processes and behaviours.

Neurogenesis: The body's ability to grow new neurons.

Neuron: A cell that transmits signals throughout the brain and body.

Neuroplasticity: The brain's ability to change chemically, structurally and functionally as a result of experience.

Neuropsychology: The study of the brain and behaviour.

Neuroscientist: A scientist that studies relationships between the brain and behaviour.

Neurotransmission: The process of neurotransmitters being fired from one neuron to the next (from the presynaptic to the postsynaptic neuron).

Neurotransmitter: A chemical messenger that is transmitted through neurons.

Non-participant observation: When the researcher remains an outsider of the group they are observing.

Non-representative sampling: Gathering participants without the assumption they will necessarily represent the wider population.

Normative social influence: A type of social influence that changes a person's behaviour because they are afraid of standing out from the group; they feel pressured to follow the established social norms.

Null hypothesis: A hypothesis that predicts that there will be no effect of the IV on the DV.

Obedience training: In Barry et al. (1959), this was an aspect of parenting that encouraged obedience in children.

Obedience: Following orders or instructions.

Olfactory system: The part of the sensory system that helps us to smell.

One-tailed test: A statistical test for an effect in one direction.

Operational definition: A specific definition of a variable in a study that clearly shows how it's being manipulated or measured.

Opportunity sample (a.k.a. convenience sample): Gathering participants who happen to be available at the time of the study.

Order effects: When the order of completing tasks in a repeated measures design affects the results.

Out-group homogeneity: An effect that has been observed in social psychology whereby out-group members are perceived as being more similar to one-another than in-group members.

Overt observation: An observation that happens with the subjects' knowledge.

Ovulation: The time in a female's cycle when eggs are released and can be fertilized. This is when females are most likely to become pregnant after copulation.

Participant expectancy effect: When participants are aware of the expected aims or outcomes of a study and this affects their behaviour (thus, influencing the validity of the results).

Participant observation: When the researcher becomes a member of the group they are observing.

Participant variability: A potential confounding variable that refers to the differences between individual participants.

Perception: The act of becoming aware of an external stimulus.

Peripheral nervous system: The name given to the connected neural pathways beyond the brain and the spinal cord.

Phenomenon: An umbrella term referring to anything that can be observed to occur, especially something that may have questions surrounding its origins or causes.

Phenotype: Whereas the genotype refers to the genetic make-up of an organism, phenotype is the observable characteristics that are a result of the genotype (and the environment).

Pheromone: A type of hormone that is transmitted through the air from one organism to another.

Phonological loop: The name given to the system in our working memory that processes auditory information. It is sub-divided into the phonological store (inner ear) and articulatory process (inner voice)

Phonological store: A sub-section of the phonological loop, this is also known as our "inner-ear." It's where auditory information is stored in working (i.e. short-term) memory.

Physiological arousal: The term used to describe what happens in the body after the activation of the stress response (e.g. increased heart rate, blood pressure, skin temperature and breathing).

Physiological response: The way our body changes internally in reaction to a stimulus.

Physiology: our body's internal processes, including blood flow, hormones, neurotransmission, etc.

Placebo Effect: When a placebo has an effect not because of the properties of the placebo, but due to the psychological processes of the person taking the placebo.

Placebo: A medicine or procedure that has no physiological effects.

Population density: The amount of people living per square km/mi in a particular area.

Population validity: The extent to which the participants in the study are representative of a wider group of people; population validity affects generalizability and is a component of external validity.

Positive correlation: As one variable increases so does the other.

Positive distinctiveness: An aspect of social identity theory that describes the desire for individuals in the in-group to establish and maintain superiority over other out-groups.

Positron Emission Tomography (PET): Much like fMRIs, this technology enables researchers to see different areas of the brain as various cognitive processes are being performed.

Post-mortem operation: Dissecting an organism after it's dead.

Post-traumatic stress disorder (PTSD): A psychological disorder that occurs as a result of exposure to one or more traumatic events. It's characterized by symptoms related to memory and emotion.

Poverty: Not having enough money to take care of basic needs like warmth, shelter, food and clothing.

Precondition: In the study of etiologies of disorders, this refers to a characteristic of an individual (e.g. brain structure or function) that might be a risk factor for developing a disorder. A small hippocampus may be a precondition for PTSD.

Prefrontal cortex (PFC): The particular area of the frontal lobe located at the very front of the forehead.

Prejudice: To pre-judge based on a preconceived idea or belief about someone. In social psychology, this refers to how individuals form opinions of others based on superficial qualities (e.g. group membership), as opposed to characteristics of the individual.

Prevalence: How common a disorder is in a given population. The prevalence rate is the % of a population that has a diagnosis of that disorder, and the lifetime prevalence rate is the % of the population that will be diagnosed with the disorder at some point in their lives.

Probability sampling: Gathering participants (a sample) with a high probability of representing the wider population.

Probability value (p value): A value that is calculated by inferential statistical tests and conveys the probability that the measure of the dependent variable was a result of the effects of the manipulation of the IV. The further below the significance level of the p value, the more statistically significant the results are.

Procedural memory (a.k.a. implicit memory): The memory of how to perform tasks and procedures.

Procedure: In psychology studies, this is how a study is carried out and data gathered.

Processing: Processing in humans has been equated to information processing in computers. It involves considering individual components of information.

Procreate: To produce offspring (i.e. to have babies).

Prosocial behaviour: Behaving in a way that benefits others.

Psychology: The scientific study of individual behaviour and mental processes.

Psychotherapy: An umbrella term that refers to any form of therapy that aims to address etiologies and/or treating symptoms by focusing on internal, cognitive processes (as opposed to biological therapies that target physiological processes). CBT is a type of psychotherapy.

Publication bias: Only statistically significant research is published, which means that the psychological (and wider) community only learn about these studies. This limited perspective of phenomena could influence our perception of what we know in psychology.

Purposive sample: A sample that has been gathered because they have a particular set of characteristics that make them suitable for study.

Qualitative methods: Research methods in psychology that gather descriptive data; the purpose of qualitative research is not to investigate effects of variables, but to understand subjective experiences of phenomena.

Quantitative methods: Research methods in psychology that gather numerical data. The purpose of quantitative methods is to investigate relationships between variables and behaviour.

Quasi-experiment: An experiment that has a treatment (i.e. an IV) but when one or more characteristics of a true experiment are not met (e.g. participants cannot be randomly allocated).

Questionnaire: A set of written questions.

Random allocation: Assigning participants to different conditions of an experiment using randomization.

Random sample: When all participants have an equal chance of being asked to participate in a study.

Rationalization: According to Bartlett's schema theory, this is the process of details of memory being changed or omitted (left out) because they are inconsistent with existing schema.

Reconstructive memory: The term used to describe the nature of memory as being susceptible to manipulation because it's a product of conscious reconstructing processes.

Reductionist: Oversimplifying a complex phenomenon by reducing it to its most basic parts.

Regulated and non-regulated couples: An operational definition used by Gottman and Levenson, a regulated couple is one whose ratio of positive to negative interactions gradually increases throughout observed discussions. A non-regulated couple is any couple that doesn't match this description.

Reliability: The extent to which a study's results have been repeated.

Religious extremism: Holding religious views that are not shared by the majority of the members of that religious group.

Rememberol™: My invented, fictional drug for memory.

Repeated measures: An experimental design that involves all participants experiencing all conditions of the experiment.

Replicate: To copy. In psychological studies it means to copy the experiment to see if the same results can be achieved.

Representative sampling: Gathering participants with the aim of using them to represent the wider population.

Reproducibility crisis (a.k.a. replicability crisis): A term used to describe a recent discovery that findings from a lot of published psychology may lack test-retest reliability.

Research (experimental) hypothesis: A prediction of how a manipulation of an IV will affect the DV.

Research design: The type of method used in the study (e.g. lab experiment, case study, etc.). See also experimental design.

Researcher bias: When a researcher's pre-existing beliefs, ideas or opinions influence the research process.

Researcher triangulation: Having more than one researcher involved in the research process, e.g. by having more than one researcher gather and/or analyse data.

Resident-intruder paradigm: A test used in experiments on rodents to measure aggression. It involves one rat (the intruder) being placed in a cage with another (the resident) and timing to see how long it takes one to attack the other.

Responsibility training: A type of parenting practice relevant to Barry et al.'s (1959) study on economic systems and enculturation. It involves teaching kids to be responsible.

Results: What the study found out; the analyzed data.

Retrospective consent: Obtaining consent to use, analyze and publish data after the data has been gathered. This is most relevant for covert observations.

Reuptake: The process of neurotransmitters in the synapse being reabsorbed by the pre-synaptic neuron.

Rich data: In qualitative research this refers to data that is detailed and has a lot of relevant and useful information that enables researchers to understand participants' experiences of phenomena.

Sample: The group of participants in a study. How the sample is obtained is called the sampling method.

Sampling bias: When some members of the population are more (or less) likely than others to be included in the sample.

Schema theory: The hypothesis that we have cognitive frameworks that organize our memories and knowledge. Schema theory also includes the characteristics and different types of schema, and how they can influence our mental processes and behaviour. While schema theory has been contributed to by many researchers over the past 100 years, Jean Piaget's (1929) and Frederic Bartlett's (1932) works were the earliest and most prominent contributions.

Schema: A cognitive framework that organizes our stored memories and clusters of knowledge.

Schematic processing: The use of existing schema when processing new information.

Script schema: A particular type of schema related to a sequence of events (e.g. attending a wedding/funeral, going to a restaurant, etc.) Other examples of types of schema are self-schemas and social schemas.

Secondary sex characteristics: Physical traits that characterize males and females but aren't directly related to reproduction. Examples include voice pitch, facial hair, jawline, etc.

Seed: An initial participant in a study that is asked by researchers to recruit other participants.

Selective serotonin reuptake inhibitor (SSRI): A type of drug that blocks reuptake and increases available serotonin in the synapse. Paroxetine, Prozac and Zoloft are SSRIs and are commonly prescribed to treat disorders related to mood and anxiety (e.g. depression and PTSD).

Self-efficacy: One's belief in their ability to be able to do something.

Self-esteem hypothesis: A central tenet of social identity theory that proposes in-group bias and other behaviours are performed with the goal of increasing one's self-esteem.

Semantic memory: A type of declarative (explicit) memory which refers to memory of facts (as opposed to memory of events, which is episodic memory).

Semi-structured interview: An interview that has an interview schedule that outlines particular topics or questions to ask, but still enables flexibility.

Sensory information: Signals that are detected, received and processed by our sensory organs, such as sound, light, taste, heat, etc.

Sensory organs: Parts of our body that detect and process sensory information, such as our eyes, skin, mouth, nose and ears.

Sensory overload: Milgram's theory that attempts to explain why people in cities are less helpful than those in the countryside – our senses are overloaded so we are less sensitive to the needs of others (similar in concept to inattentional blindness).

Separation: An acculturation strategy that involves maintaining one's heritage culture but not integrating with the new culture.

Serotonin: A neurotransmitter associated with mood, aggression and antisocial behaviour, among other things. If something is described as being serotonergic it means it is related to the transmission of serotonin (e.g. serotonergic neural pathways, serotonergic dysfunction, etc.).

Sham surgery: A placebo surgery that controls for the extraneous variable of having an operation.

Significance level: The level at which we reject or accept the null hypothesis in inferential statistical tests. In psychology, the significance level is usually set at 0.05 (5%), which means that any p value that is under 0.05 suggests the results were more than 95% likely to be the result of the manipulation of the independent variable.

Significance loss: A term coined by Lyons-Padilla et al. to describe a lack of self-worth, value and significance that comes about as a result of marginalization.

Simple experiment: An experiment that has only one independent variable (two conditions) and one dependent variable.

Single blind design: When the subject doesn't know which condition in an experiment they're in (i.e. the treatment or control condition).

Slave systems: The name given to the phonological loop and the visuospatial sketchpad in the working memory model. They are slaves to the central executive.

Snowball sample: A snowball that gradually increases in size after a small number of seeds originally selected ask more people to participate. Purposive sampling may include an element of snowball sampling.

Social categorization: The cognitive processes of categorizing people into different groups.

Social cognition: An umbrella term referring to how we think about other people and other aspects of our social environment.

Social comparison: The cognitive process of comparing one's in-group with other out-groups.

Social defeat: Being beaten by a competitor in a social setting.

Social desirability effect: When an individual changes their behaviour in order to have others view them more favourably. This could be a confounding variable, especially in social psychology studies.

Social dominance: The ability to assert leadership, authority and control over others.

Social identity theory (SIT): A theory proposed by British psychologists Henri Tajfel and John Turner that attempts to explain the many ways that belonging to, and identifying with, a group can influence our thinking and behaviour. It was developed to explain intergroup conflict, prejudice and discrimination.

Social identity: How we view ourselves when we consider our social roles and relationships with other people.

Social norm: A way of thinking or acting that is commonly accepted by a social group.

Social schema: A schema that is related to other people or social situations. Stereotypes are an example of a social schema.

Social status: An individual's rank within a social structure.

Social threat: A threat to an individual that comes from another person.

Socioeconomic status: This is a general term that refers to the position one holds in society when many factors are considered, such as income, occupation, education, housing, etc.

Span-board task: A measure of working memory capacity that requires remembering the order in which the experimenter points to a series of objects.

Statistical significance: If results of an experiment are statistical significant, it means that there was less than 5% chance they were due to chance or luck.

Stereotype: A widely held and oversimplified generalization about a group of people.

Stigma: Something that signifies disgrace or other negative qualities.

Strain: In genetics research on animals, this is a particular sub-species of animal that has been created by a process of selective breeding.

Stress hormone: A hormone released during the stress response. Cortisol (and other glucocorticoids) and adrenaline are the most commonly studied.

Stress response: see Fear response

Stressor: Anything that causes stress. When discussing PTSD, a stressor could be the traumatic event and/or a more recent stimulus that triggers an emotional response.

Structured interview: Used to make quantitative measurements, such as in the diagnosis of PTSD with the Clinically Administered PTSD Scale (CAPS), it asks a long series of narrowly-focused and closed questions.

Subordinate male/female: A member of the group who is lower in social rank than the alpha male/female.

Subsistence economy: A way of living that involves producing only enough to live on a day-to-day basis.

Superordinate goal: In Sherif's realistic group conflict theory, this is a goal that is shared by two or more different groups that requires co-operation to achieve.

Survey: A survey involves the use of interviews and/or questionnaires to gather data from a large number of participants.

Symptomatology: A set of symptoms.

Synapse: The space between neurons (between the axon terminal of the presynaptic neuron and the dendrite of the postsynaptic neuron) where neurotransmitters are fired across.

Temporal lobe: The part of the brain located around the side of the brain.

Testosterone: A particular type of hormone associated with competition, social dominance and aggression.

Test-retest reliability: A study can be said to have test-retest reliability if other researchers replicate the study and get the same or very similar results.

Thalamus: Another part of the brain in the limbic system that processes sensory information (as well as performing other functions).

The right to withdraw: Giving participants the right to stop participating in a study. It could also be applied to giving participants the right to remove specific aspects of their data (e.g. in qualitative studies).

Threat perception: Becoming aware that there is a threat in the environment.

Top-down processing (of emotional stimuli): When emotion is generated from our thoughts.

TPH-2 Gene: A gene that facilitates the building of the neurotransmitter, serotonin, from the amino acid, tryptophan.

Transferability: Applying the findings from one study to another context. It is the qualitative research equivalent of generalizability and is very similar in nature.

Treatment group: The group in an experiment that are experiencing the condition of the IV that the researchers anticipate will have an effect on the DV.

Trephining: A form of treatment for psychological disorders that involves drilling holes in one's head.

Triangulation: The use of more than one data point in the gathering or analysing of data. See also methodological, data and researcher triangulation.

True experiment: Another name for a laboratory experiment. The term laboratory experiment is best used when the experiment takes place in a lab, and true experiment otherwise.

Two-tailed test: In statistical tests, this is a test that measures for significance in both directions. A common practice is to always conduct two-tailed tests, regardless of the hypothesis.

Understanding: Thematic Education's definition of understanding is the ability to apply significant relationships of two or more units of information in response to a question or problem.

Unstructured interview: An interview that may have a limited range of topics to explore, but the direction of the interview evolves based on participant responses.

Validity: The quantitative research equivalent of credibility, validity refers to the accuracy of the methods in achieving the desired aims. See internal and external, as well as construct, population, and ecological validity.

Variable: A factor that can vary or change. In experimental research, variables are the things that can effect, or be affected by, one another.

Ventromedial PFC (vmPFC): A particular part of the prefrontal cortex, located within the middle of both hemispheres of the PFC. It is associated with working memory, executive functions, system two processing, fear extinction and top-down processing of the amygdala.

Violence: As with aggression, this can be defined in many ways, but I would define it as any action that has the intention of causing harm or suffering to another individual, especially if it involves physical assault.

Violent crime: Violent crimes are those that involve violence of some kind, such as assault, rape, murder, arson, armed robbery, etc.

Virtual Reality Exposure Therapy (VRET): A form of therapy that involves being exposed to stressors through virtual reality.

Visuospatial sketchpad: A component of the working memory model, also called the inner-eye. It enables us to visualize visuo-spatial information.

Volume: In brain research, this refers to the capacity of the part of the brain. It is a more accurate term than saying the "size" of the brain, because often brains are the same size but their capacity is different because of the density of dendrites and synaptic connections between neurons.

Vomeronasal organ (a.k.a. Jacobson's organ): A group of sensory cells in the nose of mammals that detects pheromones. There is a debate as to whether or not the vomeronasal organ functions in humans.

Warrior Gene: The name commonly given to the MAOA gene as variations of this gene (collectively known as MAOA-L genes) have been correlated with violent and antisocial behaviour.

Working memory capacity: How many units of information can be kept in our working memory at any one time. Modern research suggests that our working memory capacity maybe less than the original 7 ± 2 as was originally proposed by Miller (1956).

Working memory: "The term working memory refers to a brain system that provides temporary storage and manipulation of the information necessary for such complex cognitive tasks as language comprehension, learning, and reasoning." (Baddeley, 1992.)

References

Adams PB, Lawson S, Sanigorski A, Sinclair AJ. "Arachidonic to eicosapentaenoic acid ratio in blood correlates positively with clinical symptoms of depression". *Lipids* 1996; 31: S-167–76.

Addy, Lois. *Speed up! A kinaesthetic programme to develop fluent handwriting.* LDA Publishers. 2004.

Åhs, Fredrik, Anna Pissiota, Åsa Michel, et al. "Disentangling the Web of Fear: Amygdala Reactivity and Functional Connectivity in Spider and Snake Phobia." *Psychiatry Research: Neuroimaging* 172.2 (2009): 103-08.

Albert, D. J., M. L. Walsh, B. B. Gorzalka, et al. "Testosterone Removal in Rats Results in a Decrease in Social Aggression and a Loss of Social Dominance." *Physiology & Behavior.* U.S. National Library of Medicine.

Allport, Gordon W. *The Nature of Prejudice: Abridged.* Garden City, NY: Doubleday, 1958. Print.

Amaral, David, and Ralph Adolphs. *Living without an Amygdala.* New York: Guilford, 2016. Print.

Annemoon, M.M. van Erp and Klaus A., Miczek. "Aggressive Behavior, Increased Accumbal Dopamine, and Decreased Cortical Serotonin in Rats." *Journal of Neuroscience* 15 December 2000, 20 (24) 9320-9325

Aronson, Elliot, Beverley Anne Fehr, Robin M. Akert, and Timothy D. Wilson. Social *Psychology: Eighth Edition.* Toronto: Pearson Canada, 2013. Print.

Asch, Solomon E. "Opinions and Social Pressure." *Scientific American* 193.5 (1955): 31-35.

Atkinson, R.C., and R.M. Shiffrin. "Human Memory: A Proposed System and Its Control Processes." *Psychology of Learning and Motivation* (1968): 89-195.

Baddeley, A. "Working Memory." *Science* 255.5044 (1992): 556-59. Web.

Baddeley, Alan. "Working Memory, Reading and Dyslexia." *Advances in Psychology* (1986): 141-52.

Baddeley, Alan. "Working Memory: Theories, Models, and Controversies." *Annual Review of Psychology* 63.1 (2012): 1-29.

Baker, Laura A., Kristen C. Jacobson, Adrian Raine, et al. "Genetic and Environmental Bases of Childhood Antisocial Behavior: A Multi-informant Twin Study." *Journal of Abnormal Psychology* 116.2 (2007): 219-35.

Bandura, A. (1989). "Social cognitive theory." In R. Vasta (Ed.), *Annals of child development. Vol. 6. Six theories of child development* (pp. 1-60). Greenwich, CT: JAI Press.

Bandura, Albert, and Robert W. Jeffrey. "Role of Symbolic Coding and Rehearsal Processes in Observational Learning." *Journal of Personality and Social Psychology* 26.1 (1973): 122-30.

Bandura, Albert, Dorothea Ross, and Sheila A. Ross. "Imitation of Film-mediated Aggressive Models." *The Journal of Abnormal and Social Psychology* 66.1 (1963): 3-11.

Bandura, Albert. "Vicarious Processes: A Case of No-Trial Learning." *Advances in Experimental Social Psychology* (1965): 1-55.

Bandura, Albert. "Vicarious and Self-Reinforcement Processes." *The Nature of Reinforcement.* Academic Press. 1971.

Banister, Peter, Bunn, Geoff, Burman, Erica, et al. *Qualitative Methods in Psychology: A research guide. 2nd ed.* McGraw-Hill, Open University Press. 2011.

Barkley, Russell A. "Behavioral Inhibition, Sustained Attention, and Executive Functions: Constructing a Unifying Theory of ADHD." *Psychological Bulletin* 121.1 (1997): 65-94.

Barry, Iii Herbert, Irvin L. Child, and Margaret K. Bacon. "Relation of Child Training to Subsistence Economy." *American Anthropologist* 61.1 (1959): 51-63.

Bartlett, Frederic. *Remembering.* Cambridge University Print. 1932. Print (Available Online).

Batrinos, Menelaos L. "Testosterone and Aggressive Behavior in Man." *International Journal of Endocrinology & Metabolism* 10.3 (2012): 563-68.

Batson, C. Dani, and Et Al. "Is Empathic Emotion a Source of Altruistic Motivation?" *Journal of Personality and Social Psychology* 40.2 (1981): 290-302.

Bechara, A., D. Tranel, H. Damasio, R. Adolphs, C. Rockland, and A. Damasio. "Double Dissociation of Conditioning and Declarative Knowledge Relative to the Amygdala and Hippocampus in Humans." *Science* 269.5227 (1995): 1115-118.

Bechara, Antoine, Daniel Tranel, and Hanna Damasio. "Characterization of the Decision-making Deficit of Patients with Ventromedial Prefrontal Cortex Lesions." *Brain.* Oxford University Press, 01 Nov. 2000.

Bechara, H, Clark, L., A.. Damasio, M. R. F. et al. "Differential Effects of Insular and Ventromedial Prefrontal Cortex Lesions on Risky Decision-making." *Brain* 131.5 (2008): 1311-322.

Becker, A. E. "Eating Behaviours and Attitudes following Prolonged Exposure to Television among Ethnic Fijian Adolescent Girls." *The British Journal of Psychiatry* 180.6 (2002): 509-14.

Bernhardt, Paul C., James M Dabbs Jr, Julie A. Fielden, and Candice D. Lutter. "Testosterone Changes during Vicarious Experiences of Winning and Losing among Fans at Sporting Events." *Physiology & Behavior* 65.1 (1998): 59-62.

Berry, John W. "Acculturation: Living Successfully in Two Cultures." *International Journal of Intercultural Relations* 29.6 (2005): 697-712.

Berry, John W. "Immigration, Acculturation, and Adaptation." *Applied Psychology* 46.1 (1997): 5-34.

Berry, W John, Poortinga, Ype H, Segall, Marshall H, Dasen, Pierre R., *Cross-cultural Psychology: Research and Applications.* Cambridge: Cambridge UP, 2002. Print.

Bickman, Leonard. "The Social Power of a Uniform1." *Journal of Applied Social Psychology* 4.1 (1974): 47-61.

Blair, R. J. R. "Psychopathy, Frustration, and Reactive Aggression: The Role of Ventromedial Prefrontal Cortex." *British Journal of Psychology* 101.3 (2010): 383-99.

Bond, Rod, and Peter B. Smith. "Culture and Conformity: A Meta-analysis of Studies Using Asch's (1952b, 1956) Line Judgment Task." *Psychological Bulletin* 119.1 (1996): 111-37.

Bradbury, Thomas N., Frank D. Fincham, and Steven R. H. Beach. "Research on the Nature and Determinants of Marital Satisfaction: A Decade in Review." *Journal of Marriage and Family* 62.4 (2000): 964-80.

Bransford, John D., and Marcia K. Johnson. "Contextual Prerequisites for Understanding: Some Investigations of Comprehension and Recall." *Journal of Verbal Learning and Verbal Behavior* 11.6 (1972): 717-26.

Braun, Kathryn A., Rhiannon Ellis, and Elizabeth F. Loftus. "Make My Memory: How Advertising Can Change Our Memories of the past." *Psychology and Marketing* 19.1 (2002): 1-23.

Breakwell, Glynis M., Hammond Sean, and Fife-Schaw, Chris. *Research Methods in Psychology: Second Edition.* Sage Publications, 2001.

Breakwell, Glynis M., Jonathan A. Smith, and Daniel B. Wright. *Research Methods in Psychology.* Los Angeles: SAGE, 2012. Print.

Bremner JD, Randall P, Scott TM., et al., "MRI-based Measurement of Hippocampal Volume in Patients with Combat- Related Posttraumatic Stress Disorder." *American Journal of Psychiatry* 152.7 (1995): 973-81.

Bremner JD, Vermetten E, Schmahl C, et al. *Positron emission tomographic imaging of neural correlates of a fear acquisition and extinction paradigm in women with childhood sexual-abuse-related post-traumatic stress disorder.* Psychol Med. 2005;35:791–806.

Breslau, Naomi, Howard D. Chilcoat, Ronald C. Kessler, and Glenn C. Davis. "Previous Exposure to Trauma and PTSD Effects of Subsequent Trauma: Results From the Detroit Area Survey of Trauma." *American Journal of Psychiatry* 156.6 (1999): 902-07.

Bridgeman, Diane L. "Enhanced Role Taking through Cooperative Interdependence: A Field Study." *Child Development* 52.4 (1981): 1231-238.

Buchanan, Tony W., and William R. Lovallo. "Enhanced Memory for Emotional Material following Stress-level Cortisol Treatment in Humans." *Psychoneuroendocrinology* 26.3 (2001): 307-17.

Bushman, B. J. "The Effects of Apparel on Compliance: A Field Experiment with a Female Authority Figure." *Personality and Social Psychology* Bulletin 14.3 (1988): 459-67.

Buss, David M. "Sex Differences in Human Mate Preferences: Evolutionary Hypotheses Tested in 37 Cultures." *Behavioral and Brain Sciences* 12.01 (1989).

Carpenter, Linda L., Audrey R. Tyrka, Nicole S. Ross, et al. "Effect of Childhood Emotional Abuse and Age on Cortisol Responsivity in Adulthood." *Biological Psychiatry* 66.1 (2009): 69-75.

Case, B. J., et al. (2011). "Behavioral and neural correlates of delay of gratification 40 years later." *Proceedings of the National Academy of Sciences*, 108(36), 14998–15003.

Caspi, Avshalom, Mclay, Joseph, Moffitt, Terrie E, et al. "Role of Genotype in the Cycle of Violence in Maltreated Children." *Science* 297.5582 (2002): 851-54. Web.

Chekroud, Adam M., Jim A. C. Everett, Holly Bridge, and Miles Hewstone. "A Review of Neuroimaging Studies of Race-related Prejudice: Does Amygdala Response Reflect Threat?" *Frontiers in Human Neuroscience* 8 (2014).

Chekroud, Adam M., Jim A. C. Everett, Holly Bridge, and Miles Hewstone. "A Review of Neuroimaging Studies of Race-related Prejudice: Does Amygdala Response Reflect Threat?" *Frontiers in Human Neuroscience* 8 (2014).

Chen, Guo-Lin, and Gregory M. Miller. "Advances in Tryptophan Hydroxylase-2 Gene Expression Regulation: New Insights into Serotonin-Stress Interaction and Clinical Implications." *American journal of medical genetics*. 159B.2 (2012): 152–171.

Christakis, D. A., F. J. Zimmerman, D. L. Digiuseppe, and C. A. Mccarty. "Early Television Exposure and Subsequent Attentional Problems in Children." *Pediatrics* 113.4 (2004): 708-13.

Cialdini, Robert B., and Et Al. "Basking in Reflected Glory: Three (football) Field Studies." *Journal of Personality and Social Psychology* 34.3 (1976): 366-75.

Cialdini, Robert B., Goldstein, Noah J., and Vladas Griskevicius. "A Room with a Viewpoint: Using Social Norms to Motivate Environmental Conservation in Hotels." *Journal of Consumer Research* 35.3 (2008): 472-82.

Clark, Russell and Hatfield, Elaine. "Gender Differences in Receptivity to Sexual Offers." *Journal of Psychology & Human Sexuality* 2.1 (1989): 39-55.

Cohen, Claudia E. "Person Categories and Social Perception: Testing Some Boundaries of the Processing Effect of Prior Knowledge." *Journal of Personality and Social Psychology* 40.3 (1981): 441-52.

Cohen, Dov, Richard E. Nisbett, Brian F. Bowdle, and Norbert Schwarz. "Insult, Aggression, and the Southern Culture of Honor: An "experimental Ethnography."" *Journal of Personality and Social Psychology* 70.5 (1996): 945-60.

Conway, Andrew R.a., Michael J. Kane, and Randall W. Engle. "Working Memory Capacity and Its Relation to General Intelligence." *Trends in Cognitive Sciences* 7.12 (2003): 547-52.

Coolican, Hugh. *Research Methods and Statistics in Psychology. Sixth Edition.* Psychology Press, UK. 2014.

Cornwell, R. E., L. Boothroyd, D. M. Burt, et al. "Concordant Preferences for Opposite-sex Signals? Human Pheromones and Facial Characteristics." *Proceedings of the Royal Society B: Biological Sciences* 271.1539 (2004): 635-40.

Cutler, Winnifred B. "Human Sex-Attractant Pheromones: Discovery, Research, Development, and Application in Sex Therapy." *Psychiatric Annals* 29.1 (1999): 54-59.

Daneman, Meredyth, and Patricia A. Carpenter. "Individual Differences in Working Memory and Reading." *Journal of Verbal Learning and Verbal Behavior* 19.4 (1980): 450-66.

Darley, John M., and Bibb Latane. "Bystander Intervention in Emergencies: Diffusion of Responsibility." *Journal of Personality and Social Psychology* 8.4, Pt.1 (1968): 377-83.

Delgado, Mauricio R., Katherine I. Nearing, Joseph E. Ledoux, and Elizabeth A. Phelps. "Neural Circuitry Underlying the Regulation of Conditioned Fear and Its Relation to Extinction." *Neuron* 59.5 (2008): 829-38.

Desbordes, G, Lobsang T. Negi, Thaddeus W. W. et al. "Effects of Mindful-attention and Compassion Meditation Training on Amygdala Response to Emotional Stimuli in an Ordinary, Non-meditative State." *Frontiers in Human Neuroscience* 6 (2012).

Dorries, Kathleen M., Elizabeth Adkins-Regan, and Bruce P. Halpern. "Sensitivity and Behavioral Responses to the Pheromone Androstenone Are Not Mediated by the Vomeronasal Organ in Domestic Pigs." *Brain, Behavior and Evolution* 49.1 (1997): 53-62.

Dovidio, John F.; Kawakami, Kerry; Gaertner, Samuel L. Oskamp, Stuart (Ed). Reducing contemporary prejudice: Combating explicit and implicit bias at the individual and intergroup level. (2000). *Reducing prejudice and discrimination*, (pp. 137-163). Mahwah, NJ, US: Lawrence Erlbaum Associates Publishers, ix, 353 pp.

Draganski, Bogdan, Christian Gaser, Volker Busch, et al. "Neuroplasticity: Changes in Grey Matter Induced by Training." Nature 427.6972 (2004): 311-12.

Drews, Frank A., Monisha Pasupathi, and David L. Strayer. "Passenger and Cell Phone Conversations in Simulated Driving." *Journal of Experimental Psychology: Applied* 14.4 (2008): 392-400.

Dutton, KP. "Writing Under Exam Conditions: Establishing a Baseline." *Handwriting Review.* Vol. 7. 1992.

Eldridge, Laura L. Barbara J. Knowlton, Christopher S. Furmanski. Et al., Remembering episodes: a selective role for the hippocampus during retrieval. *Nature Neuroscience, Volume 3 no 11*, November 2000.

Elzinga, Bernet M., Christian G. Schmahl, Eric Vermetten, et al. "Higher Cortisol Levels Following Exposure to Traumatic Reminders in Abuse-Related PTSD." *Neuropsychopharmacology* 28.9 (2003): 1656-665.

Erickson, K. I., M. W. Voss, R. S. Prakash, C. et al. "Exercise Training Increases Size of Hippocampus and Improves Memory." *Proceedings of the National Academy of Sciences* 108.7 (2011): 3017-022.

Evans, Jonathan St. B. T., and Keith E. Stanovich. "Dual-Process Theories of Higher Cognition." *Perspectives on Psychological Science* 8.3 (2013): 223-41.

Faugier, Jean, and Mary Sargeant. "Sampling Hard to Reach Populations." *Journal of Advanced Nursing* 26.4 (1997): 790-97.

Feinstein, Justin S., Adolphs, Ralph, Damasio, Antonio R, and Tramel, Daniel. "The Human Amygdala and the Induction and Experience of Fear." *Current Biology.* 2011 Jan 11; 21(1): 34–38.

Felmingham, K., A. Kemp, L. Williams, et al. "Changes in Anterior Cingulate and Amygdala After Cognitive Behavior Therapy of Posttraumatic Stress Disorder." *Psychological Science* 18.2 (2007): 127-29.

Festinger, Leon. *When Prophecy Fails: A Social and Psychological Study of a Modern Group That Predicted the Destination of the World.* New York: Harper, 1964. Print.

Fougnie, D., and R. Marois. "Dual-task Interference in Visual Working Memory: A Limitation in Storage Capacity but Not in Encoding or Retrieval." *Attention, Perception & Psychophysics* 71.8 (2009): 1831-841.

Galletly, Cherrie, C. Richard Clark, Alexander C. Mcfarlane, and Darren L. Weber. "Working Memory in Posttraumatic Stress Disorder: an Event-related Potential Study." *Journal of Traumatic Stress* 14.2 (2001): 295-309.

Gardner, Katherine L. et al. "Adverse Experience during Early Life and Adulthood Interact to Elevate tph2 mRNA Expression in Serotonergic Neurons within the Dorsal Raphe Nucleus." *Neuroscience* 163.4 (2009): 991–1001.

Garrison, Carol Z., Elizabeth S. Bryant, Cheryl L. Addy, et al. "Posttraumatic Stress Disorder in Adolescents after Hurricane Andrew." *Journal of the American Academy of Child & Adolescent Psychiatry* 34.9 (1995): 1193-201.

Geene, Judith and D'Oliveira. *Learning to use statistical tests in psychology. Third Edition.* Open University Press. McGraw-Hill, New York. 2005.

Gilbertson, Mark W., Martha E. Shenton, Aleksandra Ciszewski, et al. "Smaller Hippocampal Volume Predicts Pathologic Vulnerability to Psychological Trauma." *Nature Neuroscience* 5.11 (2002): 1242-247.

Goetz, Stefan M.m., Lingfei Tang, Moriah E. Thomason, et al. "Testosterone Rapidly Increases Neural Reactivity to Threat in Healthy Men: A Novel Two-Step Pharmacological Challenge Paradigm." *Biological Psychiatry* 76.4 (2014): 324-31.

Gonzales, Amy L., and Jeffrey T. Hancock. "Mirror, Mirror on My Facebook Wall: Effects of Exposure to Facebook on Self-Esteem." *Cyberpsychology, Behavior, and Social Networking* 14.1-2 (2011): 79-83.

Gottman, John M., and Lowell J. Krokoff. "Marital Interaction and Satisfaction: A Longitudinal View." *Journal of Consulting and Clinical Psychology* 57.1 (1989): 47-52.

Gottman, John M., and Levenson, Robert W. "Marital Processes Predictive of Later Dissolution: Behavior, Physiology, and Health." *Journal of Personality and Social Psychology* 63.2 (1992): 221-33.

Gottman, John M., Levenson, Robert. "Assessing the Role of Emotion in Marriage." *Behavioural Assessment* 8, 31-48, 1986.

Gottman, John Mordechai. *What Predicts Divorce? The Measures.* Mahwah, NJ: Lawrence Erlbaum Associates, 1996.

Gottman, John Mordechai. *What Predicts Divorce? The Relationship between Marital Processes and Marital Outcomes.* New York: Psychology, 2009. Print.

Gould, Felicia, Jennifer Clarke, Christine Heim, et al. "The Effects of Child Abuse and Neglect on Cognitive Functioning in Adulthood." *Journal of Psychiatric Research* 46.4 (2012): 500-06.

Grafman, J., K. Schwab, D. Warden, et al. "Frontal Lobe Injuries, Violence, and Aggression: A Report of the Vietnam Head Injury Study." *Neurology* 46.5 (1996): 1231.

Green BL, Grace MC, Lindy JD, Leonard AC. Race differences in response to combat stress. *Journal of Traumatic Stress.* 1990;3:379–393.

Grove, William M., Elke D. Eckert, Leonard Heston, et al. "Heritability of Substance Abuse and Antisocial Behavior: A Study of Monozygotic Twins Reared Apart." *Biological Psychiatry* 27.12 (1990): 1293-304.

Herpertz, MD Sabine C. "Emotion in Criminal Offenders with Psychopathy and Borderline Personality Disorder." *Archives of General Psychiatry. American Medical Association,* 01 Aug. 2001. Web. 05 June 2017.

Hoagwood, Kimberly Eaton, Juliet M. Vogel, et al. "Implementing an Evidence-Based Trauma Treatment in a State System After September 11: The CATS Project." *Journal of the American Academy of Child & Adolescent Psychiatry* 46.6 (2007): 773-79.

Hogg, Michael A., Janice R. Adelman, and Robert D. Blagg. "Religion in the Face of Uncertainty: An Uncertainty-Identity Theory Account of Religiousness." *Personality and Social Psychology Review* 14.1 (2010): 72-83.

Holley, Sarah R., Claudia M. Haase, and Robert W. Levenson. "Age-Related Changes in Demand-Withdraw Communication Behaviors." *Journal of Marriage and Family* 75.4 (2013): 822-36.

Horne, Robert, L. Graupner, Susie Frost, et al. "Medicine in a Multi-cultural Society: The Effect of Cultural Background on Beliefs about Medications." *Social Science & Medicine* 59.6 (2004): 1307-313.

Hwang, W., H. Myers, J. Abekim, and J. Ting. "A Conceptual Paradigm for Understanding Culture's Impact on Mental Health: The Cultural Influences on Mental Health (CIMH) Model." *Clinical Psychology Review* 28.2 (2008): 211-27.

Irish, Leah, Beth Buckley-Fischer, William Fallon, et al. "Gender Differences in PTSD: An Exploration of Peritraumatic Factors." *J Anxiety Disord.* 2011 Mar; 25(2): 209–216.

Jamshed, Shazia. "Qualitative Research Method-interviewing and Observation." *Journal of Basic and Clinical Pharmacy* 5.4 (2014): 87.

Jimenez, Daniel E., Stephen J. Bartels, Veronica Cardenas, et al. "Cultural Beliefs and Mental Health Treatment Preferences of Ethnically Diverse Older Adult Consumers in Primary Care." *The American Journal of Geriatric Psychiatry* 20.6 (2012): 533-42.

Johnston, Victor S., Rebecca Hagel, Melissa Franklin, et al. "Male Facial Attractiveness: Evidence for Hormone-mediated Adaptive Design." *Evolution and Human Behavior* 22.4 (2001): 251-67.

Kahneman, Daniel. "A Perspective on Judgement and Choice: Mapping Bounded Rationality." September 2003, *American Psychologist.* Vol. 58, No. 9, 697–72.

Kandel, E. R., and L. Tauc. "Heterosynaptic Facilitation in Neurones of the Abdominal Ganglion of Aplysia Depilans." *The Journal of Physiology* 181.1 (1965): 1-27.

Kandel, Eric Â R., Yadin Dudai, and MarkÂ R. Mayford. "The Molecular and Systems Biology of Memory." *Cell* 157.1 (2014): 163-86.

Kane, Michael J., Leslie H. Brown, Jennifer C. Mcvay, et al. "For Whom the Mind Wanders, and When." *Psychological Science* 18.7 (2007): 614-21.

Kearney, David J., Kelly Mcdermott, Carol Malte, et al. "Association of Participation in a Mindfulness Program with Measures of PTSD, Depression and Quality of Life in a Veteran Sample." *Journal of Clinical Psychology* 68.1 (2011): 101-16.

Kessler R. C., Sonnega A., Bromet E., Hughes M., Nelson C. B. (1995). *Posttraumatic stress disorder in the national comorbidity survey. Arch.* Gen. Psychiatry 52, 1048–1060.

Kiefer, Markus, Stefanie Schuler, Carmen Mayer, et al. "Handwriting or Typewriting? The Influence of Penor Keyboard-Based Writing Training on Reading and Writing Performance in Preschool Children." *Advances in Cognitive Psychology 11* (2015): 136-46.

Kiehl, Kent A., Andra M. Smith, Robert D. Hare, et al. "Limbic Abnormalities in Affective Processing by Criminal Psychopaths as Revealed by Functional Magnetic Resonance Imaging." *Biological Psychiatry* 50.9 (2001): 677-84.

Kim, Hyoun S. et al. "From the Mouths of Social Media Users: A Focus Group Study Exploring the Social Casino Gaming–online Gambling Link." *Journal of Behavioral Addictions* 5.1 (2016): 115–121.

Kim, Souyoun and Lee, Daeyeol. "Prefrontal Cortex and Impulsive Decision Making." *Biological Psychiatry.* 2011 Jun 15; 69(12): 1140–1146.

Kistin, Caroline J., Jenny Radesky, Yaminette Diaz-Linhart, et al. "A Qualitative Study of Parenting Stress, Coping, and Discipline Approaches Among Low-Income Traumatized Mothers." *Journal of Developmental & Behavioral Pediatrics* 35.3 (2014): 189-96.

Klingberg, Torkel, Elisabeth Fernell, Pernille J. Olesen et al. "Computerized Training of Working Memory in Children With ADHD-A Randomized, Controlled Trial." *Journal of the American Academy of Child & Adolescent Psychiatry* 44.2 (2005): 177-86.

Klingberg, Torkel, Olesen, Pernille J., and Helena Westerberg,. "Increased Prefrontal and Parietal Activity after Training of Working Memory." *Nature Neuroscience* 7.1 (2003): 75-79.

Klingberg, Torkel. "Training and Plasticity of Working Memory." *Trends in Cognitive Sciences* 14.7 (2010): 317-24.

Klobuchar, Amy, Mehrkens Steblay, Nancy K, and Lindell Caligiuri, Hilary. "Improving Eye-witness Identifications: Hennepin County's Blind Sequential Lineup Pilot Project." *Law, Policy and Ethics Journal.* Vol 4:381. 2006.

Koenen K. C., Stellman S. D., Sommer J. F., Jr., Stellman J. M. (2008). "Persisting posttraumatic stress disorder symptoms and their relationship to functioning in vietnam veterans: a 14-year follow-up." J. Trauma. *Stress* 21, 49–57.

Koenigs, Michael, and Jordan Grafman. "Posttraumatic Stress Disorder: The Role of Medial Prefrontal Cortex and Amygdala." *The Neuroscientist* 15.5 (2009): 540-48.

Labar, Kevin S., J.christopher Gatenby, John C. Gore, Joseph E. Ledoux, and Elizabeth A. Phelps. "Human Amygdala Activation during Conditioned Fear Acquisition and Extinction: A Mixed-Trial FMRI Study." *Neuron* 20.5 (1998): 937-45.

Lane, Richard D. and Nadel, Lynn. *Cognitive Neuroscience of Emotion.* New York, N.Y.: Oxford UP, 2006. Print.

Latane, Bibb, and John M. Darley. "Group Inhibition of Bystander Intervention in Emergencies." *Journal of Personality and Social Psychology* 10.3 (1968): 215-21.

Lazar, Sara W., Catherine E. Kerr, Rachel H. Wasserman, et al. "Meditation Experience Is Associated with Increased Cortical Thickness." *NeuroReport* 16.17 (2005): 1893-897.

Ledoux, Joseph E., Morgan, Maria A., Jay Schulkin. "Ventral Medial Prefrontal Cortex and Emotional Perseveration: The Memory for Prior Extinction Training." *Behavioural Brain Research* 146.1-2 (2003): 121-30. Web.

Levine, R. V., A. Norenzayan, and K. Philbrick. "Cross-Cultural Differences in Helping Strangers." *Journal of Cross-Cultural Psychology* 32.5 (2001): 543-60.

Levine, R., S. Sato, T. Hashimoto, and J. Verma. "Love and Marriage in Eleven Cultures." *Journal of Cross-Cultural Psychology* 26.5 (1995): 554-71.

Levine, Robert V., Todd Simon Martinez, Gary Brase, and Kerry Sorenson. "Helping in 36 U.S. Cities." *Journal of Personality and Social Psychology* 67.1 (1994): 69-82.

Lexchin, J. "Pharmaceutical Industry Sponsorship and Research Outcome and Quality: Systematic Review." *Bmj* 326.7400 (2003): 1167-170.

Lieberman M. D., Hariri A., Jarcho J. M., et al. "An fMRI investigation of race-related amygdala activity in African-American and Caucasian-American individuals." *Natural Neuroscience.* (2005). 8, 720–722.

Lillard, A. S., and J. Peterson. "The Immediate Impact of Different Types of Television on Young Children's Executive Function." *Pediatrics* 128.4 (2011): 644-49.

Little, A. C., B. C. Jones, and L. M. Debruine. "Facial Attractiveness: Evolutionary Based Research." *Philosophical Transactions of the Royal Society B: Biological Sciences* 366.1571 (2011): 1638-659.

Loftus, Elizabeth F., and Hunter G. Hoffman. "Misinformation and Memory: The Creation of New Memories." *Journal of Experimental Psychology: General* 118.1 (1989): 100-04.

Loftus, Elizabeth F., and John C. Palmer. "Reconstruction of Automobile Destruction: An Example of the Interaction between Language and Memory." *Journal of Verbal Learning and Verbal Behavior* 13.5 (1974): 585-89.

Loftus, Elizabeth F., David G. Miller, and Helen J. Burns. "Semantic Integration of Verbal Information into a Visual Memory." *Journal of Experimental Psychology: Human Learning & Memory* 4.1 (1978): 19-31.

Luby, Joan. Andy Belden, Kelly Botteron, et al. "The Effects of Poverty on Childhood Brain Development." *JAMA Pediatrics* 167.12 (2013): 1135.

Lyons-Padilla, Sarah, Michele J. Gelfand, Hedieh Mirahmadi, et al. "Belonging Nowhere: Marginalization & Radicalization Risk among Muslim Immigrants." *Behavioral Science & Policy* 1.2 (2015): 1-12.

Macnamara, Annmarie, Christine A. Rabinak, Amy E. Kennedy, et al. "Emotion Regulatory Brain Function and SSRI Treatment in PTSD: Neural Correlates and Predictors of Change." *Neuropsychopharmacology* 41.2 (2015): 611-18.

Maguire, Eleanor A., Katherine Woollett, and Hugo J. Spiers. "London Taxi Drivers and Bus Drivers: A Structural MRI and Neuropsychological Analysis." Hippocampus 16.12 (2006): 1091-101.

Mahan, Amy L., and Kerry J. Ressler. "Fear Conditioning, Synaptic Plasticity, and the Amygdala: Implications for Posttraumatic Stress Disorder." *Trends in Neurosciences* 35.1 (2012): 24–35.

Mason, R. "Handwriting following transfer to secondary school – some interim notes." *Handwriting Review*, 1991.

Matud, M.pilar. "Gender Differences in Stress and Coping Styles." *Personality and Individual Differences* 37.7 (2004): 1401-415.

Mazur, Allan, Alan Booth, and James M. Dabbs Jr. "Testosterone and Chess Competition." *Social Psychology Quarterly* 55.1 (1992): 70.

McEwen BS. "Stress and hippocampal plasticity." *Annu Rev Neurosci.* 1999;22:105–122.

Mcintyre, Christa, and Benno Roozendaal. "Adrenal Stress Hormones and Enhanced Memory for Emotionally Arousing Experiences." *Neural Plasticity and Memory Frontiers in Neuroscience* (2007): 265-83.

Mendel, R., E. Traut-Mattausch. E. Jonas, S. et al. "Confirmation Bias: Why Psychiatrists Stick to Wrong Preliminary Diagnoses." *Psychological Medicine* 41.12 (2011): 2651-659.

Meyer-Lindenberg, Andreas, Joshua W. Buckholtz, et al., "Neural Mechanisms of Genetic Risk for Impulsivity and Violence in Humans." *Focus* 4.3 (2006): 360-68.

Milad, Mohammed R., Christopher I. Wright, Scott P. Orr, Roger K. Pitman, et al. "Recall of Fear Extinction in Humans Activates the Ventromedial Prefrontal Cortex and Hippocampus in Concert." *Biological Psychiatry* 62.5 (2007): 446-54.

Mischel, Walter, Ozlem Ayduk, Marc G. Berman, et al. "Willpower' over the Life Span: Decomposing Self-regulation." *Social Cognitive and Affective Neuroscience.* Oxford University Press, 18 Sept. 2010.

Mischel, Walter, Shoda, Yuichi, and Rodriguez, Monica L. "Delay of Gratification in Children." Science; May 26, 1989; 244, 4907; *Research Library* pg. 933.

Moore T, Scarpa A, Raine A. A Meta-Analysis of Serotonin Metabolite 5-HIAA and Antisocial Behavior. *Aggressive Behavior.* 2002;28:299–316.

Mosienko, V et al. "Exaggerated Aggression and Decreased Anxiety in Mice Deficient in Brain Serotonin." *Translational Psychiatry* 2.5 (2012).

Muller, N.G., and Knight, R.T. "The Functional Neuroanatomy of Working Memory: Contributions of Human Brain Lesion Studies." *Neuroscience* 139.1 (2006): 51-58.

Murphy, Dominic, and Walter Busuttil. "PTSD, Stigma and Barriers to Help-seeking within the UK Armed Forces." *Journal of the Royal Army Medical Corps* 161.4 (2014): 322-26.

Murrough, James W. "The Effect of Early Trauma Exposure on Serotonin Type 1B Receptor Expression Revealed by Reduced Selective Radioligand Binding." *Archives of General Psychiatry* 68.9 (2011): 892.

Nairne, James S., Howard L. Whiteman, and Matthew R. Kelley. "Short-Term Forgetting of Order Under Conditions of Reduced Interference." *The Quarterly Journal of Experimental Psychology* A 52.1 (1999): 241-51.

Nelson, Alan R. "Unequal Treatment: Report of the Institute of Medicine on Racial and Ethnic Disparities in Healthcare." *The Annals of Thoracic Surgery* 76.4 (2003).

Neria, Yuval, Laura DiGrande, and Ben G. Adams. "Posttraumatic Stress Disorder Following the September 11, 2001, Terrorist Attacks: A Review of the Literature Among Highly Exposed Populations." *The American Psychologist* 66.6 (2011): 429–446. PMC.

Nixon, Reginald D.v., and Richard A. Bryant. "Are Negative Cognitions Associated With Severe Acute Trauma Responses?" *Behaviour Change* 22.01 (2005): 22-28.

Norris, Fran H. "Disaster Research Methods: Past Progress and Future Directions." *Journal of Traumatic Stress* 19.2 (2006): 173-84.

North, Carol S., Carissa J. Barney, and David E. Pollio. "A Focus Group Study of the Impact of Trauma Exposure in the 9/11 Terrorist Attacks." *Social Psychiatry and Psychiatric Epidemiology* 50.4 (2014): 569-78.

Nosek, Brian. Open Science Collaboration: "Estimating the Reproducibility of Psychological Science." *Science* 349.6251 (2015).

Oberle, Eva, and Kimberly A. Schonert-Reichl. "Stress Contagion in the Classroom? The Link between Classroom Teacher Burnout and Morning Cortisol in Elementary School Students." *Social Science & Medicine* 159 (2016): 30-37.

Ochsner, Kevin N., Rebecca R. Ray, Brent Hughes, et al. "Bottom-Up and Top-Down Processes in Emotion Generation: Common and Distinct Neural Mechanisms." *Psychological Science* 20.11 (2009): 1322-331.

Ogihara, Yuji, and Yukiko Uchida. "Does Individualism Bring Happiness? Negative Effects of Individualism on Interpersonal Relationships and Happiness." *Frontiers in Psychology* 5 (2014).

Oortmerssen, G. A. Van, and Th. C. M. Bakker. "Artificial Selection for Short and Long Attack Latencies in WildMus Musculus Domesticus." *Behavior Genetics* 11.2 (1981): 115-26.

Oppenheimer, Daniel M., and Pam A. Mueller. "The Pen Is Mightier than the Keyboard: Longhand and Laptop Note-Taking." *Psychological science.* Vol 25, Issue 6, 2014

Oskamp, Stuart. Reducing Prejudice and Discrimination. New York: *Psychology*, 2008. Print.

Ostrom, Thomas M., and Constantine Sedikides. "Out-group Homogeneity Effects in Natural and Minimal Groups." *Psychological Bulletin* 112.3 (1992): 536-52.

Palinkas, Lawrence A., Sarah M. Horwitz, Carla A. Green, et al. "Purposeful Sampling for Qualitative Data Collection and Analysis in Mixed Method Implementation Research." *Administration and Policy in Mental Health and Mental Health Services Research* 42.5 (2013): 533-44.

Pardini, Dustin A., Adrian Raine, Kirk Erickson, and Rolf Loeber. "Lower Amygdala Volume in Men Is Associated with Childhood Aggression, Early Psychopathic Traits, and Future Violence." *Biological Psychiatry* 75.1 (2014): 73-80.

Park, Bernadette, and Myron Rothbart. "Perception of Out-group Homogeneity and Levels of Social Categorization: Memory for the Subordinate Attributes of In-group and Out-group Members." *Journal of Personality and Social Psychology* 42.6 (1982): 1051-068.

Parsons, Thomas D., and Albert A. Rizzo. "Affective Outcomes of Virtual Reality Exposure Therapy for Anxiety and Specific Phobias: A Meta-analysis." *Journal of Behavior Therapy and Experimental Psychiatry* 39.3 (2008): 250-61.

Passamonti, Luca, Molly J. Crockett, Annemieke M. Apergis-Schoute, et al. "Effects of Acute Tryptophan Depletion on Prefrontal-Amygdala Connectivity While Viewing Facial Signals of Aggression." *Biological Psychiatry* 71.1 (2012): 36-43.

Pattij, T., and L. Vanderschuren. "The Neuropharmacology of Impulsive Behaviour." *Trends in Pharmacological Sciences* 29.4 (2008): 192-99.

Perez DJ, Fortuna L, Alegria M. "Prevalence and correlates of everyday discrimination among U.S. Latinos." *Journal of Community Psychology.* 2008;36:421–433

Perry, BD and Pollard, D. "Altered brain development following global neglect in early childhood." *Society for Neuroscience: Proceedings from Annual Meeting,* New Orleans, 1997.

Pettigrew, Thomas F., and Linda R. Tropp. "A Meta-analytic Test of Intergroup Contact Theory." *Journal of Personality and Social Psychology* 90.5 (2006): 751-83.

Pettigrew, Thomas F., and Linda R. Tropp. "How Does Intergroup Contact

Reduce Prejudice? Meta-analytic Tests of Three Mediators." *European Journal of Social Psychology* 38.6 (2008): 922-34.

Phelps, Elizabeth A., Kevin J. O'connor, William A. Cunningham, E. et al. "Performance on Indirect Measures of Race Evaluation Predicts Amygdala Activation." *Journal of Cognitive Neuroscience* 12.5 (2000): 729-38.

Piliavin, Irving M., Judith Rodin, and Jane A. Piliavin. "Good Samaritanism: An Underground Phenomenon?" *Journal of Personality and Social Psychology* 13.4 (1969): 289-99.

Prowse, C.E. *Defining Street Gangs in the 21st Century: Fluid, Mobile, and Transnational Networks.* New York, NY: Springer New York, 2012. Print.

Qureshi, S. U., M. E. Long, M. R. Bradshaw, et al. "Does PTSD Impair Cognition Beyond the Effect of Trauma?" *Journal of Neuropsychiatry* 23.1 (2011): 16-28.

Radke, Sina, Inge Volman, Pranjal Mehta, et al. "Testosterone Biases the Amygdala toward Social Threat Approach." *Science Advances. American Association for the Advancement of Science. Vol 1*, No5, June, (2015).

Raine, Adrian, Monte Buchsbaum, and Lori Lacasse. "Brain Abnormalities in Murderers Indicated by Positron Emission Tomography." *Biological Psychiatry* 42.6 (1997): 495-508.

Raine, Adrian. "From Genes to Brain to Antisocial Behavior." *Current Directions in Psychological Science* 17.5 (2008): 323-28.

Raine, Adrian. *Anatomy of Violence - the Biological Roots of Crime.* Penguin, 2014. Print.

Rehman, Uzma S., and Amy Holtzworth-Munroe. "A Cross-cultural Examination of the Relation of Marital Communication Behavior to Marital Satisfaction." *Journal of Family Psychology* 21.4 (2007): 759-63.

Ressler, Kerry J. "Amygdala Activity, Fear, and Anxiety: Modulation by Stress." *Biological Psychiatry* 67.12 (2010): 1117-119.

Robbins, T. W., E. J. Anderson, A. D. Baddeley, et al. "Working Memory in Chess." *Memory & Cognition* 24.1 (1996): 83-93.

Rosenzweig, Mark R., and Edward L. Bennett. "Psychobiology of Plasticity: Effects of Training and Experience on Brain and Behavior." *Behavioural Brain Research* 78.1 (1996): 57-65.

Rothbaum, Barbara O., Larry F. Hodges, David Ready, et al. "Virtual Reality Exposure Therapy for Vietnam Veterans with Posttraumatic Stress Disorder." *The Journal of Clinical Psychiatry* 62.8 (2001): 617-22.

Rothgerber, Hank. "External Intergroup Threat as an Antecedent to Perceptions in In-group and Out-group Homogeneity." *Journal of Personality and Social Psychology* 73.6 (1997): 1206-212.

Sapolsky, RM. "Glucocorticoids and hippocampal atrophy in neuropsychiatric disorders." *Arch Gen Psychiatry.* 2000;57:925–935.

Sapolsky, Robert M., Uno, Hideo, Rebert, Charles S., et al. "Hippocampal Damage Associated with Prolonged Glucocorticoid Exposure in Primates." *The Journal of Neuroscience*, September 1990, Ye(g): 2897-2902.

Savic, Ivanka, Hans Berglund, Balazs Gulyas, and Per Roland. "Smelling of Odorous Sex Hormone-like Compounds Causes Sex-Differentiated Hypothalamic Activations in Humans." *Neuron* 31.4 (2001): 661-68.

Saxton TK, Lyndon A, Little AC, et al. "Evidence that androstadienone, a putative human chemosignal, modulates women's attributions of men's attractiveness." *Horm Behav.* 2008; 54:597–601.

Schlenger W, Fairbank J. "Ethnocultural considerations in understanding PTSD and related disorders among military veterans: Ethnocultural Aspects of PTSD: Issues, Research, and Clinical Application." *Washington DC: American Psychological Association*; 1996. pp. 529–538.

Scoville, W. B., and B. Milner. "Loss Of Recent Memory After Bilateral Hippocampal Lesions." *Journal of Neurology, Neurosurgery & Psychiatry* 20.1 (1957): 11-21.

Shallice, T., and Elizabeth K. Warrington. "Independent Functioning of Verbal Memory Stores: A Neuropsychological Study." *Quarterly Journal of Experimental Psychology* 22.2 (1970): 261-73.

Sherif, Muzafer, Sherif, Carolyn, W. Harvey O.J., et al., *Intergroup Conflict and Cooperation: The Robber's Cave Experiment."* Oklahoma University, Institute of Group Relations. 1954/1961. Available from psychclassics. yorku.ca.

Sherif, Muzafer. *The Robbers Cave Experiment: Intergroup Conflict and Cooperation.* Middletown, CT: Wesleyan UP, 1988. Print.

Shin, Lisa M., and Israel Liberzon. "The Neurocircuitry of Fear, Stress, and Anxiety Disorders." *Neuropsychopharmacology* 35.1 (2009): 169-91.

Siegal, Harvey A., Bibb Latane, and John Darley. "The Unresponsive Bystander: Why Doesn't He Help?" *Contemporary Sociology* 1.3 (1972): 226.

Simons, Daniel J., and Christopher F. Chabris. "Gorillas in Our Midst: Sustained Inattentional Blindness for Dynamic Events." *Perception* 28.9 (1999): 1059-074.

Simons, Daniel. Walter R. Boot, Neil Charness, , et al. "Do "Brain-Training" Programs Work?" *Psychological Science in the Public Interest* Vol 17, Issue 3, pp. 103 – 186. First published: October-02-2016

Slavin, Robert E. "Synthesis of Research of Cooperative Learning." *Educational Leadership*, v48 n5 p71-82 Feb 1991.

Smith, Sean and Vale, Wylie. "The role of the hypothalamic-pituitary-adrenal axis in neuroendocrine responses to stress." *Dialogues Clinical Neuroscience.* 2006 Dec; 8(4): 383–395.

Solomon, Z., Gelkopf, M., & Bleich, A. (2005). "Is terror gender blind?" *Social Psychiatry and Psychiatric Epidemiology*, 40, 947-954

Sparrow, B., J. Liu, and D. M. Wegner. "Google Effects on Memory: Cognitive Consequences of Having Information at Our Fingertips." *Science* 333.6043 (2011): 776-78.

Squire, Larry R., and John T. Wixted. "The Cognitive Neuroscience of Human Memory Since H.M." *Annual Review of Neuroscience* 34.1 (2011): 259-88.

Steblay, Nancy M. "Helping Behavior in Rural and Urban Environments: A Meta-analysis." *Psychological Bulletin* 102.3 (1987): 346-56.

Steimer, Thierry. "The Biology of Fear- and Anxiety-related Behaviours." *Dialogues in Clinical Neuroscience.* 2002 Sep; 4(3): 231–249.

Stein, Dan J., Soraya Seedat, Geoffrey Jh Van Der Linden, et al. "Selective Serotonin Reuptake Inhibitors in the Treatment of Post-traumatic Stress Disorder: A Metaanalysis of Randomized Controlled Trials." *International Clinical Psychopharmacology* 15 (2000).

Stone, Jeff, Zachary W. Perry, and John M. Darley. ""White Men Can't Jump": Evidence for the Perceptual Confirmation of Racial Stereotypes Following a Basketball Game." *Basic and Applied Social Psychology* 19.3 (1997): 291-306.

Sulaiman-Hill, Cheryl Mr, and Sandra C. Thompson. "Sampling Challenges in a Study Examining Refugee Resettlement." *BMC International Health and Human Rights* 11.1 (2011).

Sutan, Rosnah, and Hazlina Mohd Miskam. "Psychosocial Impact of Perinatal Loss among Muslim Women." *BMC Women's Health* 12.1 (2012).

Sutker PB1, Winstead DK, Galina ZH, Allain AN. "Cognitive Deficits and Psychopathology among Former Prisoners of War and Combat Veterans of the Korean Conflict." *American Journal of Psychiatry* 148.1 (1991): 67-72.

Suzanne Corkin, David G. Amaral, R. Gilberto González, et al. "H. M.'s Medial Temporal Lobe Lesion: Findings from Magnetic Resonance Imaging." *Journal of Neuroscience* 15 May 1997, 17 (10) 3964-3979.

Tajfel, Henri, M. G. Billig, R. P. Bundy, and Claude Flament. "Social Categorization and Intergroup Behaviour." *European Journal of Social Psychology* 1.2 (1971): 149-78.

Tajfel, Henry and Jonathan, Turner. An Integrative Theory of Intergroup Conflict. Taylor and Francis *Psychology Press*, 1979.

Takahashi, Aki, and Klaus A. Miczek. "Neurogenetics of Aggressive Behavior: Studies in Rodents." *Neuroscience of Aggression Current Topics in Behavioral Neurosciences* (2013): 3-44.

Takeuchi, H., Y. Taki, H. Hashizume, K. Asano, et al. "The Impact of Television Viewing on Brain Structures: Cross-Sectional and Longitudinal Analyses." *Cerebral Cortex* 25.5 (2013): 1188-197.

Talhelm, T, Zhang, X, Oishi, S, et al., "Large-Scale Psychological Differences Within China Explained by Rice Versus Wheat Agriculture." *Science* 09 May 2014:Vol. 344, Issue 6184, pp. 603-608

Taylor, Ann Gill, Lisa E. Goehler, Daniel I. Galper, et al. "Top-Down and Bottom-Up Mechanisms in Mind-Body Medicine: Development of an Integrative Framework for Psychophysiological Research." *EXPLORE: The Journal of Science and Healing* 6.1 (2010): 29-41.

Toril, Pilar, Josa, M. Reales, Julia Mayas, and Soledad Ballesteros. "Video Game Training Enhances Visuospatial Working Memory and Episodic Memory in Older Adults." *Frontiers in Human Neuroscience* 10 (2016).

Torres, Lucas, Mark W. Driscoll, and Maria Voell. "Discrimination, Acculturation, Acculturative Stress, and Latino Psychological Distress: A Moderated Mediational Model." *Cultural Diversity and Ethnic Minority Psychology* 18.1 (2012): 17-25.

Toth, K., and M. Kemmelmeier. "Divorce Attitudes Around the World: Distinguishing the Impact of Culture on Evaluations and Attitude Structure." *Cross-Cultural Research* 43.3 (2009): 280-97.

Trickett, Penelope K. et al. "Attenuation of Cortisol across Development for Victims of Sexual Abuse." *Development and psychopathology* 22.1 (2010): 165–175.

Tsay, M., & Brady, M. (2010). "A case study of cooperative learning and communication pedagogy: Does working in teams make a difference?" *Journal of the Scholarship of Teaching and Learning*, 10(2), 78– 89

Turvey, Carolyn L., Gerald Jogerst, Mee Young Kim, and Elena Frolova. "Cultural Differences in Depression-related Stigma in Late-life: A Comparison between the USA, Russia, and South Korea." *International Psychogeriatrics* 24.10 (2012): 1642-647.

Urry, H. L. "Amygdala and Ventromedial Prefrontal Cortex Are Inversely Coupled during Regulation of Negative Affect and Predict the Diurnal Pattern of Cortisol Secretion among Older Adults." *Journal of Neuroscience* 26.16 (2006): 4415-425.

Veltmeyer, Melinda D., C. Richard Clark, Alexander C. Mcfarlane, et al. "Working Memory Function in Post-traumatic Stress Disorder: An Event-related Potential Study." *Clinical Neurophysiology* 120.6 (2009): 1096-106.

Venkatesh, Sudhir Alladi. *Gang Leader for a Day: A Rogue Sociologist Crosses the Line.* London: Penguin, 2008. Print.

Verhaeghe, J., R. Gheysen, and P. Enzlin. "Pheromones and Their Effect on Women's Mood and Sexuality." *Facts, Views & Vision in ObGyn* 5.3 (2013): 189–195.

Watson, John B., and Rosalie Rayner. "Conditioned Emotional Reactions." *Journal of Experimental Psychology* 3.1 (1920): 1-14.

Waza, K. "Comparison of Symptoms in Japanese and American Depressed Primary Care Patients." *Family Practice* 16.5 (1999): 528-33.

Wedekind, C., T. Seebeck, F. Bettens, and A. J. Paepke. "MHC-Dependent Mate Preferences in Humans." *Proceedings of the Royal Society B: Biological Sciences* 260.1359 (1995): 245-49.

Weiskrantz, Lawrence. "Behavioral changes associated with ablation of the amygdaloid complex in monkeys." *Journal of Comparative and Physiological Psychology*, Vol 49(4), Aug 1956, 381-391.

Williams L. M., Liddell B. J., Rathjen J., Brown K. J., Gray J., Phillips M., et al. (2004a). *Mapping the time course of nonconscious and conscious perception of fear: an integration of central and peripheral measures. Human Brain Mapping.* 21 64–74.

Williams, David R.; Spencer, Michael S.; Jackson, James S., et al., (1999). "Race, stress, and physical health: The role of group identity: Self, social identity, and physical health: Interdisciplinary explorations." (pp. 71-100). *New York*, NY, US: Oxford University Press.

Wingfield, John C., Robert E. Hegner, Alfred M. Dufty, and Gregory F. Ball. "The "Challenge Hypothesis": Theoretical Implications for Patterns of Testosterone Secretion, Mating Systems, and Breeding Strategies." *The American Naturalist* 136.6 (1990): 829-46.

Wood, Ruth I., and Steven J. Stanton. "Testosterone and Sport: Current Perspectives." *Hormones and Behavior* 61.1 (2012): 147-55. Web.